A Legacy of
RELIGIOUS EDUCATORS

Historical and Theological Introductions

Edited By:

ELMER L. TOWNS & BENJAMIN K. FORREST

"Dr. Elmer Towns and Dr. Benjamin Forrest should be highly commended for co-editing *A Legacy of Religious Educators: Historical and Theological Introductions*. This marvelous book constitutes a genuine treasure trove of insightful Christian reflection by some of the finest minds in the history of the Christian Church. Their insights help us address a very pertinent question: What is the role of Biblically faithful Christian education in a resolutely secular culture? The co-editors challenge readers to identify at least one educator in the book whose thinking can inspire him or her to "take the Word of God and communicate it effectively in this world." For this reason alone, this book should belong in the libraries of every pastor, Christian educator and church, so rich in wisdom and inspiring are many of its pages."

— JOHN D. WOODBRIDGE, Research Professor of Church History
and Christian Thought, Trinity Evangelical Divinity School

"Professors Towns and Forrest have succeeded in editing a historically comprehensive book that cogently examines the educational ideas of the major figures who have shaped Western Civilization's religious tradition. Written by an international array of noted scholars, the book's chapters will engage readers in a theological and educational journey that begins with the fathers of the early Christian Church, moves through the Medieval, Reformation, Post-Reformation and Enlightenment periods, and leads to the contemporary era. Employing a biographical approach, the authors have created the contexts in which the ideas of Augustine, Aquinas, Luther, Calvin, Edwards, Raikes, Pestalozzi, and other leading religious educators originated. The authors bring the narrative forward to the present as they skillfully explore the contemporary meaning of significant theologically-grounded concepts for schools and curriculum and for teachers and learners. The chapters on William James, John Dewey, and C.S. Lewis will be especially illuminating for all who are concerned with examining and educating for the spiritual dimension of human experience."

— GERALD L. GUTEK, Professor Emeritus of Education,
Loyola University Chicago and the author of
Historical and Philosophical Foundations of Education

"A Legacy of Religious Educators insightfully discusses a very helpful selection of religious educators from a wide variety of orientations. A well-planned volume, it will inform the novice and in many cases the expert. An added value is exposure to several influential educators not generally included in such collections. I highly recommend it as both a textbook and a good read for those who want to explore the field."

— GEORGE R. KNIGHT, Professor Emeritus, Andrews University, author of *Philosophy & Education: An Introduction in Christian Perspective*

"One of the real challenges of education in our day is that every few years a new theory surfaces, with new promises and possibilities. Unfortunately, just as quickly new challenges and concerns arise, and it becomes hard for one to every find a place to rest. Amid the fluid view of education in our day, it is a gift to read about Christian views of education through the ages. In this volume we learn from the past so that we might be better informed about how we should approach the present. That, it seems to me, is a wonderful gift."

— KELLY M. KAPIC, Professor of Theological Studies at Covenant College, author of *A Little Book for New Theologians: Why and How to Study Theology*

"This new volume is a welcome contribution for understanding many of those who have shaped the formal and non-formal educational efforts of the church over the last 2,000 years. The essays that have been pulled together provide insight into the lives, ideas, passions, and efforts of various theologians, church leaders, and educational leaders, all of whom sought to faithfully lead others to know God more fully, and follow Him more faithfully in all of life. In this volume you will meet new heroes, role models, and mentors who will encourage and challenge you as you consider your own opportunities and efforts in educational ministry."

— KEVIN E. LAWSON, Director of Ph.D. and Ed.D. programs in Educational Studies at Talbot School of Theology, Biola University, editor of the Christian Education Journal, and director of the Christian Educators of the 20th Century project (www.christianeducators20.com)

"A Legacy of Religious Educators provides a well-researched and comprehensive historical overview of key religious educators and thinkers across the centuries that have significantly shaped the thought and practice of Christian educators in their formal, nonformal and informal ministries. Professors Towns and Forrest have assembled a noteworthy host of authors who insightfully analyze historical contexts and the theology of the selected thinkers who have influenced lasting innovations and have been spokespersons for broader intellectual movements. This work is worthy of a wide readership by those called to teach the Christian faith in the twenty-first century while lovingly honoring the legacy of the ages."

— ROBERT W. PAZMIŃO, Valeria Stone Professor of Christian Education, Andover Newton Theological School, author of *Foundational Issues in Christian Education*

"A Legacy of Religious Educators takes us back to selected Christian pioneers who developed practical ways to extend congregational worship into small groups of age-appropriate Bible study, mutual ministry, and Christian action around the world. The life stories of these leaders anchor their visions for spiritual formation in local congregations. The biblical commands that energized their efforts have not changed. Recapture a vision for the power of Christian Education in the local church. Hear their voices. Rediscover the legacy."

— WILLIAM R. YOUNT, Professor of Foundations of Education, New Orleans Baptist Theological Seminary, author of *Created to Learn* and *The Teaching Ministry of the Church*

ISBN 13: 978-0-997682-84-7
First print edition, January 2017
Published by Liberty University Press
Printed in the U.S.A.

Library of Congress Preassigned Control Number: 2017933409
Liberty University Press
Lynchburg, VA

Liberty.edu/LibertyUniversityPress

DEDICATION

This book is dedicated to my father, Dr. Bruce K. Forrest, who taught me
that education is a key to the door that unlocks opportunity.
He was my first teacher and from him I learned the "way I should go."

ACKNOWLEDGEMENTS

We would first like to thank the contributing authors who gave of their time, research, and mental efforts to commit to joining such a text. Their hard work and commitment toward research and writing will carry forth fruit to multiple generations of educators, researchers, and scholars. We would also like to thank LU Press and specifically Sarah Funderburke for her assistance in the editorial process. Leo Percer and Linda Elliot were editors extraordinaire who took hundreds of pages of material and made sure they would be of consistent value to those engaging in the learning and teaching process. In addition to their assistance we would also like to thank Mark Lamport for his encouragement throughout this book and for his role as recommender and sounding board. In addition to these, we would both like to personally thank our families.

Elmer would like to thank God for his wife Ruth who was living when this project was started. She passed away December 11, 2013, and was the inspiration when the original volume was written: History of Religious Educators, Baker Book House, 1975.

Ben would like to thank his wife Lerisa for her willingness to listen to all of the challenges and joys that came with such a project. She is a blessing and saint! He also wants to thank his children, Reagan, Hudson, and Graham who allowed his focus to be distracted from-time-to-time as he jumped through the hoops of trying to keep this text from stretching beyond a five-year project.

TABLE *of* CONTENTS

FOREWORD

Theological education has become an exotic and mysterious enterprise, at least to the general public. Most Americans seldom think of theological seminaries, if at all, and most conceive of them as something like graduate schools for religious professionals—teaching religious people to do whatever it is that religious people do.

Even inside the church, some confusion about theological education clouds the picture. Laypersons often assume that the seminary exists as a factory to turn out preachers — freshly minted and ready for immediate call —ready to be wound up and set in motion. The view from the pew is of interest, for it reveals the widespread impression that seminaries can do everything necessary for the preparation of ministers, even if the churches have given little attention to their own responsibility.

The most malignant confusion about theological education exists within the seminaries, and is *writ large* across the accrediting agencies and coalitions of seminaries. This is not a recent development. Writing in 1954, H. Richard Niebuhr found little clarity as he presented a survey of theological education in America: "Great confusion prevails in some quarters about theological education. What, it is asked, is the meaning of this ministry? For what purpose are we educating? The situation in some circles of theological educators seems to be similar to the one found among certain foreign missionaries and sponsors of foreign missions. They know what they are doing is important, but an understanding of the strategy of their work, a relatively precise and definite understanding of its meaning, is lacking."

Richard Niebuhr, like his brother Reinhold, was one of the paladins of American Protestantism at mid-century. The confusion he found among theological educators was, he noted, the same as that found among missionaries. They were not at all certain of their mission, their task, or their message.

Liberal Protestantism had lost confidence in the Bible, in the Gospel, and in the unique mission of the church. Progressively, its theological schools grew less and less theological; its missionaries grew less and less evangelistic; its bureaucracies grew larger and more powerful, and theological education became the engine for doctrinal dissipation, moral relativism, cultural revolution, and the death of once-great denominations.

If the evangelical church is going to respond to this crisis and confusion in theological education, we must go forward by first going backward. A fresh look at the lessons of church history would awaken us to the rich heritage of theological education that upholds the integrity of God's word and the supremacy of the Gospel. In the apostolic and post-apostolic period, Christian churches had to learn to how to educate their people. In fact, the New

Testament, echoing themes found in the Old Testament, honors the priority of the teaching ministry of the church.

The task of Christian teaching is woven throughout the Bible. In light of this, the church both became a school and it established schools. As even secular historians of education must admit, the western educational tradition is a Christian tradition and it owes its existence to the church. In early catechetical schools, the church taught its people the rudiments of the Christian faith. Early Christian academies arose out of the church.

The monasteries in the so-called "dark ages" kept the light of education alive. In these monasteries, men, whose names are known only to God, spent their lives copying documents no one cared any longer to read. God blessed their efforts by protecting their stewardship of those documents so that we might have them even now.

The university also owes its life to the church. The medieval structure of church authority established the university—an institution dedicated to study the unity of the "transcendentals," i.e. the good, the true, and the beautiful. At the core of this unity of all knowledge was the fact that God Himself is the source of knowledge and is the author of coherence in the world.

The current proletariat of the academic culture demands naturalism and excludes supernaturalism. All views are tolerated except any view that will not tolerate all things and call all things true. Postmodernism has degenerated into a circus of moral relativism, sexuality majors, gender feminism, semiotics, and fictionalized history.

Against this tide, the Christian scholar must engage the academy without compromising Christian truth, and without conforming to the prevailing worldview. This is no easy task, but it is a necessary one.

In an age of accelerated cultural, moral, and intellectual change, we must be sober and clear-minded regarding the task of education. Authentic Christian education, if it is to be recovered in this generation, must be characterized by doctrine and the pursuit of a comprehensive Christian worldview. It must be marked by diligence and academic excellence. It must refuse to follow the fads of the day and the moral relativism of our culture. It must raise up a generation of Christian counter-revolutionaries.

To accomplish this task Christian educators and scholars must not only set a vision for faithful education in the future, we must look backward to the biblical foundations of true Christian education. We must look backward with a profound sense of appreciation and stewardship for the rich heritage we have inherited from the history of the church. This revised publication is a helpful resource to that end. *A Legacy of Religious Educators* will remind us of the incredible stewardship that has been placed into our hands by men who upheld the Word of God and the centrality of the Gospel as theological educators. These men—Augustine, Luther, Calvin, Edwards, and many others—remind us by the testimony of their lives that the task of theological education is both serious and profound.

Paul reminds us in Romans 12:1-2: "Do not be conformed to this world, but be transformed by the renewal of your mind, that by testing you may discern what is the will of God, what is good and acceptable and perfect."

Disciples of the Lord Jesus Christ must be thinkers whose minds are captive to the Word of God, and whose entire intellectual structure is shaped and determined by biblical truth. Our captivity to the Word of God is a scandal in the secular culture, and among the Christians enamored with that culture. The secular intellectuals are blind to their own intellectual captivity to the spirit of the age. We, on the other hand, must wear our captivity to the Word of God as a badge of intellectual honor and integrity.

This intellectual transformation is a spiritual reality meant to demonstrate the power and the wisdom of God even in the midst of a fallen world. This is our spiritual service of worship.

R. Albert Mohler, Jr.
The Southern Baptist Theological Seminary

INTRODUCTION

Developing a theology of education is an undertaking that is both simple and challenging at the same time. As an educator, I hope that my action in the classroom (wherever that is or however that may be defined) is rooted in scripture. Yet, I know that the intent of scripture was not to create a pedagogical textbook. The simplicity of developing a theology of education is that our task is explicitly laid out before us in the pages of scripture, therefore we can easily theologize about what is to be done. We are to "teach them to observe all the things that [Jesus] commanded" (Matt. 28:20); we should also "teach them diligently to [our] children" (Deut. 6:7); to those "weaned from the milk and take from the breast" (Is. 28:9-10). Cognitively this charge is a simple task to understand. We are to transmit the knowledge of our faith from one generation to the next and from mature to the immature; however, the challenge of this task comes in understanding how this is done *and* how it is done in a Christian-ly manner.

Admitting that this task is a challenge is by no means an attempt to discourage the attempt, rather our goal is encourage educators to recognize the worthiness of such a goal. A theology of education will look differently based on various factors such as the era in which an educator lived, their own personal education as well as their socioeconomic, religious, and personal background. Each of these factors will encourage an educator in a specific manner as they act or react to their own experiences. Therefore, Christian educators interpret and impart the Scripture according to the various contexts that surround their lives. This is why we have offered such a wide variety of educators to sample and set before students as examples (to an extent). In this way, we hope that students are able to find those who have come to the task of educating with a similar background/context and they can then translate the actions, disciplines, and experiences of these teachers to their own teaching framework. "Copying and pasting" a methodology from an earlier time and place is not our goal. Instead, we believe that what has worked in the pats can work again if an educator is committed to the task of cultural translation – that is the translating of the methods, means, and mechanisms for education from a previous era to their own.

Each author in this text has attempted to analyze the historical background and the theology of education for a specific religious educator. The historical background is biographical information the contextualized their life. Their theology of education is an attempt to analysis how theology informed their role as an educator. You will notice that the authors of each chapter vary just like the subjects of each chapter. Some of the educators explored here were professionally trained educators; however, many were more formally trained as theologians, pastors, or authors, and their theology of education was more of an implicitly developed understanding of how education *should* take place rather than a fully developed pedagogical treatise. Like the educators explored here, the authors chosen for this text are not all professionally trained educators; instead, some are philosophers, historians, theologians, and missiologists. However, their value and theological insights regarding the practice of education are of great benefit because they expand education beyond the walls of a classroom (which is similar to Moses' theology of education – as it takes place when a student sits, rises, lies down, and goes out c.f., Deut. 6). These authors will point out aspects of theology unique to each educator because education extends beyond formalized classroom experiences. Each author chosen here has wide experiences in formalized schooling, but their training is more than what took place in a classroom, and as you will see many of the educators surveyed here taught in locations primarily not contained in a classroom. Because each author has a unique educational background their approach to this task at hand will vary. I am sure that readers of this text will find themselves specifically drawn to chapters, authors, and approaches to analyzing an educators theology of education. This is part of the goal of this text to reveal to readers first how broadly an educator's theology can impact their role as an educator and secondly the extensive ways that can be used to analyze a theology of education.

CHOOSING THE EDUCATORS

It was a challenge and a task to choose educators to be explored in this text. History will judge the accuracy of this list and while it is not fully comprehensive we did attempt to analyze key educators throughout the major historical segments of church history. In weighing who to include and not include in this text we examined the following four aspects of an educator's influence on religious education. If an educator fit one of these categories then we considered them for inclusion and then balanced their historical value to the field of religious education: (1) we wanted the educator to introduce innovation(s) into the body of Christ that became influential on a wide scale, (2) we wanted educators who offered some sort of summarization to a movement that became influential, (3) their innovations were both qualitative in that they influenced both the thinking and action of Christians in general and quantitative in that they influenced a great number of people within the body of Christ, and lastly (4) the educator was acceptably recognized within the greater scope of religious education as an influential character within the field and by educators throughout church history. This meant that we needed to make difficult challenges about who to include and who to leave out of the text. Some of those we wanted to include, but were unable to include in order to keep the book at a manageable length were John Knox, Nikolaus Ludwig von Zinzendorf, Abraham Kuyper, Lois and Mary Lebar, J. Edwin Orr, Kenneth Kantzer, Paulo Freire, Kenneth Gangel, Ted Ward, John Westerhoff, James Fowler, and Howard Hendricks. Perhaps leaving these educators out of this text will inspire students to take up this charge and examine these educators on their own, through independent research.

RELIGIOUS EDUCATORS VS. CHRISTIAN EDUCATORS

We could have titled this book the historical and theological foundations of Christian education; however, we did not want to limit the text to only "Christian" educators. While the majority of educators would fall within a historically Christian description, there were a few authors that we felt like we must include to be comprehensive in the field and yet we as the editors would not inherently describe them as "Christian" educators. Those included that fit this mold are John Dewey and William James. Those not making this table of contents, but also perhaps fitting this description would be James Fowler and Paulo Freire.

In addition to this delimitation, we also did not want to open the table of contents to influential educators of a different religious background. There are many that have had significant impact in the world from other religious veins, but our interest lies specifically in Christian and "religious" educators of a Judeo-Christian worldview.

ORGANIZATION OF TEXT

There are six eras explored in this text. An attempt was made to find the major influences of an era that had something to offer in the history of education that was unique to their setting and time. As you read through you will either agree or disagree with our choice of educators, and we hope that this inspires students and readers to find additional educators of the church that have had profound impact and who need to be studied today so that we can benefit from their wisdom and insight.

In addition to this, we sought to have a similar outline to each chapter so that readers could expect uniformity of chapter organization. No two chapters are exact, but there is a rough outline that readers can expect. Each chapter begins with the historical background of the educator followed by the theology of education. Following the theology of education, we sought to explore the contributions that this educator gave to the field of education and religious education. These contributions were often contributions to the role of the teacher, the role of the learner, and the role of curriculum in the educative process; however, not all educators were explicit in each of these areas and so some chapters highlight one or two of these contributions while leaving out the remaining sections. Lastly, we have tried to include a primary source sample of each of the educators with regards to their views on education. Most of the chapters has a primary source sample as we think it is valuable for students to read the educators in their own words and language.

OUR CHALLENGE

We would like to challenge, you the reader, with one concluding thought. Find at least one educator in this book that can be used to inspire your ministry as you seek to take the Word of God and communicate it effectively in your world. When you find a kindred spirit in this text, search out their writings and work to read them in their own context. Use their history and success as inspiration as you seek God's calling on your life. Elmer has been involved with Christian education for over fifty years, Benjamin has just started his academic ministry in education over the past five years; however, we are both committed to spending the time the Lord has given us to shape, instruct, and disciple students so they are equipped to train the saints for the work of the ministry (Eph. 4:11-16). We want to challenge you to spend your lives in the same direction – invest in learning so that you may teach!

Soli Deo Gloria
Elmer L. Towns
Benjamin K. Forrest

PART I

Educators in Early Church through the Middle Ages

(A.D. 1-1500)

Education is integral to the life of the Christian church, just as it was to the Hebrew nation. According to the *Shema* of Deuteronomy, every Israelite was to be instructed in the law of God, given at Mt. Sinai: "And these words that I command you today shall be on your heart. You shall teach them diligently to your children, and shall talk of them when you sit in your house, and when you walk by the way, and when you lie down, and when you rise. You shall bind them as a sign on your hand, and they shall be as frontlets between your eyes. You shall write them on the doorposts of your house and on your gates." (6:6-9, ESV) Since the Christian church was born and nurtured in the Hebrew milieu, it is natural that the church strongly emphasize the ministry of teaching.

The apostle **Paul**, who claimed to have seen Jesus in the flesh (II Cor. 5:16), was first an evangelist who carried the Christian message throughout Asia Minor and finally to Rome, but he was also an educator concerned about second- and third-generation Christians. In one letter he challenges a pupil to replicate what he was taught saying, "What you have heard from me in the presence of many witnesses entrust to faithful men[a] who will be able to teach others also." (II Tim. 2:2, ESV). The Great Commission, for Paul, was an educational endeavor to pass on the revelation he received from Christ (Gal. 1:11-12) to future generations.

Early in the third century a catechumenal system of instruction was instituted by which converts were prepared for Christian baptism in a third-year course. These schools evolved into centers for the defense of the gospel and the training of young men for the ministry. **Augustine** (354-430), the bishop of Hippo who greatly influenced the doctrinal development of the Western church, was also a master of catechizing, an art which he demonstrated in his book *The First Catechetical Instructor*.

1

Christianity began as a seemingly obscure movement, one among many in the Roman world. Its object of reverence, Jesus Christ, had been put to death by the Roman government. That same government tried first to contain Christianity and then to destroy it through severe persecution. But the faith was spread by the early Christians, who fervently evangelized and then educated the heathen. Not only did Christianity survive, but in the first half of the fourth century, it was adopted as the official religion of the Roman Empire. While Christianity came to be overly identified with the empire and its civilization, it survived both. In 410 the city of Rome was burned and sacked, and in 476 the last of the Roman emperors was overthrown. In 496 Clovis, King of the Franks, was baptized. Thus began the era in which the Germans were the champions of the faith in the West.

The next one thousand years of church history, from 500 to 1500, saw a number of significant external developments, many of them related to the founding of Islam in Arabia in the early seventh century and to Islam's challenge to Christianity. Islamic armies occupied much of the Mediterranean world, including Palestine, during its first century of existence. The Crusades in the twelfth and thirteenth centuries were devoted primarily to freeing the Middle East from Islamic control, but the Ottoman Turks reestablished Islamic control in the fifteenth century. The most significant ecclesiastical development during this period was the division between Western and Eastern Christendom in 1054, and the exacerbation of that division during the Crusades. The British Isles were largely untouched by these developments, and it was on the island of Iona that an Irish monk, **Columba** (521-597), established a significant educational center which was at once a monastery and a training ground for foreign missionaries. Even more important theologically was the educational endeavors of **Anselm of Canterbury** (1033-1109) and the scholasticism of **Thomas Aquinas** (1225-1274). Scholasticism attempted to support Christian theology and to stem rising intellectual doubts about it with Greek — and particularly Aristotelian — philosophy and science. It attempted to bring Christianity into harmony with modern civilization. Scholasticism reached its apex in Aquinas, whose emphasis on reason as the interpreter of truth had a lasting impact on the course of Christian education.

CHAPTER 1

The Apostle Paul:

Educator of the Early Church

PHIL HOWARD &
STEVE WOODWORTH

The Apostle Paul

Paul was not a teacher by calling, but rather an educator by necessity. His ministry in the context of the early church was to impart the message that he received from Christ (Gal. 1:11-12), not only in the New Testament era, but to the church universal throughout all time and in all places. Paul was not a classical educator in the sense of having a fully developed pedagogy, but through his writings we can extrapolate valuable information regarding his beliefs about education and about passing the baton of faith to future generations.

CONSIDERING PAUL AS A RELIGIOUS EDUCATOR

The Apostle Paul was a notably educated man, given largely to his capacious religious, educational and cultural heritage. In fact, these three elements of his heritage were inextricably woven together. He was a Roman citizen by birth (Acts 22:27-28), enriched by elements of Greek culture and philosophy, and his religious heritage was worthy of boasting (Phil. 3:4-6). Paul's impressive heritage was most likely shaped at home and included extensive rabbinical schooling including, at least for a time, Gamaliel's influence.[1] This matrix of spiritual, cultural and educational experience was noteworthy at several levels. Not only was this heritage interpreted as important in Paul's mind, it was obvious that strategically invoking his background established his credibility in the minds of his audience, providing political and intellectual capital when needed (Acts 21: 37ff).

Paul's encounter with the resurrected Christ on the Road to Damascus (Acts 9) utterly reinterpreted this heritage. As important as Paul's early development was on his thoughts about educational philosophy and practice, the Damascus Road encounter caused him to re-evaluate his heritage in light of the surpassing greatness of knowing Christ Jesus (Phil. 3:8). In the fullest sense of the phrase, Paul was introduced to change of epic proportions on the Road to Damascus; in fact, a case can be made that he was not simply changed or even "converted" — he was transformed (Gal. 1:13-24). To press this point, it has been suggested that there are "at least three shades of meaning associated with conversion: (1) a gradual change of life that grows out of the past is an 'alteration'; (2) a sudden change of life that rejects the past and takes on a new direction is a 'conversion'; and (3) a cognitive change of life that reconceives the past is a 'transformation' […] No one would contest that what Paul experienced was a transformation."[2] Pazmino reinforces this point in suggesting that "The so-called Pauline paradigm as described by Luke in Acts 9:1-19, 22:1-23, and 26:1-23 emphasizes conversion as an event that is radical and life-transforming in nature."[3]

Corely's description of transformation as reconceptualizing the "cognitive change of life" is particularly insightful for Christian educators who interpret their role as addressing the deepest expressions of their own lives and those of their students. While Paul was not the only

---

[1] Richard N. Longenecker, "Paul" in *A History of Religious Educators*, ed. Elmer L. Towns (Grand Rapids: Baker Book House, 1985).

[2] Bruce Corley, "Interpreting Paul's Conversion – Then And Now" in *The Road From Damascus: The Impact of Paul's Conversion on His Life, Thought and Ministry*, ed. Richard N. Longenecker (Grand Rapids: Eerdmans, 1997), 15.

[3] Robert W. Pazmino, *Principles and Practices of Christian Education: An Evangelical Perspective* (Grand Rapids: Baker, 1992), 40.

biblical character confronted with such a life-transforming experience, he serves as a model of one who fully embraced the process of his own transformation. Interpreted metaphysically, Paul's Damascus Road encounter served as a catalyst for "an interior shift of the imagination, a radical reconceptualizing of reality ... This paradigm shift didn't create more reality; it made it possible for (him) to be adequate to far more of the reality already there."[4] Consequently, the impact of Paul's Damascus Road encounter cannot be overstated; it is important to point out that, "Men and women, at their deepest level, are motivated by metaphysical beliefs. They are willing to live and die for these convictions, and they desire to create educational environments in which these most basic beliefs will be taught."[5] A case can be made that, in the zeal of his early life, Paul was already willing to die for something. The Damascus Road served as an unanticipated, and initially uninvited, context for the most radical of shifts in what (who) Paul was willing to die and live for. Paul's capacity to say, "for me to live is Christ and to die is gain" (Phil. 1:21) is reflective of an educator's personal transformation and is a fundamental shift in what and how he would teach.

Thus, as an educator and leader, Paul's invocation of an entirely new set of metaphors, and specifically his use of the "father" metaphor, was ultimately birthed on the Damascus Road framed by this life-altering, radical re-conceptualizing of reality. Jesus of Nazareth, for whom Paul was now willing to live and die for shaped what, why, and how he taught. Consequently, Paul's meaningful self-depiction as the "father" of the Corinthian church, which were his "children" (I Cor. 4:14-15), intentionally conjured images of his familial commitment and responsibility toward them. Paul was always an educator, but after the Damascus Road he was an educator transformed.

PAUL AND TRANSFORMATIONAL EDUCATION

Some popular contexts see Paul's ministry as not concerned with seeing bad people become good or good people become better. Rather, the orienting value of his ministry was to help dead people become alive. From a spiritual and anthropological perspective, it is also significant that he intentionally identified himself with this transformative dynamic, "As for you, you were dead in your transgressions and sins in which you used to live […] *all of us* also lived among them at one time […] But, because of His great love for us, God who is rich in mercy, made us alive with Christ even when we were dead in our transgressions" (Eph. 2:1-2, 4-5).

---

[4] Eugene H. Peterson, *Under the Unpredictable Plant: An Exploration in Vocational Holiness* (Grand Rapids: Eerdmans, 1992), 175.

[5] George Knight, *Philosophy and Education: An Introduction in Christian Perspective* (Berrien Springs: Andrew University Press, 1998), 17.

Similarly, Paul presents his own transformation as a model to be emulated, stating that he has been crucified in Christ, that he no longer lives, and that his life is now characterized as "Christ lives in me" (Gal. 2:20). Thus, Paul's personal, spiritual transformation led to a transformation of his educational intent. Paul's objective was not to present simply a quantitative increase of information about Jesus of Nazareth, but to facilitate a qualitative reorientation in a person's relationship with God as Father, Son, and Holy Spirit. The distinction is significant; the former perspective would be akin to "cognitive dump," an educational orientation practiced in many Christian contexts, including many churches, which is primarily concerned with transmitting more information to the learner. In this context, the educational dynamic is transactional in nature; an exchange of information is made in which the teacher, who is active, communicates the information in some fashion, and the learner, who is essentially passive, simply receives that information. On the other hand, the latter perspective reflects a movement, incorporating the active engagement of both the teacher and learner toward a complex and inner transformation. Thus, from the standpoint of Christian education, Paul's command to "Be transformed, by the renewing of your minds" (Rom. 12:2) involved the active engagement of Paul as the teacher, the readers as the learners, and the work of the Holy Spirit in the teacher, learners, and the full expression of the transformative process. In a phrase, Paul's new educational mission involved the ongoing, integrative transformation of one's identity in Christ.

His definitional concept of transformation stemmed from the Greek word, *metamorphoo*. Elsewhere, this word, suggests an outward, visible change, as in the case of Jesus' transfiguration (Matt. 17:2); however, in this context the nature of the "transformation" to which Paul refers is "invisible to the physical eye,"[6] suggesting an inner, qualitative, transformative change, a "continuing process of transformation."[7] For Paul, this transformation was a normative aspect of the Christian life.

While this transformation is what Paul was after as an educator, it is clear that he respected and advocated the educator's cooperative relationship with the student and the Holy Spirit. As such, Christian education is not a transaction between two parties, one active (the educator) and one passive (the learner). Properly understood, the learner is an active participant in this relationship, not a passive receiver, and the educator brings his or her intellectual, spiritual, and emotional engagement to foster learning. This is precisely what

---

[6] William F. Arndt, and F. Wilbur Gingrich, *A Greek-English Lexicon of the New Testament and Other Early Christian Literature,* 4th ed. (Chicago: The University of Chicago Press, 1968), 513.

[7] Collin Brown, ed., *The New International Dictionary of New Testament Theology*, Vol. 3 (Grand Rapids: Zondervan Publishing House, 1971), 864.

occurred on the Damascus Road; Paul, at that point Saul, was anything but passively involved in those moments; he was an active participant cooperating with the intent of the "educator" (the resurrected Christ). Paul's early life development, reoriented by his transformative experience on the Damascus Road, forged a deep commitment to, and often an intimate relationship with, the individuals he taught to be ministry leaders. Consequently, Paul believed that Christian education involves an intentional relationship among teachers and learners in facilitating the transformative learning of each person in a particular context. In this transformative context, everyone learns — student and teacher. This perspective of Christian education is both powerful and risky, for "When people critically examine their habitual expectations, revise them, and act on the revised point of view, transformative learning occurs."[8] Thus, as an educator, Paul demonstrates for us a sobering dependence on the Holy Spirit, and at the same time a personal and often sacrificial commitment to his students. It is for these reasons that the familial metaphor of "father" employed by Paul captures his educational intent and methodologies.

THEOLOGICAL HERMENEUTIC: CHRISTIAN COMMUNITY AS FAMILY

Due to the sheer breadth of Paul's theological writing, it would be difficult, if not nearly impossible, to pinpoint a central theological hermeneutic which framed his pedagogy. Strong cases could be made for his emphasis on the resurrection of Jesus Christ (1 Cor. 15), the sovereignty of God (Rom. 9), justification by faith (Eph. 2:8), or his foundational belief in the sinfulness of mankind (Rom. 3:23). While space prevents us from exploring each of these themes comprehensively, suffice to mention here that we recognize each and every one of these options as entirely orthodox as well as potentially correct observations in regards to Paul's theological hermeneutic. Nonetheless, for the sake of this particular chapter we would like to suggest that an often overlooked theological hermeneutic which shaped Paul's pedagogy was his firm belief in the familial nature of Christian commitment and ongoing formation as evidenced by his strong and consistent reliance on familial metaphors to describe the Christian life and his own role as a leader and teacher.

To highlight the unique role metaphors often play in our lives, Erazim Kohak notes rather dramatically that metaphors serve to "shape the context of our experience as a meaningful whole, deciding in the process not only what is primary and what derivative, but also who we ought to

---

[8] Patricia Cranton, *Understanding and Promoting Transformative Learning: A Guide for Educators of Adults,* 2nd ed. (San Francisco: Jossey-Bass, 2006), 19.

be and how we ought to act ... a metaphor is a mask that molds the wearer's face."[9] Clearly biblical writers understood this same principle and employed a myriad of metaphors to describe various roles in the early church, including shepherd, ambassador, witness, athlete, architect, and mother (Cf. Jer 3:15; 2 Cor 5:20; Acts 1:8; 2 Tim 4:7; I Cor 3:10; 1 Thess 2:7). David Bennett highlights the dominant role of the family metaphor above each of these when he refers to it as "one of the most common" and "one of the most important metaphors in the New Testament."[10] The Apostle Paul clearly understood the potential potency of metaphors and employed them frequently, borrowing from the metaphors listed above and combining them with the use of the father metaphor as well to describe his role among the fledgling churches (1 Cor 4:15; 1 Thess 2:11). The term "father" would prove to be so potent and apt for the role that it would survive for centuries as a term applied to the religious leaders of these new faith communities and employed well into the early centuries of the Christian movement by the church fathers.

TEACHERS AS TUTORS AND FATHERS

Paul emphasized the paternal aspect inherent in his role as a teacher through a number of additional familiar metaphors that he employed to demonstrate the unique identity- forming nature of the relationship between teacher and student. In his letter to the Corinthians, Paul embraces highly familiar household terminology when he writes to the church at Corinth, "For if you were to have countless tutors in Christ, yet you would not have many fathers" (1 Cor. 4:15). Here Paul employs a unique familial metaphor with direct ties to education when he contrasts his own role among the Corinthians to that of a *paidagogos* ("tutor"). In Hellenistic culture a *paidagogos*, often translated as "guardian" or "tutor," was an older slave in a household who was charged with the task of overseeing the education of a child.[11] The *paidagogos* was appointed by a child's father and was responsible for the accompaniment of a child to school each day where the *paidagogos* would assist the child in his or her educational endeavors.[12] While the *paidagogos* played a significant role in a child's life, they were often portrayed in art and literature as harsh taskmasters who were viewed less than favorably throughout Greco-Roman culture.

---

[9] Erazim Kohak, "Of Dwelling and Wayfaring: A Quest for Metaphors," in Leroy S. Rouner, ed., *The Longing for Home*, Boston University Studies in Philosophy and Religion, vol. 17 (Notre Dame: University of Notre Dame Press, 1996), 31.

[10] David W. Bennett, *Metaphors of Ministry: Biblical Images for Leaders and Followers* (Eugene: Wipf & Stock, 2004), 73.

[11] Gordon Fee, *The First Epistle to the Corinthians, NICNT* (Grand Rapids: Eerdmans, 1987), 185.

[12] Leon Morris, *The First Epistle of Paul to the Corinthians, TNTC* (Grand Rapids: Eerdmans, 1958), 83.

In 1 Cor. 4, Paul utilizes the term *myrios* ("ten thousand") as a hyperbolic phrase contrasting an innumerable number of assistants in the faith to the uniqueness of his own, exclusive role, as the one who has brought them to faith in Christ, their spiritual progenitor. Despite the fact that a *paidagogos* spent significant time with the children under their care, his influence was always subordinate to that of a father who always retained ultimate responsibility for his children's welfare. In the same way, Paul's founding of the church in Corinth places him in a role unique among anyone else who may assist the Corinthians in their spiritual journey, permitting him the opportunity to explicitly assert what he has already said implicitly, "for in Christ Jesus I became your father through the gospel (1 Cor. 4:15)."

Bengt Holmberg asserts that Paul makes reference to his parental role in every one of his letters except the letter to the Romans to "express the fact that he had begotten them or given them life by the transmission of the Gospel of Christ."[13] Walter Orr and James Walther agree adding, "By establishing the new church in a pagan city the apostle became the father of the believers; he was the only one who could actually claim that relation to them. This fatherly authority gave him the right to instruct them, and it also laid on them an obligation to heed what he said, wrote and did."[14] Paul as a teacher had significant influence on the personal identity formation of those he taught.

METHODOLOGY

Much in the same way that determining a single or obvious theological hermeneutic for Paul is a fairly elusive task for scholars, so too is the ability to pinpoint a defining educational methodology. As Richard N. Longenecker rightly observes, "It would be difficult to assert that the apostle Paul had a consciously and precisely formulated philosophy of education. Indeed, the very expression would have sounded foreign to him, but a system of educational approach is found in his writings. As a Hebrew, Paul thought more theologically than philosophically, and his teaching was more a declaration of faith than the proposal of a theory."[15]

Despite this difficulty, inherent in any discussion of Paul and his particular pedagogical views, his use of familial metaphors, and the father metaphor in particular, does suggest specific, relevant educational methods for Christian educators including instruction, identity formation, and modeling.

---

[13] Bengt Holmberg, *Paul and Power: The Structure of Authority in the Primitive Church as Reflected in the Pauline Epistles* (Philadelphia: Fortress Press, 1978), 78.

[14] William F. Orr and James Arthur Walther, *1 Corinthians: A New Translation*, AB (Garden City: Doubleday and Company, 1976), 182.

[15] Longenecker, "Paul," 26.

ROLE OF INSTRUCTION

While the responsibility to procreate was foremost among the responsibilities of a Jewish father, Philo also notes that parents are: Also in the position of instructors because they impart to their children from the earliest years everything that they themselves may happen to know, and give them instruction not only in various branches of knowledge which they impress upon their young minds, but also in the most essential questions of what to choose and avoid, namely to choose virtues and avoid vices and the activities to which they lead.[16]

Despite the fact that many of the duties of parenthood were shared by both parents, instruction was a specific and primary responsibility of the father in the Jewish community.[17] As W.A. Strange observes, "to secure the future of the Jewish community it was not enough to have children; they had to be educated in the ancestral faith. It was a proud and justifiable boast of the Jewish people that their education of the young was unsurpassed in its thoroughness and comprehensiveness."[18] Likewise, Josephus also claimed that the instruction of its children was a distinguishing characteristic of the Jewish tradition considering it "the most important duty in life."[19] This parental priority on instruction is encompassed in the Deuteronomical mandate to:

> Fix these words of mine in your hearts and minds; tie them as symbols on your hands and bind them on your foreheads. Teach them to your children, talking about them when you sit at home and when you walk along the road, when you lie down and when you get up. Write them on the doorframes of your houses and on your gates, so that your days and the days of your children may be many in the land that the LORD swore to give your forefathers, as many as the days that the heavens are above the earth. (Deut 11:18-21)

It is clear from his writing that Paul recognized this unique responsibility he possessed as a spiritual father to instruct his church. Distinguishing himself from among the thousands of teachers the church would have throughout its life, his words carried greater weight due

---

[16] Philo, *Spec. Leg.*, 2.228 in Trevor Burke, *Family Matters: A Socio-Historical Study of Kinship Metaphors in 1 Thessalonians, JSNT* 247 (New York: T&T Clark International, 2003), 51.

[17] Trevor Burke, *Family Matters: A Socio-Historical Study of Kinship Metaphors in 1 Thessalonians, JSNT* 247 (New York: T&T Clark International, 2003), 58. See also Daniel J. Estes, *Hear, My Son: Teaching & Learning in Proverbs 1-9* (Grand Rapids: Eerdmans, 1997).

[18] W. A. Strange, *Children in the Early Church: Children in the Ancient World, the New Testament and the Early Church* (Waynesboro: Paternoster Press, 1996), 13

[19] Josephus, *Contra Apion*, 1.60-61 in Trevor Burke, *Family Matters*, 52.

to his role in the congregation's creation (1 Cor 4:15). Again, in ancient society, while the mother's role was synonymous with producing, caring for, and nurturing offspring,[20] the responsibility of instruction was laid primarily on the shoulders of the father. Given such realities, it is not surprising that in his writing "Paul understands his didactic role as a paternal obligation, one that is carried out in the tenderness of a Greek father."[21] In describing the way in which Paul instructed the community, he discusses both his methods as well as his manner.

In his letter to the Thessalonians, Paul points out that he did not merely teach to the masses but to individuals, "each one of you" (1 Thess. 2:11). Leon Morris points out the significance of this by writing, "In other words, he had not contented himself with giving the message in general terms to the Thessalonian public at large, but had been sufficiently interested in individuals to bring it home to them one by one, evidently in private."[22] This insight casts further light on Paul's inference to himself as a father, for in his genuine and tender care for each member of the community, Paul was not content to teach them as a philosopher would in the city square but as father would his own children, taking into consideration the uniqueness of each child and adapting his teaching accordingly.

Second, Paul reveals the manner of his teaching by the use of three verbs *exhorting, comforting and imploring*. The first of the three verbs *parakaleo* ("*exhorting*"), is the one which Paul uses the most frequently throughout his letters.[23] While used in isolation, the word *parakaleo* would normally carry the weight of exhortation and instruction associated with urging a person to follow a specific code of moral behavior,[24] here Paul joins it with the verb *paramytheomai* ("*encouraging*") to emphasize that Paul's exhortations were designed as tools of "comforting" or "consoling."[25]

Paul's goal was not merely to command obedience from the Thessalonians, but to also empower them to be obedient. In this, Paul does not shrink back from the seriousness of his message, but purposefully joins the two verbs in order to suggest one who is comforting in times of distress, "which is in keeping the 'father and his own children' imagery with which the sentence began"[26] (1 Thess. 2:11).

---

[20] Joseph H. Hellerman, *The Ancient Church as Family* (Minneapolis: Augsburg Fortress Press, 2001), 33-35.

[21] Gene L. Green, *The Letters to the Thessalonians, PNTC* (Grand Rapids: Eerdmans, 2002), 135.

[22] Leon Morris, *1 and 2 Thessalonians: An Introduction and Commentary, TNTC* (Grand Rapids: Eerdmans, 1984), 60.

[23] Gordon D. Fee, *The First and Second Letters to the Thessalonians, NICNT* (Grand Rapids: Eerdmans, 2009), 82.

[24] Green, *Letters to the Thessalonians*, 135.

[25] F.F. Bruce, *1 & 2 Thessalonians, WBC Vol. 45* (Nashville: Thomas Nelson, 1982), 36.

[26] Green, *Thessalonians*, 82.

Finally, Paul uses the word *martyromai* ("imploring"). Paul uses this verb sparingly in his letters, appearing only here and two additional times in all of his letters (Gal 5:3, Eph 4:17). It is undoubtedly the strongest of the three verbs listed here and while there is little agreement regarding the precise meaning of this word,[27] scholars do agree that the essence of it carries with it the notion of insistence or requirement.[28]

Scholars agree that by joining together these three separate aspects of instruction, exhorting, encouraging and imploring, Paul intended for his audience to identify a single, unified thought that conveyed Paul's commitment to the overall duties of a father to his children in keeping them on the path of righteousness.[29]

Paul ultimately recognizes his responsibility to instruct his congregations as a call to reorient them into a new reality in which old definitions, loyalties, and paradigms are replaced and reorganized by the radical message of the gospel. In essence, one of Paul's foremost responsibilities to the communities he founded was to reorient them toward their new identities in Christ.

MODELING AND IMITATION

A second aspect of Paul's methodology was his continual stress on the importance of teachers serving as models for their students. It was understood that Jewish fathers were expected to serve as role models for their children. According to Hasidic teaching, "Every Jew should conduct himself in such a way that his sons will rejoice to say: 'The God of my Father.'"[30] In addition, "The Law orders that they [i.e. children] be taught to read, and shall learn both the laws and deeds of their forefathers, in order that they may imitate the latter."[31] Particularly as it relates to education and leadership development, this aspect of fathering was one that had clear implications for leadership within the larger community. Not only were children expected to imitate their fathers, but members of the community were also expected to imitate their leaders. Burke states, "The imitation of the father is one that is specifically tied and extended to the imitation of the 'fathers,' that is, the fathers of the people or nation."[32] These observations bring clarity to Paul's own desire to be imitated by his followers (1 Cor

[27] Ibid.

[28] Ibid., 136.

[29] Fee, *Thessalonians*, 82.

[30] Louis Newman, *Hasidic Anthology: Tales and Teaching of the Hasidim* (New York: Shocken Books, 1963), 117.

[31] Josephus, *Apion* 1.204 in Trevor Burke, *Family Matters,* 50.

[32] Ibid.

4:16). The responsibility of the leader to live a life worth imitating is the noteworthy emphasis here instead of the obligation of the followers.

It is instructive to note that the emphasis here is not as much on the obligation of the followers as it is on the responsibility of the leader to live a life worth imitating. As noted earlier, Paul is not merely a teacher among thousands, he is the unique teacher who has founded the Corinthian church and to whom the community can trace their birth. Far from instilling fear, Paul's claim of paternity is intended to be a call to return to their true identity as heirs to the kingdom. In essence Paul draws attention to the fact that the behavior of the Corinthians is not fitting as members of his family. If they are his children, their values and behavior should match his own.

What Paul states implicitly by use of the father metaphor in 1 Corinthians 4:15 he states explicitly in v. 16 when he exhorts the Corinthians to "be imitators of me." Despite the fact that a Western audience may easily misconstrue Paul's words here as egotistical, his first-century audience would have quickly understood his true intention. As Joseph Hellerman writes, "In contrast to contemporary American practices, the ideal son in the ancient world was typically expected to adopt his father's general lifestyle, including, among other things, his father's religious orientation, means of a livelihood, and place of residence."[33] For Paul to refer to himself as a father and simultaneously call on the community he has begotten to imitate him is nearly redundant, but fitting. To be a child in the first century was to follow in the footsteps of one's father. As Clement of Alexandria once wrote, "The man who has produced of himself one like him has achieved fulfillment – even more when he sees the other having followed in his footsteps too, in other words, when he has established a child in the same natural place as the father."[34]

Paul's exhortation that the Corinthians "imitate" him (I Cor. 4:16) reflects the complementary dynamics of informal learning portrayed in Deuteronomy 6:4-9 and perspectives found in contemporary social learning theory. Deuteronomy 6 is instrumental in illustrating the power of exposure of learners to mature role models, in this case parents, in non-structured yet highly intentional contexts that educate through "teachable moments." Similarly, classic social learning theory suggests that a learner's "capacity to learn by observation enables him to acquire large, integrated units of behavior by example without having to build up the patterns gradually by tedious trial and error [...] Much social learning occurs on the basis of

[33] Hellerman, *The Ancient Church as Family*, 102.
[34] Clement of Alexandria, *Stromata* 2.139.6.

casual or studied observation of exemplary models."[35] Framed in the context of Deuteronomy 6, social learning occurs when parents, for instance, intentionally or unintentionally model to their child faithful prayer in a moment of difficulty. Learning occurs not due to a class on prayer, or going through a prescribed curriculum related to prayer; rather, the child develops his own pattern of prayer by his observation of parents as exemplars of the faith.

Furthermore, socialization is premised on an integrated view of life. Thus, while involving a concern for behavioral change, Paul's emphasis on imitation is rooted in passing on biblical character through intentionally watching and interacting with him as a transformed role model, albeit at times from a distance. Many contemporary educators understand the correlation between the modeling of the teacher and socialization of the learner. This is a potentially transformative relationship in the educational process. "In fact, socialization is often the most life-changing learning format in any setting."[36] This is not to minimize the role of instruction as discussed above, however, if nothing else, the power of example is demonstrated in the observation that "Most of the behaviors people display are learned, either deliberately or inadvertently, through the influence of example" […] indeed "Some complex behaviors, of course, can only be produced through the influence of models."[37]

Paul was not hesitant to point to himself as an exemplary model. In fact, he invited the kind of "studied observation" referenced above in his relationship with the church leaders whom he was developing. In addition to his encouragement that the Corinthians "imitate" him, he implored them to "Follow my example, as I follow the example of Christ" (I Cor. 11:1), and he invited the church in Philippi to scrutinize his life as others had already done, "Join with others in following my example, brothers, and take note of those who live according to the pattern we gave you" (Phil. 3: 17). Reinforcing his strongly stated instruction against idleness, Paul once again unflinchingly entreats the Thessalonian believers to follow his example (II Thess. 3: 6-9).

In support of this sentiment, Derek Prime and Alistair Begg state emphatically, "*Whatever else* a shepherd and teacher provides for God's people, he is to give them an example to follow."[38] Later, Paul would echo this same mandate to his successor Timothy when he charged him to conduct himself in such a way so as to, "show yourself an example of those who believe" (1 Tim 4:12).

---

[35] Albert Bandura, *Social Learning Theory* (New York: General Learning Corporation, 1971).

[36] Michael J. Anthony, "The Nature of Theology and Education," in *A Theology for Christian Education,* eds. James R. Estep, Michael J. Anthony, and Gregg R. Allison (Nashville: B&H Publishing Group, 2008), 17.

[37] Ibid, 5.

[38] Derek Prime and Alistair Begg, *On Being Pastor: Understanding Our Calling and Work* (Chicago: Moody Publishers, 2004), 35 (emphasis mine).

Perhaps to the ears of a modern audience, the thought of a teacher urging others to imitate their lives is suspicious at best and at worst, megalomaniacal. Yet, as the Stoic philosopher Seneca, a contemporary of the Apostle Paul, once wrote, wise people seek the counsel of those who "teach us by their lives, who tell us what to do, then prove it by practice, who show us what we should avoid, and then are never caught doing that which they have ordered us to avoid."[39]

IDENTITY FORMATION

Finally, Paul embraces his role as a father to the Thessalonian community by recognizing that a primary aspect of his pastoral responsibilities is to establish and reinforce his congregation's identity. In the close of the second chapter of his first letter to the Thessalonians, Paul calls on his community to "walk in a manner worthy of the God who calls you into His own kingdom and glory" (v.12). As Charles Wanamaker asserts, "perhaps the most important contribution of Paul to the formation of the Christian community in Thessalonica was that he gave his converts a new sense of identity as converts."[40] According to Wayne Meeks, Paul accomplished this through his use of language that spoke of both "belonging" and "separation."[41]

Of particular importance is Paul's emphasis of identity through belonging. By way of Christian conversion, Paul, like Jesus, uses familial metaphors to highlight a convert's identity as a member of a new spiritual family. In order to do so, Paul consistently refers to members in the Christian community throughout each of his letters as "children," (cf. Rom 8:14; 2 Cor 6:13; Gal 3:7, 4:7) "brothers" (cf. 2 Cor 1:1; 1 Cor 1:1; 1 Thess. 3:2) and "sisters" (Rom 16:1).

As noted earlier, both Jewish and Greco-Roman cultures affirmed key aspects of the father role, including the conviction that the patriarch was the one to whom the primary responsibility of socialization fell. For the Apostle Paul, this meant that an essential aspect of his apostolic duty was to orient his new churches toward a fuller understanding of their new citizenship within the Kingdom of God. Just as parents were charged with the responsibility of initiating their children into the cultural, political, and religious life of the Roman or Jewish cultures, so now Paul was charged, as a spiritual father, to *re*-establish the values and perspectives of members of the new Christian movement.

---

[39] Seneca, *Epistulae morales ad Lucilium*, 52.

[40] Charles Wanamaker, *The Epistles to the Thessalonians: A Commentary on the Greek Text*, *NIGTC* (Grand Rapids: Eerdmans, 1990), 16.

[41] Wayne Meeks, *The First Urban Christians: The Social World of the Apostle Paul* (New Haven: Yale University Press, 1983), 84-96.

In every religious conversion, individuals are confronted by a radically new worldview in which former perspectives of identity, purpose, and meaning are imbued with new definitions and implications for life. "In a religious conversion experience a person becomes engaged with a new set of significant others who possess an alternative understanding of life and participate in an alternative social world with its own distinctive knowledge, roles, values, and attitudes."[42]

Certainly this was no less true for the community at Thessalonica who had been significantly influenced by their Jewish upbringing. Faced with ongoing persecution and hedonistic temptations, Paul reminds his audience that they are indeed a peculiar people who have been "called" by God himself into new relationships, with God, with each other, and with the world. The church at Thessalonica, Paul reminds them, is invited into a new kingdom where they are privileged to behold God in all his glory. Within this new kingdom framework Paul's use of the father metaphor makes the most sense. In his commentary on Thessalonians, Gene Green notes, "These new believers were at variance with their compatriots in the city (2:14) and the conflicts likely descended to the members of their families as well. Those who are alienated and outcast now find their identity in this new family of God, both in Thessalonica and in other cities of Macedonia (4:9-10), with the "mothers/fathers" who love them, the apostles themselves."[43]

In God's kingdom, relationships are reorganized. Under God's new economy, kinship is defined less by blood than by fidelity to the King (cf. Matt 10:37; 12:50) causing "the early Christians to self-consciously define the church as a surrogate kinship group [that] implicitly demand[ed] of community members a loyalty that excluded every competing social entity in the surrounding culture — including a convert's natural family."[44]

CONCLUSION

As an Apostle of Jesus Christ, Paul provides us with tremendous insight into the impact his relationship with Jesus had on what, who, and why he taught as he did. Inspired by the Holy Spirit, he provided a theological framework to inform and guide the beliefs, practices, and

---

[42] Charles Wannamaker, "Like a Father Treats His Own Children," *JTSA* 92 (September 1995), 46-55.

[43] Gene L. Green, *The Letters to the Thessalonians*, PNTC (Grand Rapids: Eerdmans, 2002), 129. See also Abraham J. Malherbe, "Paul and the Thessalonians: The Philosophic Tradition of Pastoral Care," *The Anchor Bible*, vol. 32B (New York and London: Doubleday, 2000), 48-52.

[44] Hellerman, *Ancient Church as Family*, 24.

values of the first century church. He humbly, yet intentionally, opened his life for scrutiny and as a model for what he believed to be normative Christian living. And, through instruction and modeling, he encouraged new believers to embrace the impact of their radically reconceptualized kingdom identity all-the-while living in this world "in order to please God" (I Thess. 4:1). As one who experienced this same transformation, and now served Jesus Christ with ardent commitment, Paul became "all things to all men so that by all possible means I might save some" (I Cor 9:22). Yet, perhaps most significantly, as an apostle and educator, he was a "father" to many. In that regard, Paul serves as an exemplar of a Christian educator at his best.

PRIMARY SOURCE SAMPLE: 2 TIMOTHY 4:1-8 (ESV)

I charge you in the presence of God and of Christ Jesus, who is to judge the living and the dead, and by his appearing and his kingdom: preach the word; be ready in season and out of season; reprove, rebuke, and exhort, with complete patience and teaching. For the time is coming when people will not endure sound teaching, but having itching ears they will accumulate for themselves teachers to suit their own passions, and will turn away from listening to the truth and wander off into myths. As for you, always be sober-minded, endure suffering, do the work of an evangelist, fulfill your ministry.

For I am already being poured out as a drink offering, and the time of my departure has come. I have fought the good fight, I have finished the race, I have kept the faith. Henceforth there is laid up for me the crown of righteousness, which the Lord, the righteous judge, will award to me on that Day, and not only to me but also to all who have loved his appearing.

BIBLIOGRAPHY

Arndt, William F., and F. Wilbur Gingrich. *A Greek-English Lexicon of the New Testament and Other Early Christian Literature.* 4th ed. Chicago: The University of Chicago Press, 1968.

Bandura, Albert. *Social Learning Theory.* New York: General Learning Corporation, 1971.

Bennett, David W. *Metaphors of Ministry: Biblical Images for Leaders and Followers.* Eugene, OR: Wipf & Stock, 2004.

Brown, Collin, ed. *The New International Dictionary of New Testament Theology.* Grand Rapids: Zondervan, 1971.

Bruce, F. F. *Paul, Apostle of the Heart Set Free.* Grand Rapids, MI: Eerdmans, 1977.

Burke, Trevor. *Family Matters: A Socio-Historical Study of Kinship Metaphors in 1 Thessalonians, JSNT* 247. New York, T&T Clark International, 2003.

Corley, Bruce. "Interpreting Paul's Conversion – Then And Now." In *The Road From Damascus: The Impact of Paul's Conversion on His Life, Thought and Ministry,* edited by Richard N. Longenecker, 1-18. Grand Rapids: Eerdmans 1997.

Estes, Daniel J. *Hear, My Son: Teaching & Learning in Proverbs 1-9.* Grand Rapids: Eerdmans, 1997.

Hellerman, Joseph H. *The Ancient Church as Family.* Minneapolis, MN: Augsburg Fortress Press, 2001.

Holmberg, Bengt. *Paul and Power: The Structure of Authority in the Primitive Church as Reflected in the Pauline Epistles.* Philadelphia, PA: Fortress Press, 1978.

Knight, George. *Philosophy and Education: An Introduction in Christian Perspective.* Berrien Springs: Andrews University Press, 1998.

Longenecker, Richard N. "Paul." In *A History of Religious Educators*, edited by Elmer L. Towns, 39-53. Grand Rapids: Baker Book House, 1975.

McRay, John. *Paul: His Life and Teaching.* Grand Rapids: Baker, 2003.

Meeks, Wayne. *The First Urban Christians: The Social World of the Apostle Paul.* New Haven: Yale University Press, 1983.

Pazmino, Robert W. *Principles and Practices of Christian Education: An Evangelical Perspective.* Grand Rapids: Baker, 1992.

Peterson, Eugene H. *Under the Unpredictable Plant: An Exploration in Vocational Holiness.* Grand Rapids: Eerdmans, 1992.

Strange, W. A. *Children in the Early Church: Children in the Ancient World, the New Testament and the Early Church.* Waynesboro, GA: Paternoster Press, 1996.

Thiselton, Anthony C. *The Living Paul: An Introduction to the Apostle's Life and Thought.* Downers Grove: IVP Academic, 2009.

Wenham, David. *Paul: Follower of Jesus or Founder of Christianity?* Grand Rapids: Eerdmans, 1995.

Zuck, Roy B. *Teaching as Paul Taught.* Grand Rapids: Baker, 1998.

CHAPTER 2

Augustine:
Teacher as Mentor

EDWARD L. SMITHER

Augustine of Hippo (354-430)

Augustine wrote at the end of the Patristic Era of church history, laying a foundation of theology that would permanently influence Western Christianity. As the Roman Empire began falling apart, Augustine wrote the *City of God,* indicating that the Roman Catholic Church was distinctly different from the earthly city of Rome. He uniquely identified the church with the doctrine of Trinity, as expressed in the councils of Nicaea and Constantinople. However, many Protestants have looked to Augustine during the Protestant Reformation because of his teaching on original sin, salvation, divine grace, eternal security, and predestination. No other theologian from the Patristic Era extended his influence into the Middle Ages and beyond as Augustine did.

HISTORICAL BACKGROUND

"I feed you on what I am fed on myself ... I set food before you from the pantry which I too live on."[1] In many ways, these words from a sermon that Augustine (354-430) preached in the church at Hippo toward the end of his life capture his approach to Christian education. Following his conversion, Augustine was enamored with the Scriptures and spent the last forty years of his life studying them, writing about them, and communicating them to others through preaching and teaching. Though Augustine developed into a teacher for others — including the faithful at Hippo, Christian correspondents, and other ordained church leaders — he remained a lifelong learner. Augustine was a mentor who always remained a disciple.[2]

In this chapter, I will argue that Augustine was an innovative Christian educator who left his mark on the church and many Christian teachers who followed him. Following a brief biographical sketch and a discussion of his biblical hermeneutics, which certainly shaped his views on education, I will describe his approach to Christian teaching. Building on these forms, I will conclude by articulating the major points of his philosophy of education.

BACKGROUND

Aurelius Augustinus was born in 354 in Tagaste (modern Souk Ahras, Algeria) — a small, insignificant town in Roman Africa. Though ethnically Punic-Berber, Augustine was culturally Roman and spoke only Latin. His father Patricius, a functionary in the local Roman administration at Tagaste, was an adherent to the traditional Roman deities, though he converted to Christianity at the end of his life. Augustine's mother Monica was a committed Christian who instructed her son informally in the Scriptures during Augustine's formative years. Though his parents differed on religious views for much of his formative years, they agreed that the key to Augustine's future was education and they sacrificed to send him away to study. Eventually, Augustine completed his studies in rhetoric (communication) in Carthage, after which he taught the art of speaking in Carthage, Rome, and eventually Milan.

While in Milan, Augustine, who had been a hearer in the Manichean sect for

---

[1] Augustine, *Sermon,* 339.3.4. Unless otherwise noted, all English translations of Augustine's works in this chapter will be taken from the *Works of Augustine (WSA)* series (Hyde Park, NY: New City Press, 1990-2013).

[2] Cf. Edward L. Smither, *Augustine as Mentor: A Model for Preparing Spiritual Leaders* (Nashville: B&H Academic, 2008), 222-32.

nine years, came under the influence of Bishop Ambrose's (337-397) preaching and was converted to Christianity in late 386. He was baptized on Easter of the following year. Resolved to renounce the world and serve God, Augustine resigned his teaching post in Milan and returned to Tagaste in 388, intending to live out his days in the "holy leisure" *(otium sanctum)* of study, prayer, and contemplation.

Augustine's life course drastically changed in 391 when he agreed to be ordained as a priest at the church of Hippo (modern Annaba) in response to the urging of Valerius, the church's aging bishop. In 395, Augustine was ordained as co-bishop of Hippo and then in 396 or 397, he became the church's sole bishop when Valerius passed away. Though Augustine's intent had been to pursue a life of monastic withdrawal in community with like-minded friends, he clearly took the call to ministry seriously and remained Hippo's bishop until his death in 430. That said, Augustine continued to live as a monk while serving as a priest and bishop. Upon his ordination in 391, he established a monastery in Hippo and when he became bishop, he turned the bishop's house into a monastery for the clergy. In this way, Augustine joined the ranks of a growing group of fourth and fifth century monk-bishops that included the likes of Basil of Caesarea (329-379) and John Chrysostom (347-407).

Today, Augustine is largely remembered and studied as a philosopher and theologian, though others have also explored the significance of his pastoral ministry as well. Arguably, his most significant legacy to the church was his writings, which included nearly 1000 surviving sermons, around 300 letters, and 117 books.[3]

AUGUSTINE'S HERMENEUTICS

How did Augustine regard the Bible and interpret it? Augustine was an active participant at the councils of Hippo (393) and Carthage (397), two fourth-century venues where the books of the canonical Scriptures were affirmed.[4] Augustine believed that the canonical Scriptures were inspired, authoritative, and the basis for sound doctrine. In fact, he often used the terms canonical Scriptures and sound doctrine interchangeably.[5] Practically speaking, the Scriptures were the basis for his preaching in the worship assembly and also for his instruction of new believers.

Augustine was quite concerned with interpreting the Scriptures faithfully, and his

---

[3] For a concise list see "Augustine's Works," in Fitzgerald, *Augustine Through the Ages* (Grand Rapids, MI: Eerdmans, 1999), xxxv-il. Cf. Possidius, trans. John E. Rotelle, *Life of Saint Augustine* (Villanova, PA: Augustinian Press, 1988), 11.5.

[4] See his discussion of the canon in Augustine, *Teaching Christianity*, 2.8.13.

[5] Cf. Smither, *Augustine as Mentor*, 238-44.

hermeneutics were characterized by a number of values and principles which are largely found in his work *Teaching Christianity (On Christian Doctrine)*. In terms of values, Augustine insisted that the preacher must first be spiritually prepared before beginning to study the Scriptures. He writes, "First of all, then, it is necessary that we should be led by the fear of God to seek the knowledge of His will ... Next it is necessary to have our hearts subdued by piety, and not to run in the face of Holy Scripture."[6] In addition to this spiritual foundation, Augustine emphasized the use of certain tools in interpretation. For example, he commended a knowledge of biblical languages (Hebrew and Greek) in addition to knowledge of biblical geography, natural history, chronology, numbers, science, history, and philosophy.[7] One of the most striking aspects of Augustine's hermeneutics was the value of love. Though not preferable, Augustine went so far as to argue that misinterpreted scripture resulting in love was an acceptable use of the text. He writes: "Whoever, then, thinks that he understands the Holy Scriptures, or any part of them, but puts such an interpretation upon them as does not tend to build up this twofold love of God and our neighbor, does not yet understand them as he ought."[8] Augustine's warning — one that is very relevant for today — is clear: we have not truly understood the Bible until we have applied it in such a way that our love for God and neighbor is evident. In short, Augustine's hermeneutics were *agape*-driven.

Regarding his hermeneutical principles, Augustine was first persuaded that Scripture interprets Scripture. He believed that the Bible ultimately had one divine author and that there was continuity between the Old and New Testaments. Asserting that we interpret the obscure in light of the clear, he adds: "Now from the places where the sense in which they are used is more manifest we must gather the sense in which they are to be understood in obscure passages."[9] If clarity was still lacking, Augustine added that interpretive help could come through the rule of faith, the manner in which the church had been interpreting the Bible and summarizing it through creedal statements since the apostolic period. Defined by Bryan Litfin as "a confessional formula ... that summarized orthodox beliefs about the actions of God and Christ in the world,"[10] the rule of faith in Augustine's day was best articulated through the Nicene Creed.[11]

---

[6] Augustine, *Teaching Christianity*, 2.7.9.

[7] Ibid., 2.16.

[8] Ibid., 1.36.

[9] Ibid., 3.26.

[10] Bryan Litfin, "Learning from Patristic Use of the Rule of Faith," in *The Contemporary Church and the Early Church*, ed. Paul A. Hartog (Eugene: Pickwick, 2010), 79.

[11] Augustine, *Teaching Christianity*, 3.2.2.

Augustine is also remembered for his allegorical interpretation of Scripture. He believed that each text held a literal meaning, a moral meaning, and most importantly a hidden spiritual meaning. Augustine was certainly not alone in this approach to Scripture, as eastern fathers such as Clement (d. 200) and Origen (185-254) and western pastors like Ambrose and Gregory the Great (540-604) interpreted Scripture in this way. In fact, it was Ambrose's allegorical exegesis that attracted Augustine to the Scriptures and ultimately the gospel in Milan. Augustine believed that allegory was necessary, because the fall had marred man's ability to apprehend the Scriptures.[12] Also, like the other fathers mentioned, Augustine was certainly influenced by neo-Platonic philosophy, which rejected the idea of God having human-like qualities or emotions like anger. Augustine believed that a text referring to the "arm of the Lord" or God's wrath must have another spiritual interpretation. One final benefit of allegory for Augustine was that it allowed the preacher to reach multiple interpretations of a single passage of Scripture. Though Augustine embraced allegorical readings of Scripture, at times, he also opted for a more literal hermeneutic. For instance, after writing more allegorical commentaries on Genesis (*On Genesis Against the Manicheans* and in Books 11-13 of his *Confessions),* he later produced a *Literal Commentary on Genesis.*

A final key principle of Augustine's hermeneutics was that Scripture should be interpreted in a Christo-centric manner. He presupposed that the overall narrative of Scripture was Christological, even if it was not explicit in the text. Hence, for Augustine, every passage of Scripture ought to be read in light of Christ's person and work. Augustine was also convinced that Christians grew in their faith because ultimately, Christ was the church's great teacher. Augustine expressed this well in *Sermon* 301A: "Now just when I speak to you from this elevated place [in the basilica], that does not mean that I am your teacher. That One — Christ — is the teacher of us all, the One whose professional chair sits above all the heavens. Under that One we come together, convening as a single school. And you and I — we are fellow students. But I'm here to advise you, just the way older students tend to do."[13]

APPROACHES TO TEACHING
MONASTERY

As noted, Augustine was a monk-bishop and effectively merged these two vocations. Friendship and community were important features of Augustine's life before his conversion

---

[12] Ibid., 2.1.1.

[13] Augustine, *Sermon* 301A, "Augustine in His Own Words" cited in *Harmless* (Washington, DC: Catholic University Press of America, 2010), 162.

and call to ministry as his *Confessions* attest. While teaching rhetoric in Milan, he and a group of like-minded friends attempted to form a philosophical community; however, the initiative failed because it required some of the men to leave their wives and family. After Augustine's conversion in the fall of 386, he retreated with his mother, son, and close friends to a friend's farm at Cassiciacum where they spent a few months in prayer, reading and discussing the Scriptures, contemplating philosophy, and also performing manual labor on the farm.[14]

Augustine's monastic itinerary continued after his return to Africa in 388 as he established a similar community with like-minded friends on his family's estate in Tagaste. A typical day in the Tagaste community included prayer, fasting, singing Psalms, and reading Scripture as well as other spiritually nourishing books. Augustine's monastic labor at this point largely involved writing and, over time, these theological and exegetical works benefited African church leaders.[15]

Though Augustine believed in Christian friendship and community, he probably did not establish an authentic monastery — one that served the church and was accountable to it — until his consecration as priest in Hippo in 391. In the garden monastery at Hippo, "the day consisted of Scripture reading as well as reading from other spiritually nourishing books ... Everyone in the monastery had work to do each day. The clergy were occupied with church work, and the laymen were involved in physical labor ... the entire monastery took each meal together."[16]

As shown, Augustine continued to live as a monk while serving as Hippo's bishop. To accommodate both vocations, he turned the bishop's house into a monastery for clergy (*monasterium clericorum*). We get a sense of this experiment through one of Augustine's sermons: "I saw that the bishop is under the necessity of showing hospitable kindness to all visitors and travelers; indeed, if a bishop didn't do that he would be said to be lacking in humanity. But if this custom were transferred to the monastery it would not be fitting. And that's why I wanted to have a monastery of clergy in the bishop's residence."[17] Though the clergy house was open to visitors, the daily life in this monastic community was quite similar to Augustine's previous monastery in Hippo. The biggest difference was that the monastic labor performed in the new monastery was considered church ministry as each of its members were ordained ministers.

How did Augustine teach or mentor in the monastic context, especially in the clergy

---

[14] Cf. Smither, *Augustine as Mentor,* 134-39.

[15] Ibid., 139-44.

[16] Ibid., 146.

[17] Augustine, *Sermon 355.2 (WSA).*

house? First, Augustine had daily opportunities to instruct his monastic brothers from the Scripture. Some of this teaching was probably academic in nature, as the community wrestled with presenting the gospel and Scriptures in a pagan, philosophical, and at times heretical context. Augustine also led the community in dialogue, particularly during common meals as the group discussed church ministry, exegesis, and theology. It is believed by some scholars that some of Augustine's books, including his significant work *On the Trinity*, were birthed around table discussions in the monastery. Finally, as Augustine involved the monks in the work of the ministry at Hippo, he ultimately released others to serve as church leaders around Africa.[18] Augustine's biographer Possidius claimed that as many as ten church leaders came from Augustine's clerical monastery.[19]

PREACHING

A second observable way that Augustine taught was through his preaching. His audience for preaching was primarily the believing community at Hippo, although Augustine preached in other towns and cities as well, especially Carthage.[20] Trained in the art of rhetoric, Augustine believed that a preacher could use rhetorical skills to persuade, influence, and convict.[21] However, he also was convinced that a sermon must be rich in biblical and theological content. William Harmless argues that Augustine's sermons were so saturated with the words of Scripture, that he "spoke Bible."[22] Though Augustine was well educated and has been regarded as elite by some observers, he still managed to connect with his audience and use sermon illustrations related to daily life in Hippo. Frederick Van der Meer adds, "In the pulpit he never used language that was above his hearers' heads, but always chose his words in such a fashion that everyone would understand him."[23] The surviving corpus of Augustine's sermons contains some 1000 messages. However, based on what we know of his preaching schedule, which included multiple sermons, what remains is merely a fraction of what he actually preached. At least one historian has estimated that he preached 8000 sermons during his lifetime.[24]

---

[18] Cf. Smither, *Augustine as Mentor*, 148-57.

[19] Possidius, *Life of Augustine*, 11.2-3.

[20] Smither, *Augustine as Mentor*, 128-29.

[21] Cf. "Augustine in His Own Words," *Harmless*, 135-40.

[22] Ibid., xxi.

[23] Frederick Van der Meer, *Augustine the Bishop*, B. Battershaw and G.R. Lamb, trans. (London: Sheed and Ward, 1961), 258.

[24] "Augustine in His Own Words," *Harmless*, 124, n. 8.

LETTERS

While serving as a priest and bishop of Hippo, Augustine wrote 236 letters. One hundred five of those were written to other ordained clergy serving in Africa and around the Mediterranean, including some of Augustine's disciples who had left the clergy house at Hippo to serve elsewhere in ministry. Of the 105 letters sent to church leaders, most of them contained some aspect of mentoring or instruction.[25] For instance, Augustine used these letters to answer theological and exegetical questions, to encourage some leaders to pursue sound doctrine, to offer guidance in practical ministry and church related matters, and to exhort others toward spiritual growth and reconciliation. In some letters, Augustine did a combination of these things.[26] For example, in 401, Augustine wrote *Letter 64* to the priest Quintianus of Carthage, admonishing him to read only the canonical Scriptures in worship assemblies. Augustine further reminded him of the decisions at the church councils of 393 and 397, which affirmed the books of the canonical Scriptures.[27]

BOOKS

While Augustine's significant literary output is acknowledged by most students of history, what might be easily missed are the occasions for his writing. Michele Pellegrino asserts that many of Augustine's works were "written at the request (often repeated and insistent) of persons who wished to be enlightened on various points of doctrine; or they arose out of the urgent demands of polemical controversy with heretics and pagans."[28] So it was the motivation to instruct the greater church — beyond his own context in Hippo — that led Augustine to write many of his works. In *Letter 151*, Augustine expressed his desire to use free time afforded to him to write, a ministry that would benefit the church. He relates: "I have resolved to devote the time entirely, if the Lord will, to the labor of studies pertaining to ecclesiastical learning; in doing which I think that I may, if it please the mercy of God, be of some service even to future generations."[29]

Let us consider some representative examples of his writing that was intended to mentor or instruct.[30] One of Augustine's earlier works, *On Faith and the Creed,* was originally an address given to the gathered bishops at the Council of Hippo of 393. In his teaching, Augustine gave a

---

[25] Cf. Smither, *Augustine as Mentor,* 157-85.

[26] Ibid., 159.

[27] Ibid., 171.

[28] Michele Pellegrino, *The True Priest: The Priesthood as Preached and Practiced by St. Augustine*, Arthur Gibson, trans. (Langley, UK: St. Paul Publications, 1968), 46.

[29] Augustine, *Letter* 151.13 *(WSA).*

[30] For a more thorough discussion, see Smither, *Augustine as Mentor,* 185-95.

line-by-line explanation of a Latin version of the Nicene Creed while also challenging Manichean thought. Later, this message was revised into a book that would continue to be a theological resource for African church leaders.[31]

In 426, Augustine completed the final installments of his work *On the Trinity*. Begun around 399 and probably the fruit of meal-time discussions in the monastery, the work was released in installments and was initially intended as a theological resource for Bishop Aurelius of Carthage. In letters to church leaders Evodius, Deogratias, and Theodorus, Augustine also recommended *On the Trinity* in response to some of their questions on the Godhead.[32]

Finally, around 399, Augustine wrote *On the Instruction of Beginners* as a response to Deogratias, a deacon in Carthage who asked for help on how to teach catechumens preparing for baptism. After laying out some principles for teaching, Augustine included two model messages in the latter part of the work.[33]

Church Councils. A final way in which Augustine instructed others was through his participation in some twenty-two African church councils between 393 and 427. As the most influential voice at these gatherings, Augustine certainly influenced the gathered bishops on issues such as the canon of Scripture, the Nicene Creed, the doctrine of the church in the face of Donatism, and the doctrines of grace in response to Pelagius. What is even more remarkable though is that after 401, the most influential church leaders at the African councils were Augustine's former disciples from the Hippo monasteries. The most prominent voices heard in councils at Carthage in 411 (against the Donatists) and 418 (against the Pelagians) were those of Augustine's disciples. In short, it seems that the African church councils were a context in which Augustine involved and released his disciples to ministry.[34]

AUGUSTINE'S THEOLOGY OF EDUCATION
SOUND DOCTRINE

Stemming from the influence of his mother Monica, who kicked him out of the house when Augustine joined the Manicheans as a youth, Augustine's teaching was greatly influenced by the value of sound or healthy teaching. Augustine used the term sound teaching *(sana doctrina)* over thirty times in his writings often as a challenge to heretical teaching, but also as a basis for holy, Christian living. As shown, Augustine often used the terms canonical

---

[31] Ibid., 186-87.

[32] See Augustine, *Letters* 174; 162; 173A; cf. Smither, *Augustine as Mentor,* 188-89.

[33] Ibid., 192-94.

[34] Ibid., 195-207.

Scriptures and sound teaching interchangeably. So his commitment to the Scriptures in weekly preaching and his affirmation of the canonical Scriptures at the Councils of Hippo and Carthage revealed his conviction for sound teaching. Finally, the purpose of many of his letters, books, sermons, and actions at church councils was to uphold and emphasize sound teaching.[35]

Community. Another key element of Augustine's educational approach was community. While Augustine was constantly around friends from before his conversion to Christ, his vision for discipleship as a monk, pastor, and mentor to other spiritual leaders continued to be shaped by community. Augustine taught in a group context as his monastic vision developed from Cassiciacum to Hippo. He also mentored church leaders in a group context during church councils, on visits to former disciples, and even through writing letters and books together.[36] Not unlike Basil and Pachomius (292-348) before him, Augustine believed that Christian community was an essential means for spiritual growth.

RELEASING TO MINISTRY

Augustine's philosophy of education was also quite practical in that he involved disciples in ministry and later released them to their own places of service. In the monastery, he assigned administrative tasks to some monks, while in the church he involved other ordained ministers in ministries such as reading Scripture in worship, serving communion, and even preaching. As shown, Augustine's disciples took an increased role in the African church councils. Finally, in Augustine's day, an increasing number of church leaders — bishops, priests, and deacons — were trained by him in the Hippo monastery.[37]

MENTORS ARE DISCIPLES

A final element of Augustine's teaching philosophy was the value that a mentor or teacher always remained a disciple.[38] Though he was the most influential African pastor and theologian of his day, Augustine remained accountable to the Hippo monastery community. In letters to Jerome and Paulinus of Nola, Augustine demonstrated a humble learner's posture on matters of theology.[39] Augustine asserted that he made progress in his spiritual life on

---

[35] Ibid., 238-44.

[36] Ibid., 214-22.

[37] Ibid., 245-54.

[38] Ibid., 222-32.

[39] See Augustine, *Letters* 28; 40; 67; 71; 73; 82; 31; 37; 41; 80; 95; 149.

his grasp of theology through the process of writing.[40] Discussing the relationship between learning and teaching, Augustine added, "I for my part ... like it better to learn than to teach ... the sweetness of truth then should invite us to learn, the necessities of charity should force us to teach."[41] Finally, in a letter to Jerome, Augustine suggested that spiritual leaders, including those who are aging, should remain learners: "Although it is more fitting that old men should be teachers than learners, it is nevertheless more fitting for them to learn than to continue ignorant of that which they should teach to others."[42]

CONCLUSION

In this chapter, after discussing Augustine's biblical hermeneutics, it has been argued that some of Augustine's key approaches to Christian education included mentoring in a monastic context, preaching, writing letters and books, and mentoring other spiritual leaders during church councils. Further, I have shown that his key teaching principles included sound doctrine, community, releasing others to ministry, and that a mentor is always a disciple.

Given these approaches and principles, what was Augustine's legacy as a Christian educator? First, he infused Roman classical learning and its trivium of grammar, logic, and rhetoric with a Christian worldview. In effect, he merged classical and Christian learning. Second, and related, through his magnum opus *City of God,* he introduced a Christian philosophy of history; that is, history could be understood through the lenses of Scripture and God's providence. Third, he continued the tradition of Ambrose and others, demonstrating that one could be a thinking Christian. Thinking Christians could be trained in philosophy, math, and communication skills and put those to good use in ministry. Fourth, his allegorical approach to biblical interpretation left a large imprint on exegesis throughout the medieval period. Finally, his monastic vision — that monasteries could include clergy, that they could be centers of learning, and that learning happened in community — influenced later monastic movements such as the Benedictines and the Augustinians.

---

[40] Smither, *Augustine as Mentor,* 224.

[41] Augustine, *On Eight Questions from Dulcitus,* 2.6 cited in Gerhart B. Ladner, *Ideas of Reform* (New York: Harper & Row, 1967), 338.

[42] Augustine, *Letter,* 166.1.1 *(WSA)*; On Augustine's teaching methods, Howard Grimes concluded, "It seems fair to say that Augustine would approve a theory of religious education which thinks of it as fundamentally a life of dialogue – dialogue between teacher and learner, between learning and learner, between learner and teacher and the biblical faith, but most of all between God and man." See Howard Grimes, "Augustine," in *A History of Religious Educators,* ed. Elmer L. Towns (Grand Rapids: Baker Book House, 1975), 59.

PRIMARY SOURCE SAMPLE: TEACHING BY EXAMPLE[43]

[Augustine's] legacy to the church was a very numerous clergy and monasteries filled with men and women vowed to continence under the guidance of their superiors, as well as libraries containing his own books and discourses and those of other holy men ... From the writings of this priest [Augustine], so pleasing and dear to God, it is clear as far as the light of truth allows humans to see, that he led a life of uprightness and integrity in the faith, hope, and love of the catholic church. This is certainly acknowledged by those who read his writings on the things of God. I believe, however, that they profited even more who were able to hear him speaking in church and see him there present, especially if they were familiar with his manner of life among his fellow human beings. Not only was he a teacher learned in the kingdom of heaven, who brings forth things new and old from his storeroom (Matthew 13:52), and one of those merchants who on finding a precious pearl sells what he has and buys it (Matthew 13:45-46). He was also one of those regarding whom it was written: So speak and so act (James 2:12), and of whom the Savior says, He who does these things and teaches them to others will be called great in the kingdom of heaven (Matthew 5:19) ... Pray for me that after having by God's gift lived with this man for almost forty years, without bitterness or dissension and in sweet familiarity, I may emulate and imitate him in the present world and enjoy the promises of almighty God with him in the world to come.

BIBLIOGRAPHY

Augustine. *Letters. Works of Saint Augustine, Part II, Volumes 1-4.* Translated by Edmund Hill . Hyde Park, NY: New City Press, 2001-2005.

Augustine. *Sermons. Works of Saint Augustine, Part III, Volumes 1-11.* Translated by Edmund Hill. Hyde Park, NY: New City Press, 1990-1997.

Augustine. *Teaching Christianity. Works of Saint Augustine.* Translated by Edmund Hill. Hyde Park, NY: New City Press, 1996.

Demacopoulos, George. *Five Models of Spiritual Direction in the Early Church.* South Bend, IN: University of Notre Dame Press, 2006.

Fitzgerald, Allan. *Augustine Through the Ages: An Encyclopedia.* Grand Rapids, MI: Eerdmans, 1999.

Grimes, Howard. "Augustine." In *A History of Religious Educators.* Edited by Elmer L. Towns, 54-59. Grand Rapids: Baker Book House, 1975.

Harmless, William. ed. *Augustine in His Own Words.* Washington, DC: Catholic University Press of America, 2010.

Ladner, Gerhart B. *The Idea of Reform: Its Impact on Christian Thought and Action in the Age of the Fathers.* New York: Harper & Row, 1967.

---

[43] This excerpt is from the writings of Augustine's disciple and co-laborer Possidius of Calama. It illustrates Augustine's value as a teacher and mentor. See Possidius, *The Life of St. Augustine,* 31.8-11.

Liftin, Bryan, "Learning from Patristic Use of the Rule of Faith," 76-99, *The Contemporary Church and the Early Church: Case Studies in Ressourcement.* Edited by Paul A. Hartog. Eugene, OR: Pickwick, 2010.

Pellegrino, Michele. *The True Priest: The Priesthood as Preached and Practiced by St. Augustine.* Translated by Arthur Gibson. Langley, UK: St. Paul Publications, 1968.

Possidius. *Life of Augustine.* Translated by John E. Rotelle. Villanova, PA: Augustinian Press, 1988.

Smither, Edward L. *Augustine as Mentor: A Model for Preparing Spiritual Leaders.* Nashville, TN: B&H Academic, 2008.

Van der Meer, Frederick. *Augustine the Bishop. Church and Society at the Dawn of the Middle Ages.* Translated by B. Battershaw, and G.R. Lamb, G.R. London: Sheed and Ward, 1961.

CHAPTER 3

Columba:

An Inadvertent Teacher of Wild Peoples

GWENDOLYN SHELDON

Columba (c. 521-597)

Columba's educational ministry took place among the people of Ireland and Western Scotland. Unlike his predecessor, Patrick, it does not seem like he sought his missionary role. Rather, as a result of his life circumstances and of his desire to deepen his own, private relationship with God, he found himself ministering to the only recently converted Gaels and preaching to the unconverted Picts. Despite the unexpectedness of the challenges with which this role presented him, Columba bore up well, relying on his insight into others' levels of understanding in order to tailor his approach and the lessons he wished to convey to the individual.

35

HISTORICAL BACKGROUND

St. Columba, known in Gaelic as *Colum Cille* or "Dove of the Church," was born *c.* 521 and died in 597. Over the course of his lifetime, he became a figure of enormous importance to the Gaels — the people of Ireland and western Scotland. He also worked to convert the Picts of eastern Scotland. In later times, monks from his monastery of Iona would convert the northern English. Over the next few centuries, monks from Iona and from amongst the newly converted English would move into the still heathen lands of the Frisians, the Germans, and even the Scandinavians. Thus, in founding a monastery, in seeking to build a sanctuary from the world where he and a few others could devote themselves to their private relationships with God, Columba inadvertently came to influence his own people and other peoples across Europe in ways he could never have foreseen. Nevertheless, it is among his own people in Ireland and Scotland that his memory has always been strongest; over the centuries, they have lovingly woven one myth after another around his name in an attempt to fill out his life story. The Book of Kells, now considered Ireland's premier national treasure, was almost certainly made in part on Iona and later brought to Iona's daughter-house at Kells.[1] The year 1997 — the fourteen hundredth anniversary of Columba's death — was marked in Ireland, Scotland, and to a lesser extent England both by huge displays of commemoration and by the launching of various research projects into Columba's life and legacy. If there was any doubt as to his importance today, such events testify to the abiding place Columba has in the spirituality and identity of these nations.

THE HISTORICAL SOURCES

Of St. Columba, J. F. Kenney once wrote that he "stands out as a clear-cut historical personality against a background wherein his associates in sanctity ... move as shadows in a land of twilight."[2] For most sixth-century Irish saints, the earliest works we have purporting to tell us about their lives date from the high or even late Middle Ages. By comparison, Columba's life comes across as well documented, having already been commemorated in poetry within a few years of his death and been the subject of a lengthy biography written only a century after his death by one of his successor abbots. Despite the information provided in these sources, our knowledge of Columba's life is still extremely limited. Columba, unfortunately, left no written

---

[1] Bernard Meehan, *The Book of Kells: An Illustrated Introduction to the Manuscript in Trinity College Dublin* (London: Thames and Hudson Ltd., 1994), 90.

[2] J. F. Kenney, *The Sources for the Early History of Ireland: Ecclesiastical* (New York: Octagon Books, 1929; repr. 1966), 425-6.

works that we can attribute to him with any certainty (although a number of religious poems have been attributed to him), nor do we have any descriptions of Columba written during his lifetime.

A vernacular poem, the *Amra Coluim Cille*, or "Eulogy of Colum Cille", is widely accepted as the earliest source of information on Columba's life. Although the oldest surviving copy dates to the eleventh century, linguistic evidence indicates that it was probably written *c.* 600, a fact that makes it quite plausible that the poem was indeed, as it claims, composed upon news of the saint's death.[3] As would be expected from any work of early medieval Irish praise-poetry, the *Amra* tells us of Columba's noble ancestry; unlike other works of its genre, however, it acclaims its subject not for his success on the battlefield, but for his upholding of Christian ideals. Unfortunately for the modern scholar, the *Amra*'s composer assumed that his audience was already familiar with the details of Columba's life and he therefore provides us with precious little specific information. Study of the *Amra* is made particularly difficult by its language, which was already so antiquated and obscure by the eighth century that Gaelic-speaking copyists appear to have felt the need to re-edit and update it.[4]

Historians have turned with relief to our most useful source of information on Columba, the *Vita Columbae*, or "Life of Columba", written in Latin by Adomnán, Iona's ninth abbot. Like Columba, Adomnán was a member of a kin group called the Cenél Conaill. Adomnán was not only Columba's successor and kinsman, but also a man of great intellectual curiosity. His *De Locis Sanctis*, a description of the holy places of the Bible, leaves little doubt that he tried in a conscientious and scholarly manner to report only what he could demonstrate from a thorough study of his own sources of information. Throughout the *Vita Columbae*, Adomnán's consciousness of his need to establish his credibility is obvious; in his second preface, he states that he got his information "from the account handed down by our elders" and that he writes "what [he] could find already in writing or from what [he] heard recounted without a trace of doubt by informed and reliable old men."[5] Though Adomnán does not name any written works on which he relied, it is likely that he made use of an earlier *vita* of Columba written by Cuimíne Ailbe, also known as Cumméne or Cummeneus Albus,

---

[3] Máire Herbert, *Iona, Kells, and Derry: The History and Hagiography of the Monastic Familia of Columba* (Oxford: Clarendon Press, 1988), 9-10.

[4] Kenney, *Early History of Ireland*, 427.

[5] Adomnán of Iona, *The Life of St. Columba*, trans. Richard Sharpe (New York: Penguin Books, 1995), 105. Sharpe's edition of the *Vita Columbae* is the best, most recent, and most readily available English translation. In addition to the translation of Adomnán's Latin work, Sharpe provides a lengthy introduction. For the convenience of readers who may not read Latin, I shall use this translation when making reference to Adomnán's work throughout the rest of this chapter.

Iona's seventh abbot who led from 657 to 669. An extraction from this work, of which no copy survives, is found within the oldest copy we have of Adomnán's *Vita*.[6] Assuming that Adomnán read this other *vita*, then he had access to an account of Columba's life written only about 70 years after the saint's death, just within living memory. While Adomnán never mentions Cuimíne Ailbe's work, he does frequently state throughout his writing how he got his information and on ten occasions, he details the chain of people through whom the information was passed from Columba's time to his own. Given Adomnán's unusual attention to documentary sources, his nearness in time and place to his subject, and the scholarly abilities demonstrated his *De Locis Sanctis*, Adomnán's *Vita Columbae* is generally considered a valuable source of information about both Columba and early medieval Ireland and Scotland.

Writing only a few decades after Adomnán, the Venerable Bede discusses Columba and monks from Iona frequently in his *Historia Ecclesiastica Gentis Anglorum*, or "Ecclesiastical History of the English People," written *c.* 731.[7] Bede mentions Columba usually in connection with missionary work done amongst the Picts or Northumbrians. While such notice certainly suggests that monks from Iona were an important presence amongst these peoples during Bede's own lifetime, historians have generally viewed Bede's information on Columba himself as unreliable.[8] After Bede, a number of Latin and Gaelic sources from the later Middle Ages and early modern period claim to give an account of Columba's life.[9] These sources appear to have drawn heavily on Adomnán's *Vita*. The material in these sources that does not reflect Adomnán's work is generally considered to reveal more about the folk traditions that gradually built up about Columba than about Columba himself.[10]

COLUMBA'S LIFE

Like St. Patrick, St. Columba has long been one of the Gaelic-speaking world's most popular saints; historians trying to clarify what we can actually say with some certainty of his life have had to sort through nearly a millennium and a half of accumulated traditions in both

---

[6] Kenney, *Early History of Ireland*, 428.

[7] Richard Sharpe, introduction to *The Life of St. Columba* by Adomnán of Iona, trans. Richard Sharpe (New York: Penguin Books, 1995), 7.

[8] Sharpe, introduction, 7.

[9] Kenney, *Early History of Ireland*, 434-441.

[10] For a description of one such source, read Brian Lacey's introduction to Manus O'Donnell's sixteenth-century *Betha Colaim Chille*. Brian Lacey, introduction to *The Life of Colum Cille*, by Manus O'Donnell, trans. Brian Lacey (Dublin: Four Courts Press, 1998), 14.

Ireland and Scotland. In doing so, they have relied almost entirely on the *Amra Coluim Cille* and Adomnán's *Vita Columbae*, turning occasionally to the Irish annals in order to align the events of Columba's life with other historical happenings. Based on these sources, it is thought that Columba was born between 520 and 522. His kin group, the Cenél Conaill, was a subset of the Uí Néill, who in the sixth and seventh centuries lived in what is now Donegal and Tyrone.[11] Like other Uí Néill families, the Cenél Conaill would remain powerful for more than another thousand years.[12] Adomnán states that Columba was of noble lineage,[13] and later events in his life make more sense if we see Columba as politically well-connected. As a child, he was fostered by a priest[14] and as a young deacon, he studied divine wisdom in Leinster.[15] More specifically, Adomnán mentions that the young deacon studied Scripture with a bishop called Uinniau,[16] a man probably of British origin who wrote a book on penance and who seems to have been a leader of the early monastic movement in Ireland.[17]

These basic facts are all that we can glean from Adomnán's chance remarks about Columba's childhood and early adulthood. The event that would have lasting consequences for the history of Christianity not only in the British Isles, but also in much of Europe, was Columba's departure from Ireland in 563 and founding of a monastery on Iona. Bede tells us that Columba "came to Britain to preach the word of God to the kingdoms of the northern Picts,"[18] but Bede's ascription of a missionary purpose to Columba is not confirmed by the Irish sources. Adomnán tells us only that he "sailed away from Ireland to Britain choosing to be a pilgrim for Christ."[19] The Irish practice of travelling abroad for devotional purposes in order, for instance, to join a British monastery, appears to have already been well established by the mid-sixth century and would grow stronger over the next few centuries. Despite the prevalence of this custom, it has often been suggested that Columba left Ireland as a penance for his supposed role in the battle of Cúl Drebene. This suggestion perhaps arose from the way Adomnán dates

---

[11] Sharpe, introduction, 8.

[12] Brian Lacey, *Colum Cille and the Columban Tradition* (Dublin: Four Courts Press, 1997), 12.

[13] Adomnán of Iona, *Life*, 105.

[14] Ibid., 206.

[15] Ibid., 174.

[16] Ibid., 110, 208.

[17] For more on this bishop, known variously as Uinniau, Finnio, or Finnbarr, see Pádraig Ó Riain, "St. Finnbarr: A Study in a Cult," *Journal of the Cork Historical and Archaeological Society* 82 (1977): 63-82.

[18] Bertram Colgrave and R. A. B. Mynors, eds. and trans., *Bede's Ecclesiastical History of the English People* (Oxford: Clarendon Press, 1969), 223.

[19] Adomnán of Iona, *Life*, 105.

Columba's journey; despite the fact that he expresses no connection between the two events, Adomnán twice describes Columba's departure as taking place two years after this battle.[20] At a much later point in the *Vita*, Adomnán says that Columba was once excommunicated at the Synod of Teltown for some trivial offenses, a sentence that was later overturned.[21] What Columba's offenses were, or even when the Synod of Teltown occurred, remain unknown. The northern Uí Néill — Columba's kinsmen — won the battle of Cúl Drebene, but there is no reason to believe that Columba played a strong role in it or that he left Ireland to expiate any sin committed in connection with it. Most likely, Columba left Ireland simply in order to engage in a devotional and ascetic lifestyle. He was one of many Irishmen to do so.

There is some debate as to whether Columba established a monastery on Iona immediately after leaving Ireland or whether he spent time in other parts of Scotland first.[22] Adomnán says only that "two years after the battle of Cúl Drebene", that is, when Columba left Ireland, he prophesied "in the presence of King Conall mac Comgaill."[23] Regardless of when he settled there, it is most likely that Iona was given to him by one of the local kings — probably Conall mac Comgaill — of Scottish Dál Riata, a collection of kingdoms stretching from northern Ireland across the sea to much of western Scotland.[24] This implies that Gaelic-speaking Scotland had been largely converted by this point, though Columba's prominent northern kinsmen might also have contributed to his success in gaining a foothold. However the community was established, it soon became popular, such that, as the *Vita* makes clear, the monks of Iona controlled several surrounding islands.

Though Columba probably left Ireland in order to engage in a more devotional lifestyle, Adomnán depicts Columba, in his role as head of a monastic community, as a busy man, dispensing advice and assigning penances to laymen who arrived from Ireland or western Scotland, copying manuscripts, giving orders to his monks, prophesying, journeying widely throughout both the Gaelic-speaking and Pictish areas, baptizing, preaching, engaging

---

[20] Ibid., 105, 118. It is because Adomnán references this battle in dating Columba's departure that we can say with some certainty that Columba set sail in 563.

[21] Ibid., 207.

[22] Alfred P. Smyth, for instance, suggests that Columba might not have settled on Iona for ten years after arriving in Scotland. See A. P. Smyth, *Warlords and Holy Men, Scotland, 80-1000 A. D.* (Edinburgh: Edinburgh University Press, 1984), 100.

[23] Adomnán of Iona, *Life*, 118-19.

[24] Seán Mac Airt and Gearóid Mac Niocaill, eds. and trans., *The Annals of Ulster (to A.D. 1131)* (Dublin: Dublin Institute for Advanced Studies, 1983), 574. The *Annals of Ulster*, in recording Conall mac Comgaill's death in 574, credit him with the donation of Iona. Whether the annals can be relied on for information about this extremely early period is a matter of debate.

in diplomatic endeavors, consecrating, Áedán mac Gabráin, as king. Adomnán never clarifies what kind of pastoral relationship the monks of Iona had with the surrounding Gaelic-speaking population, though he indicates that the people of Dál Riata were Christian and quite devoted to their local holy man.[25] Upon Conall mac Comgaill's death, for instance, Columba consecrated his successor.[26] In contrast, he depicts Pictland as a hostile, non-Christian area. Adomnán portrays Columba as visiting a Pictish king's fortress, perhaps indicating that his trips to Pictland initially had a diplomatic purpose.[27] In Pictland, Columba argued for the release of Irish slaves, engaged in contests with heathen wizards and, most importantly for the later history of the region, preached through an interpreter.[28] The *Amra* confirms that Columba engaged in evangelical work while faring into Pictland, calling him "the teacher who would teach the tribes of the Tay" and claiming, "his blessing turned them, the mouths of the fierce ones who lived on the Tay, to the will of the King."[29] It is unclear how many trips back to Ireland Columba made after settling on Iona. The only trip back to Ireland that Adomnán mentions Columba making was to Druim Cett, a hill outside Derry, where Columba participated in a meeting between the king of Dál Riata and the overlord of the northern Uí Néill.[30] Otherwise, once he left his homeland in 563 at about the age of 41 or 42, he spent his whole life in Scotland, probably mostly on Iona and on a few nearby islands. By medieval standards, he was long-lived. According to Adomnán, Columba died in the church on Iona at midnight on a Sunday in 597.[31] Assuming he was born in 521, he lived to be about 76 years old. Those who later gave accounts of Columba's death to Adomnán claimed that the event was accompanied by a variety of miracles. Adomnán notes that by the time he was writing, Columba's fame had "reached the three corners of Spain and Gaul and Italy beyond the Alps, and even Rome itself, the chief of all cities."[32]

---

[25] Gilbert Márkus, "Iona: Monks, Pastors, and Missionaries," in *Spes Scotorum — Hope of Scots: Saint Columba, Iona, and Scotland*, ed. Dauvit Broun and Thomas Owen Clancy (Edinburgh: T&T Clark, Ltd., 1999), 115-38, 126-32.

[26] Adomnán of Iona, *Life*, 209.

[27] Ibid., 184.

[28] Ibid., 179-84.

[29] The most readily available reconstruction of the Old Irish text of the *Amra*, accompanied by an English translation, is found in Thomas Owen Clancy and Gilbert Márkus, *Iona: The Earliest Poetry of a Celtic Monastery* (Edinburgh: Edinburgh University Press, 1995).

[30] Adomnán of Iona, *Life*, 151.

[31] Ibid., 225-31.

[32] Ibid., 233.

COLUMBA AS MISSIONARY EDUCATOR

Bede, inspired by Gregory the Great's mission to the English and acquiring most of his information about Columba from peoples who had been evangelized by monks from Iona, depicts Columba primarily as a missionary.[33] Neither the *Amra* nor Adomnán see Columba's monastery as a center of pastoral activity. They see it, rather, as an ascetic retreat from the world, where laymen frequently appeared but did not stay for long. Those who were assigned penances were sent to Tiree, to the unidentified island of Hinba, or even to Britain to perform them.[34] The baptisms that Columba performed did not take place on Iona. Columba's consecration of Áedán mac Gabráin as king took place on Iona, but such a consecration was hardly part of routine pastoral work. Bishops were essential to pastoral work in the Middle Ages, but while Iona sent bishops elsewhere in the seventh century, we do not read of any bishop of Iona itself before 712.[35] During Columba's lifetime, Iona seems to have been a "monastic appendage" to an already existing church structure in Dál Riata.[36] In short, when Columba acted as an evangelist, he generally did so while travelling. Occasionally, we see him acting as a teacher amongst his own monks. It is worth noting these facts for the sake of recognizing that Columba seems never to have seen himself as having a pastoral calling. He did his evangelical work incidentally, as an outgrowth of his own private but intense relationship with God.

COLUMBA AS A MONASTIC TEACHER

There is no way of knowing whether Columba ever read what would come to be Western Europe's principle guide to the monastic life — the *Rule of St. Benedict*, which St. Benedict put together probably between 535 and his death in 550.[37] Adomnán does not say that Columba, working in the mid- to late-sixth century, consciously structured his monastic community according to any rule, though it is possible that he had read Benedict's work or at least heard of its ideas. In any event, it is clear from reading the *Vita* that Columba's monastery had many of the features that St. Benedict prescribes: the monks' days were spent in a mixture of prayer, work, and study. We read of the monks working to acquire

[33] Woodbridge argued that evangelism was closely tied to Columba's understanding of Christian education. See John Woodbridge, "Columba," in *A History of Religious Educators*, ed. Elmer L. Towns (Grand Rapids: Baker Book House, 1975), 66.

[34] Ibid., 134, 189, 127, 129.

[35] Márkus, "Iona: Monks, Pastors, and Missionaries," 123-24.

[36] David Dumville, *Saint Patrick: A.D. 493-1993* (Woodbridge: Boydell Press, 1993), 188.

[37] C. H. Lawrence, *Medieval Monasticism: Forms of Religious Life in Western Europe in the Middle Ages*, 3rd ed. (Harlow, England: Pearson Education Limited, 2001), 18-22.

the necessities of life, engaging in regular, communal prayer, reading, and copying texts. Adomnán presents Columba's abbatial authority as taken for granted not only by his monks, but also by outsiders who came to Iona to seek Columba's advice or to make a confession. During Columba's lifetime, his monastery seems to have had no formal system by which it ministered to the Christian, Gaelic-speaking population surrounding it or preached to the non-Christian, Pictish population in eastern Scotland. Nonetheless, Adomnán always portrays monks from Iona as working and travelling with Columba, and it is possible that the community's eventual propensity for sending monks to recently-converted areas was prompted partially by Columba's journeys.

Columba's approach to teaching his own monks obviously differed greatly from his approach to teaching the heathen Picts or even the illiterate Christian laymen of Dál Riata. Amongst the picts he had to preach through an interpreter, but amongst his own monks, he could rely on their literacy and familiarity with the interpretation of Scripture in order to convey subtle lessons about the fullness of Scripture and its ability to contain all the divine mysteries. We see this particularly in one incident in which Columba corrected the young monk Baithéne, who would eventually succeed Columba as Iona's abbot. Adomnán writes that Baithéne came to Columba and asked that one of the monks go through a psalter that Baithéne had just copied and correct any mistakes. Columba immediately foretold that that one letter "i" would be missing and when they examined Baithéne's psalter, they found that it was so.[38] It would be a mistake to read this incident as simply a demonstration of Columba's understanding. As we shall see, to anyone familiar with the culture of the monastic interpretation of Scripture, this incident was far more meaningful than it appears to us.

Jennifer O'Reilly points out that by Columba's time, there was already a long tradition of viewing Scripture as a unified whole, of which no part can be understood individually.[39] Origen, for instance, describes "the whole range of inspired Scripture, even to the mere letter" as expressing "the wisdom of God."[40] Based on Christ's reference to the *iota* in Matthew 5:18, Origen even identifies the merest letter as the *iota*, the Greek form of "i".[41] Jerome interpreted Christ's words as indicating that even those aspects of the law that seem to be

---

[38] Adomnán of Iona, *Life*, 129-130.

[39] Jennifer O'Reilly, "The Wisdom of the Scribe and the Fear of the Lord in the *Life of Columba*," in *Spes Scotorum — Hope of Scots: Saint Columba, Iona, and Scotland*, ed. Dauvit Broun and Thomas Owen Clancy (Edinburgh: T&T Clark, Ltd., 1999), 159-211, 174-85.

[40] George Lewis, trans., *The Philocalia of Origen* (Edinburgh: T & T Clark, 1911), 2:4.

[41] Christ's words in Matthew 5:18, familiar to us in English translations as "one jot or one tittle," appear in the Latin Vulgate as *iota unum aut unus apex*.

of least significance are filled with "spiritual sacraments" and that all things are expressed in the gospels.[42] In foretelling that an "i" would be found missing from Baithéne's psalter, Columba was therefore drawing on an exegetical tradition that he could expect the other monks to understand. According to this tradition, Scripture must be interpreted holistically, since every part of Scripture ultimately points to the same spiritual truth. Furthermore, even the tiniest part of Scripture has spiritual meaning and must not be forgotten. Columba was thus suggesting that Baithéne's spiritual understanding was less than perfect. The fact that Baithéne had been making a copy of the Book of Psalms must have made this message especially obvious to those in a monastic setting, as the Psalms were often used as a primer in the teaching of literacy. This was particularly true in monasteries, where the Book's opening image — that of a blessed man ruminating over the Lord's law day and night — was often seen as a model of monastic life.[43] Moreover, the monastic offices that monks chanted daily allowed them to complete all the Psalms on a regular basis. The psalter was thus a powerful image of monastic life and monastic learning. Columba's prediction drew on a wealth of traditions to suggest that Baithéne had much to learn.

Throughout the *Vita*, we see Baithéne becoming a better and more respected monk. Columba clearly recognized this, as is shown shortly before his death in his words to the younger monk. According to Adomnán, on the day of his death, Columba was writing a copy of the Psalms. Upon reaching the verse in the thirty-fourth Psalm that says, "They that seek the Lord shall not want for anything that is good," Columba announced, "Here at the end of the page I must stop. Let Baithéne write what follows."[44] Given that the Psalms were seen as a symbol of monastic life, the implication of Columba's words was that it was time for Baithéne to take Columba's place in the life of this particular monastery. This message was emphasized by the verse before which Columba stopped, the first verse that he would have Baithéne copy: "Come, my sons, hear me; I shall teach you the fear of the Lord." Just in case the readers fail to understand what Columba's actions implied, Adomnán says, "This [verse] is appropriate for Baithéne, his successor, a father and teacher of spiritual sons, who as his predecessor enjoined, followed him not only as a teacher but also as a scribe."[45]

In these interactions with Baithéne, we do not see Columba teaching through

---

[42] Jerome, *Commentary on Matthew*, trans. Thomas P. Scheck (Washington, D. C.: The Catholic University of America Press, 2008), 78.

[43] O'Reilly, "Wisdom of the Scribe," 185-88.

[44] Adomnán of Iona, *Life*, 228.

[45] Ibid., 228.

lecture, reasoned argument, or exegesis, but through taking existing circumstances and giving them an allegorical interpretation that was appropriate to the learner's level of understanding. Likewise on other occasions, Columba responded to others' actions in ways that would impress upon them a deeper lesson than the one that initially met the eye. According to Adomnán, Columba was sometimes given visions of the divine light. On one such occasion, Fergnae, a young monk, chanced upon Columba beholding the divine light. Fergnae, not understanding what was happening, was startled by the brightness and therefore lowered his eyes and left. Columba later commended Fergnae for lowering his eyes, saying that the light would have blinded him.[46] It is at first tempting to take literally Columba's statement that the light would have blinded Fergnae. There was already, however, a long tradition, established both in the Bible and in Patristic writings, of seeing divine mysteries as being so unintelligible to the human mind as to be harmful to it. Augustine, for example, famously pictured John as being alone in his ability to contemplate the light of the divine, just as the eagle is alone in his ability to look directly at the sun's rays.[47] Columba's intention seems to have been to reassure the young monk that his natural fear of such a bright light revealed great wisdom; that is, Fergnae was wise enough to realize that he had been confronted with mysteries that he could not understand. In addition to being a compliment, Columba's words were also a warning to Fergnae — a suggestion that Fergnae should not try to understand mysteries that were not given to him to understand. Columba's message to Fergnae reveals his acceptance of a tradition according to which Scripture and its mysteries can be interpreted at many levels. Furthermore, Columba clearly accepted and was trying to convey to Fergnae the idea that people whose understanding is at one level should not try to understand Scripture's mysteries at a higher level. Origen says that for those at the very highest level of understanding, the written word is no longer even needed, but that for those at a lower level, it is edifying.[48] As with Baithéne, Columba was able to rely on Fergnae's familiarity with Patristic writings and his way of teaching Fergnae was therefore subtle.

One final example is enough to show Columba's delicate use of others' ability to see symbolism as a means of teaching. One Sunday, Columba understood that he was dying and tried to tell his monks so, though they did not catch his meaning. Exactly six days later, Columba took his servant to the barn in order to bless two heaps of grain, telling the servant

---

[46] Ibid., 220-21.

[47] Augustine of Hippo, "The Harmony of the Gospels," in *Nicene and Post-Nicene Fathers, First Series*, ed. Philip Schaff, trans. S.D.F. Salmond (Buffalo, NY: Christian Literature Publishing Co., 1888), 4:10.

[48] Lewis, *Philocalia*, 1:11.

that it was good to know that if he (Columba) had to leave, the monks would still have enough food for a year.[49] The parallels with Exodus 16 are striking: on the sixth day of each week, the Israelites gathered a double portion of manna to tide themselves over during their period of rest. Columba was gently telling his servant that he (Columba) was about to rest. Columba spelt out his meaning more clearly to the servant, giving us a rare instance of his own exegesis. He told the servant, "Scripture calls this day the Sabbath, which means 'rest'. Today is truly my Sabbath, for it is my last day in this wearisome life, when I shall keep the Sabbath after my troublesome labours."[50] It is hard to find a clearer example of Columba's spontaneous use of the symbolism of actions and events in order to convey a message to others.

COLUMBA AS A TEACHER OF PICTS AND SCOTS

In these examples, we see that Columba's method of teaching his monks was in some ways much like his preaching to the Picts or his giving of advice and penances to laymen from Ireland and Scotland: it was spontaneous and inadvertent and it relied on Columba's ability to turn events into spiritual allegories that the learners in question would understand. Amongst the literate monks of Iona, such allegories could involve references to Scripture and to the writings of the Church Fathers. In Pictland, Columba had to be somewhat less academic in his approach. In front of the Picts, for instance, Columba repeatedly placed himself and his monks in danger, seemingly in order to demonstrate the Christian God's ultimate power.[51] On one occasion, for example, a Pictish wizard challenged Columba, saying that he would call forth an adverse wind and a thick mist in order to prevent Columba from travelling. Columba took the opportunity to tell the wizard, "the almighty power of God rules all things," a statement that, in its assertion of a single power in the universe, introduced the wizard to an aspect of Christian belief that is generally foreign to polytheistic religions. Columba then had some (presumably Pictish) sailors ferry him across a lake in stormy weather, allowing the sailors to see his prayers and his trust in God.[52]

In his dealings with the Christian laymen of Scottish Dál Riata, Columba taught as he did amongst his own monks or amongst the Picts — he taught spontaneously, as the situation allowed. Again, he does not seem to have set out to be a teacher; his teaching came about as a

---

[49] Adomnán of Iona, *Life*, 226.

[50] Ibid., 227.

[51] Ibid. 175-84.

[52] Ibid. 183.

result of his own strong relationship with God, which often drew people to him. Throughout the *Vita*, we read of laymen arriving on Iona both to confess their sins to Columba and to seek his advice, prompting Columba to call on his Scriptural knowledge and understanding of human nature to provide on-the-spot lessons. One layman, for example, told Columba that his wife spurned him, causing Columba to ask the wife why she behaved so and to remind her of Jesus' words that two shall be in one flesh.[53] When the wife explained that she would rather enter a convent than remain with her husband, Columba suggested that the three of them fast and pray together. Eventually, the wife announced a change of heart. In this example, we see that although Columba could not expect Christian laymen in Ireland and Scotland to have the same knowledge of Scripture and Patristic writings that a monk would, he could use a quotation of Jesus' words to have more effect on them than those words would have on the Picts. He tailored his lessons to Christian laymen accordingly. In short, whether dealing with monks, Picts, or Christian laymen, Columba's approach was spur of the moment and often relied on others' ability to discern the symbolism of events and of Columba's words and actions.

COLUMBA'S LEGACY IN THE WRITTEN WORD

Columba's way of teaching reflected his own personality and relationship with God. It, perhaps, could not be copied by others. His legacy to Christian education lies in the fact that, as a founder of monasteries in a region that had only recently been introduced to Christianity, Columba helped to spread copies of Christian Scriptures and probably of Patristic works amongst peoples who had never been part of the Roman Empire, peoples for whom this literature was still very new. Indeed, the first books to arrive in Ireland had probably done so only in the fifth century with the spread of Christianity.[54] In the early Middle Ages, monasteries were centers of book production, not only because only monks were likely to have the skills necessary for book copying, but also because, in the remote and thinly populated areas of northern Europe, monasteries were the only communities big enough to bring together such resources as parchment and ink out of which books could be made. Adomnán often describes Columba as being in the process of copying out a text and indeed, he was copying a psalter on the day he died.[55] The importance of copying manuscripts at Iona can be seen in Adomnán's remark that "as his predecessor had

---

[53] Ibid., 194-95.

[54] Timothy O'Neill, "Columba the Scribe," in *Studies in the Cult of Saint Columba*, ed. Cormac Bourke (Dublin: Four Courts Press, 1997), 69-79, 69.

[55] Adomnán of Iona, *Vita*, 228.

enjoined," Baithéne "followed [Columba] not only as a teacher but also as a scribe."[56] Indeed, the Book of Kells (an illuminated copy of the gospels made mostly on Iona) and the Book of Durrow (another illuminated copy of the gospels made either on Iona or at one of Iona's daughter-houses in Ireland or England) were for centuries regarded as personal relics of Columba himself; it was largely due to his status that they survived.[57] Perhaps it is fitting that they were regarded as his, for they would not have been made if he had never lived. Again, Columba's importance in spreading the written word was likely inadvertent; there is no evidence in the *Vita* that the books that the monks made were intended for any use outside the monastery. By copying Christian religious works, however, the monks of Iona and of other monasteries gradually introduced these works into places that were very far, both culturally and geographically, from the places where those works were written.

CONCLUSION

In brief, by seeking a refuge from the world where he could cultivate his own relationship with God, Columba inadvertently became an exemplar of the Christian life to the monks who followed him, to the Christian Gaels, and to the non-Christian Picts. The fact that he did not set out to be a teacher is shown by the frequent subtlety of his approach. As this approach was geared, however, to others' levels of understanding and ability to read spiritual allegory, it was possibly more effective than more explicit methods of teaching. Among his own monks, Columba could reference centuries of Biblical interpretation. Among the Picts, he made use of natural events occurring before their eyes. His approach was obviously successful, for monks from Iona and its daughter-houses would spread across much of Europe.

BIBLIOGRAPHY

Adomnán of Iona. *The Life of St. Columba*. Translated by Richard Sharpe. New York: Penguin Books, 199.

Augustine of Hippo. "The Harmony of the Gospels." In *Nicene and Post-Nicene Fathers, First Series*. Edited by Philip Schaff. Translated by S.D.F. Salmond. Buffalo, N.Y.: Christian Literature Publishing Co., 1888.

Clancy, Thomas Owen and Gilbert Márkus. *Iona: The Earliest Poetry of a Celtic Monastery*. Edinburgh: Edinburgh University Press, 1995.

Colgrave, Bertram and R. A. B. Mynors, eds. and trans. *Bede's Ecclesiastical History of the English People*. Oxford: Clarendon Press, 1969.

Dumville, David. *Saint Patrick: A.D. 493-1993*. Woodbridge: Boydell Press, 1993.

---

[56] Ibid., 228.

[57] O'Neill, "Columba the Scribe," 69.

Herbert, Máire. *Iona, Kells, and Derry: The History and Hagiography of the Monastic* Familia *of Columba*. Oxford: Clarendon Press, 1988.

Jerome. *Commentary on Matthew*. Translated by Thomas P. Scheck. Washington, D. C.: The Catholic University of America Press, 2008.

Kenney, J. F. *The Sources for the Early History of Ireland: Ecclesiastical*. New York: Octagon Books, 1929; repr. 1966.

Lacey, Brian. *Colum Cille and the Columban Tradition*. Dublin: Four Courts Press, 1997.

_____. *Introduction to The Life of Colum Cille*, by Manus O'Donnell, 7-15. Translated by Brian Lacey. Dublin: Four Courts Press, 1998.

Lewis, George, trans. *The Philocalia of Origen*. Edinburgh: T & T Clark, Ltd., 1911.

Mac Airt, Seán and Gearóid Mac Niocaill, eds. and trans. *The Annals of Ulster (to A.D. 1131)*. Dublin: Dublin Institute for Advanced Studies, 1983.

Márkus, Gilbert. "Iona: Monks, Pastors, and Missionaries." In *Spes Scotorum — Hope of Scots: Saint Columba, Iona, and Scotland*, edited by Dauvit Broun and Thomas Owen Clancy, 115-38. Edinburgh: T&T Clark, Ltd., 1999.

Meehan, Bernard. *The Book of Kells: An Illustrated Introduction to the Manuscript in Trinity College Dublin*. London: Thames and Hudson Ltd., 1994.

O'Neill, Timothy. "Columba the Scribe." In *Studies in the Cult of Saint Columba*. Edited by Cormac Bourke, 69-79. Dublin: Four Courts Press, 1997.

O'Reilly, Jennifer. "The Wisdom of the Scribe and the Fear of the Lord in the *Life of Columba*." In *Spes Scotorum — Hope of Scots: Saint Columba, Iona, and Scotland*, edited by Dauvit Broun and Thomas Owen Clancy, 159-211. Edinburgh: T&T Clark, Ltd., 1999.

Ó Riain, Pádraig. "St. Finnbarr: A Study in a Cult." *Journal of the Cork Historical and Archaeological Society* 82 (1977): 63-82.

Sharpe, Richard. Introduction to *The Life of St. Columba*, by Adomnán of Iona, 1-99. Translated by Richard Sharpe. New York: Penguin Books, 1995.

Smyth A. P. *Warlords and Holy Men, Scotland, 80-1000 A. D.* Edinburgh: Edinburgh University Press, 1984.

Woodbridge, John. "Columba." In *A History of Religious Educators*, edited by Elmer L. Towns, 60-65. Grand Rapids: Baker Book House, 1975.

Anselm *of* Canterbury:

Educating for the Love of God

BYARD BENNETT

Anselm of Canterbury (1033-1109)

Anselm of Canterbury, though not typically studied as an educator, developed a unique approach to education. His theology of education is based on the idea that education should help both teacher and student to arrive at a greater love of God. Anselm's work provided an important bridge between the Benedictine monastic spirituality of the early Middle Ages and the scholastic theological tradition of the later Middle Ages. In continuity with earlier monastic writers, Anselm argued that education can never be an end in itself, only a means to knowing the love of God and being formed by it. At the same time, Anselm was deeply interested in the study of logic, an emerging discipline that would dominate late medieval education, leading to the rise of scholastic theology. Anselm was able to hold together the monastic and scholastic models of education by creating a new educational synthesis based on the ideas of *right order* and *faith seeking understanding*.

HISTORICAL BACKGROUND

Anselm was born in Aosta in northern Italy in 1033. After his mother's death, he quarreled bitterly with his father and renounced his patrimony, setting off across the Alps with a single servant in 1053. He subsequently spent several years traveling in France. During these years, Anselm was unsure whether he should dedicate himself to the monastic life of simplicity and prayer or aspire to become an eminent scholar. Since, during Anselm's lifetime, monasteries were the place one went to receive an education (universities were founded at a later date), Anselm was able to defer any final decisions about his future while pursuing advanced education in a monastic environment.

By 1059, Anselm had decided to settle at the monastery of Bec in central Normandy (France) to study under the prior of the monastery, Lanfranc of Pavia (c. 1005-1089). In 1060, at the age of 27, Anselm chose to become a monk at that monastery. When Lanfranc left the monastery in 1063, Anselm served as the principal teacher at Bec, becoming abbot in 1078.

After Lanfranc's departure, Anselm changed the way that the monastery provided education. While Lanfranc was at Bec, the monastery permitted "wandering scholars" (i.e. young noblemen seeking an advanced education) to live at the monastery and study under Lanfranc (as Anselm himself had done). Educating these young noblemen provided a steady stream of revenue that allowed the monastery to build new buildings and purchase or produce books.

Anselm discontinued this practice and focused all his attention upon teaching his fellow monks, who, for the most part, were not of noble background but came from local families of modest means. This new approach meant that Anselm needed to create a strong system of foundational education that was carefully linked back to the religious context. In his teaching, Anselm sought to show how the disciplines of grammar, rhetoric, and logic could help one to understand the biblical text and resolve doubts and questions that arose from reading and reflecting on the text.

Anselm's first two works, the *Monologion* (1075-1076) and the *Proslogion* (1077-1078), were written after the monks he taught asked him to commit his teaching to writing. The *Monologion* is a meditation on the nature of the divine essence while the *Proslogion* explores the connection between faith and reason. Though these early treatises include reflection upon philosophy, grammar, and dialectic, they actually formed part of an introduction in the monastic curriculum to the disciplined reading of the Bible. Anselm's treatises came to be highly regarded by other contemporary monks and scholars and, by 1085, were being read throughout Europe.

Anselm was elected Archbishop of Canterbury in 1093, succeeding his teacher Lanfranc (the first Archbishop of Canterbury under Norman rule), who had died in 1089. During the four years prior to Anselm's appointment, the morally challenged English king (William Rufus) had plundered the church's estates, leaving the church's finances in disarray. As a monastic teacher, Anselm was unhappy with the administration and politics required by his new job as archbishop. He had a tense relationship with the king, who expected the Archbishop, as a feudal landholder, to contribute significant funds and troops to support the king's military campaigns. Anselm felt this placed an intolerable financial burden upon the tenant farmers who worked the land on the church's estates. This tension between the two figures was exacerbated by the fact that the king and most of the English bishops did not recognize Urban II as pope, whereas Anselm did.

These disagreements continued to be a source of friction, leading Anselm to leave England in 1097 and not return until after the king's death in 1100. Around this time, Anselm produced his other two major works, *Why God Became Man* (written 1094-1098) and *On the Virgin Conception and Original Sin* (written 1099-1100).

After his return to England in 1100, Anselm continued to experience tension with the new king (Henry I). Much of the conflict arose from a disagreement over the respective roles played by the Pope and king in selecting bishops and investing them with temporal and spiritual authority. Anselm again went into exile over this question from 1103 until 1106, when the king and pope were able to reach a compromise. After two years of frail health, Anselm died on April 21, 1109.

THEOLOGY OF CHRISTIAN EDUCATION

For Anselm and other representatives of early medieval monastic theology, the goal of all forms of education and study was to arrive at a greater love of God and neighbor, an idea that has roots in the teaching of Jesus (Mk. 12:30-31) and Paul (1 Cor. 13:1-3,13). Monastic writers believed that if education was to end in love, it must begin with careful, meditative reading of Scripture (*lectio divina*, "sacred reading"). This type of reading sought to discern the fullness of meaning present within the biblical text. Meditative reading allowed the biblical text to engage the reader not only at the level of historical narration (informing the reader of past events) or moral instruction (what is to be done), but also shows the reader future events (producing hope in the promises of God) and actively draws the reader's mind up toward God (increasing faith and love toward God). Any literary documents produced after such meditation (i.e. a sermon or biblical commentary) should invite the hearer or reader into this same process of discernment and elevation of the mind toward God.

Monastic education thus focused less on the receiving of *information* (intellectual mastery of content) and more on an ongoing process of *formation* (being affected and changed through one's encounter with the biblical text, due to the action of God). For monastic writers this was an important distinction, since they did not see knowledge or education as spiritually neutral matters.

Studying and learning, they believed, are always the beginning of a trajectory, an adoption of a certain stance toward the future and life's larger projects. The value of any form of learning lies in the attitudes and habits of mind that it cultivates and reinforces in the student. Following Paul's teaching that "knowledge puffs up, but love builds up" (1 Cor. 8:1), monastic educators believed that careful study and meditation on the biblical text could help one remain open to God and respond to God and one's neighbor with appropriate attitudes and emotions (such as humility, awe, gratitude, and ultimately, love). Acquiring worldly knowledge, they argued, gives one the appearance of intelligence and power but ultimately produces arrogant pride, dismissive attitudes, and all-or-nothing public competition.

Given such reservations about worldly knowledge, it is always remarkable to see the tenacity with which monastic educators pursued the study of the liberal arts and philosophy. This apparent contradiction can be resolved when one comprehends the peculiar way in which monastic theology understood God, the divine plan, the created order, and human reason to be connected.

For monastic writers, God's reason is responsible for bringing all created things into existence, giving each its peculiar character, and providentially ordering all things in relation to one another so that each plays a role in achieving the divine purpose. A certain hierarchy therefore exists within the world, with creatures on a lower level being ordered in a way that appropriately serves those on a level above it. Grass provides food for cows and cows provide food for human beings. Children have a debt of love and obedience that is owed toward their parents; all human beings owe a similar (but even greater) debt toward God.

Because human beings have been created in the image of God, their minds reflect divine reason and are informed and ordered by it. This allows the created mind to grasp divine matters and to understand the patterns, causes, and purposes God's reason has established within the created order. To observe the created world and investigate its order is thus natural for the mind and necessary to the well-being of all rational creatures, for such observation directs the mind upward toward God, who is the source and goal of all life.

LANGUAGE

The mind can investigate order within the created realm in different ways, namely *language, order, and reference* and *language, order and truth.*

Language, Order and Reference

Anselm's early works (e.g., the minor work *On Truth*) try to understand how the order in language maps onto the order within the created world. As learners, we understand the world through signs associated with language (spoken words and written symbols, which have meaning by referring back to prior concepts). The relation between sign and reality is nonetheless more complicated than it first appears. The word "man," for instance, is ambiguous, since it could refer either to an individual human being or to the human race. In some cases, there is no one-to-one relation between words and things in the external world; for example, to amuse a child, one could tell a story about wild animals that talk, but no such things actually exist in the external world. A more serious and disturbing departure from reality occurs when one tells a lie; in this case, the words one uses have meaning and describe a certain state of affairs as present when it is not, based on an intention to deceive.

Language, Order and Truth

Language, Anselm argues, was intended to communicate truth and fulfills its natural function when it does this, inviting us to enter into the truth and become wise. The study of language (grammar and rhetoric) alerts us to the fact that language can also create misunderstanding when it is used improperly and can even be abused to deceive and manipulate others. One must therefore carefully consider the conditions for truthfulness in speech; in Anselm's view, speech is rightly ordered when it affirms that what is so is so (or that what is not so is not so). Here again, Anselm is trying to emphasize the connection in education between intellectual study and moral and spiritual formation, using the primary organizing concept of "right order" to link these together — truth is the right order of knowledge and leads on to divine wisdom and the blessedness of life with God.

REASON

A second way that the mind can investigate the created order is by using reason to analyze aspects of God's nature and God's action in creation that are hard to understand. In Anselm's view, human reason, unaided by revelation, was insufficient to understand divine matters. Anselm held that one must begin by accepting what the church teaches. Having accepted *that* matters are so, one can then begin to ask *how* they are so; faith can thus move on to seek understanding. In the beginning of the *Proslogion*, Anselm summarized his position this way: "I do not try, Lord, to attain Your lofty heights, because my understanding is in no way equal to it. But I do desire to understand your truth a little, that truth that my heart believes and loves. For I do not seek to understand so that I may believe; but I believe so that I may understand. For I believe this also, that "unless I believe, I shall not understand" [Is. 7:9]."[1] In a work written a few years later, *On the Incarnation of the Word*, Anselm similarly asserted: "Indeed no Christian ought to argue how things that the Catholic Church sincerely believes and verbally professes are not so, but by always adhering to the same faith without hesitation, by loving it, and by humbly living according to it, a Christian ought to argue how they are, inasmuch as one can look for reasons. If one can understand, one should thank God; if one cannot, one should bow one's head in veneration."[2]

Arriving at a deeper understanding of the faith requires more than simply citing biblical passages or accepted ecclesiastical authorities. One must grasp how matters are intrinsically ordered in such a way that something *must* be so, i.e., why it is right for something to be this way and it is not fitting for it to be some other way. Insofar as reason strictly requires things to be this way, no further objections can be raised. Through this process of inquiry, even without invoking the authority of Scripture, one can develop a compelling case for the truths of the Christian faith, one that should be acceptable to all rational people, even opponents of the faith: "I composed these works [sc. the *Monologion* and the *Proslogion*] especially to show that compelling arguments apart from the authority of Scripture can establish things that we by faith hold about the divine nature and the divine persons besides the incarnation. If someone wanted to read them ... I think that they will discover in them regarding this matter things that they will neither be able to disprove nor wish to make little of."[3]

Such inquiry will be of the greatest benefit to the person who has faith. When a person who already believes understands the reasons underlying the faith, he or she will gain greater certainty and confidence; having hungered to know more, he or she will delight in knowing the order and reasons for God's actions. Anselm's treatise *Why God Became Man* is an example of this process of inquiry. In the preface to that work, he explains that the aim of the treatise is to prove

> [in the] first book ... by unavoidable logical steps, that, supposing Christ were left out of the case ... it is impossible that, without him, any member of the human race could be saved ... In the second book, similarly, the supposition is made that nothing were known

---

[1] *Proslogion* 1; trans. Brian Davies and G.R. Evans, *Anselm of Canterbury: The Major Works* (Oxford: Oxford Univ. Press, 1998), 87.

[2] *On the Incarnation of the Word* 1, trans. Davies and Evans, 235.

[3] *On the Incarnation of the Word* 6; trans. Davies and Evans, 246.

about Christ, and it is demonstrated with no less clear logic and truth: that human nature was instituted with the specific aim that at some stage the whole human being should enjoy blessed immortality ... that it was inevitable that the outcome concerning mankind which was the reason behind man's creation should become a reality, but that this could only happen through the agency of a Man-God; and that it is from necessity that all the things which we believe about Christ have come to pass.[4]

Anselm wanted the reader to see that there is nothing arbitrary or contingent about God assuming humanity in the incarnation. Given what God had previously willed to happen, it was both fitting and necessary that God should proceed in this particular way and no other; God's commitment to complete his plans should also inspire in us the greatest confidence and hope.

CONTRIBUTION TO EDUCATION AND CHRISTIAN EDUCATION
TEACHER AND LEARNER

For Anselm, the teacher must be a person who has genuinely understood truth and personally responded to it, aligning his or her mind and will with the divine order. Anselm finds this state of rectitude (conformity with truth) exemplified in St. Benedict of Nursia, the founder of the monastic tradition to which Anselm belonged. Anselm, addressing Benedict, describes himself as having been "drawn to that same blessedness, wondering at your life, stirred by your kind admonitions, [and] instructed by your gentle doctrine."[5] The teacher, having personally responded to the truth, embodies rectitude in a way that attracts the student's mind and heart toward the same goal, so that both may "be conscious of, understand, and love the supreme good."[6]

To respond to the truth as an educator also requires forbearance toward the students' present defects of character and the obstacles that these currently pose to the learning process. Eadmer, in his *Life of Anselm*, describes Anselm's interactions with Osbern, a young monk of noble birth who regularly opposed Anselm's authority and enjoyed interrupting and troubling him.[7] Instead of reacting to this challenge, Anselm was grieved that Osbern's keenness of

---

[4] *Why God Became Man*, Preface; trans. Davies and Evans, 261-262.

[5] In Anselm's *Prayer to St. Benedict*, lines 6-9; trans. Benedicta Ward, *The Prayers and Meditations of St. Anselm* (New York: Penguin, 1973), 196.

[6] *Monologion* 68; trans. Davies and Evans, 73.

[7] Eadmer, *Life of Anselm* 10; ed. and trans. R.W. Southern, *The Life of St. Anselm, Archbishop of*

mind was not matched with a rightly ordered character. By dealing with Osbern patiently and kindly, Anselm was able to win him over to the truth. On that basis, Anselm was then able to show Osbern what justice and right order required, thus addressing issues pertaining to Osbern's character. Anselm's patience as a teacher not only leads to Osbern's own change and growth, but also this turning of teacher and student toward God upholds the honor of God, fulfilling the goal of the Benedictine rule, "that in all things God might be glorified."[8]

Anselm assumed that the one who teaches was called to a life of teaching, a pattern of specific service by which one carries out the broader calling to love and benefit not only the neighbor, but also the enemy. By accepting and working through the difficulties associated with this calling, one is able to be perfected in love and render honor to God.

CURRICULUM AND METHODS

In the monastery, time was set aside during the day for various forms of study and instruction.[9] All forms of monastic study made extensive use of repetition to facilitate the memorization of large amounts of information. This included not only material related to instruction in Latin, but also the prayers used in daily worship and passages from Scripture and patristic works (particularly early Christian commentaries on Scripture and the writings of Augustine and Gregory the Great).

Opportunities for instruction existed even apart from the formal curriculum.[10] In regular addresses given to the whole community, the abbot reinforced the monks' understanding of the biblical story by inviting the monks to reflect upon simple, clear analogies from contemporary life. These analogies typically involved images that would be immediately familiar to all and did not depend upon a chain of reasoned argument; thus, for example, the teacher might "compare God with a great feudal lord, and the Devil with his enemy, the human soul with the lord's man," and so on.[11]

Anselm also devoted considerable time to writing prayers and meditations that could

---

Canterbury (Oxford: Clarendon, 1972), 16-17.

[8] *Rule of Benedict* 57.9.

[9] See G.R. Evans, "The Meaning of Monastic Culture: Anselm and His Contemporaries," in *The Culture of Medieval English Monasticism*, ed. James G. Clarke (Rochester, N.Y.: The Boydell Press, 2007), 77.

[10] On monastic instruction during the time of Anselm, see G.R. Evans, "St. Anselm and Teaching," *History of Education* 5 (1976): 89-101.

[11] Ibid., 97; for a more detailed discussion, see Evans, "St. Anselm's Analogies," in *Vivarium* 14, (1976): 81-93.

be used by the student outside the formal process of instruction. The presence and voice of the teacher thus extended beyond the classroom to structure the private activities and spiritual formation of the student.

The first stage of the monastery's formal curriculum focused on the reading of Latin authors (like Virgil and Ovid) combined with grammatical studies (which introduced the student to the basic elements of literary criticism). This initial level of study involved reading selected texts under the guidance of a teacher. The manuscripts containing these texts often included a gloss, a series of brief annotations written in the margin of the manuscript. These annotations (which were often culled from different pre-existing sources) explained difficult or unfamiliar words in the text and sometimes commented briefly on matters of etymology, lexical choice, or syntax when the thread of the argument needed clarification or explanation. As students gained a greater understanding of Latin literary style and how to read, interpret, and evaluate literary works, they were encouraged to experiment by writing their own compositions, particularly religious verse. These practices of studying, interpreting, and composing texts were intended to help the student read the Bible more carefully, understanding how grammar, genre, and rhetoric might shape the interpretation of difficult passages.

The second stage of the formal curriculum, which existed only in a limited number of monasteries, involved the study of logic. This, however, was not necessarily the first time in the curriculum that the student had been exposed to philosophy. During the previous study of grammar, the student might have already begun to consider philosophical themes related to learning, knowing, and the organization of knowledge by reading through Priscian's *Foundations of Grammar* and works of Augustine such as *On the Teacher*.[12]

Like grammatical studies, logic was intended to help the student analyze language and clarify arguments. To achieve this goal, logic introduced new concepts and more specialized methods of analysis that had been developed by the Neoplatonic commentators on Aristotle during the fourth to sixth centuries A.D. In Anselm's time, the principal works read were Boethius' translations and commentaries on Aristotle's *Categories* and *On Interpretation* and on Porphyry's *Isagoge*, sometimes supplemented by Cicero's *Topics*.[13]

---

[12] For further discussion, see Anneli Luhtala, *Grammar and Philosophy in Late Antiquity: A Study of Priscian's Sources* (Amsterdam: John Benjamins, 2005).

[13] Peter Boschung, *From a Topical Point of View: Dialectic in Anselm of Canterbury's De Grammatico* (Leiden: Brill, 2006), 23-24.

The guidance of the teacher played a crucial role in the study of logic. At first, the teacher would offer a commentary to explain difficult passages in the text being read. The teacher would then guide the student through a series of questions, inviting the student to discover where the argument under consideration might lead. In guiding students by the use of questions, the teacher needed to constantly adapt his teaching and questions to the varying abilities and specific needs of the students he was teaching, seeking always to show the students the relevance of the material, so as to awaken in students a desire for this type of knowledge.

As students gained confidence, they were invited to ask questions; this often took the form of pointing out an apparent contradiction in the material being studied. (Thus, for example, Anselm's *De grammatico* begins with the student asking the teacher to resolve an apparent conflict between Priscian and Boethius as to whether *literate* is a substance or a quality.) The teacher would then show how this quandary could be resolved, modeling the procedures students would need to use to solve similar problems in the future. (The problems investigated might eventually include even complex theological issues like the nature of Trinitarian relationships, the necessity of the Incarnation, and the relationship between divine foreknowledge, predestination, grace, and free will.)

In responding to a student's question, the teacher sought to show how the proposed solution precisely fit the problem, so that the student might sense the rightness (rectitude) of the solution and take delight in it.[14] Anselm emphasizes the pleasure that accompanies intellectual discovery and makes learning intrinsically enjoyable in spite of the hard work involved. In the preface to the *Proslogion*, Anselm describes the intensity of his intellectual quest, the flash of insight that showed him the right and fitting answer to his question, and the great delight and joy he experienced: I began to wonder if perhaps it might be possible to find one single argument that required no other save itself, and that by itself would suffice to prove that God really exists, that He is the supreme good needing no other and is He whom all things have need of for their being and well-being, and also to prove whatever we believe about the Divine Being. But as often and as diligently as I turned my thoughts to this, sometimes it seemed to me that I had almost reached what I was seeking, sometimes it eluded my acutest thinking so completely, so that finally in desperation, I was about to give up what I was looking for as something impossible to find. However, when I had decided to put aside this idea altogether … in spite of my unwillingness and resistance to it, it began to force itself upon me more and more pressingly.

---

[14] For further discussion, see G.R. Evans, "Insight in the Thought of St. Anselm," *Reading Medieval Studies* 1 (1975): 1-15.

So ... when I was quite worn out with resisting ... there came to me ... what I had despaired of finding ... Judging, then, that what had given me such joy to discover, would afford pleasure, if it were written down to anyone that might read it, I have written the following ... [15]

Given the mind's restless desire to understand and the pleasure the mind experiences when it gains insight, seekers of wisdom will naturally band together in a community of learners. In the beginning of *Why God Became Man*, Anselm describes this common quest that binds him to others:

> I have often been asked most earnestly ... to set down a written record of the reasoned explanations with which I am in the habit of answering people who put enquiries to me about a certain question of Our Faith. For they say that these explanations please them, and they think them satisfactory. They make this request, not with a view of arriving at faith through reason, but in order that they may take delight in the understanding and contemplation of the things which they believe ... [16]

This common thirst to understand the wisdom of God unites one to others in bonds of spiritual friendship; such friendship plays an essential role in one's return to God and union with God.[17]

> If it is wisdom, the very Wisdom of God will show itself to them. If it is friendship, they will love God more than themselves and one another as themselves, and God will love them more than they love themselves because it is through Him that they love Him and themselves and one another ... Therefore in that perfect and pure love of the countless angels and holy men where no one will love another less than himself, each will rejoice for every other as for himself ... to the degree that each one loves some other, so he will rejoice in the good of that other.[18]

The search for wisdom thus begins and ends with love, transcending the limitations of the formal curriculum; since love contains within itself a natural drive toward relationship and community, learning can never be a purely solitary individual activity.

---

[15] *Proslogion*, Preface, trans. Brian Davies and G. R. Evans, 82.

[16] Anselm, *Why God Became Man* 1.1; trans. Brian Davies and G. R. Evans 265.

[17] Cf. Julian Haseldine, "The Monastic Culture of Friendship," in Clarke, 182: "Friendship in this view finds its value not in personal emotional growth within particular relationships but rather in its capacity to extend beyond any such instances and to enrich the community experience and lead to God... Furthermore, this type of community was for them not the result of mere historical circumstance but represented the inheritance of a sure path to salvation and the highest human vocation."

[18] *Proslogion* 25; trans. Brian Davies and G. R. Evans, 103.

CONCLUSION

Because Anselm published no theoretical treatise on education, his contributions to teaching and learning have often been overlooked. Anselm's approach to education can nonetheless be reconstructed from his logical works and theological treatises. These texts show that Anselm stood at the intersection of two different worlds, Benedictine monasticism and an emerging scholastic tradition centered on Aristotelian logic.

In Benedictine monasticism, although study was required, it was clearly and consistently subordinated to the goal of spiritual formation. Education was not pursued for its own sake and could be justified only insofar as it supported the broader Benedictine project of learning obedience, reading the Scriptures rightly, and being perfected in love.

Where more advanced studies, such as logic, existed, they remained the concern of an elite few. The use of logic, in particular, had to be defended against suspicions that it aimed to pronounce judgment on the faith (and might find the faith wanting).

The genius of Anselm was to propose a way of reconciling and connecting these two worlds. God's will, Anselm argued, has ordered the world in a way that reflects the commitments of God. Because God has bound himself to a certain ordered way of proceeding in the world, he has made it possible for us to seek out and grasp why things must be as they are. Far from being an imposition upon the faith, such enquiries are supremely reverent in character, reflecting a disposition to seek and love the truth and, in loving the truth, we find ourselves loving God.

PRIMARY SOURCE SAMPLE [19]

I have often been asked most earnestly, both by word of mouth and in writing, by many people, to set down a written record of the reasoned explanations with which I am in the habit of answering people who put enquiries to me about a certain question of Our Faith. For they say that these explanations please them, and they think them satisfactory. They make this request, not with a view to arriving at faith through reason, but in order that they make take delight in the understanding and contemplation of the things which they believe, and may be, as far as they are able, 'ready always to give satisfaction to all who ask the reason for the hope that is in us' [1 Peter 3:15]. The question is one which unbelievers, deriding Christian simplicity as foolish, are in the habit of raising as an objection against us, and many

---

[19] This primary source sample is quoted from Anselm, *Why God Became Man*, 1.1, trans. Brian Davies and G.R. Evans, 265.

believers too are in the habit of pondering it in their hearts. The question is this: By what logic or necessity did God become man, and by his death, as we believe and profess, restore life to the world, when he could have done this through the agency of some other person, angelic or human, or simply by willing it? About this issue not only people who are literate, but many also who are unlettered, ask questions and long for a rational explanation. Many people, then, are asking for a treatment of this subject, and, although it is one which in the course of enquiry appears very difficult, in its solution it is intelligible to all, and appealing because of its utility and the beauty of its logic. With this in mind, I grant that what has been said about the matter by the holy Fathers ought to be sufficient, but I will nevertheless undertake to make plain to enquirers what God shall see fit to reveal to me about this subject. And since matters which are explored by means of question and answer are clearer to many people, particularly to slower intellects, and are correspondingly more pleasing, I will take, from among the people who importune me with this request, the one who is the most insistent of them all in goading me on to undertake this endeavor, and I shall have him dispute with me. And so, let Boso ask the questions, and let Anselm answer ...

BIBLIOGRAPHY

Anselm, *The Prayers and Meditations of St. Anselm.* Translated by Benedicta Ward. New York: Penguin, 1973.

Boschung, Peter. *From a Topical Point of View: Dialectic in Anselm of Canterbury's De Grammatico.* Leiden: Brill, 2006.

Davies, Brian and G.R. Evans, trans. *Anselm of Canterbury: The Major Works.* Oxford: Oxford University Press, 1998.

Evans, G.R. "Insight in the Thought of St. Anselm." *Reading Medieval Studies* 1 (1975): 1-15.

_____. "St. Anselm and Teaching," *History of Education* 5 (1976): 89-101.

_____. "St. Anselm's Analogies," *Vivarium* 14 (1976): 81-93.

_____. "The Meaning of Monastic Culture: Anselm and His Contemporaries." In *The Culture of Medieval English Monasticism*, edited by James G. Clarke, 75-85. Rochester, N.Y.: The Boydell Press, 2007.

Haseldine, Julian. "The Monastic Culture of Friendship." In *The Culture of Medieval English Monasticism*, edited by James G. Clarke, 177-202. Rochester, N.Y.: The Boydell Press, 2007.

Luhtala, Anneli. *Grammar and Philosophy in Late Antiquity: A Study of Priscian's Sources.* Amsterdam: John Benjamins, 2005.

Southern, R.W. *The Life of St. Anselm, Archbishop of Canterbury.* Oxford: Clarendon, 1972.

ADDITIONAL RECOMMENDED WORKS

Baumstein, Paschal. "Benedictine Education: Principles of Anselm's Patronage," *American Benedictine Review* 43, no. 1 (March 1992): 3-11.

Biff, Inos, Costante Marabelli, and Stefano Maria Malaspina, eds. *Anselmo d'Aosta Educatore Europeo.* Milan: Jaca Book, 2003.

Evans, G.R. *Anselm.* London: Continuum, 1989.

Southern, R.W. *Saint Anselm. A Portrait in Landscape.* Cambridge: Cambridge University Press, 1990.

Thomas Aquinas:

Teaching Theology in the Age of Universities

DANIEL FĂRCAȘ

Thomas Aquinas (1225-1274)

Thomas Aquinas was the most important theologian in the Middle Ages and — along with Plato, Aristotle, Descartes, Kant, Hegel, and Heidegger — one of the major philosophers in the history of the Western world. As an instructor of theology, he both illustrated the medieval curricula and teaching methods and offered an Aristotelian framework to explain teaching in general and the teaching of Christian theology in particular. Aquinas' philosophy of teaching can be found in a short writing titled *On the Teacher*, where he defines teaching in terms of bringing into *act* the *potency* of knowledge which is in the soul of the pupil. There is an apologetic aspect of Aquinas' philosophy of education, which is profoundly Christian and partially directed against pagan understandings of teaching. In this regard, Aquinas paradoxically uses Aristotelian philosophical categories to build up a Christian philosophy of education. Through his activity as a theology instructor, Aquinas tried to build bridges between the pagan philosophy and Christian doctrines, while preserving theology within an orthodox framework.

HISTORICAL BACKGROUND

The theological background of Aquinas' century was quite complex. There was a shift in the way theologians used to speak about God due to a change in the philosophical context of his century. The thirteenth century was known as the Century of Scholasticism. There were three main directions that defined this century. The first of them was a philosophy inspired by a Christian Platonism and was mainly influenced by the Augustinian tradition. Considered to be one of the sources of Scholasticism, Augustine's (354-430) theology survived over the centuries within a Christian context. The theology of Augustine included a distinctive Platonic ingredient, moderately welcomed by the Fathers of the Church as well as by most medieval authors. The Platonic categories were believed to offer the conceptual material for Christian philosophy, and this partially explains its success in the Christian world. The other two directions were related to Aristotelian philosophy, whose writings on natural philosophy and metaphysics were finally retrieved and translated into Latin after centuries when only his writings on logic had been known. But these two directions were quite different in their purposes and in their conclusions. One was the so-called "Heterodox Aristotelism," or "Latin Averroism"[1] represented by Siger of Brabant (ca. 1265-1281/1284) and Boethius of Dacia, masters of the Parisian faculty of arts. Their teaching was based on Aristotle's philosophy but was read and interpreted through the lens offered by the commentaries of the Muslim philosopher Averroes (1126-1198).[2] While the Parisian Averroists supported philosophical ideas conflicting with the Christian worldview (such as the eternity of the world — *i.e.* there is no creation and no end of this world — as well as the unity of the intellect — *i.e.* there is no personal intellect but the sole divine intellect manifested in humans, so there is no individual soul to survive after the death of the body), the other Aristotelian trend of the thirteenth century was represented by Christian theologians such as Albert the Great (ca. 1200-1280) and Thomas Aquinas (1225-1274), a master and his student. These two Dominican theologians were the breakthrough of Aristotelism in Christian medieval theology. So far, theologians had resisted Aristotelism because it was seen as conflicting with the Scriptures, and they preferred Platonic concepts (considered more mystical and appropriate to theology) to support their doctrine.[3] Albert and Aquinas strived to accommodate Aristotelian

---

[1] See Fernand Van Steenberghen, *La philosophie au XIIIᵉ siècle* (Louvain: Publications universitaires, Paris: Béatrice-Nauwelaerts, 1966), 11.

[2] Averroes was widely known as the "Commentator," because of his extensive commentaries on all of Aristotle's writings.

[3] Platonism, as well as Aristotelism represented the two main philosophical directions of the classical philosophy, which highly influenced medieval thought. They are not unvarying philosophical directions, so any description is limited. Based on Plato's philosophy, Neo-Platonists came up with a

philosophy to the biblical revelation and so they were the first theologians to write a Christian theology using Aristotelian terminology.

In brief, putting the Heterodox Aristotelism aside, one could conclude that the two alternative approaches of the thirteenth century Christian theology were made up by a combination of philosophical categories, but each approach included a dominant aspect, which was either a Neo-Platonic or an Aristotelian element. While we can identify a certain amount of Christian Platonism in Aquinas' writings (no theologian was secured against an authoritative patristic tradition which included Augustine's and Pseudo-Dionysius' theological books!), Aquinas' theology was modeled mainly by Aristotelism. Indeed, the major challenge of the thirteenth century education was a question over Aristotle's use in theology. The difference between Aquinas and his contemporaries can be found in the way they phrased the question over Aristotle. While most of Aquinas' contemporaries tried to find out why Aristotle's philosophy was not suitable for the study of theology, Aquinas rephrased the question over Aristotle and answered it accordingly: How can Aristotle's pagan philosophy serve Christian theology?

A PLACE FOR QUESTIONING: AQUINAS
AND THE AGE OF UNIVERSITIES

Aquinas' century was the century of universities. While the origin of universities can be found in the twelfth century, it is in the thirteenth century that the university became a well-rounded institution in medieval society and started to develop at an accelerated pace.

---

hierarchical image of the world and usually defined God as the One beyond Being (or as the Good beyond Being). There is an Idea (or a model) for every single thing in this world, and Ideas are placed in the divine intellect. Also, most Neo-Platonists contended that human souls should try to reach God through a mystical experience. There are also some philosophical ideas blatantly conflicting with the Christian theology (such as the preexistence of the souls, which are thought to be uncreated divine spirits, as well as the dualistic worldview, which involves the idea that matter and body are considered to be evil as opposed to God, who is good). According to Aristotle (who was Plato's main disciple), there are no separated Ideas of the things. On the contrary, a thing is made up of matter and form and it comes into being when the form (existing in the matter as potency) is brought into act. In brief, Aristotelism explains the world in terms of concepts such as matter and form, potency and act. All the medieval philosophers and theologians used categories from both these philosophical systems, so we can't speak of pure Platonic or pure Aristotelian philosophies in the Middle Ages. Nevertheless, medieval authors used Platonic and Aristotelian philosophical categories in different amounts, so we can speak of a philosopher's dominantly Platonic or dominantly Aristotelian philosophical or theological systems. Albert the Great and Aquinas were the first two major theologians to create theological systems dominantly inspired by Aristotle's philosophy.

The University of Paris was the second university (after Bologna) to come into being and was officially recognized by the pope in 1215. Universities brought together people and ideas that shaped the destiny of philosophical and theological education. Universities were corporations of schools (*universitas facultatum*),[4] as well as corporations of instructors and students (*universitas magistrorum et scholarum*); they were, also academic guilds where students were apprentices of their masters (*magistri*).

Aquinas studied and taught at the University of Paris. At the time Aquinas became a student, the University of Paris included four different faculties: the faculty of arts, the faculty of medicine, the faculty of law (*i.e.* canon law), and the faculty of theology. The faculty of arts was considered the "inferior faculty" (as opposed to the three "superior faculties"), because the access to the study of medicine, jurisprudence, or theology was opened only for the faculty of arts graduates, known as masters of arts (*magistri artium*). In other words, the study of theology was conditioned on the study of arts as a preliminary study (consisting of seven liberal arts, which included the so-called *trivium* – grammar, logic, and rhetoric — and *quadrivium* — arithmetic, geometry, music, and astronomy). As the study of liberal arts was based on Greek and Latin knowledge, in Aquinas' century, it included the study of Aristotelian philosophy (including natural philosophy and metaphysics), sometimes read based on Arabic commentaries (namely those of Averroes). This situation generated a deep conflict between the faculty of arts and the faculty of theology; it was a clash between two worldviews. The University of Paris was profoundly marked by this conflict, which shaped both the philosophy and theology of the thirteenth and fourteenth centuries, and Aquinas was directly involved in the debate over the writings of the Latin Averroists. This conflict produced an interesting debate between theologians and philosophers, which was a conflict between Christian and non-Christian worldviews. But it was an academic conflict as well, which generated an important number of polemic writings. Aquinas had his own contribution to this debate, with his treatises *On There Being Only One Intellect: Against the Averroists* and *On the Eternity of the World* (1270); each essay addressing one of the two major non-Christian ideas the Averroists held.

Within the faculty of theology of the Parisian university, there were two theological chairs: one was held by Franciscan monks and the other by Dominican theologians (the Franciscan and Dominican orders being the most important intellectual orders of that time). Among the various differences between Franciscans and Dominicans was the question on the

---

[4] Hastings Rashdall, *The Universities of Europe in the Middle Ages*, vol. 1 (Cambridge: Cambridge University Press, 2010), 6.

highest power of the soul: for Franciscans, it was by means of will (*i.e.* of love) whereby we can relate to God, while for Dominicans it was by means of the intellect whereby humans are able to know God. Besides the academic conflict between the faculty of arts and that of theology, there was another academic conflict within the faculty of theology. Theological differences between the masters of the Parisian school generated controversies, which resulted in academic disputations known as *quaestiones disputatae* ("disputed questions"). They were not only a new theological genre, but a teaching method as well. In Aquinas' century, it became a tradition as well as an academic duty for the scholars or students to engage in theological disputations before the masters and students on a weekly basis. These disputations were not only tournaments between academic knights, but also a pattern for the modern academic debate. Teaching theology was performed by asking good questions and striving to provide clear answers.

AUTHORSHIP AND TEACHING:
AQUINAS' CONTRIBUTION TO EDUCATION

In his history of medieval philosophy, Étienne Gilson contended that Aquinas' most important works (with the exception of *Summa contra Gentiles*) were generated from his teaching activity.[5] In fact, Aquinas' writings, as well as the writings of most of his major Parisian contemporaries, were the result of an academic activity. Aquinas was born in a noble family at Roccasseca Castle in the area of the town of Aquino (in the Lazio region of Italy), and he lived, learned, and worked in an academic setting. He lived his early years at the Montecassino Abbey, where he received his elementary education. At the age of fourteen, he went to the University of Naples as a student of the faculty of arts (1239). Around 1244, Aquinas became a Domincan monk, where he learned education and apologetic preaching from the Dominican Order, the Order of Preachers. In 1245, he began studies at the University of Paris under the Dominican monk Albert the Great, whom he joined at the Dominican *studium generale* of Cologne in 1248. In 1252, he returned to Paris to earn his master of theology (which he completed in 1256). From 1252-1273, Aquinas taught theology in different schools or universities including Agnani, Orvieto, Rome, Viterbo, Paris, and Naples. He continued teaching until several months before his death in 1274. Most of his writings were intended for academic purposes: some of them were treatises he wrote as a student before earning his academic degrees in theology, according to the academic requirements of that time; some others were books and treatises he wrote as an academic and instructor of theology. He is considered by the Roman Catholic Church as a *doctor ecclesiae* (a "doctor or teacher of the Church") — an

---

[5] Étienne Gilson, *La philosophie au Moyen-Âge*, vol. 1 (Paris: Payot, 1922), 139.

important honorary title awarded to the most famous theologians of the Church[6] — and as the *doctor angelicus* ("angelic doctor").

A survey of Aquinas' most important works will help us understand both the curricula and the methods used in thirteenth century theological university education, as well as Aquinas' teaching content and methods.

AQUINAS' CURRICULUM AND METHODS

Aquinas' teaching resulted in an impressive number of writings. Based on these writings, we can identify Aquinas' curricula and teaching methods, which are quite similar to the curriculum and methods used in the thirteenth century.

THE COMMENTARY

Each theological genre Aquinas explored involves a specific theological method. One of the theological genres he used was the *commentary*. According to the academic tradition of his time, every student in theology was supposed to work a number of years as "bachelor of the Bible" (*baccalaureus biblicus*), reading the Bible. The "reading" (*lectio*) of the Bible was a public activity consisting of teaching the Bible.[7] Beginning in his early years as *baccalaureus biblicus* and continuing throughout his life, Aquinas wrote an impressive number of biblical commentaries: on Isaiah, on Jeremiah, on Lamentations, on the gospel according to Matthew, on the gospel according to John, on Paul's epistles, on Job, and on the Psalms. He also wrote the *Golden Chain*, a work dedicated to the four gospels, which consists of a collection of paraphrases from various Church Fathers on each verse of the gospels. However, most of Aquinas' biblical commentaries are known as expositions. An "exposition" was no longer a liturgical or devotional reading of the Bible (as it used to be in previous centuries), but it reflected an effort to provide an academic approach to the sacred text based on its literal meaning rather than on its allegorical one, as well as Scripture is reflected on holistically.

Aquinas commented on other theological books credited with theological authority at that time. One of his first commentaries was on Peter Lombard's books

---

[6] This title was shared by Aquinas with some other medieval theologians, such as: Anselm of Canterbury (also known as the "Magnificent Doctor"), Albertus Magnus (also known as the "Universal Doctor"), Bonaventure (known as the "Seraphic Doctor"), Duns Scotus (the "Subtle Doctor") or John of the Cross (honored by the Catholic Church as the "Mystic Doctor").

[7] Marie-Dominique Chenu, *Introduction à l'étude de saint Thomas d'Aquin* (Paris: Vrin, 1950), 207.

of *Sentences*.[8] Commenting and teaching Lombard's *Sentences* was a requirement for every student who stood for a master's degree in theology. At this stage, the student was a "bachelor of the *Sentences*" (*bacalaureus sententiarum*). Aquinas' commentary on the *Sentences* is an original theological masterwork and his first attempt to provide a systematic approach to the Christian doctrines. Aquinas' theological commentaries include commentaries on Pseudo-Dionysius' *On the Divine Names* and on Boethius' *On the Trinity*.

The two stages that a student had to complete in order to earn a master's degree in theology correspond to the two sources of authority in the Catholic Church — Scripture and Tradition. Also, while we cannot speak yet about a biblical theology and a systematic theology in the modern sense (because the reading of the Bible is here less exegetical and the reading of the *Sentences* is quite philosophical), we can identify the two major branches of theology: an analytical approach of the sacred text and a systematic approach of the doctrines.

DISPUTED QUESTIONS

Another theological genre illustrated by Aquinas was the *disputed question,* a teaching and training method. This method purposed for masters to engage in academic disputation on different theological subjects. At the University of Paris, these disputations were customarily conducted between Dominicans and Franciscans. With the disputed questions, theology goes into the era of universities: doctrine is debated and theological solutions are questioned. A disputed question began with a list of pros and cons (usually, the cons or the objections were listed first), continued with a solution offered by the master, and ended with the rejection of the cons according to the solution already provided. Among Aquinas' various disputed questions, we mention: *On Truth* (where he strives to define truth and knowledge from a theological and philosophical standpoint and, in the second part, the concept of good); *On the Power of God* (Aquinas defines the power of God based on two Aristotelian correlative concepts: power – *i.e.* possibility – and act); *On Evil*; *On the Soul* (here again, Aquinas uses Aristotle's treatise *De anima*) etc.[9]

---

[8] The four books of the *Sentences* (*Sententiarum libri quatuor*) were a twelfth century collection of patristic quotes gathered and edited by Peter Lombard (1095-1160), a bishop of Paris; the quotations were grouped according to the different theological doctrines, in order to form a textbook of theology.

[9] Jan A. Aertsen, "Aquinas's philosophy in its historical setting," in *The Cambridge Companion to Aquinas*, eds. Norman Kretzmann and Eleonore Stump (Cambridge: Cambridge University Press, 1999), 17.

SERMONS

A third theological genre was the *sermon*. Preaching was viewed as a teaching activity at university, as masters were supposed to preach "before the University" (*coram universitate*),[10] *i.e.* before the masters of theology and the students. As a teaching activity, academic sermons (*sermones*) were sometimes assimilated with conferences (*collationes*) on different theological topics. A small number of Aquinas' sermons have survived. However, we mention Aquinas' sermons (and conferences) on the Child Jesus, on the Feast of Pentecost, on the prayer "Our Father," on the Parable of the Sower, on the false prophets, on the Ten Commandments, etc. While their influence was little, it is important to note that Aquinas illustrated this genre (which was mandatory for every master of theology), and used it in his teaching.

THEOLOGICAL SYNTHESIS

The theological synthesis, a fourth theological genre, were intended to be either catechetical or dogmatic writings. Aquinas' commentary on Peter Lombard's *Sentences* is more than a mere commentary: as Lombard intended his *Sentences* to cover all Christian doctrines, Aquinas' commentary is a contribution to systematic theology as well (which includes the doctrine of God, the doctrine of creation, including angels, humans and the doctrine of sin; the doctrines of incarnation and salvation, as well as a review of virtues; the doctrine of the sacraments, and the doctrine of sin). The *Compendium of Theology* is a catechetical writing, which includes reflections both on dogmatic and practical theology. It is intended to be a brief summary of the Christian doctrine divided into three main sections, according to the three "theological virtues," as they are called by the Catholic Church: faith (the doctrines of God, of the works of God, of creation, of the Last Days, and of the eternal life, as well as hamartiology, Christology, etc.), hope (on prayer), love (on virtues, on love, and on sin). Maybe the most known of Aquinas' works are the two *summae*: the *Summa contra Gentiles* and the *Summa Theologiae*. The latter, *Summa Theologiae*, includes three parts (or even four, because the second part is divided in two). The first one (*I^a pars*) deals with the doctrine of God, Trinity, creation, and image of God; the second one (*I^a II^{ae}* and *II^a II^{ae}*) deals with concepts such as law, grace, virtue, and sin, and contemplative life; finally, the third one (*III^a pars*) deals with Christology and sacraments. The outline of all of Aquinas' theological syntheses is quite the same: it begins with God as transcendent, his relation to the world, and

---

[10] Jean-Pierre Torrel, *Initiation à saint Thomas d'Aquin. Sa personne et son œuvre* (Fribourg: Éditions universitaires Fribourg (Paris: Éditions du Cerf, 1993), 104.

finishes on some practical aspect of Christian theology (Christian life, sacraments etc.).

Some of these theological genres can also be viewed as teaching methods. Aquinas' *Sentences* are more than an exposition of Peter Lombard's writings — they are a systematic approach of the doctrine. As M. D. Chenu noted, Aquinas included large commentaries of different scriptures in his *Summa Theologiae*, and two examples include the creation narrative from Genesis (*Summa Theologiae*, I, q. 65-74) and the life of Jesus Christ (*Summa Theologiae*, III, q. 27-59).[11] Also, Aquinas used questions (*quaestiones*) as divisions of his different systematic treatises, such as his commentary of the *Sentences*, *Summa contra Gentiles* and his *Summa Theologiae*.

The theological genres Aquinas used to illustrate his curriculum were founded on Scripture; however, his study of the Old and New Testaments must be understood within its medieval context, when access to the original languages was rare, and interpretation was highly influenced by tradition. Secondly, Aquinas taught dogmatic theology and his teaching was shaped by the medieval worldview and philosophical categories in use at that time. Lastly, as the thirteenth century was marked by the presence of muslims in Europe, including their influence on Christian thought, Aquinas provided an apologetic approach: not only were his writings apologetic, but his preaching was also (in fact, the Dominican Order — also known as the Order of Preachers — was an apologetic order: since their beginnings, Dominicans had set their goal to defend the gospel against the pagans). In short, Aquinas' teaching was biblical, doctrinal, and apologetic. We should also add that all these three aspects of Aquinas' curriculum were influenced by his interest in Aristotle's metaphysics and its potential in offering a philosophical support for theology. (Aquinas was probably the most important theologian who produced a *philosophical theology*.) In other words, the fourth feature of Aquinas' theological teaching is philosophical.

ON THE TEACHER: AQUINAS' THEOLOGY OF EDUCATION

The question on how teaching and discipleship are possible was not one of Aquinas' favorite topics. In fact, Aquinas was a celebrated educator rather than a theorist of teaching and education. His main contribution to the philosophy of education is a short disputed question, namely *On Truth*, XI (which is known as *On the Teacher* or, in Latin, *De magistro*).

Some other references to the same topic can be found in: Summa contra Gentiles, II, 75, 14-17; Summa Theologiae, I, q. 117, a. 1 and a. 2, to which we should add some incidental references to the topic of teaching, such as II Sentences, d. 9, a. 2, ad 4 and d. 28, a. 5, ad 3; Sermon on the Child Jesus etc.

[11] Chenu, *Introduction à l'étude de saint Thomas d'Aquin*, 222.

It is hard to answer the question of why Aquinas was not interested in this topic, but we should notice that there is a more basic aspect which underlies the problem of education — the question of knowledge: Can we know anything at all? What can we know? How can we know? Aquinas' theory of knowledge can be found in all of his writings, either explicitly developed or implicitly involved in the text, and is inspired by Aristotelian philosophy. As a general rule, for Aristotle, knowledge is the actualization of the general concepts in the intellect, based on the data from the external world reported by senses. Inspired by Aristotle, Aquinas elaborated on a theory of knowledge dependent on abstraction (*i.e.* our intellect generates abstract concepts based on the diversity of objects reported to us by our five senses).[12] In other words, general concepts (which are a matter of teaching) are based on our interaction with the outside world. General concepts are not in a (divine) "intelligible place" (*topos noetos*, as Plato stated), but they are generated by our intellect based on the information produced by our senses. The contact with the outside world is a basic principle Aquinas applies to theology: creation provides a lot of information about its creator, because God naturally revealed himself in his creation. Thus, every created reality includes a likeness of God or God's "traces" (*vestigia dei*), and humans are made in the image and likeness of God. The existence of God was proved by Aquinas using five arguments based on the relation of the creation with its creator or, to put it philosophically, based on the relation of the effects to their cause.[13] Also, the attributes of God we find in the Bible should be understood, according to Aquinas, as analogies[14] (creation is good because God is good, so, based on the good aspects of the created world, we can get an idea of what God's goodness means[15]).

TEACHING

Are teaching and learning possible? According to Aquinas, they are possible under two circumstances.[16] First of all, learning is possible for humans provided that humans are individuals endowed with intellect. While this might sound strange, Aquinas had to defend human ability to learn and teach against Averroes, who stated that individuals do not possess a personal intellect. We have already seen that one of the major theological inquiries of the

---

[12] For Aquinas's theory of knowledge by abstraction, see Peter S. Eardley and Carl N. Still, *Aquinas: A Guide for Perplexed* (London, UK: Continuum, 2010), 51-66.

[13] Thomas Aquinas, *Summa Theologiae*, I, q. 2, a. 3.

[14] On the complex topic of the "analogy of being", see Bernard Montagnes, *The Doctrine of the Analogy of Being according to Thomas Aquinas* (Milwaukee: Marquette University Press, 2004).

[15] Aquinas, *Summa Theologiae*, I, q. 13.

[16] Aquinas, *On the Teacher*, a. 1, *reply*.

thirteenth century concerned the oneness of the intellect (or, in other words, the Arabian philosophy of Averroes according to which there was a sole intellect, common to all human beings). Aquinas makes a plea for the Christian *personalism*: this means that every human being is an individual person, endowed with his or her own intellect. (On the contrary, one can't be a person unless he or she possesses an individual intellect.) In other words, teaching and learning is a process which concerns two different people — a teacher and a learner — who do not share the same intellect, but will possibly possess a common science, as the teacher is able to *cause* the science in his pupil.[17] This approach concerns another Arabian philosophy as well — Avicenna's conception of the "giver of forms" (*dator formarum*), which is the divine agent intellect which generates a flow of knowledge toward humans. In a personalist setting such as Aquinas', this approach is useless and even ambiguous.[18] Secondly, learning and teaching are possible provided that knowledge is not deposited in the human soul (or in its highest part, which is the intellect). If it were so, learning would not be more than remembering what one already knows; in this case, learning would not be a real process. Of course, Aquinas has in mind various philosophies of knowledge inspired by Plato. Indeed, according to Plato, learning was considered to be the act of remembering what human souls (pre-existent to the body and identified with divinities, which means they were not created but have always existed) have already known before their incarnation. If it were so, states Aquinas, teaching would not be possible (it would be a mere illusion consisting in remembering what one already knows).

If an actual knowledge is not infused by a "giver of forms," nor is it already deposited in the human soul, how is learning still possible? Aquinas uses Aristotelian concepts (act and potency, effect and cause, etc.) to define knowledge:

> For certain seeds of knowledge pre-exist in us, namely, the first concepts of understanding, which by the light of the agent intellect are immediately known through the species abstracted from sensible things. These are either complex, as axioms, or simple, as the notions of being, of the one, and so on, which the understanding grasps immediately. In these general principles, however, all the consequences are included as in certain seminal principles. When, therefore, the mind is led from these general notions to actual knowledge of the particular things, which it knew previously in general and, as it were, potentially, then one is said to acquire knowledge.[19]

---

[17] Aquinas, *Summa contra Gentiles*, II, 75, 14.

[18] Aquinas, *On the Teacher*, a. 1, *reply*.

[19] Aquinas, *On the Teacher*, a. 1, *reply* (trans. James V. McGlynn, 1953).

There are several aspects we should mention on knowledge: knowledge is the actualization of a potency by abstraction (*i.e.* the actualization of general and intellective principles — the seeds of knowledge, which are already in the human soul as potency — in the presence of particular and material realities or, more accurately, in the presence of the abstracted species of particular realities); this actualization is an effect determined by a double cause (*i.e.* an inner cause, which is the agent intellect of each person, and an outer cause, which is the sensible reality). Based on the knowledge of general principles, one can reason because the conclusions are included in general principles. This is already a learning process, but is conducted individually. This variety of knowledge acquisition is known as "discovery."

A more complex variety of knowledge acquisition is based on the "teaching" process and follows a similar pattern based on actualization and causality. Teaching consists of the actualization of potential knowledge, not by abstraction but by using "signs" which pass on to the pupil the reasoning process of the teacher.[20] The outer cause of knowledge is, in this case, the teacher himself. Common sense and the teacher are similar in that they are outer causes of knowledge and they mediate knowledge. The major difference teaching involves is the way it operates, *i.e.* by signs (there is a semiotic aspect of teaching).

As the agent intellect is thought to be the image of God in the human being, Aquinas contends that it is through the natural light of the intellect that God operates in us. Through the intellect, "God alone teaches interiorily and principally."[21] Consequently, we can say that the two causes of learning are the external teacher (a human instructor) and the internal teacher (God, who operates by the intellect).

THE TEACHER AND THE LEARNER

Then who can be a teacher? It is clear that, for Aquinas, God is a teacher (*magister*), because He teaches us inside our soul by the agent intellect which illuminates the seeds of knowledge in our soul. However, God's presence in our soul is not supernatural, but is based on a natural power of the human soul which is the intellect. Indeed, Aquinas' theological system focuses on the natural revelation (it is a natural theology), because Aquinas intended to prove that there is no contradiction between faith and natural reason. Consequently, God as creator of the world is at the core of Aquinas' theology and Aquinas' theory of knowledge is based on this metaphysical understanding of theology. Just as he

---

[20] Aquinas, *On the Teacher*, a. 11, ad 11.

[21] Aquinas, *On the Teacher*, a. 11, *reply*.

causes the world to be, he also causes the knowledge in our souls.[22] He is both the agent that calls things into being and the agent that determines knowledge of the created world. Following Aristotle, Aquinas called God the "first mover" (*primum movens*) because, as he is the creator, God is the ultimate and highest agent who causes movement and change in the world.[23] Through the agent intellect he planted in us to be his image in man (*imago dei*), God is the mover which causes knowledge in us.

Man can be a teacher based on his resemblance to God. Man also can cause knowledge and so he is also a mover. This is seen in when he said, "The teacher furnishes the pupil's intellect with a stimulus to knowledge of the things which he teaches, as an indispensable mover, bringing the intellect from potentiality to actuality."[24]

While the learning process is possible without an external teacher through discovery, one can't be called his own teacher. In contrast with discovery, teaching is the best way to acquire knowledge, because a teacher possesses the detailed knowledge of the science and can guide his pupil faster and easier to the knowledge.[25]

But not only is God the internal teacher and man the external teacher. Angels can be teachers as well. In the hierarchical worldview professed by the Scholastic philosophers, angels are in the intermediary position between God and humans. Angels can't provide man general principles or axioms on which reasoning is based, as God does, nor can they propose to man sensible signs, as man can do when he teaches somebody, but angels can reinforce the light of the human intellect.[26] Man can teach angels, not on the divine realities, but on his own thoughts,[27] and angels can teach angels as well.[28]

CURRICULUM AND THE CONTENT OF TEACHING

When it comes to theology, what can be taught? Like all theologians of Scholasticism, Aquinas maintained that theology is a science, which is an important aspect for theology in the age of universities: while the sacred doctrine is given by revelation, it can be taught

---

[22] "To create implies first causality, which belongs to God alone; to make implies causality in general; to teach implies the same general causality with reference to knowledge". Cf. *On the Teacher*, a. 3, ad 16, translated by James V. McGlynn (Chicago: Henry Regnery Company), 1953.

[23] Aquinas, *Compendium of Theology*, I, 4.

[24] Aquinas, *On the Teacher*, a. 1, ad 12 (trans. James V. McGlynn, 1953).

25 Aquinas, *On the Teacher*, a. 2, ad 4.

[26] Aquinas, *On the Teacher*, a. 3.

[27] Aquinas, *Summa Theologiae*, I, q. 117, a. 2.

[28] Aquinas, *II Sentences*, d. 9, q. 1, a. 2, ad 4.

and learned. Theology is based on the wisdom provided by the divine revelation not by the human reason, but as Aquinas continues, theology instructs not only on truths which can be known by revelation but also on the truths covered by different philosophical disciplines.[29] Nevertheless, there is no contradiction between the truth of faith and the truth of reason, so the principles of knowledge implanted in us are also contained in the divine wisdom[30] and the created "sensible things, from which human reason takes its knowledge, retain within themselves some sort of trace of likeness to God."[31] We have already shown that, based on these traces, Aquinas provided his arguments for the existence of God, in addition to his theory of the language of theology (*i.e.* the theory of the "analogy of being").

The general pattern of teaching (which includes an internal teacher and an external one) is obvious here, too. While the light of grace is infused over us to teach us by revelation, Aquinas places the preacher in the position of the external teacher: "But because, apart from the infused light, the habit of faith is distinguished by determinate beliefs by the teaching of the preacher according to what is said in Romans 10:14 — 'And how are they to believe him whom they have not heard?'" — just as the understanding of principles naturally instilled is determined by the sensibles received, so the truth of the preacher is confirmed by miracles.[32] In addition to this, the use of metaphors, symbols, and parables is meant to supply the sensible basis to our knowledge of God.[33]

Theology is an argumentative science and, as the argument of authority is the most appropriate, theology uses not only the authority of revelation or tradition, but also the authority of philosophers.[34] The arguments are the method of conveying the sacred doctrine both to believers and non-believers. The method of inquiring of the authorities (present or ancient ones) is mentioned by Aquinas, because wisdom must be sought from a teacher or from those who are wiser than us.[35]

CONCLUSION

In his writings, Aquinas made a plea for theology as a science. Accordingly, if this belief in theology as a science is true, then theology is teachable! In this regard, Aquinas

---

[29] Aquinas, *Summa Theologiae*, I, a. 1, ad 2.

[30] Aquinas, *Summa contra Gentiles*, I, 7, 3.

[31] Aquinas, *Summa contra Gentiles*, I, 8, 1 (trans. Anton C. Pegis).

[32] Aquinas, *I Sentences*, q. 1, a. 5, sol. (trans. Joseph Kenny).

[33] Aquinas, *I Sentences*, q. 1, a. 5; *Summa Theologiae*, I, q. 1, a. 9.

[34] Aquinas, *I Sentences*, q. 1, a. 5, *reply*; *Summa Theologiae*, I, q. 1, a. 8.

[35] Aquinas, *Sermon on the Child Jesus*, collatio, 10.

retrieved Aristotle's philosophy in order to use it to substantiate his theological teachings. According to Aquinas, teaching is a natural process. The process of teaching is explained in Aristotelian metaphysical terms, such as causality, actualization, agent, form, etc. Besides, Aquinas introduces two Augustinian concepts — the internal teacher and the external teacher — which are interpreted through an Aristotelian lens: they are the two causes of teaching — God, as the principal teacher, and man, as a second and instrumental teacher. In brief, Aquinas' understanding of teaching involves that teaching is a rational and natural process, even when it is about teaching theology. As a major representative of Scholasticism, Aquinas offered a reflection on education based on what were the scientific authorities of his time, consistent with the new era theology had just entered — the age of universities.

PRIMARY SOURCE SAMPLE[36]

Now knowledge is acquired in man, both from an interior principle, as is clear in one who procures knowledge by his own research; and from an exterior principle, as is clear in one who learns (by instruction). For in every man there is a certain principle of knowledge, namely the light of the active intellect, through which certain universal principles of all the sciences are naturally understood as soon as proposed to the intellect. Now when anyone applies these universal principles to certain particular things, the memory or experience of which he acquires through the senses; then by his own research advancing from the known to the unknown, he obtains knowledge of what he knew not before. Wherefore anyone who teaches, leads the disciple from things known by the latter, to the knowledge of things previously unknown to him; according to what the Philosopher says (Poster. I, 1): "All teaching and all learning proceed from previous knowledge."

Now the master leads the disciple from things known to knowledge of the unknown, in a twofold manner. Firstly, by proposing to him certain helps or means of instruction, which his intellect can use for the acquisition of science: for instance, he may put before him certain less universal propositions, of which nevertheless the disciple is able to judge from previous knowledge: or he may propose to him some sensible examples, either by way of likeness or of opposition, or something of the sort, from which the intellect of the learner is led to the knowledge of truth previously unknown. Secondly, by strengthening the intellect of the learner; not, indeed, by some active power as of a higher nature, as explained above

---

[36] Thomas Aquinas, *The Summa Theologiae of St. Thomas Aquinas* Translated by the Fathers of the English Dominican Province, vols. 1-5 (Notre Dame/New York: Christian Classics/Benziger Bros., 1981), I, q. 117, a. 1.

(q. 106, a. 1; q. 111, a. 1) of the angelic enlightenment, because all human intellects are of one grade in the natural order; but inasmuch as he proposes to the disciple the order of principles to conclusions, by reason of his not having sufficient collating power to be able to draw the conclusions from the principles. Hence the Philosopher says (Poster. I, 2) that "a demonstration is a syllogism that causes knowledge." In this way a demonstrator causes his hearer to know.

BIBLIOGRAPHY

Aertsen, Jan A. "Aquinas's Philosophy in its Historical Setting." In *The Cambridge Companion to Aquinas*, edited by Norman Kretzmann and Eleonore Stump, 12-37. Cambridge: Cambridge University Press, 1999.

Aquinas, Thomas. *The Catena Aurea.* Volume III, Part I: "The Gospel of St. Luke." Translated by John Henry Newman, New York: Cosimo Inc., 2007.

————. *Compendium of Theology.* Translated by Cyril Vollert, St. Louis & London: B. Herder Book Co., 1947.

————. *The Disputed Questions on Truth.* Questions I-IX, Translated by Robert W. Mulligan, 1952; Questions X-XX, translated by James V. McGlynn, 1953; Questions XXI-XXIX, translated by Robert W. Schmidt, Chicago: Henry Regnery Company, 1954.

————. "On There Being only One Intellect." In *Aquinas Against the Averroists*, edited by Ralph McInnerny, 17-146. Purdue University Research Foundation, 1993.

————. *Sancti Thomae de Aquino Opera Omnia*, issu Leonis XIII P.M. edita. Tomus XXII: "Quaestiones Disputatae de Veritate," volumen II, fasc. 1 (qq. 8-12), Romae: ad Sanctae Sabinae, 1970.

————. *Summa contra Gentiles.* Translated by Anton C. Pegis, James C. Anderson, Vernon J. Bourke, Charles J. O'Neil, New York: Hanover House, 1955-1957.

————. *Summa Theologiae of St. Thomas Aquinas.* Translated by the Fathers of the English Dominican Province, vol. 1-5, Notre Dame/New York: Christian Classics/Benziger Bros., 1981.

Chenu, Marie-Dominique. *Introduction à l'étude de saint Thomas d'Aquin.* Paris: Vrin, 1950.

Dominican House of Studies. "St. Thomas Aquinas' Works in English." Accessed October 30, 2013. http://dhspriory.org/thomas/.

Eardley, Peter S. and Carl N. Still. *Aquinas: A Guide for Perplexed.* London (UK), New York (USA): Continuum, 2010.

Fundación Tomás de Aquino. "S. Thomae de Aquino Opera Omnia." Accessed October 30, 2013. http://www.corpusthomisticum.org/iopera.html.

Gilson, Étienne. *La philosophie au Moyen-Âge.* Paris: Payot, 2 vol., 1922.

McInnerny, Ralph, ed. *Thomas Aquinas: Selected Writings.* Penguin Classics, 1999.

Montagnes, Bernard. *The Doctrine of the Analogy of Being according to Thomas Aquinas.* Translated by E. M. Macierowski, Milwaukee: Marquette University Press, 2004.

Ozoliņš, Janis Talivaldis. "Aquinas and His Understanding of Teaching and Learning." In *Aquinas, Education and the East*, edited by Thomas Brian Mooney and Mark Nowacki, 9-25. Dordrecht: Springer, 2013.

Rashdall, Hastings. *The Universities of Europe in the Middle Ages.* Vol. 1: "Salerno, Bologna, Paris." Cambridge: Cambridge University Press, 2010.

Torrell, Jean-Pierre. *Initiation à saint Thomas d'Aquin. Sa personne et son œuvre*. Fribourg: Éditions universitaires Fribourg, Paris: Éditions du Cerf, 1993.

Van Steenberghen, Fernand. *La philosophie au XIIIe siècle*. Louvain: Publications universitaires, Paris: Béatrice-Nauwelaerts, 1966.

Velde, Ruedi A. te. "Natural Reason in the *Summa contra Gentiles*." In *Thomas Aquinas. Contemporary Philosophical Perspectives*, edited by Brian Davies, 117-140. Oxford: Oxford University Press, 2002.

PART II

Reformation Educators

(A.D. 1500-1650)

Various attempts to reform the church characterized the period from 1500 to 1650, and each movement contributed something to the development of Christian education. Reformers ranged from Christian humanists to pietists, and from Protestants to Counter Reformation Catholics. **Erasmus** (1466-1536), the most eminent Christian humanist, wanted to restore the Roman church, which had lost its spiritual moorings, to its ancient purity. But he also had a decisive influence on European education, encouraging better teaching methods and a greater understanding of the student. Erasmus was educated in a school in Deventer operated by the Brethren, part of the heterogeneous pietist movement that was to produce a number of significant educators.

The Protestant Reformation in Europe had a significant impact on all aspects of society, including education. Its primary leaders were **Martin Luther** (1483-1546) and **Philip Melanchthon** (1497-1560) in Germany, **Huldreich Zwingli** (1484-1531) and **John Calvin** (1509-1564) in Switzerland. The Protestants repudiated the authority and corruptions of the papacy, recognizing as their sole authority the Bible. Luther, who was a teacher throughout his career, wrote more about education than any of the rest. He helped to strengthen and establish schools' and to set up new curricula. He encouraged secular authorities to take an active role in the education of their constituency, and both secular and spiritual leaders from all of Germany sought his advice on educational matters. He was assisted by Melanchthon, who eventually became known as the "teacher of Germany." Melanchthon organized, developed, and refined Luther's ideas, including those concerning education. The educational efforts of Zwingli at Zurich and Calvin at Geneva were integral to their religious reforms. Zwingli was concerned with the education of all the people, seeing it as something to be conducted within a community of caring individuals. Calvin's gymnasium was a product of his experience at Strasbourg and became a training ground for young ministers. It was grounded in the principles of Calvin's Institutes of the Christian Religion and was organized just as logically and methodically. Calvin's academy became the pattern for Reformed education.

83

One of the leading figures of this Counter-Reformation was **Ignatius of Loyola** (1491-1556), founder of the Society of Jesus and its system of schools. Using his genius for organization and adapting the best educational theories and methods then available, he created an integrated curriculum which was graded but which also provided for the individual advancement of brighter students. He stressed the educational value of self-activity. His aim was to instill in students a Christian outlook on life and thus to influence society for good.

CHAPTER 6

Erasmus:

A Return to the Sources of Education

JASON J. GRAFFAGNINO

Desiderius Erasmus (1466-1536)

Erasmus' enduring legacy encourages educators today to recognize the value of a "humanistic" education that returns to classical and timeless sources of education rather than focusing on that which has yet to prove effective for training students in the Christian faith. In a letter to Christian Northhoff (1497), Erasmus wrote, "A constant element of enjoyment must be mingled with our studies, so that we think of learning as a game rather than a form of drudgery, for no activity can be continued for long if it does not to some extent afford pleasure to the participant." This view of education provides a picture of Erasmus' views on education and clarifies why he is worth studying today as an educator. He was concerned with not only the content of education, but the pedagogy and results found in a classroom as well. It is this intentionality that should resonate with teachers who seek to train up the next generation of Christian leaders.

HISTORICAL BACKGROUND

Desiderius Erasmus was born in Rotterdam, Netherlands as the illegitimate son of a priest.[1] After becoming orphaned at a young age, he was schooled under the tutelage of the Brethren of the Common Life and was influenced by the *Devotia Moderna*. He eventually entered an Augustinian monastery at Steyn. Being a brilliant student, Erasmus earned a secretary's post for a rising bishop that allowed him to exit his lowly monastic endeavor in favor of traveling throughout Europe in the highest of societal circles. After studying at the University of Paris, where he opposed the scholasticism of his day, he traveled to England where he became tutor of the children of Henry VII's court physician, Giovanni Barerio. Barerio took Erasmus to live in Italy with his family for two years, and it was in Turin where Erasmus earned his Doctor of Theology.[2]

Erasmus would ultimately influence the early lives of Henry VIII, Charles V, and Ferdinand of Spain.[3] He developed friendships with John Colet and Thomas More in England, and lectured in Greek and Theology at the University of Cambridge. His publication of a Greek New Testament in 1516 may have also emboldened future reformers who wanted greater access to scripture. A dispute between Erasmus and Luther over free will garnered the former strong support among the most radical of the reformers, the Anabaptists.[4] Erasmus spent his final years in Basle, where he sought the restoration of Christian peace and tranquility. The Roman Church that he sought to "purify" throughout his life eventually found his works to be heretical.[5]

---

[1] The exact day and year of Erasmus' birth in Holland are uncertain. He may have been embarrassed by the circumstances of his birth, since he later tried to cover over the matter by shifting the year of his birth. His father was said to be Roger Gerard, a skilled copier of manuscripts and a priest, and his mother, Margaret, the daughter of a physician. He had an elder brother named Pieter, born also of the same parents out of wedlock. Scholars have noted the apparent date of Erasmus' birth was either 27 or 28 October 1466, 1467, or 1469. Most surmise the year of his birth was actually 1466. See Léon E. Halkin, *Erasmus: A Critical Biography*, trans. John Tonkin (Oxford: Blackwell Publishers, 1994), 1; John P. Dolan, *The Essential Erasmus* (New York: New American Library, 1964), 17; Albert Rabil, Jr., "Desiderius Erasmus," in *Renaissance Humanism: Foundations, Forms, and Legacy*, vol. 2, *Humanism Beyond Italy* (Philadelphia: University of Pennsylvania Press, 1988), 216-17.

[2] Dolan, *The Essential Erasmus*, 17-19.

[3] Desiderius Erasmus, *The Education of a Christian Prince*, trans. and ed. Lester K. Born (New York: Columbia University Press, 1936), 4. In fact, Erasmus wrote this work to Charles V when the latter was only sixteen years of age.

[4] Abraham Friesen, *Erasmus, the Anabaptists, and the Great Commission* (Grand Rapids, MI: William B. Eerdmanns, 1998), 20-42; Jason J. Graffagnino, "The Shaping of the Two Earliest Anabaptist Catechisms" (PhD diss., Southwestern Baptist Theological Seminary, 2008), 10, 61-69, 148-55.

[5] Dolan, *The Essential Erasmus*, 20-23.

THEOLOGY OF CHRISTIAN EDUCATION
THEOLOGICAL HERMENEUTIC: A FAITH TO BE TAUGHT AND LEARNED

Erasmus was called "The Prince of the Humanists" and epitomized the idea of a "Christian" humanist.[6] He was certain that both religion and classical letters had deteriorated since the age of the last classical writers and the Church Fathers.[7] He desired to restore "both classical letters and classical Christianity by reestablishing culture and Christianity upon their ancient sources."[8] Erasmus focused on a recovery of an ancient, but in some ways new "method of learning," which re-examined the classical Latin and Greek authors and the Bible in its original languages. Erasmus often used *ad fontes*, meaning "to the sources" (literally "to living springs"), to call for a return to a "golden age" of Christianity before the dominance of popes and Church tradition. His desire was to recover the "distant age in which *real* culture and *real* Christian authenticity could be found."[9]

In this call for a revival of classical letters, Erasmus had concerns, which he shared in a letter to Wolfgang Capito[10] written on twenty-sixth of February 1517, eight months before

---

[6] Renaissance historians have tried to differentiate between secular humanism (specifically in the Italian cities) and "Christian" humanism. The implication was that one version of humanism was mainly pagan and the other specifically Christian. This thesis was dependent on what or who exactly was defined as a Christian humanist. Kristeller pointed out that if Christian humanists comprised those scholars who acknowledged the teachings of Christianity and were members of one of the Christian churches, but did not necessarily discuss religious or theological topics, then virtually all Renaissance humanists *were* Christian humanists, since the supposed cases of explicitly pagan or atheistic beliefs were atypical and ambiguous. However, in adequately discussing Christian humanism, one must use the term in a more specific manner, by identifying Christian humanists as "those scholars with a humanist classical and rhetorical training who explicitly discussed religious or theological problems in all or some of their writings." See Paul Oskar Kristeller, *Renaissance Thought and Its Sources*, ed. Michael Mooney (New York: Columbia Press, 1979), 86; Wallace K. Ferguson, *The Renaissance in Historical Thought: Five Centuries of Interpretation* (Cambridge, MA: Riverside Press, 1948), 41; Johan Huizinga, *Erasmus and the Age of the Reformation*, trans. Frederick J. Hopman and Barbara Flower (New York: Harper, 1957), 40.

[7] Ferguson, *Renaissance in Historical Thought*, 41. In Erasmus' day the major Church Fathers were Tertullian, Irenaeus, Origen, Jerome, Ambrose, Augustine, Chrysostom, Gregory of Nyssa, Gregory of Nazianzus, and Basil, among others. The title "Church Fathers" was not a static one, but rather a popular title that has been widely interpreted throughout Christian history.

[8] Bard Thompson, *Humanists and Reformers: A History of the Renaissance and Reformation* (Grand Rapids, MI: William B. Eerdmans, 1996), 30-31.

[9] Ibid., 31.

[10] Capito (1478-1541) was a Protestant Reformer and Old Testament scholar. In 1515 at Basle, he

Luther nailed his famous theses:

> In a word, all seems to me to promise the greatest success. There is still one misgiving in my mind: that under cover of the reborn literature of antiquity paganism may try to rear its ugly head, for we know that even among Christians some scarcely acknowledge Christ in more than name, and under the surface are rank heathens; or that the rebirth of Hebrew studies may give Judaism its cue to plan a revival, the most pernicious plague and bitterest enemy that one can find to the teaching of Christ. For such is the nature of human affairs: never was good so successful that something in the way of evil did not try to creep under the cover of it. I could wish that those frigid sophistries could either be quite cut out or at least were not the theologians' only concern, and that Christ pure and simple might be planted deep into the minds of men; and this I think could best be brought about if, aided by the support of the three tongues, we drew our philosophy from the true sources.[11]

The "Judaism" of which Erasmus assailed as "the most pernicious plague and bitterest enemy that one can find to the teaching of Christ" was religious legalism. He was concerned that if the study of Hebrew became popular outside of the circle of biblical scholarship then it may lead to a revival of legalism. Erasmus saw "Judaism" as a spiritual rather than social issue within the walls of Christendom. He witnessed many who had replaced personal faith in Christ with legalism and repetitive formal observances. This attitude of Erasmus reflected a fervent Paulinism especially in his *Paraphrasis in Epistolam Pauli ad Romanos* (*Paraphrase on Romans*, 1517).[12]

Erasmus called for a quasi-primitivism in his desire "that Christ pure and simple

---

came into contact with Erasmus. He later sympathized with Lutheran views, except towards the Eucharist, in which he followed the "memorialism" of Zwingli. In 1523, he settled in Strasbourg and worked along with Martin Bucer to reform the city. He was exceptionally tolerant towards the Anabaptists and other radicals. He wrote a Hebrew grammar and commentaries on several books of the Old Testament. See James M. Kittelson, *Wolfgang Capito: From Humanist to Reformer*, Studies in Medieval and Reformation Thought (Leiden: Brill Academic Publishers, 1975), 23-51, 112-42, 171-206.

[11] Desiderius Erasmus, *The Collected Works of Erasmus*, trans. and ed. Robert D. Sider (Toronto: University of Toronto Press, 1974-2004), 4:266-67, hereafter CWE; Desiderius Erasmus, *Opus Epistolarum Des. Erasmi Roterodami*, ed. P. S. Allen (Oxford: Clarendon Press, 1910), 2:491.

[12] CWE, 4:266, footnote 149. Throughout his NT writings, Paul presented a distinct contrast between the freedom one has in Christ and the legalism of the Judaizers. Erasmus expounded upon Rom 4:17 and stated, "The Jews think that they are alive and that they amount to something. They detest the Gentiles as if dead and worthy of nothing good. But the summons of God accomplishes more for the Gentiles than their own ancestry accomplishes for the Jews." See CWE, 42:30;

might be planted deep into the minds of men," and that this could best be done by a return to "the true sources."[13] He believed that most "so-called" Christians did not comprehend the basics of Christianity, nor did they crave to learn about their ostensible faith. He called those Christians "rank heathens" and blamed their ignorance on the Church itself.[14] In the *Pio Lectori* (Foreword to his third edition New Testament, 1522), he interjected, "Now the fact that we have today many Christians so ignorant that they possess less knowledge of the faith than even its worst enemies, I attribute mostly to the priests."[15] Erasmus' use of the phrases "minds of men," "ignorant," and "knowledge of faith" indicated that he perceived true Christianity was a faith which must be *taught* and *learned*, and not simply *asserted*. It was at this point that Erasmus succeeded beyond all other humanists in amalgamating the classical ideal of *humanitas* (human culture) and the Christian ideal of *pietas* (devotion to God).[16] In summarizing the crux of Erasmus' thought, Albert Rabil, Jr. assessed, "The classical was the ideal of eloquence combined with deep learning; the Christian was the ideal of devotion born of understanding. Erasmus instilled eloquence and learning into Christianity and piety into paganism."[17]

HERMENEUTICAL INFLUENCE: PHILOSOPHIA CHRISTI

The melding of *pietas* and *humanitas* may be seen in what Erasmus called *philosophia Christi* (the philosophy of Christ). In the *Paraclesis* (Preface to his first edition New Testament, 1516) Erasmus spoke of the *philosophia Christi* and stated, "For what I seek to declare is nothing but the truth itself, the simplest expression of which is always the most forceful."[18] He began by questioning the *pietas* of those who identified themselves as Christians by pointing out that the "Platonists, Pythagoreans, Academics, Stoics, Cynics, Peripatetics, and Epicureans all know the

---

Desiderius Erasmus, *Desiderii Erasmi Roterodami Opera Omnia* (London: Gregg Press, 1962), 7:790, hereafter OPERA.

[13] CWE, 4:266-67; Erasmus, *Opus Epistolarum*, 2:491.

[14] Ibid.

[15] Desiderius Erasmus, "Foreword," *Novum Testamentum* (1522), in *The Praise of Folly and Other Writings*, trans. and ed. Robert M. Adams, *Norton Critical Editions in the History of Ideas* (New York: Norton, 1989), 135, hereafter *EFNT*.

[16] Rabil, Jr., 216; *Cassell's Latin Dictionary* (1897), s. v. "humanitas, pietas."

[17] Ibid.

[18] Desiderius Erasmus, *Paraclesis*, in *The Praise of Folly and Other Writings*, ed. and trans. Robert M. Adams, Norton Critical Editions in the History of Ideas (New York: Norton, 1989), 119, hereafter *Paraclesis*; OPERA, 5:139.

doctrines of their particular sects, they learn them by heart, and fight fiercely for them, ready to die rather than abandon the cause of their particular patron."[19] However, he then asked of Christians, "Why then don't we stand up even more spiritedly on behalf of our maker and our leader, Christ?" He added, "Beyond doubt, only Christ was a teacher descended from heaven, only he (who was eternal wisdom itself) could teach positive certainties, only he (the unique author of human salvation) could teach us saving doctrine, only he could exemplify what he taught and grant us whatever he promised."[20] Christ deserved the devotion of his followers and yet the opportunity to follow him required a conscious choice that Erasmus believed few had made. Erasmus explained, "The path is direct and ready for anyone to take. Only bring a pious, alert mind and above all one imbued with a pure and simple faith. Simply make yourself teachable, and you have made long strides in this philosophy."[21]

Another aspect of Erasmus' *philosophia Christi* dealt with *humanitas*. His focus on a return to the classics was epitomized by a return to Scripture. He desired that the written Word be translated into the spoken language of the people. He declared that "Christ wanted his mysteries to be disseminated as widely as possible" and Erasmus disagreed with those who wanted to prevent Scripture from being "read in translation by the unlearned." He even broke the social mores of his day when he preferred "that all women, even of the lowest rank, should read the evangelists and the epistles of Paul." He desired that Scripture would be "translated into all the languages of the human race, so they could be read and studied" even by non-Christians.[22] Erasmus saw the truest example of *humanitas* as being the written Scriptures. He declared:

> But it's my opinion — and a proper one, unless I'm badly mistaken — that the pure and genuine philosophy of Christ is drawn from no other source than the evangelical books and the letters of the apostles. Any man who piously reflects on these writings, praying rather than disputing, and seeking to be transformed within rather than armed for battle, will certainly find that there is nothing pertaining to the felicity of man, nothing relating to our conduct in this world, nothing about the great problems of life, that is not treated here [in the Scriptures], explained and resolved. If we want to learn something, why should any author be more agreeable than Christ himself?[23]

Erasmus believed that the written Scripture fulfilled part of Christ's promise that he would be

---

[19] Erasmus, *Paraclesis*, 119-20; OPERA, 5:139.

[20] Erasmus, *Paraclesis*, 120; OPERA, 5:139.

[21] Ibid.

[22] Erasmus, *Paraclesis*, 121; OPERA, 5:140.

[23] Erasmus, *Paraclesis*, 124-25; OPERA, 5:141.

with believers until the end of time (Matt. 28:20). According to Erasmus, not only would Christ's promise be realized through the indwelling Holy Spirit in the life of the believer, but also the Christian would experience Christ through the written Word. Erasmus stated that "he [Christ] is present most especially in these writings [Scripture] in which even now he lives, breathes, and speaks to us, more forcefully (I might almost say) than when he lived among men."[24]

Erasmus wanted to see the *philosophia Christi* realized in transformed lives of believers. He desired faith in action, a faith that had been *learned*. He declared, "Happy the man whom death overtakes in the act of meditating [on] this philosophy of Christ. Let us all, then, immerse ourselves in it, embrace it, practice it night and day, kiss it greedily, and die in it after we have been transformed into it ... "[25] Quoting Christ's words from John 14 Erasmus noted:

> "Who loves me," he [Christ] said, "keeps my word;"[26] it is the very mark that he himself designated. Well, then, if we are really Christians in our hearts, if we actually believe he was sent from heaven to teach us what the philosophers could not, if we really expect from him rewards such as no prince however opulent could ever give us, why is anything more precious to us than this text?[27]

According to Erasmus, transformed Christians, out of "love" (*diligere*) of Christ, would keep his word through loving others. In his *Enchiridion Militis Christiani* (*Handbook of the Christian Soldier*, 1503) he cited Paul's words in Galatians 5:13-14, "For you were called to freedom, brethren; only do not turn your freedom into an opportunity for the flesh, but through love serve one another. For the whole Law is fulfilled in one word, in the statement, '*You Shall Love Your Neighbor as Yourself.*'"[28] Referring to the love of one another borne out of one's love for Christ, Erasmus continued:

> This was the greatest commandment in the Mosaic law, and this is what Christ repeats and perfects in the gospel. For this reason above all he was born and died, to teach us not to act like Jews, but to love. After the Last Supper, with what anxiety and emotion he orders his apostles not observe prescriptions about food and drink but about mutual charity! What else does John, fellow initiate

---

[24] Erasmus, *Paraclesis*, 125; OPERA, 5:142.

[25] Erasmus, *Paraclesis*, 127; OPERA, 5:144.

[26] John 14:15, 23.

[27] Erasmus, *Paraclesis*, 123; OPERA, 5:141.

[28] Gal. 5:13-14; CWE, 66:78; OPERA, 5:35, emphasis original.

in Christ's mysteries, teach, or rather demand, but that we love one another? While Paul commends charity throughout the Epistles, as I said, in writing to the Corinthians he puts charity before miracles and prophecy and the tongues of angels.[29]

Erasmus believed that this kind of love epitomized *philosophia Christi*. From the written words of Scripture he saw faith in action. Christ *taught* his followers how to love, according to Erasmus. Sincere *pietas* consequently resulted in *humanitas*. Stated simply, Erasmian Christian humanism, in essence *philosophia Christi*, may be seen in Christ's words:

> "And you shall love the Lord your God with all your heart, and with all your soul, and with all your mind, and with all your strength ...   You shall love your neighbor as yourself." There is no other commandment greater than these.[30]

The "Love the Lord your God" was the *pietas* or devotion to God fulfilled, while the "Love your neighbor as yourself" was the *humanitas* or love of human classicism implemented.[31]

Erasmus saw *philosophia Christi* exemplified in the amalgamation of *pietas* and *humanitas*. Christ's purpose in life and death was not to teach believers a list of rules, but rather to teach them to love. Erasmus believed that "the love of God and neighbor" signified the essence of true Christian faith. He surmised that this kind of "faith" was atypical among many who called themselves "Christians" because they had not been instructed properly as to the quintessence of authentic Christianity.

---

[29] CWE, 66:79; OPERA, 5:35.

[30] Mark 12:30-31. The first part of the text referred to Deut 6:5 also called the *Shema*, and the second part of the text referred to Lev 19:18. This quotation by Christ was also included in Matt 22:37-9 and Luke 10:27.

[31] The Greek word for "love" in this passage was *agapaō*, defined as love which was "spontaneous and unmotivated." *Agapaō* was not a type of love that was the result of an impulse of feelings or the consequence of natural inclinations. Christian love was seen as "uncalculating, unlimited, and unconditional." It was a "reflection of God's love" borne out of one's true "fellowship with God." See Anders Nygren, *Agape and Eros*, trans. Philip S. Watson (London: Society for Promoting Christian Knowledge, 1932; reprint, London: SPCK, 1953), 91-102.

CONTRIBUTION TO EDUCATION
AND CHRISTIAN EDUCATION
ERASMUS THE EDUCATOR: THE ROLE OF THE TEACHER

Erasmus believed the greatest concern of his time was that many individuals who considered themselves to be Christians were ignorant of true faith, and in actuality were "rank heathens."[32] In *Enchiridion* Erasmus proclaimed, "Yet we are living in a world that has grown alien to the world of Christ both in doctrine and in practice."[33] In the forward to his third edition Greek-Latin New Testament, he stated the specific reason for the failures of his day, "Now the fact that we have today many Christians so ignorant that they possess less knowledge of the faith than even its worst enemies, I attribute mostly to the priests."[34] He accused theologians and teachers of making matters "worse by adapting the words of Scripture to the justification of their own crimes."[35] Instead, he urged the leaders of the Church to hold Scripture in the highest regard: "In truth Scripture should be a source of that norm of behavior that can correct them."[36] Furthermore, the terms "Pope" and "Abbot" were to mean "love, not power."[37]

In perhaps his most famous work, *Moriae Encomium* (*The Praise of Folly*, 1510), Erasmus continued his assault on the leaders of the church. He declared that the most pernicious enemies of the church were "impious popes, who by their silence allow Christ to be forgotten, ... contaminate his teachings with their interpretations, and murder him with their atrocious manner of life."[38]

The problem, according to Erasmus, was that many Church leaders had "never seriously considered what it is to be truly a Christian."[39] He turned to the Old Testament prophets to illustrate the grave situation of the Church in his day:

> In name, in customs, in ceremonies we are Christian, rather than in our minds. Either for lack of knowledge we don't have anything to teach the people, or else, being corrupted with worldly lusts, we consult our own advantage rather than that of Jesus Christ. What

---

[32] CWE, 4:266-67; Erasmus, *Opus Epistolarum*, 2:491.

[33] Erasmus, *Enchiridion*, 74.

[34] *EFNT*, 135; OPERA, 7:**3c.

[35] Erasmus, *Enchiridion*, 75.

[36] Ibid.

[37] Ibid., 74.

[38] Erasmus, *The Praise of Folly and Other Writings*, ed. and trans. Robert Martin Adams, 71.

[39] *EFNT*, 137; OPERA, 7:**3c.

wonder, then, if the people are sunk in darkness, when those who should be the light of the world are also hidden in gloom? When those who should be the salt of the earth know nothing worthy of Christ? When those who should be a shining light for the entire house are themselves blind? When those who should be as a strong city atop a lofty mountain, showing others the way, are themselves bogged down in the filth of greed and lust? And would there were not so many to whom that saying of Isaiah could be applied: "his watchmen are blind; they are all ignorant, they are all dumb dogs, they cannot bark, sleeping, lying down, loving to slumber. Yea, they are greedy dogs which can never have enough, and they are shepherds that cannot understand; they all took their own way, every one for his gain, from his quarter."[40] And also from Jeremiah: "My people hath been lost sheep: their shepherds have caused them to go astray."[41] Again, Ezekiel declaims with great boldness against shepherds turned to wolves, who feed themselves but let their flock scatter and be slaughtered.[42] In passage after passage the prophets recur to this charge, saying that from the shepherds arise the calamities that befall the sheep. So says Zechariah the prophet: "They were troubled because there was no shepherd."[43]

Erasmus indicated that the external aspects of Christianity were being carried out in the form of "customs" and "ceremonies," but there was nothing happening in the "minds" ("*animo*") of the followers.[44] He declared that because of a "lack of knowledge we don't have anything to teach the people," or because of "being corrupted with worldly lusts, we consult our own advantage rather than that of Jesus Christ."[45] Erasmus depicted a state of affairs in which Christ's great commandment — to love of God and neighbor — had been forgotten. Because of a lack of devotion to God and an unwillingness to return to the classics in education, there was no "real" Christianity, but rather a faith only "in name."[46]

THE ROLE OF THE LEARNER
IN EDUCATION AND LEARNING

Not only did Erasmus call for the young people to be educated, but he required them to be tested following that instruction as well. The children had to "be carefully examined in

---

[40] Isa 56:10.

[41] Jer 50:6.

[42] Ezek 22:25-28.

[43] Zech 10:2; *EFNT*, 137; OPERA, 7:**3d.

[44] *EFNT*, 137; OPERA, 7:**3c-d.

[45] *EFNT*, 137; OPERA, 7:**3d.

[46] *EFNT*, 137; OPERA, 7:**3c.

private by men of authority, to make sure they know and recall" what they were taught.[47] For Erasmus, the key element in the reform of the church was proper instruction. In his *Institutio Christiani Matrimonii* (*Institution of Christian Matrimony*, 1526), Erasmus discussed the subjects of baptism and teaching, in which he clearly stated, "Rebirth is really brought about less by baptism than by teaching."[48] Instruction in the faith, more than baptism, was the means by which one became a Christian. Erasmus stressed the inward commitment that instruction promoted against the external rite of baptism. According to him, the apostle Paul said as much when he wrote those "to whom he had preached the gospel" but "had not baptized" and declared, "My little children, to whom I give second birth until Christ is formed in you."[49] Erasmus continued his discussion of Paul's emphasis on teaching as the source of rebirth and added, "And elsewhere (in the New Testament, Paul wrote): 'For in Christ Jesus I have begotten you through the gospel.'"[50] Erasmus also referred to Philemon 10, where Paul called "Onesimus his son, whom he had 'begotten in his bonds,' obviously by means of teaching."[51] Paul was not referring to those he had baptized, but rather those he had instructed. Erasmus emphasized instruction as being essential in salvation. In a sense he was correcting an overemphasis on the external rite of baptism and instead emphasized an internal belief — in keeping with the Augustinian heritage.

The instruction of the gospel led to the rebirth of humanity, therefore for Erasmus, the instructor or "catechist" was more of a "father" to the young convert than the godparent that stood at his or her baptism.[52] Erasmus asserted: "The word of God is the seed by which humanity is reborn, and thus spiritual kinship is established between all who listen to the same evangelist — between pupil and teacher...In my opinion, those who are called catechists have more right to be called fathers than the godparents, provided they live up to their name."[53]

If the catechumen was able to give a complete account of what his or her sponsor

---

[47] *EFNT*, 135; OPERA, 7:**3c.

[48] CWE, 69:280. "Non enim proprie generat qui baptizat, sed qui docet." OPERA, 5:643.

[49] CWE, 69:280. "Paulus enim ita scribit iis, quos non baptizarat, sed quibus praedicarat Euangelium: *Filioli mei quos iterum parturio, donec formetur Christus in vobis.*" OPERA, 5:643-44; Gal 4:9.

[50] CWE, 69:280. "Atque iterum: *Nam in Christo Jesu per Euangelium ego vos genui.*" OPERA, 5:644; 1 Cor 4:15.

[51] CWE, 69:280. "Et Onesimum appellat *silium*, quem in vinculis genuerat, utique doctrina." OPERA, 5:644; Phil 10.

[52] CWE, 69:280; OPERA, 5:644.

[53] CWE, 69:280. "Sermo Dei semen est quo renascitur homo. Nascitur igitur spiritualis cognatio

had "promised in their name at their baptism," and he or she was also able to explain "what was actually involved in the baptismal ceremony" as a result of the instruction of the catechist, then the catechumen may "renew their promises in public assemblies." Erasmus compared these would-be ceremonies to those of the monks presenting their vows before the public. He described dramatic presentations of the monks, which drew "tears from the onlookers," and concluded that "enacting this promise" of the catechumens "not to men, but to God" would be even more powerful. [54] With regards to this public presentation by the catechumens Erasmus pronounced:

> In this way it might actually come about that young people would understand what duties they owe their Prince and what exertions may raise them to true piety. When they are older it will help them realize in how many ways they have wandered from their first profession...How truly magnificent would be this spectacle if one could hear the voices of many young people dedicating themselves to Jesus Christ, many new recruits pledging loyalty to his cause, and renouncing this...We should see many new Christs, bearing on their brows the insignia of their Prince; we should see the flock of candidates advancing from the holy fount, and hear the voices of a united society acclaiming Christ's recruits and wishing them well. These ceremonies I should wish to be publicly performed, so that the young may not simply receive the faith passively and in their cradles, but receive it publicly, before everyone, ... and if it is carried out as it should be, we'll have many more genuine Christians than we do now, or I'm much mistaken. [55]

The phrases "what duties they owe their Prince and what exertions may raise them to true piety, ... dedicating themselves to Jesus Christ, ... and bearing on their brows the insignia of their Prince" all reveal a *pietas* that was the result of a renewed life. As the young people came to understand what Christ had done for them, and they realized where they had fallen short, they would be able to hear "the voices of a united society" urging them to profess "publicly, before everyone" their loyalty to Christ and one another resulting in a *humanitas* lived out before the world. Thus Erasmus' *philosophia Christi* fused *pietas* and *humanitas* — the love of God and neighbor — so that the church and the

---

inter omnes qui eumdem audiunt Euangelistam, inter Discipulum & Praeceptorem ...   Jam qui dicuntur Catechistae, mea sentential, justius deberent appellari Patres quam Susceptores, si modo vere sunt quod dicuntur." OPERA, 5:644.

[54] *EFNT*, 136; OPERA, 7:**3c. It should be noted that Thomas Aquinas called the monastic vows a "second baptism." See Roland H. Bainton, *Here I Stand: A Life of Martin Luther* (New York: Abingdon-Cokesbury, 1950), 33.

[55] *EFNT*, 136; OPERA, 7:**3c.

world would be filled with "many more genuine Christians."[56]

Erasmus appeared to be calling for a return to the substance of pre-baptismal catechization in the early churches where the instruction of the catechumens would occur prior to the public ceremony in which "we should see the flock of candidates advancing from the holy fount."[57] Erasmus implied a second baptism ceremony of the catechumens once they demonstrated that they openly lived reborn lives due to an inward commitment to follow Christ.

In 1522, Erasmus seems to have envisioned an immersion ceremony as the completion of the initial infant baptism. This two stage water baptism began with the primary baptism of the infant in order to remove original sin. The process was completed through a secondary baptism as the confessor rose from the baptismal fount, professing spiritual rebirth in a public declaration of faith.

In his *Paraphrasis in Evangelium Matthaei* (*Paraphrase on Matthew*, 1522), Erasmus gave clear detail as to the instruction given to the would-be believer regarding the Trinity, the essentials about the church, and the resurrection of saints, which was to take place prior to a literal second baptism.[58] He plainly affirmed:

> After you have taught them these things (*Haec ubi illos docueritis*), and they believe what you have taught them (*si crediderint quae docuistis*), have repented their previous lives and are ready to embrace the doctrine of the gospel [in their life], then immerse them in water (*tum tingite illos aqua*), in the name of the Father, the Son, and the Holy Ghost, so that by this holy sign they may believe that they have been delivered freely through the benefit of my death from the filthiness of all their sins and now belong to the number of God's children.[59]

The order, according to Erasmus, was: instruction, belief, repentance, baptism. The teacher was to instruct the pupil in the "things" of the faith, which would lead to conviction, followed by repentance, and finally resulting in baptism.[60]

Two years later in his *Paraphrasis in Acta Apostolorum* (*Paraphrase on the Acts of the Apostles*, 1524), Erasmus continued his emphasis on instruction *prior* to baptism. He declared: "Teach those who are to be baptized the rudiments of the evangelical

---

[56] Ibid.

[57] Ibid.

[58] Friesen, *Erasmus*, 50; OPERA, 7:146.

[59] Friesen, *Erasmus*, 50-51; OPERA, 7:146.

[60] Ibid.

philosophy; unless one believes these he will in vain be baptized with water. Teach those who have been baptized to live according to my teaching and always to progress to more perfect beings."[61] Erasmus proposed an order to Christian development. Correct teaching led to personal repentance and faith. This teaching of the "rudiments of the evangelical philosophy" (*Euangelicae Philososphiae rudimenta*) was followed subsequently by secondary baptism through immersion. Following immersion was further instruction of the believer toward a life lived out in Christ in order "to progress to more perfect beings (*simper ad perfectiora proficient*)."[62]

In the foreword to his third edition Greek-Latin New Testament Erasmus recommended that the catechumens would advance from "the holy fount," after "pledging loyalty" to the cause of Christ and giving an account of "what their sponsors promised in their name at their [initial infant] baptism." He acknowledged his concerns about the apparent repetition of baptism. Immediately after detailing the post-catechization public ceremony, which Erasmus himself said would result in "many more genuine Christians," he stated that "the ceremony of baptism seems to be repeated, which is not right." However, Erasmus proposed a solution to that problem if it was made clear "that the second ceremony does nothing but ratify the first."[63]

Erasmus called for a pre-confirmation catechization which was modeled after the pre-baptismal catechization approach of the early church. He reinterpreted the significance of water baptism with his ratification of initial baptism through subsequent immersion. He suggested that new birth was a two-phase process. Initially, the objective in the sacrament of the first water baptism was subjective appropriation of personal repentance and faith upon the child. Secondarily, personal faith was affirmed or declared through the subsequent public immersion (*tinguĕre*) by the believer.[64]

Erasmus' comparison of the public catechization ceremonies to those of the monks' presentations eventually led the doctors at the Sorbonne in Paris, in their analyses in 1526 of Erasmus' propositions, to censure his work and to declare that to "rebaptize" children would lead ultimately "to the destruction of the Christian religion."[65] By 1559 all of Erasmus' works were on the *Roman Index*. The Inquisition had succeeded in removing the famous humanist's name from

---

[61] CWE, 50:24; OPERA, 7:674.

[62] CWE, 50:24; OPERA, 7:674.

[63] *EFNT*, 135-36; OPERA, 7:**3c.

[64] Friesen, *Erasmus*, 50-51; OPERA, 7:146.

[65] Friesen, *Erasmus*, 35.

Catholic Europe; however, in Protestant cities his works were still being printed and were still influencing many who sought to "learn."[66]

CURRICULAR APPROACH: THE ROLE OF ERASMUS' LATIN CATECHISM (1513/14)

In 1513, John Colet[67] summoned his friend Erasmus to compose a Latin version of his *Cathechyzon in Englysh* (1512) for use by the young students at his St. Paul's School.[68] Colet's English text was in a rustic style and gained little attention outside of the walls of St. Paul's. However, Erasmus' *Christiani hominus institutum* (*Basic Principles of Christian Conduct*, 1513/14), with its elegant and refined Latin poetic verse was adopted quickly by other schools and broadly disseminated throughout all of Europe.[69] *Christiani hominus institutum* was translated back into English by Thomas Berthelet (*The Godly and Pious Institution of a Christen Man*, 1537) thus providing evidence that Erasmus' Latin version eclipsed Colet's English original.[70]

Erasmus' Latin catechism followed Colet's outline, and covered the *Apostles' Creed*, and the seven sacraments of the Catholic Church. The largest section of Erasmus' Latin edition was entitled *Amor dei* (Love of God), in which he described Jesus' atonement as a sacrifice that set the

---

[66] H. R. Trevor-Roper, *Men and Events: Historical Essays* (New York: Harper and Brothers, 1957), 51. Within seven years of Erasmus' call for further catechetical instruction, catechisms appeared from the pens of the *Unitas Fratrum* (1522), the Anabaptists (1526), and the Lutherans (1529). Ironically, the Catholics later produced an "official" catechism following the Council of Trent in 1566.

[67] John Colet (ca. 1466-1519) was the Dean of St. Paul's Cathedral in London. He was known for a series of lectures on Paul's epistles, given at Oxford during the last decade of the fifteenth century. The lectures were notable for their humanist critical approach and their plea for a return to the discipline of the primitive Church. Colet met Erasmus in 1499, while Erasmus was in England, and the two remained close friends. Upon his father's death, Colet gained a large fortune and founded St. Paul's School in the face of opposition. One hundred fifty-three boys, without restriction as to nationality and at no cost to themselves, studied Greek and Latin as well as the basics of the Christian faith in order to develop learned Christians through the study of human art and literature. See J. H. Lupton, *A Life of John Colet, D. D.: Dean of St. Paul's and Founder of St. Paul's School — With an Appendix of Some of His English Writings* (London: George Bell and Sons, 1887; reprint, Hamden, CT: Shoe String Press, 1961), 156-77; John B. Gleason, *John Colet* (Berkeley, CA: University of California Press, 1989), 93-125; 217-34.

[68] Lupton, *Life of John Colet,* 279. For the complete text of Colet's catechism see Lupton, 285-89.

[69] Gleason, *John Colet,* 231. For the complete text of Erasmus' catechism see CWE, 85:92-107 (English and Latin) and OPERA, 5:1357-59 (Latin).

[70] William H. Woodward, *Desiderius Erasmus Concerning the Aim and Method of Education*, Burt Franklin: Research & Source Works Series 714, History of Education 3 (Cambridge: Cambridge University Press, 1904; reprint, New York: Lenox Hill, 1971), 238.

human race free and "paid our ransom like a friend."[71] The use of "friend" (*amico*) in reference to Jesus Christ, paying the ransom on behalf of humanity, was another example of Erasmus' emphasis on the "love of God and neighbor" and the importance of a believer's personal relationship with the Savior.[72]

Towards the Holy Spirit, Erasmus stressed the personal relationship between Christ and the believer with the statement of "*enriching* the innermost recesses of *my mind*" and that the Holy Spirit "*recreates me* with his life-giving spirit."[73] Erasmus perceived the relationship between the authentic Christian and Jesus to be personal and intimate. This kind of personal language by Erasmus may have resulted from his prior exposure to the "Brethren of the Common Life" tradition and the *Devotio Moderna* of Thomas à Kempis.

After his own emphasis on fleeing from pride, envy, anger, gluttony, lust, sloth, and avarice, Erasmus moved on to the second largest section of his catechism, "*Amor proximi*" or "Love of neighbor."[74] Once again, he followed Colet's catechism, and yet developed the message by elaborating his own thought. Erasmus added more detail and avowed:

> And just as I am dear to myself, I will love all my neighbours — and unless I am mistaken, anyone who is a human being is my neighbour — and I will do so in such a way that my love for a friend is referred to Christ and to a holy life and to true salvation. Therefore, whenever it is needful and necessary, I will assist him in body and mind, eagerly and dutifully, just as I would wish to be helped if I should lack for something.[75]

He mentioned that he "will love all my neighbours" and followed that declaration with a clear reference to Christ's response to the lawyer's question, "And who is my neighbor?"[76] It was in Luke 10 where the lawyer replied to Jesus that the essence of the Law was to "love God and neighbor" and Christ responded, "You have answered correctly; Do this and you will live."[77] Jesus answered the lawyer's question, "And who is my neighbor?" with the story of the "Good

---

[71] CWE, 85:98-99; OPERA, 5:1358.

[72] The word *amico* came from the root *amare*, meaning "to love from inclination or passion." Again, the same word was used to describe the "love" toward the Father and the Son. See *Cassell's*, s. v. "amicus, amare."

[73] CWE, 85:100-01; OPERA, 5:1358-59. Italics added for emphasis.

[74] CWE, 85:104-05; OPERA, 5:1359.

[75] Ibid.

[76] ". . . amabitur omnis proximus . . ." CWE, 85:104-05; OPERA, 5:1359; Luke 10:29.

[77] Luke 10:28.

Samaritan,"[78] which signified faith in action. Erasmus plainly referred to Christ's answer to the lawyer with his own statement, " ... and unless I am mistaken, anyone who is a human being is my neighbour ... "[79] For Erasmus loving his neighbor meant to love "in such a way that my love for a friend is referred to Christ and to a holy life and to true salvation."[80] Erasmus' desire to live "a holy life" and one that possessed "true salvation" for himself and for all who identified themselves as Christians was clear in his correspondence with a friend in following the writing of this catechism.[81] His concern was for those "Christians" who "scarcely acknowledge Christ in more than name," but were truly "rank heathens."[82] As a direct result of his "love of God and neighbor," he yearned to educate "ignorant Christians" and transform them into Christians who possessed "holy lives" and "true salvation."[83]

The continental popularity of Erasmus' name led to the reproduction and wide use of *Christiani hominis institutum* well into the early stages of the Reformation even after Luther's catechisms became predominant among Protestants after 1529.[84] In fact, Erasmus' Latin catechism gained popularity among both Protestants and Catholics throughout Europe. Petrus Tritonius Athesinus, a Tyrolian,[85] Protestant humanist educator, composed his own catechism in which

---

[78] Luke 10:30-37.

[79] " . . . (est autem, ni fallor, proximus ille quisquis homo est)." CWE, 85:104-05; OPERA, 5:1359.

[80] " . . . ac sic ut amor referatur amici in CHRISTUM vitamque piam veramque salutem." CWE, 85:104-05; OPERA, 5:1359.

[81] CWE, 4:266-67; Erasmus, *Opus Epistolarum*, 2:491.

[82] CWE, 4:266-67; Erasmus, *Opus Epistolarum*, 2:491.

[83] " . . . vitamque piam veramque salutem." CWE, 85:104-05; OPERA, 5:1359.

[84] Gleason, *John Colet,* 231. Prior to Erasmus' Catholic catechisms, the most widely published catechism was a work by Franciscan Dietrich Kolde (1435-1515) whose catechism entitled *Der Kerstenen Spiegel* (*A Fruitful Mirror*) was published in 1470 with more than forty-five editions in German, Dutch, and Latin. Kolde earned a reputation of caring for plague victims, promoting peace, and reforming convents. Erasmus met Kolde in the early 1490s, and noted his reputation as a skilled preacher and a consummate Christian. Erasmus and other humanists admired the Franciscan's piety and lifestyle; however they remained silent as to the accuracy of his written words. Nevertheless, Erasmus viewed Kolde's work as too traditional. Erasmus' opinion of Kolde may be gleaned from two letters, one written to Charles Utenhove on 9 August 1532 and the other written to Jodocus Gaverius on 1 March 1533, in which Erasmus reminisced about his meeting that took place with Kolde roughly forty years earlier. Erasmus, *Opus Epistolarum*, 1:589; 5:237-50, 10:79-83; Bert Roest, *Franciscan Literature of Religious Instruction before the Council of Trent*, Studies in the History of Christian Traditions, ed. Robert J. Bast, vol. 117 (Leiden: Brill, 2004), 90-91.

[85] Modern-day southern Austria and northern Italy.

he used Erasmus' entire Latin text as the second half of his two-part work.[86] In Catholic Cracow (Poland), Nicholas Barbonius utilized Erasmus' text in his own *Pedagogium seu morum puerilium praecepta Christiana.* Johannes Sulpitius, in Protestant Utrecht (The Netherlands), followed suit in his *De moribus puerorum carmen,* and in England, Erasmus' Latin catechism was employed from 1558 onward.[87]

METHODS OF CHRISTIAN EDUCATION:
THE ROLE OF PUBLIC CATECHIZATION

Erasmus believed that a personal following of Christ was crucial in the development of genuine faith. Proper training and education would remedy the problem of superficial Christians both inside the Church and in civil society, but the solution could only come as the result of genuine instruction by true believers.

In *Institutio principis Christiani* (*The Education of A Christian Prince,* 1516) Erasmus continued his assault on the external rituals of the church:

> Do not think that the profession of a Christian is a matter to be lightly passed over, entailing no responsibilities unless, of course, you think the sacrament which you accepted along with everything else at baptism is nothing. And do not think you renounce just for the once the delights of Satan which bring pain to the Christ. He is displeased with all that is foreign to the teachings of the Gospel. You share the Christian sacrament alike with all others — why not its teachings too? You have allied yourself with Christ — and yet will you slide back into the ways of Julius and Alexander the Great? You seek the same reward as the others, yet you will have no concern with His mandates.
>
> But on the other hand, do not think that Christ is found in ceremonies, in doctrines kept after a fashion, and in constitutions of the church. Who is truly a Christian? Not he who is baptized or anointed, or who attends church. It is rather the man who has embraced Christ in the innermost feelings of his heart, and who emulates Him by his pious deeds.[88]

In his examination of the externals of the faith, Erasmus demanded that the Christian not only

---

[86] Ferdinand Cohrs, "Der humanistische Schulmeister Petrus Tritonius Athesinus," *Mitteilungen der Gesellschaft für deutsche Erziehungs — und Schulgeschichte,* 8 (1898): 264-65; cited in Gleason, *John Colet,* 231, 379.

[87] Cohrs, *Die evangelischen Katechismusversuche vor Luthers Enchiridion,* 418-19.

[88] Erasmus, *The Education of a Christian Prince,* 153.

"share the Christian sacraments," but that the true believer must uphold "its teachings too."[89] He affirmed that the Christian must "not think that Christ is found in ceremonies, in doctrines ... and in constitutions of the church." The true "Christian," according to Erasmus, was not the one outwardly "baptized or anointed" or "who attends church." He identified the "true Christian" as the one "who has embraced Christ in the innermost feelings of his heart, and who emulates Him by his pious deeds."[90]

Erasmus recommended reform of the church of his day, regarding the ignorance of the people:

> And I think I see a way in which we can render somewhat fewer of our people completely unfit for reading the scriptures. That would be if every year the substance of our Christian faith and doctrine could be proposed, briefly, clearly, and with learned simplicity, to the entire population. And lest the substance be adulterated by crafty preachers, it would be well to have a booklet composed by learned and judicious men, which could be recited by the assembled priests unanimously. I should like preaching to be done, not from the defective inventions of human minds, but from the evangelical sources, from the apostolic letters, from the creed, which — though I don't know whether it was produced by the apostles — certainly carries on it the marks of apostolic majesty and purity. The substance of our faith might, I think, be discussed not inappropriately at Eastertime.[91]

What Erasmus apparently called for was a kind of *public* catechization or the use of a catechism as a means of instruction in a public setting. He called for a "booklet composed by learned and judicious men, which could be recited by the assembled priests unanimously."[92] He was not calling for more external rituals, but rather a presentation of the essence of the Christian faith in a simple, understandable manner. Again, true to his Christian humanist views, he demanded a return to "the evangelical sources... the apostolic letters" and "the creed" with regard to preaching. He alluded to the baptismal practice in the early churches of baptizing candidates at Easter when he suggested that the "substance of our faith might, I think, be discussed not inappropriately at Eastertime."

---

[89] Ibid.

[90] Ibid.

[91] *EFNT*, 135; OPERA, 7:**3c.

[92] Ibid. It should be noted that Erasmus made these remarks in 1522, in the foreword to the third edition of his New Testament. By this time his Latin catechism, written in 1513/14, had circulated throughout Europe, and yet he apparently called for another simple catechetical work to be written for the purpose discussed above.

With his inclusion of "the creed" Erasmus affirmed his intention for public catechization.[93]

In addition to the "public catechization," Erasmus proposed another reform of the church:

> In addition, I think it would help in no small degree toward the end we desire if children who have been baptized, when they reach the age of puberty, should be ordered to attend sessions in which it would be made clear to them what was actually involved in the baptismal ceremony. Then let them be carefully examined in private by men of authority, to make sure they know and recall what the priest has taught them.[94]

Evidently Erasmus called for a sort of *post*-baptismal catechization. In order to see Christianity only "in name" abated, he suggested that "children who have been baptized" should be taught "what was actually involved in the baptismal ceremony."[95] Erasmus' desire was to eradicate the possibility of "ignorant Christians," and he saw education in the essence of the faith as the only way to solve the problem.

CONCLUSION

Desiderius Erasmus believed that "nominal" Christianity was the result of unlearned subjects. He desired to return "to the sources" of education in order to combat such failures through the melding of *pietas* and *humanitas* that resulted in *philosophia Christi*. This theological hermeneutic led Erasmus to not only author his own catechism, but also to call on others to do likewise. He saw "public" catechization as a way to "test" the acumen of the students and assure that effective Christian education had been realized. For Erasmus, Christianity became "real" once it had been effectually *taught* and *learned*. In order for Christian education to thrive Erasmus resolved to turn back "to the sources."

PRIMARY SOURCE SAMPLE[96]

Just as one who poisons the public fountain from which all drink deserves more than one punishment, so he is the most harmful who infects the mind of the prince with base ideas, which later produce destruction of so many men. If anyone counterfeits the prince's

---

[93] *EFNT*, 135; OPERA, 7:**3c.

[94] Ibid.

[95] Ibid.

[96] Erasmus, *The Education of a Christian Prince*, 146-48, 212-13.

coinage, he is beaten about the head; surely he who corrupts the character of the prince is even more deserving of that punishment. The teacher should enter at once upon his duties, so as to implant the seeds of good moral conduct while the senses of the prince are still in the tenderness of youth, while his mind is furthest removed from all vices and tractably yields to the hand of guidance in whatever it directs. He is immature both in body and mind, as in his sense of duty. The teacher's task is always the same, but he must employ one method in one case, and another in another. While his pupil is still a little child, he can bring his teachings through pretty stories, pleasing fables, clever parables. When he is bigger, he can teach the same things directly....

Before all else the story of Christ must be firmly rooted in the mind of the prince. He should drink deeply of His teachings, gathered in handy texts, and then later from those very fountains themselves, whence he may drink more purely and effectively. He should be taught that the teachings of Christ apply to no one more than to the prince....

Therefore, the tutor should first see that his pupil loves and honors virtue as the finest quality of all, the most felicitous, the most fitting a prince; and that he loathes and shuns moral turpitude as the foulest and most terrible of things....

A prince who is about to assume control of the state must be advised at once that the main hope of a state lies in the proper education of its youth. This Xenophon wisely taught in his Cyropaedia. Pliable youth is amenable to any system of training. Therefore the greatest care should be exercised over public and private schools and over the education of girls, so that the children may be placed under the best and most trustworthy instructors and may learn the teachings of Christ and that good literature which is beneficial to the state. As a result of this scheme of things, there will be no need for many laws or punishments, for the people will of their own free will follow the course of right.

BIBLIOGRAPHY

Cohrs, Ferdinand. "Der humanistische Schulmeister Petrus Tritonius Athesinus." In *Mitteilungen der Gesellschaft für deutsche Erziehungs — und Schulgeschichte*, 8 (1898): 264-5. Cited in Gleason, John B. *John Colet*. Berkeley, CA: University of California Press, 1989.

Dolan, John P. *The Essential Erasmus*. New York: New American Library, 1964.

_____. Review of *Erasmus, the Anabaptists and the Problem of Religious Unity*, by I. B. Horst. *MQR* 43 (Oct 1969): 343-44.

Erasmus, Desiderius. *Christian Humanism and the Reformation: Selected Writings of Erasmus with His Life by Beatus Rhenanus and a Biographical Sketch by the Editor*, Third edition. Edited by John C. Olin. New York: Fordham University Press, 1987.

_____. *The Collected Works of Erasmus*. Vols. 1-84. Translated and edited by Robert D. Sider. Toronto: University of Toronto Press, 1974-2004.

_____. *The Colloquies of Erasmus*. Translated and edited by Craig R. Thompson. Chicago: University of Chicago Press, 1965.

_____. *Desiderii Erasmi Roterodami Opera Omnia*. Vols. 1-10. London: Gregg Press, 1962.

_____. *The Education of a Christian Prince*. Translated by Lester K. Born. New York: Columbia University Press, 1936.

_____. *Enchiridion Militis Christiani: An English Version*. Edited by Anne M. O'Donnell. Oxford: Oxford University Press, 1981.

_____. *The Essential Erasmus*. Translated and edited by John P. Dolan. New York: New American Library, 1964.

_____. *Inquisitio de Fide*. Translated and edited by Craig R. Thompson. New Haven: Yale University Press, 1950.

_____. *Der Katechismus des Erasmus von Rotterdam (1512/13)* in *Evangelische Katechismen der Reformationszeit vor und neben Martin Luthers Kleinem Katechismus*, ed. Ernst-Wilhelm Kohls. Gütersloher: Gerd Mohn, 1970.

_____. *Novum Testamentum Graeco-Latin Interprete Desiderio Erasmo, Roterodamo*. Frankfurt: Balth. Christoph. Wustium, 1673.

_____. *Opus Epistolarum Des. Erasmi Roterdami*. Edited by P. S. Allen. Oxford: Oxford Press, 1906-58.

_____. *The Praise of Folly and Other Writings*. Translated and edited by Robert Martin Adams. New York: Norton, 1989.

Ferguson, Wallace K. *The Renaissance in Historical Thought: Five Centuries of Interpretation*. Cambridge, MA: Riverside Press, 1948.

Friesen, Abraham. *Erasmus, the Anabaptists, and the Great Commission*. Grand Rapids, MI: William B. Eerdmans, 1998.

Gleason, John B. *John Colet*. Berkeley, CA: University of California Press, 1989.

Graffagnino, Jason J. "The Shaping of the Two Earliest Anabaptist Catechisms." Ph.D. diss., Southwestern Baptist Theological Seminary, 2008.

Halkin, Léon-E. *Erasmus: A Critical Biography*. Translated by John Tonkin. Oxford: Blackwell Publishers, 1993.

Huizinga, Johan. *Erasmus and the Age of Reformation*. Translated by Frederick J. Hopman and Barbara Flower. New York: Harper, 1957.

_____. *The Waning of the Middle Ages: A Study of the Forms of Life, Thought and Art in France and The Netherlands in the XIVth and XVth Centuries*. Translated by Frederick J. Hopman. London: Edward Arnold, 1924.

Kittelson, James M. *Wolfgang Capito: From Humanist to Reformer*. Studies in Medieval and Reformation Thought. Leiden: Brill, 1975.

Kristeller, Paul Oskar. *The Classics and Renaissance Thought*. Cambridge, MA: Harvard University Press, 1955.

_____. *Renaissance and Thought and Its Sources*. Edited by Michael Mooney. New York: Columbia Press, 1979.

Lupton, J. H. *A Life of John Colet, D. D.: Dean of St. Paul's and Master of St. Paul's School — With an Appendix of Some of His English Writings*. Hamden, CT: Shoe String Press, 1961.

Nygren, Anders. *Agape and Eros*, trans. Philip S. Watson. London: Society for Promoting Christian Knowledge, 1932; reprint, London: SPCK, 1953.

Rabil, Jr., Albert. "Desiderius Erasmus." In *Renaissance Humanism: Foundations, Forms, and Legacy*, vol. 2, *Humanism Beyond Italy*. Philadelphia: University of Pennsylvania Press, 1988, 216-64.

Roest, Bert. *Franciscan Literature of Religious Instruction Before the Council of Trent.* Studies in the History of Christian Traditions, ed. Robert J. Bast, vol. 117. Leiden: Brill, 2004.

Thompson, Bard. *Humanists and Reformers: A History of the Renaissance and Reformation.* Grand Rapids, MI: William B. Eerdmans, 1996.

Trevor-Roper, H. R. *Men and Events: Historical Essays.* New York: Harper and Brothers, 1957.

Woodward, William H. *Desiderius Erasmus Concerning the Aim and Method if Education*, Burt Franklin: Research & Source Works Series 714, History of Education 3. Cambridge: Cambridge University Press, 1904. Reprint, New York: Lenox Hill, 1971.

CHAPTER 7

Martin Luther:

Education for the Preservation of the Gospel and Society

WILLIAM M. MARSH

Martin Luther (1483-1546)

Martin Luther fought for the reform of Christendom in its entirety. This task included a reformation of not only the church and theology, but also the temporal world. Luther labored as an educator for the full span of his career as a Reformer, and from this role, he cast a vision for the indispensability of education to ensure the preservation of the integrity of the gospel and the maintenance of an ordered and healthy society.

HISTORICAL BACKGROUND

On November 10, 1483, Martin Luther was born to Hans and Margarete Luther in Eisleben, a small mining town in Thuringia, Germany. He came from peasant stock, yet his father Hans, a miner and smeltermaster, always had aspirations to increase the Luther family's status within society.[1] Eisleben would be Luther's childhood home for only a short while until his parents relocated as early as 1484 to Mansfield, the city where his education would begin, and the place he considered his hometown.[2] At the age of seven, young Martin entered the Latin school in Mansfield, where his educational career launched with the *trivium* (grammar, logic, rhetoric).[3] In these "trivial" schools, music also played a significant role among the other areas of reading, writing, and arithmetic, and so, Luther became familiar with music theory and how to sing. Additionally, students were required to participate in special services, and through these events, Luther was exposed to the church's liturgy. Most likely, it was at this same time where he first encountered the basics of the Christian faith.[4] Despite positives from his early childhood schooling (such as developing a love for music and establishing a foundation in the liberal arts), Luther's initial educational experience left a negative imprint that is manifest in later reflections. For instance, in his 1524 treatise, *To the Councilmen of all Cities in Germany that They Establish and Maintain Christian Schools*, Luther reminisced, "Today, schools are not what they once were, a hell and purgatory in which we were tormented with *casualibus* and *temporalibus*, and yet learned less than nothing despite all the flogging, trembling, anguish, and misery."[5]

When Luther was fourteen years old, Hans sent his teenage son to the urban city of Magdeburg, accompanied by his friend Hans Reinicke, to find advanced educational opportunities.[6] Little, if anything, is known about the nature of Luther's education in Magdeburg

---

[1] Luther biographer, Martin Brecht, gives an informative look into Luther's parents' ancestry and economic status, along with Hans' determination to succeed in business to move his family out of their peasant conditions. See Martin Brecht, *Martin Luther: His Road to Reformation, 1483-1521*, trans. James L. Schaaf (Philadelphia: Fortress Press, 1985), 1-11.

[2] Ibid., 9.

[3] Ibid., 12.

[4] Ibid., 15.

[5] *Casualibus* and *temporalibus* are grammatical terms for "cases" and "tenses". Martin Luther, *To the Councilmen of all Cities in Germany that They Establish and Maintain Christian Schools*, in *Luther's Works [LW]*, eds. Jarsolav Pelikan (vols. 1-30) and Helmut T. Lehmann (vols. 31-55), vol. 45, *The Christian in Society II*, ed. Walther I. Brandt, trans. Albert T. W. Steinhaeuser and rev. Walther I. Brandt, (Philadelphia: Fortress Press, 1999), 369.

[6] Gustav M. Bruce, *Luther as an Educator* (Westport, CT: Greenwood Press, 1928), 61.

besides that the school he attended was possibly under the care of the Brethren of Common Life.[7] A year later, Luther transferred to Eisenach, though the cause is not certain. There he enjoyed fellowship with many of his relatives, and made strides in ascending beyond his lower class economic ranking.[8]

By the time Luther completed his early education and turned eighteen, Hans Luther's financial situation had increased considerably so that he was able to provide a promising future for his son.[9] So, Luther enrolled in the University of Erfurt in 1501 with a career as a lawyer in sight. As was customary before studying law, he received a baccalaureate degree in philosophy in 1502, followed by matriculating at Erfurt with a Masters of Liberal Arts in 1505.[10] Here at Erfurt is where Luther intensively studied and was influenced by Aristotle, nominalism, and humanism, all three of which would figure prominently in the development of his thought and theology later in life, especially in his career as a Reformer.[11]

The next stage of Luther's education was unexpectedly cut short. Only a few weeks of studying law had transpired before Luther brought his promising career path to an abrupt end. As the story goes, Luther was near Stotternheim when a lightning bolt struck close by, filling him with the fear of death which led to his cry for help and promised vow, "Help, St. Anne, I will become a monk!" Shortly, thereafter, Luther abandoned his law books and garb for a cowl on July 17, 1505, and joined the monastery of the Augustinian Hermits.[12] In 1507, he was consecrated a priest whereupon Johann von Staupitz, the vicar general of

---

[7] Some biographers assume that the school in Magdeburg was run by the Brethren; however, Martin Brecht doubts that such a school ever existed there. Nevertheless, he concedes that Luther, indeed, lived with the Brethren to some degree while attending the nearby cathedral school. See his comments in Brecht, *Road to Reformation*, 16-17.

[8] In a letter to George Spalatin on January 14, 1520, Luther discloses various details about his background. Referencing Eisenach, he remembers, "My parents moved there from [a place] near Eisenach. Nearly all my kinfolk are at Eisenach, and I am known there and recognized by them even today, since I went to school there for four years, and there is no other town in which I am better known" (*LW* 48:145). Brecht recounts that Luther succeeded at befriending the Shalbe family, a high society family of whom the father, Heinrich Schalbe, had served as mayor of Eisenach. Additionally, he developed a close relationship with Priest Johannes Braun, the vicar at the foundation of St. Mary. Through these two relationships, Luther entered a new class of society while also finding substantial exposure to the "spiritual" life of the heavily saturated monastic setting of Eisenach. Brecht, *Road to Reformation*, 17-21.

[9] Bruce, *Luther as Educator*, 66.

[10] Ibid., 72.

[11] Heiko A. Oberman, *Luther: Man between God and the Devil* (New Haven, CT: Yale University Press, 1989), 113-24.

[12] Ibid., 124-25.

the Augustinian Hermits and Luther's mentor, quickly dispatched him to the University of Wittenberg to teach moral philosophy.[13]

While balancing teaching duties at Wittenberg, Luther's theological education progressed. In March, 1509, Luther earned a Bachelor of the Bible, rapidly followed by his completion of a Bachelor of the Sentences in the fall of the same year.[14] Upon completion of these two degrees, Luther was summoned back to Erfurt to lecture on Lombard's *Sentences* and did not return to Wittenberg University until 1511. On October 19, 1512, the ceremony commenced to award Martin Luther with a doctorate in theology, thereby accepting him onto the theological faculty at Wittenberg.[15] From this point onwards until his death in 1546 (strangely enough at his birthplace, Eisleben) Luther served his entire academic career as a "Doctor of Holy Scripture" and professor at his "Little Wittenberg," though against his will as Luther would later recount.[16] Significant for consideration, as Marilyn Harran has keenly noted, is that all of Luther's Reformation activities happened in the midst of an educational setting.[17] Therefore, it comes as no surprise to see Luther labor during his tumultuous life to bring about reform, not only within the church or society, but even within the world of education.

THEOLOGY OF CHRISTIAN EDUCATION
THEOLOGICAL HERMENEUTIC

Perhaps one of Martin Luther's greatest contributions to Christianity as a monumental figure in church history is his impact on biblical interpretation. The significance of Luther's advances in hermeneutics cannot be understated. Gerhard Ebeling has even argued the case that Luther's Reformation discovery of justification by faith was ultimately the product of the

---

[13] Brecht, *Road to Reformation*, 72, 92.

[14] Luther's degree, bachelor of the sentences, is in reference to Peter Lombard's (ca. 1100-1160) four-volume work called the *Sentences*. As Brecht notes, Lombard's *Sentences* was the standard textbook for theological instruction in the Middle Ages. Ibid., 93.

[15] Helmar Junghans, "Luther's Wittenberg," in *The Cambridge Companion to Martin Luther*, ed. Donald K. McKim (Cambridge: Cambridge University Press, 2003), 24.

[16] At the end of his *Commentary on the Alleged Imperial Edict* from 1531, Luther declared, "However, I, Dr. Martinus, have been called to this work and was compelled to become a doctor, without any initiative of my own, but out of pure obedience. Then I had to accept the office of doctor and swear a vow to my most beloved Holy Scriptures that I would preach and teach them faithfully and purely." *LW* 34:103.

[17] Marilyn J. Harran, "Introduction," in *Luther and Learning*, ed. Marilyn J. Harran (Cranbury, NJ: Associated University Presses, 1985), 15. C.f. David W. Lotz, "Sola Scriptura: *Luther on Biblical Authority*," *Interpretation* 35 (1981): 258, "The Lutheran Reformation was thus the work of a professor of biblical theology..."

Reformer's hermeneutical development as he transitioned away from the traditional Medieval fourfold method towards a "new hermeneutic."[18] Many scholars in the past century or more have labored to bring the principles of Luther's hermeneutics together into a coherent synthesis. Though diverse renderings exist, a fair amount of consistency can be observed among the more pronounced principles of biblical interpretation associated with Luther.[19] For the purpose of illuminating the effects of Luther's theological hermeneutic on his educational philosophy, three features that most pertain to this relationship will be treated: the authority of Scripture (*sola Scriptura*), Christ-centered interpretation, and law and gospel.[20]

SOLA SCRIPTURA

The Reformation saw the recovery and establishment of many evangelical

---

[18] Gerhard Ebeling, "The New Hermeneutics and the Early Luther," trans. Mrs. James Carse, *Theology Today* 21 (1964): 34-46; idem., "The Beginnings of Luther's Hermeneutics," trans. Richard B. Steele, *Lutheran Quarterly* 7 (1993): 129-58. Although his work is meant to counter Ebeling's classic thesis on the nature of Luther's hermeneutical shift in the *First Lectures on the Psalms*, James Preus, nonetheless, similarly contends that it was the Reformer's early hermeneutic that laid the groundwork for his Reformation theology. See James S. Preus, "Old Testament *Promissio* and Luther's New Hermeneutic," *Harvard Theological Review* 60 (1967): 145.

[19] Research on Luther's approach to biblical interpretation and hermeneutics is voluminous. Samplings of some of the key contributions are: Karl Holl, "Luther's Bedeutung für den Fortschritt der Auslegungskunst," in *Gesammelte Aufsätze zur Kirchengeschicte*, vol. 1: *Luther* (Tübingen: J. C. B. Mohr (Paul Siebeck), 1927), 544-82; Gerhard Ebeling, *Evangelische Evangelienauslegung: Eine Untersuchung zu Luthers Hermeneutik* (Wissenschaftliche Buchgesellschaft: Darmstadt, Germany, 1942); Heinrich Bornkamm, *Luther and the Old Testament*, trans. Eric W. and Ruth C. Gritsch, ed.Victor I. Gruhn (Philadelphia: Fortress Press, 1969); James S. Preus, *From Shadow to Promise: Old Testament Interpretation from Augustine to the Young Luther* (Cambridge, MA: Harvard University Press, 1969); Christine Helmer, "Luther's Trinitarian Hermeneutic and the Old Testament," *Modern Theology* 18 (2002): 49-73; Mark D. Thompson, *A Sure Ground on Which to Stand: The Relation of Authority and Interpretive Method in Luther's Approach to Scripture*, Studies in Christian History and Thought (Waynesboro, GA: Paternoster Press, 2004).

[20] To some degree, this tripartite sequence could be considered a cogent display of how Luther's doctrine of Scripture normed his interpretive method. He intended his hermeneutic to conform to the nature and purpose of the Bible as the written Word of God. In terms of the German Reformer's bibliology, the "authority of Scripture" could represent the "formal principle;" his Christ-centered interpretation the "material principle;" and the law and the gospel dialectic as what Scripture *does*. Most recently, Reformation and Lutheran scholar, Timothy Wengert, has penned a wonderfully short guide to Luther as a biblical interpreter under the title, *Reading the Bible with Martin Luther*. Similarly, he divides his threefold account of Luther's approach to the Scriptures as authority (*sola Scriptura* and Christ as the interpretive key), method (distinguishing law and gospel), and interpretation (application of the "theology of the cross"). See Timothy J. Wengert, *Reading the Bible with Martin Luther: An Introductory Guide* (Grand Rapids: Baker Academic, 2013), vii-viii, 1.

commitments, but perhaps foremost among them all was the reassertion of the supreme authority of Scripture (*sola Scriptura*) over all other theological, ministerial, or practical norms. Luther himself vigorously sought to dethrone the papacy and church tradition from their lofty placement above and against Holy Scripture.[21] In one of his colorful displays from 1539 in the treatise *On Councils and the Church*, Luther rejected the notion that Scripture endorses the papacy's office of which they strove to leverage biblical support in texts such as Ephesians 4:11, claiming equivalence to "apostles and prophets." Even if Paul, indeed, prescribed their offices from this verse (which he rejected), Luther denied the papacy's adequate fulfillment of these spiritual vocations insofar as "they are acquainted with more human doctrine, and also with more villainy" than Scripture and true Christian doctrine "because ... true apostles, evangelists, and prophets *preach God's word*, not *against God's word*."[22]

Although Luther's doctrine of the Word of God is multi-faceted, and many scholars regard it to extend beyond mere reference to the Bible, one must certainly not minimize the significance that Luther, nonetheless, believed that Scripture was the written revelation of God.[23] Moreover, *sola Scriptura* is a fitting description for Luther's position on the authority of Scripture even if he never used the phrase. He firmly upheld the belief that the Bible was God's Word(s) with the Holy Spirit as its ultimate author, and thus, it alone was the place where God's voice was to be heard with full certainty and authority.[24] From his sermon, "The Gospel for the Sunday after Christmas" on Luke 2:33-40, Luther utilized the idea of the "temple" as the habitation of God for an analogous purpose to say that "it also signifies Holy

---

[21] "The fundamental characteristic of all Protestant theologies was the categorical disavowal of the primacy of the Roman pontiff. No matter what else is to be said about Protestant theology, one fact is clear: all Protestant churches, without exception, renounced their allegiance to the pope in Rome. That was the common bond. A pope, who held judicial and theological primacy, was neither needed nor wanted." See Hans J. Hillerbrand, *The Division of Christendom: Christianity in the Sixteenth Century* (Louisville, KY: Westminster John Knox Press, 2007), 383.

[22] Italics mine. *LW* 41:157.

[23] Mark D. Thompson provides a helpful survey of scholars' various perspectives on what Luther means by the "Word of God" in relation to the Bible and scriptural authority in Thompson, *A Sure Ground on Which to Stand*, 47-53.

[24] In Robert Kolb and Charles P. Arand, *The Genius of Luther's Theology: A Wittenberg Way of Thinking for the Contemporary Church* (Grand Rapids: Baker Academic, 2008), 167, they explain that Luther's high view of Scripture was not novel in church history. So to some degree, he took it for granted and mainly argued for it in view of its abuse or negligence rather than as a proposal for a new doctrinal position altogether. C.f. Vítor Westhelle, "Luther on the Authority of Scripture," *Lutheran Quarterly* 19 (2005): 375, "The *sola scriptura* principle is not an invention of the Reformation. It was inherited, as were many other theologuemna, from late medieval theologians, preachers, and philosophers."

Scripture wherein one finds God as in his proper place."[25] In his reflection upon God's words to David in Isaiah 59:17, he identified the Holy Spirit as the origin of Christian Scripture: "My spirit which is upon you, and My words which I have put in your mouth. *My Spirit, who has spoken in the prophets and apostles.*"[26] Likewise, in his treatise, *On the Last Words of David*, Luther wrote, "Thus we attribute to the Holy Spirit all of Holy Scripture."[27]

Scriptural authority, for Luther, was certainly connected to how it bore witness to Christ, but as a written document, the Bible's authority over popes, councils, and traditions was self-evident, given that the "prophets and apostles" alone were the ones through whom God had revealed his Word and will definitively. This aspect of *sola Scriptura* is reflected especially in polemical passages such as his 1521 treatise on *The Misuse of the Mass*. Luther pleaded that if his opponents were to cease from their "lunacy" for at least one hour, they would see clearly that their erroneous teachings on the ordinances of the church "are not depending upon divine sayings [the Word of God], but only upon human ones."[28] He, then, continued, "Thus it is contrary to human reason, not to mention the divine Scriptures, to found and build an article of faith on human fancies, for the holy sacraments and articles of faith rightly demand that they be founded and preserved *only through the divine Scriptures*, as Moses abundantly testifies in Deuteronomy."[29] Similarly, from his famous 1535 commentary on Galatians in his exposition of Gal 1:9, Luther remarked, "Nevertheless, we are presented here with an example that enables us to know for a certainty that it is an accursed lie that the pope is the arbiter of Scripture or that the church has authority over Scripture."[30] In response, he charged everyone to follow Paul's example in this verse to subordinate oneself to "Sacred Scripture" as "witnesses, disciples, and confessors" rather than as "masters, judges, or arbiters."[31] In closing, he stated, "Nor should any doctrine be taught or heard in the church except the pure Word of God. Otherwise, let the teachers and the hearers be accursed along with their doctrine."[32]

---

[25] *LW* 52:105.

[26] Italics mine. *LW* 17:308. Here Luther is using the formula of the "prophets and apostles" to speak holistically of the two Testaments.

[27] *LW* 15:275. The complete quotation from Luther adds, "Thus we attribute to the Holy Spirit all of Holy Scripture and the external Word and the sacraments, which touch and move our external ears and other senses."

[28] *LW* 36:135.

[29] Italics mine. Ibid., 135-36.

[30] *LW* 26:57. In Galatians 1:9, Paul warns the believers, "As we have said before, so now I say again: If anyone is preaching to you a gospel contrary to the one you received, let him be accursed" (ESV).

[31] Ibid.

[32] Ibid. In this passage, the context demonstrates that Luther clearly is using "Word of God" synonymous

CHRISTOCENTRIC THEOLOGY

A second main component of Luther's theological hermeneutic is his Christocentric reading of Scripture. Ultimately, for Luther, all of the Bible's particulars meet at Christ, its center. As Paul Althaus recognized, "[Luther] knows that the rich content of the Bible includes laws, historical accounts, prayers, proclamation, prophecy, etc. However, taken theologically, and that means in terms of its essential theme, Luther sees the Bible as a great unity. It has only one content. That is Christ."[33] Therefore, David Lotz has argued, "this 'christological concentration' is the decisive element in Luther's interpretation and use of Scripture. It is also the key to his concept of biblical authority."[34] Luther himself expressed this notion of the Bible's hermeneutical key in his *Preface to the Epistles of St. James and St. Jude*, when he contended, "All the genuine sacred books agree in this, that all of them preach and inculcate Christ. And that is the true test by which to judge all books, when we see whether or not they inculcate Christ. For all the Scriptures show us Christ."[35] In this way, Luther considered Scripture a "servant" and Jesus Christ its "Lord and King."[36] To frame the hermeneutical situation negatively, Luther asked in *The Bondage of the Will* in response to Erasmus' preface from *On the Freedom of the Will*, "Take Christ out of the Scriptures, and what will you find left in them?"[37] For Luther, Christ was the plain sense subject matter of Scripture, and therefore, the Bible's meaning could not be regarded as ultimately obscure in reply to Erasmus' indictment. If, however, Erasmus' vision of scriptural meaning was correct, then Luther's argument was that the Bible's voice would be silenced and rendered impotent no matter whatever else a reader could make of or glean from it.

Luther's conception of Christ as the essential meaning (i.e., *sensus literalis*) of the Bible is multi-dimensional, just as his theology of the Word of God. Yet at a basic level, Luther asserted that "all the Scriptures point to Christ alone" because of the biblical text's authorial intent from both its human and divine author.[38] Among other aims, Luther envisioned the ultimate task of the prophetic and apostolic offices of the human writers as one given to set the biblical audience's hope and faith upon the long-promised Messiah (OT), who is the crucified and resurrected Son of God and Son of David (NT), Jesus Christ. Along these lines,

---

with "Sacred Scriptures."

[33] Paul Althaus, *The Theology of Martin Luther*, trans. Robert C. Schultz (Philadelphia: Fortress Press, 1966), 74.

[34] Lotz, "Sola Scriptura: *Luther on Biblical Authority*," 270.

[35] *LW* 35:396.

[36] *LW* 26:295.

[37] *LW* 33:26.

[38] *LW* 35:132.

Gary Simpson argued that Luther was always careful to establish an "intrascriptural warrant" for his view that the entirety of the Bible is meant to show Christ.[39] For example, in his *Preface to the Prophet Isaiah*, Luther said that "[Isaiah] is concerned altogether with the Christ, that his future coming and the promised kingdom of grace and salvation shall not be despised or be lost and in vain because of unbelief and great misfortune and impatience amongst his people."[40] Likewise, in the New Testament, Luther considered that it is "the office of a true apostle to preach of the Passion and resurrection and office of Christ, and to lay the foundation for faith in him, as Christ himself says in John 15:[27], 'You shall bear witness to me.'"[41] In other words, Holy Scripture's prime subject matter is Christ due to the purpose of both the prophetic and apostolic offices as witnesses to Jesus, who together constitute the Spirit-inspired authors of the Old and New Testaments.[42]

LAW AND GOSPEL

A third feature of Luther's theological hermeneutic that impacted his philosophy of education is law and gospel. Luther regarded a true theologian as one who can "distinguish the Gospel from the Law," and furthermore, he declared that "knowledge of this topic, the distinction between the Law and the Gospel, is necessary to the highest degree; for it contains a summary of all Christian doctrine."[43] According to Gerhard Ebeling, law and gospel is "the basic guiding principle of theological thought" for Luther.[44] In his earlier years, Luther focused on the traditional delineation of letter and spirit borrowed from the Apostle Paul's antithesis in Second Corinthians 3:6; however, as Luther's hermeneutic matured, the letter/spirit division grew into Luther's classic law/gospel dialectic insofar as the emphasis shifted

---

[39] Gary M. Simpson, "'You shall bear witness to me': Thinking with Luther about Christ and the Scriptures," *Word and World* 29 (2009): 383.

[40] *LW* 35:277.

[41] Ibid., 396.

[42] Additionally, recent studies have sought to expose the Trinitarian basis for Luther's messianic/Christological interpretation of Scripture. See, for instance, Christine Helmer, "Luther's Trinitarian Hermeneutic and the Old Testament," *Modern Theology* 18 (2002): 49-73; Mickey L. Mattox, "Luther's Interpretation of Scripture: Biblical Understanding in Trinitarian Shape," in *The Substance of the Faith: Luther's Doctrinal Theology for Today*, Dennis Bielfeldt, Mickey L. Mattox, and Paul R. Hinlicky (Minneapolis, MN: Fortress Press, 2008), 11-57; John T. Slotemaker, "The Trinitarian House of David: Martin Luther's Anti-Jewish Exegesis of 2 Samuel 23:1-7," *Harvard Theological Review* 104 (2011): 233-54.

[43] *LW* 26:115-17.

[44] Gerhard Ebeling, *Luther: An Introduction to His Thought*, trans. R. A. Wilson (Philadelphia: Fortress Press, 1970), 113.

from using these dualisms to refer to what the Old and New Testaments *are* and into what Holy Scripture *does* to its readers/hearers.[45] The main subject of theology in Luther's thought, therefore, is "the *sinning* human being and the *justifying* God."[46] Law and gospel is the effect of Scripture's witness to Christ upon the creaturely sinner who encounters the divine reality of the biblical text through the ministry of the Word and the Spirit. Lutheran theologian Robert Kolb has taught that Luther's view of what it means to be human at the most basic level is summed up in the human person's identity as one whom God considers to be righteous.[47] It is Scripture as the living and active Word of God that creates this creature-Creator relationship where the sinner will hear God's performative speech across both Testaments in either the condemning verdict of his law or the promise of forgiveness of sins and justification by faith alone in the gospel of his Son.[48]

HERMENEUTICAL INFLUENCE ON LUTHER'S THEOLOGY OF EDUCATION

Luther's hermeneutic had both a direct and indirect impact upon his theology of

---

[45] Ebeling helpfully shows how what began as the letter and the spirit in Luther's earlier writings later transformed into the law and the gospel distinction. See Ebeling, *Luther*, 93-124. For a study that sees Luther's law/gospel formulation at the heart of the letter/spirit contrast, see also Randall C. Gleason, "'Letter' and 'Spirit'" in Luther's Hermeneutics, *Bibliotheca Sacra* 157 (2000): 468-85.

[46] In Oswald Bayer, *Martin Luther's Theology: A Contemporary Interpretation*, trans. Thomas H. Trapp (Grand Rapids: Eerdmans, 2008), 37, Bayer explains that Luther comes to this view of the "subject of theology" because of how the Reformer understands what occurs when the creature encounters the Creator God in the Scriptures, whether the reader is a theologian or not. The study of Scripture for *scientia* (knowledge) or *sapientia* (wisdom) is always an experience of the Holy God, who speaks through Scripture his divine word of law or gospel upon his audience. Bayer bases his interpretation of Luther's "subject of theology" upon the near same expression found in Luther's commentary on Psalm 51, when he contends, "The proper subject of theology is man guilty of sin and condemned, and God the Justifier and Savior of man the sinner. Whatever is asked or discussed in theology outside this subject, is error and poison. All Scripture points to this." *LW* 12:311.

[47] Robert Kolb, *Luther and the Stories of God: Biblical Narratives as a Foundation for Christian Living* (Grand Rapids: Baker Academic, 2012), 66.

[48] Robert Kolb, "Reality Rests on the Word of the Lord: Martin Luther's Understanding of God's Word," *Reformation & Revival* 9 (2000): 53. For a more expansive study of Kolb's argument about the connection between Luther's anthropology and righteousness, see Robert Kolb, "God and His Human Creatures in Luther's Sermons on Genesis: The Reformer's Early Use of His Distinction of Two Kinds of Righteousness," *Concordia Journal* 33 (2007): 166-84. Additionally, for indispensable studies on the law and gospel in Luther, see Robert Kolb, "'The Noblest Skill in the Christian Church': Luther's Sermons on the Proper Distinction of Law and Gospel," *Concordia Theological Quarterly* 71 (2007): 301-18; Gerhard O. Forde, "Law and Gospel in Luther's Hermeneutic," *Interpretation* 37 (1983): 240-52.

education. When considering Luther's theological hermeneutic, an instance of its direct influence would be his commitment to the supremacy of Holy Scripture for all levels of education. *Sola Scriptura* is definitely at work when Luther asserted in *To the Christian Nobility of the German Nation* (1520), "The universities only ought to turn out men who are experts in the Holy Scriptures, men who can become bishops and priests, and stand in the front line against heretics, the devil, and all the world."[49] Furthermore, canon law must be displaced because "it only hinders the study of the Holy Scriptures."[50] Luther even regarded "secular law" as underneath the authority of Scripture. "Surely, wise rulers," he remarks, "side by side with Holy Scripture, would be law enough."[51] For the sake of Christendom, the supremacy of Scripture needed to be reinstituted throughout the full scope one's educational journey, whether in pursuit of a ministerial or a secular office.[52] Hence, Luther's comprehensive recommendation, "Above all, the foremost reading for everybody, both in the universities and in the schools, should be Holy Scripture."[53]

An example of indirect influence from Luther's theological hermeneutic upon his theology of education comes through his doctrine of the two kingdoms. The hermeneutical effect is "indirect" since this particular teaching of Luther's finds its ground in the law and gospel distinction, which was identified previously as a primary component of the Reformer's approach to biblical interpretation. In his 1523 political treatise, *Temporal Authority: To What Extent It Should Be Obeyed*, Luther divided humanity into two classes: Christians, who belong to the kingdom (*reich*) of God, and non-Christians, who belong to the kingdom (*reich*) of the

---

[49] *LW* 44:207.

[50] Ibid., 202.

[51] Ibid., 203.

[52] One must not forget throughout this analysis that Luther's views of education were articulated within the context of Christendom. Luther's Reformation program never had in mind only the church. "Christendom" as an "all-embracing political, social, and religious phenomenon" was also in need of drastic Christian reform and separation from the clutches of the papacy in addition to the church (Hillerbrand, *The Division of Christendom*, 11). For Luther, joint effort from both the temporal and spiritual estates was necessary to preserve the integrity of the gospel. Thus, reform of education was integral to his vision so that a new generation of Christians could arise "freed" from Rome's captivity in order to permeate society with faith and love. For more from this perspective of the Reformation, Scott Hendrix has offered a compelling vision of Luther's "reforming agenda" as one that was holistically aimed at Christendom rather than at mere ecclesial concerns in his book *Recultivating the Vineyard: The Reformation Agendas of Christianization* (Louisville, KY: Westminster John Knox Press, 2004), 37-68.

[53] *LW* 44:205-6.

world.[54] And with these two kingdoms, "God has ordained two governments (*regiment*): the spiritual, by which the Holy Spirit produces Christians and righteous people under Christ; and the temporal, which restrains the un-Christian and wicked so that — no thanks to them — they are obliged to keep still and to maintain an outward peace."[55] God rules the former by the gospel and the latter by the law.[56] The gospel and the law each assigned to its own "kingdom" are, according to Ebeling, "two different ways in which God encounters the sinful world."[57] So, the doctrine of the two kingdoms cannot be reduced merely to political theology. For Luther, this viewpoint constitutes the full realm of the Christian's earthly existence.[58]

Luther consistently held that the gospel and law respectively rule over the two kingdoms, which is evident from his two primary writings on education. Both treatises include sections pointed towards the spiritual and temporal estates independently and in that order. For example, several years later in 1530, Luther sharply divided *A Sermon on Keeping Children in School* into a twofold address to both realms. At the start, he disclosed his aim that "I propose, therefore, to take up the question of what is at stake in this matter in the way of gains and losses, first those that are spiritual or eternal, and then those that are temporal or worldly."[59] Beginning with the spiritual estate, Luther considered it as the office that "helps to further and sustain this temporal life and all the worldly estates."[60] Furthermore, he added, "Indeed, it is only because of the spiritual estate that the world stands and abides at all; if it were not for this estate, the world would long since have gone down to destruction."[61] Parents, thus, must beware in ceasing from sending and keeping their children in school to become what is the true "spiritual estate," namely, one is a minister of the Word and sacraments.[62] Because God has instituted this office by the blood of his own Son, Luther

---

[54] *LW* 45:88.

[55] Ibid., 91.

[56] Ibid., 88-90.

[57] Ebeling, *Luther*, 185.

[58] David C. Steinmetz explains in his essay, "Luther and the Two Kingdoms," from *Luther in Context*, 2nd ed. (Grand Rapids: Baker Academic, 2002), 118-19, that the two kingdoms doctrine encompasses both spheres of human relationship. The first and antecedent realm is where one is in relation to God justified by faith in Christ. The secondary or consequent realm is where one is in relation to society, which becomes the place where Luther assigns the role of "good works," namely, the locus of faith exercising itself in the deeds of love for the good of one's neighbor.

[59] *LW* 46:219.

[60] Ibid., 220.

[61] Ibid.

[62] Ibid.

believed it to be the most honored vocation within God's economy.[63] Fathers and mothers ought to rejoice to discover that God has chosen their young one to be "a good Christian pastor, preacher, or schoolmaster, . . . There is no dearer treasure, no nobler thing on earth or in this life than a good and faithful pastor and preacher."[64] Hence, to neglect education for the spiritual estate is to doom the temporal order. The pastor's public role (and derivatively the schoolmaster's) is a necessary one because he "informs and instructs the various estates on how they are to conduct themselves outwardly in their several offices and estates, so that they may do what is right in the sight of God."[65] In short, Luther envisioned the preacher from within the spiritual estate as the one responsible for giving ultimate "direction to all the temporal estates and offices."[66]

When Luther turned his focus to the temporal estate, he presented an equally compelling case for the indispensability of education to maintain the integrity and stability of the world order. Although he admitted that the temporal office is not conferred with the same nobility as the spiritual since "it is not purchased at so dear a price as the preaching office, by the blood and dying of the Son of God," he still regarded it as "a glorious ordinance and splendid gift of God, who has instituted and established it and will have it maintained as something men cannot do without."[67] If the spiritual estate exists to make sinners saints, then Luther contended that the function of the temporal government is "to make men out of wild beasts and to prevent men from becoming wild beasts."[68] With a hint of Pauline rhetoric,

---

[63] Ibid., 221-22.

[64] Ibid., 223. In the full quotation, Luther said that the one whom God raises up to fill these offices is "a special servant" unto the Lord and for the world. This language echoes the paradoxical Christian life he unfolded in his 1520 treatise, *The Freedom of a Christian*. In his "outer man," a Christian is a "dutiful servant of all, subject to all" (*LW* 31:344). As the believer inhabits the kingdom of the world, he "does not live for himself alone in this mortal body to work for it alone, but he lives also for all men on earth" (*LW* 31:364). The Christian is foremost a "servant" insofar as Luther said that faith works through love always with the primary consideration of how "he may serve and benefit others in all that he does, considering nothing except the need and the advantage of his neighbor" (*LW* 31:365). In sum, Luther concluded "that a Christian lives not in himself, but in Christ and in his neighbor. Otherwise he is not a Christian. He lives in Christ through faith, in his neighbor through love" (*LW* 31:371). Education, then, is a necessary means by which the Christian is prepared to be the proper "servant" for his or her "neighbor," that is, one's fellow human within the church, the household, and society.

[65] *LW* 46:226.

[66] Ibid.

[67] Ibid., 237.

[68] Ibid.

Luther then asked, "And what men are capable of doing it?" His answer rejected the notion that the maintenance of peace and order in the worldly government can be accomplished by those who "rule only with the fist."[69] Rather, as Solomon instructs in Proverbs 8, Luther asserted that wisdom and reason must be supreme in a secular authority's armament, not force.[70]

In sum, the gospel rules over the spiritual estate through the ministry of the Word and Spirit to grant true knowledge of the will of God for all things under creation, while the law rules over the temporal estate through the ministry of wisdom and reason to restrain evil, to protect one's neighbor from all injustices, and to preserve peace and tranquility within Christendom. Alas, as Luther sighed, "Yet it cannot possibly be maintained unless people keep their children studying and in school; there is no doubt about that."[71]

LUTHER'S CONTRIBUTION TO EDUCATION AND CHRISTIAN EDUCATION
PARENTS AS TEACHERS

A pervasive theme in Luther's writings on education is parental responsibility to raise children well for the sake of church and state. As early as 1519 in *A Sermon on the Estate of Marriage*, Luther encouraged parents to remember that they "can do no better work and do nothing more valuable either for God, for Christendom, for all the world, for themselves, and for their children than to bring up their children well."[72] There is "no greater tragedy in Christendom," according to Luther, when parents spoil their children.[73] The right raising of children is what the Reformer regarded as perhaps "the end and chief purpose of marriage."[74] Moreover, parents who emulate the biblical model will make certain to care for both their child's body *and* soul.[75] In this context, education is required for the proper development of the whole person, which Luther believed was essential for the total Christian life as it exists for the integrity and health of the two kingdoms.

Not only did Luther challenge parents to raise their children in a biblical manner

---

[69] Ibid., 238.

[70] The connection between "rule by wisdom" instead of "rule by force" to education is bound up for Luther with the conception of the law as the worldly government's "wisdom and reason." Ibid., 239.

[71] Ibid., 241-42.

[72] *LW* 44:12.

[73] Ibid.

[74] Ibid.

[75] Ibid., 13.

because of how God has purposed marriage for this end, but also he told them plainly that to supply their children with an education is the Lord's mandate. In *To the Councilmen* (1524), the "third consideration" he offered parents to support Christian schooling finds its ground in scriptural commands and expectations from the Pentateuch and the Psalms. Furthermore, Luther said this responsibility ought to be self-evident because "nature itself should drive us to do this and even the heathen afford us abundant examples of it."[76] After listing three reasons for why he suspected parents fail to fulfill their duty, Luther turned to the temporal government to take up this role, since they were entrusted with the welfare of the city.[77] In doing so, Luther reminded them that a "city's best and greatest welfare, safety, and strength consist rather in its having many able, learned, wise, honorable, and well-educated citizens."[78] "It therefore behooves," said Luther, "the council and the authorities to devote the greatest care and attention to the young."[79]

Another way that Luther charged was to encourage mothers and fathers to be good stewards of their child's "gifts" or abilities. For fear of the spiritual estate's demise, Luther warned, "If God has given you a child who has the ability and the talent for this office, and you do not train him for it but look only to the belly and to temporal livelihood, ... you are making a place for the devil and advancing his kingdom."[80] Likewise, when sharing the same concerns about the temporal estate, Luther declared, "Now if you have a son who is able to learn, and you are in a position to keep him at it, but do not do so, ... then you are doing all in your power to oppose worldly authority."[81]

---

[76] *LW* 45:353.

[77] Luther submitted three reasons for parental neglect of their educational duty towards children: First, some parents lack the sheer goodness and decency to fulfill it. Using an image from the animal kingdom, Luther calls these parents "ostriches," who are content to lay eggs and bring children into the world, but have no desire to provide further for their young. Second, a majority of parents are simply ignorant of the task and its necessity. These parents are oblivious to this responsibility, and Luther considered their own lack of training and discipleship as a partial cause for this mindset. In other words, no one has "educated" the parents with a proper theology of marriage and parental duty to fit them for this task. And third, many parents have the ability and inclination, yet lack the time and opportunity. Luther's realism showed in this third reason as he acknowledged that the "common man" has several obstacles in his way, poverty most of all, that prevent the fulfillment of any educational aspirations for one's children. Also in mind at this point are orphans entrusted to guardians without means for proper provision. Each scenario, Luther demanded, is a justifiable case within which the government for its own sake should take responsibility for the education of children. Ibid., 354-55.

[78] Ibid., 355.

[79] Ibid.

[80] *LW* 46:229.

[81] Ibid., 242.

Luther increased the severity of these cautions through eschatological accountability. In *A Sermon on the Estate of Marriage* (1519), Luther informed the father that "at his death and on the day of judgment he will be asked about his child and will have to give a most solemn account."[82] And if he has not been a good steward of his own child's abilities and talents, then he could hear God reply, "For you could have helped. I gave you children and material means for this purpose, but you wantonly allowed me and my kingdom and the souls of men to suffer want and pine away — and you thereby served the devil and his kingdom instead of me and my kingdom. Well, let him be your reward. Go with him now into the abyss of hell."[83]

CHILDREN AS LEARNERS

One of Luther's driving convictions about the importance of education that repeatedly manifests itself was his zeal for the well-being of children. It is evident throughout his comments on education that Germany's "wild boar" had a tender heart for the little ones.[84] Luther took interest in the education of both boys and girls. During his appeal to the German princes to reform universities and schools in *To the Christian Nobility* (1520), he recommended that the primary reading should be the Scriptures. In addition to the younger boys who would focus on the Gospels, Luther wished, "And would to God that every town had a girls' school as well, where the girls would be taught the gospel for an hour every day either in German or in Latin."[85] In general, Luther had a high estimation for what the young ones were capable of learning at school besides "praying and singing."[86] He asked, "Is it not only right that every Christian man know the entire holy gospel by the age of nine or ten? ... A spinner or a seamstress teaches her daughter her craft in her early years. But today even the great, learned prelates and the very bishops do not know the gospel."[87]

---

[82] *LW* 44:13

[83] *LW* 46:230. Additionally, in A *Sermon on Keeping Children in School* (1530), Luther rebuked those who refused to give their children a proper education as specifically poor stewards of the child's God-given talents and skills: "Yet you are such an accursed, ungrateful wretch that you will not give a son into training for the maintenance of these gifts of God" (*LW* 46:254).

[84] In the Papal Bull, *Exsurge Domine*, issued on June 15, 1520 for the excommunication of the one Martin Luther, Pope Leo X described the Reformer as a "wild boar" who had invaded the Lord's vineyard. For accounts of this narrative, see chapter eight of Roland Bainton's classic biography, *Here I Stand: A Life of Martin Luther* (Peabody, MA: Hendrickson Publishers, 2009), 125-41; cf., Hillerbrand, *The Division of Christendom*, 49-63.

[85] *LW* 44:206.

[86] Ibid.

[87] Ibid.

Furthermore, in response to parents who assume that discipline and training in the household is sufficient to raise boys and girls properly for the enduring future of Christendom, Luther exposed that the "net result" would be nothing more than "enforced outward respectability; underneath, they are nothing but the same old blockheads, unable to converse intelligently on any subject, or to assist or counsel anyone."[88] Parents were fooling themselves if they thought that a simple trade/skill and corrective, behavioral discipline at home were all that was needed to maintain the temporal estate. Rather, "the very best schools for both boys and girls" are essential so that the world might "have good and capable men and women, men able to rule well over land and people, women able to manage the household and train children and servants aright. Now such men must come from our boys, and such women from our girls. Therefore, it is a matter of properly educating and training our boys and girls to that end."[89]

To prevent any excuses such as financial burdens from hindering a child's education, Luther even appealed for the state to establish government aid and scholarships. If the temporal authorities see "a promising boy" who is in need, then "the resources of the church should be used to assist." As for scholarships, Luther also offered ideas for estate planning:

> Let the rich make their wills with this work in view, as some have done who have established scholarship funds. This is the right way to bequeath your money to the church, for this way you do not release departed souls from purgatory but, by maintaining God's offices, you do help the living and those to come who are yet unborn, so that they do not get into purgatory, indeed, so that they are redeemed from hell and go to heaven; and you help the living to enjoy peace and happiness. That would be a praiseworthy Christian testament. God would have delight and pleasure in it, and would bless and honor you in return by giving you pleasure and joy in him.[90]

As for his philosophy of education, Luther proffered a balanced approach between education as spiritual/character formation and training for vocation.[91] In *To the Councilmen*

---

[88] *LW* 45:368.

[89] Ibid.

[90] *LW* 46:257.

[91] What has not yet been stated is the significance of the development of Luther's doctrine of the priesthood of all believers and its effect on how the Reformer understood "vocation" and/or "calling." The priesthood of all believers doctrine was explicitly articulated in *To the Christian Nobility* (1520), and afterwards, became the fuel for fanning the flame of service in the two realms of Christian existence. In a challenging and illuminating article, Marilyn Harran traces the impact of Luther's doctrine of the priesthood of all believers throughout the expressions of his educational vision. She

(1524), Luther suggested that young boys "attend such a school for one or two hours during the day, and spend the remainder of the time working at home, learning a trade, or doing whatever is expected of them."[92] Likewise, "a girl can surely find time enough to attend school for an hour a day, and still take care of her duties at home."[93] Several years later in *A Sermon on Keeping Children in School* (1530), Luther acknowledged that the stability of the world required more vocations than simply pastors and preachers. Since God is God of both of the two kingdoms, "Every occupation has its own honor before God, as well as its own requirements and duties."[94] Education, therefore, must continue to thrive and be upheld as a priority in the land in order to provide a ready reserve for the pastoral office (spiritual estate) and to ensure that a king or emperor has the vocations requisite for the temporal estate's peace and health such as chancellors, jurists, counselors, clerks, scholars, schoolmasters, soldiers, writers, and physicians.[95] Without society's commitment to education of the young, "theologians and jurists [will not] remain," and "everything else will go down to destruction with us; you can be sure of that."[96]

CURRICULUM AND METHODS

Luther's "reforming agenda" for Christendom also extended to curriculum and pedagogy because, as historian Scott Hendrix notes, the Reformer saw the need for "schools that would undo the training he and others had received in the monasteries and universities of their youth. These new schools would teach 'true Christianity,' preparing the young for

---

argues that Luther's broadened views of education and vocation were made possible because theology was the ground for the Reformer's pedagogy. As she reflects, "While I think it remains an open question whether our largely secular culture can reestablish the link between theology and pedagogy, we cannot fail to see that a concept of education that is not rooted in a larger sense of purpose and connected to the goal of service will ultimately fail its greatest challenge and opportunity. If we reject theology as the foundation for pedagogy, can we find another foundation that will adequately address both the purposes and methods of education?" See Marilyn J. Harran, "The Contemporary Applicability of Luther's Pedagogy: Education and Vocation," *Concordia Journal* 16 (1990): 319-32.

[92] *LW* 45:370.

[93] Ibid.

[94] *LW* 46:246. On interpretations of Luther's theology of "vocation," see Gustaf Wingren, *Luther on Vocation*, trans. Carl C. Rasmussen (Eugene, OR: Wipf & Stock Publishers, 2004); Karlfried Froehlich, "Luther on Vocation," *Lutheran Quarterly* 13 (1999): 195-207; Robert Kolb, "Called to Milk Cows and Govern Kingdoms: Martin Luther's Teaching on the Christian's Vocations," *Concordia Journal* 39 (2013): 133-41.

[95] *LW* 46:231, 243-54.

[96] Ibid., 251.

service both in the church and in the civil realm."[97] An initial step towards that goal, for Luther, was the removal of the substance of Aristotle's writings from the university program. In *To the Christian Nobility* (1520), Luther issued the call for Aristotle's *Physics*, *Metaphysics*, *Concerning the Soul*, and *Nicomachean Ethics* to be entirely discarded "along will all the rest of his books that boast about nature, although nothing can be learned from them either about nature or the Spirit."[98] On the other hand, he conceded that Aristotle's books on *Logic*, *Rhetoric*, and *Poetics* along with Cicerco's *Rhetoric* could be retained for benefit.[99] Luther's problem at this level was, of course, that the spiritual estate in particular seemed to be trained in everything but Holy Scripture, even in material that contradicted the Bible's own doctrine concerning man's nature, will, and good works. In his continued appeal for curriculum reform, Luther fought for the recovery of the languages (Hebrew, Greek, Latin) while requesting that canon law be "completely blotted out, from the first letter to the last, especially the decretals."[100] In Luther's view, "Every institution that does not unceasingly pursue the study of God's word becomes corrupt."[101]

Luther's zeal for religious education coupled with his humanist affinity for the liberal arts carried over into his 1524 treatise *To the Councilmen*.[102] A country that cherishes the languages and the arts adorns itself with great "ornament, profit, glory, and benefit, both for the understanding of Holy Scripture and the conduct of temporal government."[103] Luther advocated that school be a pleasurable experience, instead of the "hell and purgatory" he

---

[97] Hendrix, *Recultivating the Vineyard*, 63.

[98] *LW* 44:200.

[99] Ibid., 201.

[100] Ibid., 202.

[101] Ibid., 207.

[102] For a sustained introspection into Luther's view of the liberal arts and its relevance for today's educational philosophy, see John S. Reist, "The Knife that Cuts Better than Another: Luther and Liberal Arts Education," *Perspectives in Religious Studies* 21 (1994): 93-113; cf, Gene Edward Veith, Jr., "Classical Education as Vocational Education: Luther on the Liberal Arts," *Logia* 21 (2012): 23-26.

[103] *LW* 45:358. See also the Reformer's compelling case for the utter importance of languages in education made in the same treatise, "And let us be sure of this: we will not long preserve the gospel without the languages. The languages are the sheath in which this sword of the Spirit [Eph. 6:17] is contained; they are the casket in which this jewel is enshrined; they are the vessel in which this wine is held; they are the larder in which this food is stored; and, as the gospel itself points out [Matt. 14:20], they are the baskets in which are kept these loaves and fishes and fragments. If through our neglect we let the languages go (which God forbid!), we shall not only lose the gospel, but the time will come when we shall be unable either to speak or write a correct Latin or German." Ibid., 360.

experienced, and so set forth that he "would have them study not only languages and history, but also singing and music together with the whole of mathematics."[104] Four years later in 1528, Luther also initiated and endorsed while Melanchthon wrote, *Instructions for the Visitors of Parish Pastors in Electoral Saxony*, which included a detailed syllabus for schools for the young. It was split into three divisions. The first division focused on children who were beginning to read and write. Latin was the only language required, "not German or Greek or Hebrew as some have done hitherto and troubled the poor children with so many languages. This is not only useless but even injurious."[105] In addition, these children would learn "the primer," which consisted of the alphabet, the Lord's Prayer, the Creed, and other prayers. The second division added grammar to the reading and writing skills.[106] Many of the activities for this division featured practice in music, expounding *Aesop's Fables*, declining nouns and conjugating verbs, studying selections from classic writings within the liberal arts curriculum, memorizing Scripture, and reciting the Lord's Prayer, the Creed, and the Ten Commandments.[107] The third division was made up of "the more excellent ones" in grammar from the second division.[108] These students would spend the afternoons in intensified study of more music, grammar, and liberal arts material such as writings from Cicero and Virgil.[109] Once grammar was mastered, then the children would move into dialectic and rhetoric. Again, Latin was the preferred language, and these "more excellent ones" would be required to speak it alone with one another and the schoolmaster.[110]

Luther not only oversaw syllabi revision, but also made recommendations for library

---

[104] Ibid., 369.

[105] *LW* 40:315.

[106] The syllabus instructs, "The hours before noon shall always and everywhere be so ordered that only grammar be taught. First, etymology. Then, syntax. Next, prosody. When this is finished, the teacher should start over again from the beginning, giving the children a good training in grammar. For if this is not done all learning is lost labor and fruitless. The children are to recite these grammatical rules from memory, so that they are compelled and driven to learn grammar well." Ibid., 317-18.

[107] *LW* 40:316-19.

[108] Ibid., 319. This third division is the fruition of Luther's idea already stated in *To the Councilmen* (1524), when he suggests, "The exceptional pupils, who give promise of becoming skilled teachers, preachers, or holders of other ecclesiastical positions, should be allowed to continue in school longer, or even be dedicated to a life of study" in contrast to the boys and girls who attended school briefly to return home for the development of a skill or household duties (*LW* 45:370).

109 After several hours of music in the afternoon, "[t]hen one should expound Virgil to them, and when this is finished one may read Ovid's *Metamorphoses* with them. In the evening: Cicero's *Officia* or *Familiar Letters*. In the morning: Virgil is to be repeated, and in grammar the pupils are to be required to explain, decline, and indicate the various forms of discourse." *LW* 40:319-20.

[110] Ibid., 320.

reform. Near the end of his writing, *To the Councilmen* (1524), Luther expressed that any nation that desires to retain the languages and the liberal arts should resolve that "no effort or expense should be spared to provide good libraries or book repositories, especially in the larger cities which can well afford it."[111] The Reformer discouraged that libraries "heap together all manner of books indiscriminately and think only of the number and size of the collection."[112] Instead, more judicious selections should be made "for the right sort of books, consulting with scholars as to my choice."[113] In the extended selection below, one can see how Luther considered even the contents of a library as one small piece of a larger picture of a reformed and restored Christendom:

> First of all, there would be the Holy Scriptures, in Latin, Greek, Hebrew, and German, and any other language in which they might be found. Next, the best commentaries, and, if I could find them, the most ancient, in Greek, Hebrew, and Latin. Then, books that would be helpful in learning the languages, such as the poets and orators, regardless of whether they were pagan or Christian, Greek or Latin, for it is from such books that one must learn grammar. After that would come books on the liberal arts, and all the other arts. Finally, there would be books of law and medicine; here too there should be careful choice among commentaries.

> Among the foremost would be the chronicles and histories, in whatever languages they are to be had. For they are a wonderful help in understanding and guiding the course of events, and especially for observing the marvelous works of God.[114]

From start to finish, in both *To the Councilmen* (1524) and *A Sermon on Keeping Children in School* (1530), Luther pleaded for widespread financial support to ensure the future of a priceless education for children. First, from *To the Councilmen*, Luther challenged citizens to consider educational investments as significant contributions for the betterment of the spiritual and temporal estates:

> My dear sirs, if we have to spend such large sums every year on guns, roads, bridges, dams, and countless similar items to insure the temporal peace and prosperity of a city, why should not much more be devoted to the poor neglected youth — at least enough to engage one or two competent men to teach school?

---

[111] *LW* 45:373.

[112] Ibid., 375.

[113] Ibid., 376.

[114] Ibid.

Moreover, every citizen should be influenced by the following consideration. Formerly he was obliged to waste a great deal of money and property on indulgences, masses, vigils, endowments, bequests, anniversaries, mendicant friars, brotherhoods, pilgrimages, and similar nonsense. Now that he is, by the grace of God, rid of such pillage and compulsory giving, he ought henceforth, out of gratitude to God and for his glory, to contribute a part of that amount toward schools for the training of the poor children. That would be an excellent investment.[115]

Second, in *A Sermon on Keeping Children in School,* Luther made repeated attempts to inspire financial support for the schools. He says at one point, "A man ought to be willing to crawl on his hands and knees to the ends of the earth to be able to invest his money so gloriously well."[116] In another place he laments:

Formerly, when people served the devil and put the blood of Christ to shame, all the purses stood wide open. There was no limit to men's giving to churches, schools, and all sorts of abominations. Children could be driven, pushed, and forced into monasteries, churches, foundations, and schools at unspeakable cost — all of which was a total loss. But now when men are to establish real schools and real churches — no, not establish them but just maintain them in a state of good repair, for God has established them and also given enough for their maintenance — and we know that in so doing we keep God's word, honor Christ's blood, and build the true church, now all the purses are fastened shut with iron chains.[117]

One final noteworthy highlight is Luther's vision for compulsory education. Once again, near the close of *A Sermon on Keeping Children in School* (1530), Luther advocated that it was the duty of the government to compel its young, especially the exceptional ones, to remain in school. No different than the state's practice of compulsory military service for those best-suited, so also should the temporal estate compel its promising subjects to continue in education, "For here there is a worse war on, a war with the very devil, who is out to secretly sap the strength of the cities and principalities, emptying them of their able persons until he has bored out the pith and left only an empty shell of useless people whom he can manipulate and toy with as he will."[118]

---

[115] *LW* 45:350-51.

[116] *LW* 46:228.

[117] Ibid., 256.

[118] Ibid., 257.

CONCLUSION

Justification for Martin Luther as a religious educator goes without saying. From 1512 until his death on February 18, 1546, Luther fulfilled the role of Doctor of Holy Scripture at Wittenberg University. In addition, he served for a period as the dean of the theological faculty.[119] His entire Reformation career was spent as an educator as a member of an educational institution. Moreover, Luther modeled what he proposed insofar as he was an active educator within both the spiritual (preacher) and temporal estates (professor). Furthermore, his incessant appeals to the secular authorities caused him to be a contributor to society, rather than merely a critic. As Luther historian James Kittelson has characterized him, "Luther was the pacesetter" for educational reform in Germany.[120] And as many scholars have shown, Luther's work for change within education was more than an incidental effect from his labors as a religious Reformer.[121] In fact, Luther went so far as to say on several occasions that if he were able to lay aside his calling as a Doctor of Holy Scripture, "there is no other office I would rather have than that of schoolmaster or teacher of boys; for I know that next to that of preaching, this is the best, greatest, and most useful office there is."[122]

---

[119] Marilyn J. Harran, "Luther as Professor," in *Luther and Learning*, ed. Marilyn J. Harran (Cranbury, NJ: Associated University Presses, 1985), 42.

[120] James M. Kittelson, "Luther the Educational Reformer," in *Luther and Learning*, ed. Marilyn J. Harran (Cranbury, NJ: Associated University Presses, 1985), 99.

[121] In Gustav Bruce's classic analysis of *Luther as an Educator*, he provides an insightful evaluation of Luther's lasting impact upon education for subsequent generations in Germany and in the Western world. See Bruce, *Luther as an Educator*, 285-99. See also Christopher D. Jackson, "Educational Reforms of Wittenberg and their Faithfulness to Martin Luther's Thought," *Christian Education Journal 10.1* (2013):71-87, who argues the claim that the educational reforms carried out by Melanchthon under the influence of his humanistic leanings was consistent with Luther's theology and vision; therefore, the legacy of Lutheran education would be distinctively Lutheran. If granted, Jackson's thesis works towards the dismissal of the proper place of Luther within the history of education as an open question.

[122] *LW* 46:253; cf., a recording by John Mathesius in *Table Talk*, "In a city as much depends on a schoolmaster as on a minister. We can get along without burgomasters, princes, and noblemen, but we can't do without schools, for they must rule the world. One sees that there are no rulers today who aren't compelled to let themselves be guided by a lawyer or a clergyman. They don't know anything of themselves and are ashamed to study, and so advisers must come from the school. *If I weren't a preacher I know no position on earth I'd rather fill [than that of schoolmaster].*" (*LW* 54:404; italics mine).

PRIMARY SOURCE SAMPLE[123]

From Martin Luther to all my dear friends, pastors, and preachers who truly love Christ: Grace and peace in Christ Jesus, our Lord.

My dear sirs and friends, you see with your own eyes how that wretch of a Satan is now attacking us on all sides with force and guile. He is afflicting us in every way he can to destroy the holy gospel and the kingdom of God, or, if he cannot destroy them, at least to hinder them at every turn and prevent them from moving ahead and gaining the upper hand. Among his wiles, one of the very greatest, if not the greatest of all, is this—he deludes and deceives the common people so that they are not willing to keep their children in school or expose them to instruction. He puts into their minds the dastardly notion that because monkery, nunning, and priestcraft no longer hold out the hope they once did, there is therefore no more need for study and for learned men, that instead we need to give thought only to how to make a living and get rich.

This seems to me to be a real masterpiece of the devil's art. He sees that in our time he cannot do what he would like to do; therefore, he intends to have his own way with our offspring. Before our very eyes he is preparing them so that they will learn nothing and know nothing. Then when we are dead, he will have before him a naked, bare, defenseless people with whom he can do as he pleases. For if the Scriptures and learning disappear, what will remain in the German lands but a disorderly and wild crowd of Tartars or Turks, indeed, a pigsty and mob of wild beasts? But he does not let them see this now. He blinds them in masterly fashion so that, when it comes to the point where their own experience compels them to see it, he can laugh up his sleeve at all their weeping and wailing…

Now because it is a part of our duty as pastors to be on guard against these and other wicked wiles, we must not shut our eyes to a matter of such great importance. On the contrary, we must advise, exhort, admonish, and nag with all our power and diligence and care, so that the common people may not let themselves be so pitifully deceived and deluded by the devil. Therefore let each of us look to himself and remember his office so that we do not go to sleep in this matter and allow the devil to become god and lord. For if we are silent about this and shut our eyes to it, and the young people are neglected and our offspring become Tartars or wild beasts, it will be the fault of our own silence and snoring, and we shall have to render full account for it.

---

[123] A selection from the second of Luther's two introductory sections to *A Sermon on Keeping Children in School* (1530). *LW* 46:217-18.

BIBLIOGRAPHY
PRIMARY SOURCES

Luther, Martin. *Luther's Works: American Edition*. 55 vols. Edited by Jaroslav Pelikan and Helmut T. Lehmann. St Louis: Concordia Publishing House; Philadelphia: Fortress Press, 1955-56.

WORKS CITED

Althaus, Paul. *The Theology of Martin Luther*. Translated by Robert C. Schultz. Philadelphia: Fortress Press, 1966.

Bayer, Oswald. *Martin Luther's Theology: A Contemporary Interpretation*. Translated by Thomas H. Trapp. Grand Rapids: Eerdmans, 2008.

Brecht, Martin. *Martin Luther: His Road to Reformation, 1483-1521*. Translated by James L. Schaaf. Philadelphia: Fortress Press, 1985.

Bruce, Gustav M. *Luther as an Educator*. Westport, CT: Greenwood Press, 1928.

Ebeling, Gerhard. *Luther: An Introduction to his Thought*. Translated by R. A. Wilson. Philadelphia: Fortress Press, 1970.

_____. *Evangelische Evangelienauslegung: Eine Untersuchung zu Luthers Hermeneutik*. Wissenschaftliche Buchgesellschaft: Darmstadt, Germany, 1942.

_____. "The New Hermeneutics and the Early Luther." Translated by Mrs. James Carse. *Theology Today* 21 (1964): 34-46.

_____. "The Beginnings of Luther's Hermeneutics." Translated by Richard B. Steele. *Lutheran Quarterly* 7 (1993): 129-58, 315-38, 451-68.

Froehlich, Karlfried. "Luther on Vocation." *Lutheran Quarterly* 13 (1999): 195-207.

Forde, Gerhard O. "Law and Gospel in Luther's Hermeneutic." *Interpretation* 37 (1983): 240-52.

Gleason, Randall C. "'Letter' and 'Spirit' in Luther's Hermeneutics. *Bibliotheca Sacra* 157 (2000): 468-85.

Harran, Marilyn J. "Introduction." In *Luther and Learning*, ed. Marilyn J. Harran, 15-25. Cranbury, NJ: Associated University Presses, 1985.

_____. "Luther as Professor." In *Luther and Learning*, ed. Marilyn J. Harran, 29-51. Cranbury, NJ: Associated University Presses, 1985.

_____. "The Contemporary Applicability of Luther's Pedagogy: Education and Vocation." *Concordia Journal* 16 (1990): 319-32.

Helmer, Christine. "Luther's Trinitarian Hermeneutic and the Old Testament." *Modern Theology* 18 (2002): 49-73.

Hendrix, Scott H. *Recultivating the Vineyard: The Reformation Agendas of Christianization*. Louisville, KY: Westminster John Knox Press, 2004.

Holl, Karl. "Luther's Bedeutung für den Fortschritt der Auslegungskunst." In *Gesammelte Aufsätze zur Kirchengeschichte*, vol. 1: *Luther*, 544-82. Tübingen: J. C. B. Mohr (Paul Siebeck), 1927).

Jackson, Christopher D. "Educational Reforms of Wittenberg and their Faithfulness to Martin Luther's Thought." *Christian Education Journal* 10 (2013):71-87.

Junghans, Helmar. "Luther's Wittenberg." In *The Cambridge Companion to Martin Luther*, ed. Donald K. McKim, 20-35. Cambridge: Cambridge University Press, 2003.

Kittelson, James M. "Luther the Educational Reformer." In *Luther and Learning*, ed. Marilyn J. Harran, 95-114. Cranbury, NJ: Associated University Presses, 1985.

Kolb, Robert and Charles P. Arand. *The Genius of Luther's Theology: A Wittenberg Way of Thinking for the Contemporary Church*. Grand Rapids: Baker Academic, 2008.

Kolb, Robert. *Luther and the Stories of God: Biblical Narratives as a Foundation for Christian Living*. Grand Rapids: Baker Academic, 2012.

_____. "Reality Rests on the Word of the Lord: Martin Luther's Understanding of God's Word." *Reformation & Revival* 9 (2000): 47-63.

_____. "'The Noblest Skill in the Christian Church': Luther's Sermons on the Proper Distinction of Law and Gospel." *Concordia Theological Quarterly* 71 (2007): 301-18.

_____. "God and His Human Creatures in Luther's Sermons on Genesis: The Reformer's Early Use of His Distinction of Two Kinds of Righteousness." *Concordia Journal* 33 (2007): 166-84.

_____. "Called to Milk Cows and Govern Kingdoms: Martin Luther's Teaching on the Christian's Vocations." *Concordia Journal* 39 (2013): 133-41.

Lotz, David W. "Sola Scriptura: *Luther on Biblical Authority*." *Interpretation* 35 (1981): 258-73.

Mattox, Mickey L. "Luther's Interpretation of Scripture: Biblical Understanding in Trinitarian Shape." In *The Substance of the Faith: Luther's Doctrinal Theology for Today*, Dennis Bielfeldt, Mickey L. Mattox, and Paul R. Hinlicky, 11-57. Minneapolis, MN: Fortress Press, 2008.

Oberman, Heiko A. *Luther: Man between God and the Devil*. Translated by Eileen Walliser-Schwarzbart. New Haven, CT: Yale University Press, 2006; reprint, New Haven, CT: Yale University Press, 1989.

Preus, James S. *From Shadow to Promise: Old Testament Interpretation from Augustine to the Young Luther*. Cambridge, MA: Harvard University Press, 1969.

_____. "Old Testament *Promissio* and Luther's New Hermeneutic." *Harvard Theological Review* 60 (1967): 145-61.

Reist, John S. "The Knife that Cuts Better than Another: Luther and Liberal Arts Education." *Perspectives in Religious Studies* 21 (1994): 93-113.

Simpson, Gary M. "'You shall bear witness to me': Thinking with Luther about Christ and the Scriptures." *Word and World* 29 (2009): 380-88.

Slotemaker, John T. "The Trinitarian House of David: Martin Luther's Anti-Jewish Exegesis of 2 Samuel 23:1-7." *Harvard Theological Review* 104 (2011): 233-54.

Steinmetz, David C. "Luther and the Two Kingdoms." In *Luther in Context*, 2nd ed., 112-25. Grand Rapids: Baker Academic, 2002.

Thompson, Mark. *A Sure Ground on Which to Stand: The Relation of Authority and Interpretive Method in Luther's Approach to Scripture*. Studies in Christian History and Thought. Waynesboro, GA: Paternoster Press, 2004.

Veith, Gene Edward, Jr. "Classical Education as Vocational Education: Luther on the Liberal Arts." *Logia* 21 (2012): 23-26.

Wengert, Timothy J. *Reading the Bible with Martin Luther: An Introductory Guide*. Grand Rapids: Baker Academic, 2013.

Westhelle, Vítor. "Luther on the Authority of Scripture." *Lutheran Quarterly* 19 (2005): 373-91.

Wingren, Gustaf. *Luther on Vocation*. Translated by Carl C. Rasmussen. Eugene, OR: Wipf & Stock Publishers, 2004.

ADDITIONAL SCHOLARLY RESEARCH

Brecht, Martin. *Martin Luther: His Road to Reformation, 1483-1521*. Translated by James L. Schaaf. Philadelphia: Fortress Press, 1985.

_____. *Martin Luther: Shaping and Defining the Reformation, 1521-1532*. Translated by James L. Schaaf. Minneapolis, MN: Fortress Press, 1990.

_____. *Martin Luther: The Preservation of the Church, 1532-1546*. Translated by James L. Schaaf. Minneapolis, MN: Fortress Press, 1993.

Eby, Frederick. *Early Protestant Educators*. New York: AMS Press, 1971.

Everist, Norma. "Luther on Education: Implications for Today." *Currents in Theology and Mission* 12 (1985): 76-89.

Grimm, Harold J. "Luther on Education." In *Luther and Culture*, George W. Forell, Harold J. Grimm, and Theodore Hoelty-Nickel, 73-142. Decorah, IA: Luther College Press, 1960.

Harran, Marilyn J. *Martin Luther: Learning for Life*. Concordia Scholarship Today. St. Louis: Concordia Publishing House, 1997.

Kolb, Robert. *Martin Luther: Confessor of the Faith*. New York, NY: Oxford University Press, 2009.

_____. *Martin Luther as Prophet, Teacher, Hero: Images of the Reformer, 1520-1620*. Texts and Studies in Reformation and Post-Reformation Thought. Grand Rapids: Baker Academic, 1999.

Lohse, Bernhard. *Martin Luther's Theology: Its Historical and Systematic Development*. Translated and edited by Roy A. Harrisville. Minneapolis: Fortress Press, 1999.

Noll, Mark A. "The Earliest Protestants and the Reformation of Education." *Westminster Theological Journal* 43 (1980): 97-131.

Oberman, Heiko A. *The Harvest of Medieval Theology: Gabriel Biel and Late Medieval Nominalism*, 3rd ed. Grand Rapids: Baker Academic, 2000; reprint Cambridge, MA: Harvard University Press, 1963.

_____. *The Dawn of the Reformation: Essays in Late Medieval and Early Reformation Thought*. Grand Rapids: Eerdmans Publishing, 1992; reprint, Edinburgh, Scotland: T&T Clark, 1986.

Painter, F.V. N. *Luther on Education*. St. Louis: Concordia, 1928.

Rosin, Robert. "Luther on Education." *Lutheran Quarterly* 21 (2007): 197-210.

Strauss, Gerald. *Luther's House of Learning: Indoctrination of the Young in the German Reformation*. Baltimore, MD: The Johns Hopkins University Press, 1978.

Watson, Philip S. *Let God be God! An Interpretation of the Theology of Martin Luther*. Eugene, OR: Wipf and Stock Publishers, 2000; reprint, London: The Methodist Bookroom, 1947.

CHAPTER 8

Huldrych Zwingli:
A Christian Humanistic Educator

DONGSUN CHO

Huldrych Zwingli (1484-1531)

Zwingli wrote the first fully protestant work on pedagogy in 1523 when he wrote *Christian Education of Youth*. In 1525, Zwingli became the Latin master at the Grossmünster and established a new Christian institution called *Prophezei* (Prophecy) in order to train ministers and lay leaders who had to lead the church and the state according to the will of God. This *Prophezei* later became a model for the theological institutions of other Reformed churches in Germany, the Netherlands, and England. From the very beginning of his reform of the church, Zwingli knew that there would be no genuine reform of worship unless one reformed the education system of the church leaders and of society, as well.

HISTORICAL BACKGROUND

Compared to Luther and Calvin, Zwingli has been unknown to many Protestant churchmen. People have known him simply as a Swiss theologian who opposed Luther's doctrine of Communion, as well as his refutation of the Anabaptists. However, one should recognize that Zwingli was a first-generation Protestant Reformer like Luther and the first Reformed theologian prior to Calvin. The Swiss Reformer Zwingli (1 January 1484–11 October 1531) was born in Wildhaus, Switzerland about two months after Luther. Switzerland's political, social, and religious situations were ripe for Zwingli's Protestant Reformation. Zwingli's higher education came from the institutions where humanism was thriving. He went to Berne and later matriculated at the University of Vienna. Ultimately, he earned his Master of Arts degree at the University of Basel (1506). Here the future Reformer of Zurich already learned about the problems of indulgence and faith in Christ alone for forgiveness from Wyttenbach, professor of theology at Basel.[1]

While serving as a parish pastor of Glarus (1505-1516), Zwingli began to cultivate his friendship with Erasmus. Erasmus' influence on Zwingli is conspicuous in the latter's respect for pagan classics, his strong desire for moral reform of the church, and his emphasis on biblical exegesis based on linguistic and textual studies. Nonetheless, later Zwingli proved that he was not a mere disciple of Erasmus. Unlike the Catholic humanist, the Reformer of Zurich strongly advocated the doctrine of predestination and could not tolerate Erasmus' "semi-Pelagianism."[2] In 1512, 1513, and 1515, Zwingli joined the Swiss mercenary campaigns as a chaplain, to assist the interests of the Papacy against the French monarchy. This chaplain experience led him to realize that the Swiss mercenary service badly damaged the moral integrity of Swiss society.

In 1516 he became a preacher in an abbey in Einsiedeln and began to preach against the practice of pilgrimages, which medieval Catholicism promoted as a means of salvific grace. Nonetheless, Zwingli had not yet become a Protestant Reformer during his ministry at Einsiedeln. He still served his community as a humanist reformer who remained in a good relationship with the Papacy, and even received financial aid from Rome annually for five years (1515-1520).

Zwingli began his new preaching ministry at Grossmunster in 1519. Instead of preaching famous passages, according to the lectionary of the church, he did expository preaching of the entire Book of Matthew, because every part of the Bible came from the mouth of God. Zwingli attacked the moral and spiritual corruptions of the church leaders, while preaching Christocentric

---

[1] Philip Schaff, *Modern Christianity. The Swiss Reformation*, vol. 8 of *History of the Christian Church*, rev. 3rd ed. (Grand Rapids: Eerdmans, 1953), 7.

[2] Ibid., 25-26.

messages promised in the Old Testament and fulfilled in the New Testament. He preached all of the New Testament books, except Revelation, in four years. Interestingly, it was the scandal of sausages in 1522 that officially launched Zwingli's Reformation movement in Zurich. The printer Froschauer cooked sausages, and Leo Jud, priest and one of Zwingli's close friends, broke the Lenten abstinence regulation. In opposition to the bishop of Constance, which governed the parish of Zurich, Zwingli defended his friends by appealing to the freedom of Christians in Christ and to the *sola fide* principle. In response to the bishop's request for the punishment of Zwingli's circle, the Zurich Council released him from the obligations of a Catholic priest, but made a preaching position for him, so he would continue his evangelical sermons freely.

In January 1523, under the supervision of the Zurich Council, a public theological disputation between Zwingli and the party of the Catholic representatives took place. The final verdict on the case in debate came from the judgment of the audience, but more realistically from the city Council. The Council agreed with Zwingli's argument for the independence of Zurich in theological matters and, therefore, supported his reform. Zwingli issued *67 Articles,* which contained many of Protestant doctrines such as *sola fide*; *sola scriptura*; the headship of Christ in the church; the right of clerical marriage; rejection of the intercession of saints and the rejection of purgatory. In 1524, the Council ordered the removal of images and the prohibition of mass from taking place in the church.

Zwingli's Reformation program had challenges not only from Catholics but also from other Protestants. Beginning in 1523, some of Zwingli's disciples asked him for more biblical and, therefore, more radical reform of the church. Later, this small group of brethren, known as the Swiss Brethren, became known as Anabaptists who refused infant baptism and the governing role of the magistrates in the matter of religion. For Zwingli, the Anabaptist vision that excluded infant baptism and separated the church from the state was very dangerous to his vision that the church and the state should make a theocratic government similar to Old Testament Israel. Zwingli's other theological challenge came from his fellow German Reformer in Wittenberg, Germany. In order to resolve a theological difference between Luther and Zwingli on the Lord's Supper, they met in Marburg in 1529. Luther taught the real physical presence of Christ in the Lord's Supper, and Zwingli presented the symbolic presence of Christ. Unfortunately, their meeting failed to produce theological and political alliance between the Lutherans and the other magisterial Reformers. The five Catholic cantons of Swiss attacked Zurich in October 9, 1531. Zwingli fought against the Catholic army as a patriotic chaplain of the Protestant Zurich but fell in the battle in October 11, 1531. After the death of Zwingli, Bullinger succeeded Zwingli in Zurich and refined his teacher's legacy.

THEOLOGY OF CHRISTIAN EDUCATION
THEOLOGICAL HERMENEUTIC

One can detect Zwingli's five major hermeneutical principles within his writings, in relation to his theology of Christian education. The first hermeneutical principle is a humanistic approach to biblical interpretation. As a humanist, Zwingli highlighted the studies of "languages, genres, literary forms of the Bible" in order to discern the will of God in the Bible correctly.[3] As a result, Zwingli prioritized the natural or literal sense among the "various [natural, moral, and mystical or allegorical] senses" of the biblical texts.[4] Therefore, all the professors of the *Prophezei* were basically humanistic philologists who studied words as a scientific analysis. Zwingli was convinced that the correct exegesis of a biblical text in its cultural and historical contexts could liberate people from many superstitious religious practices and the idolatrous liturgy that medieval Roman Catholicism created.[5]

The second hermeneutical principle is *sola scriptura*. Zwingli did not hesitate to show his opposition to any human authoritative doctrines, whether they were church fathers or medieval theologians that would not be in harmony with the Bible.[6] Zwingli's *sola scriptura* also entails 'Scripture by Scripture.' According to him, the orthodox church fathers could refute heresies because they let Scripture interpret itself without imposing their own ideas upon it.[7] Zwingli and his supporters knew how to "develop a consistent argument from scripture alone, while their opponents had to fall back on tradition and authority of the church."[8]

The third hermeneutical principle is the distinction between the material and the spiritual in experiencing the grace of God. Through such a distinction, people could understand the proper

[3] I. L. Snavely Jr., "Ulrich Zwingli," in *Historical Handbook of Major Biblical Interpreters*, ed. Donald K. McKim (Downers Grove, IL: InterVarsity Press, 1998), 253.

[4] W. Peter Stephens, "The Theology of Zwingli," in *the Cambridge Companion to Reformation Theology*, eds., David Bagchi and David C. Steinmetz (New York: Cambridge University Press, 2004), 83.

[5] Bruce Gordon, *The Swiss Reformation* (New York: Manchester University Press, 2002), 231.

[6] "I began to try every doctrine by this touchstone [the word of God], and if I saw that the stone reflected the same colour or rather that the doctrine could bear the brilliancy of the stone, I accepted it; if not, I rejected it." See Ulrich Zwingli, *The Latin Works and the Correspondence of Huldreich Zwingli: Together with Selections from his German Works*, ed. Samuel Macaulay Jackson, trans. Henry Preble, Walter Lichtenstein, and Lawrence A. McLouth, Vol. 1: 1510-1522 (New York: G. P. Putnam's Sons, 1912), 204.

[7] Ulrich Zwingli, *Selected Works of Huldreich Zwingli (1483-1531): The Reformer of German Switzerland*, ed. Samuel Macauley Jackson (Philadelphia: University of Philadelphia, 1901), 105.

[8] Gordon, *The Swiss Reformation*, 69.

role of biblical signs. For Zwingli, the material signs in the believer's mind, such as baptismal water and the elements of the Eucharist, represented their spiritual realities that the Holy Spirit alone could illuminate.[9] As "God in his freedom," however, the Holy Spirit cannot be "bound to" any material of his creation.[10] The materials of the sacraments could not carry spiritual power to transform the souls at all.[11] Nonetheless, Luther's critique that Zwingli's commemoration of the Lord's Supper presented biblical signs merely as meaningless forms is not tenable. Zwingli simply denied their sacramental efficacy, while admitting the necessity of the material signs.[12]

The fourth hermeneutical principle is the illumination of the Holy Spirit as the ultimate interpreter of the Bible. Due to the total depravity of humanity, man cannot have true knowledge of God unless he realizes his sinfulness and the necessity of his savior Christ, whose righteousness was imputed to believers for their justification before the holy God.[13] Only then could the Holy Spirit, not by a theologian or the church or even the council, make those biblical truths believable to the readers of the Bible. And faith alone could enable one to appreciate the illumination of the Holy Spirit. However, not all readers could have faith since the elect alone receive faith.[14] Therefore, the illuminating work of the Holy Spirit is not available to everyone who reads the Bible.

The fifth hermeneutical principle is the concept of covenant. The Zurich Reformer strongly espoused the continuity between the old covenant and the new covenant in a way that insisted Christians must have only one covenant of God. Therefore, Zwingli refuted Luther's antithetical understanding of the relationship between the law and the gospel. The law demonstrates not only how much we are hopeless and helpless in the matter of our salvation but also how we should live according to the revelation of God. Locher asserts that

---

[9] Lee Palmer Wandel, "Zwingli and Reformed Practice," in *Educating People of Faith: Exploring the History of Jewish and Christian Communities*, ed. John H. Van Engen (Grand Rapids: Eerdmans, 2004), 292.

[10] Gottfried Wilhelm Locher, *Zwingli's Thought: New Perspectives* (Leiden: E. J. Brill, 1981), 179.

[11] Ulrich Zwingli, *Commentary on True and False Religion*, ed. Samuel Macauley Jackson (Durham: Labyrinth Press, reprint, 1981), 182.

[12] Wandel, "Zwingli and Reformed Practice," 292.

[13] Ulrich Zwingli, *The Christian Education of Youth*, trans. Alcide Reichenbach (Collegeville, PA: Thomson Brothers, 1899), 61-64.

[14] G.W. Bromiley, ed., *Zwingli and Bullinger*, vol. 24 of *Library of Christian Classics* (Philadelphia: Westminster, 1953), 33: "The sole causality of God necessarily involved for Zwingli a rigorous doctrine of the divine predestination and election, for all that is good in man derives from God, and faith itself is possible only where God himself has sovereignly decreed to give it."

Zwingli's most important contribution to the Reformation was his concept of covenant.[15] Zwingli's covenant theology that refused the Lutheran antithesis of the law and the gospel presented a new and positive perspective of the law. If God revealed what he wanted from us through the law, the law itself is good news in our imitation of Christ. Since the entire Bible is given to us in order to reform both individuals and the corporate community, then, "integrating the church into the political governance of the state" was not optional but necessary.[16] On the other hand, Zwingli also refuted the Spiritualists who appealed to the New Testament alone, while excluding the Old Testament as authority for the church.

EDUCATION IMPLICATIONS OF THEOLOGY

Due to Zwingli's strong emphasis on the illumination of the Holy Spirit, his hermeneutic could face the Spiritualists' danger of a radically privatized spirituality that undermines the objective authority of the Bible. However, the Reformer's humanistic training in language skills and analysis of literary genres and forms kept him from being one of these Spiritualists.[17] Zwingli's zeal for a humanistic study of the Bible helped the education system of the *Prophezei* not to fall into a mere pietistic discipleship training program, which would end up memorizing some selected Bible verses and uncritically meditating on them.[18] However, there was one fundamental difference between Zwingli and his contemporary humanists in relation to their humanistic interest in languages and literature. For the humanists, the purpose of studying ancient languages was first, either for ascetic satisfaction, political advantages, or economic successes, which were also primary goals for learning languages among socio-political elites. For Zwingli, the study of languages was not to obtain personal benefits but to serve God and others through the knowledge of the Bible.[19] Without a proper Hebrew and Greek education, one cannot learn about the will of God from the Bible. Both Zwingli's humanism and his Protestant theology of *sola scriptura* urged his students to commit themselves to the

[15] Locher, *Zwingli's Thought*, 29: "This [the concept of covenant] passed from Zwingli via Bullinger to Piscator at Herborn and to Olevian and Franciscus Junius at Heidelberg, thence to the Netherlands where it came to full flower in the shape of Federal Theology."

[16] Gordon, *The Swiss Reformation*, 78.

[17] Peter Stotz, "Heinrich Bullinger (1504-1575) and the Ancient Languages," in *Scholarly Knowledge: Textbooks in Early Modern Europe*, eds. Emidio Campi, Simone De Angelis, Anja-Silvia Goeing, and Anthony T. Grafton (Genève: Librairie Droz S. A. , 2008), 114.

[18] Ernst Gerhard Rüsch, "*Die humanistischen Vorbilder der Erziehungsschrift Zwinglis,*" *Theologische Zeitschrift* 22 (1966): 147.

[19] Ibid., 137-38.

study of biblical languages. People suffered long superstitious practices such as the Mass, and the cult of saints and Mary because of their lack of biblical languages. Zwingli also encouraged his students to study Latin because it was still the language of scholarship, and Latin biblical manuscripts could be useful in textual criticism.

Based on the distinction between the material and the spiritual, Zwingli considered the materialization of the spiritual nature of God in the worship of him as idolatry. For Zwingli, the material also included the printed copy of the Bible and the sermons of evangelical preachers. Zwingli's radical dualism of the spirit and matter could weaken the objective authority of the incarnation and the canonical writings by overemphasizing the sovereignty and freedom of the Holy Spirit, as if the Holy Spirit could work apart from the Bible. It is not surprising that Zwingli considered some pagan philosophers such as Socrates as a pre-incarnational Christian.[20] It would imply Christian education could take place without the church context and apart from the gospel. In addition, the Zurich Reformer's antithesis between the material signs and their spiritual realities left a dilemma concerning the role of a school in Christian education. He did not clarify how such a materialized educational agency should operate as a means of prophetic ministry of the Holy Spirit.

Zwingli's doctrine of total human depravity and the illumination of the Holy Spirit led him to reject the Catholic humanistic optimism of education as "the way to the Christian life."[21] The Catholic humanists, such as Erasmus, who presented Christian education as a matter of cultivating human reason, failed to recognize that even cultivated human reason was utterly depraved due to sin. Definitely, this does not mean that Zwingli was anti-intellectual in his Reformation program. He never denied the usefulness of a classical theological education as a means to study the will of God. Zwingli's point is that the human efforts to educate students cannot replace the role and power of the Holy Spirit in Christian education. A good education or even the preaching of the word of God cannot make people believe the veracity of the Bible unless the Holy Spirit works within their souls.[22] Therefore, a Christian education should start with a prayer of invocation to the Holy Spirit. Despite Zwingli's theological theory of education, based on a more realistic observation of human reason, for some modern Zwingli readers, this radically negative position of human reason and capability in education could "undermine the institutional basis of the Christian society Zwingli strove to establish."[23]

---

[20] Bromiley, *Zwingli and Bullinger*, 242, 275.

[21] Gordon, *The Swiss Reformation*, 80.

[22] Rüsch, *"Die humanistischen Vorbilder der Erziehungsschrift Zwinglis,"* 133–34.

[23] Gordon, *The Swiss Reformation*, 81.

Zwingli's covenant theology, in association with the concept of the kingdom of God, required all Christians of Zurich to be actively involved in political affairs. In the old covenant, God required Israel to obey his commandments and promised his blessings for the obedient, but punishments for the disobedient. Zwingli considered the sufferings of the Swiss as the consequences of the divine punishment upon her sins. Zwingli had no expectation of the restoration of biblical Christianity without the Christianized state whose magistrates supervise the lives of her members. Education was "the preferable means" for Zwingli to accomplish the "oneness" of Zurich as a covenantal body.[24] Therefore, the Zurich Reformer determined to provide Christian education to not only all kinds of ministers but also lay leaders who should lead the state according to the will of God in the Bible. In addition, all common folks of Zurich were one of the targeted audiences of the *Prophezei*, because they also consisted of the Zurich society. Unlike Erasmus, whose primary target audience for his philosophy of education was princes and socio-political elites, Zwingli saw all civic members of Zurich as the necessary object of Christian education and produced the democratization of education.[25] Since the nature of Zwingli's reform was religious and also socio-political, his reformation of Christian education could not be as radical and fast as the radical Anabaptist movement wanted.[26]

CONTRIBUTION TO EDUCATION AND CHRISTIAN EDUCATION
TEACHER

Zwingli left some insights regarding the role of the teacher in his *Christian Education,* although he did not write a treatise on being a teacher. Fortunately, Mykonius, disciple and colleague of Zwingli, also left other interesting information about the Reformer as a teacher. Zwingli saw the ministry of a prophetic teacher as "prescriptive rather than predictive."[27] Teachers should guide their students to realize their sinfulness, the necessity of Christ, their savior, and the way of cultivating the Christian life.[28] Not only biblical scholars but also

---

[24] H. Wayne Pipkin, "Huldreich Zwingli," in *A History of Religious Educators*, ed. Elmer L. Towns (Grand Rapids: Baker, 1975), 126.

[25] Ibid. See also Rüsch, *"Die humanistischen Vorbilder der Erziehungsschrift Zwinglis,"* 138 and 146.

[26] Pipkin, "Huldreich Zwingli," 125.

[27] Snavely, "Ulrich Zwingli," 249.

[28] Samuel Macauley Jackson, *Huldreich Zwingli: The Reformer of German Switzerland 1484-1531,* rev.. 2nd ed. (New York: G. P. Putnam's Sons, 1972), 400.

teachers of languages have to assist their students to learn more about the biblical doctrines of Christ and his gospel.[29] Without spiritual regeneration, one cannot expect many fruits from Christian education. Therefore, teachers must pray that God would open their students' minds and hearts to realize and accept the truth of God by the illumination of the Holy Spirit based on the word of God.[30] Since God predestined some to salvation, Christian educators cannot instill faith in their students' souls. If students would have faith in Christ, their faith resulted from the presence of the sovereign God in their souls, not from teachers' excellent pedagogy. Rather, teachers should aim to prepare their students to understand the right meanings of biblical texts and to clarify what the Bible reveals, because faith comes by hearing the word of God as Paul teaches in Romans 10:17.[31] Teachers cannot cause faith in the souls of their students. The Holy Spirit alone can bring out faith in them. However, the Holy Spirit works through the word of God in order to produce faith in its hearers. Therefore, a correct interpretation of the Bible is an inevitable means for successful Christian education. This is why Zwingli emphasized the humanistic study of languages, literature, and even rhetoric.

Interestingly, Mykonius made an appealing report of Zwingli's teaching methodology. Mykonius did not appreciate the unorganized pedagogy of medieval theology classes. However, Zwingli's theology classes were different. In contrast, Mykonius praised Zwingli for presenting his lesson in a very organized way. Due to his clear and well-organized presentation, both the most intellectual and the simplest were enabled to understand his lessons easily.[32] Zwingli's succinct and systematic organization of lessons was a key to his success as a preacher and teacher. Mykonius also praised Zwingli's own academic training course. According to Mykonius, Zwingli studied liberal arts, poetics, and philosophy in sequence before finally studying theology.[33] Zwingli's learning experience of language and classics also enabled him to be a good communicator of knowledge.

---

[29] Zwingli, *Christian education*, 71.

[30] Ibid., 57.

[31] Zwingli, *Christian Education*, 57: "First of all, let me say that, although man can in no wise draw his own heart to faith in the only true God, even if one could surpass in power of speech the celebrated and eloquent Pericles, but only our heavenly Father who draws us to Himself can do these things; yet faith comes, according to the apostle Paul, by hearing, in so far as such hearing is the hearing of the Word of God."

[32] Anja-Silvia Goeing, "Establishing the Modes of Learning: Old and New Hebrew Grammars in the 16th century," in *Scholarly Knowledge: Textbooks in Early Modern Europe*, ed. Emidio Campi (Geneva: Librairie Droz, 2008), 165.

[33] Ibid.

LEARNER

The sooner students received Christian education with regard to the things that pleased God, the better they could imitate Christ in their lives.[34] As a Christian, every student has an obligation to help and love his neighbors. But he cannot assist them effectively unless he knows the will of God. Therefore, a Christian student needs to study the word of God without ceasing. Here comes the importance of knowledge of languages. One's knowledge of biblical languages definitely guides the student to discern what the will of God is in a particular situation.[35] Students should also learn Latin, although it is not a biblical language because of its universal use among scholars and in other areas of life. However, Zwingli warned his students not to use their knowledge of languages for personal desires to be rich and powerful. Since knowledge of languages is a gift of the Holy Spirit, students should not abuse or misuse that sacred gift.[36] Students must make sure that their study of languages should not make them drift away from the biblical truths of God. Therefore, Zwingli warned students not to take advantage of language skills in order to satisfy personal sinful desires such as "wantonness, ambition, love of power, deceitfulness, vain philosophy, etc."[37]

Students must also obtain "the highest type of Christian manhood" as a result of Christian education.[38] They need to learn about the importance of modesty and decency in speech, the consumption of food and drink, as well as dress in order to reflect their Christlikeness. [39] In particular, the youth need to learn about sexual purity. Students must also keep themselves from the love of money. Covetousness destroys not only individual souls but also the state where they live. Idleness is to be condemned. All students, particularly candidates for ministry, should work diligently as if they must earn at least one trade skill for making a living as a result of their education. Christian learners could participate in public festivals and parties with moderation since there is no biblical prohibition of such a public meeting, and the public meeting would reduce sins and hypocrisy that a secret meeting might cause. Students should govern their tempers with self-control, while also honoring their parents. The ultimate goal of learning in Christian education is that students live "a

---

[34] Zwingli, *Christian Education*, 67-68; 84.

[35] Ibid., 69.

[36] Ibid., 70.

[37] Jackson, *Huldreich Zwingli*, 400.

[38] Ibid., 399.

[39] Zwingli, *Christian Education*, 81-84.

sober, God-fearing, earnest, and useful life."[40] They need to see the ultimate purpose of their lives and education as their services for their neighbors, as their Redeemer Christ did with his own life.[41] Character training to imitate Christ would enable students to be beneficial to their personal neighbors and political community as well.

CURRICULUM & METHODS

Zwingli did not write a curriculum for Christian education in a modern sense. From his treatises on youth Christian education and his instructions for the *Prophezei*, however, we can summarize what subjects he wanted his students to study and how they were expected to accomplish their education. With regard to curriculum, Zwingli's students should study Christian theology, ancient languages, homiletic preaching for the Christian life, and basic science.[42] Knowledge of three ancient languages (Hebrew, Greek, and Latin) was essential to learn the true meaning of a biblical text. Therefore, the *Prophezei* had a very strong emphasis on linguistic skills. Students should study Latin first, then Greek, and finally Hebrew, which was considered as the most difficult language among the three.[43] But the purpose of the *Prophezei* was specifically to study the Old Testament by reading all three ancient manuscripts of the same biblical text. An hour was assigned to the linguistic study of each ancient biblical text.

Students met at seven o'clock AM (during summer) eight o'clock AM (during winter) every day except Fridays and Sundays in the choir of the Grossmünster. Students had to learn how to do biblical exegesis along with the doctrinal and pastoral implications. The Reformer expected students to be instructed in Christian ethics through their study of the word of God.

The exegetical classes began with prayer for the illumination of the Holy Spirit in their reading and interpreting of the biblical manuscripts. After prayer, someone read a text for the day from the Latin Vulgate. Then, a Hebrew professor read the same text from the Hebrew Bible and explained the Hebrew text in Latin. After the exegesis of the Hebrew text, Zwingli read the same text from the Septuagint, translated it into Latin, and compared the Greek and the Latin texts.[44] The purpose of a comparative reading of the two different texts

---

[40] Jackson, *Huldreich Zwingli*, 401.

[41] Zwingli, *Christian Education*, 84.

[42] Gordon, *The Swiss Reformation*, 62.

[43] Ulrich Gäbler, *Huldrych Zwingli: His Life and Work*, trans. Ruth C. L. Gritsch (London: T. & T. Clark, 1998), 100.

[44] Fritz Büsser, "Théorie et pratique de l'éducation sous la Réforme a Zurich," in *La Réforme et l'éducation: sous la direction de J. Boisset*, ed. Jean Boisset (Toulouse: Privat, 1974), 159.

was to learn the subtle nuances of words in the Greek text. Every reader of ancient biblical texts should explain the meaning of his text exegetically, doctrinally, and practically. If someone, whether faculty or students, discovered something new or better in a process of a comparative study of ancient biblical manuscripts, he had the privilege to present it to the entire audience.[45] After all of the analysis on three ancient biblical texts was completed, someone presented his mediation on the text in Latin. After this, Zwingli or one of the other professors preached in German for the common folks who would be present by that time. Although the clergy and students of Latin had to attend the daily exposition of the Bible, the laity, including lay women, were invited and could learn about the Bible. After the morning devoted to the study of the Old Testament, there was a study of classical Latin and Greek by a sort of faculty of Arts. Students received lessons in Latin grammar, dialectic, and rhetoric and had to memorize and read aloud the best phrases of great ancient writers such as Virgil, Cicero, and Homer.[46]

On the other hand, Myconius, disciple and close friend of Zwingli, offered his New Testament exegesis classes at Fraumünster, another Latin school of Zurich. In order to avoid a schedule conflict with the *Prophezei*, Myconius offered his classes in the afternoon at three o'clock. Like the *Prophezei*, the Fraumünster school also invited both students and lay people who wanted to listen to expository preaching. At Fraumünster, Zwingli got more actively involved in the expository preaching of the New Testament in which he had expertise. The learning process at the *Prophezei'* and the Latin school of Fraumünster was a communal work of all faculty members and students. The format of the exegetical classes was a seminar rather than a lecture.[47]

ZWINGLI AS A CHRISTIAN EDUCATOR

The Reformer could not consider education as a purely academic discipline.[48]

---

[45] Zwingli, *Christian Education*, 48.

[46] Ibid., 49.

[47] Büsser, "Théorie et pratique de 1'éducation sous la Réforme a Zurich," 160.

[48] Accordingly, games could be of educational value because games could make the body strong and the mind sharp. In this sense, the old Swiss exercises such as running, jumping, putting the stone, fencing, and wrestling could be recommendable. Chess games are also permissible because they train a player's mind to have foresight. However, students should play only for an appropriate amount of time and avoid spending too much time which would prevent them from acquiring vocational skills. Without the capability to accomplish his vocation successfully, one would be a burden to a society. Therefore, cards and dice games must be avoided because they have nothing to do with the training of the body or the mind but with chance. See Zwingli, Christian Education, 90-91.

Education must be associated with the Christian life, certainly for Christian character development. For Zwingli, "the knowledge of God" must be "forged – tested and strengthened – in the praxis of faith."[49] Therefore, Zwingli pointed to Christ as the model of the Christian life, as Erasmus did. The difference between Zwingli and Erasmus is that the former utilized neither ancient pagan people nor Christian saints as a model for Christian education, because Christ alone is sufficient to be the model for all Christian learners.[50]

Zwingli presented a model of Christian pedagogy in his treatise *Christian Education of Youth* (1523), which later Protestants, in particular Reformed Christians, studied continually.[51] His work received much appreciation from the beginning of its publication to the early twentieth century. K. Fulda, the editor of the 1524 South-German edition, described it as "the first Protestant treatise on pedagogy."[52] Zwingli wrote this work for Gerald Meyer who was initially his student but later became his stepson by marriage. The Reformer demonstrated his genuine pastoral desire for rescuing a Christian young man from the social and religious corruptions of the medieval Zurich that marred his moral and intellectual life by bringing him up with the word of God. Not only Zwingli's contemporary but also later Christian educators greatly appreciated this writing. Numerous editions of this work display how much his philosophy of youth education has been influential.[53]

The *Prophezei* that Zwingli founded in the Grossmünster (1525) was "the first chapter of Reformed higher education."[54] As the Greek *Prophezei* implies, this new Protestant educational institution was to produce the Christian leaders who could do the work of prophets in not only ecclesiastical but also in civic areas of Zurich (1 Cor 14:26-33). Zwingli's reformed school became a model for the theological institutions of other Reformed

---

[49] Wandel, "Zwingli and Reformed Practice," 274.

[50] Zwingli, *Christian Education*, 72. For Zwingli, Christ is "the complete and perfect pattern of all virtues."

[51] This work was originally written in Latin with the title *Quo pacto ingenni adolescents informandi sint, Praeceptiones pauculae, Huldrich Zwinglio autore* [In what way noble youth must be instructed, a few precepts, Ulrich Zwingli author].

[52] Zwingli, *Christian Education*, 43.

[53] Jackson, *Huldreich Zwingli*, 212 n. 1. In 1524 the same work was also published in Zurich. Augsburg published it along with Erasmus' treaties on children. In the same year the first German translation of Zwingli's treaties appeared and was reprinted in 1844. *Christian Education of Youth* was also found in a collection of essays on pedagogical themes in 1541. Zwingli's own translation into the Zurich German dialect was republished in 1879 and 1884. The English translation was made by Alcide Reichenbach in 1899.

[54] Gordon, *The Swiss Reformation*, 232.

churches in Germany, the Netherlands, and England. The same institution made a significant contribution to Protestant biblical scholarship in Switzerland by producing a German Bible translation, although this Bible was heavily indebted to Luther's German translation. In addition, the *Prophezei* published many biblical commentaries. Some of them became a model for Calvin when he made his own commentaries.[55] Zwingli's other contribution to Christian education was his desire to provide education for all Christians who belonged to different kinds of social classes. [56]

CONCLUSION

Zwingli's concept of education was basically humanistic in his pedagogy but profoundly Christian in the ultimate purpose and praxis of education. As a humanist, he highlighted the importance of language skills and scientific textual analysis in obtaining the knowledge of truth. His humanist perspective also granted that education is a sacred means of transforming the souls of individuals and their society. Unlike his contemporary secular and Catholic humanists, for Zwingli, the true and primary educator is not a human teacher, but the Holy Spirit who could enlighten the sinful minds of students. Zwingli urged Christian teachers to pray for the illuminating ministry of the Holy Spirit before their class and to depend on Him as the true teacher during the class. According to the Zurich Reformer, the ultimate goal of Christian education is neither to satisfy personal aesthetic taste nor to increase power and wealth but to serve God and others, as Jesus did. Christlikeness in every aspect of the Christian life, whether it is in a private or public setting, was Zwingli's aim in his reformation of the educational system of Zurich. Zwingli's school education was not a personal enterprise but a communal project. All faculty members worked together in order to enhance the students' understanding of the will of God revealed in the Bible and to have them apply their knowledge of the Bible in their daily lives. For Zwingli, Christian education is not a purely academic but a very practical discipline, which results in a life-changing experience according to the word of God. In Zwingli's classroom not only teachers, but also students, were expected to make a contribution to Christian education by sharing what they had learned with one another by the help of the Holy Spirit.

---

[55] Locher, *Zwingli's Thought*, 29.

[56] Wandel, "Zwingli and Reformed Practice," 288. Zwingli's desire to educate all citizens of Zurich does not necessarily mean that all citizens had equal opportunities for education. "…women had less access to the study of Scripture and its languages than men; artisans had less access than the sons of the merchants; those intended for the clergy had fullest access. Each Christian, however, was to have access to some of that education, and all were to have access of one kind or another to its core: God's Word."

PRIMARY SOURCE SAMPLE[57]

It is not my purpose to set out the directions which ought to be given from the cradle or during the earliest years at school, but those which are suitable for young men who have already attained to discretion and can stand on their own feet. I count you amongst this number. You will, I hope, diligently read these directions and so model yourself upon them that you will be a living example to others. May God himself do this work in you. Amen.

First and chiefly, it is beyond our human capacity to bring the hearts of men to faith in the one God even though we had an eloquence surpassing that of Pericles. For that is something which only our heavenly Father can do as he draws us to himself. Yet it is still the case, in the words of St. Paul, that "faith cometh by hearing, and hearing by the Word of God," though this does not mean that very much can be accomplished by the preaching of the external word apart from the internal address and compulsion of the Spirit. Therefore it is necessary not merely to instil faith into the young by the pure words which proceed from the mouth of God, but to pray that he who alone can give faith will illuminate by his Spirit those whom we instruct in his Word.

BIBLIOGRAPHY
PRIMARY SOURCES

Zwingli, Ulrich. *Commentary on True and False Religion*. Edited by Samuel Macauley Jackson. Durham: Labyrinth Press. Reprint, 1981.

_____. *Selected Works of Huldreich Zwingli (1483-1531): The Reformer of German Switzerland*. Edited by Samuel Macauley Jackson. Philadelphia: University of Philadelphia, 1901.

_____. *The Latin Works and the Correspondence of Huldreich Zwingli: Together with Selections from his German Works*. Edited by Samuel Macauley Jackson. Translated by Henry Preble, Walter Lichtenstein, and Lawrence A. McLouth, Vol. 1: 1510-1522. New York: G. P. Putnam's Sons, 1912.

_____. *The Christian Education of Youth*. Translated by Alcide Reichenbach. Collegeville, PA: Thomson Brothers, 1899.

SECONDARY SOURCES

Bromiley, G.W. ed. *Zwingli and Bullinger*. Vol. 24 of *Library of Christian Classics*. Philadelphia: Westminster, 1953.

Büsser, Fritz. "Théorie et pratique de l'éducation sous la Réforme a Zurich." In *La Réforme et l'éducation: sous la direction de J. Boisset*. Edited by Jean Boisset, 153-69. Toulouse: Privat, 1974.

Gordon, Bruce. *The Swiss Reformation*. New York: Manchester University Press, 2002.

Locher, Gottfried Wilhelm. *Zwingli's Thought: New Perspectives*. Leiden: E. J. Brill, 1981.

Gäbler, Ulrich. *Huldrych Zwingli: His Life and Work*. Translated by Ruth C. L. Gritsch. London: T. & T. Clark, 1998.

---

[57] Ulrich Zwingli, "Of the Education of Youth," in *Zwingli and Bullinger* ed. G. W. Bromiley, vol. 24 of *Library of Christian Classics* (Philadelphia: Westminster Press, 1953), 102-108.

Goeing, Anja-Silvia. "Establishing the Modes of Learning: Old and New Hebrew Grammars in the 16ᵗʰ Century." In *Scholarly Knowledge: Textbooks in Early Modern Europe.* Edited by Emidio Campi, 157-82. Geneva: Librairie Droz, 2008.

Jackson, Samuel Macauley. *Huldreich Zwingli: The Reformer of German Switzerland 1484-1531.* Revised. 2ⁿᵈ ed. New York: G. P. Putnam's Sons, 1972.

Pipkin, H. Wayne. "Huldreich Zwingli." In *A History of Religious Educators,* 124-135. Edited by Elmer L. Towns. Grand Rapids: Baker, 1975.

Rüsch, Ernst Gerhard. *"Die humanistischen Vorbilder der Erziehungsschrift Zwinglis."* *Theologische Zeitschnft* 22 (1966): 122-47.

Schaff, Philip. *Modern Christianity. The Swiss Reformation.* Vol. 8 of *History of the Christian Church,* rev. 3ʳᵈ ed. Grand Rapids: Eerdmans, 1953.

Snavely Jr., I. L. "Ulrich Zwingli." In *Historical Handbook of Major Biblical Interpreters.* Edited by Donald K. McKim, 249-55. Downers Grove, IL: InterVarsity Press, 1998.

Stephens, W. Peter. "The Theology of Zwingli." In *the Cambridge Companion to Reformation Theology.* Edited by David Bagchi and David C. Steinmetz, 80-99. New York: Cambridge University Press, 2004.

Stotz, Peter. "Heinrich Bullinger (1504-1575) and the Ancient Languages." In *Scholarly Knowledge: Textbooks in Early Modern Europe.* Edited by Emidio Campi, Simone De Angelis, Anja-Silvia Goeing, and Anthony T. Grafton, 113-38. Genève: Librairie Droz S. A., 2008.

Wandel, Lee Palmer. "Zwingli and Reformed Practice." In *Educating People of Faith: Exploring the History of Jewish and Christian Communities.* Edited by John H. Van Engen, 270-93. Grand Rapids: Eerdmans, 2004.

152

CHAPTER 9

Ignatius Loyola:
Soldier of the Exercised Mind and Disciplined Spirit

GEORGE THOMAS KURIAN
MARK A. LAMPORT

Ignatius of Loyola (1491-1556)

In 2013, for the first time, a Jesuit by the name of Jorge Mario Bergoglio was elected Pope of the Roman Catholic Church. Ignatius of Loyola (1491-1556), a contemporary of Martin Luther, was instrumental in the founding and rapidly expansive growth of the influential Society of Jesus, or the Jesuits. Following is a brief account of the life and mission of this man, considered to be one of the most important Christians of the sixteenth century. In addition, this chapter will detail the religious conditions in the Church, and describe the most acclaimed contributions of Ignatius Loyola and the Jesuits to Christian education.

HISTORICAL BACKGROUND
LIFE AND MISSION

Ignatius[1] was a Basque (northern Spain) whose given name was Don Inigo Lopez de Recalde, but took the name of Loyola from his ancestral estate. Born into a wealthy and culturally religious family, Ignatius, was the youngest of thirteen children. His mother died shortly after his birth. As a young man, he developed a quick temper and self-confessed prideful countenance. More than once he engaged in duels and became a competent swordsman. Once, as the story goes, he ran his weapon through the chest of a Moor because denied the divinity of Jesus.

At seventeen years of age Ignatius Loyola became knight in the Spanish kingdom of Navarre. After a career of thirteen years as a soldier, he was severely injured by the French at the siege of Pamplona in 1521. While recovering in his castle, he read the *Lives of the Saints* and was moved by the example of Jesus and those who had suffered hardship for their Christian faith. As is the case of many, serious injury caused him to reevaluate his life: priorities, postures, and practices. These seeds of religious awakening sparked an emerging openness to the immanent reality of God. He would later profoundly write: "If God causes you to suffer much, it is a sign that He has great designs for you, and that He certainly intends to make you a saint. And if you wish to become a great saint, entreat Him yourself to give you much opportunity for suffering; for there is no wood better to kindle the fire of holy love than the wood of the cross, which Christ used for His own great sacrifice of boundless charity."[2]

This was certainly the case in God's designs on the life-calling of Ignatius Loyola. Flush with transcendent sensitivities, he experienced a vision of the Virgin Mary at the Shrine of Our Lady of Montserrat in 1522. From his extraordinary event Loyola dedicated his life to the service of the Church. Called by God, he was still not clear as to what his energies and his new urging would drive him to do. In lieu of clarity, he decided to go on an evangelistic pilgrimage to Jerusalem, but while there he found that the doors to further advancement for ministry in the Church were closed because he lacked a formal education. Returning from Jerusalem at the age of thirty-three, and desiring to be equipped for his calling, so even at his relatively advanced age, Loyola entered the grammar school at Barcelona. Having his educational aspirations whetted, he doggedly pursued a comprehensive and arduous education at the universities of Alcala, Salamanca, and Paris, respectively.

---

[1] We wish to limit our use of only the single name "Ignatius" so as to avoid possible confusion with the great Ignatius of Antioch.

[2] Joseph A. Munitiz and Philip Endean, eds. and trans., *Personal Writings by St. Ignatius of Loyola* (New York: Penguin Classics, 1997), 147.

RELIGIOUS FERMENT

During this time as Ignatius Loyola experienced formal liberal arts and theological education, the Protestant Reformation was advancing in response to ecclesiastical devices in the Roman Catholic Church. As a result of these frontal attacks on traditional beliefs and practices, Catholics responded in kind with an equally formidable rejoinder: the so-called Counter Reformation.

The "Counter Reformation" is an infelicitous and clumsy term to describe one of the most transformative movements in Christian history, one that modernized the Catholic Church and made it a global rather than a purely European institution. The Counter Reformation suggests a defensive and reactionary movement, whereas it was really the culmination of a centuries-old effort on the part of dedicated Catholics to bring the Church out of its medieval torpor. It was not led by any one man but was energized by several generations of Catholic thinkers, cardinals, theologians, and evangelists.[3] It was a tidal wave that carried the church from its medieval moorings and expanded its reach across five continents. Protestant Reformers called the movement derisively as the "Counter Reformation" and since Catholic historians never disowned it, the name stuck. But a more proper name would be "Catholic Renewal." From this religious fermentation emerged the innovative contributions of Ignatius of Loyola. One of the many organizations that spearheaded Catholic Renewal was the order known as Society of Jesus, founded by Ignatius of Loyola. What follows is the genesis of this innovation.

While studying in Paris, he formed close friendships with six fellow students: Francis Xavier, Diego Laynez, Bobadilla, Faber, Salmeron, and Rodriguez. These seven friends were instrumental in conceiving the *Societas Jesu* (Society of Jesus). Its motto was "Defend and Advance," and it had a double mission: to combat Protestantism and to convert the heathen.[4] (To be fair, it should be noted Loyola devoted himself more to reforming the Catholic Church from within than to combatting the Protestants.) The society was formed in 1534 with Ignatius at the helm, and six years later was officially approved by Pope Paul III. Later popes added many privileges to the order and it became one of the most militant defenders of the Catholic faith. From 1522 to 1524 Ignatius Loyola wrote his classic *Spiritual Exercises*, a simple two hundred page set of meditations, prayers, and various other

---

[3] For further information, see Michael Mullett, *The Catholic Reformation* (New York: Routledge, 1999); John C. Olin, *The Catholic Reformation: Savonarola to St. Ignatius Loyola* (New York: Fordham University Press, 1993).

[4] See John O'Malley, S.J. *The First Jesuits* (Cambridge: Harvard University Press, 1993), 57.

mental exercises. [5] The exercises of the book were designed to be carried out over a period of twenty eight to thirty days. He died in Rome on July 31, 1556, as a result of the Roman Fever, a severe case of malaria that recurred in Rome, Italy, at different points in history. Loyola was beatified in 1609, and canonized in 1622.

THEOLOGY OF CHRISTIAN EDUCATION

Ignatius Loyola's ideas on Christian education and spiritual formation were echoed in a number of later Papal encyclicals. In *Divini Illius Magistri* (The Christian Education of Youth) Pope Pius XI wrote: "The subject of Christian Education is man, whole and entire, soul united to body in unity with all his faculties, natural and supernatural, such as reason and revelation, fallen but redeemed by Christ. The Christian teacher will gather and turn profit whatever there is of real worth in the systems and methods of modern times." [6]

Loyola embraced this approach to learning and contended the proper and immediate end of Christian education is to cooperate with divine grace in forming the true and perfect Christian. Christian education, in his view, takes in the whole scope of human life, not with a view to constraining it in any way but in order to elevate, regulate, and perfect it, in accordance with the example and teaching of Christ. The true Christian, then, does not renounce the activities of this life, but develops and perfects them by coordinating them with the supernatural. These clear goals were guided by equally clear rationale.

THEOLOGICAL HERMENEUTIC

Palpable, deep-seated characteristics illuminate the signature, guiding principles of theological outworking of the mission of Ignatius Loyola. First, he was an austere, rather strict, person, who, at various points in his life, lived in caves, practiced asceticism, begged for food during his theological education, and lived very modestly. This seems an extreme opposite of his wealthy upbringing and heritage, yet it was this complete abandonment to the cause of Christ that motivated his life. Second, there was also a pronounced inborn intellectual and physical rigor within his existence as observed from his days as a professional soldier, then later as an adept academic. And third, life is not to be compartmentalized into discrete realms of human knowing. No, this world is superintended by the God who unifies truth throughout the various disciplines. As later Christian philosophers would expound,

---

[5] Anthony Mottola, trans., *Spiritual Exercises of Saint Ignatius: St. Ignatius' Profound Precepts of Mystical Theology*, Reissue ed. (New York: Doubleday, 1989).

[6] Libreria Editrice Vaticana, "Divini Illius Magistri: Encyclical of Pope Pius XI on Christian Education to the Patriarchs, Primates, Archbishops, Bishops, and Other Ordinaries in Peace and Communion with the Apostolic See and to All the Faithful of the Catholic World," http://www.vatican.va/holy_father/ pius_xi/encyclicals/ documents/hf_p-xi_enc_31121929_divini-illius-magistri_en.html (accessed May 4, 2014).

all truth is God's truth, whatever it may be found.[7] These three factors are prominent in informing Loyolas' hermeneutic in his faith experience and educational philosophy and practices. Understandably, then, these tenets are most visibly observed as one reads the self-discipline inherent in his noted "spiritual exercises," to which we now turn our attention. These exercises are the key to understanding Ignatius Loyola and Jesuit education.

THEOLOGICAL ORIENTATION AND EDUCATIONAL PRACTICES

In terms of the influence of the Jesuit Order on post-tridentine history of the Church (i.e., events occurring after the Council of Trent, 1545–1563), Loyola was perhaps one of most influential figures in Catholic history. He was not merely an educator in the strict sense of the term; he was also spiritual director whose *Spiritual Exercises* is still considered an important manual for the religious life; secondly, he was an organizer and great visionary, and thirdly, a towering intellect. Education is only one of the fields of endeavor on which he left an indelible mark. He was also at the same time a soldier, who approached his calling with the single-mindedness of an ascetic. His goal was not merely to educate but to change the very character of education and to transform it into a vocation. One of the legacies of Jesuit education and one that is enshrined in its Constitution is religious obedience.[8] It was one virtue that Loyola consistently exhibited in his personal life and demanded from all his associates. Obedience meant that there would be smooth sequacious flow of ideas from the top to bottom, from superior to inferior, and from teacher to student. Learning was ultimately an act of obedience to God.

Perhaps the work of the Society of Jesus begun by Ignatius Loyola that is best known is that of education, yet it is interesting that he initially had no intention of including teaching among the Jesuits' works. As already mentioned, the purpose of the first members was to be at the disposal of the Pope to go where they would be most needed. Before 1548 Loyola had opened schools in Italy, Portugal, the Netherlands, Spain, Germany, and India, but they were intended primarily for the education of the new young Jesuit recruits. Ten such colleges within six years indicated the rapid growth of the Jesuits. But in 1548 at the request of the magistrates of Messina in Sicily, Loyola sent five men to open a school for laypersons as well as Jesuit students. It soon became clear by requests for schools from rulers, bishops,

---

[7] This idea is fully developed in Arthur Holmes, *All Truth is God's Truth* (Downers Grove, IL: InterVarsity Press, 1983).

[8] Published originally in 1540, "Constitution of the Jesuits, http://www.bibliotecapleyades.net/vatican/esp_vatican13.htm (accessed October 28, 2013).

and cities that this work was truly one of the most effective ways to correct ignorance and corruption among the clergy and faithful, to stem the decline of the Church in the face of the Reformation, and to fulfill the motto of the Society of Jesus, *"Ad Majorem Dei Gloriam,"* — to the greater glory of God.

Loyola was among the first educators to divide a school into grades and classes. There were two degrees of teaching: one superior, embracing theology, law and medicine, and the other preparatory. He arranged courses in a series and coordinated definite learning sequences with their respective syllabi. Each grade included several divisions according to the number of students. The Jesuits sought to identify talent and spared no means in pursuit of this goal. Learning was conceived as a race in which every student was competing. This metaphor was reinforced by prizes and awards for the victor as in ancient Greece. There was no discrimination against students of lower classes. Even Descartes, no friend of the Church, noted the equality with which Jesuits treated those "who are illustrious and those who are not."[9]

Loyola realized that education is a counterword that, historically, has multiple purposes and definitions.[10] In primary terms, it is a means of preparing students to earn a living. On another level, it is a means of developing the mind and body to make sense of the world and to solve problems. On a third level, it is a means of transmitting knowledge and creating new forms of knowledge through study and research. In a Christian education, of course, there is a fourth level, which is to know God intimately. Sometimes these purposes are in conflict with each other and it is the task of the educator to resolve these conflicts. Loyola was an innovator who created new institutions of learning but he was also a mediator who mediated the interdisciplinary conflicts in an age when hundreds of new disciplines were being created. The taxonomy of subjects and disciplines itself became a crucial element in educational thought.

Loyola was an early promoter of the democratization of education which began in the later Middle Ages. Education was not merely a privilege conferred on the children of noble classes; neither was it the privilege of the few brilliant and talented pupils. Everyone was entitled to a sound education, and Loyola was among the first educators to promote free and universal education.

---

[9] Decartes was educated by the Jesuits and his experiences are detailed in Rene Fulop-Miller, *Descartes And The Jesuits* (Whitefish, MT: Kessinger Publishing, 2010), 36.

[10] A fuller treatment of Ignatius Loyola's educational ideas can be found in George W. Traub, ed., *A Jesuit Education Reader* (Chicago: Loyola Press, 2008); Joseph N. Tylenda, ed. and trans., *A Pilgrim's Journey: The Autobiography of St. Ignatius of Loyola*, rev. ed. (San Francisco: Ignatius Press, 2001).

EDUCATIONAL PHILOSOPHY OF THE JESUIT SYSTEM

The Jesuits first emerged as one of the champions of the Papacy, and their loyalty to the institution and the person of the pope has been one of their distinguishing characteristics. Winning back Protestants through political means would be difficult because it would mean further conflicts and wars (of which there had been too many). So the chief weapon in the Jesuit armory was *education*, which had become one of the rationales (*ratio essendi*) of Protestantism. The Jesuits, thus, were among the first to use education as a tool to achieve a specific end or goal, and the teacher as a master craftsman shaping human minds.

The outline of the Jesuit system and organization was first conceived by Loyola with the assistance of Diego Laynez, one of his fellow Parisian students, in the provincial of Italy. Loyola headed the order for sixteen years – under the pope's sanction of the order – until his own death in 1556. However, the *Constitution* of the order was not promulgated until two years after Loyola's death. Its principal architect was Laynez who took over as superior general after Loyola's death. The *Ratio atque Institutio Studiorum Societas Jesu* (*The Method and System of Studies of the Society of Jesus*), which was an expansion of part four of the *Constitution*, described school administration in detail, was not published until 1599 when Claudio Aquaviva became superior general. [11] The *Ratio Studiorum* thus covers Jesuit management of their educational enterprise over a course of sixty years under three superiors general and not merely the ideas of Loyola.

It is in the *Constitution* that the military character of the Jesuit Order is most evident. Loyola was first and foremost a soldier and he had instilled in him the instincts and habits of a soldier. Implicit obedience to one's superior, in this case the pope, was the primary call on a soldier of Christ. Below the pope, the order was headed by a general (again a military term). His powers were similar to those of the pope and his decisions were never questioned. As the society spread, each country was divided into provinces and each of these provinces or districts (corresponding to dioceses) was headed by a provincial who was chosen by the general for three-year terms. In each province the Jesuit educational system was headed by a rector. The rector also was appointed by the general for three-year terms but was directly responsible to and reported to the provincial. In each institution there was a prefect of studies under the rector and the provincial and under him there were professors or preceptors assisted by monitors. It was a finely tuned system that has worked harmoniously for centuries.

---

[11] For more on the educational system of the Jesuits see Robert Schwickerath, "Ratio Studiorum: The Educational System of the Jesuits," *The Original Catholic Encyclopedia*, 2013, http://oce.catholic. com/index.php?title=Ratio_Studiorum_(accessed October 29, 2013).

The Jesuits never engaged in elementary education. Jesuit colleges required students to be literate before admission. This is due not to a disinterest in primary education but to a shortage of trained teachers at this level. The Constitution limits Jesuit education to *Studia Inferiora* (Lower Colleges) and *Studia Superiora* (Universities and higher education).

The most numerous class is the former. Boys (only) were admitted to these lower colleges from ten to fourteen years of age and spend five or six years there. After finishing the secondary curriculum, boys spent two years in religious studies. During the university course, those training to be Jesuits were known as *Scholastici* while all others were known as *externi*. A full university course lasted seven or nine years, excluding the five or six years spent in teaching in the lower college. At the end of university training, the students became either *coadjutors spiituales* (spiritual assistants) or *professi* (professors). The former took monastic vows of chastity, poverty, and obedience and bound themselves to teaching and preaching. The latter took an additional oath to place themselves at the disposal of the pope and to travel on assigned missions. They formed the legislative body of the order who elected the superior general and the provincials. A complete Jesuit training took up to twenty three years to gain appointment to the full office of a professor.

Loyola was an intensely practical man and no detail, however small, escaped his attention. He insisted that no Jesuit college should be without proper buildings and equipment, or located in places without political and social stability. The Jesuits accepted donations from the faithful but did not charge any tuition fees. The Constitution of the order charged them *"Gratis Accepistis, Gratis Date"* (Freely you have received, freely give.) Originally the school curriculum was modified by Hieronymian, partly humanistic and partly religious and owed much to Johann Sturm, the founder of a gymnasium at Strasburg. Sturm had a definite set of ideals for his school, which he described as follows: "A wise and persuasive piety should be the aim of our studies. The student should be distinguished from the unlettered by scientific culture and the art of diction. Hence knowledge, purity and the eloquence of diction should be the aim of scholarship."[12]

In the schools the eloquence of diction referred to was limited to Ciceronian Latin. All study of the vernacular was forbidden and only Latin was allowed to be spoken at school. The first three years were devoted to Latin classics and grammar, and classical authors were studied in the last two years. It was not until 1832 that the curriculum included mathematics, natural sciences, history and geography.

---

[12] Lewis W. Spitz, *Johann Sturm on Education* (Minneapolis, MN: Concordia Publishing House, 1993), 243.

The core of the curriculum, however, was devoted to moral, social, and religious training. In boarding colleges called *convictus*, established under Laynez, students were constantly under the watchful eye of the fathers. Students were required to participate in daily mass, confession, prayer, meditation and Christian instruction. If a curriculum is judged by the quality of the students and their training, then Jesuit education had one of the best track records of any educational system. Despite the narrow scope of its courses of study, it was a rigorous discipline that was uncompromising in its adherence to the best educational traditions of both the classical and the Christian worlds. It was a Catholic education that was also catholic, in the universal sense.

The curriculum of the Jesuit universities offered three years in philosophy followed by six years in theology. The philosophy curriculum included logic, metaphysics, psychology, ethics, as well as algebra, geometry, trigonometry, calculus, mechanics, natural science, physics, chemistry, geology, astronomy, together with other electives. This lead to the Master of Arts degree following successful completion and examination. In the theology curriculum, four years were devoted to the study of the Scriptures, Hebrew, Latin, and Oriental languages, along with church history, canon law, and dogmatic theology. It was further followed by a two-year training, and concluded with a public examination and a defense of the thesis. The culmination of this study led to the Doctor of Divinity degree.

SIGNIFICANT CONTRIBUTIONS OF JESUIT EDUCATION TO CHRISTIAN EDUCATION
TEACHER

What distinguished Jesuit education was not so much the scope of the subjects but the training of the teacher and their professionalism. Over the course of some twenty years, the Jesuit teacher was subjected to the most rigorous and unforgiving training program, and the theological underpinnings of Jesuit education gave teachers a motivation that was not mercenary or measurable in monetary terms. It was selfless in its dedication to students. The ability of the teacher to communicate orally was honed by constant practice. In earlier times, the Jesuits emphasized memorization but the most common form of instruction was the *Prelectio* in which each passage or idea was explained in detail. This method had six stages: lexical meaning, nuance or subtle gradations in meaning, analogy with similar ideas in other works or subjects, information and commentary, rhetorical subtleties, and moral importance.

LEARNER

Such an elaborate system required intense training on the part of the teacher and an equally intense desire to learn on the part of the student. Repetition was the key to both learning and memorization. Although four and a half hours were spent each day in the classroom, teaching was limited to one Latin author and one continuous repetition. Ignatius Loyola's motto was *Pluribus die bus fere singula precepta inculcanda sunt* (*Usually each rule must be reinforced for several days*). The number of subjects learned was less important than the thoroughness with which they are assimilated. Another Jesuit motto was *Repetitio mater studiorum* (*Repetition is the mother of learning*). Each day began with a review of the preceding day's work and each week ended with a repetition of all that had been learned during that period. The last month of every year reviewed the course of the year, except in the three lowest classes where the whole last half of the year was a repetition of the first half. Students were also required to teach in the *studia inferiora*.

CURRICULUM AND METHODS

The curriculum of Jesuit colleges was not broad but was systematic and designed to stimulate student interest. They offered a variety of incentives to the students, including prizes that constantly rewarded talent and virtue. Learning was not a chore incidental to life; it was life itself. Education was a process of edification in which knowledge was built brick by brick, as in architecture and then cemented by the *magisterium* of the professors. One device used was that in which the brightest students were selected as *decuriones* who worked in *decuriae* or squads encouraging other students to excel in their studies. Other students were arranged in pairs as *emuli* or rivals, challenging their peers to better performance. In addition, public *disputationes* or contests were held each week between two sides, one known as Rome and the other as Carthage. They employed a form of disputation called *concertatio*. Teachers and prefects served as judges, and prizes were awarded to the victors. More advanced discussions were held by voluntary societies known as *academiae*.

Jesuit education differed from other systems in another remarkable respect: discipline did not include corporal punishment. Pupils were led, not driven, and Jesuit teachers were noted for their unfailing kindness and diplomacy. Occasionally, a corrector, usually from outside the school, was employed to deal with the more refractory pupils but these were infrequent.

Jesuit success in education provoked much criticism from non-Catholics. Among the strictures was the inflexibility of their creed which brooked no opposition. No Jesuit teacher could teach anything against the doctrines of the church. Unorthodoxy was condemned and regimentation was the order of the day. Although this was considered a failing by secular educators, it was a strength that contributed to the institutional vitality and stability of the church.

From the sixteenth to the eighteenth century, and even perhaps through the twentieth, Jesuit education was celebrated as one of the most effective in the world. The growth of their schools was phenomenal. When Loyola died, there were already 100 colleges and universities not merely in Europe, but also India, Japan, China and Ethiopia. Under Aquaviva, the number of colleges grew to 372 and within 150 years to 769. Most had a student body numbering in the thousands. Paris had fourteen colleges with fourteen thousand students and the College at Clermont had three thousand. Among their alumni in France were Corneille, Moliere, Bossuet, Diderot, Cardinal Richelieu, and Duc de Luxembourg, Marshal of France. Perhaps the best testimony to the Jesuits came from Voltaire, the arch enemy of the Church, who said, "During the seven years I lived in the house of the Jesuits, what did I see among them? The most laborious, frugal, and regular life, all their hours divided between the care they spent on us and the exercises of their austere profession. I attest the same as thousands of others brought up by them, like myself, not one will be found to contradict me."[13]

Within the next century, Jesuits faced serious reverses as they were expelled from many European and Latin American countries. In 1773 Pope Clement XIV dissolved the Society "Recognizing that the members of the society have not a little troubled the Christian commonwealth, and that for the welfare of Christendom it were better that the order should disappear."[14] However, most countries readmitted the Jesuits within a century.

CONTRIBUTIONS TO CHRISTIAN EDUCATION

Ignatius Loyola's "spiritual exercises" were means to prepare and entice the soul to separate itself from disorderly desires and then to seek and find God's will for one's life. The Exercises recognize not only the intellect but also that emotions and feelings can help us to come to knowledge of the action of the Spirit in our lives. Loyola recommended this prayer to penitents seeking to forfeit their will to be superintended by God: "Receive, Lord, all my liberty, my memory, my understanding, and my whole will. You have given me all that I have, all that I am, and I surrender all to your divine will, that you dispose of me. Give me only your love and your grace. With this I am rich enough and I have   no more to ask"[15] Then the will is properly aligned, one's education in godliness is more readily conceived.

---

[13] Thomas Hughes, *Loyola and the Educational System of the Jesuits* (Charleston, SC: BiblioLife, 2009), 152.

[14] For a good introduction to this topic see John Hungerford Pollen, "The Suppression of the Jesuits, 1750-1773," *The Catholic Encyclopedia*, vol. 14, *Simony-Tournon,* (New York: Robert Appleton Company, 1912), http://www.newadvent.org/cathen/14096a.htm (accessed October 29, 2013).

Characteristically, Loyola saw means and ends arranged in a hierarchy of values. The lower ends subserved in the intermediate ones and they in turn led up to the higher ends in life, and his task was to devise means of achieving them. The highest goal in education was the truth, in this case, the truth as revealed in the Bible and in the person of Jesus Christ. Jesuits would provide the environment, personnel, and content for education, while the students would provide the willing minds. Loyola always expressed his desire that students should strive for true excellence in their fields of study.

For Loyola the primary intellectual objective was not intricate mastery of the subject matter but the very discipline of learning.[15] In other words, education was a tool, apart from the contents. But he also realized that when properly used the tool can lead to a mastery of the subject. Loyola's insights defined *mathesis* or the process of acquiring knowledge which lies at the heart of education. He identified six key essentials: motivation of the student, magisterium of the teacher, repetition of the subject matter, classification of ideas, and rewards for excellence. He regarded the development of the mind in the same terms as development of the body and uses his favorite term Exercises (as used in the title of his book, *Spiritual Exercises*) to describe training of the body, mind and spirit. Learning was also an exercise with its own rubrics. Loyola's writings are characterized by a spirit of innovation and experimentation. He preserved much of the Thomist legacies in Catholic education, while at the same time discarding the dog-eared and moth-eaten ideas that plagued medieval educators. To appreciate his true stature, his work must be judged against the backdrop of medieval culture which was already moribund by the sixteenth century. To eliminate the stereotypes associated with medieval monks, he discouraged his associates from wearing the monastic cowl and dress. Instead he had them dress like diocesan priests.

LEGACY AND JUSTIFICATION FOR INCLUSION

The *Spiritual Exercises* remain an integral part of the Novitiate training period of the Roman Catholic religious order of Jesuits. Also, many local Jesuit outreach programs throughout the world offer retreats for the general public in which the *Exercises* are employed. Beginning in the 1980s, Protestants have had a growing interest in the *Spiritual Exercises*. There are recent (2006) adaptations that are specific to Protestants that emphasize the exercises as a school of contemplative prayer.

Loyola's most notable achievement may well be the restoration of the primacy of teaching in education. He provided his teachers with a *Ratio docendi*, a reason for teaching,

---

[15] More on these ideas can be found in Traub, *A Jesuit Education Reader,* 2008.

which is to be found in their ability to mold the elastic minds of the young, and thus enhance their ability to engage and interact with the world around them. For the world is not "natural," but supernatural; the world is not to be feared, but engaged.

Finally, Loyola's gifts were many. His ideas were perhaps most clearly spelled out in his prolific writings and letters. Our attempts to summarize them follow. First, education was a means to an end, not an end in itself. Second, learning and faith are compatible and, in fact, complement each other. Third, the goal of education is excellence. Fourth, education should promote virtue and intellect together. Fifth, there is a hierarchy of subjects, disciplines and faculties, with theology preeminent among them. Sixth, students should be encouraged to exercise constantly both their minds and their bodies. Seventh, teachers should take a personal interest in the growth of their pupils. Eighth, students should be constantly engaged in the discovery of new ideas and in testing them to see if they are true. Ninth, training should be age-specific, or suitable to the age level of the student. Tenth, education must be adaptable, and must not shun ideas because of innate prejudice; neither should they fail to discard obsolete ideas because they are comfortable. Lastly, education must be free and universal.[16]

Ignatius Loyola, whose love it was to be actively involved in teaching catechism to children, directing adults in the Spiritual Exercises, and working among the poor and in hospitals, would, for the most part, sacrifice this love for the last fifteen years of his life to work out of two small rooms, his bedroom and next to it his office, directing this new society throughout the world. He would spend years composing the Constitutions of the Society and would write thousands of letters to all corners of the globe to his fellow Jesuits dealing with the affairs of the Society and to lay men and women directing them in the spiritual life. From his tiny quarters in Rome he would live to see in his lifetime the Society of Jesus grow from eight to a thousand members, with colleges and houses all over Europe and as far away as Brazil and Japan. Some of the original companions became the Pope's theologians at the Council of Trent, an event which played an important role in the Catholic Counter Reformation.

His legacy includes many Jesuit schools and its system of Christian schools and educational institutions worldwide. In the United States alone there are twenty-eight Jesuit colleges and universities and more than fifty secondary schools. Worldwide the Jesuits today have over five hundred universities and colleges, 30,000 members, and teach over 200,000 students each year. It is the nature, content, discipline, and rigor of his innovative educational advancements that has rippled throughout all branches of Christian world. From

---

[16] James Brodrick, *The Origin of the Jesuits* (Chicago: Loyola Press, 1997).

this relentlessly devoted Christian educator, we have benefitted by principled exercises for spiritual maturity and organized studies in secondary and tertiary education from Christian perspectives. Yet, while some in Western Christian world may be making headway on the disciplined life of the spirit, lesser progress – we argue with dismay – has been made in the vigorous refinement of the Christian mind. May we be soldiers in the spirit of Ignatius in the disciplined exercise of our Christian minds.

BIBLIOGRAPHY

Brodrick, James. *The Origin of the Jesuits*. Chicago: Loyola University Press, 1986.

Fulop-Miller, Rene. *Descartes and the Jesuits*. Whitefish, MT: Kessinger Publishing, 2010.

Hughes, Thomas. *Loyola and the Educational System of the Jesuits*. Charleston, SC: BiblioLife, 2009.

Holmes, Arthur. *All Truth is God's Truth*. Downers Grove, IL: InterVarsity Press, 1983.

Mottola, Anthony, trans. *Spiritual Exercises of Saint Ignatius: St. Ignatius' Profound Precepts of Mystical Theology*. Reissue ed. New York: Doubleday, 1989.

Munitiz, Joseph A. and Philip Endean, eds. and trans. *Personal Writings by St. Ignatius of Loyola*. New York: Penguin Classics, 1997.

Mullett, Michael. *The Catholic Reformation*. New York: Routledge, 1999.

Olin, John C. *The Catholic Reformation: Savonarola to St. Ignatius Loyola*. New York: Fordham University Press, 1993.

O'Malley, John. *The First Jesuits*. Cambridge: Harvard University Press, 1993.

Spitz, Lewis W. *Johann Sturm on Education*. Minneapolis: Concordia Publishing House, 1993.

Traub, George W., ed. *A Jesuit Education Reader*. Chicago: Loyola Press, 2008.

Tylenda, Joseph N, ed. and trans. *A Pilgrim's Journey: The Autobiography of St. Ignatius of Loyola*. Rev. ed. San Francisco: Ignatius Press, 2001.

FURTHER RECOMMENDED RESOURCES

Caraman, Philip. *Ignatius Loyola*. New York: Harper & Row, 1990.

De Dalmases, Candido. *Ignatius of Loyola, Founder of the Jesuits*. St. Louis: Institute of Jesuit Sources, 1985.

Magevney, Eugene. *The Jesuit as Educators*. Charleston, SC: BiblioLife, 2010.

Rahner, Hugo, and Leonard von Matt. *St. Ignatius of Loyola: A Pictoral Biography*. Translated by John Murray. Chicago: Henry Regnery Company, 1956.

Ravier, Andre. *Ignatius Loyola and the Founding of the Society of Jesus*. San Francisco: Ignatius Press, 1987.

CHAPTER 10

Philip Melanchthon:
Christian Education in the German Reformation

MARTIN I. KLAUBER

Phillip Melanchthon (1497-1560)

Philip Melanchthon was one of the most important pioneers of the Reformation. As one of the major founders of the Lutheran movement (along with Martin Luther), he was actively involved in Christian education, and fifty-six cities and eight universities sought his advice in reforming their educational systems. In addition to this he also helped found four universities, and as a result he gained the nickname the "Preceptor of Germany."

HISTORICAL BACKGROUND

Philip Melanchthon was the son of a master-armorer in Bretton in the Palatinate. His father died when he was only eleven and he was sent to live with his two brothers with his grandfather and later was sent to the home of his great-aunt, who was the sister of the famous Hebrew scholar, Johann Reuchlin. When the great scholar visited his nephew, Reuchlin was impressed with young Philip's language skills and noted that he was something of a prodigy. Reuchlin gave him a Bible and a Greek grammar text and later changed his last name from the German Schwartzerd to the Greek form, Melanchthon.

Melanchthon displayed a passion for classical texts from authors such as Cicero, Vergil, and Livy. His name change symbolized his adherence to humanism since its followers often considered themselves to have Greek and Roman roots, so they could use either the Latin or the Greek version of their names.[1] As early as 1518, he gained the attention of the great Erasmus for his book *Rudiments of the Greek Language* (1518). So it is proper to characterize Melanchthon as a humanist. However, one must be careful not to assume that the term refers to an ideology that glorifies man over God. As Paul Oskar Kristeller has shown, the term "humanist" in this context refers primarily to the study of the humanities, an adherence to an academic curriculum that emphasized a return to original sources and the study of original languages. One can clearly see, therefore, that this emphasis on sources and languages contributed in many ways to the Reformation movement.[2]

Reuchlin, a great humanist scholar in his own right, encouraged his nephew to pursue the study of the original languages, and also helped him to gain a position at the fledgling University of Wittenberg in 1518. Melanchthon arrived at an auspicious time just after the posting of the *Ninety-five Theses* and began to teach Greek and Hebrew. While there he gained an immense interest in the study of theology. In his inaugural lecture "On Correcting the Studies of Youth," he declared his commitment to a pure, classical education. He expressed his disdain for the scholastic methodology in favor of humanism, with an emphasis on the study of the Bible in its original languages. He also emphasized the study of the *trivium*, grammar, rhetoric, and logic. He did not totally reject dialectics, but advocated a form of dialects that could be informed and sharpened by rhetoric. In addition to this, Melanchthon also stressed the study of history as essential for both theologian and pastor. He believed it

---

[1] Clyde L. Manschreck, *Melanchthon, the Quiet Reformer* (New York: Abingdon Press, 1958), 33.

[2] Paul Oskar Kristeller, *Renaissance Thought: The Classic, Scholastic and Humanist Strains*, (New York: Harper & Row, 1955), 10.

could prevent one from falling into theological error as those in the past had done.[3]

Upon his arrival at Wittenberg, he immediately poured his energy into the classroom and lectured on the writings of Homer, the epistle of Titus, and other biblical books. He also taught the biblical languages with such vigor and enthusiasm that his classes were packed with students. Melanchthon's influence on education was so pervasive that he gained the moniker, "the preceptor of Germany." The preceptor soon became a major draw for the University of Wittenberg, which saw its student body grow quickly by leaps and bounds.[4]

In 1519, he accompanied Luther to Leipzig where Luther debated the Roman Catholic polemicist Johann Eck. Originally it was Luther's colleague Andrea Karlstadt who was tapped to lead the debate, but Luther quickly had to rush to his aid. Melanchthon's presence propelled him into the skirmish with Johann Eck over issues such as indulgences, penance, purgatory, and the authority of the pope. It also led him to unabashedly support the cause of the Reformation and resulted in his break with Reuchlin. The years 1520 and 1521 were pivotal for the Reformation and included Luther's famous confrontation with Charles V at the Diet of Worms, his exile at the Wartburg Castle, and culminated in Luther's formal excommunication from the Roman Catholic Church. During Luther's time at the Wartburg, Melanchthon remained in Wittenberg and witnessed the radicalization of the Protestant movement led by Carlstadt. It was also in 1521 that Melanchthon published his *Loci Communes,* a major systematic theology text based on the book of Romans, focusing on the key issues of sin, law, and grace. Translated "common places," he divided the text into subtopics, which became a very helpful organizational tool for teaching theology. Luther gave the work his highest degree of praise saying: "Next to Holy Scripture, there is no better book."[5]

After Luther returned and routed the radicals, the Reformation began in earnest and that included the process of what scholars refer to as "confessionalization." Once the Duke of Saxony proclaimed the duchy to be Evangelical, the laity had to be taught what that really meant. In a state-church context, the monarch or the Duke could control the religion of the realm, but that did not mean that everyone would automatically follow his lead. The

---

[3] An English translation of this text is contained in Ralph Keen, ed., *A Melanchthon Reader* (New York: Peter Lang, 1988). For the original Latin edition see *Corpus Reformatorum: Philippi Melanthonis opera quae supersunt omnia*, ed. Karl Bretschneider and Heinrich Bindseil, 28 vols. (Halle: Schwetschke, 1834-1860), vol. 11.

[4] Eric Frank, "Philip Melanchthon: Scholar and Reformer" *WRS Journal* (August, 1996), 38.

[5] Wilhelm Pauck, *From Luther to Tillich: The Reformers and Their Heirs* (New York: Harper Collins, 1985), 57.

people had to learn the nature of the new faith and this required education. According to Melanchthon, reforming the educational system would be foundational to raising a new generation of Lutherans and he assumed the leadership of these reforms. He focused his efforts on the founding of public schools and the reorganization of the university system. He trained an entire generation of teachers, and Manschreck claims that by the time of Melanchthon's death there was "hardly a city in Germany which did not have a teacher who was trained by him."[6]

THEOLOGY OF CHRISTIAN EDUCATION

For Melanchthon, Scripture served as the foundation of his educational system and he geared every subject to lead one to a better understanding of the nature of God. The study of the liberal arts and the original languages would enable the student to exegete the Bible in an adequate manner and to understand proper Christian teaching. In this way, students could use the pagan classics as preparatory for the higher level study of divine revelation. This was innovative and avoided the narrow approach that shunned the use of the classics in favor of the study of Scripture alone. He outlined this vision in his "Plan for the Studies of a Student of Theology," circulated in manuscript form from 1529 until its official publication in 1537.[7]

THEOLOGICAL HERMENEUTIC

Melanchthon's theological hermeneutic developed out of his *loci* method as epitomized in his *Loci Communes*. This was more than just a method for discussing theological topics, but also focused on key issues such as soteriology and anthropology and here he showed how his thinking differed from his medieval forbears. The doctrines of *sola fide* and *sola scriptura* provided the foundation of his approach, and the entire curriculum was designed to lead one to the proper study of Scripture, which would inevitably lead to a rejection of Roman Catholic teaching on such core areas of theology.[8]

---

[6] Manschreck, *Melanchthon*, 131.

[7] Robert Kolb, "The Pastoral Dimension of Melanchthon's Pedagogical Activities for the Education of Pastors," in *Philip Melanchthon: Theologian in Classroom, Confession, and Controversy*, eds. Irene Dingel, Robert Kolb Nicole Kuropka, and Timothy J. Wengert (Göttingen: Vandenhoeck & Ruprecht, 2012), 31.

[8] Timothy J. Wengert, *Human Freedom, Christian Righteousness: Philip Melanchthon's Exegetical Dispute with Erasmus of Rotterdam* (Oxford: Oxford University Press, 1998), 650.

CURRICULUM AND METHODS

With his theology of education founded upon scripture, he faced the challenging task of turning his theology into a methodology. He published a plan for reforming German schools called the *Visitation Articles* in 1528. This plan proposed how to create a public school system to be implemented in Saxony. Most of the eighteen articles were doctrinal in nature, covering such issues as the sacraments, prayer, the Ten Commandments, marriage, confession, and the freedom of the will. The idea was to ensure proper Christian theology as the basis for education and to provide for its proper application. The articles also contained instructions for those inspecting the public schools in order to reform them along evangelical lines, emphasizing a classical educational model.[9] This was a major development and was the first public school system since the days of the Roman Empire. The groundwork for the 1528 plan was Melanchthon's establishment of public schools at Eisleben and Nuremburg in 1524 and 1525. In 1527 he visited the schools in Thuringia and conceived the plan to reform all the schools in Saxony. Melanchthon outlined the curriculum and in many cases nominated the teachers for these schools. Such education was necessarily based on the principles of *sola scriptura* and the priesthood of all believers, as all followers of Christ had to be able to read in order to understand Scripture. Accordingly, a basic understanding of the principles of evangelical theology was also essential for promoting social order and Melanchthon could point to the example of Thomas Müntzer and the Peasants' Revolt of 1525.[10]

One major reason for the establishment of the public schools was the closing of the monasteries and therefore the closing of the monastic schools. In addition to the need for new schools, there was the problem of recruiting competent teachers who typically received relatively low pay. Melanchthon complained that cattle herders were paid more than the teachers and lamented the necessity of teachers to find alternative sources of income, which were sometimes questionable such as manufacturing and the selling alcoholic beverages

---

[9] *Corpus Reformatorum: Philippi Melanthonis opera quae supersunt omnia*, ed. Karl Bretschneider and Heinrich Bindseil, 28 vols. (Halle: Schwetschke, 1834-1860), vol. 26, 8-28,

[10] Manschreck, *Melanchthon*, 132. The Peasants' Revolt took place from 1524 to 1525 in the German-speaking areas of Europe and was ruthlessly repressed by the aristocracy, which included both Roman Catholic and Lutheran forces. In addition to the traditional economic concerns that typified similar revolts throughout Europe in the late-medieval and early modern era, there was a significant amount of apocalyptic imagery in this particular revolt led by the radical reformer, Thomas Müntzer. The culmination of the revolt was the battle of Frankenhausen in 1525 that led to the wholesale slaughter of thousands of peasants and included the capture of Müntzer who was then tortured and executed. For more information see Michael G. Baylor, *The German Reformation and the Peasants' War: A Brief History with Documents* (Boston: Bedford/St. Martin's, 2012).

on school grounds. Teachers, he argued, should be paid at a fair level out of public funds. His influence was so pervasive that nearly all of the Protestant primary Latin schools and gymnasia in the evangelical territories of Germany were founded on Melanchthon's principles of education.[11]

There was obviously a strong emphasis on the study of biblical languages and classical Latin, as he believed that the study of languages served as the building blocks of a good liberal arts education. He believed that Latin as the first step for further studies should be taught first and that younger students should not move on to Greek, Hebrew, or even German until they had achieved some mastery of Latin.[12]

As for the teaching of theology, he teamed with Luther to provide such basic tools as the catechism, which could be memorized and provide the rudimentary elements of proper Christian doctrine. Teaching children should obviously start with reading and a basic manual containing the alphabet, the Apostles creed, and the Lord's Prayer. He encouraged the schoolmasters to require a daily writing assignment along with the memorization of Latin vocabulary. He summarized his position in 1528: "Parents should send their children to school, and prepare them for the Lord God so that he may use them for the service of others."[13]

Once the children were able to read basic Latin, they should be taught proper grammar and study of classical texts. They should also be taught music, which was one of the major disciplines of the *quadrivium*. In addition, he advocated that one day each week should be devoted to the study of the Christian faith. He explained: "Let the schoolmaster hear the whole group, making them, one after the other, repeat the Lord's Prayer, the creed, and the ten commandments."[14] Once grammar had been mastered, the student could concentrate on reading the important classics such as Virgil, Ovid, and Cicero. At this stage the students could be taught to write Latin on their own. Melanchthon emphasized that grammar was crucial for everything else that followed in one's education. If the students were unable to master the basics of grammar they could never effectively advance in their education. It was the key to unlocking the meaning of Scripture and of classical knowledge. To this end he published his own grammar text. His Latin grammar went through more than fifty editions and continued to be used until the eighteenth century. In addition to these, he also composed texts for other topics such as

---

[11] Clyde Manschreck, "The Bible in Melanchthon's Philosophy of Education," *The Journal of Bible and Religion*, Vol. 23, No. 3 (July, 1955), 202-203.

[12] Manschreck, *Melanchthon*, 142.

[13] Ibid., 140.

[14] Ibid., 141.

rhetoric, logic ethics, history, physics, and psychology.[15]

Melanchthon also encouraged the students and teachers to conduct their classes speaking only Latin. His three stages of primary education outlined above did not necessarily take three years to complete; instead, advancement would only be allowed after the student could demonstrate competence on the previous level.[16]

The next level of education for the boys was the gymnasium where they would work on Greek and Hebrew. There was a heavy emphasis on reading classical Greek texts such Xenophon and Plutarch. Dialectics, Rhetoric, Mathematics, and Cosmology were key topics for study. To facilitate instruction, Melanchthon composed textbooks on virtually every subject. His Greek grammar went through forty-three editions by 1622. His *Elements of Rhetoric and Dialectics* became the standard for instruction. Even Roman Catholic schools used some of his textbooks.[17]

The next level of education was the university and Melanchthon considered them foundational since the teachers for the secondary schools would be trained there. He reformed or contributed to the reform of seven universities in Germany including the University of Wittenberg, where he composed the basis for reorganizing the curriculum and setting up a method of studying theology focused on exegesis of the text rather than relying upon scholastic authorities. In addition to his reforming roles, he also was instrumental in founding major universities as Königsberg, Jena, and Marburg.[18]

The reform of the University of Wittenberg began while he was rector from 1523-1524. In his new curricular approach, the old dependence on the writings of Aristotle was replaced with an emphasis on original languages. He introduced a new form of academic debate, the declamation, which emphasized the art of rhetoric over the old dependence on logic. In a declamation, the orator was to defend a point of view using the art of persuasive discourse, while in the disputation, the speaker made more extensive use of logic by defending every major objection to an argument. The declamations took place twice a month, the first by a teacher specializing in rhetoric and grammar and the second was to be performed by a student under the supervision of the instructor.[19] He composed a great number of

---

[15] Ibid., 141-150.

[16] Ibid., 142.

[17] James William Richard, *Philip Melanchthon, the Protestant Preceptor of Germany* (London: G. P. Putnam's Sons, 1898), 136.

[18] Manschreck, *Melanchthon*, 145.

[19] Philip Melanchthon, *Orations on Philosophy and Education*, ed. Sachiko Kusukawa (Cambridge: Cambridge University Press, 1999), xv.

these declamations, some of which he delivered himself and many were presented by various colleagues.[20] The declamations provided the student with important practice in the art of speaking well and in a clear fashion. The academic disputation continued to be practiced, but as a companion to what Melanchthon believed to be the higher art form of rhetoric.[21]

Mathematics and Natural Philosophy were major topics to be taught at the University, and Melanchthon utilized Euclid's Elements for the former and Pliny's *Natural History* for the latter. At Wittenberg, faculty held two disputations a month on these topics.[22]

An additional major change in educational approach was the rejection of the dependence on Peter Lombard's *Sentences* the *Libri Quattuor Sententiarum,* which had been the textbook for systematic theology in the late-medieval period. The *Sentences* were compiled by Lombard around 1150 and consisted of a compilation of citations from Scripture and the Church Fathers and organized around various theological topics. A comprehensive study of the *Sentences* was required for a Master's degree in theology and it served as the basis for the academic disputation in which the student would debate a theological proposition using dialectics or logic. Melanchthon replaced the study of the *Sentences* with a thorough study of Scripture. In fact, his *Loci Communes* was largely based on his exegesis of Romans. This was a significant development in educational pedagogy, as the vast majority of great medieval theologians had written a commentary on the *Sentences.* Logic, therefore, became a preparatory study for the more important mastery of rhetoric and study of original texts such as the Pauline corpus, rather than a compilation of patristic sources.[23]

Furthermore, Melanchthon dropped the use of Aristotle's *Metaphysics* because he believed that the topic would better be taught in the area of theology, which he saw as a divine science. He replaced it with Cicero's *De Oratore* and the writings of Virgil and Quintilian. This did not mean that he disparaged the use of Aristotle; rather, he made extensive use of him.[24] Philosophy, especially Aristotelianism, remained an essential handmaiden to the study of theology. Furthermore, Melanchthon viewed the study of philosophy as foundational to

---

[20] Timothy J. Wengert, "The Biblical Commentaries of Philip Melanchthon," in *Philip Melanchthon: Theologian in Classroom, Confession, and Controversy,* 49.

[21] Timothy J. Wengert, "Philip Melanchthon and Wittenberg's Reform of the Theological Curriculum" in *Church and School in Early Modern Protestantism: Studies in Honor of Richard A. Muller on the Maturation of a Theological Tradition,* eds. Jordan J. Ballor, David S. Systma, and Jason Zuidema (Leiden: Brill, 2013), 17-18.

[22] Melanchthon, *Orations,* xv.

[23] Richard, *Philip Melanchthon,* 95-96.

[24] Melanchthon, *Orations,* xv.

the entire study of the liberal arts. He preferred Aristotle as more systematic and consistent a method than that of Plato.[25] He explained this in his "Dedicatory Letter to the *Epitome of Moral Philosophy:*"

> False beliefs also harm morals, and the very habit of sophistry is destructive in many ways: it corrupts one's judgment, lures minds away from the love and study of propriety and simple truth, and accustoms the intellect to loving monstrous beliefs, and to striving to obfuscate rather than explain things. In Aristotle, however, method governs the disputation and, so to speak, forces it within boundaries, so that it does not stray from demonstrations and the right path. For that reason it elicits true opinions and explains them in order and properly. Therefore, Peripatetic philosophy is more useful, because of both the true opinions and the example of method. Aristotle himself said that beliefs that have no usefulness for life or morals should be rejected.[26]

CONTRIBUTIONS TO CHRISTIAN EDUCATION

In 1527, the Elector of Saxony commissioned a group of scholars and pastors to visit the churches in the duchy in order to determine what areas needed improvement. Melanchthon participated and conducted a tour of the churches in Thuringia. During this trip he encountered Anabaptist teaching. So when he returned to Wittenberg, he composed a set of instructions for the inspectors called the *Visitation Articles*. The *Articles* included an important section on refuting heterodoxy. In 1528 his plan for reforming the schools in Saxony became the law of the land.[27]

In 1533, after the death of the Elector John of Saxony, Melanchthon formally composed a new set of theological statutes for the University of Wittenberg based in part on the *Augsburg Confession* (1530) and his *Apology of the Augsburg Confession* (1531). It is interesting that these reforms did not take place in the 1520's. This can be explained, in part, by the upheavals that took place during that decade including the development of the Anabaptist movement and the Peasants' Revolt of 1525. The statutes were built upon a defense of the gospel against the *Confutation of the Augsburg Confession* and against anti-Trinitarian heresies that also threatened it. Melanchthon emphasized that the statutes were in harmony with Scripture and the decision of the first four ecumenical councils of the early church. They also emphasized lectures on biblical books with requirements to teach Romans, John, Psalms, Genesis, and Isaiah. Melanchthon

---

[25] Melanchthon, *Orations*, xvxii; see also Nicole Kuropka, "Philip Melanchthon and Aristotle" in *Philip Melanchthon: Theologian in Classroom*: 19-29.

[26] Melanchthon, *Orations*, 141.

[27] Manschreck, *Melanchthon*, 136-37.

also commended lectures on Augustine's *De litera et spiritu*. The Wittenberg reforms set the pattern for other evangelical universities in the German-speaking territories. These were state institutions where the faculty was bound by confessional norms. Here, Melanchthon's textbooks were commonly used and his methodology ranged far beyond philology and theology, but also included the sciences and medicine.[28]

CONFESSIONALIZATION

Educating the young was but the first step to changing society as a whole based on the Lutheran form of theology. Included here was the training of a new generation of evangelical pastors who could reach the adults. Melanchthon believed that the study of the humanities was essential to the proper training of the clergy. The Reformation changed the emphasis from the administration of the sacraments to the preaching and teaching of the Word of God. A good pastor would have to possess a thorough knowledge of the biblical languages. Furthermore, they would also need training in the art of rhetoric in order to communicate the gospel in a clear way. Lastly, he commended the *loci* method, epitomized in his *Loci Communes*, as the best way to teach the new, evangelical theology to the laity. The *loci* would point the believer to the essential doctrines of the faith and a clear presentation of the gospel that all could easily understand.[29]

The process of confessionalization assumed that the pastors received a proper university education. The education of the clergy was a gradual process, so it made sense that the percentage increased from the first to the second half of the sixteenth century. The Peasants' War had decimated the rural parishes and it took a while for them to be properly replaced.[30] Susan-Karant Nunn shows that from 1521 to 1550 in several districts in Germany including Electoral Saxony, only 96 of 361 pastors had received a university education. The vast majority of these finished their degrees before 1517. According to Nunn, this shows that for the areas studied, very few clergy benefited from the educational reform. Most of the pastors had started their careers as Roman Catholic priests. So, it makes sense that it took decades for the educational reforms to take hold on the parish level.[31]

---

[28] Robert Kolb, "Pastoral Education in the Wittenberg Way" in *Church and School in Early Modern Protestantism*, 69.

[29] Joon-Chul Park, "Philip Melanchthon's Reform of German Universities and its Significance: a Study on the Relationship between Renaissance Humanism and the Reformation" (Ph.D. dissertation: Ohio State University, 1995), 99.

[30] Park, "Philip Melanchthon's Reform of German Universities," 192.

[31] Susan Karant-Nunn, *Luther's Pastors: The Reformation in the Ernestine Countryside* (Philadelphia: Amer Philosophical Society, 1979), 14-18.

LEGACY OF MELANCHTHON AS AN EDUCATOR

Most scholars would affirm the success of Melanchthon's educational reform, but Gerald Strauss argues that he did not succeed in confessionalizing the German people toward the Protestant faith. In fact those who participated in the new educational system continued to think and act in the same way as those students who were schooled in the previous system.[32] Strauss made significant use of the Visitation Records to show that there was no significant difference between the typical behavior of laymen under both Roman Catholic regimes. For example, in Strasbourg, the study of the Lutheran catechism was mandatory, yet it was almost universally ignored by 1598. In the countryside, the level of Christian piety and knowledge of the basic truths of the faith were even worse than in the cities, according to Strauss. His argument is based in part on the lack of Lutheran schools in the small villages. Most of the children could not even recite the Ten Commandments.[33] Strauss concludes: "A century of Protestantism had brought little or no change in the common religious conduct and in the ways in which ordinary men and women conducted their lives. Given people's nebulous grasp of the substance of their faith, no meaningful distinction could have existed between Protestants and Catholics."[34]

Strauss's conclusions have been the subject of significant criticism.[35] Geoffrey Parker points out that the use of Visitation Records as the sole source of evidence of the success or failure of the Lutheran educational system is by itself insufficient to come to any final conclusions. First, the visitors were looking for areas that needed improvement, so it makes sense that they would focus on shortcomings rather than successes, and second, the records were inconclusive for urban areas where one would assume that the level of Protestant education had achieved a greater measure of success.[36]

Lewis Spitz argues that one has to expand the use of sources well beyond mere Visitation Records to come to any significant conclusions. He notes as well that the Visitation Records had the inherent weakness of looking for misbehavior. He also recommends the use

---

[32] Gerald Strauss, *Luther's House of Learning: Indoctrination of the Young in the German Reformation* (Baltimore: Johns Hopkins University Press, 1978), 299.

[33] Ibid., 298.

[34] Ibid., 299.

[35] A recent M.A. thesis by Anna Lynch includes a very helpful survey of the literature on Strauss's arguments. See Anna Lynch, "Early Lutheran Education in the Late Reformation in Mecklenburg" (M.A. Thesis, University of Iowa, 2013).

[36] Geoffrey Parker, "Success and Failure During the First Century of the Reformation," *Past & Present*, no. 136 (1992): 43–82.

of other sources such as well-worn copies of devotional literature used in the home. If one could show that families actually used such material, it would go a long way to disproving Strauss' claims. One could also add personal diaries, wills, marriage and estate records to the list, which could indicate a higher level of personal piety among the laity.[37]

Strauss' study also provides important fodder for further study of the impact of the Reformation in rural parishes. C. Scott Dixon, for example, examines the impact of the Reformation in the German margravate of Brandenberg-Ansbach-Kulmbach. He notes that the Reformation made slow inroads into the rural parishes where the majority of the people lived and he points to a significant level of resistance to the new beliefs. In contrast to the cities, in rural areas the teachers were relatively poor on quality and attendance at school was, at best, uneven.[38]

James Kittleson uses the same type of sources as Strauss in his study of the Reformation in Strasbourg, but he comes to a different conclusion. He agrees with Strauss that education was at the core of the Reformation, but his use of the Visitation Records show, in his view, that the people of Strasbourg did experience a significant change in their lives as a result of Lutheran teaching.[39]

CONCLUSION

The debate over the relative effectiveness of the Lutheran educational reforms spearheaded by Melanchthon reflects the age-old problem of the difference between belief and behavior, especially in a state-church environment. One can enforce confessional compliance, but that does not always translate into devotional habit. The Pietist Movement that followed the Lutheran Age of Orthodoxy reflects the need for an emphasis on the practical aspects of the faith. The pendulum has swung back and forth ever since between theological orthodoxy and a living, personal faith. Melanchthon showed that both are needed.

---

[37] Lewis W. Spitz, "Review: Luther's House of Learning: Indoctrination of the Young in the German Reformation by Gerald Strauss," *The American Historical Review* 85, no. 1 (February 1, 1980): 143.

[38] C. Scott Dixon, *The Reformation and Rural Society: The Parishes of Brandenburg-Ansbach-Kulmbach, 1528-1603* (Cambridge: Cambridge University Press, 1996).

[39] James Kittelson, "Successes and Failures in the German Reformation: The Report from Strasbourg," *Archif für Reformationgeschiichte*, 73 (1982): 153-75.

PRIMARY SOURCE SAMPLE[40]

I embrace the science known as philosophy of nature, the reasons and examples of customs. With this, if he is properly endowed, one builds his way to the top. He will take up causes from which he builds up an abundance of topics and ample oratory, he will administer the state, where he will seek formulas for equality, goodness and justice. Doubtless this usefulness of philosophy was seen by that most famous orator Demosthenes, and why he so correctly commanded each young man: But think! Read the rest in the Eroticus yourself. Marcus Cicero never failed to give the first prize to philosophy; and I think you have heard, from the conversation of the lawyers Servius Sulpicius and Quintus Scaevola, that the Romans called someone sophos when they admired his rich knowledge of philosophical things.

In what truly pertains to the sacred, consider particularly how it refers to the spirit. For if, as a class of studies, the sacred things are the most powerful for the mind, work and care are necessary. For the odor of the ointments of the Lord is far sweeter than the aromas of the human disciplines: with the spirit as leader, and the cult of our arts as ally, we may approach the holy. Just as Synesius writes to Herculianus: when it is healthy, in good spirits, and well-practiced, philosophy is admirably used in the pursuit of the divine.

BIBLIOGRAPHY

Dixon, C. Scott. *The Reformation and Rural Society: The Parishes of Brandenburg-Ansbach-Kulmbach, 1528-1603.* Cambridge: Cambridge University Press, 1996.

Frank, Eric. "Philip Melanchthon: Scholar and Reformer" *WRS Journal* (August, 1996): 36-41.

Karant-Nunn, Susan. *Luther's Pastors: The Reformation in the Ernestine Countryside.* Philadelphia: Amer Philosophical Society, 1979.

Keen, Ralph, ed. *A Melanchthon Reader.* New York: Peter Lang, 1988.

Kittelson, James. "Successes and Failures in the German Reformation: The Report from Strasbourg" *Archif für Reformationgeschiichte*, 73 (1982): 153-75.

Kolb, Robert. "The Pastoral Dimension of Melanchthon's Pedagogical Activities for the Education of Pastors," in *Philip Melanchthon: Theologian in Classroom, Confession, and Controversy*, eds. Irene Dingel, Robert Kolb, Nicole Kuropka, and Timothy J. Wengert. Göttingen: Vandenhoeck & Ruprecht, 2012: 29-42.

_____. "Pastoral Education in the Wittenberg Way" in *Church and School in Early Modern Protestantism: Studies in Honor of Richard A. Muller on the Maturation of a Theological Tradition*, eds. Jordan J. Ballor, David S. Systma, and Jason Zuidema. Leiden: Brill, 2013: 67-79.

Kristeller, Paul Oskar. *Renaissance Thought: The Classic, Scholastic and Humanist Strains.* New York: Harper & Row, 1955.

---

[40] From Philip Melanchthon, "On Correcting the Studies of Youth" (1518), in *A Melanchthon Reader*, ed. Ralph Keen (New York: Peter Lang, 1998), 54-55.

Kuropka, Nicole. "Philip Melanchthon and Aristotle" in *Philip Melanchthon: Theologian in Classroom Confession, and Controversy*, eds. Irene Dingel, Robert Kolb, Nicole Kuropka, and Timothy J. Wengert. Göttingen: Vandenhoeck & Ruprecht, 2012: 19-28.

Lynch, Anna. "Early Lutheran Education in the Late Reformation in Mecklenburg." M.A. Thesis, University of Iowa, 2013.

Manschreck, Clyde, L. "The Bible in Melanchthon's Philosophy of Education" *The Journal of Bible and Religion*, Vol. 23, No. 3 (July, 1955): 202-207.

_____. *Melanchthon, the Quiet Reformer*. New York: Abingdon Press, 1958.

Melanchthon, Philip. *Corpus Reformatorum: Philippi Melanthonis opera quae supersunt omnia*, ed. Karl Bretschneider and Heinrich Bindseil, 28 vols. Halle: Schwetschke, 1834-1860, vols. 1-28.

_____. *Orations on Philosophy and Education*, ed. Sachiko Kusukawa. Cambridge: Cambridge University Press, 1999.

Park, Joon-Chul "Philip Melanchthon's Reform of German Universities and its Significance: A Study on the Relationship between Renaissance Humanism and the Reformation." PhD diss., Ohio State University, 1995.

Parker, Geoffrey. "Success and Failure During the First Century of the Reformation," *Past & Present*, no. 136 (1992): 43–82.

Pauck, Wilhelm. *From Luther to Tillich: The Reformers and Their Heirs*. New York: Harper Collins, 1985.

Richard, James William. *Philip Melanchthon, the Protestant Preceptor of Germany* London: G. P. Putnam's Sons, 1898.

Spitz, Lewis W. "Review: Luther's House of Learning: Indoctrination of the Young in the German Reformation by Gerald Strauss," *The American Historical Review* 85, no. 1 (February 1, 1980): 143.

Strauss, Gerald. *Luther's House of Learning: Indoctrination of the Young in the German Reformation*. Baltimore: Johns Hopkins University Press, 1978.

Wengert, Timothy J. "The Biblical Commentaries of Philip Melanchthon," in *Philip Melanchthon: Theologian in Classroom, Confession, and Controversy*, eds. Irene Dingel, Robert Kolb, Nicole Kuropka, and Timothy J. Wengert. Göttingen: Vandenhoeck & Ruprecht, 2012: 43-76.

_____. *Human Freedom, Christian Righteousness: Philip Melanchthon's Exegetical Dispute with Erasmus of Rotterdam*. Oxford: Oxford University Press, 1998.

_____. "Philip Melanchthon and Wittenberg's Reform of the Theological Curriculum" in *Church and School in Early Modern Protestantism: Studies in Honor of Richard A. Muller on the Maturation of a Theological Tradition*, eds. Jordan J. Ballor, David S. Systma, and Jason Zuidema. Leiden: Brill, 2013: 17-48.

CHAPTER 11

John Calvin:

Teacher in the School of Christ

DUSTIN BRUCE

TIMOTHY PAUL JONES

MICHAEL WILDER

John Calvin (1509-1564)

John Calvin's impact in the realm of theology would be difficult to overestimate — but his impact extended far beyond theology. A frequently overlooked aspect of his impact has been in the field of Christian education. For Calvin, learning played a central role in the life of the church; this centrality was evidenced through one of his favorite metaphors for the church, the *schola Christi* or "school of Christ." In this school, Scripture serves as the primary textbook. God's people enter as pupils into the school of Christ, in which all are encouraged to read Scripture privately and to hear Scripture expounded corporately. The pursuit of this ideal required Calvin to function not only as a theological reformer but also as an educational reformer.

HISTORICAL BACKGROUND

Born Jean Cauvin (1509–1564) to a middle-class family in Noyon, Picardy, Calvin received education through his father's efforts to secure aristocratic patronage.[1] Around the age of eleven or twelve, Calvin was sent to Paris to attend *Collége de la Marche*, a preparatory school that housed the preeminent humanist scholar, Mathurin Cordier (1479–1564).[2] Cordier emphasized the importance of learning to read and write proficiently out of concern for his students' spiritual well being. Calvin understood his time at *de la Marche* to have been foundational for his mastery of Latin, eventually dedicating his First Thessalonians commentary to Cordier.[3]

Desirous of a more conservative and pious education, Calvin soon transferred to *Collége de Montaigu*, a monastery school designed to prepare young men for the priesthood.[4] At *de Montaigu*, Calvin studied with the faculty of the arts, which prepared young men for further study by focusing on foundational disciplines of rhetoric, logic, culture, languages, and nature.[5] Known as a place that combined rigorous academics with an austere lifestyle, the students of *de Montaigu* rose at four to begin a hard day of study, punctuated by times for prayer and simple meals — a schedule Calvin would maintain throughout his life.[6]

At his father's insistence, Calvin transferred from Paris to the University of Orléans near the end of 1527 or the beginning of 1528. While Paris had a fine school for an aspiring priest, Orléans boasted a renowned program in civil law. At Orléans, Calvin studied under the greatest French lawyer of his age, Pierre de l'Estoile. Despite the quality of teaching at Orléans, Calvin transferred to Bourges around May of 1529.[7] Under the protection of the sister of King

---

[1] Bruce Gordon, *Calvin* (New Haven: Yale University Press, 2009), 5.

[2] Cordier, along with Calvin, was associated with a movement known as Renaissance Humanism. This movement, which helped pave the way for the Reformation, insisted on the worth of humankind in light of being created in the image of God, as well as the importance of human creativity. Scholars involved in Renaissance Humanism promoted the liberal arts as a course of study, as well as a return to the study of classical Greek and Roman sources. Desiderius Erasmus was the most influential humanist scholar in Calvin's day. The philological tools that proved helpful for the study of ancient literature, likewise proved helpful for studying the Scriptures.

[3] Herman J. Selderhuis, *John Calvin: A Pilgrim's Life*, trans. Albert Gootjes (Downers Grove, IL: IVP Academic, 2009), 12–13.

[4] Burk Parsons, ed., *John Calvin: A Heart for Devotion, Doctrine, and Doxology* (Lake Mary, FL: Reformation Trust, 2008), 20.

[5] Selderhuis, *John Calvin: A Pilgrim's Life*, 14.

[6] Gordon, *Calvin*, 7–8.

[7] Selderhuis, *John Calvin: A Pilgrim's Life*, 15.

Francis I of France, Bourges served as "a sort of center for reform-minded critics."[8] Here, Calvin studied under an Italian lawyer, Andrea Alciati. De l'Estoile in Orléans and Alciati in Bourges represented two approaches to the humanism that so greatly influenced Calvin. De l'Estoile embraced a humanist methodology "wedded to the medieval tradition of legal commentary."[9] In this method, the French lawyer organized material topically, with little attention being paid to historical development.[10] Alciati, on the other hand, advocated an interpretation of the same body of Roman law by examining the words and phrases "stylistically (rhetorically) and with regard to particular circumstances (historically) in order to discern particular meanings."[11] While Calvin preferred de l'Estoile as a person and teacher, his mature hermeneutic would share greater similarities with Alciati's method.

Calvin returned to Orléans in October 1530 to finish his education, receiving his bachelor's in law in February 1531. The recent graduate then planned a trip to Paris in order to secure a publisher for his first book, a commentary on Seneca's classic work *De Clementia*.[12] While detouring through Noyon, Calvin found his father gravely ill. Upon his father's death in May 1531, Calvin was free to abandon law for the study of theology. He soon set out for a new place of learning, the *Collége Royal*.

Established and protected by King Francis I, the *Collége Royal* served as an important hub of humanist learning. Keen interest in the study of the Hebrew, Greek, and Latin languages promoted an atmosphere conducive to reformation.[13] "Calvin was surrounded there by scholars who wanted to work, learn, and teach from original sources, including the Bible, which was exactly in line with his own interests."[14] Calvin's growing humanist interest led him to publish his first book in 1532, not on Scripture, but a critical edition with commentary of Seneca's *De Clementia*. The work never found the success for which Calvin had hoped. Still, the work was impressive for a young man of twenty-three and proved something of a forerunner to the extensive literary labors that were to come.

---

[8] Ibid.

[9] Gordon, *Calvin,* 20.

[10] Ibid.

[11] Ibid.

[12] Selderhuis, *John Calvin: A Pilgrim's Life,* 17.

[13] Ibid.

[14] Ibid.

CONVERSION

Calvin's interest would soon shift from pagan classics to Holy Scripture, when, in 1533, the young scholar underwent a "sudden conversion."[15] Previously devoted to the Roman Catholicism in which he was raised, Calvin testifies, "God by a sudden conversion subdued and brought my mind to a teachable frame … Having thus received some taste and knowledge of true godliness I was immediately inflamed with so intense a desire to make progress therein, that although I did not leave off other studies, I yet pursued them with less ardour."[16]

Calvin's conversion was not only spiritual in nature; it meant a radical shift in allegiances as well.[17] The writings of Martin Luther had proven instrumental in Calvin's conversion.[18] While Calvin was not content for Luther to remain the dominant influence of the Protestant movement, he did recognize Luther as his father in the faith and as a key catalyst in the movement for reform.[19]

MINISTRY

Calvin's early educational path and interests prepared him well for a life of theological, ecclesiological, and educational reform. Calvin participated "in two distinct but related movements of restoration in the sixteenth century: the restoration of arts and letters by the recovering of classical literature, and the restoration of the church by the recovery of the genuine meaning of Scripture."[20] The two, however, were not unrelated. "Calvin used the gifts of teaching and interpretation developed as a student of classical texts to restore both the doctrine and genuine interpretation of Scripture to the teachers, pastors, and ordinary

---

[15] Some scholarly debate exists as to the actual date of Calvin's conversion, with guesses ranging from 1527 to 1534. Bruce Gordon argues convincingly for 1533 in his masterful biography. What is clear is that 1533 marked a significant shift in Calvin's interest, ambition, and trajectory. Gordon, *Calvin*, 33.

[16] Guilielmus Baum, Eduardus Cunitz, and Eduardus Reuss, eds., *Ioannis Calvini Opera Quae Supersunt Omnia* (Brunsvigae: C. A. Schwetschke, 1863), 31:13–35. Quoted in Gordon, Calvin, 33.

[17] Alister E. McGrath, *A Life of John Calvin: A Study in the Shaping of Western Culture* (Oxford, UK: Wiley-Blackwell, 1993), 70.

[18] John Calvin, "Calvin to Martin Luther, January 21, 1545," in *The Letters of John Calvin*, trans. Jules Bonnet, vol. 1, 4 vols. (New York: Burt Franklin, 1972), 440.

[19] Randall Zachman, "John Calvin," in *The Reformation Theologians: An Introduction to Theology in the Early Modern Period*, ed. Carter Lindberg (Oxford, UK ; Malden, Mass: Wiley-Blackwell, 2001), 185–87.

[20] Ibid., 184.

Christians."[21] First in Basel, then more famously Geneva, Calvin would seek to realize this theological project.

On All Saints Day in 1533, Calvin's friend, Nicholas Cop, delivered a mildly evangelical convocation address, much to the dismay of the Roman Catholic authorities. Since Cop was not a theologian by training, Calvin was soon implicated as the man behind the speech and forced to flee Paris.[22] By 1534, Calvin was on his way to Basel, which had already broken from Rome. In Basel, Calvin vigorously studied the languages, attempting to pursue the quiet life of a scholar. Though seeking to avoid controversy with the Roman Catholic Church, even using a pseudonym, Calvin soon found himself engaging in the preaching and teaching that would mark his career.[23] In 1535, Calvin was publishing again, this time penning the preface to Robert Olivétan's French translation of the New Testament. In the same year, Calvin penned a simple prototype of what would become his most famous work, *Institutes of the Christian Religion*. The *Institutes*, intended to provide an overview of biblical doctrine for French Protestants, would increase in size and depth through many revisions, just as Calvin's importance and popularity as a Reformer would.

Though Calvin's first version of the *Institutes* proved wildly successful, Calvin was not well-known in Basel. In 1536, while traveling on family business, Calvin was forced to spend a night in Geneva, a city only recently led to embrace Protestant ideals by Guillaume Farel. Hearing of Calvin's presence, Farel tracked the Frenchman down and bursting into his room, appealed for Calvin to remain in Geneva to lead reforms.[24] Calvin attempted to rebuff the fiery Reformer by sharing his desire for a life of scholarship. In response, Farel thundered down a curse upon Calvin's head if the gifted young theologian refused the difficult work of reform. Calvin, much to his surprise, had been apprehended for the cause of the Genevan reformation.

Calvin, the reluctant prophet, accepted the call to become a teacher and then a preacher in the newly reformed church in Geneva. With little training for the public ministry, Calvin learned the work of the pastor from Farel and Pierre Viret.[25] During his first tenure in the Swiss city, Calvin saw his first catechism and a statement of faith adopted, but problems over the discipline of the church led to his removal after less than two years.

After being expelled, along with Farel, from Geneva in 1538, Calvin took refuge in the city of Strasbourg, the home of Martin Bucer. During his three-year stay in Strasbourg, Calvin

---

[21] Ibid.

[22] Timothy George, "Glory Unto God: John Calvin," in *Theology of the Reformers*, Rev. (Nashville: B & H Academic, 2013), 183.

[23] Selderhuis, *John Calvin: A Pilgrim's Life*, 44.

[24] Gordon, *Calvin*, 64.

[25] Zachman, "John Calvin," 86.

subjected himself to the authority and tutelage of Bucer, who Calvin referred to as a father in the ministry.[26] Timothy George refers to this period as the happiest period of Calvin's life and also the most important for his "development as a reformer and a theologian."[27] Echoing this sentiment, Selderhuis explains, "It was in Strasbourg that Calvin was born...as a theologian and a church leader."[28] Five developments mark Calvin's Strausburg ministry:[29]

(1) Calvin served as a pastor of a French-speaking congregation.

(2) Calvin developed as a teacher, serving as "lecturer in Holy Scripture" at the Strausburg Academy, which had been established by Johannes Sturm.

(3) He developed as a writer, publishing the 1539 edition of the *Institutes*, which was three times larger than the previous edition.

(4) He served as a church statesman, attempting to mend the schism between the Protestants of Switzerland and Germany.

(5) Calvin married Idelette de Bure, the French-speaking widow of an Anabaptist. In Strasbourg, Calvin had made a life. When Geneva beckoned him to return, he was understandably hesitant.

Despite great reservation, on September 13, 1541, Calvin returned to Geneva. Calvin proposed several reforms, but he made no fuss regarding his treatment three years prior. On his first Sunday, Calvin described the situation,

> When I went to preach again for the first time, there was not a soul that did not sit up straight, full of curiosity. However, I completely passed over everything that had happened and that they surely were curious to hear about, and devoted a few words to explaining the essence of my ministry. Thereafter I gave a short testimony of my faith and the sincerity of my intentions. Then I chose to expound the passage to which I had come before my banishment. In this way I hoped to show that I had not put down my teaching office, but had only interrupted it for a while.[30]

Calvin chose to forego lambasting his now defeated opponents in order to focus on the Word of God preached. Such was the tenor of Calvin's ministry in Geneva. Soon after his arrival, the consistory of Geneva began to meet, finalizing the struggle over the discipline of the church. The consistory would exercise church discipline and the organization of the various

[26] Ibid., 187.
[27] George, "Glory Unto God: John Calvin," 188.
[28] Selderhuis, *John Calvin: A Pilgrim's Life*, 86.
[29] The five categories are taken from George. George, "Glory Unto God: John Calvin," 188–90.
[30] Quoted in Selderhuis, *John Calvin: A Pilgrim's Life*, 118.

church offices. As such, it was a key component for Calvin's "school of Christ." On Christmas Day 1559, Calvin was granted Genevan citizenship. Five years later, on May 27, 1564, Calvin died. The next day, a Sunday, this teacher in the "school of Christ" was buried in an unknown grave, desiring no adulation after his death.

THEOLOGY OF CHRISTIAN EDUCATION

For Calvin, Christian education had entered a time of crisis during the pre-Reformation era.[31] Much of the pastoral leadership of the Medieval Roman Church lacked both the skill and desire to interpret or to teach the Bible effectively. Calvin describes it this way, "Those who were regarded as the leaders of the faith neither understood thy Word, nor greatly cared for it. They drove unhappy people to and fro with strange doctrines, and deluded them with I know not what follies."[32] Calvin responded by centralizing Scripture in the life of the church, emphasizing the teaching of the Word of God as the foundation of theological education.

THEOLOGICAL HERMENEUTIC

In order to better understand Calvin's approach to theological education, it is helpful to grasp his unending resolve that God has made Himself known — both through creation itself and through His word. Calvin believed that it was imperative that those who are redeemed study God's word diligently that they may know Him and His ways more deeply.

The Knowledge of God

The knowledge of God and of humanity forms a crucial thread throughout Calvin's theology.[33] The *Institutes* begin with the famous words, "Nearly all the wisdom we possess, that is to say true and sound wisdom, consists of two parts: the knowledge of God and of ourselves."[34] These are not two distinct types of knowledge, but they function together, so that to gain one is necessarily to gain the other. Paul Helm comments, "Calvin's point is that the

---

[31] Zachman points out that both Protestants and many Roman Catholics felt the ministry of the church to be in crisis. Zachman, *John Calvin as Teacher, Pastor, and Theologian*, 11.

[32] John Calvin and Jacob Sadoleto, *A Reformation Debate: Sadoleto's Letter to the Genevans and Calvin's Reply*, ed. John C. Olin (Grand Rapids: Baker, 1976), 82.

[33] Eberhard Busch, "God and Humanity," in *The Calvin Handbook*, ed. Herman J. Selderhuis, trans. Judith J. Guder (Grand Rapids: Eerdmans, 2009), 224.

[34] John Calvin, *Institutes of the Christian Religion*, ed. John T. McNeil, trans. Ford Lewis Battles (Philadelphia: Westminster Press, 1960), 1.1.1.

knowledge of God and of ourselves are *immediately reciprocal.*"[35] Anthropology, for Calvin, "has no independent status."[36]

God's revelation is twofold. "First," Calvin stated, "as much in the fashioning of the universe as in the general teaching of Scripture the Lord shows himself to be simply the Creator. Then in the face of Christ he shows himself the Redeemer." God has, from the beginning, revealed himself as Creator. By emphasizing knowledge, Calvin highlighted God as revealer. Unable to penetrate into the "being" or "essence" of God, man stands desperate for God to reveal himself. "Calvin's thought has its whole existence within the realm of God as revealer and man as knower."[37]

God graciously chooses to reveal himself, but man is by nature a knower. Calvin stated, "There is within the human mind, and indeed by natural instinct, an awareness of divinity [*sensus divinitatis*]."[38] This serves to leave men without excuse before God. Calvin continued on, "To prevent anyone from taking refuge in the pretense of ignorance, God himself has implanted in all men a certain understanding of divine majesty."[39] While some claim to not believe in God, even they "from time to time feel an inkling of what they desire not to believe."[40] Calvin emphasized, "Men of sound judgment will always be sure that a sense of divinity which can never be effaced is engraved upon men's minds."[41]

If humanity possesses within itself a sense of divinity, why do men fail to perceive God rightly and respond accordingly?[42] Calvin elaborated on the problem, "While some may evaporate in their own superstitions and others deliberately and wickedly desert God, yet all degenerate from the true knowledge of him." He concluded, "And so it happens that no real piety remains in the world."[43]

Despite the testimony provided by creation, humanity is ultimately unwilling to

---

[35] Paul Helm, *Calvin: A Guide for the Perplexed* (New York: T & T Clark, 2008), 24. Emphasis original.

[36] T.F. Torrance, *Calvin's Doctrine of Man* (Westport, CT: Greenwood Press, 1957), 13.

[37] Edward A. Dowey, *The Knowledge of God in Calvin's Theology*, 3rd. ed. (Grand Rapids: Eerdmans, 1994), 3.

[38] Calvin, *Institutes of the Christian Religion*, 1.3.1.

[39] Ibid.

[40] Ibid., 1.3.2.

[41] Ibid., 1.3.3.

[42] For a helpful discussion of Calvin's anthropology in relation to this discussion, see Timothy Paul Jones, "John Calvin and the Problem of Philosophical Apologetics," *Perspectives in Religious Studies* 23 (Winter 1996).

[43] Ibid., 1.4.1.

receive any productive knowledge regarding God. Due to the Fall, humanity is no longer willing to desire, to receive, or to believe God's truth.[44] Calvin lamented, "It is in vain that so many burning lamps shine for us in the workmanship of the universe to show forth the glory of its Author. Although they bathe us wholly in their radiance, yet they can of no way lead us into the right path. Surely they strike some sparks, but before their fuller lights shine forth these are smothered."[45]

In a fallen world, the revelation of God in creation leaves humanity without excuse. The problem is, however, with humanity not creation. Calvin commented, "But although we lack the natural ability to mount up unto the pure and clear knowledge of God, all excuse is cut off because the fault of dullness is within us."[46] The knowledge of God in creation, then, functions similar to the first use of the law in exposing idolatry and showing a need for redemption.[47] From the testimony of creation, any self-knowledge one gains is of the humbling variety, which exposes deficiencies and weakness and leaves one desperate for God. For Calvin, the two-fold knowledge of God and self leaves humanity humbled and God glorified.

A Theology of the Word of God

Calvin's theology has been described as "a theology of the Word of God."[48] For Calvin, Scripture presents God's unified testimony concerning himself. Humanity gains a reliable knowledge of the Creator exclusively through God's special revelation found in the Bible. Though God reveals himself through the natural world, the fallen nature of humanity prevents correct interpretation and leaves humanity dependent on God's Word as found in the Bible.

For Calvin, Scripture must be accepted as the Word of God for it to have any spiritual benefit. Inherent to Scripture's divine quality is its self-authenticating quality. External proofs of Scripture's reliability may be useful, but ultimately do not bring about belief in Scripture.[49] The same Spirit, who carried inspired human beings along to write the Scripture, convinces his chosen children of its divine nature.[50]

---

[44] Michael Horton, *Calvin on the Christian Life, Theologians of the Christian Life* (Wheaton, IL: Crossway, 2014), 50.

[45] Calvin, *Institutes of the Christian Religion*, 1.5.14.

[46] Ibid., 1.5.15.

[47] Horton, *Calvin on the Christian Life*, 51.

[48] R. S. Wallace, "Calvin, John," *New Dictionary of Theology* (Downers Grove, IL: InterVarsity Press, 1988), 121. Wallace presents a concise, but helpful summary of Calvin's theology.

[49] Calvin, Institutes of the Christian Religion, 1.7.4.

[50] Ibid.

Because Christ is the source of all revelations, both the New and Old Testament "comes from Christ, is mediated through him, and at the same time points to Christ in all its parts."[51] Drawing from Pauline texts, Calvin emphasizes that Christ is both the "goal" and the "soul" of the law.[52] It is through right interpretation of Scripture that hearers can know Christ and his benefits.[53]

HERMENEUTICAL INFLUENCES ON THEOLOGY AND PRACTICE

Calvin's emphasis on the Word of God as the primary textbook in the school of Christ worked itself out in a number of ways related to education both within the local church and more broadly. Calvin's Protestantism emphasized the need to distribute biblical truths through the means of preaching, writing, and reading.[54] The central role of Scripture demanded a literate laity able to study the Bible and access help in the form of commentaries and other works, such as his *Institutes*. Contrary to the Roman Catholic Church, Calvin envisioned a future where the godly of all classes and ages possessed the ability to read the very words of God in their own language.

Calvin the teacher cannot be understood apart from his all-encompassing desire to make the actual words of Scripture accessible to and understood by all people. "From the very beginning of his adherence to the evangelical movement, Calvin above all else sought to restore the proper and fruitful reading of Scripture to every Christian, no matter how unlearned that person might be."[55] Part of Calvin's aspiration involved making the Bible available to all through translating and producing copies of God's Word into the common languages. This, of course, required a literate laity. To have all the people of God growing in their knowledge of God's word was no less than prophetic fulfillment. Calvin claimed, "When, therefore, we see that there are people from all classes making progress in God's school, we acknowledge his truth which promised a pouring forth of his Spirit on all flesh [Joel 2:28; Acts 2:17]."[56]

---

[51] Peter Optiz, "Scripture," in *The Calvin Handbook*, ed. Herman J. Selderhuis, trans. Rebecca A. Giselbrecht (Grand Rapids: Eerdmans, 2009), 242.

[52] Ibid., 243.

[53] R. Ward Holder, *John Calvin and the Grounding of Interpretation: Calvin's First Commentaries, Studies in the History of Christian Traditions* 127 (Leiden and Boston: Brill, 2006), 139.

[54] Gerald L. Gutek, *Historical and Philosophical Foundations of Education: A Biographical Introduction*, 5th ed. (New York: Pearson, 2011), 119.

[55] Zachman, *John Calvin as Teacher, Pastor, and Theologian*, 56.

[56] Jean Calvin, *Institutes of the Christian Religion, trans. Ford Lewis Battles*, 1536 ed. (Grand Rapids:

Calvin understood that making the Bible available was not sufficient. God's people would also need the church with her trained teachers for guidance in reading and understanding Scripture. If "faith comes from hearing, and hearing through the word of Christ" (Rom 10:17 ESV), then the language of the preacher must be the language of Scripture concerning Christ.[57] The pastor teaches doctrine drawn from Scripture, while the laity reads the Bible for themselves, confirming the pastor's faithfulness. The "school of Christ," then, was to be a community of preaching and teaching.[58] Whereas the Roman Church had removed the Scripture from the people, Calvin sought to build a community sustained by the Word of God.[59] This commitment required Calvin to undertake a comprehensive theological and educational project, complete with publications of various sorts, a particular ecclesiological structure, and educational reforms to establish a literate society.

CONTRIBUTION TO EDUCATION
AND CHRISTIAN EDUCATION

Had it been up to Calvin, his primary contribution to Christian education would have been as a secluded author, spending long hours churning out theological treatises. However, Calvin's future did not rest solely in his own hands. Late in life, Calvin would pontificate, "whilst my one great object was to live in seclusion without being known, God so led me about through different turnings and changes, that he never permitted me to rest in any place, until, in spite of my natural disposition, he brought me forth to public notice."[60] Led into a position of public prominence, Calvin used it to not only advance his theological beliefs, but also influence other important aspects of society, such as government, and education.[61]

ROLE OF THE TEACHER

Since the church exists as the school of Christ for Calvin, it must be filled with instructors who stand as godly interpreters of the Scripture. Upon returning to Geneva, Calvin worked with the elders and magistrates to draft the *Ecclesiastical Ordinances*, which not only established the relationship between church and state, but also outlined four offices within

---

Eerdmans, 1975), 374.

[57] Zachman, *John Calvin as Teacher, Pastor, and Theologian*, 192.

[58] Ibid.

[59] Gordon, Calvin, 276.

[60] John Calvin, *Commentary on the Psalms*, trans. Anderson, James, Calvin Translation Society Edition., Calvin's Commentaries (Grand Rapids: Baker, 1979), xli.

[61] Michael J. Anthony and Warren S. Benson, *Exploring the History and Philosophy of Christian Education: Principles for the 21st Century* (Grand Rapids: Kregel, 2003), 210.

the church – pastor, doctor, elder, deacon.[62] The first two of the offices involved teaching and Calvin understood himself as called to both.[63]

Pastor

Pastors, also referred to as elders and ministers, are charged to "proclaim the Word of God, to instruct, admonish, exhort, and censure, both in public and private, ... "[64] The aim of the pastor was the instruction of ordinary Christians within a local congregation, most of whom had no knowledge of the original languages of Scripture, if literate at all.[65] Calvin served as a pastor himself for twenty-seven years, leading J.D. Benoit to claim, "Though he may be first thought of as a theologian, he was even more a pastor of souls."[66]

The primary task of the pastor was preaching, a priority which resulted in the restructuring of parish life and the development of other aspects of Calvin's educational infrastructure.[67] As Bernard Cottret notes, "For Calvin, therefore, preaching was not just one literary genre among others; it was the very essence of the Reformation."[68] As a pastor in the school of Christ, the text of Scripture provided the content for the sermon. Calvin writes, "A rule is prescribed to all God's servants that they bring not their own inventions, but simply deliver, as from hand to hand, what they have received from God."[69]

As a pastor, Calvin provided an inimitable example with his preaching schedule. Theodore Beza notes, "Besides preaching every day from week to week, usually and as often as

---

[62] David L. Puckett, "John Calvin as Teacher," *Southern Baptist Journal of Theology* 13, no. 4 (Winter 2009): 45. John Calvin, *Calvin: Theological Treatises*, ed. J. K. Reid (Philadelphia: Westminster, 1954), 69.

[63] Zachman, *John Calvin as Teacher, Pastor, and Theologian*, 13.

[64] Calvin, *Calvin*, 58.

[65] Zachman, *John Calvin as Teacher, Pastor, and Theologian*, 13.

[66] J.D. Benoit, "Pastoral Care of the Prophet," in *John Calvin: Contemporary Prophet*, ed. Jacob T. Hoogstra (Grand Rapids: Baker, 1959).

[67] Scott M. Manetsch, *Calvin's Company of Pastors: Pastoral Care and the Emerging Reformed Church*, 1536-1609 (New York: Oxford University Press, 2013), 148.

[68] Bernard Cottret, *Calvin: A Biography, trans. M. Wallace McDonald* (Grand Rapids: Eerdmans, 2000), 295.

[69] John Calvin, *Commentaries on the Book of the Prophet Jeremiah and Lamentations*, trans. John Owen, vol. 1 (Grand Rapids: Baker, 1979), 43.

he could he preached twice every Sunday."[70] Calvin, however, understood himself as fulfilling another function besides that of pastor.

Doctor

The office of doctor, or teacher, was aimed at the education of future pastors of the church, both locally and throughout Christendom. The doctor was to focus on teaching without concerning himself with the duties associated with pastoring a local congregation. This office sought to ensure that pure doctrine was being taught in the churches. The *Ecclesiastical Ordinances* set forth, The office proper to doctors is the instruction of the faithful in true doctrine in order that the purity of the gospel be not corrupted either by ignorance or by evil opinions. As things are disposed today, we always include under this title aids and instructions for maintaining the doctrine of God and defending the Church from injury by the fault of pastors and ministers.[71]

The office was referred to in the *Ecclesiastical Ordinances* as the "order of the schools," with the stated purpose of training future pastors.[72] It was suggested to maintain at least two doctors: one to lecture in Old Testament and another for the New Testament. This would provide pastoral candidates with the requisite training for preaching the whole counsel of God.

Calvin understood the office of doctor as essential for the health of the church as a whole. Zachman explains the relationship of doctors to pastors as a move from the universal to the particular. "Doctors teach the doctrines of piety and the true understanding of Scripture to the universal church and its pastors," he explains. Afterwards, "pastors preach such doctrine, and interpret Scripture, both in general to the whole congregation and in particular to each individual therein."[73] Though Calvin filled both offices, it was his work as doctor that has proved influential far beyond his lifetime.[74]

Learner

For Calvin, all who belong to the church sit as pupils in the school of Christ with the Word of God as their primary textbook. This has profound implications for the Christian

---

[70] This was amid the duties associated with his office of teacher. Beza continues, "he lectured three times a week on theology; he gave remonstrances in the consistory, and delivered as it were an entire lesson every Friday in the conference on Scripture that we call a congregation, . . ." Theodore Beza, *L'historie de La Vie et Mort de Calvin* (1565), vol. 21, Ioannis Calvini Opera quae supersunt omnia (Brunswick and Berlin: Braunschweig, 1863), col. 33., quoted in Cottret, Calvin, 289.

[71] Calvin, *Calvin*, 62.

[72] Puckett, "John Calvin as Teacher," 46.

[73] Zachman, *John Calvin as Teacher, Pastor, and Theologian*, 62–63.

[74] Puckett, "John Calvin as Teacher," 46.

as learner and would largely determine Calvin's educational program. The ideal church is comprised of godly interpreters who encourage one another in their pursuit of the knowledge of God, which results in genuine transformation.

Calvin's vision demands, not only a learned clergy, but a literate laity as well. Zachman comments on Calvin's goal, "Calvin worked to create a church in which all Christians — teachers, pastors, and ordinary Christians — would be reading Scripture for themselves and would also be hearing and receiving instruction from others to guide their reading."[75] Thus, both pastor and layman continue to feed on the Word of God throughout their lives, even while instructing one another. Calvin's emphasis was on a community of learners, being formed by their increasing knowledge of Christ.[76]

CURRICULUM AND METHODS

For Calvin, the reform of education was just as necessary as the reform of religion. Only by renovating the educational system could the people overcome the religious and civic errors that Roman Catholicism had instilled. He understood Reformed Protestantism to be a pedagogical religion and sought to employ a variety of curriculum and methods to educate both the clergy and laity.[77]

THE INSTITUTES

Central to Calvin's educational program was his most famous work, *The Institutes of the Christian Religion*. First appearing in 1536, the *Institutes* went through eight Latin editions, appearing in its final form in 1559.[78] Calvin's pedagogical intention changed over time as the *Institutes* developed from edition to edition. The 1536 edition closely resembled a catechism, wherein Calvin sought to inform readers regarding true piety.[79] By the time Calvin released the second edition in 1539, the *Institutes* had expanded threefold. The 1539 edition retained the catechetical scheme, but shifted from an emphasis on piety to presenting biblical doctrine for theological students.[80] In Calvin's own words, the *Institutes* consisted of "a sum of religion in all its parts."[81]

---

[75] Zachman, *John Calvin as Teacher, Pastor, and Theologian*, 65.

[76] Holder, *John Calvin and the Grounding of Interpretation: Calvin's First Commentaries*, 173.

[77] Gutek, *Historical and Philosophical Foundations of Education*, 119.

[78] George, "Glory Unto God: John Calvin," 193.

[79] Wulfert De Greef, "Calvin's Writings," in *The Cambridge Companion to John Calvin*, ed. Donald K. McKim (New York and Cambridge: Cambridge University Press, 2004), 43.

[80] Ibid.

[81] Calvin, *Institutes of the Christian Religion*, 1:4.

The *Institutes*, as a "summary of Evangelical doctrine," necessitated brevity. For Calvin, brevity was a mark of clarity and effectiveness in teaching.[82] At the same time, he sought to be comprehensive by covering all topics contained within the Christian religion.[83] Finally, Calvin placed great importance on the order and method contained in the *Institutes*. Since the work was primarily a teaching tool for Protestant theology, Calvin began with the most agreed upon aspects of theology and moved to the more controversial. By organizing the material in this way, Calvin hoped to be more persuasive in his presentation of Reformation doctrine.[84]

Calvin's intention regarding the *Institutes* was never to replace Biblical exposition with a study of theology, but to provide a theological companion that would assist readers in their interpretation of Scripture. In the 1541 edition, Calvin encouraged "all who revere the word of the Lord to read this and impress it in their memory with diligence, if they want first to have a summary of Christian teaching and then an entry point to profit well in reading the Old as well as the New Testament."[85] Furthermore, the *Institutes* can be tied to no lectures, as Calvin did not lecture in theology, but engaged only in lectures regarding biblical exposition.

COMMENTARIES

Comparable only with Martin Luther as a Reformer, Calvin stands above all the men of his generation as a biblical exegete, for only his commentaries remain comparable to what is produced today.[86] Fulfilling the office of doctor, Calvin constantly delivered lectures to ministerial candidates by working exegetically through books of the Bible. The material from these lectures would be transcribed by students and edited by Calvin. As such, there stands a strong link between Calvin's teaching ministry as a doctor and his commentaries.[87] Calvin's first commentary, on the book of Romans, was published in 1540 while he served at Strasbourg. After establishing his ministry in Geneva, Calvin returned to the production of commentaries, publishing on nearly the entire New Testament and much of the Old Testament.

Calvin's commentaries were meant to work hand in hand with his *Institutes*. The

---

[82] Zachman, *John Calvin as Teacher, Pastor, and Theologian*, 87.

[83] Ibid.

[84] Ibid., 88.

[85] Jean Calvin, *Institutes of the Christian Religion: 1541 French Edition*, trans. Elsie Anne McKee (Grand Rapids: Eerdmans, 2009), 3–4.

[86] Gerald Bray, *Biblical Interpretation: Past & Present* (Downers Grove, IL: InterVarsity Press, 1996), 177.

[87] Puckett, "John Calvin as Teacher," 49.

commentaries would focus on the biblical text and avoid getting sidetracked by theological disputes and commonplaces, which would be handled in the *Institutes*.[88] In pursuit of his ideal of brevity, Calvin sought to treat the text thoroughly, but not exhaustively.[89] His commentaries reveal his commitment to understanding the Scripture according to its "natural sense" or derived grammatically in a straightforward and literal manner.[90] Alongside the *Institutes*, Calvin's commentaries served an important role in his program of theological education by transmitting his oral teaching on the proper interpretation of Scripture.

CATECHISM

In Reformed Geneva, Calvin saw a great need to supplement the religious training of parents with official instruction administered by the church.[91] Calvin understood the church to bear a particular "obligation for a program of religious education in order to inspire and guide children to lives of piety."[92] Out of concern that parents were ill equipped to teach the rudiments of the faith or would teach their former Roman Catholic beliefs, Calvin and his colleagues formed catechism classes in each of the Genevan churches.[93] Catechism as a method of instruction was so important to the Genevan Reformer, he made the use of his catechism one of two conditions for returning to Geneva the second time.[94]

According to the ecclesiastical ordinances, children were to attend classes at noon on Sunday in the parish in which the child lived. The classes were known as catechisms due to the particular method of instruction used. In a catechism, a pastor or other teacher asked a number of simple questions that have set answers to be memorized.[95] For Calvin, catechisms functioned

---

[88] Richard A. Muller, *The Unaccommodated Calvin: Studies in the Foundation of a Theological Tradition, Oxford Studies in Historical Theology* (Oxford and New York: Oxford, 2000), 140–145.

[89] Raymond A. Blacketer, "Commentaries and Prefaces," in *The Calvin Handbook*, ed. Herman J. Selderhuis (Grand Rapids: Eerdmans, 2009), 184.

[90] Ibid.

[91] Prior to the Reformation, religious instruction in Geneva consisted of memorizing prayers and the Apostle's Creed, and occasionally the Ten Commandments. The majority of this instruction was carried out by illiterate mothers. Robert M. Kingdon, "Catechesis in Calvin's Geneva," in Educating People of Faith (Grand Rapids: Eerdmans, 2004), 295.

[92] Barbara Pitkin, "The Heritage of the Lord," in *The Child In Christian Thought*, ed. Marcia J. Bunge (Grand Rapids: Eerdmans, 2001), 186.

[93] Kingdon, "Catechesis in Calvin's Geneva," 300. This is not to say Calvin did not place the responsibility of instructing children in the home. See Pitkin, "The Heritage of the Lord," 171.

[94] Ibid., 303.

[95] The concept of catechizing existed before the Reformation, but seems to have experienced a dramatic growth in popularity during the Reformation. Ibid., 301.

in a two-fold manner, to instruct the uneducated in sound doctrine and equip with the means to discern false and corrupt doctrine. In a letter to Edward Seymour, Duke of Somerset, he instructs, "make provision for the children being instructed in a good Catechism, what may show them briefly, and in language level to their tender age, wherein true Christianity consists. The Catechism will serve two purposes, to wit, as an introduction to the whole people, so that everyone may profit from what shall be preached, and also to enable them to discern when any presumptuous person puts forward strange doctrine."[96]

Calvin proposed the requirement of catechism, first in the 1537 *Articles Concerning the Organization of the Church* and then in the 1541 *Ecclesiastical Ordinances*. His initial 1537 catechism saw limited use and went through a major revision before publication in 1545.[97] The 1545 catechism consisted of six questions per week for an entire year.[98] Rotating only six questions would allow for memorization by students.[99] Calvin's pedagogical tool was divided into four sections: faith, which contained a study of the Apostle's Creed; law, which covered the Ten Commandments and portions of New Testament sayings; prayer, which offered general instructions on prayer before focusing on the Lord's Prayer; and the sacraments, which Calvin limited to baptism and communion.[100] After completing the catechism process, a child would have memorized the Apostle's Creed, the Ten Commandments, portions of the New Testament, and the Lord's Prayer.[101] Furthermore, the Apostle's Creed and the Lord's Prayer were recited during each worship service, serving as useful aids in retention.[102]

THE GENEVAN ACADEMY

Calvin's plan for Geneva included the founding of two schools, a college and an academy, for the education of the citizens of the Protestant city. For the Reformer, educational institutions were "essential to the building of a Christian society."[103] Calvin envisioned a college that would offer Hebrew, Latin, and Greek and prepare students for service in the

---

[96] Baum, Cunitz, and Reuss, *Ioannis Calvini Opera Quae Supersunt Omnia*, 13, 72; ET: Letters, II, 191.

[97] The second edition of Calvin's catechism was completed as a draft by 1542 and distributed in prepublication form.

[98] The Genevan Catechism consisted of 55 weeks, rather than the usual 52.

[99] Kingdon, "Catechesis in Calvin's Geneva," 303.

[100] Ibid., 304.

[101] Ibid.

[102] Ibid., 306.

[103] Gordon, Calvin, 299.

state or the church.[104] Studies were to be infused with religious activities, including prayer, Psalm singing, and daily recitations of the Apostle's Creed and Decalogue.

After living in Geneva for years with this unrealized dream, Calvin finally witnessed success when, in 1559, the Academy at Geneva opened under the rectorship of Calvin's friend and colleague, Theodore Beza.[105] The Academy, committed to the humanist vision of education shared by Calvin and Beza, operated with two schools. The *schola privata* instructed the Genevan children. The *schola publica* educated the future ministers. Calvin's involvement with the Academy was extensive, lecturing three-times weekly on biblical books. Unfortunately, the establishment of the Academy came near the end of Calvin's life, but it proved an enduring part of his legacy. Michael Horton summarizes Calvin's massive contribution to education well:

> Many students of the Geneva Academy went on to other Reformed universities like Heidelberg, Leiden, and Basel, as well as Oxford and Cambridge, the two English universities having been reformed by Vermigli and Bucer respectively. A number of English students, exiles during Mary's reign, returned to become leaders in church and state under Elizabeth. If the Renaissance was an unwitting carrier of the Reformation, the influence worked also in reverse. Wherever Reformed convictions gained a foothold, there was a revival of classical learning and interest in the arts and sciences — not only among the highly educated, but even among the daily laborer, who also had more access to basic education. Indeed, with "the new learning," as critics called it, spiritual and cultural rebirth usually went hand in hand. In short, Calvin's significance lies in the fact that he helped to shape a tradition that existed before and after him.[106]

CONCLUSION AND ANALYSIS

Calvin's theological contributions cannot be separated from his educational contributions. The Genevan Reformer was a theological educator in the deepest sense of the term. Committed to a theological program influenced by humanist ideology and Reformation principles, Calvin dreamed of a literate society in which every citizen had access to the written Word. Through his preaching and teaching, Calvin served as a model instructor. By authoring the *Institutes* and biblical commentaries, Calvin established himself as an educator of Christians that he never met face to face on this earth. By creating catechisms and championing educational institutions, Calvin demonstrated a forward-thinking adaptability that continues to shape Christian education today.

---

[104] Gutek, *Historical and Philosophical Foundations of Education*, 119.

[105] Gordon, *Calvin*, 300.

[106] Horton, *Calvin on the Christian Life*, 237.

PRIMARY SOURCE SAMPLE[107]

Letter to the Reader

It has always been a practice and diligent care of the Church, that children be rightly brought up in Christian doctrine. To do this more conveniently, not only were schools formerly opened and individuals enjoined to teach their families properly, but also it was accepted public custom and practice to examine children in the Churches concerning the specific points which should be common and familiar to all Christians. That this be done in order, a formula was written out, called Catechism or Institute....

Since it is proper for us by every means to endeavor to make the unity of faith shine forth among us which is so highly commended by Paul, the solemn profession of faith which is joined to our common baptism ought to be directed chiefly to this end. It might therefore be wished, not only that there exist a perpetual consent by all in pious doctrine, but that there be also a single form of Catechism for all Churches. But since for many reasons it will hardly ever be otherwise than that each Church have its own Catechism, we should not too strenuously resist it; provided, however, that the variety in the kind of teaching be such that we are all directed to the one Christ, by whose truth, if we be united in it, we may grow together into one body and one spirit, and with one mouth also proclaim whatever belongs to the sum of the faith....

...There are other kinds of writing to show what are our views in all matters of religion; but what agreement in doctrine our Churches had among themselves cannot be observed with clearer evidence than from the Catechisms. For in them there appears not only what someone or another once taught, but what were the rudiments with which both the learned and the unlearned among us were from youth constantly instructed, all the faithful holding them as the solemn symbol of Christian communion. This indeed was my chief reason for publishing this Catechism.

BIBLIOGRAPHY

Anthony, Michael J., and Warren S. Benson. *Exploring the History and Philosophy of Christian Education: Principles for the 21st Century*. Grand Rapids: Kregel, 2003.

Baum, Guilielmus, Eduardus Cunitz, and Eduardus Reuss, eds. *Ioannis Calvini Opera Quae Supersunt Omnia*. 59 vols. Brunsvigae: C. A. Schwetschke, 1863.

---

[107] A selection from John Calvin, "The Catechism of the Church of Geneva: That Is a Plan for Instructing Children in the Doctrine of Christ," in *Calvin: Theological Treatises*, trans. J.K.S. Reid, vol. XXII, Library of Christian Classics (Philadelphia: The Westminster Press, 1954), 88–139.

Benoit, J.D. "Pastoral Care of the Prophet." In *John Calvin: Contemporary Prophet*, edited by Jacob T. Hoogstra. Grand Rapids: Baker, 1959.

Beza, Theodore. *L'historie de La Vie et Mort de Calvin (1565)*. Vol. 21. Ioannis Calvini Opera quae supersunt omnia. Brunswick and Berlin: Braunschweig, 1863.

Blacketer, Raymond A. "Commentaries and Prefaces." In *The Calvin Handbook*, edited by Herman J. Selderhuis, 181–192. Grand Rapids: Eerdmans, 2009.

Bray, Gerald. *Biblical Interpretation: Past & Present*. Downers Grove, IL: InterVarsity Press, 1996.

Busch, Eberhard. "God and Humanity." In *The Calvin Handbook*, edited by Herman J. Selderhuis, translated by Judith J. Guder, 224–235. Grand Rapids: Eerdmans, 2009.

Calvin, Jean. *Institutes of the Christian Religion*. Translated by Ford Lewis Battles. 1536 ed. Grand Rapids: Eerdmans, 1975.

———. *Institutes of the Christian Religion: 1541 French Edition*. Translated by Elsie Anne McKee. Grand Rapids: Eerdmans, 2009.

———. *Calvin: Theological Treatises*. Edited by J. K. Reid. Philadelphia: Westminster, 1954.

———. "Calvin to Martin Luther, January 21, 1545." In *The Letters of John Calvin*, translated by Jules Bonnet, 1:440. New York: Burt Franklin, 1972.

———. *Commentaries on the Book of the Prophet Jeremiah and Lamentations*. Translated by John Owen. Vol. 1. Grand Rapids: Baker, 1979.

———. *Commentary on the Psalms*. Translated by Anderson, James. Calvin Translation Society Edition. Calvin's Commentaries. Grand Rapids: Baker, 1979.

———. *Institutes of the Christian Religion*. Edited by John T. McNeil. Translated by Ford Lewis Battles. 2 vols. Philadelphia: Westminster Press, 1960.

———. "The Catechism of the Church of Geneva: That Is a Plan for Instructing Children in the Doctrine of Christ." In *Calvin: Theological Treatises*, translated by J.K.S. Reid, XXII:88–139. Library of Christian Classics. Philadelphia: The Westminster Press, 1954.

Calvin, John, and Jacob Sadoleto. *A Reformation Debate: Sadoleto's Letter to the Genevans and Calvin's Reply*. Edited by John C. Olin. Grand Rapids: Baker, 1976.

Cottret, Bernard. *Calvin: A Biography*. Translated by M. Wallace McDonald. Grand Rapids: Eerdmans, 2000.

Dowey, Edward A. *The Knowledge of God in Calvin's Theology*. Third. Grand Rapids: Eerdmans, 1994.

George, Timothy. "Glory Unto God: John Calvin." In *Theology of the Reformers*, 179–264. Revised. Nashville: B&H Academic, 2013.

Gordon, Bruce. *Calvin*. New Haven: Yale University Press, 2009.

De Greef, Wulfert. "Calvin's Writings." In *The Cambridge Companion to John Calvin*, edited by Donald K. McKim, 41–57. New York and Cambridge: Cambridge University Press, 2004.

Gutek, Gerald L. *Historical and Philosophical Foundations of Education: A Biographical Introduction*. 5th ed. Pearson, 2011.

Haroutunian, Joseph, and Louise Pettibone Smith. *Calvin: Commentaries*. Philadelphia: Westminster Press, 1958.

Helm, Paul. *Calvin: A Guide for the Perplexed*. New York: T & T Clark, 2008.

Holder, R. Ward. *John Calvin and the Grounding of Interpretation: Calvin's First Commentaries*. Studies in the History of Christian Traditions 127. Leiden and Boston: Brill, 2006.

Horton, Michael. *Calvin on the Christian Life*. Theologians of the Christian Life. Wheaton, IL: Crossway, 2014.

Jones, Timothy Paul. "John Calvin and the Problem of Philosophical Apologetics." In *Perspectives on Religious Studies*, 23 (Winter 1996): 387-403.

Kingdon, Robert M. "Catechesis in Calvin's Geneva." In *Educating People of Faith*, 294–313. Grand Rapids: Eerdmans, 2004.

Manetsch, Scott M. *Calvin's Company of Pastors: Pastoral Care and the Emerging Reformed Church, 1536-1609*. New York: Oxford University Press, 2013.

McGrath, Alister E. *A Life of John Calvin: A Study in the Shaping of Western Culture*. Oxford, UK: Wiley-Blackwell, 1993.

Muller, Richard A. *The Unaccommodated Calvin: Studies in the Foundation of a Theological Tradition*. Oxford Studies in Historical Theology. Oxford and New York: Oxford, 2000.

Optiz, Peter. "Scripture." In *The Calvin Handbook*, edited by Herman J. Selderhuis, translated by Rebecca A. Giselbrecht, 235–244. Grand Rapids: Eerdmans, 2009.

Parsons, Burk, ed. *John Calvin: A Heart for Devotion, Doctrine, and Doxology*. Lake Mary, FL: Reformation Trust, 2008.

Pitkin, Barbara. "The Heritage of the Lord." In *The Child in Christian Thought*, edited by Marcia J. Bunge, 160–193. Grand Rapids: Eerdmans, 2001.

Puckett, David L. "John Calvin as Teacher." *Southern Baptist Journal of Theology* 13, no. 4 (Winter 2009): 45–48.

——— . *John Calvin's Exegesis of the Old Testament*. Columbia Series in Reformed Theology. Louisville, KY: Westminster John Knox Press, 1995.

Selderhuis, Herman J. *John Calvin: A Pilgrim's Life*. Translated by Albert Gootjes. Downers Grove, IL: IVP Academic, 2009.

Torrance, T.F. *Calvin's Doctrine of Man*. Westport, CT: Greenwood Press, 1957.

Wallace, R. S. "Calvin, John." *New Dictionary of Theology*. Downers Grove, IL: Inter-Varsity Press, 1988.

Zachman, Randall. "John Calvin." In *The Reformation Theologians: An Introduction to Theology in the Early Modern Period*, edited by Carter Lindberg, 184–197. Oxford, UK ; Malden, Mass: Wiley-Blackwell, 2001.

——— . *John Calvin as Teacher, Pastor, and Theologian*. Grand Rapids: Baker, 2006.

PART III

Puritan Era Educators

(A.D. 1650-1750)

The Brethren, part of the pietist movement that produced Erasmus also produced **John Amos Comenius** (1592-1670) and **August Hermann Francke** (1663-1727). The pietists emphasized a return to devout living, personal Christianity, the sending of missionaries to proclaim the gospel, and serious yet practical Bible study. Comenius was a pastor who was forced to leave his homeland during the Thirty Years' War. His emphasis on universal education and his scientific approach to the education of the Young make him it, a real sense the precursor of much modern educational theory and practice. He influenced, at least indirectly, such notables as Rousseau, Pestalozzi, and Herbart. Francke founded the famous orphanage and school at Halle, which served as a pattern for later educational institutions. He advocated such things as small classes, instruction in manual skills, and scientific demonstrations in the classroom, and he was the first to establish an institution for the training of teachers. His influence is apparent in the writings of, among others, Wesley and Zinzendorf.

Two of the most prolific Puritan authors were **Richard Baxter** (1651-1691) author of *The Reformed Pastor,* and **Jonathan Edwards** (1703-1758), the greatest American theologian in the eighteenth century. Baxter built upon Calvin's theology in his own work in education for the sake of discipleship and provides educators today with a picture of how pastoral discipleship can work in a biblically illiterate culture. On the other hand, Edwards had a great impact on education in America as he sought to educate for the affections rather than remaining content to educate purely for the mind. He helped broaden the audience for the gospel as we ourselves see its inclusiveness, by re-thinking how Native Americans were to be evangelized, rather than ignored or relocated. We learn how to simplify and yet teach the same "greater light" to others. He, and his to-be son-in-law, David Brainerd loved the Indians (of Stockbridge) and Edwards adapted his sermons for the separate services he held for this non-white congregation. Here was education married to evangelism, and he even spoke of

203

"great awakenings" among the leadership of the Indians to which they ministered. Before he died, Edwards was named the third president of the College of New Jersey (Princeton). However, he served in this capacity for only two months before he died due to complications from a smallpox inoculation.

CHAPTER 12

John Amos Comenius:
Teaching All Things to All People

DAVID I. SMITH

JOAN L. H. DUDLEY

John Amos Comenius (1592 – 1670):
John Amos Comenius was one of the most important and influential educational thinkers in
the Western tradition, helping to shape modern schooling. He worked to reform schools and
improve instructional materials and, as a bishop in the Moravian Brethen, sought to ground
his educational work in a comprehensive theological and philosophical vision that united
erudition, virtue, and piety in the service of wisdom. His work remains widely studied and
an important source for Christian reflection on education.

HISTORICAL BACKGROUND

The scholar and reformer who would become known as the father of modern education began his life in obscurity. John Amos Comenius[1] was born to Martin and Anna Komenský on March 28, 1592, the youngest of five children. It is uncertain whether he was born in Komňa, Nivnice, or Uherský Brod, but all three were located in southeastern Moravia, in what is today the Czech Republic. His family were members of the Church of the United Brethren, a small Christian group that emerged in the mid-fifteenth century from the Hussite movement. Commonly known as the Moravian Brethren, these believers were characterized by practical piety, a high view of biblical authority, and a strong history of education in the Scriptures.

A combination of humble origins and the loss of his parents and two sisters in quick succession before his teens limited Comenius' educational opportunities as a child. He spent some years at the village school in Strasnitz, recalling later the harshness and poor quality of the education provided. At the age of sixteen, he enrolled in the Latin grammar school of Přerov. There he nurtured a love of learning alongside a critical eye toward instructional methods. Being older than his fellow students created perspective, and he soon concluded that the lack of progress was due to the inefficiency of the teachers rather than the defects of students. Here began Comenius' interest in devising new methods of classroom instruction and better schemes of study, particularly in relation to the study of Latin.

In 1611, he matriculated into the Reformed Gymnasium at Herborn, where the staff included the theologian and educator John Henry Alsted, who influenced Comenius' thinking about education. In 1613, he moved on to complete his studies at the Calvinist University of Heidelberg, returning to Přerov in 1614 on foot, due to lack of funds. He took up a teaching position in the school of his childhood and was ordained two years later, adding duties as a pastor to his work. He soon turned his energies to improving educational

---

[1] Comenius is the adopted Latin name of Jan Amos Komenský, and John is the Anglicized version of his first name. The biographical sketch that follows is indebted to Daniel Murphy's biographical portrait in Daniel Murphy, *Comenius: A Critical Reassessment of His Life and Work* (Portland, OR: Irish Academic Press, 1995), which is an excellent introduction to Comenius' work. It also draws from the following sources: William Boyd, *The History of Western Education* (New York: Barnes & Noble, 1966); Klaus Goßmann and Henning Schröer (eds.), *Auf den Spuren des Comenius: Texte zu Leben, Werk und Wirkung* (Göttingen: Vandenhoek & Ruprecht, 1992); Simon S. Laurie, *John Amos Comenius Bishop of the Moravians His Life & Educational Works.* (Philadelphia: Burt Franklin, 1973); Will Monroe, *Comenius and the Beginnings of Educational Reform* (New York: Charles Scribner's Sons, 1900); John Sadler, *Comenius* (London: Collier-MacMillan Company, 1969); L. Glenn Smith and Joan Smith, *Lives in Education* (New York: St. Martin's Press, 1994); Matthew Spinka, *John Amos Comenius: That Incomparable Moravian* (New York: Russell & Russell, 1967).

practice; in 1616, he produced his first school textbook, *Principles of a Simpler Approach to Grammar*. By this point, his lifelong trajectory, which was found at the intersection between the church and the school, was set. He began a prodigious program of writing on religious and social issues, language learning, theology, and history, and embarked upon a projected encyclopedia; he would eventually produce some 250 works.[2]

WAR AND EXILE

During his time in Přerov, he married Magdalena Vizovská and was soon the father of two young children. These happy years were short-lived. In 1620, the Thirty Years' War (1618-1648) came to Fulneck, where Comenius was now living with his family. Catholics were pitted against Protestants, ministers in Protestant denominations were forced to flee, and books deemed heretical were burned. Intense religious intolerance and persecution were specifically directed toward the Moravian Brethren. When Spanish troops arrived in Fulneck, Comenius' house was destroyed. Though he at first managed to move his books to the city hall, that too was destroyed and he was forced into hiding on the estate of the sympathetic Count de Zerotin. After two years, his wife and two children, who had sought shelter at her mother's home, died from the plague that spread alongside the fighting.

Comenius continued to write, preach, and minister to his fellow Moravians. During these years, he translated the Psalms into Czech and completed *The Labyrinth of the World and the Paradise of the Heart*, a classic allegory in the vein of (and predating) Bunyan's *Pilgrim's Progress*. After a period of grief for his family that found expression in written laments, he remarried in 1624. Pressure on the displaced community continued to increase, however. An edict of 1627 required all inhabitants of the Kingdom of Bohemia to embrace Catholicism or leave, and this rendered further protection of the Moravian clergy by sympathetic nobles untenable. The Brethren were forced to scatter. Comenius left in 1628 for Leszno, Poland, and was never to see his homeland again.

EDUCATIONAL REFORM

In Leszno, Comenius gained a position at the gymnasium and began to test his educational ideas. He invested three years in the creation of a new Latin textbook for beginners, the *Janua Linguarum Reserata*. This celebrated text was a radical departure, turning from the customary literary excerpts to a collection of words and phrases drawn

---

[2] Klaus Schaller, *Johann Amos Comenius: Ein pädagogisches Porträt* (Weinheim: Beltz Verlag, 2004), 13-17.

from everyday experience and marked by playful humor. Widely applauded, the book was translated into more than a dozen languages, including Arabic, Turkish, and Mongolian. He also reformed the daily operation of the school, emphasizing formation in faith and virtue, grounding learning in students' experiences, and setting time aside for regular recreation. Meanwhile, his ecclesial work continued; in 1632, the year in which the *Janua* appeared, he was elected to the position of bishop in the United Brethren.

Alongside his theological and pedagogical work, Comenius shared the seventeenth century passion for universal schemes of knowledge; alongside his textbooks, his "pansophic" writings attempted to express the unity and harmony of all knowledge in Christian terms, and this became a second pillar of his growing fame. His pansophic work informed his educational efforts not only by providing a vision of a comprehensive, meaningfully integrated curriculum, but also in tandem with his deep conviction that all human beings should have access to such knowledge – his passion for universal education became a hallmark of his work. As his reputation spread, international invitations to participate in educational reform began to arrive. In England, Samuel Hartlib, a philanthropist and associate of Oliver Cromwell, asked Comenius to join an English parliamentary committee for the implementation of educational reform and the establishment of a pansophic college. The project was interrupted by the outbreak of civil war in 1642. During his stay in England, it appears he was invited to become head of Harvard College, later to become Harvard University, but he declined and instead moved to Sweden to engage in school reform. En route, he met and debated with René Descartes in the Netherlands. They parted with apparent mutual respect but significant differences, Descartes regarding Comenius as mixing theology and philosophy too readily and Comenius urging "all human knowledge, such as derives from the senses alone and reasonings thereon, to be imperfect and defective."[3]

Comenius hoped that his work improving school curriculum in Protestant Sweden would foster support for the United Brethren, with a view to their eventual repatriation. Nicolaus Drabik, a lifelong friend, had nurtured this hope through prophecies foretelling the imminent return of the Brethren to their homeland. Comenius not only clutched at these prophecies, but also published them, and both their failure and his association with what the Enlightenment would regard as superstition tarnished his later historical reception. His hopes of Swedish intervention proved to be in vain, and he returned to the exiled Brethren community in Leszno in 1646, a journey further darkened by the death of his second wife. Two years later, he was elected Senior Bishop. In the same

---

[3] See Nicolette Mout, 'Comenius, Descartes and Dutch Cartesianism,' *Acta Comeniana* 3 (1972), 239-243.

year, the Treaty of Westphalia ended the Thirty Years' War but proved disastrous for the Brethren, as the freedom of religion granted to other Protestant groups was not extended to them and their return home became impossible.

In 1650, Comenius moved to Sáros Pátak, Hungary, for further school reform work, leaving behind his son and third wife in Leszno. He was given generous resources by Prince Sigismund of Hungary and opened a model school in 1651. Friction with the rector and teachers, who objected to the increased demands on their energies and the learner-focused pedagogy, was initially overcome through Prince Sigismund's support; but with his death in 1654, the tensions recurred. Comenius was able to win many over to his emphasis on play through the success of his use of theatrical performances, and he produced important works during these years including *Schola Ludus* (School as Play) and the *Orbis Sensualium Pictus* (World of Things in Pictures). The latter achieved particular fame after its printing in 1658 with its innovative use of woodcut illustrations to connect language learning to children's interests and his pansophic vision. Nevertheless, he finished his time in Hungary in 1655 somewhat disillusioned with the amount of progress made, and returned to work as a pastor in Leszno.

HIS FINAL YEARS

In 1655, tragedy struck once more. Protestant Sweden invaded Catholic Poland, enjoying vocal support from local Protestants, including Comenius and the Brethren. When Poland emerged victorious, Comenius and his fellow Brethren were caught up in Catholic reprisals as Leszno was burned to the ground. Comenius, now 63, lost everything – his savings, his possessions, and his library, including the manuscripts of various major works over which he had been laboring for decades. As the surviving Brethren scattered, Comenius fled first to Silesia before finding refuge in Amsterdam, where he remained until his death. Friends took up collections for him and the city provided him with a salary which enabled him to focus on preparing his writings for publication. His *Opera Didactica Omnia* (Collected Educational Works) appeared in 1657, running to over 1000 pages.[4]

Alongside educational writings, he continued his efforts toward promoting ecumenical understanding between denominations, urging "in all things essential unity; in those less needful ... freedom; and in all things love to all."[5] He became involved in the Peace Conference

---

[4] The principal Latin texts are available in Dmitrij Tschizewskij and Klaus Schaller (eds.), *Ausgewahlte Werke: Johann Amos Comenius*, 3 vols. (Hildesheim: Olms, 1973).

[5] Murphy, *Comenius*, 43, citing Comenius's *Unum Necessarium* ('The One Thing Necessary'). Cf. Eve Chybova Bock, "Seeking a Better Way," *Christian History* January 1, 1987, https://www. christianhistoryinstitute.org/magazine/article/seeking-a-better-way/ (accessed December 10, 2013).

that ended the Anglo-Dutch war, supervised a translation of the Bible into Turkish, and worked on the seven volumes of his final pansophic project, *De Rerum Humanorum Emendatione Consultatio Catholica* (Universal Deliberation on the Reform of Human Affairs). Work on this final synopsis of his thinking was interrupted by his death on November 15, 1670; it was not to be published until 1966.

Throughout his life, Comenius was not one to dwell in defeat. He faced personal tragedies and difficulties with faith and hope and urged posterity to take up the task of transforming the wilderness of the world into an arena for human flourishing and love of God and neighbor.

THEOLOGY OF CHRISTIAN EDUCATION

In the *Great Didactic*, Comenius wrote, "All that does not relate to God and to the future life is nothing but vanity"[6] In his allegory, *The Labyrinth of the World and the Paradise of the Heart*, Comenius' pilgrim views the vanity and vice distorting all human callings before encountering Christ, who invites him to "transfer and turn over to me whatever you have seen in the world, whatever human efforts you have witnessed for the sake of earthly goods."[7] For Comenius, this led not to a withdrawal from the world into pious escapism or a disparagement of that which is of this world, but rather to a concerted engagement with the world in confidence that all things could in the end find their dignity in relation to God. Comenius' vision of the Christian life and education is marked by a constant effort to refer the parts to the whole, to refer all things to God in such a way as to achieve harmony between faith, learning, and proper living. Comenius grounded his thinking in a high view of the authority of the Bible while also embracing empirical sources of understanding in the name of an ultimate unity of truth. Placing God at the center meant not that the things of this world grew strangely dim, but that the Christian's life in the world should be marked by a passion for the reform and renewal of all things.

At the start of the *Pampaedia*, which contains his mature reflection on pedagogy, Comenius declares his intent as follows, *"Firstly,* the expressed wish is for full power of development into full humanity not of one particular person, but of *every single individual*, young and old, rich and poor, noble and ignoble, men and women – in a word, every being born on earth, with the ultimate

---

[6] John Amos Comenius, *The Great Didactic of John Amos Comenius*, trans. M. W. Keatinge (New York: Russell & Russell, 1967), 226 (XXIV:24).

[7] John Comenius, *The Labyrinth of the World and the Paradise of the Heart*, trans. Howard Louthan and Andrea Sterk (New York/Mahwah: Paulist Press), 190.

aim of providing education to the entire human race regardless of age, class, sex and nationality."[8] Comenius advocated that educational provision should be made with a view to serving "every being born on earth" without favoritism based on ability, socioeconomic status, gender, or ethnicity. As he went on to comment, "There is no exception from human education except for non-humans."[9] This universality of provision was to go hand in hand with a holistic approach to educational content, focused on broad-based development into "full humanity" rather than on a narrower range of knowledge or skills. This focus was reflected in Comenius's commitment to the ideal of *pansophism*, or universal wisdom, whereby human understanding is brought to grasp God's ordering of the full panoply of creation, drawing together truths revealed through sciences and through the Scriptures, and led to live wisely and virtuously within it. The expansive vision expressed here is elsewhere summarized as *omnes omnia omnino*, or teaching all things to all people with reference to the whole.[10]

ERUDITION, VIRTUE, PIETY

His vision for education both undergirded and was grounded in an account of the learner that refused to separate the cognitive, the moral, and the spiritual. In the *Great Didactic*, Comenius summarized his educational anthropology saying,

> ... it is plain that man is situated among visible creatures so as to be (i.) a rational creature. (ii.) The Lord of all creatures. (iii.) A creature which is the image and joy of its Creator. These three aspects are so joined together that they cannot be separated ... From this it follows that man is naturally required to be: (1) acquainted with all things; (2) endowed with power over all things and over himself; (3) to refer himself and all things to God, the source of all. Now if we wish to express these three things by three well-known words, these will be (i.) Erudition. (ii.) Virtue and seemly morals. (iii.) Religion or piety.[11]

Comenius insists firmly and repeatedly that these three elements are not to be understood as separate modules or compartments. He does not join faith, experience, and reason so much by allocating each its circumscribed sphere of operation as by refusing to conceive of any as functioning properly apart from the others. Rationality that fails to be oriented to the whole (and therefore to the revealed truths of the Scriptures as well as the empirical deliverances of science) or that does not consider its relationship to how we treat our neighbor and the

---

[8] A. M. O. Dobbie, *Comenius's Pampaedia or Universal Education* (Dover: Buckland, 1986), 19.

[9] Ibid., 31.

[10] Comenius, *Great Didactic*, 76 (XI:1).

[11] Comenius, *Great Didactic*, 36-38 (IV:1-6).

wider creation falls short of its proper role and purpose.[12] Similarly, if we focus on Comenius' account of piety, we find a fractal effect as mind, will, and spirit again appear in concert. Piety then means, "that (after we have thoroughly grasped the conceptions of faith and of religion) our hearts should learn to seek God everywhere ... and that when we have found Him we should follow Him, and when we have attained Him we should enjoy Him. The first we do through our understanding, the second through our will, and the third through the joy arising from the consciousness of our union with God."[13] The goal is not to apply reason to some things and faith to others, but rather to seek the full development of each in harmony with the other.

Pious reflection was to be worked out (and emerge from) virtuous action. The reference to humanity as "Lord of all things" derives from Genesis 1:28 and its image of human dominion over the natural world. For Comenius, this points to the need for virtue and the exercise of understanding and will in self-control for the sake of service and the flourishing of other creatures:

> To be the lord of all creatures consists in subjecting everything to his own use by contriving that its legitimate end be suitably fulfilled; in conducting himself royally, that is gravely and righteously, among creatures ... [not being] ignorant where, when, how, and to what extent each may prudently be used, how far the body should be gratified, and how far our neighbour's interests should be consulted. In a word, he should be able to control with prudence his own movements and actions, external and internal, as well as those of others.[14]

Just as the characterization of piety ended in joy, so growth in virtue is oriented to delight in one's neighbor and the shared delight of creation. We are, says Comenius (playing on Proverbs 8:30-31), "sent into the world ... that we may serve God, his creatures, and ourselves, and that we may enjoy the pleasure to be derived from God, from his creatures, and from ourselves."[15] The goal of a

---

[12] Contrast the then nascent Royal Society's declaration of "Divinity, Metaphysicks, Morals, Politics, Grammar, Rhetorick or Logicks" as falling outside of empirical inquiry. Cited in John Edward Sadler, *J.A. Comenius and the Concept of Universal Education* (London: George Allen & Unwin, 1966), 148. Compare John Amos Comenius, *The Way of Light*, trans. Ernest Trafford Campagnac (Liverpool: University Press, 1938).

[13] Comenius, *Great Didactic*, 218 (XXIV:2).

[14] Comenius, *Great Didactic*, 37 (IV:4).

[15] Comenius, *Great Didactic*, 72 (X:8). The pleasure derived from ourselves is defined as "that very sweet delight which arises when a man, who is given over to virtue, rejoices in his own honest disposition, since he sees himself prompt in all things which the order of justice requires." (p.73; X:13.)

properly formed education is that those shaped by it will exert their power in the world in such a manner that the "hope and longing of creatures should be fulfilled, and that everything everywhere should advance correctly, and that all creatures should have cause to join us in praising God."[16]

HARMONY

One who possesses not just knowledge, but also virtue and wisdom may, Comenius contends, attain harmony both inwardly and outwardly, becoming able to live the good life on earth while being prepared for eternal salvation. The emphasis on the underlying harmony of all things extends from the capacities of the self (reason, virtue, and faith in harmonious concert) outward to the self's relation to the world (understanding of, service to, and rejoicing in one's neighbor and the wider creation). This leads Comenius to resist further lines of division: "Bias towards persons, nations, languages and religious sects must be totally eliminated if we are to prevent love or hatred, envy or contempt, or any other emotion from interfering with our plans for happiness ... How utterly thoughtless ... to hate your neighbour because he was born in another country or speaks a different language."[17]

In Comenius's vision, the divisions within the self, within knowledge, and within and between religious denominations and human societies were all to be overcome by orienting everything back to God in Christ. Although Comenius exhibits a strong focus on the needs and well-being of the learner, he also insisted that the purpose of schooling included social needs and the promotion of a peaceful, fruitful, and just society. In a recurring biblical image echoing Genesis, the Wisdom literature, Isaiah 5 and John 15, Comenius pictured the self, the social world, and the school as "gardens of delight" (places of beauty, harmony, justice, and piety) that have descended to the state of "wild and horrible wilderness" but are to be restored through human cooperation with the renewing work of the spirit of God. Spiritual growth, disciplined learning, moral formation, and social justice thus become organic parts of the same educational vision.[18]

---

[16] Dobbie, *Pampaedia*, 26 (I:13).

[17] John Amos Comenius, *Panegersia, or Universal Awakening*, trans. A. M. O. Dobbie (Shipston-on-Stour: Peter I. Drinkwater, 1990), 70.

[18] David I. Smith. "Biblical Imagery and Educational Imagination: Comenius and the Garden of Delight," in David Lyle Jeffrey and C. Stephen Evans (eds), *The Bible and the University* (Scripture and Hermeneutics Series 8) (Milton Keynes/Grand Rapids: Paternoster/Zondervan, 2007): 188-215.

213

CONTRIBUTIONS TO CHRISTIAN EDUCATION

Comenius characterized the schools of his youth as the "terror of boys and slaughterhouses of the mind," "grinding houses of torment and torture."[19] He lamented the loss of time and opportunity for learners: "For five, ten, or more years they detained the mind over matters that could be mastered in one. What could have been gently instilled into the intellect was violently impressed upon it, nay rather stuffed and flogged into it. What might have been placed before the mind plainly and lucidly, was treated of obscurely, perplexedly, and intricately, as if it were a complicated riddle."[20]

These systemic defects were exacerbated by the sinful tendencies of those educating and being educated, for "owing to our corrupt nature, evil clings to us readily."[21] While, on the one hand, efforts to remove evil apart from the work of Christ in taking away the sins of the world are futile, on the other hand, "it is clear from Scripture that piety itself is teachable," and "since the Holy Spirit usually employs natural agencies, and has chosen parents, teachers, and ministers who should faithfully plant and water the grafts of Paradise (1 Cor. 3:6-8), it is right that these should appreciate the extent of their duties."[22] Reform of education was to involve the efforts of the various members of the Christian community rather than being left in the hands of teachers alone. The following is a more detailed synopsis of what Comenius can teach us regarding the role of the teacher, the learner, and the curriculum.

THE ROLE OF THE TEACHER: MORAL EXEMPLARS

Comenius' vision of holistic growth required that teachers be more than technically competent for they were to serve as exemplars of erudition, virtue, and piety. In teaching language, for instance, the teacher's utterances must be grammatically correct, suited to the learner's developmental stage, cognizant of the particular relationship of the patterns of the learner's native tongue to the second language being learned, and also reflective of virtue in the content and manner of speaking.[23] Comenius hoped that by the teacher's godly example, care in removing bad associations and temptations, and disciplined but supportive instruction students

[19] Nash, *The Educated Man,* 183, quoting from *Great Didactic* XI:7; John Amos Comenius, *The School of Infancy* (Chapel Hill: University of North Carolina Press, 1956), 68.
[20] Comenius, *Great Didactic,* 78 (XI:9).
[21] Comenius, *Great Didactic,* 216 (XXIII:17)
[22] Dobbie, *Pampaedia,* 46 (III:46); Comenius, *Great Didactic,* 218, 229-230 (XXIV:1,30).
[23] David I. Smith and Barbara Carvill, *The Gift of the Stranger: Faith, Hospitality, and Foreign Language Learning* (Grand Rapids: Eerdmans, 2000), 46-48.

would be encouraged to act in such a way that the use of force would be unnecessary. Youth were to be instructed to be prudent, self-controlled, strong, truthful, responsible, just, and ready to serve others. These virtues were to be ingrained through constant practice ("Virtue is practiced by deeds and not by words") accompanied by examples of well-ordered lives and presentation of precepts and rules of conduct.[24] Parents were admonished to likewise display faith in their children's learning potential, provide godly models, and delight in their children's learning.

In his curricular recommendations, Comenius criticized the pagan morality of the classics, complaining that classical writers were now more studied than the Scriptures and that works shaped by idolatry would "blind the intelligence by the plausibility of their carnal wisdom."[25] "A good and honest life," he insisted, "can only be formed if those things are loved which ought to be loved, that is to say, God and our neighbor."[26] Classical writers taught a set of virtues contrary to those of Christ: "Christ teaches self-abnegation, they teach self-love. Christ teaches us to be humble, they to be magnanimous. Christ demands meekness, they inculcate self-assertion."[27] Nonetheless, selective use of classical learning was affirmed provided it occurred after a student's Christian formation had progressed.

THE ROLE OF THE LEARNER:

Two aspects of Comenius' thought are important for understanding the role of the learner. First, learning should be a lifelong pursuit. Second, the nature of the learner should be taken to account before starting the teaching or learning process.

Lifelong Learning

Comenius's educational vision encompassed lifelong learning for all.[28] He envisaged a cradle-to-grave educational process divided according to stages of maturation, thus laying the groundwork for later developmental theories of learning and the organization of modern

---

[24] Comenius, *Great Didactic*, 213 (XXIII:9); 215-216 (XXIII:15-16). Cf. Jan Hábl, "Character formation: A forgotten theme of Comenius's didactics," *Journal of Education and Christian Belief* 15:2 (2011), 141-153.

[25] Comenius, *Great Didactic*, 237 (XXV:12).

[26] Comenius, *Great Didactic*, 241 (XXV:18).

[27] Comenius, *Great Didactic*, 243 (XXV:19).

[28] Dobbie, *Pampaedia*, 103-191 (VIII). The eight stages of education from birth to death are tied to the eight "worlds" of Comenius' pansophic scheme; see ibid., 191, and Dagmar Čapková, Jaromír Cervenka, Pavel Floss and Pavel Kalivoda, "The Philosophical Significance of the Work of Comenius," *Acta Comeniana* 8 (1989), 5-17.

schooling around age-based grade levels.[29] From birth through the age of six, the child learned at home at the knee of the mother.[30] From the ages of six through twelve, the child would attend the local primary school where senses and imagination were to be stimulated and memory fostered. Youths aged twelve through eighteen attended the grammar school where subject disciplines would be studied "with a view to the fuller and clearer use of reasoning."[31] Those particularly gifted would then proceed to the university, with the remaining students entering the world of work; university students were to focus their undivided attention on the particular subject for which they were most clearly gifted.[32] Learning was to continue throughout adulthood and into old age, with a focus at the end on preparing to die well. There were to be no distinctions based on social standing or intellectual capabilities. Both boys and girls were both to be educated (as equally formed in the image of God), although the chief end in view for girls was that they would be able to teach their own children.[33]

Nature

Comenius sought to ground his recommendations in the "nature of things." As nature cannot be hurried, children were not to be presented with material or be required to perform in ways for which they were neither mentally nor physically ready. As nature's growth and maturation progress from the simple to the complex, the child's lessons sequence from general to specific, near to far, known to unknown. As nature provides those elements necessary for survival and growth, so, too, the student must be prepared and provided with what is needed for further learning. Appeal to nature did not imply leaving matters to take their course; plants require hoeing, tending, and pruning if they are to bring forth sweet fruit, and human learners require discipline and the "engrafting" of virtue and piety for

---

[29] Cf. Jean Piaget, "The significance of John Amos Comenius at the present time," introduction to John Amos Comenius on Education, *Classics in Education Series* No. 33, (New York: Teachers College Press Columbia University, 1967), 1-31.

[30] According to Comenius, learning was actually to begin before the child was born with training for motherhood and admonitions to maintain physical, mental, emotional, and spiritual health during pregnancy. See Comenius, *School of Infancy*, 76-84.

[31] Dobbie, *Pampaedia*, 145 (XI).

[32] Comenius, *Great Didactic*, 281-281 (XXXI).

[33] See Christine Reents, "Comenius' Impulse zur Mädchenbildung? Oder: Die Gleichheit von Mann und Frau als Ausdruck ihrer Gottebenbildlichkeit," in Klaus Goßmann and Christoph Th. Scheilke, *Jan Amos Comenius 1592-1992: Theologische und pädagogische Deutungen* (Gütersloh: Gütersloher Verlagshaus Gerd Mohn, 1992), 49-69.

proper maturation to occur.[34] Cultivation does not threaten or spoil nature, but rather brings it from an unformed beginning to its intended fruitfulness.[35] Comenius specifies that "by the word nature we mean, not the corruption which has laid hold of all men since the Fall (on which account we are naturally called the children of wrath, unable by ourselves to have any good thoughts), but our first and original condition, to which as a starting-point we must be recalled."[36] Our human "nature" as those called to be images of God is a potential now spoiled but capable of fresh realization through grace, including the operation of grace through educational means.

THE ROLE OF CURRICULUM

Comenius was particularly interested in sensory learning and language acquisition. This section will focus briefly on how he understood the role of the curriculum as it relates to these two types of learning.

Turn to Experience

Comenius turned from the traditional focus on classical texts to an emphasis on the world of experience and learning through the senses. The natural world, human society, and the scriptures were to be studied as representing books in which truth was revealed. Learners were to be brought into contact with creation, working from sensory experience back to imagination, expression, and understanding, and in turn applying the learning to virtuous living in the world:

> The objects should first be placed before the organs of sense on which they act. Then the internal senses should acquire the habit of expressing in their turn the images that result from the external sensation, both internally by means of the faculty of recollection, and externally with the hand and tongue. At this stage the mind can begin to operate, and, by the processes of exact thought, can compare and estimate all objects of knowledge. Last of all the will (which is the guiding principle in man) makes its power felt in all directions. To attempt to cultivate the ... intellect before the imagination ... is a waste of time.[37]

---

[34] Comenius, *Great Didactic*, 52-3 (VI:3), 57 (VII:1). Comenius cites examples of children who were raised by wild animals and whose human faculties remained undeveloped. cf. *Pampaedia* II:3: "nature ... should not be allowed to lie neglected and contribute neither to the glory of God nor to man's salvation" (p.22).

[35] See e.g. Comenius, *Great Didactic*, 123-124 (XVI:48); also Klaus Schaller, "Erziehung zur Menschlichkeit, Komenskys kritischer Beitrag zu Gegenwartsproblemen der Erziehung," in Klaus Goßmann and Christoph Th. Scheilke, *Jan Amos Comenius 1592-1992: Theologische und pädagogische Deutungen* (Gütersloh: Gütersloher Verlagshaus Gerd Mohn, 1992), 17-30.

[36] Comenius, *Great Didactic*, 40 (V:1).

[37] Comenius, *Great Didactic*, 257 (XXVII:7).

217

Knowledge acquired through sense and reason alone was defective, and what was learned through the senses had to be related back to the theological vision of the whole mediated through Scripture.[38] Conversely, a focus on words alone without grounding in practical experience was empty. Comenius urged:

> The task of the pupil will be made easier, if the master, when he teaches him anything, show him at the same time its practical application in every-day life. This rule must be carefully observed in teaching languages, dialectic, arithmetic, geometry, physics, etc. If it be neglected, the things that you are explaining will seem to be monsters from the new world, and the attitude of the pupil, who is indifferent whether they exist or no, will be one of belief rather than of knowledge. When things are brought under his notice and their use is explained to him, they should be put into his hands that he may assure himself of his knowledge and may derive enjoyment from its application. Therefore, those things only should be taught whose application can be easily demonstrated.[39]

Comenius compared a teacher who does not provide sufficient explanation and preparation to a nurse who forces a child to walk before it is ready and beats it for failing.[40] Concepts were to be explained by the shortest and most practical rules, with few well-chosen words, and accompanied by appropriate examples with visual support. The curriculum was to be broad in scope, ranging across scientific knowledge, human callings, arts and languages, and biblical teaching. The goal was for the student to learn responsibility and to enjoy an independent and productive life, one that glorifies God, serves society, and prepares for heaven.

Schools were to provide a secure, active, satisfying, and interactive environment. Rote memorization and meaningless repetition were to be avoided, for a human learner "is not a block of wood from which you can carve a statue which is completely subject to your will; he is a living image, shaping, misshaping and reshaping itself according to opportunity."[41] Students recorded their discoveries in notebooks, which they then shared with their classmates.

---

[38] Eetu Pikkarainen, "Signs of Reality: The Idea of General *Bildung*" by J. A. Comenius, in Pauli Siljander, Ari Kivelä, and Ari Sutinen, *Theories of Bildung and Growth: Connections and Controversies between Continental Educational Thinking and American Pragmatism* (Rotterdam: Sense, 2012), 19-30.

[39] Comenius, *Great Didactic*, 140 (XVII:44).

[40] Comenius, *Great Didactic*, 139 (XVII:40)

[41] Vladimir Jelinek, *The Analytical Didactic of Comenius* (Chicago: University of Chicago Press, 1953), 108 (XXXIII).

Periods of play, exercise, and rest were essential, and while Comenius repeatedly affirmed the dangers of idleness and the value of industriousness, he also noted that students should never be over-pressured.[42] Blocks, games, art activities, and theatrical performances were seen as having educational value. Grounded in his vision of delight in God, creation, and one another as basic to wisdom, Comenius pioneered the conception of play as having educational value and insisted that from the earliest age "parents ought to be especially careful never to allow their children to be without delights."[43]

Language Learning

Comenius' impact as a developer of curriculum was most celebrated in the realm of second language learning.[44] He broke with the tradition of using Latin as the medium of instruction, insisting that the mother tongue be studied first, with Latin and vernacular languages to follow as needed. Language texts were founded upon familiar topics and taught via a sensory approach tailored to student readiness. In place of compendia of classical texts, he turned to concrete vocabulary, real-world content, and active verbs presented visually and in context to be acquired conversationally. Students read the text, conversed with the teacher in the target language, studied grammatical form, and responded in writing.

His most lasting language text was the innovative *Orbis Pictus*,[45] the first illustrated schoolbook, a work both encyclopedic and oriented to students' contemporary experience. The contents range across the personal, familial, societal, global, and theological, encompassing all areas of learning and their interdependence – animals, occupations, toys, virtues, sciences, God, and also physical deformities, war, sickness, and death. The topics are organized with some progression from simple to complex, from concrete to abstract, but also with an eye toward telling a meaningful and comprehensive overall story. On each page, above the text, the student sees a picture (a new development based on advances in printing technology) coded with numbers corresponding to words within the text, which places the vernacular alongside the language being studied in parallel columns. The chapter texts proceed with

---

[42] Comenius, *Great Didactic*, 214 (XXIII:11).

[43] Comenius, *School of Infancy*, 84.

[44] See L. G. Kelly, *25 Centuries of Language Teaching 500 BC – 1969* (Rowley: Newbury House Publishers, 1976); Jean-Antoine Caravolas, "Comenius (Komensky) and the Theory of Language Teaching," *Acta Comeniana* 10 (1993), 141-170.

[45] For a more thorough analysis of the *Orbis Pictus* see Joan L. H. Dudley, *One Picture is Worth a Thousand Words: A Pictorial Word Journey Through the Orbis Pictus of J. A. Comenius* (PhD diss., St. Louis University, 2010).

increasing length and complexity of syntax, fostering vocabulary acquisition through meaningful reading. Embedded in the pictures and texts are moral and spiritual truths, social contexts, and cultural values, and the whole sequence traces a path from God as the point of origin through the panoply of creation and human experience to the final day of judgment. Characteristically, the task of learning words and sentence structures is thoroughly embedded in a vision of the harmony of the whole and the inseparability of learning, social well-being, moral formation, and life lived before God.

CONCLUSION

The influence of Comenius on the subsequent development of education was considerable, and his educational thought is still studied and discussed, especially in Europe. As Klaus Schaller has noted, the urge to make Comenius modern has resulted in him being claimed as the father of various modern movements in education, often at the expense of retaining the integrity of his own thinking; recent Comenius research has been concerned to locate Comenius more carefully in his own times.[46] He worked with the intellectual tools and social currents available to him, and sought to reform the schools of his day. It is not surprising that some of his ideas now seem overly optimistic, misinformed, or simply quaint. Nevertheless, the degree to which his educational vision retains its power almost four centuries later is remarkable.

Many details of Comenius' educational recommendations retain contemporary force. His embrace of new educational technologies, his focus on meaningful learning and careful gradation of learning, his affirmation of play, of the sensory and visual, and of children's own experience, his interdisciplinary focus on curricular integration, his refusal to separate knowledge from values, his quest for justice through universal educational provision without discrimination based on gender, wealth, or ability, and his interest in the relationship between schooling and the health of society are all examples of features of his thinking that have lost none of their relevance.

What held his many interests and diverse recommendations together, however, was his theological vision of all things made new through Christian engagement in the reform of schools and society. Despite a life filled with troubles, he worked tirelessly to reshape the education of his day and to articulate a Christian vision capacious enough to guide such a

---

[46] Klaus Schaller, "The influence of modern Comenius studies on the philosophy of education in the Federal Republic of Germany," *History of Education* 12:2 (1983), 87-92.

project. Comenius' parting shot was an exhortation to those who would follow to continue the project. In the final volume of the *Consultatio*, he addressed himself to posterity, writing of his lifelong reform efforts:

> I chose this line of action to avoid doing nothing, that is to say, I preferred to weave certain inventions for the benefit of a new generation and to unravel them when I discovered better ones. But since my Ulysses is now arriving in the form of the everlasting Bridegroom, my heart rejoices to have kept faith with him, and behold! I am now ceasing from unraveling my life's work. Let this be my final fabric for the use of all who may desire it. But those who long for a better one (being now awakened to its importance) must be free to weave it. [47]

PRIMARY SOURCE SAMPLE (WITH COMMENTARY): THE *ORBIS PICTUS*[49]

The *Orbis Pictus* begins with *Chapter I: Invitation*. The figure of an elderly formally dressed man dominates this woodcut. On his journey, the gentleman comes upon a young lad. Their encounter occurs in an open area; in the distant background is a vague outline of a village complete with a church as evidenced by the steeple. The figures are dressed as travelers upon the same well-traveled road. Although the bodies face the reader, their faces are turned toward each other, their facial expressions capturing the curiosity of Comenius's young audience.

The elderly, God-fearing, and gentle master invites the lad to join him and thus, learn on the path to wisdom. Wisdom is defined not as an inexhaustible body of knowledge, but as an understanding of how to act and to speak "rightly" (in correct grammar and syntax as well as righteously) all that is "necessary." The courteous young lad, who has doffed his hat in respect, now will not be left alone, but rather guided through his journey, "only by God's help."

---

[47] John Amos Comenius, *Pannuthesia or Universal Warning*, Trans. A. M. O. Dobbie (Shipston-on-Stour, UK: Peter Drinkwater, 1991), 19 (I:6).

From here the journey will proceed through the alphabet, God and his creation, human callings and technologies, arts, virtues, social structures, and comparative religion, ending at "The Last Judgment." Here, having traveled the road to wisdom, the young reader is once again presented with the woodcut image from *Chapter I: Invitation.* This is *Chapter CLI: The Close,* which exhorts the student to continue to learn through reading "other good *Books*" so as to become *"learned, wise, and godly."* "Remember these things," the teacher exhorts, "fear God, and call upon him, that he may bestow upon thee the *Spirit of Wisdom.*"

BIBLIOGRAPHY

Bock, Eve Chybova. "Seeking a Better Way." *Christian History* January 1, 1987. Accessed December 10, 2013. https://www.christianhistoryinstitute.org/ magazine/article/seeking-a-better-way/.

Boyd, William. *The History of Western Education.* New York: Barnes & Noble, Inc., 1966.

Čapková, Dagmar, Jaromír Cervenka, Pavel Floss and Robert Kalivoda. "The Philosophical Significance of the Work of Comenius." *Acta Comeniana* 8 (1989): 5-17.

Caravolas, Jean-Antoine. "Comenius (Komensky) and the Theory of Language Teaching." *Acta Comeniana* 10 (1993): 141-170.

Comenius, John Amos. *John Amos Comenius on Education.* New York: Teachers College Press, 1967.

_____. *Orbis Pictus.* Translated by Charles Hoole and edited by C. W. Bardeen. Syracuse: C.W. Bardeen, 1887.

_____. *Panegersia, or Universal Awakening.* Trans. A. M. O. Dobbie. Shipston-on-Stour: Peter I. Drinkwater, 1990.

_____. *Pannuthesia or Universal Warning.* Trans. A. M. O. Dobbie. Shipston-on-Stour, UK: Peter Drinkwater, 1991.

_____. *The Great Didactic of John Amos Comenius.* Trans. M. W. Keatinge. New York: Russell & Russell, 1967.

_____. *The Labyrinth of the World and the Paradise of the Heart.* Trans. Howard Louthan and Andrea Sterk. New York/Mahwah: Paulist Press.

_____. *The Way of Light.* Translated by Ernest Trafford Campagnac. Liverpool: University Press, 1938.

Dobbie, A. M. O. *Comenius's Pampaedia or Universal Education.* Dover: Buckland, 1986.

Dudley, Joan L. H. "One Picture is Worth a Thousand Words: A Pictorial Word Journey Through the *Orbis Pictus* of J. A. Comenius." PhD diss., St. Louis University, 2010.

Hábl, Jan. "Character formation: A forgotten theme of Comenius's didactics." *Journal of Education and Christian Belief* 15:2 (2011): 141-153.

Jelinek, Vladimir. *The Analytical Didactic of Comenius.* Chicago: University of Chicago Press, 1953.

Kelly, L. G. *25 Centuries of Language Teaching 500 BC – 1969.* Rowley: Newbury House Publishers, 1976.

Laurie, Simon S. *John Amos Comenius Bishop of the Moravians His Life & Educational Works.* Philadelphia: Burt Franklin. 1973.

Monroe, Will. *Comenius and the Beginnings of Educational Reform.* New York: Charles Scribner's Sons, 1900.

Mout, Nicolette. "Comenius, Descartes and Dutch Cartesianism." *Acta Comeniana* 3 (1972): 239-243.

Murphy, Daniel. *Comenius: A Critical Reassessment of his Life and Work*. Portland, OR: Irish Academic Press, 1995.

Nash, Paul. *The Educated Man*. New York: John Wiley & Sons, Inc., 1965.

Pešková, Jaroslava, Josef Cach, and Michal Svatoš, eds. *Homage to J. A. Comenius*. Prague: Charles University in Publishing House Karolinum, 1991.

Pikkarainen, Eetu. "Signs of Reality: The idea of general Bildung by J. A. Comenius." In Pauli Siljander, Ari Kivelä, and Ari Sutinen (eds). *Theories of Bildung and Growth: Connections and Controversies between Continental Educational Thinking and American Pragmatism*. Rotterdam: Sense, 2012.

Reents, Christine. "Comenius' Impulse zur Mädchenbildung? Oder: Die Gleichheit von Mann und Frau als Ausdruck ihrer Gottebenbildlichkeit." In Klaus Goßmann and Christoph Th. Scheilke. *Jan Amos Comenius 1592-1992: Theologische und pädagogische Deutungen*. Gütersloh: Gütersloher Verlagshaus Gerd Mohn, 1992: 49-69.

Sadler, John. *Comenius*. London: Collier-MacMillan Company, 1969.

————. *J. A. Comenius and the Concept of Universal Education*. London: George Allen & Unwin Ltd, 1966.

Schaller, Klaus. "The influence of modern Comenius studies on the philosophy of education in the Federal Republic of Germany." *History of Education* 12:2 (1983): 87-92.

————. "Erziehung zur Menschlichkeit, Komenskys kritischer Beitrag zu Gegenwartsproblemen der Erziehung." In Klaus Goßmann and Christoph Th. Scheilke, *Jan Amos Comenius 1592-1992: Theologische und pädagogische Deutungen*. Gütersloh: Gütersloher Verlagshaus Gerd Mohn, 1992: 17-30.

————. *Johann Amos Comenius: Ein pädagogisches Porträt*. Weinheim: Beltz Verlag, 2004.

Smith, David I. "Biblical Imagery and Educational Imagination: Comenius and the Garden of Delight." In David Lyle Jeffrey and C. Stephen Evans (eds). *The Bible and the University* (Scripture and Hermeneutics Series 8) Milton Keynes/Grand Rapids: Paternoster/Zondervan, 2007: 188-215.

Smith, David I. and Barbara Carvill. *The Gift of the Stranger: Faith, Hospitality, and Foreign Language Learning*. Grand Rapids: Eerdmans, 2000.

Smith, L. Glenn, and Joan Smith. *Lives in Education*. New York: St. Martin's Press, 1994.

Spinka, Matthew. *John Amos Comenius: That Incomparable Moravian*. Chicago: University of Chicago, 1943 or Russell & Russell, 1967.

CHAPTER 13

Richard Baxter:

Educating Through Pastoral Discipleship

BOB R. BAYLES

TIMOTHY K. BEOUGHER

Richard Baxter (1615-1691)

Richard Baxter was a pastor, educator, author, and reformer who significantly challenged the theological and educational landscape of seventeenth century England with lasting implications. The state of theological and biblical education in the twenty-first century American church is not radically different from that of his era in England. In both cultures there is a decline in biblical and theological literacy and a lack of consistent discipleship by those in the church. Thus, Baxter can provide an example for pastors today to envision and practice pastoral discipleship in a culture that struggles with biblical literacy and implementation.

HISTORICAL BACKGROUND

The seventeenth century in Western history was an amazing century, a virtual "who's who" of the historically influential. Foremost among the names are Elizabeth I, Cromwell, James I and II, Anne of Austria, and Louis XIV, Bach, Scarlatti, Descartes, Bacon, Locke, Rembrandt, Milton, Shakespeare, Galileo, Newton, Kepler, Leibnitz, John Owen, and the list goes on. Suffice it to say, Richard Baxter's world was an explosive one where new technologies, new thoughts, new art forms, new sciences, new religious insights, and new educational theories abounded. The Reformation of the previous century gave birth to a host of new ideas that explored on the landscape of seventeenth century Europe. In this *sitz im Leben*, Baxter emerges as a significant force in English history, particularly its religious life.

Richard Baxter was born in 1615 and died in 1691. He lived in a time of revolution and religious persecution. He witnessed the English Civil War, the beheading of Charles I, the Commonwealth under Oliver Cromwell, the restoration of the monarchy under Charles II in 1660, the Great Ejection from the Church of England of two thousand Puritan pastors in 1662, the subsequent persecution of these nonconformists and their followers, and the return of toleration in 1689. His autobiography, *Reliquiae Baxterianae* (1696), serves as a firsthand reflection on these tumultuous events.

Baxter is best known as a Puritan pastor,[1] one who shepherded his flock in Kidderminster, England with great passion and skill. When viewed in light of his later influence, Baxter's early years were far from auspicious. No one could have guessed that this boy, born to Richard and Beatrice Baxter, would amount to much of anything. He was forced to live until the age of ten with his maternal grandfather because of his father's gambling debts. However, after his father's conversion, young Richard returned to his parental home at Eaton Constantine. Through his father's example and particularly by the reading of Edmund Bunny's *Resolution*, Baxter in turn experienced his own conversion at the age of fifteen. Baxter desired university training but instead pursued private tutoring under Richard Wickstead. During his tutoring, Wickstead neglected Baxter but allowed him use of his excellent library. This "self-education" process no doubt contributed to Baxter developing some rather eccentric theological positions.[2]

[1] For overviews of Puritan life, see, John E. Adair, *Founding Fathers: The Puritans in England and America* (London: Dent, 1982); J. I. Packer, *A Quest for Godliness: The Puritan Vision of the Christian Life* (Wheaton: Crossway, 1990); Leland Ryken, *Worldly Saints: The Puritans as They Really Were* (Grand Rapids: Zondervan, 1986); and Stephen Foster, *The Long Argument: English Puritanism and the Shaping of New England Culture, 1570-1700* (Chapel Hill, NC: University of North Carolina Press, 1991).
[2] See Timothy K. Beougher, *Richard Baxter and Conversion: A Study of the Puritan Concept of Becoming a Christian* (Tain, Scotland: Christian Focus Publications, 2007).

After his ordination in the Church of England, Baxter served as a schoolmaster in Dudley and then as a curate in Bridgnorth. While Baxter was at Bridgnorth, the parishioners of Kidderminster threatened to petition Parliament against their vicar and his curate on charges of incompetence and drunkenness. To avoid the looming scandal, the vicar agreed to dismiss the curate and offered to give up his pulpit to any lecturer whom the parishioners might select. In March, 1641, the church called Baxter as their lecturer.

In Kidderminster, a town of approximately two thousand persons, Baxter exercised his pastoral ministry for fifteen months before a five-year interruption due to the English Civil War (1642-1647), then again for fourteen years. He became seriously ill near the end of the Civil War and languished near death at the estate home of some friends. Thinking he was about to die, Baxter meditated on heaven. He eventually recovered from the serious illness (though he would remain in poor health the remainder of his life) and published his meditations on heaven. The resulting book, *The Saints Everlasting Rest,* was a run-away bestseller, bringing Baxter immediate fame.

Most significantly, Baxter claims that his illness, "made me study and preach things necessary, and a little stirred up my sluggish heart to speak to sinners with some compassion, *as a dying man to dying men.*"[3] This phrase became his motto, a guidepost for his life and ministry. He uses the phrase over and over in his works. His life was a continual struggle against death. He was harassed by a constant cough, frequent bleedings from the nose, migraine headaches, digestive ailments, kidney stones, gall stones, etc. He has been called a virtual "museum of diseases."[4] Living in an era before painkillers, Baxter tells us that from the age of twenty-one onwards that he was "seldom an hour free from pain."[5]

After the civil war, he returned to his ministerial duties at Kidderminster in June 1647, where his life became a model of ministerial consistency and faithfulness. In addition to his regular parish work between 1647 and 1660, he still found time to write and publish fifty-seven books, including *The Reformed Pastor*, *A Treatise on Conversion*, and *A Call to the Unconverted*.[6] He labored successfully by visiting his parishioners in their homes, giving

---

[3] *The Autobiography of Richard Baxter*, ed. by N.H. Keeble (London: J.M. Dent & Sons, 1974), 26 [emphasis added].

[4] Timothy Beougher and J. I. Packer, "Go Fetch Baxter," *Christianity Today* (December 16, 1991): 27.

[5] *Autobiography*, 76.

[6] The *Treatise on Conversion* and *Call to the Unconverted* were originally preached. Baxter wrote his pulpit notes in shorthand. Thomas Baldwin, who lived with him and took over the ministry at Kidderminster when Baxter was ejected, learned to decipher Baxter's shorthand notes, and transcribed many of his sermons for the printer.

them public and private instruction, and becoming their friend as well as their pastor.[7]

The political and religious landscape changed following the period of the English Commonwealth when Charles II became king. The Act of Uniformity was passed on May 19, 1662, establishing the extreme Episcopal polity as orthodoxy and threatening removal from their places of ministry all who disagreed and refused to "conform." Baxter left the Church of England six days later, officially embracing non-conformity.

In the earlier period of his ministry, Baxter had resolved not to marry so that he might pursue his pastoral and ministerial duties without interruption.[8] However, after "leaving" the Church of England, he married Margaret Charlton[9] on September 10, 1662. While Baxter used the Prayer Book, he did not utilize the aspects that he and many other Puritans felt were unscriptural elements. However, when the Act of Uniformity mandated full compliance with the Prayer Book, Baxter and some two thousand other Puritan pastors left the Church of England rather than sacrifice their theological integrity.

THEOLOGY OF CHRISTIAN EDUCATION

Possessing a Bible does not mean understanding the Bible. Baxter discovered this reality in a harsh way. When he entered pastoral ministry in Kidderminster, biblical and theological illiteracy was paramount among his parishioners. He determined he would correct this problem. Through a process of preaching biblically and theologically sound

---

[7] See Richard Baxter, *The Reformed Pastor* (Carlisle, PA: Banner of Truth reprint, 1974).

[8] E.g., in his *Christian Directory*, Baxter claims that while it is not "unlawful" for ministers to marry, "so great a hinderance [sic] ordinarily is this troublesome state of life to the sacred ministration which they undertake, that a very clear call should be expected for their satisfaction." *The Practical Works of Richard Baxter*. Vol. 1, (London: George Virtue, 1838), 400. Though this work was not published until after his marriage (1673), it may be taken to be representative of his thought throughout his life.

After his marriage he not only recorded his belief that for himself at Kidderminster "my single life afforded me much advantage" but he also continued to commend celibacy for ministers in general. He says that even Margaret "lived and died in the same mind." *Breviate*, 101.

See also Timothy K. Beougher, "The Puritan View of Marriage: The Nature of the Husband/Wife Relationship in Puritan England as Taught and Experienced by a Representative Puritan Pastor, Richard Baxter," *Trinity Journal* 10 n.s. (Fall 1989): 131-58.

[9] Margaret had been converted under Baxter's preaching at Kidderminster. Baxter tells the story of their marriage in his tribute to her titled, *A Breviate of the Life of Margaret, the Daughter of Francis Charlton, of Apply in Shropshire, Esq; and Wife of Richard Baxter. For the use of all, but especially of their Kindred* (London: B. Simmons, 1681). It was reprinted in 1928 as *Richard Baxter and Margaret Charlton: A Puritan Love Story*, ed. by John T. Wilkinson (London: George Allen & Unwin Ltd.) and in 1997 as *A Grief Sanctified: Passing Through Grief to Peace and Joy*, ed. by J. I. Packer (Ann Arbor, Mich.: Servant Publications).

sermons and his commitment to teaching every family in his parish in their homes, Baxter reversed this illiteracy and brought to his congregation in Kidderminster a deeper understanding of the Bible and God. Thus, he believed that the role of the shepherd was personal discipleship and in this discipleship he intentionally taught each family in his fold – biblical and practical truths about scripture. Indeed, part of the Puritan passion was a deep understanding of God, the Bible, and his world.

THEOLOGICAL HERMENEUTIC

The task of "hermeneutics" is to explain or interpret the Scriptures. For Baxter, hermeneutics had a historical commitment in that an author interprets a passage for others in the context of his/her historical setting. We may attempt to divorce ourselves from our context and attempt to arrive at a purely objective view of the text, but that is not completely possible – even for the best of scholars. Baxter recognized this challenge and accepted the charge to assist seventeenth Century Englishmen/women to translate the scriptures from Palestinian to an English context.

On this topic of translating context to truth, one author explained that Baxter was an astute "exegete of his culture as well as of his church."[10] This statement that *he was an exegete of his culture* reveals our task at hand and how studying Baxter can encourage readers to understand the task of teaching and discipline in their own ministerial context. His historical setting forced his interpretation of Scripture. Baxter had a burden for evangelism, discipleship, and pastoral oversight of his congregation which he felt the Church of England had neglected. We clearly see his Puritan roots in his passion to pastor his church members in Kidderminster, for their conversion and education in biblical principles.

THEOLOGY OF THE PURITANS

In essence, Baxter's theological hermeneutic was the hermeneutic of his puritanism. He interpreted scripture as if it were the word of God spoken years ago for the culture of his day. This Word was to be applied in everyday life, as Christians were to live out their faith in a practically similar fashion as the Apostle Paul lived out his faith. However, in order to fully understand Baxter, one must gain insight into these "Puritan" roots that formed the basis of his theology.

---

[10] Lynell Friesen, "The Work and Thought of Richard Baxter," *Third Millennium Ministries: IIIM Magazine,* July 3, 2000.

The Puritans were above all else a "Bible movement."[11] Puritanism is a spiritual movement that began in Protestant Reformation England. Following Henry VIII's decision to sever ties with Rome (following Pope Clement VII's refusal to grant Henry a divorce from Catherine of Aragon), the English Church went from Protestant (under Edward VI), back to Catholic (under Mary, whose putting to death of Protestants earned her the nickname "Bloody Mary"), to what became known as the Great Compromise under Elizabeth I. Elizabeth I desired to end the religious turmoil, so her compromise was the formation of the Anglican Church — a church with basically Protestant beliefs (though some doctrinal statements were purposely ambiguous) but with some elements of religious practice (endorsed by the Anglican Prayer Book) that made "high church" proponents feel more comfortable. The Puritans desired to rid the Prayer Book of those practices they found unbiblical and superstitious.

Baxter's thinking was thoroughly entrenched in Puritanism, particularly of the seventeenth century. Shaw argues that Baxter's hermeneutic, or theological method, can be traced to the concept of "delighting in God."[12] The essence of this delight to is to "live for the pleasure of God" and to "glorify him by enjoying him forever."[13] Further, Shaw explains that the theological framework of Puritanism which Baxter worked within, sought to reform many aspects of church life, including worship, piety, and morals in accordance with scriptural principles.[14] Chief among these principles for Baxter was "delighting in God." For Baxter, this was not " ... fantasizing about God or having private visions. It is not ecstasy or excitement, some sort of religious shiver that goes up and down the spine. It is not the absence of sorrow or fear ... "[15] Rather, in Baxter's own words, delight in God is "...a solid, rational complacency [satisfaction] of the soul in God and holiness, arising from the apprehensions of

---

[11] J. I. Packer, *Among God's Giants* (Eastbourne, England: Kingsway, 1991), 129.

[12] Mark Shaw, *10 Great Ideas from Church History* (Downers Grove, IL: InterVarsity Press, 1997), 95. Shaw also borrows from John Piper in order to offer a synonymous understanding of delighting in God with Piper's terminology, "Christian Hedonism." Shaw defines Christian Hedonism saying, "A hedonist is someone who lives for pleasure. A Christian hedonist is someone who lives for the pleasures of God. For a Christian hedonist the chief end of humankind is to glorify God by enjoying him forever. Christian hedonism seeks not to make a god out of pleasure but to make God our highest pleasure and treasure. In fact, Christian hedonism sees increasing delight in God as the essential key to breaking the hold of Faustianism [secular mindedness] in our churches and our culture and unleashing a new spirit of true worship." For more on delighting in God see John Piper, *Desiring God: Meditations of a Christian Hedonist* (Portland, OR: Multnomah Press, 2011).

[13] Shaw, *10 Great Ideas,* 95.

[14] Ibid.

[15] Ibid., 100.

that in him which is justly delectable to us."[16] In short, this means to be satisfied with God in every aspect of life with no need to draw from secular sources. Shaw states that Baxter's great idea is that "... our worship of God is at its best when our delight in God is at its height."[17] This theology should greatly extend our understanding of worship as more than the musical aspects of a Sunday morning service. For Baxter, this great idea extended into his pastoral ministry as a means of getting people to know God and live out the Christian life in everyday, practical living.[18] This was done by Baxter through the intensive discipling of the people of Kidderminster. If Shaw is correct, then delighting in God becomes a primary lens through which Baxter saw his work and ultimately frames his theological hermeneutic.

CONTRIBUTIONS TO CHRISTIAN EDUCATION

While Baxter was a pastor and theologian, it is his contributions to theological education that draws our attention. Packer writes about Baxter saying, "A schoolmaster by instinct, Baxter usually called himself his people's teacher, and teaching was to his mind the minister's main task." [19] As a pastor, Baxter was intensely committed to the discipleship (he called this catechizing) of every one of the eight-hundred families in his parish of Kidderminster. He accomplished this task by visiting at least fifteen families per week, going into their homes and personally teaching them the principles of scripture. Associates aided Baxter in this monumental task, but it was a task he was firmly committed to and to which he was successful. He explained the spiritual condition of this flock at his arrival saying, "When I came thither first, there was about one family in a street that worshipped God and called on his name, and when I came away there were some streets where there was not passed one family in the side of a street that did not do so; and that did not by professing serious godliness, give us hopes of their sincerity ... "[20]

In *The Reformed Pastor,* he described his approach and the response of his parishioners.

---

[16] Baxter, *Christian Directory,* in *Practical Works,* I:158.

[17] Shaw, 96. For an excellent treatment on worship, see Harold Best, *Unceasing Worship: Biblical Perspectives on Worship and the Arts* (Downers Grove, IL: IVP, 2003).

[18] J. I. Packer, *Knowing God* (Downers Grove, IL: IVP, 2003). This great idea could very well be the impetus for Packer's book.

[19] J. I. Packer, "Introduction" to Richard Baxter, *The Reformed Pastor* (Carlisle, PA: Banner of Truth reprint, 1974), 12.

[20] Baxter, *Reliquiae Baxterianae,* I, 84-85.

We spend Monday and Tuesday, from morning almost to night in the work, taking about fifteen or sixteen families in a week, that we may go through the parish, in which there are upwards of eight hundred families, in a year; and I cannot say yet that one family hath refused to come to me, and but few persons excused and shifted it off. And I find more outward signs of success with most that come, than from all my public preaching to them.[21]

The key to Baxter's pastoral method was personal care of individuals, based upon intimate knowledge of their daily lives, prompted and sustained by an unaffected and impartial love for all. At first, he was content to catechize only those in the Church, and to talk with individuals now and then. He discovered, however, that for his preaching to be fruitful he must follow it up with direct personal discourse with every family in his parish. He urged pastors to take up this ministry of personal instruction with this heartfelt plea.

I study to speak as plainly and movingly as I can, and yet I frequently meet with those that have been my hearers eight or ten years, who know not whether Christ be God or man, and wonder when I tell them the history of his birth and life and death, as if they had never heard it before. . . . I have found by experience, that some ignorant persons, who have been so long unprofitable hearers, have got more knowledge and remorse of conscience in half an hour's *close discourse*, than they did from ten years' public preaching. I know that preaching the gospel publicly is the most excellent means, because we speak to many at once. But it is usually far more effectual to preach it privately to a particular sinner, as to himself: for the plainest man this is, can scarcely speak plain enough in public for them to understand; but in private we may do it much more.

I conclude, therefore, that public preaching alone will not be sufficient ... Long may you study and preach to little purpose, if you neglect this duty [of personal instruction].[22]

He felt compelled to disciple his parishioners during the week so that they had a basic framework of theology to understand his sermons. Baxter's concern was that everyone in his parish was to be educated in the faith. Baxter's admission that such daily attention to his church members reaped more reward than the sermons he preached. This provides great insight regarding his vision of education and discipleship.

As Baxter emphasizes throughout *The Reformed Pastor*, in order for him to be able to preach theologically sound sermons on Sunday, the people must understand Monday-

---

[21] Baxter, *The Reformed Pastor*, 43.
[22] Ibid., 196.

Saturday. His emphasis on teaching his members throughout the week reveals a great deal regarding how the goals of Christian education should be accomplished. He taught throughout the week so that he could preach theologically on Sunday – and so they could understand the theology of these sermons.

THE ROLE OF THE TEACHER

Early in *The Reformed Pastor,* Baxter lays the groundwork for the purpose of his writing this book by sharing a parable.

> If thousands of you were in a leaking ship, and those that should pump out the water, and stop the leaks, should be sporting or asleep, or even but favouring themselves in their labours, to the hazarding of you all, would you not awaken them to their work and call on them to labour as for your lives? ... Would you not say, "The work must be done, or we are all dead men. Is the ship ready to sink, and do you talk of reputation? Or had you rather hazard yourself and us, than hear of your slothfulness?" This is our case, brethren. The word of God must needs be done! Souls must not perish while you mind your worldly business or worldly pleasures, and take your ease, or quarrel with your brethren! Nor must we be silent while men are hastened by you to perdition, and the Church brought into greater danger and confusion ... [23]

Baxter's specific cry was to pastors, but one can see the seedbed for greater responsibility that he later references and locates in the role of the parent. [24] His charge was a similar to Paul's charge in 2 Timothy 2:4-6; however, here Baxter argues that pastors and educators must not worry about world pursuits and in so doing neglect the spiritual care of those in our charge. While Baxter may not have an explicit treatise on teaching in an educational setting, he provides readers with enough information to extrapolate foundational tenets he had regarding the role of a teacher in the shepherding of pupils toward godliness. "You, that are schoolmasters and tutors, begin and end with the things of God. Speak daily to the hearts of your scholars those things that must be wrought into their hearts, or else they are undone. Let some piercing words fall frequently from your mouths, of God, and the state of their souls, and the life to come. Do not say, they are too young to understand and entertain

---

[23] Ibid., 39-40.

[24] Baxter devoted a section of his *Christian Directory* to instruct parents, especially fathers, on their role as spiritual leaders in the home. That section from the *Christian Directory*, including the duties of fathers, mothers, and children, was published in a single volume edited by Randall J. Pederson: Richard Baxter, *The Godly Home* (Wheaton, IL: Crossway, 2010).

them. You little know what impressions they may make." [25] His reference to the teacher is also his advice to pastors who take part in discipleship. Repeatedly, he warns the pastor of his solemn duties to the congregation. Education seems to be central to his thought and processes of making disciples. "Doth not a careful shepherd look after every individual sheep? And a good schoolmaster after every individual scholar? And a good physician after every particular patient? And a good commander after every individual solder? Why then should not the shepherds, the teachers, the physicians, the guides of the churches of Christ, take heed to every individual member of their charge?" [26] Moving his attention from the church to the home, Baxter transitions his focus from the teacher as pastor to the teacher as parent. On family education he says,

> We must have a special eye upon families, to see that they are well ordered, and the duties of each relation performed. The life of religion, and the welfare and glory of both the Church and State, depend much on family government and duty. If we suffer the neglect of this, we shall undo all … If any good be begun by the ministry in any soul, a careless, prayerless, worldly family is like to stifle it, or very much hinder it … Neglect not, I beseech you, this necessary part of your work. Get masters [fathers] of families to do their duty, and they will not only spare you a great deal of labour, but will much further the success of your labours. If a captain can get the officers under him to do their duty, he may rule the soldiers with much less trouble, than if all lay upon his own shoulders. *You are not like to see no general reformation, till you procure family reformation.* [27]

It is this emphasis on the discipleship of families where Baxter provides modern educators with important insights into various educational endeavors. Similar to Baxter's time period, the evidence of biblical illiteracy surrounds us, but he provides specific instructions to pastors for teaching families to have a greater awareness and investment in their faith.

> (1) Get information on how each family is ordered, that you may know how to proceed in your endeavours for their further good. (2) Go occasionally among them, when they are likely to be most at leisure, and ask the master of the family whether he prays with them, and reads the Scripture, or what he doth? Labour to convince such as neglect this, of their sin; and if you have opportunity, pray with them before you go, and give them an example of what you would have them do. (3) If you find any, through ignorance and want of practice, unable to pray, persuade them to study

---

[25] Baxter, *The Reformed Pastor*, 60.

[26] Ibid., 91.

[27] Ibid., 100-102, emphasis added.

their own wants, and to get their hearts affected with them, and, in the meanwhile, advise them to use a form of prayer, rather than not to pray at all. (4) See that in every family there are some useful moving books, beside the Bible. (5) Direct them how to spent the Lord's day; how to dispatch their worldly business, so as to prevent encumbrances and distractions; and when they have been at church, how to spend the time in their families. The life of religion dependeth much on this ... Persuade the master of every family to cause his children and servants to repeat the Catechism to him, every Sabbath evening, and to give him some account of what they have heard at church during the day.[28]

THE ROLE OF CURRICULUM

For Baxter, all study and thus all curricular investment should integrate a study of God. For, "nothing can be rightly known, if God be not known; nor is any study well managed, nor to any great purpose, where God is not studied."[29] He explained that the Christian faith is learned in order saying,

> How can you build, if you first not lay a good foundation? Or how can you set on the top-stone, while the middle parts are neglected? 'Grace makes no leaps,' any more than nature. The second order of Christian truths have such a dependence upon the first, that they can never be well learned till the first are learned ... The most godly people, therefore, in your congregations, will find it worth their labour to learn the very words of a catechism. If, then, you would safely edify them, and firmly establish them, be diligent in this work.[30]

The context of Baxter's educational investment was as the pastor of Kidderminster. There, he recognized that the parishioners under his care were not aware of scriptural or theological truths; therefore, he believed that all study should do a better job of making pupils aware of the truths therein. According to Baxter, studying "some little knowledge of the works of God, and of some of those names which the divided tongues of the nations have imposed on them, and not to know God himself, nor exalt him in their hearts" is "poor business."[31] Therefore, education and the teaching of God should not be in an abstract sense or for the sake of knowledge, but for the knowledge of God in a relational sense. For, "this is the sanctification of your studies, when they are devoted to God, and when he is the end, the object, and the life of them all."[32]

---

[28] Ibid., 100-101.

[29] Ibid., 56.

[30] Ibid., 176-177.

[31] Ibid., 56.

[32] Ibid., 58.

CONCLUSION

We have, as did Baxter, a biblically and theologically illiterate populace. This includes those within the church. So where do we begin applying Baxter and his approach? Baxter's pastoral theology cannot be simply reduced to a discipleship model. His approach resists the twenty-first century tendency to develop a twelve-step process. His approach was a philosophical one, an educational philosophy that aligned itself with sound biblical and theological principles. Certainly there were methods he used. He utilized other ministers around him in this task. The Bible was the primary curriculum he used. The outcome he desired was a more biblically and theologically minded parishioner. These he accomplished. But we must resist the effort to label all he did as a method.

What we can surmise from reading Baxter are two important lessons that transcend time and location. First, Baxter himself was a thinker, a pastor, and a disciple-maker. It has been noted that congregations typically do not rise higher than the person in the pulpit. So we begin with the local pastor. This person should be biblically and theologically trained. It does not mean they must possess advanced degrees before pastoring, but neither should beginners and theologically unaware persons be in a pastoral/leadership role.[33]

Second, we must embrace Baxter's emphasis on family ministry. Baxter shares what he has learned through experience: "You are not like to see any general reformation, till you procure family reformation. Some little religion there may be, here and there; but while it is confined to single persons, and is not promoted in families, it will not prosper, nor promise much future increase."[34] This is a profound theological statement for today. We must find ways to train families and make them biblically and theologically literate. The trend of biblical and theological illiteracy today is eerily reminiscent of Baxter's Kidderminster congregation. He knew that without a reformation of the family – a reformation that held biblical and theological literacy as central – there could be no reformation of his church and ultimately no reformation of society.

PRIMARY SOURCE SAMPLE[35]

We must study to build up those who are already truly converted. In this respect our work is various, according to the various states of Christians.

---

[33] Note Paul's qualifications for elders in Titus 1:9, "holding fast the faithful word which is in accordance with the teaching, that he may be able both to exhort in sound doctrine and to refute those who contradict" and in 1 Timothy 3:6, "and not a new convert, so that he will not become conceited and fall into the condemnation incurred by the devil."

[34] Baxter, *The Reformed Pastor*, 102, emphasis added.

[35] Ibid., 97-98.

There are many of our flock that are young and weak, who, though they are of long standing, are yet of small proficiency or strength. This, indeed, is the most common condition of the godly. Most of them content themselves with low degrees of grace, and it is no easy matter to get them higher. To bring them to higher and stricter opinions is easy, that is, to bring them from the truth into error, on the right hand as well as on the left; but to increase their knowledge and gifts is not easy, and to increase their graces is the hardest of all ...

Now, seeing the case of weakness in the converted is so sad, how diligent should we be to cherish and increase their grace! The strength of Christians is the honour of the Church. When they are inflamed with the love of God, and live by a lively working faith, and set light by the profits and honours of the world, and love one another with a pure heart fervently, and can bear and heartily forgive a wrong, and suffer joyfully for the cause of Christ, and study to do good, and walk in-offensively and harmlessly in the world, are ready to be servants to all men for their good, becoming all things to all men in order to win them to Christ, and yet abstaining from the appearance of evil, and seasoning all their actions with a sweet mixture of prudence, humility, zeal, and heavenly mindedness — oh, what an honour are such to their profession! What an ornament to the Church; and how serviceable to God and man! Men would sooner believe that the gospel is from heaven, if they saw more such effects of it upon the hearts and lives of those who profess it. The world is better able to read the nature of religion in a man's life than in the Bible ... It is, therefore, a most important part of our work, to labour more in the polishing and perfecting of the saints, that they may be strong in the Lord, and fitted for their Master's service.

BIBLIOGRAPHY

Adair, John E. *Founding Fathers: The Puritans in England and America.* London: Dent, 1982.

Baxter, Richard. *The Autobiography of Richard Baxter.* Edited by N.H. Keeble. London: J.M. Dent & Sons, 1974.

_____. *A Breviate of the Life of Margaret, the Daughter of Francis Charlton, of Apply in Shropshire, Esq; and Wife of Richard Baxter. For the use of all, but especially of their Kindred.* London: B. Simmons, 1681.

_____. *A Christian Directory,* Volume 1 of *The Practical Works of Richard Baxter.* London: George Virtue, 1838.

_____. *The Godly Home.* Edited by Randall J. Pederson. Wheaton, IL: Crossway, 2010.

_____. *The Reformed Pastor.* Carlisle, PA: Banner of Truth reprint, 1974.

_____. *Reliquiae Baxterianae.* London: T. Parkhurst, 1696.

Beougher, Timothy K. *Richard Baxter and Conversion: A Study of the Puritan Concept of Becoming a Christian.* Tain, Scotland: Christian Focus Publications, 2007.

_____. "The Puritan View of Marriage: The Nature of the Husband/Wife Relationship in Puritan England as Taught and Experienced by a Representative Puritan Pastor, Richard Baxter," *Trinity Journal* 10 n.s. (Fall 1989): 131-58.

Beougher, Timothy and J. I. Packer. "Go Fetch Baxter." *Christianity Today* (December 16, 1991): 27.

Best, Harold. *Unceasing Worship: Biblical Perspectives on Worship and the Arts.* Downers Grove, IL: IVP, 2003.

Foster, Stephen. *The Long Argument: English Puritanism and the Shaping of the New England Culture, 1570-1700.* Chapel Hill, NC: Univ. of North Carolina Press, 1991.

Freisen, Lynell. "The Work and Thought of Richard Baxter." *Third Millennium Ministries: IIIM Magazine,* July 3, 2000.

Packer, J. I. *Among God's Giants.* Eastbourne, England: Kingsway Press, 1991.

_____. *A Quest for Godliness: The Puritan Vision of the Christian Life.* Wheaton: Crossway, 1990.

_____. "Introduction" to Richard Baxter, *The Reformed Pastor.* Carlisle, PA: Banner of Truth reprint, 1974.

_____. *Knowing God.* Downers Grove, IL: IVP, 2003.

Piper, John. *Desiring God: Meditations of a Christian Hedonist.* Portland, OR: Multnomah Press, 2011.

Ryken, Leland. *Worldly Saints: The Puritans as They Really Were.* Grand Rapids: Zondervan, 1986.

Shaw, Mark. *10 Great Ideas from Church History.* Downers Grove, IL: Intervarsity Press, 1997.

CHAPTER 14

August Hermann Francke:

Architect of Practical Piety

TOM SCHWANDA

MARK A. LAMPORT

August Hermann Francke (1633-1727)

August Hermann Francke was a man of extraordinary accomplishments who escaped the nominal Christianity of his seventeenth-century, state-run Lutheran Church and put his newfound faith into practice – vigorous, action-oriented, disciplined, community-changing practice. His desire in ministry, which led him to create schools, an orphanage, and mission activities, was to pursue the transformation of individuals, the church, his country, and the world. If his is a name the reader would not recognize, Francke would not mind. He sought to live simply the disciplined Christian life, submitting his will to that of God, and producing great acts of faith and mercy and transmitting contribution. Following is a brief account of Francke's history, thinking, and influence on Christian education theory and practice.

HISTORICAL BACKGROUND

Germany faced numerous conflicts both politically and spiritually in the seventeenth century. The Thirty Years' War (1618-1648) between Protestants and Roman Catholics unleashed widespread devastation across Europe, destroying approximately one-third of the population and wreaking havoc with an unstable economy. Tragically, this war did not bring lasting resolution and new hostility erupted in many regions after the 1670s. Spiritually, life was also difficult as the Lutheran Church emphasized a rigid form of confessionalism that elevated preservation of theological orthodoxy at the expense of an equal recognition of a deep personal relationship with God, at least in the minds of the Pietists.

August Hermann Francke, as a Lutheran pastor, had been formed in the strict orthodoxy of his native church. Doctrinal precision was frequently elevated to specific propositions that needed to be affirmed rather than a vibrant faith in which to live out the gospel. The typical Lutheran sermon was strong on polemic and erudite quotations of abstract references to the original languages of the Bible and short on practical biblical wisdom to guide the daily activities of the German citizen. While a few leaders within the Lutheran orthodoxy recognized the necessity for change, the greater call for renewal emerged from German Pietism.[1] Some of the primary characteristics of German Pietism included the necessity of a vibrant personal faith in Jesus Christ through conversion, conventicles (i.e. small groups) that encouraged daily renewal through reading of Scripture and prayer, irenic relationships with other Christians that sought to create ecumenical networks, and acts of social compassion motivated out of love for Jesus to those in need. Until recently, Philip Jacob Spener (1635–1705), was recognized as the "father of German Pietism." More current scholarship has accorded that title to Johann Jacob Schütz (1640–1690), the Lutheran layperson best known today for his stirring hymn, "Sing Praise to God Who Reigns Above." Nonetheless, Spener's *Pia Desideria* (i.e. pious desires), written in 1675, convincingly established the vision for renewal of the Lutheran Church. His recommendations stressed a more practical use of the Bible, greater involvement of the laity, a greater reliance upon love for daily life and dealing with controversies, and that theological training should both elevate the importance of piety and equip preachers to proclaim the gospel to save souls and not just parade one's scholarship.

Francke was born in Lübeck, a village in northern Germany, near the Danish

---

[1] The best introduction to German Pietism is Douglas H. Shantz, *An Introduction to German Pietism* (Baltimore: The John Hopkins University Press, 2013). The term "German Pietism" is intentional to distinguish it from Reformed Pietism that developed earlier than its Lutheran counterpart.

border. As a young boy, Francke attended the local school in Gotha, Germany, where he became acquainted with the educational principles of Wolfgang Ratich (1571–1635) and John Amos Comenius.[2] They, in turn, had developed their own experiments of pedagogy from Francis Bacon. Francke continued his education at a number of German universities, including a significant period at Leipzig where he first came in contact with Spener.[3] Spener encouraged Francke and his classmates to transform the agenda of their *collegium philobiblicum* (i.e. weekly gathering to practice the exegesis of scripture) to become more personal and devotional in nature. Lutheran orthodox professors and clergy alike were disturbed by this non-academic approach and tension soon grew between Francke and his critics. As he attempted to integrate Spener's agenda for spiritual renewal into practice, he experienced a protracted spiritual struggle for repentance (*Busskampf*) that reached its climax in 1687 as he prepared to preach his first sermon. His study of John 20:31 ("These signs have been written in order that you may hold the faith that Jesus is the Christ, the Son of God, and that through faith you may possess life in his name.") eventually brought the desired spiritual awakening and rebirth within him. His emphasis on a vital heart experience of Jesus Christ combined with his proclivity to criticize the Orthodox Lutheran clergy created frequent controversy that occasioned a number of short-term pastorates.

As a young pastor, Francke revealed his desire to encourage a deeper understanding and application of scripture through regular usage of the catechism with children, discussion following his sermons, and inviting parishioners into his home for further dialogue on spiritual matters. He faced increased hostilities and attacks from Lutheran Orthodox pastors until late 1691 when the trajectory of his ministry radically shifted with his appointment as professor of biblical languages at the newly formed Halle University; he also pastored the church in Glaucha, a suburb of Halle.[4] Glaucha had faced numerous challenges following the Thirty Years' War that decimated half of its population of approximately two-thousand people. While it rebounded better economically than other towns in Germany, it was severely hit by a plague in 1682–1683 and massive fires in 1683–1684, both of which further decreased its size to about four-hundred residents. Glaucha had grown

---

[2] Francke was an unusual child; for example, at the age of ten, he asked his mother for a small room for study and prayer. He was also something of a child prodigy; by 16 Francke had studied philology, philosophy, Greek, logic, metaphysics, geography, history, and Hebrew. He was a linguistic genius—by his death he knew some 35 languages.

[3] Francke stayed at Hamburg with followers of Spener, and then several months with Spener as houseguest. From that time, he addressed Spener as father, and Spener addressed Francke as son.

[4] Seven years later, he was appointed professor of theology, and in 1716 he became vice chancellor at the university, where he served until his death in 1727.

to about five-hundred people when Francke arrived in 1692. The challenges of ministry were further complicated by the ratio of thirty-seven taverns to two-hundred households that not surprisingly created a reputation for drunkenness and poor morality.[5]

THEOLOGY OF CHRISTIAN EDUCATION

The End we aim at, and the Means we make use of for obtaining the same, are all of one Piece. The Word of God is instilled into the Children from their Youth up. Unfeigned Faith in our Lord Jesus Christ is laid for a Foundation, and a real Sense of Godliness, attended with a conscientious Behavior, are the most material Points, to the obtaining whereof, our earnest endeavours are constantly directed .[6]

Before Francke's conversion, he possessed little awareness of the dynamic and transformative nature of theology. Gary Sattler's translation of Francke's *Lebenslauf* (i.e. autobiography) is very revealing as Francke confesses: "My theology I grasped in my head and not in my heart, and it was more a dead science than a living understanding. I knew well what to say, what faith, rebirth, justification, renewal, etc., are, also knew well how to discern one from the other and how to prove it with texts from Scripture, but of it all I found nothing in my heart and had nothing more than what floated about in my memory and fantasy."[7] Francke recognized that conversion was essential not only to do theology properly, but also to truly grasp the revelatory meaning of scripture. Throughout his writings and ministry, this is reflected in his vision of living, preaching, and teaching so that he and others could live to God's glory and one's neighbor's good. From these organizing principles, he deemed education should be holistic and benefit every dimension of life. The seismic shift of life and faith through his conversion was immediately realized as Francke asserts, "Although I had previously made an idol of education I saw now that faith like a mustard seed is worth more than a hundred sacks full of education."[8] The effect was soon evident to his students. Instead of lecturing in Latin, the normal language for theological discourse, he spoke in the vernacular German and provided opportunities for questions and discussions at the end of each lecture.[9] Francke recognized that the impact of knowledge upon one's life

---

[5] Shantz, *An Introduction to German Pietism*, 119-120.

[6] From Francke's *Pietas hallensis* and recorded in *Abstract of the Marvelous Footsteps of Divine Providence* (London: J. Downing, 1707), pp. 35, 36.

[7] Gary R. Sattler, *God's Glory, Neighbor's Good* (Chicago: Covenant Press, 1982), 26.

[8] Ibid., 33.

[9] While this may not seem an unusual teaching methodology to twenty-first century American

was far more important than the mere accumulation of it. This transformed his pedagogy, as he placed sincere repentance as the essential foundation for any educational efforts. While he realized not all students would begin at this point, it was critical for them to experience repentance and conversion before they completed their studies. Markus Matthias summarizes Francke's conviction asserting, "to make of the student a real theologian or scholar of God, thus one [is] taught by God (John 6:45)."[10] Additionally, Francke's own conversion opened his eyes to grasp scripture more fully. In reading the Old Testament, he used the imagery of the husk and kernel of scripture to communicate the manner of finding Christological meaning. Reliance only on the historical-grammatical method would never lead one to the presence of Christ, but only the husk of the passage. According to Francke, there was a deeper message behind the literal interpretation and that only those reborn could perceive Jesus Christ (the kernel) in that text. Additionally, he realized the important partnership that was required between scripture and the Holy Spirit to comprehend and appositely apply God's word to the person's life. This was critical since it was the Holy Spirit who had placed the deeper meaning of scripture within the text. Therefore, according to Francke, unless one was reborn and guided by the Holy Spirit one would only be able to grasp the literal or technical knowledge of scripture and not the vital *cognitio spiritualis* (spiritual knowledge) of the dynamic word of God.[11]

Another significant component of Francke's theology that directly impacted his practice of education was his sensitivity to the poor of Glaucha. His 1697 sermon on "The Duty to the Poor" based on Luke 16:19–31 (the rich man and Lazarus) is most illuminating.[12] Francke reminds his listeners that there is no excuse for neglecting the poor and those with means should simplify their lives so they can help those in need. While it is wise to serve the poor with the proper motive, their service is ultimately caring for Jesus himself (Matt. 25:40). Further, due to impoverished conditions, many parents neglected to send their children to school which further diminished their moral upbringing. This, in part, inspired Francke to open an orphanage more for neglected children than strictly defined orphans.[13] This reflects another dimension of his theology; that education was the best means for lifting children out of poverty. All these efforts are reflective of Francke's emphasis upon the practical nature of

---

education, it was highly abnormal in German and most European university classrooms.

[10] Markus Matthias, "August Hermann Francke (1663–1727)" in Carter Lindberg, ed. *The Pietist Theologians* (Malden, MA: Blackwell Publishing, 2005), 109.

[11] Matthias, "August Hermann Francke," 106.

[12] See Sattler, *God's Glory, Neighbor's Good*, 155–185 for the complete sermon.

[13] Further insight into this will be discussed below.

theology as he sought to awaken whomever he could with the vital nature of piety or "true religion." One of his common ways of summarizing this has been recorded in his memoirs, "an ounce of true faith, was of more value than pounds of knowledge; and that a drop of sincere love to God and man, was to be esteemed above an ocean of learning."[14]

CONTRIBUTION TO CHRISTIAN EDUCATION

Over time, Francke created a vast and expansive network of educational institutions (*Stiftungen*). His first venture was the *Armen–Schule* (poor school) established before Easter 1695, which provided an opportunity for both boys and girls to receive instruction free of charge. By Pentecost of the same year, the progress of those children was so impressive that some parents offered to pay tuition if Francke would open a similar school for their children (i.e. *Bürger-Schule* or school for citizens). Shortly after Pentecost, Francke added a third school, *Pedagogium Regium* (school for royalty) – dedicated to children of nobility. His creative and organizational genius continued to explore new opportunities and eventually included a Latin school to prepare boys for the university, a high school for girls, and a teacher's college for training the theological students who then taught in Francke's various schools. The older students would tutor two hours a day in the schools in exchange for their meals.

In 1698, Francke began his famous orphanage with education as its primary goal. The motivation behind its construction reveals an important principle in Francke's pedagogical vision: many of the children who were carefully taught in his school quickly lost the benefit of their instruction due to the unhealthy and immoral environments in which they lived. This conviction is descriptive of Francke's understanding of Christian formation, that one should never assume that any aspect of life is neutral without in some way impacting education either for good or for ill. By establishing a controlled environment of the orphanage, Francke could monitor the larger shaping of the students' lives according to his pietistic curriculum. Significantly, unlike many orphanages at this time, Francke did not exploit the children by demanding long hours of labor but instead focused on formation and conversion. Additionally, the children in the orphanage were not allowed to remain beyond sixteen years of age. This increased both the importance of the students being good learners as well as receiving a practical education to prepare them for living responsibly on their own. Francke's fame soon spread, and his schools attracted children from across Europe.

---

[14] Rezeau Brown, ed. *Memoirs of August Hermann Francke* (Philadelphia: American Sunday School Union, 1831), 83.

Francke was keenly alert to the distinction between the false wisdom of the world and the true wisdom from God. Pietism shared the aversion of Comenius that Greek and Roman literature was dangerous because of its unchristian foundation. While that placed a heavy emphasis upon the Bible and Luther's *Catechism* as the foundational curriculum, there was an appreciation and inclusion of many subjects that one would associate with liberal arts education. For example, the boys in the *Pedagogium Regium* studied Latin, Greek, Hebrew, French, history, geography, botany, music, astronomy, mathematics, etc. The curriculum also included indoor and outdoor activities such as carpentry, drawing, and field trips to various crafts and professions in the city. Once again, Francke's insistence on the practical nature of education is evident by the emphasis placed on the young boys to master glass-cutting, copperplate engraving, and woodworking. Given the strong Pietistic foundation of Francke, it is not surprising that weekday academic studies were supplemented by daily Bible reading, morning and afternoon prayers, and times of instruction. Francke integrated spirituality into classes by concluding each day with a longer period devoted to reading scripture, hymn singing, and catechizing in small groups. On Sunday, all students were required to attend two worship services that included a sermon, hymns, and more catechization.[15]

PEDAGOGICAL INSTRUCTION FOR TEACHERS AND STUDENTS

Unfortunately none of Francke's pedagogical writings have been translated into English. However, brief sections of one of his most important works, *A Short and Simple Guide on How Children Can Be Led to Genuine Piety and Christian Wisdom* (1702) provides a clarifying introduction to his philosophy of education that centered on sound piety for the glory of God. The Bible, Luther's *Catechism*, and the disciplined use of prayer were central to his curriculum, and the Holy Spirit was essential for creating the proper attitude and space for learning. (See *Appendix 1* for typical elementary school schedule.)

Teacher

Broadly speaking, Francke stressed three key principles to his teachers: being a good example for students, examining one's self as an effective guide for others, and knowing students personally. Even more overarching than these three principles is the requirement that the love of God must be the primary motivation for all teachers. Francke also stressed the necessity of conversion for all teachers. Without being born again, one lacks the proper

---

[15] Richard L. Gawthrop, *Pietism and the Making of Eighteenth-Century Prussia* (Cambridge University Press, 1993), 157.

belief and foundation for guiding others. This elevates the biblical reminder that teachers and those in positions of authority are to set the example for those who are younger or new in the faith. Francke understood children naturally imitate those who are older than them. Since there were so few healthy models of morality in Glaucha, it was essential for teachers to demonstrate the biblical message both in and out of the classroom. Further, for Francke, since education required the joint cooperation of the home, church, and school, it was equally the responsibility of Christian parents to model a healthy Christian lifestyle. One recognizes the radical God-centered focus that was consistent with Francke's theology in these following words:

> If the teacher himself has true wisdom it will be easy for him to lead his pupils thereto. If he himself does not have nor seek it, it is just as if one would give an unwise and inexperienced physician a proven medicine which he does not know how to use according to the condition of the patient or the different symptoms of the illness. Finally, it is neither he who plants nor he who waters something, but God who gives the increase, to whom be all glory forever. Amen.[16]

Clearly teachers should, therefore, follow Christ, eschew harshness, and model love and patience to learners.

Secondly, and intimately related, teachers must monitor themselves and ensure that they are living a life that is reflective of the gospel. To ensure that each person is modeling the best example for children, Francke challenges everyone to "enter into himself, and see whether he hath laid in himself a sure and firm foundation of true piety."[17] It is only by careful self–reflection that a person can be aware of the mask of hypocrisy and live in full sincerity before their neighbor. Sattler expands this principle in his translation of Francke who said, "The teacher should not be sullen, angry, vexatious, and impatient with the children in instruction and other teaching, but rather be loving and kind. In summary, should faith and love and thus the true being which is in Jesus be awakened in such tender hearts, they must surely be introduced and led on through the sweetness of the Gospel and not the bitterness of the Law."[18]

Again the responsibility falls upon teachers and parents alike to consistently review their own lives to ensure they are maturing in Christ and reflecting Christ's love to the learner.

---

[16] Sattler, *God's Glory, Neighbor's Good*, 56.

[17] August Hermann Francke, *Pietas Hallensis: Foot-Steps of Divine Providence* (London, 1705), 192.

[18] Sattler, *God's Glory, Neighbor's Good*, 55.

Third, Francke stressed the importance that teachers must know their students. Part of this is the wisdom of being careful not to bore students and destroy their love for learning. Francke wisely counseled,

> That one not give the children books which are quite too long, but rather as short as possible, for they do not lose the joy as easily when they soon come to an end and receive something new. That one teach them Christian doctrine in the German language and have them learn it from German books, for otherwise they easily receive an unpleasantness in Christianity and do not pay attention to the doctrine, (but rather) to being able to repeat the words, albeit without understanding.[19]

The wise and sensitive educator will discover the natural talents as well as the unique God-given abilities within a child so that these might be more fully cultivated. This can best be done through careful supervision. Francke developed a careful means of record-keeping for monitoring the growth of students. Those supervising the educational process would meet weekly to discuss their observations. Additionally, Francke understood one must be sensitive to the unique temperament and needs of each person. Teachers, therefore, should seek the best way to guide each learner in their education. Again Sattler provides a helpful translation and illustration of this principle from Francke's own writing saying. "That one may not overload them too much. A teacher must herein be like a wise sower which does not sow one seed upon the other and suffocate the lower with the upper ... Some think their children and pupils are well versed in Christianity if they can read, learn, and repeat much by rote, yet ... not yet show the least fruit."[20]

LEARNER

Francke's insights from the learner's perspective can also be summarized in three principles: cultivating an attitude of self-denial, breaking the self–will of the child, and the uncommon but possible need for punishment in situations when the teacher deems it necessary. Memorization, review, and discussion of biblical texts as well as other writings (e.g. Luther's *Catechism*) filled a substantial segment of each day's studies. Much of the memorization consisted of learning three standard components of virtually any catechism, that is, the Apostles' Creed, Ten Commandments, the Lord's Prayer, and other biblical commands related to baptism. A primary purpose of this discipline was to foster an ascetic-

---

[19] Sattler, *God's Glory, Neighbor's Good*, 54.
[20] Ibid., 54.

like denial that would encourage one in the development of vocation and life beyond school. This practice was more than simply self-denial; it included affirmation of the gifts God had implanted within the person that could be refined in service to God's glory and our neighbor's good.

Second, some educators from the Enlightenment to the present day have criticized Francke for stressing the importance of "breaking the will" and conversion. According to him, and many others at this time, the will and not the intellect was the seed bed of evil. Though some might find this premise rigid and even manipulative, it is consistent with the Christian understanding that sin has affected all of humanity. More specifically, when Francke addresses "breaking the self-will" and not just the will, he does not intend to diminish the importance of the individuality of a person. Rather, he is actually seeking to bring freedom and transformation of person's self–will that is in rebellion against God and humanity. This perspective was consistent with the prevalent view that the person affected by sin was unable to express love that was not manipulative. None of this is possible without God's grace that enables humanity to bring their wills into submission of God's will. Clearly, this is reflective of the Pietistic understanding of repentance and conversion that reveals the necessity to reorient the heart toward God; without cultivating the proper obedience, one is likely to reject the wisdom of God, parents, and teachers. But once the will was under the guidance of divine authority and obedience, the student as well as teacher could live for God's glory and not selfish or personal gain.

Third, amidst German Pietism and even many Enlightenment thinkers, there was widespread acceptance of harsh discipline including physical punishment as well as university students who frequently bullied younger students. Some contemporary writers, when studying Francke, react strongly against his provision for this. However, when compared with other educators of his time, including more popular writers such as John Locke, who encouraged that problem children should be "soundly whipped," Francke displays a more compassionate and balanced approach to discipline.[21] The central issue once again relates to Francke's understanding of sin and how it warps a person's self–will and turns their heart toward self rather than God or others. This is also reflective of Francke's theology of education that the total person must be included, not just the understanding, but also the will. This holistic approach seeks to form the learner in mind and soul. Physical punishment was a

---

[21] Marcia J. Bunge, "Education and the Child in Eighteenth-Century German Pietism: Perspectives from the Work of A. H. Francke." In *The Child in Christian Thought*, ed. Marcia J. Bunge (Grand Rapids: Eerdmans, 2001), 276.

last resort and, due to the frequent abuse of beating children in the eighteenth century, Francke cautions about the potential dangers of using force. Additionally, he counsels that if punishment is necessary, the teacher should be quick to seek reconciliation with the student and thereby once again establish a healthy and compassionate example for the learner to ensure that no barriers or resentment develops to disrupt the goal of education.

LEGACY AND SIGNIFICANCE

At the time of his death in 1727, Francke's various schools were providing an education for over 2,200 boys and girls. A profound expression of the viability of his *Stiftungen* is that they are still in operation today. Further, his expansive vision gave birth to numerous other educational institutions that sought practical ways to address the needs of others, including a chemistry lab, a museum, a library, the development of a publishing house and bookstore to produce inexpensive Bibles, the first pediatric hospital in Germany, a medical dispensary, various mission efforts, and a home for widows. Beyond the local region of Halle, Francke's vision influenced the training of teachers who occupied major educational positions throughout central Europe and extended both the pedagogical and Pietistic principles of its founder. Francke's influence spread beyond Germany and Europe as well, particularly with his impressive innovations that included both girls and the poor – two groups typically neglected by others as not requiring instruction – and influenced education well into the eighteenth century by demonstrating the value of educating the mind and character of all students. Comparatively, John Locke felt that education should focus primarily on upper class boys. While Francke's theology of education was more advanced than many, he failed to appreciate the significant role of play in a child's development and education. His rigid structure throughout the various schools revealed his intensity that resembles the monastic ordering of *ora et labora* (prayer and work) of the Benedictines. For him, play was seen as disruption of a healthy Christian life and he made no provision for dance or movement.

Many future influential leaders were graduates of Halle's education institutions, including Bartholomäus Ziegenbalg (1682–1719), the father of Protestant missions long before William Carey, who established missions in southeast India, was granted that title. Henry Mühlenberg (1711–1787), a Lutheran pastor whose ministry significantly laid the foundation for the Lutheran Church in America, was a student and teacher at Halle shortly after Francke's death.

The vision of Francke's orphanage and school for poor children spread throughout Europe, including Britain and beyond. Not only did it inspire George Muller in the development of his orphanage in Bristol, England, but it also motivated George Whitefield's transatlantic journey and his first visit to Georgia in 1738 to establish an orphanage modeled after Francke's orphanage and schools for poor children.[22] Two of Francke's emissaries from Halle assisted with the development of the University of Pennsylvania.

Francke created a wide–ranging vision that arose from his Pietistic theology of experimental learning and flourished through his ministry of preaching, teaching, and creating diverse social and spiritual institutions for God's glory and the good of one's neighbor.

APPENDIX 1:

Typical Timetable of Daily Curriculum

7-8a.m.	Song, prayer, Bible reading, catechism, church service
8-9a.m.	One-half hour Bible reading, one-half hour catechism for older children
9-10a.m.	One-half hour explaining quotations and Proverbs to younger children; one-half hour study of Psalms and New Testament by older children
10-11a.m.	Writing
2-3p.m.	Prayer and Bible reading, church service
3-4p.m.	One-half hour reading by younger children; one-half hour study of quotations by older children
4-5p.m.	Catechism
5-6p.m.	Evening prayers

FRANCKE'S WRITINGS

Francke's principal contributions to theological literature are *Manuductio ad lectionem Scripturae Sacrae* (A Guide to the Reading and Study of the Holy Scriptures), 1693, translated into English in 1813; *Praelectiones hermeneuticae* (Lectures on Hermeneutics), 1717; *Commentatio de scopo librorum Veteris et Novi Testamenti* (History Books of the Old and New Testament), 1724; and *Lectiones paraeneticae* (1726-1736). Also significant to exploration of Francke's understanding of education is his preface to the German translation of FranÇois Fenelon's *Über die Mädchenerziehung* (On the Education of Girls), 1705. An account of his orphanage, entitled *Segensvolle Fußstapfen*, which subsequently passed through several editions, has also been partially translated under the title *The Footsteps of Divine Providence* or, *The bountiful Hand of Heaven defraying the Expenses of Faith.* (London, 1705).

---

[22] Arnold A. Dallimore, *George Whitefield* (Edinburgh: Banner of Truth, 1970), I: 206–07.

BIBLIOGRAPHY

Brown, Rezeau, ed. *Memoirs of August Hermann Francke*. Philadelphia: American Sunday School Union, 1831.

Bunge, Marcia J. "Education and the Child in Eighteenth–Century German Pietism: Perspectives from the Work of A. H. Francke." In *The Child in Christian Thought*, ed. Marcia J. Bunge. Grand Rapids: Eerdmans, 2001, 247–78.

Francke, August Hermann. *Biographical Dictionary of Evangelicals*. Timothy Larsen, editor. Downers-Grove, IL: Intevarsity Press, 2003.

_____. *New Schaff-Herzog Encyclopedia of Religious Knowledge*. Grand Rapids: Baker Book House, 1954.

_____. *The Oxford Dictionary of the Christian Church*. Edited by F. L. Cross and E. A. Livingstone. Oxford, 1997.

Gawthrop, Richard L. *Pietism and the Making of Eighteenth-Century Prussia*. Cambridge: Cambridge University Press, 1993, 121–222.

Matthias, Markus. August Hermann Francke (1663–1727). In Carter Lindberg, ed. *The Pietist Theologians*. Malden, MA: Blackwell Publishing, 2005, 100–114.

Pietists: Selected Writings. Edited by Peter C. Erb. New York: Paulist Press, 1983.

Sattler, Gary R. *God's Glory, Neighbor's Good*. Chicago: Covenant Press, 1982.

Shantz, Douglas H. *An Introduction to German Pietism*. Baltimore: The John Hopkins University Press, 2013.

Stoeffler, F. Ernest. *The Rise of Evangelical Pietism*. Leiden: E. J. Brill, 1965.

CHAPTER 15

Jonathan Edwards:

Influencing and Shaping the Heart

MICHAEL A.G. HAYKIN

with DUSTIN BRUCE

Jonathan Edwards (1703-1758)

Jonathan Edwards believed that the "easiest way of reforming a people in the world is by education."[1] He spent his entire life in what was then considered the frontier of the Western world — the American colonies. Though his educational opportunities were somewhat limited when compared to his counterparts in Britain, Edwards developed a range and depth of thought that placed him among the intellectual elite of the eighteenth-century transatlantic community and he rightly deserves to be regarded as America's greatest theologian.

---

[1] Kenneth P. Minkema, "'Informing of the Child's Understanding, Influencing His Heart, and Directing Its Practice': Jonathan Edwards on Education," Acta Theologica, 31, no.2 (January 2011): 163.

HISTORICAL BACKGROUND

Jonathan Edwards was born October 5, 1703, at East Windsor, Connecticut.[2] His father, Timothy Edwards (1669–1758), served as the pastor of the town's Congregational Church. His mother, Esther (1672–1770), was the daughter of Solomon Stoddard (1643–1729), the powerful pastor of the Congregational Church in Northampton, Massachusetts from 1669 until his death in 1729. The fifth of eleven children, Edwards was the only boy among ten sisters. Though he lived far from the center of the first British Empire, Edwards was not without educational opportunities. Timothy Edwards ran a preparatory school for college entrance in one of the rooms on the first floor of the parsonage and here Timothy taught local boys along with Jonathan and his ten sisters.[3] Since women were rarely given the opportunity to get an education at this time, Timothy Edwards' attitude reveals the important role learning played in the Edwards home. In fact, in his early childhood, Jonathan was tutored not only by his Puritan father, but also by his older sisters.[4] As Kenneth Minkema has noted with regard to the Edwards sisters, they were more than able to help tutor their younger brother, for they "consulted Bible commentaries in Latin, read Addison and Steele, and, ... wielded rapier-like wits."[5]

When Edwards was six, Timothy Edwards introduced Latin into his son's elementary school curriculum. By the time Edwards entered the Connecticut Collegiate School (later to become Yale University) in 1716, he was able to read Latin, Greek, and even some Hebrew. The college was based in New Haven, though Edwards studied at the branch at Wethersfield. Four years later, in 1720, Edwards graduated at the head of his class academically with a B.A. In the previous four years he had studied grammar, rhetoric, logic, arithmetic, ancient history, natural science, astronomy, and metaphysics. He would also have been introduced to the study of theology through readings in John Calvin (1509–1564), John Owen (1616–1683), and the *Marrow of Sacred Divinity* (1642) by William Ames (1576–1633).[6] Subsequent studies led to an M.A. in 1723.

---

[2] The standard critical biography of Edwards is George M. Marsden, *Jonathan Edwards: A Life* (New Haven/London: Yale University Press, 2004). Less critical, but also helpful, is Ian H. Murray, *Jonathan Edwards – A New Biography* (Edinburgh/Carlisle, PA: Banner of Truth, 1987).

[3] Kenneth P. Minkema, "'Informing of the Child's Understanding, Influencing His Heart, and Directing Its Practice': Jonathan Edwards on Education," *Acta Theologica*, 31, no. 2 (January 2011): 160. On Jonathan's sisters, see Kenneth P. Minkema, "Hannah and Her Sisters: Sisterhood, Courtship, and Marriage In the Edwards Family in the Early Eighteenth Century," *The New England Historical and Genealogical Register* 146 (January 1992): 35–56.

[4] Minkema, "Hannah and Her Sisters," 41.

[5] Minkema, "Informing of the Child's Understanding," 161.

[6] Michael J. McClymond and Gerald R. McDermott, *The Theology of Jonathan Edwards* (Oxford: Oxford University Press, 2012), 24.

Edwards' father and mother had taken great pains to encourage his personal piety, but his conversion did not come until after college in the spring of 1721, at the age of eighteen.[7] It was while he was reading 1 Timothy 1:17 that:

> There came into my soul, and was as it were diffused through it, a sense of the glory of the Divine Being; a new sense, quite different from anything I ever experienced before. Never any words of Scripture seem to me as these words did. I thought with myself, how excellent a Being that was; and how happy I should be, if I might enjoy that God, and be rapt up to him in Heaven, and be as it were swallowed up in him forever ... From about that time, I began to have a new kind of apprehensions and ideas of Christ, and the work of redemption, and the glorious way of salvation by him. An inward, sweet sense of these things, at times, came into my heart; and my soul was led away in pleasant views and contemplations of them. In my mind was greatly engaged to spend my time reading and meditating on Christ, on the beauty and excellency of his person, and a lovely way of salvation, but free grace in him.[8]

Not long after his conversion, Edwards drew up what are known as the *Resolutions* (1722–1723), a list of seventy guidelines to help him stay passionate in his pursuit of God and his glory throughout his ministry. His first resolution, for example, stated, "resolved, that I will do whatsoever I think to be most to God's glory, and my own good, profit, and pleasure, in the whole of my duration."[9] The *Resolutions* do not mention education per se, but Resolution 28 probably comes the closest to what the young Edwards understood to be the most important aspect of all learning: "Resolved, to study the Scriptures so steadily, constantly and frequently, as that I may find, and plainly perceive myself to grow in the knowledge of the same."

Edwards' conversion was followed by a call to ministry, and he briefly served as pastor of two small congregations. First, Edwards served a break-away Presbyterian congregation in what is now lower Manhattan and then a Congregationalist church in Bolton, Connecticut. Between these two pastorates, the young scholar completed his M.A. thesis, which was a defense of justification by faith alone and a critique of those who diverged from this key Reformation tenet. Edwards had already spent time studying in the college library at Yale, which contained

---

[7] For the date of Edwards' conversion, see Murray, *Jonathan Edwards*, 35.

[8] Jonathan Edwards, "Personal Narrative" in *Letters and Personal Writings*, ed. George C. Claghorn (The Works of Jonathan Edwards vol. 16 [New Haven/London: Yale University Press, 1998], 792–793).

[9] For an edition of the *Resolutions*, see Stephen J. Nichols, ed., *Jonathan Edwards' Resolutions and Advice to Young Converts* (Phillipsburg, New Jersey: P&R Publishing, 2001). The *Resolutions* can be found on pages 17–26.

volumes of some of the foremost thinkers of the day, including Isaac Newton (1642–1727) and John Locke (1632–1704);[10] these studies were formative on his thinking. These two men, along with others, represented new ways of viewing the universe and its creator that have come to be labeled "the Enlightenment." It is significant to note that Edwards was never chary of reading the latest thought and seeking to explain it from the point of view of the scriptures and even incorporating it where he could into his Calvinistic worldview.

Eventually, he found himself back in New Haven serving as a tutor at Yale, his alma mater. He later characterized his time as a tutor as a spiritually low time. It seems he was not cut out for the academic life, even though his whole approach to life was deeply intellectual. In August 1726, Edwards left New Haven and found his niche as the assistant pastor to his grandfather, Solomon Stoddard. Within a year, he had married Sarah Pierpont (1710–1758), whom he had first met while at Yale.

It is worth noting that Edwards' first mention of Sarah, whose spirituality he deeply admired, was penned in the flyleaf of his Greek grammar. Cast in the form of a "prose poem," it runs thus:

They say there is a young lady in [New Haven] who is beloved of that almighty Being, who made and rules the world, and that there are certain seasons in which this Great Being, in some way or other invisible, comes to her and fills her mind with exceeding sweet delight, and that she hardly cares for any thing, except to meditate on him — that she expects after a while to be received up where he is, to be raised out of the world and caught up into heaven; being assured that he loves her too well to let her remain at a distance from him always. There she is to dwell with him, and to be ravished with his love, favor and delight forever. Therefore, if you present all the world before her, with the richest of its treasures, she disregards it and cares not for it, and is unmindful of any pain or affliction. She has a strange sweetness in her mind, and sweetness of temper, uncommon purity in her affections; is most just and praiseworthy in all her actions; and you could not persuade her to do anything thought wrong or sinful, if you would give her all the world, lest she should offend this great Being. She is of a wonderful sweetness, calmness and universal benevolence of mind; especially after those times in which this great God has manifested himself to her mind. She will sometimes go about, singing sweetly, from place to [place]; and she seems to be always full of joy and pleasure; and no one know for what. She loves to be alone, and to wander in the fields and on the mountains, and seems to have someone invisible always conversing with her.[11]

[10] Kenneth P. Minkema, "Jonathan Edwards, America's Theologian: A Commemorative Yale Exhibition" in his and George G. Levesque, *Jonathan Edwards Tercentennial Exhibition: Selected Objects from the Yale Collections 1703–2003* (New Haven, CT: Yale University, 2003), 6.
[11] "On Sarah Pierpont" in *Letters and Personal Writings*, ed. Claghorn, 789–790. The description

At the time that this text was written, Jonathan was twenty and Sarah but thirteen. Though too young to court — New England women at this period of time were generally married in their mid-twenties, though the average marrying age for the seven Edwards sisters who married was thirty.[12] Edwards was clearly taken with Sarah's piety, spiritual maturity, and the fact that her outward deportment matched her inner spirituality. Sarah's sweetness — her sweetness of mind and temper, her sweet singing, and the "exceeding sweet delight" that she had for God — especially appealed to Edwards, for whom the adjective "sweet" and its derivatives was frequently on his lips when he spoke of God and divine things. By God's grace, Edwards had found a soulmate: her affective piety and commitment to meditation upon God and spiritual things were in perfect harmony with his spirituality. It is not surprising that he does not mention in this paragraph what others frequently remarked on, namely Sarah's physical beauty. Samuel Hopkins (1721–1803), one of Edwards' close friends and his first biographer, recalled that Sarah was "comely and beautiful."[13] For Jonathan, though, it was evidently the sweetness of her inner beauty that attracted him to her.

Upon the death of his grandfather in 1729, Edwards became the pastor of the Northampton church. The Northampton church had enjoyed a number of small revivals during Solomon Stoddard's long pastorate, the last one having been in 1718. After that time, though, Edwards judged there had been little spiritual advance. In his words:

> Just after my grandfather's death, it seemed to be a time of extraordinary dullness in religion. Licentiousness for some years prevailed among the youth of the town; they were many of them very much addicted to night-walking, and frequenting the tavern, and lewd practices, wherein some, by their example, exceedingly corrupted others. It was their manner very frequently to get together, in conventions of both sexes for mirth and jollity, which they called frolics; and they would often spend the greater part of the night in them, without regard to any order in the families they belonged to: and indeed family government did too much fail in the town. It was become very customary with many of our young people to be indecent in their carriage at meeting, which doubtless would not have prevailed in such a degree, had it not been that my grandfather, through his great

---

"prose poem" is that of Minkema, "Jonathan Edwards, America's Theologian: A Commemorative Yale Exhibition," 10.

[12] Minkema, "Hannah and Her Sisters," 45.

[13] Samuel Hopkins, "A Short Sketch of Mrs. Edwards's Life and Character," Appendix I to his *Memoirs of the Life, Experience and Character of the Late Rev. Jonathan Edwards, A.M.* in *The Works of President Edwards* (1817 ed.; repr. New York: Burt Franklin, 1968), I, 94. See also the remarks of Amanda Porterfield, *Feminine Spirituality in America: From Sarah Edwards to Martha Graham* (Philadelphia: Temple University Press, 1980), 39–40.

age (though he retained his powers, surprisingly to the last), was not so able to observe them. There had also long prevailed in the town a spirit of contention between two parties, into which they had for many years been divided; by which they maintained a jealousy one of the other, and were prepared to oppose one another in all public affairs.[14]

As Edwards notes in this text, the adults in the town were split into two factions, the "haves" and the "have-nots" — those who were wealthy and had property and those who were jealous of them and who sought to diminish their power and influence.[15] Most of these adults were taken up, not with the things of God and his kingdom, but with other cares and pursuits, especially the pursuit of material wealth. Outwardly they were orthodox, but they had no inward religion. Their orthodoxy was dry and lifeless. Not surprisingly, their children were, in Edwards' own words, "very much addicted to night-walking, and frequenting the tavern, and lewd practices." As American historian Richard Lovelace has noted, if these teens had had drugs, they would have used them.[16]

EDWARDS' THEOLOGY FOR EDUCATION

In the early 1730s, however, there began to be a growing sensitivity to sin and a willingness to listen to religious counsel.[17] A series of sermons on justification by faith alone — the doctrine that Edwards' master's thesis had been on and that had been so central to the Reformation — were particularly used of God to awaken the lost and the spiritually indifferent. The series was preached by Edwards in November and December of 1734. In the series Edwards especially stressed that God, in justifying sinners, does so on the basis of his mercy alone. Those whom God saves are not saved because God sees anything in them that would merit his favour and blessing. To quote Edwards: when God justifies a person he "has no regard to anything in the person justified, as godliness, or any goodness." In fact, Edwards went on to say, "before this act [of justification], God beholds him as an ungodly creature."[18]

---

[14] *A Faithful Narrative of the Surprising Work of God* in *Jonathan Edwards on Revival* (Edinburgh: The Banner of Truth Trust, 1984), 9. In this collection of Edwards' writings, the title has been changed to *A Narrative of Surprising Conversions*. The original title has been used here.

[15] Murray, *Jonathan Edwards*, 87.

[16] Richard Lovelace, *Dynamics of Spiritual Life: An Evangelical Theology of Renewal* (Downers Grove, IL: InterVarsity Press, 1978), 38.

[17] *Faithful Narrative* in *Jonathan Edwards on Revival*, 9–10.

[18] *Justification by Faith Alone* in *The Works of Jonathan Edwards* (1834 ed.; repr. Edinburgh: The Banner of Truth Trust, 1974), 1:622. For a study of Edwards' doctrine of justification, see Samuel T. Logan, Jr., "The Doctrine of Justification in the Theology of Jonathan Edwards," *The Westminster Theological Journal*, 46 (Spring 1984), 26–52.

Justification entails God choosing to reckon Christ's perfect righteousness to the sinner and in this way the sinner can be declared righteous.

Edwards identified the exposition of this central feature of the New Testament as the major catalyst that the Holy Spirit used to begin an extraordinary time of revival in Northampton.

> There were some things said publicly ... concerning justification by faith alone ... It proved a word spoken in season here; and was most evidently attended with a very remarkable blessing of heaven to the souls of the people in this town ... And then it was, in the latter part of December [of 1734], that the Spirit of God began extraordinarily to set in, and wonderfully to work amongst us; and there were very suddenly, one after another, five or six persons, who were to all appearances savingly converted, and some of them wrought upon in a very remarkable manner.[19]

Edwards here makes a direct link between the preaching of biblical truth and the onset of revival by his use of the connective "then." It was *after* the preaching of justification by faith alone — which Edwards also denotes as "the way of the gospel ... the true and only way"[20]— that the Spirit began to work so "wonderfully" and "suddenly." Also from an educational standpoint, it is important to emphasize what John Hannah has observed:

> Though Edwards presented argument after argument to sustain his points [in his sermons], he did not believe that rational explanations or carefully crafted sermons possessed the power in themselves to convince anyone. He felt that that was the work of the Holy Spirit through the Word of God. He wrote, "The light of reason convinces the world that it is so: the Word of God puts it past doubt." Reason can demonstrate that something is true, but only the Spirit of God can create an affectionate desire or delight in it.[21]

Soon, Edwards narrated in his account of this revival, an intense concern to be right with God and to walk with him gripped the town. The town's population was about twelve hundred people, and Edwards initially reckoned that some three hundred were saved in about

---

[19] *Faithful Narrative* in *Jonathan Edwards on Revival*, 11–12. For a discussion of other subsidiary causes of the revival, see Samuel T. Logan, Jr., "Jonathan Edwards and the 1734-35 Northampton Revival," *Preaching and Revival* (London: The Westminster Conference, 1984), 63–65.

[20] *Faithful Narrative* in *Jonathan Edwards on Revival*, 12.

[21] John Hannah, "The Homiletical Skill of Jonathan Edwards,", *Bibliotheca Sacra* 159 (January-March 2002): 98.

six months.[22] At the revival's height, in March and April of 1735, there were about thirty people a week professing conversion.[23] Edwards would later judge that there were not as many converts as he had thought during the actual time of the revival.[24] Nevertheless, he never doubted that what took place during 1734 and 1735 was a tremendous, God-wrought awakening in the town. Nor was the revival limited to the town of Northampton. It spread swiftly to thirty-two other towns throughout the Connecticut River Valley.

Revival fires cooled, but not for long. During the years 1740–1742, a second, much larger wave of revival — akin to a spiritual tsunami and thus appropriately called the Great Awakening — swept through New England and the rest of the American colonies along the Atlantic seaboard. Numerous preachers and congregations across various denominational lines were profoundly involved in a massive outpouring of the Spirit of God that transformed the colonial American landscape. And Edwards, who was deeply involved in preaching and writing about this revival, gained international fame as a sophisticated theologian of revival through works such as *Treatise Concerning Religious Affections* (1746).

However, all was not well within his own congregation. In 1748, Edwards witnessed the beginning of a controversy that engulfed the Northampton congregation and would eventually lead to his dismissal. The Northampton church had accepted the Half-Way Covenant in 1672, which allowed professedly unregenerate parents to have their infants baptized, provided the parents embraced a Christian worldview and morality. In the 1690s, Solomon Stoddard, however, had given these parents not just the right to baptize their infants, but also admission to the Lord's Supper since he believed the Lord's Supper was a converting ordinance. Known as Stoddardeanism, this theological perspective had become standard practice within Congregationalist churches in western Massachusetts.[25] Edwards had struggled with his grandfather's position for some time before declaring it unbiblical in 1748 and seeking to limit participation in the Lord's Supper to those professing a conversion

---

[22] *Faithful Narrative* in *Jonathan Edwards on Revival*, 19.

[23] Ibid., 21.

[24] Jonathan Edwards, Letter to Thomas Gillespie, 1 July 1751 in *The Great Awakening*, ed. C.C. Goen (The Works of Jonathan Edwards, vol. 4; New Haven/London: Yale University Press, 1972), 565.

[25] For the half-way covenant, see especially Robert G. Pope, *The Half-Way Covenant: Church Membership in Puritan New England* (Princeton, NJ: Princeton University Press, 1969). On Stoddardeanism in particular, see especially Thomas M. & Virginia L. Davis, ed., *Edward Taylor vs. Solomon Stoddard: The Nature of the Lord's Supper* (Boston: Twayne Publishers, 1981) and Keith J. Hardman, *The Spiritual Awakeners: American Revivalists from Solomon Stoddard to D.L. Moody* (Chicago, IL: Moody Press, 1983).

experience. The famous pastor found himself at odds with the majority of his congregation and he was dismissed in June of 1750.

After his dismissal, Edwards became the pastor of a church in what was then the frontier village of Stockbridge, Massachusetts, ministering to the Mohawk, Mohican, and Iroquois Indians of the area. There is little doubt that Edwards ultimately saw his removal from Northampton to Stockbridge in 1750 as providential, for it enabled him to address some evils that were hampering Christian witness to the Native Americans. Edwards spent the 1750s fighting the Europeans' exploitation of the Indians and "arguing for the Indians' right to a proper education by qualified teachers."[26] It was also during his seven years at Stockbridge that he had the time to write those books which established him as the "greatest Christian theologian of the eighteenth century."[27] Among these works were his notable defenses of Calvinism, *A Careful and Strict Inquiry into the Modern Prevailing Notions of that Freedom of the Will, Which is Supposed to be Essential to Moral Agency* (1754), and *The Great Christian Doctrine of Original Sin Defended* (1758).

This period of literary fruitfulness at Stockbridge came to an end in 1757, when Edwards reluctantly accepted an invitation to become president of the College of New Jersey, which is now Princeton University. Edwards had been a strong supporter of the college, and he had experience teaching young people, both at Yale many years earlier and then at Stockbridge. Thus, he was a natural choice to succeed the previous president, his own son-in-law, Aaron Burr, Sr. (1716–1757).[28] Arriving in Princeton at the beginning of 1758, Edwards assumed office on February 16. A week later he was inoculated against smallpox, which was raging in the vicinity. Though the vaccine appeared to be an initial success, complications set in. On March 22, 1758, Jonathan Edwards breathed his last. Just before his death, those gathered around his bedside were lamenting what his death would mean to the church and college. To their surprise, the dying Edwards piped up with his last recorded words, "Trust in God, and ye need not fear."[29] When Sarah, who had

---

[26] Minkema, "Jonathan Edwards, America's Theologian: A Commemorative Yale Exhibition," 7; McClymond and McDermott, *Theology of Jonathan Edwards*, 560–563.

[27] Perry Miller, in his general preface to Edwards' Works, described Edwards as "the greatest philosopher-theologian yet to grace the American scene" ("General Editor's Note," in *The Freedom of the Will*, ed. Paul Ramsey, [The Works of Jonathan Edwards, vol.1; New Haven/London: Yale University Press, 1957], viii). See also Miklós Vetö, "Book Reviews: *America's Theologian. A Recommendation of Jonathan Edwards*. By Robert W. Jenson", *Church History*, 58 (1989), 522; John F. Wilson, "Jonathan Edwards's Notebooks for 'A History of the Work of Redemption' " in *Reformation, Conformity and Dissent*, ed. R. Buick Knox (London: Epworth Press, 1977), 240.

[28] Minkema, "Jonathan Edwards, America's Theologian: A Commemorative Yale Exhibition," 7.

[29] Cited Murray, *Jonathan Edwards*, 441.

not yet joined her husband in Princeton, heard the news of her husband's demise, she responded, "O what a legacy my husband, and your father has left us!"[30] These words were truer than even she realized.

CONTRIBUTIONS TO CHRISTIAN EDUCATION

In order to understand Jonathan Edwards' contribution to Christian education, it is vital to understand his key legacy as a theologian of revival and the religious affections.[31] The fires of revival in the 1730s and 1740s had caused no little controversy in the trans-Atlantic Christian community.[32] Edwards, who was at the center of the Awakening in America, was forced to respond to questions and concerns in a series of treatises and books that culminated in his 1746 publication, *Religious Affections*.[33]

With *A Faithful Narrative of the Surprising Work of God*, Edwards established himself as a proponent of revival. Published in its final form in 1737, *A Faithful Narrative* expanded from a 1735 version of eight large sheets to a 132-page book.[34] Robert Davis Smart comments: "The dramatic increase in page count seems proportionate to the size of Edward's growing leadership role in the revival."[35] And along with this growing leadership role came a maturation of thinking in the theology of revival. This maturation in Edwards' thought was first visible in his 1741 commencement address at Yale, In *The Distinguishing Marks of the Spirit of God*. In this work, Edwards applied the command of 1 John 4:1, to "try the spirits" to the revival.[36] His work was divided into three parts. First, Edwards laid out a series of nine "negative signs" that failed to prove whether a work was of the Spirit of God or not. Next, he presented five "positive evidences," which serve as distinctive marks that a work was indeed of the Spirit of God. Finally, Edwards made a

---

[30] Ibid., 442.

[31] For Edwards as a theologian of revival, see Michael A.G. Haykin, *Jonathan Edwards: The Holy Spirit in Revival* (Webster, NY: Evangelical Press, 2005).

[32] For an historical overview of the Great Awakening, see Thomas S. Kidd, *The Great Awakening: The Roots of Evangelical Christianity in Colonial America* (New Haven/London: Yale University Press, 2007). Also see Mark A. Noll, *The Rise of Evangelicalism: The Age of Edwards, Whitefield, and the Wesleys* (Downers Grove, IL: IVP Academic, 2003).

[33] For a critical edition, see Jonathan Edwards, *Religious Affections*, ed. John E. Smith (The Works of Jonathan Edwards, vol. 2; New Haven/London: Yale University Press, 1959).

[34] Murray, *Jonathan Edwards*, 118; Robert Davis Smart, *Jonathan Edwards's Apologetic for the Great Awakening* (Grand Rapids, MI: Reformation Heritage Books, 2011), 14.

[35] Smart, *Jonathan Edwards's Apologetic for the Great Awakening*, 14.

[36] Jonathan Edwards, *The Distinguishing Marks of the Spirit of God* in *Great Awakening*, ed. Goen, 214–288.

contemporary application and inferred that the recent revival of interest in religion had been in the main a work of the Spirit of God.

In this Yale address, Edwards introduced the idea that piety can be judged through the presence of various signs.[37] Edwards readily admitted to the presence of counterfeits, especially during a time of revival. But, Edwards contended, God had not left his church without means, which are found within scripture, by which to assess the authenticity of spirituality. C. C. Goen notes the significance of *Distinguishing Marks* in this respect: "Thus began a critical but sympathetic examination of revivalism which Edwards would continually develop and refine until it issued in the mature statement of 1746, *A Treatise Concerning Religious Affections*, wherein he demonstrated that true religion necessarily involves the whole person, and that it can and must be subjected to discriminating judgment."[38] What Edwards began in *Distinguishing Marks* found its fulfillment, as it were, in *Religious Affections*.[39]

Edwards's *Religious Affections* seeks to find a *via media* between two poles: one that exalted emotion and the other that exalted reason. James Davenport (1716–1757), a minister from Southold, Long Island, is a good example of the former, while a good example of the latter was Charles Chauncy (1705–1787), the co-pastor of Boston's prestigious First Church.[40] Itinerating throughout New England in 1742 and 1743, Davenport exhibited some bizarre patterns of behavior: he claimed to have the ability to distinguish who was among the elect of God and thus divided churches; he assured people who had visions while he was preaching that this was a genuine sign of their conversion; and he claimed to receive

---

[37] "Editor's Introduction" in Edwards, *Religious Affections*, ed. Smith, 6.

[38] "Editor's Introduction" in Edwards, *The Great Awakening*, ed. Goen, 53.

[39] In between these two works, Edwards penned *Some Thoughts Concerning the Present Revival of Religion in New England*. In this work, Edwards articulated a detailed defense of the Great Awakening for those misinformed as to the events surrounding the Awakening, but not necessarily predisposed against it. Jonathan Edwards, *Some Thoughts Concerning the Present Revival of Religion in New England* in *Great Awakening*, ed. Goen, 290–530.

[40] For a discussion of Davenport's involvement in the revival, see Harry S. Stout and Peter Onuf, "James Davenport and the Great Awakening in New London," *The Journal of American History*, 71 (1983–1984): 556–578; Murray, *Jonathan Edwards*, 223–229; Robert E. Cray, Jr., "More Light on a New Light: James Davenport's Religious Legacy, Eastern Long Island, 1740–1840," *New York History*, 73 (1992): 5–27.
For a good discussion of Chauncy's life and theological position, see Conrad Cherry, *The Theology of Jonathan Edwards. A Reappraisal* (1966 ed.: repr. Bloomington/Indianapolis: Indiana University Press, 1990), 164–167; Thomas Templeton Taylor, "The Spirit of the Awakening: The Pneumatology of New England's Great Awakening in Historical and Theological Context" (Ph.D. thesis, University of Illinois at Urbana-Champaign, 1988), 335–370; Smart, *Jonathan Edwards's Apologetic for the Great Awakening*, 161–180.

direct guidance from the Spirit in dreams. Davenport's antics provided anti-revival forces, known as the "Old Lights," with a highly visible target for their attacks. To them, he came to epitomize the anarchy and destruction of church harmony that the revival had brought in its wake. The captain of these forces was Charles Chauncy. George Marsden comments that for several years, "much of Edwards' energy would be devoted to what amounted to a verbal duel with the Boston pastor Charles Chauncy, the most outspoken champion of the Old Lights."[41]

Chauncy's main attack on the revival was his *Seasonable Thoughts on the State of Religion in New-England* (1743). It continued to press home what Chauncy saw as the main work of the Spirit, the enlightenment of the mind. "An enlightened mind, and not raised affections," he stated, "ought always to be the guide of those who call themselves men; and this, in the affairs of religion, as well as other things: And it will be so, where God really works on their hearts, by his Spirit."[42] The criticism of Chauncy, coupled with the clearly outrageous character of Davenport's ministry, forced Edwards to chart a moderate course that recognized the importance of accepting doctrine, but demanded a central role for the affections.[43]

IGNITING RELIGIOUS AFFECTIONS: THE CURRICULUM OF AN EDWARDSEAN EDUCATION

At the core of Edwards' preaching and teaching was a desire to provide a vehicle by which the Holy Spirit could effect a lasting change in the affections of his listeners and that his listeners could know with a degree of certainty that the affections they experienced were real and from God. In his context in New England, he had to do this without falling into one of two extremes; passionless intellectualism or unbridled emotionalism.

Edwards' reasoning about this didactic goal — its excellence its foundations, and its character — is best seen in his *Religious Affections*, which Iain H. Murray calls "one of the most important books possessed by the Christian church on the nature of true religion." In this book, Edwards presented a thorough analysis of religious experience and articulated his mature thoughts on how the work of the Spirit in man's heart may be rightly discerned.[44] Taking 1 Peter 1:8 as his primary text, Edwards offered a Puritan plain-style treatment of the

---

[41] Marsden, *Jonathan Edwards*, 238.

[42] Charles Chauncy, *Seasonable Thoughts on the State of Religion in New-England* (1743 ed.; repr. Hicksville, NY: The Regina Press, 1975), 327.

[43] Interestingly, Chauncy's rationalistic tendencies failed to keep him tethered to orthodoxy. He increasingly moved away from Reformed and Puritan thought, eventually embracing Unitarian and Universalist doctrines. See Smart, *Jonathan Edwards's Apologetic for the Great Awakening*, 299–302.

[44] Murray, *Jonathan Edwards*, 267.

passage.[45] Edwards explained that according to 1 Peter 1:8, true religion manifested itself in two ways: love to Christ and joy in Christ, both of which were affections. From this Petrine text, Edwards thus deduced what is the foundational thesis for his entire treatise: "True religion, in great part, consists in holy affections."[46] "We see that the Apostle," Edwards explained, "in observing and remarking the operations and exercises of religion … singles out the religious affections of love and joy…wherein their religion did thus appear true and pure, and in its proper glory."[47] For Edwards, "affections," which he defined as "the more vigorous and sensible exercises of the inclination and will of the soul," provide the key for discerning true religion.[48]

After defending this thesis in Part I, Edwards worked out the consequences in two parts. In Part II, he offered twelve non-signs or tests that fail to prove the genuineness of a person's spirituality one way or another. Finally, in Part III, Edwards delineated twelve "distinguishing signs of truly gracious and holy affections."[49] At the heart of these twelve signs is the Holy Spirit, as Kyle Strobel notes:

> The Spirit's work in the heart … is the driving force of the affections. The Spirit is, Edwards claims, 'a powerful holy affection', and upon receiving the Spirit with his sanctifying and saving work, the elect are thereby baptized with fire. The Spirit's procession in the Godhead is, as it were, God's own affection. Fittingly, the effect of the Spirit's work in the hearts of the saints follows suit, vigorously inclining them to the goodness, beauty and love of God.[50]

---

[45] For a discussion of Puritan sermon form, see Stephen R. Holmes, "Religious Affections by Jonathan Edwards" in *The Devoted Life: An Invitation to the Puritan Classics*, ed. Kelly M. Kapic and Randall C. Gleason (Downers Grove, IL: InterVarsity Press, 2004), 289–290. Holmes notes that the Puritan sermonic form "was capable of almost infinite expansion."

[46] Edwards, *Religious Affections*, ed. Smith, 95.

[47] Ibid.

[48] Ibid., 96. Brad Walton has shown that Edwards' concept of religious affections is an extension of the Puritan concept of "heart religion" and not in opposition to it. Walton summarizes, "So far from representing a discontinuity with puritan traditions, Edwards's *Religious Affections* is, in fact, a conservative extension of traditional puritan "heart religion" into the context of the Great Awakening. More precisely, *Religious Affections* is a reassertion — elicited by the events of the Great Awakening — of traditional puritan "experimental" spirituality, cast largely in the same form, and using the same language and conceptualization, as seventeenth-century puritan analyses of true piety, spiritual sensation and heart religion, but differing from them chiefly in its more philosophically rigorous presentation." Brad Walton, *Jonathan Edwards, Religious Affections and the Puritan Analysis of True Piety, Spiritual Sensation and Heart Religion* (Lewiston, NY: Edwin Mellen Press, 2002), 1.

[49] Edwards, *Religious Affections*, ed. Smith, 197.

[50] Kyle Strobel, *Jonathan Edwards' Theology: A Reinterpretation* (T & T Clark Studies in Systematic Theology v. 19; London/New York: Bloomsbury T & T Clark, 2013), 214.

Understanding that no perfect system of distinguishing true believers and nominal ones exists, Edwards maintained that God has not provided men with the means to know with unassailable certainty who their fellow brothers in Christ are, but "the Scriptures do abound with rules, which may be serviceable to ministers, in counseling and conducting souls committed to their care, in this pertaining to their spiritual and eternal state."[51] Edwards' explanation of these rules makes the *Religious Affections*, in the opinion of many scholars and pastors, "the most important and accurate analysis of religious experience ever written."[52]

Thus, for Edwards, true faith entailed love. To come to faith and to truly understand and to embrace what Christ has done for sinners meant, first of all, finding Christ beautiful and attractive. Then, a heart of faith was manifested in loving, good works toward one's neighbor. Citing 1 John 5:1 as proof, Edwards could thus argue, "[S]aving faith implies in its nature divine love."[53] For Edwards, love stood as chief among the affections and was, in fact, the "fountain" from which all other affections sprung. For Edwards, then, true faith — and true understanding by extension — necessarily implied the presence of religious affections.

EDWARDS' EDUCATIONAL METHODOLOGY
TEACHING FOR UNDERSTANDING

An excellent vantage-point from which to view Edwards' affective hermeneutic in action when it comes to the subject of education is a letter that he wrote in November of 1751 to Sir William Pepperrell (1696–1759), a native of Kittery, Maine (then a part of Massachusetts), and an extremely wealthy merchant who played a key role at various times in New England military affairs.[54] Edwards had been to visit Pepperrell at his Kittery home the previous spring, and Pepperrell, in turn, had been able to raise £700 for Edwards' work at Stockbridge. Pepperrell thought Edwards' ministry would be "a means of building up the

---

[51] Edwards, *Religious Affections*, ed. Smith, 193.

[52] Sam Storms, *Signs of the Spirit: An Interpretation of Jonathan Edwards' Religious Affections* (Wheaton, IL: Crossway, 2007), 21.

[53] Jonathan Edwards, *Writings on the Trinity, Grace, and Faith*, ed. Sang Hyun Lee (The Works of Jonathan Edwards, vol. 21; New Haven: Yale University Press, 2002), 448.

[54] My attention was drawn to this letter by Kenneth P. Minkema, "Jonathan Edwards on Education and His Educational Legacy" in *After Jonathan Edwards: The Courses of the New England Theology*, ed. Oliver D. Crisp and Douglas A. Sweeney (Oxford: Oxford University Press, 2012), 31–36. This article and that of Minkema, "Informing of the child's understanding, influencing his heart, and directing its practice," 163–167, have been very helpful in what follows. For the letter, see *Letters and Personal Writings*, ed. Claghorn, 406–414.

kingdom of our glorious Redeemer," and was thus eager to support his work.[55] As Kenneth Minkema has recently noted, this letter contains "Edwards's most complete statement of his philosophy of education."[56]

Edwards had an idea for a school for both Native American boys and girls — the inclusion of girls reflects Edwards' own early educational experience of being taught with his sisters[57] — but he wanted it to be free from "the gross defects of the ordinary method of teaching among the English."[58] The major defect that Edwards had in mind was "learning without understanding." Children, he had observed, were taught to read, or to say their catechism, without understanding what they were reading or saying. Edwards thus recommended that nothing be taught without imparting some understanding of what had been taught. This entails a dialogical approach to teaching with the teacher asking the child questions and giving the child the freedom to ask questions in turn. A critical goal in this "new" way of teaching would be to make "the child's learning ... pleasant, entertaining and profitable."[59] The child's lesson will thus "cease to be a dull, wearisome task, without any suitable pleasure or benefit."[60] The child will thus acquire "an early taste for knowledge," because such acquisition is pleasurable.

Edwards' view of the importance of the affections is quite apparent here. Teaching needs to be coupled with understanding so that the learning experience might be a pleasant one. The pleasure thus derived from understanding was critical to the learning process for it stimulated the desire to learn more. As it had been Edwards' thinking about growth in spiritual maturity, so it is here: both are tied to the affections. As Edwards had argued during the controversies over the revivals, true knowledge is intimately tied to the affections.

TEACHING THE WHOLE STORY FOR RELIGIOUS AFFECTION

Another defect of New England teaching, in Edwards' mind, was the failure to provide children with "a short general scheme of the scriptural history," that is the overall narrative of Bible history from creation to the close of the history. If children were taught this, then they would be able to know where each Bible story that they subsequently learned

---

[55] *Letters and Personal Writings*, ed. Claghorn, 406–407, n.1.

[56] Minkema, "Jonathan Edwards on Education" in *After Jonathan Edwards*, ed. Crisp and Sweeney, 32.

[57] Ibid., 33.

[58] *Letters and Personal Writings*, ed. Claghorn, 407.

[59] Ibid., 409-410.

[60] Ibid., 408.

(such as the flood or the birth of Christ) fits into the larger picture. In this way, education of the whole child could ensue, in which there is an "informing of the child's understanding, influencing his heart, and directing its practice."[61] In fact, Edwards also wanted to give the children some church history — "I can see no good reason, why children can't, or mayn't, be taught something in general of ecclesiastical history"[62] — and chronology, the geography of the ancient world, and music — which has a "powerful efficacy to soften the heart into tenderness" and "to harmonize the affections."[63] Minkema draws attention to Edwards' emphasis about the importance of music in the educational curriculum. It was "a carryover" from his own devotional life and that of his family, where singing had a central part.[64]

One of Edwards' educational goals in this school for Native Americans, though, reveals Edwards as typical man of his day. Teaching them the subjects he had enumerated would speedily change their affections, "bring them off from their barbarism and brutality" and "coarseness, and filth, and degradation, of savage life" and give them "a relish for those things, which belong to civilization and refinement."[65] Edwards was further convinced that all of the education should be in English, since "Indian languages are extremely barbarous and barren, and very ill-fitted for communicating things moral and divine, or even things speculative and abstract. In short, they are wholly unfit for a people possessed of civilization, knowledge and refinement ... without their learning English, their learning to read will be in vain; for the Indians have not the Bible, nor any other book, in their own language."[66] As Minkema has noted, here Edwards shows himself "to be a person of his times."[67] For the majority of Edwards' British contemporaries, and obviously for Edwards himself, to be Christian meant the embrace of European culture and especially learning a European language, in this case English. Yet, some of Edwards' Puritan forebears would have strongly disagreed with him. For example, in his missionary work among the Narragansett Indians in Massachusetts, John Eliot (1604–1690) soon recognized that he needed to translate the scriptures into

---

[61] Edwards, *Letters and Personal Writings*, ed. Claghorn, 409–410.

[62] Ibid., 410.

[63] Ibid., 410–411.

[64] Minkema, "Jonathan Edwards on Education" in *After Jonathan Edwards*, ed. Crisp and Sweeney, 34.

[65] Edwards, *Letters and Personal Writings*, ed. Claghorn, 411.

[66] Ibid., 413.

[67] Minkema, "Jonathan Edwards on Education" in *After Jonathan Edwards*, ed. Crisp and Sweeney, 34.

Algonquian.[68] He first prepared a catechism (1654) and then turned to the Bible, which was completed and printed in 1663. A second edition came out in 1685. He also translated the Westminster Larger Catechism (1669) and drew up a grammar (1666) in Algonquian. If such texts, especially the Bible and the Westminster Catechism, could be translated into Algonquian, then Edwards' point is nullified. In fact, Edwards' opinion regarding the Native American languages was essentially groundless, for he had no personal knowledge of these languages. He always worked through translators in Stockbridge rather than taking the time to learn the languages of those he was trying to reach with the gospel.[69]

SYNTHESIZING THE SOCRATIC METHOD AND DIALOGUE

A second text regarding Edwards' thought about education can be found in his reply to the trustees of Princeton upon their offering him the presidency of the school.[70] Edwards had a number of reasons for refusing to accept the invitation, but essentially they boiled down to two. One had to do with the written corpus that he had been engaged in writing, especially *A History of the Work of Redemption*, which was "the body of divinity ... thrown into the form of an [*sic*] history," in which Edwards was looking at the various aspects of theology in relation to the "great work of redemption of Jesus Christ" and their "historical order." Edwards really did not want to abandon this project — "my heart is so much in these studies, that I cannot find it in my heart to be willing to put myself into an incapacity to pursue them any more"— where then was he to find the time needed to adequately discharge the duties of a school president. As he told the trustees, his real talent was writing: "I think I can write better than I can speak."[71]

The other reason centered upon the fact that his bodily state — which he described as one "attended with flaccid solids, vapid, sizy and scarce fluids, and a low tide of spirits" — was ill-suited for taking on the governance of a school like Princeton as well as teaching "algebra, and the higher parts of mathematics, and ... the Greek classics." Edwards knew

---

[68] On Eliot, see Sidney H. Rooy, *The Theology of Missions in the Puritan Tradition. A Study of Representative Puritans: Richard Sibbes, Richard Baxter, John Eliot, Cotton Mather, and Jonathan Edwards* (Delft: W. D. Meinema, 1965), 156–241; Ola Elizabeth Winslow, *John Eliot: "Apostle to the Indians"* (Boston: Houghton Mifflin, 1968); Richard W. Cogley, *John Eliot's Mission to the Indians before King Philip's War* (Cambridge, MA: Harvard University Press, 1999).

[69] McClymond and McDermott, *Theology of Jonathan Edwards*, 561–562.

[70] Again, Minkema has examined this text in "Jonathan Edwards on Education" in *After Jonathan Edwards*, ed. Crisp and Sweeney, 36–37. For the letter, see *Letters and Personal Writings*, ed. Claghorn, 725–730.

[71] Edwards, *Letters and Personal Writings*, ed. Claghorn, 726–729.

Greek, he went on to mention, but it was the Greek of the New Testament, which was not as difficult a study as classical Greek.[72] He did indicate he was willing to give instruction in Hebrew, because, he openly told the trustees, he wished to improve his own ability in the language of the Old Testament.[73]

He was also prepared to teach "the senior class," and "do the whole work of a professor of divinity, in public and private lectures, proposing questions to be answered, and some to be discussed in writing and free conversation, in meetings of graduates and others."[74] This short sentence reveals a lot about Edwards' preferred educational method. It involved questions being proposed by the teacher, with answers being written out by the students that were then discussed "in free conversation." There are actually two extant lists of theological questions drawn up Edwards.[75] The first is "Questions on Theological Subjects," which was drawn up around 1746 and which he may well have used with various pastors-in-training who lived with him during the 1740s and 1750s, men like Samuel Hopkins or Joseph Bellamy (1719–1790). It contains questions like, "In what sense was faith in Jesus Christ necessary in order to salvation under the old testament?"[76] The other list is found in a pamphlet entitled "The Theological Questions of President Edwards, Senior and Dr. Edwards, His Son."[77] These questions, some ninety in all, are arranged systematically and ask such things as "19. Why did God decree sin?", "44. Why was an atonement and one so necessary as the blood of Christ necessary?" and "90. In what does the happiness of heaven consist?"

Having the student prepare to discuss these questions ahead of time and then having a free discussion about them is brilliant pedagogy. The student is compelled to understand the subject at hand thoroughly and then be able to defend his perspective. The teacher, who presumably has a greater knowledge of the subject, can then deepen the student's understanding where there are lacunae. The teacher thus becomes a true mentor.

---

[72] Ibid., 726.

[73] Ibid., 729.

[74] Edwards, *Letters and Personal Writings*, ed. Claghorn, 726–729.

[75] For a discussion of these lists, see Minkema, "Jonathan Edwards on Education" in *After Jonathan Edwards*, ed. Crisp and Sweeney, 38–39.

[76] Minkema, "Jonathan Edwards on Education" in *After Jonathan Edwards*, ed. Crisp and Sweeney, 38.

[77] *Bibliotheca Sacra* 39 (1882), 367–381. The questions of the elder Edwards run from pages 367–370, while those of his son, 313 in total, occupy the rest of this article.

THE AFFECTIVE TEACHER

Edwards reminds modern-day educators that the affections are absolutely critical to the learning process, whether that learning is about God or about the rules of English grammar. Due to the fact that the human being is first and foremost a unitary being, in which mind, will, and heart all impact each other, the process of learning can never be merely a matter of the mind. Therefore, the teacher must work to ignite these affections in the student in order to equip the student to approach the task of learning with potential success. If the affection of love and pleasure is kindled in the learning process, then there will be a genuine hunger to learn. Edwards was also prepared to innovate and embrace new knowledge. This can be seen in his own learning from various Enlightenment authors and is also part and parcel of his own critique of methods of teaching in Puritan New England. Thus, the teacher is to always be a learner and at the advanced level of an educational system, the teacher is also to be a researcher. It is interesting to note that one of the reasons Edwards was hesitant to take on the presidency of Princeton was because he did not want it to negatively impact his research and writing. Finally, his Socratic or dialogic method of teaching is brilliant, for it engages the student and avoids the danger of losing him in a boring lecture. The role of the teacher should be to leave a legacy and pass a torch to the generation following. His Socratic approach was structured so that his students would be able to ask and answer the same questions to the next set of students who would one day follow.

CONCLUSION

In an ordination sermon that Edwards preached in August of 1744 for a Robert Abercrombie, he took John 5:35 ("he was a burning and a shining light") for his text and sought to drive home to his fellow pastor, and to all of his hearers, the true nature of pastoral ministry. It entailed pure teaching, but teaching that was passionate and that sought to shape and influence the heart:

> [W]hat is implied in a minister of the Gospel's being a burning light [is that] ... his heart be full of much of the holy ardour of a spirit of true piety ... True piety ... reaches the heart, is chiefly seated there, and burns there ... 'Tis by this therefore especially, that a minister of the Gospel is a burning light: A minister that is so, has his soul enkindled with the heavenly flame; his heart burns with love to Christ, and fervent desires of the advancement of his Kingdom and glory; and also with ardent love to the souls of men, and desires for their salvation ... A minister is [also] set to be a light to men's

271

souls, by teaching, or doctrine: And if he be a shining light in this respect, the light of his doctrine must be bright and full… He must be one that is *able to teach*, not one that is raw, ignorant or unlearned, and but little versed in the things that he is to teach others; *not a novice*, or one that is *unskilful in the word of righteousness*; he must be one that is well studied in divinity, well acquainted with the written Word of God, mighty in the Scriptures, and able to instruct and convince gainsayers.[78]

Here in this text we not only see Edwards' ideal minister/teacher, one that is able to teach and is skilled in the exposition and explanation of scripture, but also the essence of his educational philosophy: it sought to influence and shape the heart.

PRIMARY SOURCE SAMPLE[79]

The following questions were used by Edwards in mentoring the pastoral interns who lived in his home for periods of time. They give a good idea of the sort of things he expected future pastor-teachers both to know and to communicate.

- How does it appear that something has existed from eternity?
- How does it appear that this earth and the visible system are not from eternity?
- How does it appear that the existence of man is derived and dependent?
- How do you prove the natural perfections of God, viz. his intelligence, infinite power, foreknowledge and immutability?
- How do you prove his moral perfections, that he is a friend of virtue, or absolutely holy, true, just and good?
- How do you prove that the

scriptures are a revelation from God? And what are the evidences, internal and external?
- How do you prove the divine mission of Christ?
- How do you prove the divinity of Christ?
- How do you prove the personality and divinity of the Holy Ghost?
- How do you prove that the persons in the Trinity are one God?
- Whence arose the Manichean notion of two gods, and how is it confuted?
- Whence arose the polytheism of the Pagans, and how confuted?
- Whence was it that the

---

[78] Jonathan Edwards, *The True Excellency of a Minister of the Gospel* (Boston: W. McAlpine, 1744), 10–12, *passim*.

[79] *Bibliotheca Sacra* 39 (1882), 367–370.

- knowledge of the one true God, in which Noah was instructed, was not preserved among his posterity in all ages?
- Why are not mankind in all ages (their internal faculties and external advantages being sufficient) united in right sentiments of the one true God?
- Were the moral character of God and the moral law understood and loved, would there be any objections against revealed religion?
- What is the true idea of God's decrees?
- How do you prove absolute and particular election?
- Did God decree the existence of sin?
- Why did God decree sin?
- In what sense did he introduce sin into the university?
- How do you reconcile this with the holiness and goodness of God?
- What is necessary to constitute a moral agent?
- Are men moral and free agents?
- What is the difference between natural and moral power and inability?
- How is the absolute moral necessity, or inability, consistent with the free agency of man?
- How is the doctrine of universal, absolute decrees, consistent with the free agency of man?
- How do you prove a universal and special providence?
- What is the covenant of redemption?

- If man was created in original righteousness, how is that consistent with moral agency? It being said that a necessary holiness is no holiness.
- What was the constitution under which Adam in innocency was placed?
- Was Adam under the same necessity of falling that we are of sinning?
- Are all intelligences bound to love God supremely, sinners and devils?
- Is the law holy, just and good, and how is it proved?
- Are they who are under its curse bound to delight in it?
- How great is the demerit of sin?
- Are the torments of hell eternal?
- How do you reconcile them with the justice and infinite goodness of God?
- How do you reconcile them with those texts which say Christ died for all men, that God will not that any should perish?
- How does it appear that human nature is originally depraved?
- Whence comes that depravity?
- How is it proved to be total?
- What is the covenant of grace?
- Are the law and gospel inconsistent with each other?
- Why was an atonement, and one so precious as the blood of Christ necessary?
- In what manner did Christ atone for sin?
- To whom doth it belong to provide an atonement, God, or the sinner?
- Did Christ redeem all men alike, elect and non-elect?
- Can the offer of the gospel be made in sincerity to the non-elect?
- How is redemption applied?
- What is the office of the Holy Ghost in the work of redemption?

- What is regeneration?
- Whence arises the necessity of it?
- What is true love to God?
- What is true benevolence to men?
- What is true repentance, and how distinguished from legal?
- What is true faith?
- What is pardon and justification? What is their foundation, and what is the influence of faith therein?
- How are full satisfaction and free pardon consistent?
- Is the sinner forgiven before he repents?
- Is sanctifying grace needful at all to any man, unless with respect to that which is his duty, and in neglect of which he would be without excuse?
- What is the sum of man's duty, and what the effect produced by the sanctifying influence of the Holy Spirit?
- Can that holy volition in us, which is the effect of divine power, be wholly our act, or our duty?
- How is it proved that unbelief is sin, and that all errors in moral matters are of a criminal nature?
- Will the wicked heathens, Jews, infidels, and errorists of every kind, be without excuse at the day of judgment?
- What is the essence of true virtue, or holiness?
- Is there no virtue in the exercise of natural conscience, the moral sense, natural compassion and generosity?
- Is not self-love the root of all virtue?
- Do not the unregenerate desire to be regenerated, and can they not properly pray for regenerating grace?

- Do they not desire the heavenly happiness?
- What is the utmost the unregenerate do in the use of the means of grace?
- Is any duty done by them therein?
- Do they grow better in the use of means?
- To what are they to be exhorted?
- What is the real advantage of the assiduous use of means to the unregenerate?
- How do you prove that the institution of the Sabbath is of perpetual obligation?
- How is it that the Sabbath is changed from the seventh to the first day of the week?
- How do you prove that public worship is to be celebrated on the Sabbath?
- What is the foundation of the duty of prayer, since God is omniscient and immutable?
- How do you prove that family prayer is a duty?
- To whom are the promises of the gospel made, to the regenerate, or unregenerate?
- Are no encouragements given to the unregenerate?
- How do you prove the saints' perseverance?
- What is the nature of a Christian church?
- Who are fit for communion therein?
- What is the nature and import of baptism?
- How do you prove infant baptism?
- What is the nature of the Lord's Supper?
- What are the rules and end of church discipline?
- What is the character of a good minister of Christ?
- In what does the happiness of heaven consist?

BIBLIOGRAPHY

Chauncy, Charles. *Seasonable Thoughts on the State of Religion in New-England*. 1743 ed.; repr. Hicksville, NY: The Regina Press, 1975.

Cherry, Conrad. *The Theology of Jonathan Edwards: A Reappraisal*. Bloomington, IN: Indiana University Press, 1990.

Cogly, Richard W. *John Eliot's Mission to the Indians before King Philip's War*. Cambridge, MA: Harvard University Press, 1999.

Cray Jr., Robert E. "More Light on a New Light: James Davenport's Religious Legacy, Eastern Long Island, 1740–1840." *New York History*, 73 (1992): 5–27.

Crisp, Oliver D. and Douglas A. Sweeney. *After Jonathan Edwards: The Courses of the New England Theology*. Oxford University Press, 2012.

Davis, Thomas M. and Virginia L. Davis, ed. *Edward Taylor vs. Solomon Stoddard: The Nature of the Lord's Supper*. Boston: Twayne Publishers, 1981.

Edwards, Jonathan. *The Great Awakening*. Edited by C.C. Goen. The Works of Jonathan Edwards, vol.4. New Haven: Yale University Press, 1972.

_____. *Letters and Personal Writings*, edited by George C. Claghorn. The Works of Jonathan Edwards, vol. 16. New Haven/London: Yale University Press, 1998.

_____. *Religious Affections*. Edited by John E. Smith. The Works of Jonathan Edwards, vol.2. New Haven/London: Yale University Press, 1959.

_____. *Writings on the Trinity, Grace, and Faith*. Edited by Sang Hyun Lee. The Works of Jonathan Edwards, vol. 21. New Haven: Yale University Press, 2002.

_____. *Jonathan Edwards on Revival*. Edinburgh: Banner of Truth Trust, 1984.

_____. *Jonathan Edwards' Resolutions And Advice to Young Converts*. Edited by Stephen J. Nichols. Phillipsburg, New Jersey: P&R Publishing, 2001.

_____. *Justification by Faith Alone* in *The Works of Jonathan Edwards*, vol. 1. 1834 ed.; repr. Edinburgh: The Banner of Truth Trust, 1974.

_____. *The True Excellency of a Minister of the Gospel*. Boston: W. McAlpine, 1744.

Hannah, John. "The Homiletical Skill of Jonathan Edwards", *Bibliotheca Sacra* 159 (January-March 2002): 96–107.

Hardman, Keith J. *The Spiritual Awakeners: American Revivalists from Solomon Stoddard to D.L. Moody*. Chicago, IL: Moody Press, 1983).

Haykin, Michael A.G. *Jonathan Edwards: The Holy Spirit in Revival*. Webster, NY: Evangelical Press, 2005.

Holmes, Stephen R. "Religious Affections by Jonathan Edwards." In *The Devoted Life: An Invitation to the Puritan Classics*. Edited by Kelly M. Kapic and Randall C. Gleason, 285–297. Downers Grove, IL: InterVarsity Press, 2004.

Hopkins, Samuel. "A Short Sketch of Mrs. Edwards's Life and Character", Appendix I to his *Memoirs of the Life, Experience and Character of the Late Rev. Jonathan Edwards, A.M.* in *The Works of President Edwards*, vol. I. 1817 ed.; repr. New York: Burt Franklin, 1968.

Kidd, Thomas S. *The Great Awakening: The Roots of Evangelical Christianity in Colonial America*. New Haven/London: Yale University Press, 2007.

Logan, Jr., Samuel T. "Jonathan Edwards and the 1734-35 Northampton Revival" in *Preaching and Revival*. London: The Westminster Conference, 1984.

_____. "The Doctrine of Justification in the Theology of Jonathan Edwards." *The Westminster Theological Journal*, 46 (Spring 1984): 26–52.

Lovelace, Richard. *Dynamics of Spiritual Life: An Evangelical Theology of Renewal.* Downers Grove, IL: Inter Varsity Press, 1978.

Marsden, George M. *Jonathan Edwards: A Life.* New Haven and London: Yale University Press, 2004.

McClymond, Michael J., and Gerald R. McDermott. *The Theology of Jonathan Edwards.* New York: Oxford University Press, 2012.

Miller, Perry. "General Editor's Note." In *The Freedom of the Will*, edited by Paul Ramsey, 1:vii–viii. The Works of Jonathan Edwards, vol.1. New Haven/London: Yale University Press, 1957.

Minkema, Kenneth P. "Hannah and Her Sisters: Sisterhood, Courtship, and Marriage Int He Edwards Family in the Early Eighteenth Century." *The New England Historical and Genealogical Register* 146 (January 1992): 35–56.

————. "Jonathan Edwards, America's Theologian: A Commemorative Yale Exhibition" in his and George G. Levesque, *Jonathan Edwards Tercentennial Exhibition: Selected Objects from the Yale Collections 1703–2003.* New Haven, CT: Yale University, 2003.

————. "'Informing of the child's understanding, influencing his heart, and directing its practice': Jonathan Edwards on education", *Acta Theologica*, 31, no.2 (January 2011):159–188.

Murray, Ian H. *Jonathan Edwards–A New Biography.* Edinburgh: Banner of Truth, 1987.

Noll, Mark A. *The Rise of Evangelicalism: The Age of Edwards, Whitefield, and the Wesleys.* Downers Grove, IL: IVP Academic, 2003.

Pope, Robert G. *The Half-Way Covenant: Church Membership in Puritan New England.* Princeton, NJ: Princeton University Press, 1969.

Porterfield, Amanda. *Feminine Spirituality in America: From Sarah Edwards to Martha Graham.* Philadelphia: Temple University Press, 1980.

Rooy, Sidney H. *The Theology of Missions in the Puritan Tradition. A Study of Representative Puritans: Richard Sibbes, Richard Baxter, John Eliot, Cotton Mather, and Jonathan Edwards.* Delft: W. D. Meinema, 1965.

Smart, Robert Davis. *Jonathan Edwards's Apologetic for the Great Awakening.* Grand Rapids, MI: Reformation Heritage Books, 2011.

Storms, Sam. *Signs of the Spirit: An Interpretation of Jonathan Edwards' Religious Affections.* Wheaton, IL: Crossway, 2007.

Stout, Harry S. and Peter Onuf. "James Davenport and the Great Awakening in New London." *The Journal of American History*, 71 (1983–1984): 556–578.

Strobel, Kyle. *Jonathan Edwards's Theology: A Reinterpretation.* T & T Clark Studies in Systematic Theology v. 19. London and New York: Bloomsbury T & T Clark, 2013.

Taylor, Thomas Templeton. "The Spirit of the Awakening: The Pneumatology of New England's Great Awakening in Historical and Theological Context." PhD diss., University of Illinois at Urbana-Champaign, 1988.

Walton, Brad. *Jonathan Edwards, Religious Affections and the Puritan Analysis of True Piety, Spiritual Sensation and Heart Religion.* Vol. 74. Studies In American Religion. Lewiston, NY: Edwin Mellen Press, 2002.

Wilson, John F. "Jonathan Edwards's Notebooks for 'A History of the Work of Redemption' " in *Reformation, Conformity and Dissent*, edited by R. Buick Knox. London: Epworth Press, 1977.

Winslow, Ola Elizabeth. *John Eliot: "Apostle to the Indians."* Boston: Houghton Mifflin, 1968.

PART IV

Post-Enlightenment Educators

(A.D. 1750-1850)

During the late eighteenth century. England was the scene for the Methodist revival and the rise of the Sunday-school movement. Representatives of these forces played crucial roles in the development of Christian education. **John Wesley** (1703-1791) was at once the founder of the Methodist revival and a pioneer of popular education. He not only preached and wrote voluminously, he criticized public schools and began his own. He encouraged intellectual and moral discipline as well as self-respect. He did much to spread knowledge and culture, especially among the poorer classes, breaking down barriers of privilege and creed and making learning accessible to all. Wesley also encouraged the development of Sunday schools, and while some contend that one of the early schools he organized was the first Sunday school, the school begun by **Robert Raikes** (1735-1811) in Gloucester in 1780 was more likely the first. Raikes brought children off the streets on Sundays to instruct them in religion as well as traditional subjects. He emphasized direct study of the Bible rather than memorizing catechism, and his schools had a great impact on the morals of their students.

The Continental educators whose influence on religious education was the greatest were Switzerland's **Johann H. Pestalozzi** (1746-1827) and Germany's **Johann Friedrich Herbart** (1776-1841). Pestalozzi's most significant contributions were his sociological inquiry into education and his concern for the education of disadvantaged children. His natural theory of education was a way of cooperating with the natural development of the student's Godgiven powers. Herbart, who successfully combined the talents of a philosopher and educator, considered the fundamental goal of education to be moral men. To achieve this goal all branches of knowledge are integrated into a system, and religion, rather than being taught separately, is drawn from the other subjects.

CHAPTER 16

John Wesley:
Methodizing Christian Education

MARK A. MADDIX

JAMES R. ESTEP

John Wesley (1703-1791)

John Wesley was perhaps the most influential evangelist and social reformer of the 18th Century. John and his brother Charles were responsible for the founding of the Methodist denomination, which started from their methodical approach to spiritual formation. While predominantly known as an itinerant preacher and evangelist, Wesley was also an accomplished educator and reformer. He developed systems of small groups, purposed to foster spiritual growth and to encourage participants to pursue a holiness of heart and life. In addition to this he also began elementary and secondary schools to educate the children of his Methodist movement.

HISTORICAL BACKGROUND

John Wesley's life and ministry transformed eighteenth century England. His emphasis on the proclamation of the gospel provided freedom from sin and social liberation, which revolutionized society. Wesley's impact included his evangelistic efforts, the development of schools, reforming prisons, and establishing groups that helped individuals to grow toward "holiness of heart and life."[1] His ministry and educational efforts stemmed from his deep theological conviction that God's grace could transform humans and society. Wesley was a pastor and a practical theologian who is best known for the development and foundation of the Methodist movement.

John Wesley (1703-1791) was born on June 17, 1703 to Samuel and Susanna Wesley. Samuel was an Anglican clergyman of the Epworth church and a biblical scholar of considerable renown.[2] Susanna was a strong disciplinarian who provided six hours of education a day for her children. She devoted Thursday evenings to Wesley, and was especially careful with her ministry to him. She viewed his miraculous escape from the burning of Epworth Rectory as evidence of God's superintending providence, and an indication that the Lord had a noble purpose for John's life.[3]

Susanna and Samuel showed real concern for the spiritual well-being of their children. Samuel influenced his sons through his own devotion to scholarship. In addition, the Wesley household embraced a number of different styles of devotional literature.[4] Wesley's childhood offered a strong blend of Puritan devotion and Anglican sacramentalism with churchmanship, all of which influenced Wesley's educational practice.[5] Wesley had a strong formal education by attending the Charterhouse Boarding School at age ten, and then attending Oxford University to receive his bachelor's degree at age twenty-one and master's degree at the age of twenty-four. He was ordained deacon of the Church of England on September 19, 1725 with the blessing of Susanna and Samuel Wesley. As a student he demonstrated considerable proficiency in classical studies, but his greatest delight was logic and debate.[6] At Oxford,

---

[1] See Charles Yrigoyen, John Wesley: *Holiness of Heart and Life* (Nashville: Abingdon, 1996).

[2] Vivian H. H. Green, *The Young Mr. Wesley* (New York: St. Martin's Press, 1961), 12.

[3] Kenneth Collins, T*he Scripture Way of Salvation: The Heart of John Wesley's Theology* (Nashville: Abingdon Press, 1999), 14.

[4] Martin Schmidt, *John Wesley: A Theological Biography,* 2 vols., (Nashville: Abingdon Press, 1966), 1:63.

[5] Robert Monk, *John Wesley: His Puritan Heritage* (Nashville: Abingdon Press, 1966), 23.

[6] John Wesley, *The Works of John Wesley*, ed. Thomas Jackson, 3rd ed. (1872; repr., Peabody, MA: Hendrickson Publishers, 1986), 2:72-73.

John joined his brother Charles' Holy club comprised of young men interested in spiritual growth and the reading of classical literature and devotional classics like Thomas A' Kempis' *Imitation of Christ*, Jeremy Taylor's *Holy Living and Dying*, and William Law's *Serious Call*. This experience changed Wesley's life and the result was, after graduating from Oxford in 1729, he became a Fellow at Lincoln College and was appointed a tutor of undergraduates in both academics and spiritual progress.[7] This group also served others by visiting the sick, elderly, and imprisoned, and provided clothing and financial aid. It was through this formal educational experience that their disciplined manner was called, "The Holy Club," "The Bible Moths," or "The Methodists."[8]

John and Charles Wesley sailed for Georgia on October 21, 1735 to preach Christ to the Indians. However, their missionary efforts were abandoned, and Wesley became the pastor of the English churches at Savannah and Frederica.[9] Wesley was influenced by the religious piety of the Moravians, which forced him to ask questions about his own faith. It was during their mutual voyage to Georgia, after a succession of storms, that John found the peace he was for which he was searching. During these storms, the Moravians sang, while the English passengers were trembling with terror.[10] What Wesley learned from the Moravians was that God granted individuals salvation instantaneously. At that moment of salvation, a person is born again and could be assured of the witness of the Spirit. Through this experience Wesley desired with all his heart to find that faith which would deliver him from fear and doubt, and bring the assurance of the acceptance with God.

After a couple years in Georgia, Wesley returned to England and continued to preach, but felt defeated and disillusioned. Wesley searched the Scriptures trying to find the solution to his spiritual condition. After several weeks of relentless searching, Wesley found the answer. While attending a Moravian meeting in Aldersgate Street where someone was reading Luther's Preface to the *Epistle of the Romans*, Wesley describes his May 24, 1738, experience in his Journal: "About a quarter before nine, while he was describing the change, which God works in the heart through faith in Christ, I felt my heart strangely warmed. I felt I did trust in Christ, Christ alone, for salvation, and an assurance was given me, that He had

---

[7] Schmidt, *A Theological Biography*, 2:196-197.

[8] Luke Tyerman, *The Life and Times of the Reverend John Wesley*, M.A.(New York: Harper and Brothers, 1972), 69-70.

[9] David M. Henderson, *John Wesley's Class Meeting: A Model of Making Disciples* (Nappanee, IN: Evangel, 1997).

[10] John Telford, ed., *The Letters of the Rev. John Wesley* (England: The Epworth Press, 1960), 78-79.

taken away my sins, even mine, and saved me from the law of sin and death."[11] Wesley at once began to pray earnestly for his enemies and publicly testified to all present what he now felt. Wesley's Aldersgate experience resulted in a "heart-felt" religion that became the central thrust and aim of Methodism. His preaching and educational endeavors were centered on the transformational power of the conversion experience. The influence of the Moravian's focus on instantaneous conversation was influential in his doctrine of sanctification and "holiness of heart and life."

WESLEY AS EVANGELIST

John Wesley's primary mission was to save souls. He included this in his list of rules for his preachers stating, "You have nothing to do but to save souls. Therefore spend and be spent in this work; and go always, not only to those who want you, but to those who want you most."[12] Wesley realized early in his ministry that his mission could not be fulfilled if it was limited to conventional English parish ministry. In order to accomplish his mission he learned about "open-air preaching" from his friend, George Whitefield. Wesley was reluctant to follow Whitefield's methods, but in 1739 he began open-air preaching. He found that this method was successful in reaching men and women who did not enter most churches. As a result Wesley preached and hearers were convicted of their sinfulness. Later the famous phrase that described his life, "the world is my parish" motivated him to break from the conventional parish boundaries to preach to gospel to anyone who wanted to listen. Wesley preached in fields, barns, and even his father's grave to ensure that souls were saved. Most of his preaching was to the outcasts of society; as a result not all joined Methodist societies. He preached to crowds of 60,000 to 134,000 in 1755. He traveled 250,000 miles on a horse and preached more than 40,000 sermons, sometimes four or five times a day[13] and the result was a revivalist movement that transformed eighteenth century England. At his death in 1791, his followers numbered seventy-nine thousand in England and forty-thousand in America. Even though the Methodist movement sprung up as a renewal movement in the Church of England, Wesley never belonged to the Methodist Church. He remained an Anglican priest the entirety of his life.

---

[11] Wesley, *The Works*, 1872/1986, 1:103.

[12] *Minutes of the Methodist Conferences* (London: John Mason, 1862), 1:494, 496.

[13] Henry Abelove, *The Evangelist of Desire: John Wesley and the Methodist* (Stanford, CA: Stanford University Press, 1990), 9-10.

WESLEY AS SOCIAL REFORMER

Wesley not only preached to save souls, but he preached to liberate people from bondage and oppression from sin, and social injustices such as poverty, lack of education and health services. John Wesley's famous phrase "there is no holiness without social holiness" focused on the development of church community through societies, classes, and bands, but also included the engagement in transforming and redeeming the world. Some theologians suggest that the genius of the Wesleys and the early Methodists was their ability to transform social structures.[14] They were most effective in England's emerging manufacturing and industrial centers. Wesley's desire to reach the poor and to resist social evil was one of the cardinal tenets of his ministry.[15] His concern for the poor resulted in the development of schools, as well as prison and education reform. Wesley was able to accomplish this through the development of Methodist societies. These societies became the chief vehicle for implementing Wesley's "evangelical economics."[16] Also, as Wesley traveled he provided medical service to people without charge. He also made sure that they could also go to the back door of a nearby rectory to get food or medicine.[17] Wesley deployed genteel and open-handed charity, providing coal, bread, and clothes for the needy, especially among his followers. He visited with people house-to-house and developed close supervision of work programs for the unemployed, while also assuming the responsibility for orphans.[18]

For Wesley and Methodists, holiness was both personal and social. This was reflected in the context of Christian fellowship through his group formation and through his socio-economic influence. Wesley's described holiness as "renewal of the whole image of God,"[19] which included the renewing and transformations of people and all creation. His view of holiness was the whole world, created and recreated as Christ followers engaged in God's redemptive work on earth.

---

[14] Manfred Marquardt, *John Wesley's Social Ethics: Praxis and Principles,* trans. John E. Steely and W. Stephen Gunter (Nashville: Abingdon Press, 1992), 199-204.

[15] John R. Tyson. *"Why did John Wesley 'Fail'? A Reappraisal of Wesley's Evangelical Economics,"* Methodist History 35, no. 3 (1997): 180.

[16] Ibid.

[17] Abelove, *The Evangelist of Desire*, 9.

[18] Ibid.

[19] See chapter 2 of Armistead, M. Kathryn, Brad D. Strawn and Ronald W. Wright, eds., *Wesleyan Theology and Social Science: The Dance of Practical Divinity and Discovery* (Newcastle upon Tyne: Cambridge Scholars Publishing, 2010).

INFLUENCES ON WESLEY'S THEOLOGY ON EDUCATION

Wesley's own educational experiences are mirrored in the model of education he proposed. He was cognizant of the influence and impact it had on him, undeniably spurring him on to affirming the value of education for spiritual formation.[20]

Wesley's educational beliefs were a synthesis of ideals espoused by his religious and secular contemporaries. From these educational convictions, he not only challenged the foundations of eighteenth century English education, but called for reformation and reinvention of educational ideals and practices, particularly in homes, congregations, and schools. Wesley's educational philosophy was an integration of his theological beliefs, personal experience, his own educational experience, and appraisals of contemporary educators. Wesley's beliefs on education were indeed his own, but several contributing factors are readily identifiable as strongly influencing his views. First and foremost was the influence of his mother on his own, personal education, followed by the German Pietistic/Moravian movement, as well as the contemporary educational theories of his day.

SUSANNA WESLEY

Susanna Wesley's puritanical ideas toward behavior management and child-rearing are readily offered in Wesley's educational theory and practice.[21] In fact, Wesley even cited his mother's eight "by-laws" of parenting in his journal as being ideal for child rearing.[22] The eight "by-laws" that Susannah Wesley developed for child-rearing included: benefit of honesty, consistency, a clean slate, rewarding obedience, recognition that the it is the thought that counts, respect for others, being true to One's Word, and the importance of an education for her daughters. These by-laws impacted Wesley's own philosophy of educating children, which consisted of conquering their will and bring them to an obedient temper.

GERMAN PIETISM/MORAVIANISM

The theological influence of German Pietism[23] on Wesley, to which he was exposed

---

[20] Mark A. Maddix, "John Wesley's Formative Experiences: Foundations for His Educational Ministry Perspectives," *Didache: Faithful Teaching 9*, no. 1 (2009): 1-8.

[21] Robert C. Monk, *John Wesley: His Puritan Heritage* (Nashville: Abingdon Press, 1966), 185, 190.

[22] John Wesley, *The Works of John Wesley*, 3rd ed. (Peabody, MA: Hendrickson Publishers, 1986), I, 392-393. For further information see: John Wesley Prince, *Wesley on Religious Education: A Study of John Wesley's Theories and Methods of the Education of Children in Religion* (New York: The Methodist Book Concern, 1926), 103-115.

[23] For Wesley's own account of his encounter with the Pietists in Germany see Journal, August 21,

both in America and later Germany, was limited.[24] However, the Moravians did indeed have a profound influence on Wesley in regard to his educational theory. "It was [Count] Zinzendorf who would establish in Wesley's mind a paradigm for the Moravian ideal."[25] Wesley adopted the educational philosophy of the Moravians that emphasized an academically rigorous study of Scripture as well as the humanities, including biblical and ancient languages, with an almost equal emphasis on spiritual and moral development, all in the context of a rigidly structured academic community.[26] Wesley's emphasis on education for spiritual formation was, indeed, innate to the movement he fostered. This was a direct adaptation of the influence German pietism had on his practical theology.[27] In fact, his exposure to the Pietist educational model in Herrnhut, Germany would later be emulated at Wesley's Kingswood School in Bristol, England.[28]

CONTEMPORARY EDUCATIONAL THEORIES/THEORISTS

John Locke (1632-1704) was the leading educational philosopher of eighteenth century England, and Wesley was familiar with his "Essay on the Human Understanding and Thoughts on Education," even requiring it in the fourth year of study at his Kingswood School.[29] Locke's influence is particularly evident in the "disciplinary concept of education" maintained by Wesley.[30] Wesley's attitude toward including the family/home, even in boarding-school education, can be attributed to influence by John Milton's *Tractate on*

1738 in Works, I, 154-156.

[24] cf. F. Ernest Stoeffler, "Religious Roots of the Early Moravian and Methodist Movements," *Methodist History* 24, no. 3 (1986): 132-140; Karl Zehrer, "The Relationship between Pietism in Halle and Early Methodism," *Methodist History* 17, no. 4 (1979): 211-224; Kenneth J. Collins, "The Influence of Early German Pietism on John Wesley," *The Covenant Quarterly* 48, no. 4 (1990): 23-42.

[25] Warren Thomas Smith, "Eighteenth Century Encounters: Methodist-Moravian," *Methodist History* 24, no. 3 (1986): 150.

[26] James Riley Estep, Jr., "Wesley's Educational Ideal at Kingswood and the Modern Christian School," *Journal of Christian Education and Information Technology* (Korean), 14 (October 2008): 55-72.

[27] James Riley Estep, Jr., "Scripture and Spiritual Formation in the German Pietist Tradition," *Christian Education Journal* 3, no. 9 (Fall, 2011): S94-109.

[28] Martin Schmidt, *A Theological Biography*, 1:297.

[29] Prince, *Wesley on Religious Education*, 103; Alfred H. Body, *John Wesley and Education* (London: Epworth Press, 1936), 61.

[30] Body, *John Wesley and Education*, 33.

Education, which he read and liked.[31] In fact, Milton and Wesley "both express the same view of the true aim of education," i.e., restoration of humanity from the Fall,[32] an idea he also shared in common with William Law.[33] Likewise, John Norris' *Reflections,* written about the concept of knowledge, was edited by Wesley and an abridged edition was released in 1755, although he did not fully agree with Norris, as evidenced by his omissions from the text.[34]

The influence of contemporary educators was not always positive. In some cases, Wesley's tone even became condemnatory toward "the great triumvirate, Rousseau, Voltaire, and David Hume," whom he asserted had removed revelation from religion and the Creator from His creation.[35] For example, Wesley's *Thoughts upon Necessity* argued against Hume's view of human predetermination, denying human free will, which is a fundamental tenet to Wesley's educational philosophy.[36] Similarly, Wesley found Rousseau's *Emile* to be "most empty, silly, injudicious thing that ever a self-conceited infidel wrote,"[37] asserting that if Rousseau's educational principles were used at Kingswood School we would be "continually ruining fifty children at a time!"[38] Regardless of how one assesses Wesley's sentiment of his contemporaries, one point is evident: Wesley was not ignorant of the prevailing educational theorists or philosophies of his time. In fact, the influential factors explain Wesley's emphasis on home, congregation, and school.

THEOLOGY OF CHRISTIAN EDUCATION

Wesley "viewed education as a means of grace — as an instrument through which the Holy Spirit worked," e.g., for conversion and continual maturation.[39] The intent of education was a pietistic matter, but it also was instrumental in the advancement of his reformation.

---

[31] Wesley, Works, VIII, 16. *John Wesley, A Plain Account of Kingswood School* (1781), Works, XIII, 296. cf. Wesley Tracy, "Christian Education in the Wesleyan Mode," Wesleyan Journal of Theology 17, no. 1 (1982): 36; Prince, Wesley on Religious Education, 103.

[32] Body, *John Wesley and Education,* 34.

[33] Wesley, Works, XIV, 3; *John Wesley, A Short Account of the School in Kingswood, Near Bristol* (1768), Works, XIII, 3; Body, *John Wesley and Education,* 159.

[34] John C. English, "John Wesley's Indebtedness to John Norris," *Church History* 60, no. 1 (1991): 67.

[35] Wesley, Works, VII, 271.

[36] Albert C. Outler eds., *John Wesley* (New York: Oxford University Press, 1964), 472-473.

[37] Wesley, "A Thought on the Manner of Educating Children," (1783), Works, XIII, 475.

[38] Ibid.

[39] Gayle Carlton Felton, "John Wesley and the Teaching Ministry: Ramifications for Education in the Church Today," *Religious Education* 92, no. 1 (1997): 95.

Hence, he viewed education as a means of advancing personal piety and the Methodist movement within the Church of England. This is particularly evident in his avocation for childhood education, wherein he affirmed that children would be led to salvation through training that leads to conversion. For Wesley, his emphasis on an educational evangelism was not held in tension with his revivalistic tendencies, since "the revival methods would be necessary only where Christian nurture had failed."[40]

THEOLOGICAL HERMENEUTIC
Grace in the Theology of Wesley

John Wesley was a practical theologian. He believed that theology was for the purpose of transforming personal life and social relations. His "practical divinity" was soteriological in focus — to see human persons reconciled to God and renewed in the image of God.[41] This soteriological focus is reflected in Wesley's *ordo salutis,* which focused on salvation as a gift, and included a divine-human synergism, enabled by grace, which leads to the transformation of people into the image of God. The key to Wesley's soteriological doctrines of justification, sanctification, and Christian perfection is his understanding of grace. Wesley's view of grace included a Western theological view of grace as divine pardon and forgiveness, and the Eastern theological view of grace as the power of God working to renew our nature.[42] Thus grace, when it is received, both communicates forgiveness and makes renewal possible. Because the very nature of God is love, God's love is intended to be received, and to create that bond in order to receive and reciprocate love.[43] It is this bond that enables the creature to share in the nature of God, and thus be renewed in God's image.

The themes of God's commitment to mercy and love for creation and God's gracious identification in the incarnation were central to Wesley's "optimism of grace." Because grace is God's loving presence, it cannot be forced upon us. It is not irresistible, as some predestinarians assert.[44] Wesley's view of grace and human responsibility was what separated him from the Reformed theologians of his day. He rejected predestination by holding

---

[40] Prince, *Wesley on Religious Education*, 98.

[41] Thomas Langford, "John Wesley and Theological Method," in *Rethinking Wesley's Theology for Contemporary Methodist*, ed. Randy Maddox (Nashville: Abingdon, 1998), 35.

[42] Randy Maddox, *Responsible Grace: John Wesley's Practical Theology* (Nashville: Kingswood Books, 1994), 23.

[43] Theodore Runyon. *The New Creation: John Wesley's Theology Today* (Nashville: Abingdon Press, 1998), 26.

[44] Ibid., 27.

together divine initiative and human responsibility, which is referred to as "co-operating grace" or "responsible grace."[45] Accordingly, depriving human beings of freedom is not the nature of God's grace. Yet grace makes possible the human response by the prompting of God's Spirit at work in us, both to communicate love and to begin the process of renewal. The work of the Holy Spirit, through prevenient grace is active in our lives, even before we are aware of this activity. For Wesley, this idea of prevenient grace was an important aspect of the nature of Grace. He defined this concept as grace that comes before and provides opportunity for humans to be free will agents. Wesley's view that salvation is a gift of God, coupled with his view of human response is central to his soteriology. As we engage in service we are "co-creators" with God in the redemption of humanity and all creation.

The way people receive grace from God is through the regular participation in the "means of grace." In Wesley's sermon "The Means of Grace" he explained that these means of grace are "outward signs, words, or actions, ordained by God, and appointed for this end, to be ordinary channels whereby God might convey to men preventing, justifying and sanctifying grace."[46] Wesley used the word "means" with the word "ordinance" on occasion as an indicator that this participation was expected by God. While the Means of Grace themselves had no salvific worth, they were channels by which the Holy Spirit works in extraordinary ways. The means, like grace, were available to all, even to those who did not yet experience what Wesley calls "salvation."[47]

As grace is dynamic, so are the means of grace. The result is that there are many different forms that Wesley categorized as Instituted, Prudential, or General Means of Grace.[48] Wesley believed that the Instituted means were evident in the life of Christ. These means of grace, particularly in their corporate expressions, mirror the intended and ongoing sacramental life of the church. They include prayer, searching the scriptures, participating in the Lord's Supper (Eucharist), fasting, and Christian conferencing (spiritual conversation). The Prudential Means of Grace were designed to meet the person at his or her point of need; thus they are adaptable to a person's particular historical situation or context. They include

---

[45] Maddox, *Responsible Grace,* 92.

[46] Wesley, "The Means of Grace," in *Bicentennial Edition,* 1:381.

[47] Dean Blevins, "Worship: Formation and Discernment," *Wesley Theological Journal* 33, no. 1 (Spring, 1998): 11-27; See Henry Hawthorn Knight, *The Presence of God in the Christian Life: John Wesley and the Means of Grace* (Metuchen, NJ: Scarecrow, 1992); Ole E. Borgen, *John Wesley on the Sacraments* (Grand Rapids: Francis Asbury, 1985); Rob Staples, *Outward Signs and Inward Grace: The Place of Sacraments in the Wesleyan Tradition,* (Beacon Hill: Kansas City, 1991).

[48] Blevins, "Formation and Discernment,"121.

obeying Christ, small groups, special prayer meetings, visiting the sick, doing all the good we can to all the people we can, and reading from the devotional classics. The general means of grace include watching, denying ourselves, taking up our cross daily, and exercising the presence of God.

Wesley did not confine God's grace to just these practices. Because he understood grace to be God's loving uncreated presence, he believed many other activities could be means of grace. Thus, grace is still active even among those who have no access to specific means like Christian baptism, the Eucharist, or the study of Scripture.

However, Wesley believed that by participation in the instituted means of grace a person can be made aware of God's pardoning and empowering presence on a regular basis. Wesley's therapeutic focus is evident in his invitation for his people to meditate regularly on the affirmation that Christ "sealed His love with sacraments of grace, to breed and nourish up in us the life of love."[49] Thus, all who need further empowering by God's grace should faithfully participate in the instituted means of grace.

SCRIPTURE IN THE THEOLOGY OF WESLEY

John Wesley described himself as *homo unius libri*, "a man of one book."[50] He declared that he read the Bible "to find the way to heaven."[51] It is noteworthy that Wesley did not focus on heaven as a goal or ideal *per se,* but instead the believers were followers of the "way" and life of salvation. Thus, the Bible functions as sacred Scripture in the various ways to transform and shape the perspectives and lives of those who comprise the church, not simply in the kinds of arguments that someone may appropriate to validate the reliability of the Bible, or in the ways someone may appeal to specific data within the Bible.[52] For Wesley, he did not view Scripture in an epistemic way, so that one may assess the validity of Christian doctrine by what the Bible states. That is, the Bible functions to clarify theological information about the Christian faith. However, Wesley understood scripture to have a more formative role than an epistemic role.[53] That is, the early church appropriated and turned

---

[49] Maddox, *Responsible Grace*, 200.

[50] "Preface" to Sermons on Several Occasions, in *Works* (Bicentennial ed.), 1:105.

[51] Ibid.

[52] See Robert W. Wall, "Toward a Wesleyan Hermeneutic of Scripture," in *Reading the Bible in Wesleyan Ways: Some Constructive Proposals*, ed. Barry L. Callen and Richard P. Thompson (Kansas City, MO: Beacon Hill Press, 2004), 39-55.

[53] See William J. Abraham, *Canon and Criterion in Christian Theology* (Oxford: Oxford University Press, 1998), esp. 1-56; See Mark A. Maddix and Richard Thompson, "The Role of Scripture in

repeatedly to this particular collection of texts because of the formative ways that these texts (and not others) functioned within the Christian community. This Wesleyan understanding of the Bible as Scripture, to be pursued in (trans)formational terms, is consistent with the place of the biblical texts within the pre-canonical period of the early church.[54] Wesley's hermeneutical approach to Scripture corresponds to the early churches use of Scripture in worship, prayer, and a variety of formative practices. In other words, Wesley viewed Scripture primarily as means of forming people to live holy lives.

Wesley affirmed the Reformation idea of *sola scriptura* and the authority of Scripture, but he did not follow all the implications of this doctrine without modifications. When Wesley read "scripture alone," he believed that the Bible is the primary source of authority, but not necessarily the only religious authority.[55] As Donald Thorsen states, "John Wesley's most enduring contribution to theological method stems from his . . . [inclusion] of experience along with Scripture, tradition, and reason as genuine sources of religious authority. While maintaining the primacy of Scripture, Wesley functioned with a dynamic interplay of sources in interpreting, illuminating, enriching, and communicating biblical truths."[56] This perspective does not imply that tradition, reason, or experience can stand alone as authorities, but serve as a partner in interpreting Scripture.

Wesley's appeal to Scripture was primary in his theological method. When Scripture is silent about specific issues, the practice of tradition may be allowed. Wesley, following his Anglican tradition was highly influenced by the "Protestant theological method," which used Scripture, reason, and tradition. It is better known as the "Anglican Triad." Wesley added "experience" to the traditional Anglican Triad, which altered its substance by placing experience as a valid means of authority. He applied the familiar distinction between theoretical faith *fides quae creditor* and an existential one *fides qua creditur* so as to insist on "Heart religion" in place of all nominal Christian orthodoxy. Wesley added experience to make room for his own conversion at Aldersgate and the conversion of others.[57] Albert

---

Christian Formation," *Wesley Theological Journal* 46, no. 1 (Spring 2011): 134-149.

[54] See William J. Abraham, *Canon and Criterion in Christian Theology* (Oxford: Oxford University Press, 1998), esp. 1-56; See also Maddix and Thompson, "The Role of Scripture," 134-149.

[55] Dean Blevins and Mark A. Maddix, *Discovering Discipleship: Dynamics of Christian Education* (Kansas City: Beacon Hill Press, 2010), 65.

[56] Donald Thorsen, "Interpretation in Interactive Balance: The Authority of Scripture for John Wesley," in *Reading the Bible in Wesleyan Ways*, ed. Barry L Callen and Richard P. Thompson (Kansas City: Beacon Hill Press, 2004), 18.

[57] See Albert C. Outler, ed. *John Wesley* (New York: Oxford University Press, 1964); W. Stephen Gunter, et al. *Wesley and the Quadrilateral: Renewing the Conversation* (Nashville: Abingdon Press,

Outler coined the term "Quadrilateral" to describe Wesley's theological method, even though "quadrilateral" is not used in Wesley's writings.[58]

The quadrilateral is a methodology of theological reflection that places Scripture as the rule and as authoritative in a way that should not be ascribed to other components. Tradition, reason, and experience then form an interpretative or hermeneutical spiral in which the dialogical relationship among all the components continually enables the church to understand and apply Scripture more accurately and effectively.[59]

Wesley was a "man of one book" but he read widely in the areas of science, literature, Catholic mysticism, early church fathers, and Protestant reformers. Wesley drew on these sources when interpreting the Bible. He understood that "all truth is God's truth" and that God reveals through Scripture as His primary means of revelation, but God also reviews through natural revelation. Wesley believed that both special and natural revelation is an expression of God's gracious activity. Special revelation, then, fulfills what is started in natural revelation, and that all knowledge of God comes from God's initiative. Wesley believed that knowledge was developed through the senses, primarily from the heart, which was why Methodism was known as a "religion of the heart."

CONTRIBUTIONS TO CHRISTIAN EDUCATION

Welsey's contribution to Christian education was beyond the theological and philosophical, with the aim that the practical expression of his theology of education produced a multi-faceted, multi-tiered system of education for the church. His "educational theory not only covered the best in philosophy but also covered all levels of instruction – the home, elementary, secondary, and graduate levels and adult education."[60] He understood that education begins in the family, at home, but was not limited to familial

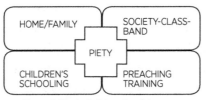
Figure 1: Wesley's Educational Avenues

instruction. He advocated education through the congregation, and formal education through schooling, but all with the aim of facilitating piety within the believer (Figure 1). This was not only for children, but for adults as well, especially those desiring to serve as lay preachers within the Methodist movement.

1997).

[58] See Outler, *John Wesley*.

[59] Gunter, et al. *Wesley and the Quadrilateral*, 142.

[60] Herbert W. Byrne, *John Wesley and Learning* (Salem, OH: Schmul's Wesleyan Book Club, 1997), 215.

CHRISTIAN EDUCATION IN THE HOME

As previously noted, Wesley's principles and practices for Christian instruction in the family was a direct inference from his mother. Wesley affirmed that children had a genuine potential for saving-faith, an authentic relationship with God, and the capacity for religious instruction.[61] He understood that education in the home took two forms: (1) Discipline, which addressed the behavioral concerns of the child, and (2) Instruction, which referred to the child's cognitive learning of the Christian faith.

In Sermon 95, "On the Education of Children," Wesley outlined several principles for parents to "train up a child" (Prov. 22:6). In it, he encouraged parents to have routine conversations about God with their children, focus on "breaking the will" of the child, not lavishing them with undue praise, and teaching them self-moderation in their diet, attire, and possessions. He likewise said that parents could teach this by not taking revenge on a child's behavior, but by modeling mercy and justice. "Use every means to give them a love of truth, — of veracity, sincerity, and simplicity, and of openness both of spirit and behaviour [sic]."[62]

Horace Bushnell's *Christian Nurture* (1846), while distinct from Wesley in terms of importance of socialization and religious instruction in the Christian home, parallels Wesley's focus on spiritual nurturing in the family.[63] To assist in facilitating familial instruction, Wesley prepared a series of tracts entitled "Lessons for Children," "Instructions for Children," and "Tokens for Children," all designed to provide guidelines and/or content for parents teaching their children.[64] Parents were likewise not alone in providing home-based Christian instruction. Wesley instructed the lay preachers within the Methodist Societies to assist families as well, requiring them to equip and train parents to lead families to worship and prayer, to teach children through regular home visits, and to develop specialized ministries within the Methodist Societies specifically for children.[65]

EDUCATIONAL METHODOLOGIES

Wesley's educational methodology is more difficult to define because in teaching children it included lectures, drilling, and memorization. However, his educational practices with adults

---

[61] James Riley Estep, Jr., "Wesley's Philosophy of Formal Childhood Education," *Christian Education Journal* NS1, no. 2 (1997): 43-52.

[62] Wesley, *Works*, III, 349-60.

[63] Mark A. Maddix, "Christian Nurture and Conversion: A Conversation between Horace Bushnell and John Wesley," *Christian Education Journal* 9, no. 2 (Fall, 2012): 309-325.

[64] Prince, 125-132.

[65] Ibid., 132-136.

included both accountability and some flexibility, depending on the level of the group. The development of classes, societies, and bands indicated that even though Wesley rejected the current educational philosophies of Rousseau, he understood the developmental needs of the learner. He placed a strong emphasis on accountability through community as a means for spiritual growth and development.

The formation of societies was the heart of Wesley's educational methodology. Wesley formed Methodist Societies for those who "wanted to 'flee from the wrath to come" by providing an interpersonal context to promote personal piety.[66] The general expectations for the Societies were provided by Wesley in "The Nature, Design, and General Rules of the United Societies."[67] The Methodist Societies were indeed the principal means of providing continuing adult education for Wesley's adherents, including an educational opportunity for women, whom he felt should have an equivalent education to men.[68]

Societies had preachers, assistants (like executive pastors), stewards to serve as treasurers, and secretaries for the Society, depending on the needs of the Society, which greatly ranged in size from small, such as thirty-two, to as large as over eight-hundred.[69] The formation of Methodist societies grew in England: for example in 1776 they had 19,267 members, which grew to 85,063 by 1801.[70]

Membership in the Societies required a ticket for admission, attesting to one's personal piety, and a penny offering to cover expenses.[71] Its curriculum included not only pietistic preaching, but Wesley "expected his printed sermons to function as curriculum in the processes of adult education, along with a range of other materials such as his two-volume 'Explanatory Notes upon the New Testament' and 'The General Rules of the United Societies.'"[72] In addition, hymnody was also a means of providing educational resource for adults, such as *A Collection of Hymns for the Use of the People Called Methodists* (1780), as was Wesley's "Arminian Magazine," started in 1778.[73] However, Wesley was not content with just the formation of Societies as larger gatherings, but divided them further into small groups called classes and even smaller units still,

---

[66] Wesley, *Works*, VIII, 250.

[67] Ibid., 269-274.

[68] Wesley, *Works*, III, 602; Volume XII, 262. Cf. Burton, 19, 44.

[69] Wesley, *Works*, I, 158; Wesley, Works, II, 49.

[70] David Lows Watson, *The Early Methodist Class Meeting: Its Origins and Significance* (Eugene, OR: Wipf and Stock, 2002), 131.

[71] Wesley, *Works*, 357; VIII, 252; XIII, 259.

[72] Felton, *Teaching Ministry*, 101.

[73] Prince, *Wesley on Religious Education*, 102.

called bands, to provide a comprehensive Christian education ministry in the Society. David Lowes Watson explains,

> Wesley practiced the concept of ecclesiola in ecclesia with integrity: the freedom of small groups, focused on the immediacy of obedient Christian discipleship; and the necessary structure of the larger church where doctrine and order were established in the realities and uncertainties of the world. The inference is clear: The structure of the larger ecclesia must be affirmed as inherently valid and necessary if the freedom of the ecclesiola is to be exercised responsibly.[74]

This organizational principle is illustrated in Figure 2 where Wesley's idea of a Methodist Society can be seen. In this model, classes and/or bands function within classes or independent of them, but all under the auspices of the Society.

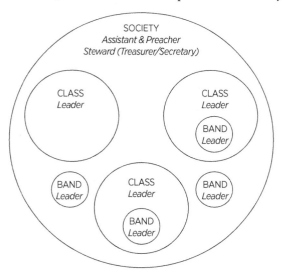

Figure 2: Methodist Societies

Classes consisted typically of twelve individuals, much like a small group today. They were formed to facilitate the "temporal and spiritual welfare of the society."[75] Class leaders were responsible for "contributions, but also to watch over the souls of their brethren," noting the classes allowed for the assessment of the spiritual maturity of individuals.[76] Leaders were to visit each class member weekly, receive the Society's offering, and meet with the Societies' Assistant and Stewards on a weekly basis,[77] which was later changed to monthly.[78]

Bands were even smaller "classes" and were designed to provide weekly spiritual accountability to members of Methodist societies, the purpose being to 'confess our faults one to another,' and pray one for another that we may be healed," outlining that they would meet at least weekly, be punctual, have singing and prayer, "to speak each of us in order, freely and plainly, the true state of

---

[74] Watson, *Early Methodist Class Meeting*, 127.

[75] Wesley, *Works*, III, 427.

[76] Wesley, *Works*, XIII, 259; see also Wesley, *Works*, VII, 253.

[77] Wesley, *Works*, III, 426-427.

[78] Wesley, *Works*, VIII, 253, 256.

our soul, with the faults we have committed in thought, word, or deed, and the temptations we have felt since our last meeting." They appointed a Leader "to speak his own state first, and then to ask the rest, in order, as many and as searching questions as may be, concerning their state, sins, and temptations."[79] To assist the band leaders, Wesley published "Rules of the Band-Societies" in 1738, including the questions for discussion and "Directions Given to Band-Societies" to guide the leader.[80]

The Society-Class-Band system was obviously successful for promoting the fledgling Methodist movement and in facilitating personal piety among its members. Yet, it was not without its critics. Some objected to it as a distraction from the mission of the church, which was identified by critics as preaching, and perceived the band leaders as "Romish Priest," i.e. their own little papacies, taking confessions, and assuming authority over the members.[81] However, these criticisms did not hinder the formation of a community of believers in Methodist Societies.

ROLE OF THE TEACHER AND EDUCATIONAL CURRICULUM

In Wesley's educational philosophy the most important element of learning was the teacher; the most important quality was his or her spirituality: "The human aspect of the teacher's role was rated higher than his technical task."[82]

Also, the teacher was the primary molder of the will of the child, thus the classroom would be highly teacher-centered. The teacher was the transmitter of knowledge and the center of the educational enterprise. The teacher was a model for students to imitate, which followed the ancient Greek view of teacher as the one who forms and shapes human character and virtue. In Wesley's estimate, the most important element of the teacher was their spirituality. This emphasis on the spiritual life of the teacher was reflected in Wesley's careful attention in "procuring Masters" to teach at Kingswood.[83]

Wesley outlined the curriculum of study for children enrolled at Kingswood, which consisted of eight classes per day. The curriculum was indeed intensive and encyclopedic, combining classical and religious instruction.[84] Figure 3 contains a description of Kingswood's course of study.[85]

---

[79] Ibid., 258.

[80] Ibid., 272-273; see also Wesley, *Works*, VI, 273-274.

[81] Wesley, *Works*, X, 351, 352.

[82] Schmidt *A Theological Biography*, 1:180.

[83] Wesley, *Works*, Plain Account of Kingswood School, XIII, 297.

[84] Wesley, *Works*, XIII, 284-289.

[85] Body, *John Wesley and Education*, 159.

One unique element in Wesley's curriculum was the inclusion of physical education at Kingswood, typically negated from Christian education, but this inclusion reflected Wesley's general concern for physical health and "is not irrational in the light of his theory of human nature and its remaking."[86] Wesley provided a comprehensive sketch of the developments within Kingswood in his Journals, but in 1768 he published "A Short Account of the Kingswood School" and later in 1781 "A Plain Account of Kingswood School," both of which restated his motivation and plan for the establishment of the school. While Kingswood was not the only school established by Wesley, it is the one that most reflects his ideals on schooling.

WESLEY'S CURRICULUM/SCHEDULE FOR KINGWOOD

HR.	CLASS 1	CLASS 2	CLASS 3	CLASS 4	CLASS 5	CLASS 6	CLASS 7	CLASS 8
7		Manners of the Ancient Christians	Primitive Christianity	Pilgrim's Progress	Life of Mr. Haliburton	Life of Mr. de Renty	Law's Christian Perfection	Law's Serious Call
8	Reading	English or Latin Grammar	Eng. or Latin Grammar	Latin Grammar	Latin Grammar	Latin Grammar	Greek Grammar or Tully and Virgil altern. Later Greek Test't	Latin Greek and Hebrew altern.
9			Corderius or Historiae Selectae	Kempis or Cornelius Nepos.	Erasmus Phaedrus or Asllust	Caesar Terence or Vell. Paterc.		
10	Writing	Writing	Writing	Writing and Arithmetic	Arithmetic	Geog.	Chron-ology	Rhetoric
1 & 2	Reading	Construe & parse	Corderius or Hist. Select.	Kempis or Nepos	Erastmus, &c.	Caesar, &c.	Greek Grammar or Tully & Virgil	Latin, Greek and Hebrew
3		Praelect Pueriles				Roman Antiquities	Greek Antiquities	Hebrew Antiquities
4	Writing	Trans. into English and Latin altern.	Trans.	Trans.	Trans.	Trans.	Trans. and Verses altern.	Trans. Verses Theme Declamation
Note: All classes except the eighth spend Saturday afternoon in Arithmetic and in transcribing what they learn on Sunday, and repeat on Monday morning.								

Figure 3: Wesley's Curriculum/Schedule at Kingswood

THE ROLE OF THE STUDENT

Wesley's theology reflected his view of human persons as being "created in the image of God" and in need of restoration. At times he viewed childhood as a "unit of salvation" instead of a time period when people grow and develop. However, Wesley's educational practices were developmentally sensitive for the most part, and he considered the uniqueness of each person.

---

[86] Prince, *Wesley on Religious Education*, 144.

His theology reflected in his concern for all people, rich and poor, and he viewed all people as equals with the capacity to learn, grow, and develop. Students were seen as rational and spiritual beings where freedom comes primarily through the discipline and development of the mind. Thus, his epistemology emerges from his view of revelation, intuition, and experience.

CHRISTIAN EDUCATION IN SCHOOLS

Wesley saw the development of schools as central to education the poor and less educated of society. His preference in schooling models reflects the eighteenth century schools in England: Grammar, Vocational, and Charity schools, which later included the Sunday school. Wesley supported all of these models, but they required something more, i.e. a pietistic focus. Wesley established his own grammar and vocational school, e.g. Kingswood, and charity schools as well, e.g. the "Old House" at Kingswood, the Foundry, and West Street, Soho; and especially the educational opportunity provided to the poor by the Sunday school.[87]

Even though Wesley had advocated children's education years earlier than Robert Raikes' Sunday school movement would even start, Wesley readily endorsed the use of the Sunday school because it was a way to revive religion in the nation. The Wesleyans even formed the Wesleyan Sunday School Union. Wesley ordered all the Methodist Societies to start Sunday Schools, primarily to address rampant poverty and due to Raikes' non-sectarian position.[88]

Before services I stopped into the Sunday school, which contains two hundred and forty children, taught every Sunday by school masters, and superintended by the curate. So, many children in one parish are restrained from open sin, and taught a little good manners, at least, as well as to read the Bible. I find these schools springing up wherever I go. Perhaps God may have a deeper end therein, that men are aware of. Who knows but some of the schools may become nurseries for Christians?[89]

By 1811 (the year of Raikes' death), the number of Sunday schools in England reached over four-hundred thousand, and by 1831 the number grew to 1,250,000, in part due to Wesley's promotion of them.[90]

---

[87] Dean G. Blevins, "To be a Means of Grace: A Wesleyan Perspective on Christian Practices and the Lives of Children," *Wesleyan Theological Journal* 43, no. 1 (2008): 47-67; Prince, *Wesley on Religious Education* 52-61; Byrne, *John Wesley and Learning*, 129.

[88] Byrne, *John Wesley and Learning*, 129.

[89] Wesley, *Works*, IV, 284.

[90] James E. Reed and Ronnie Prevost, *A History of Christian Education* (Nashville: B&H Academic, 1998), 259.

Kingswood School is considered by most to be Wesley's crowning educational achievement and legacy.[91] It was to "answer the design of Christian education," and developed sanctified intellects for use in God's service so "that they might be rational, scriptural Christians."[92] As a tuition-based boarding school established near Bristol (England), it paralleled the schedule and curriculum of Moravian schools in eastern Germany, reflecting Wesley's affirmation of the pietistic school model. Kingswood was founded May 21, 1739, along with a charity school for the children of poverty stricken miners. Later, the school expanded to four programs of study and also housed a library to support its programs.[93] The school was for boys ages six to twelve, with strict attention given to admission and enrollment standards; students studied ten hours per day. In later years, the school provided instruction and opened housing for girls.[94]

THE ROLE OF PROFESSIONAL DEVELOPMENT AND PASTORAL TRAINING

In regard to the sustaining of his movement, Wesley provided extensive training for lay leaders to serve as preachers and teachers. The equipping of these leaders was based on self-study, not seminary. "Decades after his own Oxford education for the ministry, John Wesley was faced with educating growing number of poorly educated lay preachers in his movement; he responded by designing a course of education for the lay clergy that he expected them to pursue even as they traveled and preached."[95]

Wesley "looked for signs of devotion to God, holy character, gifts of the work, and success with listeners" – these are reflected in the examination of lay preacher's candidates in 1746, "These tests focus on faith in God, love for God, and devotion to God."[96] To equip such men, Wesley utilized five methods of training: Conferences, publications, internships (which consisted of demonstration, delegation, and supervision), spiritual experiences, and active involvement in classes and bands, (small groups).[97] In so doing, Wesley was able to field lay ministers at an impressive rate and with some degree of quality assurance.[98]

---

[91] Estep, "Wesley's Educational Ideal," 55-72.

[92] Wesley, *Works*, XIII, 293.

[93] Randy L Maddox, "Kingswood School Library Holdings (ca. 1775)," *Methodist History* 41, no. 1 (2003): 342-370.

[94] Prince, *Wesley on Religious Education*, 90; Stanley Ayling, *John Wesley* (New York: William Collins Publisher 1979), 170.

[95] Burton, *Spiritual Literacy*, 110.

[96] Ibid., 109-110.

[97] Byrne, *John Wesley and Learning*, 202.

[98] Bill Temple, "Preparation for 'Beating the Devil': Uncovering the Leadership Development

He required the lay preachers to have a growing knowledge of the following areas of study: Bible, Greek and Hebrew, secular and Christian history, science, metaphysics, and natural philosophy, as well as the early church fathers and a study of behaviors expected of men, principally delivered by a regiment of reading for six to eight hours per day. He provided a "Christian Library" in the form of a fifty-five volume set of books, which contained excerpts of texts, outlines, summations.[99] In addition, the textbooks used at Kingsway were also required of lay preachers.

Itinerant preachers were expected to have spiritual exercises from four to five a.m., such as meditation, prayer, and devotional study of Scripture; and then read from six a.m. to noon prior to going to actual minister the rest of the day. To those lay preachers who rejected Wesley's voluminous reading requirement, saying "'But I have no taste for reading'," he retorted, "Contract a taste for it by use, or return to your trade."[100]

WESLEY'S EDUCATIONAL LEGACY

One does not customarily revere John Wesley as an educator. Yet, in the midst of the Great Awakening in England, Wesley sounded a voice for educational reform. Attention given to instruction in the Christian home, Methodist Societies, through schooling, e.g. the Sunday School, Kingswood, Cokesbury, and Foundry, as well as the non-formal means utilized to equip Methodist lay preachers, makes Wesley one of the more comprehensive educational theorist of his era. However, the assessment of Wesley's educational endeavors is often sharply contrasted. For example, church historian Gerald Cragg asserts that "in education his [Wesley's] lack of imagination gave him little understanding of the young."[101] On the other hand, John Gross comments that Wesley's "willingness to experiment with new ideas is seen in departures made at Kingswood and Cokesbury from the traditional programs of the English school."[102]

Wesley was a man of his time who advanced the cause of Christian education to the best of his ability. "It is only right," comments Cragg, "to remember that few men in his period

---

Paradigm and Practices of John Wesley in Early British and American Methodism," unpublished paper (Trinity Evangelical Divinity School, Deerfield, Illinois, 1994), 4.

[99] Wesley, *Works*, X, 490-492; Byrne, *John Wesley and Learning*, 200; Burton, *Spiritual Literacy*, 111.

[100] Wesley, *Works*, VIII, 315.

[101] Gerald R. Cragg, *The Church in the Age of Reason* (1648-1789) (New York: Penguin Books, 1970), 149 [emphasis added].

[102] John Owen Gross, *John Wesley: Christian Educator* (Nashville: Board of Education, the Methodist Church, 1954), 9 [emphasis added].

did more to promote the cause of education."[103] His theology (and philosophy) of education offers the contemporary Christian educator a legacy on which to follow. His voice need not be silenced by the passage of time, and though his practices may be antiquated, his principles offer us a relevant direction for Christian education today.

PRIMARY SOURCE SAMPLE[104]

"Train up a child in the way wherein he should go: And when he is old, he will not depart from it." Prov. 22:6.

1. We must not imagine that these words are to be understood in an absolute sense, as if no child that had been trained up in the way wherein he should go had ever departed from it. Matter of fact will by no means agree with this: So far from it, that it has been a common observation, "Some of the best parents have the worst children." It is true, this might sometimes be the case, because good men have not always a good understanding; and, without this, it is hardly to be expected that they will know how to train up their children. Besides, those who are in other respects good men have often too much easiness of temper; so that they go no farther in restraining their children from evil, than an old Eli did, when he said gently, "Nay, my sons, the report I hear of you is not good." This, then, is no contradiction to the assertion; for their children are not "trained up in the way wherein they should go." But it must be acknowledged, some have been trained therein with all possible care and diligence; and yet before they were old, yea, in the strength of their years, they did utterly depart from it.

2. The words, then, must be understood with some limitation, and then they contain an unquestionable truth. It is a general, though not an universal, promise; and many have found the happy accomplishment of it. As this is the most probable method for making their children pious which any parents can take, so it generally, although not always, meets with the desired success. The God of their fathers is with their children; he blesses their

---

[103] Cragg, *The Church*, 149.

[104] This primary source sample is an excerpt from *The Sermons of John Wesley*, "Sermon 95: On The Education Of Children," copyright 1999 by the Wesley Center for Applied Theology. Text may be freely used for personal or scholarly purposes or mirrored on other web sites, provided this notice is left intact. Any use of this material for commercial purposes of any kind is strictly forbidden without the express permission of the Wesley Center at Northwest Nazarene University, Nampa, ID 83686. Contact the webmaster for permission. Edited by Keith Millar with corrections by George Lyons and additional formatting by Ryan Danker for the Wesley Center for Applied Theology at Northwest Nazarene University.

endeavours; and they have the satisfaction of leaving their religion, as well as their worldly substance, to those that descend from them.

3. But what is "the way wherein a child should go" and how shall we "train him up" therein. The ground of this is admirably well laid by Mr. Law, in his "Serious Call to a Devout Life." Part of his words are, —

"Had we continued perfect as God created the first man, perhaps the perfection of our nature had been a sufficient self-instructer for everyone. But as sickness and diseases have created the necessity of medicines and physicians, so the disorders of our rational nature have introduced the necessity of education and tutors.

"And as the only end of a physician is, to restore nature to its own state, so the only end of education is, to restore our rational nature to its proper state. Education, therefore, is to be considered as reason borrowed as second-hand, which is, as far as it can, to supply the loss of original perfection. And as physic may justly be called the art of restoring health, so education should be considered in no other light, than as the art of recovering to man his rational perfection.

"This was the end pursued by the youths that attended upon Pythagoras, Socrates, and Plato, their every-day lessons and instructions were so many lectures upon the nature of man, his true end, and the right use of his faculties; upon the immortality of the soul, its relation to God; the agreeableness of virtue to the divine nature; upon the necessity of temperance, justice, mercy, and truth; and the folly of indulging our passions.

"Now, as Christianity has, as it were, new created the moral and religious world, and set everything that is reasonable, wise, holy, and desirable in its true point of light; so one would expect the education of children should be as much mended by Christianity, as the doctrines of religion are.

"As it has introduced a new state of things, and so fully informed us of the nature of man, and the end of his creation; as it has fixed all our goods and evils, taught us the means of purifying our souls, of pleasing God, and being happy eternally; one might naturally suppose that every Christian country abounded with schools, not only for teaching a few questions and answers of a catechism, but for the forming, training, and practicing children in such a course of life as the sublimest doctrines of Christianity require.

"And education under Pythagoras or Socrates had no other end, but to teach children to think and act as Pythagoras and Socrates did.

"And is it not reasonable to suppose that a Christian education should have no other end but to teach them how to think, and judge, and act according to the strictest rules of Christianity

"At least one would suppose, that in all Christian schools, the teaching them to begin their lives in the spirit of Christianity, — in such abstinence, humility, sobriety, and devotion as Christianity requires, — should not only be more, but a hundred times more, regarded that nay or all things else.

"For those that educate us should imitate our guardian angels; suggest nothing to our minds but what is wise and holy; help us to discover every false judgement of our minds, and to subdue every wrong passion in our hearts.

"And it is as reasonable to expect and require all this benefit from a Christian education, as to require that physic should strengthen all that is right in our nature, and remove all our diseases."

4. Let it be carefully remembered all this time, that God, not man, is the physician of souls; that it is He, and none else, who giveth medicine to heal our natural sickness; that all "the help which is done upon earth, he doeth it himself;" that none of all the children of men is able to "bring a clean thing out of an unclean;" and, in a word, that "it is God who worketh in us, both to will and to do of his good pleasure." But is generally his pleasure to work by his creatures; to help man by man. He honours men to be, in a sense, "workers together with him." By this means the reward is ours, while the glory redounds to him.

BIBLIOGRAPHY
PRIMARY SOURCES

Wesley, John. *A Christian Library, Consisting of Extracts from and Abridgements of the Choicest Pieces of Practical Divinity which has been Published in the English Tongue.* 30 Vols. London: T. Blanshard, 1819-1827.

_____. *A Collection of Forms of Prayer for Every Day in the Week.* 1738. Reprint, Nashville: United Methodist Publishing House, 1992.

_____. *Explanatory Notes on the New Testament.* 2 Vols. 1780. Reprint, Peabody, MA: Hendrickson Publishers, 1986.

_____. *Explanatory Notes on the Old Testament.* 1765. Reprint, Salem, OH: Schmul Publishers, 1975.

_____. *The Sunday Service of the Methodists in North America.* 1784. Reprint, Nashville: United Methodist Publishing House, 1992.

_____. *A Plain Account of Christian Perfection.* Kansas City: Beacon Hill Press, 1966.

SECONDARY SOURCES

Abraham, William J. *Canon and Criterion in Christian Theology.* Oxford: Oxford University Press, 1998.

Abelove, Henry. *The Evangelist of Desire: John Wesley and the Methodist.* Stanford, CA: Stanford University Press, 1990.

Armistead, M. Kathryn, Brad D. Strawn and Ronald W. Wright, eds. *Wesleyan Theology and Social Science: The Dance of Practical Divinity and Discovery.* Newcastle upon Tyne: Cambridge Scholars Publishing, 2010.

Ayling, Stanley. *John Wesley*. New York: William Collins Publisher, 1979.

Blevins, Dean and Mark A. Maddix, *Discovering Discipleship: Dynamics of Christian Education*. Kansas City: Beacon Hill Press, 2010.

_____. "Worship: Formation and Discernment." *Wesley Theological Journal* 33, no. 1 (Spring, 1998): 11-27.

_____. "To be a Means of Grace: A Wesleyan Perspective on Christian Practices and the Lives of Children," *Wesleyan Theological Journal* 43, no. 1 (Spring 2008):47-67.

Body, Alfred H. *John Wesley and Education*. London: Epworth, 1936.

Borgen, Ole E. *John Wesley on the Sacraments*. Grand Rapids: Francis Asbury, 1985.

Byrne, Herbert W. *John Wesley and Learning*. Salem, OH: Schmul's Wesleyan Book Club, 1997.

Burton, Vicki Tolar. *Spiritual Literacy in John Wesley's Methodism*. Waco, TX: Baylor University Press, 2008.

Collins, Kenneth. *The Scripture Way of Salvation: The Heart of John Wesley's Theology*. Nashville: Abingdon Press, 1999.

_____. "The Influence of Early German Pietism on John Wesley," The Covenant Quarterly 48, no. 4 (November 1990): 23-42.

Cragg, Gerald R. *The Church in the Age of Reason* (1648-1789). New York: Penguin Books, 1970.

Dwyer, James A. and Karl Zehrer, "The Relationship between Pietism in Halle and Early Methodism," *Methodist History* 17, no. 4 (July 1979): 211-224.

English, John C. "John Wesley's Indebtedness to John Norris," *Church History* 60, no. 1 (March 1991): 55-69.

Estep, James R. Jr., "Scripture and Spiritual Formation in the German Pietist Tradition." *Christian Education Journal* 3, no. S9 (Spring 2012): S94-S109.

_____. "Wesley's Philosophy of Formal Childhood Education," *Christian Education Journal* NS1, no. 2 (Fall 1997):43-52.

_____. *Wesley's Educational Ideal at Kingswood and the Modern Christian School, Journal of Christian Education and Information Technology* (Korean), 14 (October): 55-72.

Felton, Gayle Carlton. "John Wesley and the Teaching Ministry: Ramifications for Education in the Church Today." *Religious Education* 92, no. 1 (Winter 1997): 92-105.

Green, Vivian H. H. *The Young Mr. Wesley*. New York: St. Martin's Press, 1961.

Gunter, Stephen W., ed. *Wesley and the Quadrilateral: Renewing the Conversation*. Nashville: Abingdon Press, 1997.

Gross, John Owen. *John Wesley: Christian Educator. Nashville: Board of Education, the Methodist Church*, 1954.

Henderson, David M. *John Wesley's Class Meeting: A Model of Making Disciples*. Nappanee, IN: Evangel, 1997.

Knight, Henry Hawthorn. *The Presence of God in the Christian Life: John Wesley and the Means of Grace*. Metuchen, NJ: Scarecrow, 1992.

Langford, Thomas. "John Wesley and Theological Method," In *Rethinking Wesley's Theology for Contemporary Methodist*. Edited by Randy Maddox. Nashville: Abingdon Press, 1998.

Maddix, Mark A. "John Wesley's Formative Experiences: Foundations for His Educational Ministry Perspectives," *Didache: Faithful Teaching* 9, no. 1 (June 2009): 1-8.

_____. "Christian Nurture and Conversion: A Conversation between Horace Bushnell and John Wesley," *Christian Education Journal* 9, no. 2 (Fall 2012): 309-325.

_____. "John Wesley and a Holistic Approach to Christian Education," *Wesley Theological Journal* 44, no. 2 (Fall 2009): 76-93.

Maddix, Mark A. and Richard Thompson. "The Role of Scripture in Christian Formation." *Wesley Theological Journal* 46, no. 1 (Spring 2011): 134-149.

Maddox, Randy L. *Responsible Grace: John Wesley's Practical Theology*. Nashville: Kingswood Books, 1994.

————. "Kingswood School Library Holdings," *Methodist History* 41, no. 1(2003): 342-370.

Marquardt, Manfred. *John Wesley's Social Ethics: Praxis and Principles*. Translated by John E. Steely and W. Stephen Gunter. Nashville: Abingdon Press, 1992.

Minutes of the Methodist Conferences. London: John Mason, 1862.

Monk, Robert. *John Wesley: His Puritan Heritage*. Nashville: Abingdon Press, 1966.

Outler, Albert C., ed. *John Wesley*. New York: Oxford University Press, 1964.

Prince, John Wesley. *Wesley on Religious Education: A Study of John Wesley's Theories and Methods of the Education of Children in Religion*. New York: The Methodist Book Concern, 1926.

Reed, James E. and Ronnie Prevost. *A History of Christian Education*. Nashville: B&H Academic, 1998.

Runyon, Theodore. *The new creation: John Wesley's Theology Today*. Nashville: Abingdon Press, 1998.

Schmidt, Martin. *John Wesley: A Theological Biography*. Vols. 1 and 2. Nashville: Abingdon Press, 1966.

Smith, Warren Thomas. "Eighteenth Century Encounters: Methodist-Moravian," *Methodist History* 24, no. 3 (April 1986):141-156.

Staples, Rob. *Outward Signs and Inward Grace: The Place of Sacraments in the Wesleyan Tradition*. Kansas City: Beacon Hill, 1991.

Stoeffler, F. Ernest. "Religious Roots of the Early Moravian and Methodist Movements," *Methodist History* 24, no. 3 (April 1986): 132-140

Thorsen, Donald. "Interpretation in Interactive Balance: The Authority of Scripture for John Wesley." In *Reading the Bible in Wesleyan Ways*, edited by Barry L. Callen and Richard P. Thompson, 81-106. Kansas City: Beacon Hill Press, 2004.

Telford, John, ed. *The Letters of the Rev. John Wesley*. England: The Epworth Press, 1960.

Temple, Bill. "Preparation for 'Beating the Devil: Uncovering the Leadership Development Paradigm and Practices of John Wesley in Early British and American Methodism," unpublished paper, Trinity Evangelical Divinity School, Deerfield, Illinois, 1994.

Tracy, Wesley. "Christian Education in the Wesleyan Mode," *Wesleyan Journal of Theology* 17, no. 1 (1982): 30-53.

Tyerman, Luke. *The Life and Times of the Reverend John Wesley*, M.A. New York: Harper and Brothers, 1972.

Tyson, John R. "Why did John Wesley 'Fail'? A Reappraisal of Wesley's Evangelical Economics." *Methodist History* 35, no. 3: (1997): 176-187.

Wall, Robert W. "Toward a Wesleyan Hermeneutic of Scripture." In *Reading the Bible in Wesleyan Ways: Some Constructive Proposals*, ed. Barry L. Callen and Richard P. Thompson. Kansas City, MO: Beacon Hill Press, 2004.

Watson, David Lows, *The Early Methodist Class Meeting: Its Origins and Significance. Eugene*, OR: Wipf and Stock, 2002.

Yrigoyen, Charles. *John Wesley: Holiness of Heart and Life*. Nashville: Abingdon, 1996.

CHAPTER 17

Robert Raikes:

Author of the Sunday School Movement

RODERICK C. WILLIS II

L. PHILIP BARNES

Robert Raikes (1735-1811)

Robert Raikes was an English philanthropist and evangelical Anglican layman, noted for his promotion of Sunday schools. He funded and organized Sunday schools in eighteenth century England to enable children, who were often required to work long hours six days a week to learn to read and write, to become acquainted with Christian moral and religious teaching. The Sunday school system he started in England was widely adopted elsewhere and weekly Sunday school continues to this day to introduce young people to Christian faith and discipleship.

HISTORICAL BACKGROUND

Robert Raikes was a successful eighteenth century businessman and social reformer who is often credited with founding the modern Sunday school movement. Before outlining the details of his life and his contribution to the emergence of Sunday schools, it is useful to say something about the socio-historical context in which he lived and worked.

Class distinctions were a prominent and influential feature of British society in the eighteenth century. A small hereditary aristocracy possessed much of the national wealth and enjoyed a lifestyle of opulence and indulgence, which contrasted markedly with the poverty experienced by the majority of the population, many of whom were forced to work long hours to achieve subsistence. The aristocracy had possession of large estates and benefited financially from increased agricultural production as a result of more efficient farming methods and horticulture. The gentry, as owners of smaller estates, were not as fortunate, as they were less able to pay the taxes that were levied to fund Britain's foreign wars throughout the century, e.g., against Spain, and in the case of France on four different occasions.

More efficient and effective farming meant that fewer people were needed to "work the land," while at the same time the population was growing. The British population actually doubled in the hundred years after 1721, from 7.1 to 14.2 million people. Most of the growth occurred after 1750, and particularly after 1780. This growth can largely be attributed (predictably) to an increase in family size and a falling mortality rate: between 1810 and 1820, the average family size grew to include five or six children, the highest level of growth in any decade in modern British history. The growth of population throughout the eighteenth century is not unrelated to the emergence of Britain as a major industrial and economic world power. Some historians distinguish between a First Industrial Revolution, which began the last decades of the seventeenth century and the early decades of the in the eighteenth century, and a Second Industrial Revolution in the 1850s, which deepened and extended the process of industrialization. Technological and mechanical inventions "revolutionized" the practice of agriculture, manufacturing, mining, and transport, which in turn produced profound economic, social and cultural effects. In simple terms, a previously manual labor and draft-animal based economy gave way to a machine-based manufacturing economy. In addition to manufacturing, coal, water, and steam provided the energy to drive industry. Canals, improved roads, commercial railways and ships aided connectivity and increased the opportunity for transporting British goods to the world.[1] Although class distinctions continued throughout

---

[1] A clear and informative account of the Industrial Revolution in Britain is provided by Robert C. Allen, "The British Industrial Revolution in Global Perspective: How Commerce Created the

the eighteenth century, the period saw the emergence of a new middle class in towns and cities. Middle-class families earned their livings in trade or in professions, such as law and medicine. The production of commodities at affordable prices (alongside a growing market and monetary economy) benefited those who produced, distributed, and sold goods. The manufacture of goods centered on factories and contributed to a shift of population from the countryside to towns and cities for those searching for work. Often factories were unhealthy and dangerous places. They were dirty, poorly ventilated, and noisy. Moreover, wages were low and workers were often required to work from twelve to fourteen hours daily, six days a week. A growing social and economic divide emerged between those who labored in factories and in industry and those who owed the means of production or sold the products of industry.

During the eighteenth century, English families were not mandated by law to enroll children in school. Education was a privately funded privilege, the cost and practicalities of which excluded most families and children. At the beginning of the seventeenth century the Elizabethan Poor Law of 1601 had made it compulsory for the poor, including children, to work in order to keep them from disturbing the civil order. Disobedience to the law was punishable by fines or jail. Many families of the lowest economic standing could barely support themselves and were fined or detained in government subsidized workhouses that functioned as communal factories or farms for the "unemployed" and the "idle." Forced employment was seen as "relief" (i.e., welfare), as well as a disincentive to criminality. Work was perceived to be in keeping with the Christian moral virtues of self-sufficiency and of service to the community. Many children worked full-time from a relatively young age and were precluded from learning how to read and write.[2]

Throughout this century, the Church of England was, for the most part, religiously and politically conservative. It was the established church and enjoyed official patronage and favor. Passionate convictions in religion were frowned upon by many clergy and the heart of the gospel was equated with upright, middle class behavior. The philosopher John Locke (1632-1704) expressed the views of the political and religious establishment when he railed against religious enthusiasm in Chapter XIX of Book 4 of *An Essay Concerning Human Understanding*. He describes religious "enthusiasts" as people who "persuade themselves that they are under the peculiar guidance of heaven in their actions and opinions, especially in

---

Industrial Revolution and Modern Economic Growth," available at http://www.nuff.ox.ac.uk/users/allen/unpublished/econinvent-3.pdf (accessed on July 1, 2015).

[2] Roy Porter, *English Society in the Eighteenth Century* (Harmondsworth: Penguin Books, 1990), 143-184, and W. B. Stephens, *Education in Britain, 1750-1914* (London: Palgrave Macmillan, 1999).

those of them which they cannot account for by the ordinary methods of knowledge and principles of reason."[3] Moreover, he believed, their opinions and beliefs were "ungrounded fancies of a man's own brain."[4] Locke was not adverse to religion; he believed that the existence of God was rationally grounded. He was also prepared to accept the reality of revelation, but only if reason could first establish and confirm the credentials of revelation. The social fabric of British society was regarded as ordered by God. This belief was expressed by the hymn writer, Mrs. Cecil Alexander in "All things bright and beautiful." The third verse states:

> The rich man in his castle,
> The poor man at his gate,
> God made them high and lowly,
> And ordered their estate.

These words, although written in the nineteenth century, capture what many Christians believed in the eighteenth century: God allocated to each his or her role in society.

Although the social order may be ordered by God and the established church regarded as dispensing God's grace to the nation (factors that give some sense to speaking of British society as Christian), for the most part much of the population was "unchurched." E. W. Rice says of this period that "Christianity was dying of respectability on the one hand and confronted by a seething mass of ignorance and nameless vices on the other."[5] John Wesley (1703-1791), who along with his brother Charles and George Whitefield, initiated the Evangelical Revival, spoke negatively of "the ... character of the English nation" as "ungodliness ... Ungodliness is our universal, our constant, our peculiar character."[6] Wesley was a Church of England minister, who was not oblivious to the spiritual plight of the masses. He made it his life's work to challenge ungodliness, and in this he was joined by others. When more conservative clergy excluded him from their pulpits, Wesley began to address the public in open areas, such as fields and town centers. He is said to have preached forty-thousand

---

[3] John Locke, *An Essay Concerning Human Understanding*, (Amherst, NY: Prometheus Books, 1995), Bk. 4, Ch. 19, Section 5.; for a sympathetic yet critical discussion of religious enthusiasm, see George Mavrodes, "Enthusiasm," *Philosophy of Religion* 25 (1989), 171-186.

[4] John Locke, *An Essay Concerning Human Understanding*, Bk. 4, Ch. 18, Section 4.

[5] E. W. Rice, *The Sunday-School Movement (1780-1917) and the American Sunday-School Union (1817-1917)* (Philadelphia: American Sunday-School Union, 1917), 13.

[6] Quoted by A Skevington Wood, "Awakening" in Tim Dowley, *The History of Christianity: A Lion Handbook* (Herts: Lion Publishing, 1977), 445.

sermons and travelled 250,000 miles over the period of his ministry. Although estimates of the success of the Evangelical Revival in Britain vary, it is undeniable that it did effect major religious and social change: Many people converted to a lively form of Christianity that looked to the Christian Scriptures for inspiration and guidance, and this rediscovery of "biblical Christianity" who contributed to a new social conscience among Christians that agitated for prison reform, the end of slavery, and universal education.

LIFE AND CHARACTER

Much that was written about Robert Raikes in the nineteenth century (after his death in 1811) painted his personality and achievements in glowing terms. It should be noted, however, that this was the century when the British Empire enjoyed its greatest influence and widest rule: This was the empire upon which "the sun never set." Victorian Britain believed itself to instantiate the virtues of civilization, commerce, and Christianity, and saw its "mission" as bringing these virtues to the "uncivilized" world beyond British shores. Historians and social commentators of the period regarded the Empire as the deserved result of Britain's technological, commercial, religious, and moral superiority. Part of this sense of superiority was expressed in colorful and heroic biographies of explorers, adventurers, educators and social reformers, which served to inspire and confirm Britain's "rightful" pre-eminence among the nations. As a consequence, nineteenth century biographies of Robert Raikes and accounts of his personality and achievements are not entirely free of exaggeration and uncritical use of sources; yet, while taking account of this, a reasonably secure historical picture of his life and achievements can be gained.

All accounts of his life identify Robert Raikes as a man of strong and consistent Christian commitment who contributed personally, politically, and financially to Christian and reforming social causes. There is convincing evidence to interpret his humanitarian work as an expression of his Christian beliefs about the love and mercy of God and the demands of Christian charity. He was also "a good businessman, steady, methodical and very tenacious of purpose."[7] According to Leslie Stephen's entry for Raikes in the 63-volume first edition of *Dictionary of National Biography* (published between 1885 and 1900), Raikes "was an active

---

[7] G. L. Merrill , "Robert Raikes and the Eighteenth Century," in George R Merrill, Marion Lawrence, and Al Hartshorn, *The Development of the Sunday School 1780-1905: The Official Report of the Eleventh International Sunday School Convention*, Toronto, Canada, June 23-27, 1905 (Boston, Mass.: Executive Committee of the International Sunday School Association, Fort Hill Press, 1905), 1.

and benevolent person."[8] This description is clearly a positive tribute from one whom, while an abolitionist on the matter of slavery and a friend of William Wilberforce, was also at the time he composed this entry a vocal agnostic. Many of the biographical sources report that Raikes was devout in liturgical observance of Sunday worship and that he regularly attended early morning prayers in St. Mary de Crypt Church in Gloucester. He was unostentatious and well regarded in the community, and there is no suggestion of scandal in either his public or private life. In all respects he seems to have lived an entirely moral and exemplary life, a life inspired by Christian beliefs and values and one lived faithfully in accordance with these.

Raikes was born in Gloucester on fourteenth September, 1735, the son of the editor and owner (also called Robert) of a successful regional newspaper, the *Gloucester Journal*, and the grandson of an Anglican vicar, Timothy Raikes. On the death of his father in 1757, Robert (the Younger) inherited the family printing and publishing business. In 1767 he married Anne (d. 1828), daughter of Thomas Trigge; together they had three sons and seven daughters, of whom one son and one daughter died in infancy.

PRISON REFORM

Evidence of Raikes's developing social conscience was revealed in 1768, when the *Gloucester Journal* carried an appeal by him for funds on behalf of prisoners.[9] Interestingly, although John Howard and Elizabeth Fry are regarded as the pioneers of prison reform, Raikes was apparently active in this regard before Fry, and Raikes' work was known to Howard; he offered hospitality to Howard when he visited Gloucester in 1773 on his tour of prisons in the west of England to gather evidence of the conditions and to publicize the abuses in prisons.

Fees were traditionally extracted from prisoners to support the cost of their confinement and those who could not contribute had to rely on the gifts of others. Overcrowding and cruelty by jailers were commonplace. Raikes records: "The prisoners are locked up at night in a large apartment called the Main, with a chain run through each man's link; during the night they steal from each other, shoes, buckles, bread, or anything which it is possible to conceal ... In short, the inhabitants of this prison give a more affecting picture of the miseries entailed on mankind by the corruptions of human nature than it is

---

[8] Leslie Stephen, "Raikes, Robert," *Dictionary of National Biography*, Vol. 47, edited by Leslie Stephen and Sidney Lee (London: Smith, Elder: 1885-1900), 168.

[9] See Philip Woodfine, "Debtors, Prisons, and Petitions in Eighteenth-Century England," *Eighteenth-Century Life* 30 (2006), 1-31.

in the power of the imagination to paint."[10]According to John Ferguson, Raikes campaigned on issues relating to prison reform.[11] The first was the separation of debtors from other prisoners: While Rakes did not oppose custodial sentences for debtors, there is evidence that he frequently secured their release by paying what was owed. The second issue for which he campaigned was "the destitute," that is, those prisoners who (or whose families) could not afford food or provide for themselves in prison, unlike those with financial resources, who could pay for food and preferential treatment. Jailers were not salaried but lived off fees paid by prisoners for food, bedding, and other facilities; consequently, those without money had to beg from those who had or to serve the jailers in some way.

Raikes advanced his cause in two ways. One way was to "agitate" politically for improved conditions for the destitute; the second was to establish funds for the improvement of their conditions and situation. Raikes campaigned on behalf of such a fund through his publications and gave generously himself. Finally, he campaigned, successfully, against overcrowding in prisons and unsanitary conditions. In 1788, Fanny Burney described the results of the reforms at Gloucester jail, reforms largely initiated and achieved by the political campaign pursued by Raikes through his newspaper and advanced by his donations. He believed, "Every culprit is to have a separate cell. Every cell is clean, neat, and small, looking towards a wide expanse-of country, and, far more fitted to his speculation, a rich expanse of the heavens. Air, cleanliness, and health seem all considered but no other indulgence. The debtors also are considered, as they ought to be, with far more favor than the other offenders; and of course perfectly guarded from all intercourse with them."[12]

Unlike other social reformers, Raikes recognized that prison improvements and prison reform did not address the underlying issue of the causes of crime, and although he stressed the importance of individual choice and personal responsibility, he also appreciated that crime was related to poverty and ignorance. Ferguson has noted how Raikes's understanding of ignorance was complex and included both lack of education and lack of knowledge of Christian moral and religious teaching.[13] The role of ignorance of religion, for him, is made clear in his account in *The Gloucester Journal* of the execution of James Hawkins in 1785:

---

[10] Robert Raikes, *Gloucester Journal*; quoted from John Ferguson, "In Honour of Robert Raikes," *Baptist Quarterly* 28 (1980), 349.

[11] Ferguson, 350.

[12] Ferguson, 350.

[13] Ibid, 351-352.

Hawkins exhibited a melancholy proof of the truth of that expression, 'having the conscience seared with a hot iron' fortho' little more than twenty-one years of age, he was a shocking instance of the villainy which pervades the human heart; when the mind is destitute of every principle, and ignorance and vice are free from impose. He had never offered up a prayer to his Creator. He said he knew not how to pray. He was totally devoid of all sense of a future state.[14]

That prevalence of ignorance in society was not a new insight for Raikes, for some years earlier he had already become involved in setting up Sunday schools so that children, particularly those who were poor, could become acquainted with Christian teaching, while simultaneously learning how to read. To this topic we now turn.

RAIKES AND THE SUNDAY SCHOOL MOVEMENT

Some uncertainty surrounds the circumstances of the setting up of Sunday schools by Raikes, for although all narratives associate him with the initiative, there are differences in accounts. One story recounts that on a particular Sunday when he was in St Catherine's Meadows, on the outskirts of Gloucester, he observed children being rowdy and badly behaved, and in response to his reprimand was told there was nothing for them to do and no one to take an interest in them. Another version of the story states that Raikes was in his newspaper office one Sunday afternoon and became conscious of noisy and ill-mannered behavior of children outside. Raikes' own version, recounted in a letter to Colonel Townley of Lancaster in the *Gentleman's Magazine*, described him walking through a slum in Gloucester on a weekday and being appalled by the condition and behavior of the children in the street.

> Some business leading me one morning to the suburbs of the city, where the lowest of the people (who are principally employed in the pin factory) chiefly reside, I was struck with concern at seeing a group of children wretchedly ragged, at play in the streets. I asked an inhabitant whether those children belonged to that part of town, and admitted their misery and idleness. "Ah, sir," said the woman to whom I was speaking, "Could you take the view of this part of town on Sunday, you would be shocked indeed; for then the street is filled with multitudes of those wretches who come on release of the day of employment, spend their time in noise and riot, playing at 'chuck' and singing and swearing in a manner so horrid as to convey to any serious minded, an idea of hell rather than any other place."[15]

---

[14] Ibid, 351.

[15] Cited by Elmer L. Towns, "Robert Raikes: A Comparison with Earlier Claims to Sunday School Origins," *Evangelical Quarterly* 43 (1971), 73; original source, *The Gentleman's Magazine,* ed. by

Raikes decided to do something that would bring educational advantages to the children and further the cause of Christianity. He spoke to Rev. Thomas Stock (1749–1803), the curate of a neighboring parish, and together they engaged and paid four women to teach children in their own homes, with Stock drawing up the content for their instruction. In his Journal, Stock provided a complementary account of the beginning of the Sunday school:

> Mr. Raikes meeting me one day by accident at my door, and in the course of conversation lamenting the deplorable state of the lower classes of mankind, took particular notice of the situation of the poorer children. I had made, I replied, the same observation, and told him if he would accompany me into my parish we would attempt to remedy the evil. We immediately proceeded to the business, and procuring the names of about ninety children, placed them under the care of four persons for a stated number of hours on Sunday. As minister of the parish I took upon me the superintendence of the schools and one-third of the expense. The progress of this institution is justly to be attributed to the constant representation which Mr. Raikes made in his own paper, The Gloucester Journal, of the benefits which he perceived would probably arise from it.[16]

The Sunday school curriculum was designed to teach the children reading and writing using the Bible as a textbook, with classes before and after lunch, on occasions incorporating formal church worship. Some writers, George L. Merrill, for example, made the claim that the first Sunday school was exclusively for boys. This view has been countered by Elmer Towns who quotes from a letter to a certain Mrs. Harris from Robert Raikes in which he speaks about the organization of the first Sunday school and expressly states that "the sexes [were] kept separate" — boys and girls were in attendance. In the same letter Raikes also says that of these children, "I give some little token of my regard, as a pair of shoes, if they are barefooted, and some who are very bare of apparel, I Clothe."[17]

As the movement became more widespread there was some church opposition to the teaching of writing, particularly within sections of the Church of England, as there were those who believed that teaching the "poor" to read and write could encourage them to think of themselves as equals to their "superiors," and so "upset" the social order. Teaching the poor to read enabled them to read the Bible and appropriate its message for themselves,

---

Silvanus Urban, Vol. 303, (June, 1784): 68-81.

[16] Thomas Stork, *The Journal*, cited by W. R. Stephens, *A History of the English Church, Vol. VII* (New York: Macmillan and Company, 1906), 300-301.

[17] Letter to Mrs. Harris from Robert Raikes on organization of a Sunday school, cited by Towns, *op cit.*, 74.

for, as stated by Calvin, the Bible is "the key that unlocks the kingdom of God for us."[18]As Bebbington has commented "literacy was a precondition for reading the Bible. Reading skills ... [were] fostered primarily for that purpose throughout Protestant northern Europe."[19]It is an incontrovertible fact that widening access to education in the modern era was in part the legacy of the Protestant Reformation, which stressed that salvation was gained through one's personal response to the teaching of the Christian Scriptures and not through the sacerdotal system of Roman Catholicism. Each should read the Scriptures for himself or herself and ascertain what is required for salvation, and what is required, according to the Reformers, is plain for all to read (thus, their doctrine of the perspicuity of Scripture).[20]

Some months later Raikes set up a Sunday school in his own parish of St Mary le Crypt, which opened in July 1780. Originally the "school" was situated in Sooty Alley. A room (the kitchen) was rented in the home of a certain Mrs. Meredith and she was paid to act as school mistress (superintendent) to those who attended. Unfortunately, she was unable to cope with the bad behavior of the children and the school was transferred to the home (again the kitchen was used) of Mrs. Critchley in Southgate Street, which faced St. Mary de Crypt Church and Raikes' house, though now supervised by Mrs. Brandon. At this stage, payment was made by Raikes to those involved. Three years later he included in his paper a short anonymous notice of the success of Sunday schools, which in turn created further interest and inquiries. In all probability, over this period, Raikes was ascertaining if his "experiment" in combining literacy skills with religious education was successful. George L. Merrill, in a paper first published in 1905, quoted from an unpublished letter by Raikes in which he gave reasons for not publicizing his initiative in establishing Sunday schools: "To see whether these degraded children, when disciplined and instructed would show the same evidence of human feelings and instincts as those more favorably situated."[21] Clearly Raikes' initiative was successful and under his guidance, (in some cases) financial support, and supervision additional Sunday schools were opened. Press notices generated further activity, with more schools opening in Leeds, Manchester, and the surrounding districts.

In the early years of the 1780s the Baptist William Fox entered into correspondence

---

[18] Quoted by Peter Ovitz, "Scripture," in Herman J. Selderhuis, *The Calvin Handbook* (Grand Rapids, Michigan: Eerdmans, 2009), 236.

[19] D. W. Bebbington, *Evangelicalism in Modern Britain: A history from the 1730s to the 1980s* (London: Unwin Hyman, 1989), 123.

[20] For discussion see, Stephen R. Holmes, "Kings, Professors, and Ploughboys: On the Accessibility of Scripture," *International Journal of Systematic Theology* 13 (2011), 403-415.

[21] Merrill, "Robert Raikes and the Eighteenth Century," 3.

with Rakes and raised the idea of creating a central body to coordinate the efforts of Sunday school promoters throughout the country. In 1785 Fox put his ideas into practice and founded the *Society for the Establishment and Support of Sunday Schools throughout the Kingdom of Great Britain.* Within four more years the Sunday Schools Society was reported as having given help to 2,232 schools, catering for 200,787 children. The society gave 184,248 spelling books, 42,680 New Testaments, 6,583 Bibles and 4,112 pounds, six shillings and five pence. As a member of the established Church of England, Raikes supported Anglican initiatives and believed that it should take the lead in sponsoring and leading Sunday schools. A number of bishops supported his work, and when Samuel Glasse, a friend of Raikes, preached a sermon at Painswick, Gloucestershire, in 1786, on behalf of its schools, he claimed that 200,000 children were already being taught in Sunday schools in England. Glasse further advanced the movement through the publication of a sermon on Deut. 31: 12-13, entitled "The Piety, wisdom, and policy, of promoting Sunday-Schools" (1786) and an essay in the *Gentleman's Magazine* (1788).

Around the same time, the precursor to the "Sunday school" was increasing in popularity in America, in large part through the promotion of John Wesley, who is sometimes credited with establishing an early version of the Sunday school in Savannah, Georgia in 1737. Wesley seems to have been encouraged, however, by the emergence of Raikes' approach to Sunday schools in England in the early 1780s. Wesley made several references to Sunday school in his *Journal* (entry for July 18, 1784) saying, "Before service, I stepped into the Sunday school which contained two hundred and forty children. I find these schools springing up where ever I go."[22] As Elmer Towns has stated, "Wesley was interested in the Sunday school movement and contributed to it wherever possible."[23] In 1803, further impetus was given to the movement in England by the establishment of the Sunday School Union. It aimed to improve the educational and religious provision of schools and to encourage their adoption and growth by the churches, to supply books and stationary as cheaply as possible and where necessary to give advice and grants of money (provided voluntarily from patrons).

The financial contributions and educational service of lay supporters was essential to the success of Raikes' Sunday schools and those established by others. Within a number of years of the schools' emergence, paid teachers began to be replaced by voluntary workers. Voluntary lay teachers were recruited from local churches and were required to be of good standing in their

---

[22] Quoted by Elmer L. Towns, in "John Wesley and Religious Education," (1970). Articles. Paper 16, p. 327. http://digitalcommons.liberty.edu/towns_articles/16 (accessed July 1, 2015).
[23] Ibid..

communities and of strong Christian character. From the beginning, it seems that older pupils acted as "monitors" and assisted by teaching small groups and helping younger pupils in their learning, typically with about twenty pupils to a class. Often, but not always, teachers operated under clergy supervision. Biblical instruction was often complemented by hymn singing, a practice that required the participation of all and that traces its origins to the Reformation, principally to that of Luther, who not only translated sacred songs from Greek and Latin into the language of the common people but also wrote hymns that used rhyme and familiar folk tunes to make them easy to learn and memorize.[24]

Timothy Larsen has stated that by the mid-19th century, "Sunday school attendance was a near universal aspect of childhood,"[25] though it should be remembered that Sunday schools were a distinctively Protestant institution. Parents who did not regularly attend church often sent their children to Sunday school. Working-class families were grateful for the opportunity to receive an education and the denominational and non-denominational organizers and providers of Sunday schools were enthusiastic to maintain and encourage Christian commitment. By the 1870s, however, compulsory state education was established in both America and England and this led to Sunday schools largely relinquishing their educational role and concentrating on the exclusively religious role of providing Christian instruction and advancing the claims of Christianity. Numbers did fall, but Sunday school attendance remained a common experience for many children, and remained so, up until the 1960s. Throughout the 1960s there was a marked decline in the number of children that attended Sunday school. There are a variety of reasons for this: new progressive attitudes to parenting that allowed children to decide for themselves whether to attend or not; the impact of television and its provision of alternative forms of entertainment and interest; and greater emphasis on secular school education, which was seen as providing the means to "get on" in life and to advance socially and financially. This decline was also part of a larger process of secularization that affected the churches and institutional religion. Although most writers trace the roots of secularization back to the nineteenth century, the 1960s marked a decisive point in its "progress:" church membership declined precipitously and increasingly religion became regarded as a private affair that is irrelevant to public life and even morality. Yet Sunday schools retain some of their influence and importance, where this denotes a place

---

[24] Martin Luther, *Luther's Works: Liturgy and Hymns, Vol. 53* (Minneapolis, MN: Augsburg Fortress, 1970).

[25] Timothy Larsen, "When did Sunday Schools Start?" *Christianity Today*, August, 28, 2008, http://www.christianitytoday.com/ch/asktheexpert/whendidsundayschoolstart.html (accessed October 30, 2015).

of Christian education and learning for children that meets weekly on Sunday, even though alternative names such as Kidz Club and Sunday Morning Live are now used in various contexts.

RAIKES AS THE "FOUNDER" OF THE SUNDAY SCHOOL

While Robert Raikes is commonly regarded as the founder of Sunday schools and of the Sunday School movement, this claim is not without its detractors and there are historians that identify earlier examples. Reference has already been made to the work of John Wesley in Georgia; other writers refer to Hannah Bell of High Wycombe, England, in the late 1760s and Dr. Joseph Bellamy is credited by Joel Hauser in *Ecclesiastical History of Connecticut* with beginning a Sunday school in Bethlehem, Connecticut in 1740. The most detailed and judicious examination of these claims has been made by Elmer Towns,[26] who concludes that the traditional ascription to Raikes as the founder of the Sunday school is well attested and stands up to historical scrutiny. Towns identified five criteria that while evident in Raikes' school were missing in the earlier schools. (1) The earlier schools focused solely on religious teaching and excluded general education of the kind included by Raikes; ironically, as Sunday schools developed and their curriculum moved in a more religious direction, the impression had already been given to the public that Sunday schools were a useful and helpful complement to state schools that provided a general education. (2) Raikes' Sunday schools gained popular approval and *directly* inspired other to set up Sunday schools. (3) The earlier schools went out of existence, whereas Raikes' Sunday school inspired a movement that continues to this day. (4) The curriculum in Raikes' schools was devoted to the direct study of the Bible (and not catechisms or "secondary standards"). (5) The Sunday school, while not engaging in direct evangelism, nevertheless aimed to awaken and renew moral and religious commitment. On this basis Towns concludes that "Raikes can be said to have begun the Sunday school movement."[27]

CONCLUSION

As noted above there is debate over the origins of the Sunday school movement, and perhaps to use the term *movement* is to slant the debate in a direction that favors the conclusion that Robert Raikes is properly accredited as its founder. This is because the example of Raikes in setting up a Sunday school inspired others to copy and emulate his ideas and practice. All saw

---

[26] Elmer L. Towns, "Robert Raikes: A Comparison with Earlier Claims to Sunday School Origins," *Evangelical Quarterly* 43 (1971), 68-70.
[27] Ibid., 71.

the validity of his interpretation of Christian discipleship and, like Raikes, acted on humanitarian grounds to "relieve the plight of the poor," by providing them with a basic education, to be acquired through reading and learning from the Christian Scriptures. Yet to refer to *humanitarian grounds* in this context is somewhat misleading, for what is now understood by this term actually disguises the fact that Christian efforts to educate the poor along with efforts to improve prison conditions, to alleviate poverty, and to bring an end to slavery were pursued on exclusively religious grounds. It was commitment to the Christian gospel and Christianity that inspired Raikes not only to introduce instruction in the Bible to children in Sunday schools but also to teach them to read and write. Christian commitment embraces both love of God and love of neighbor: it is this that Raikes appreciated and so vividly illustrates.

PRIMARY SOURCE SAMPLE[28]

"My dear Madam, — Amongst the numerous correspondents which my little project for civilizing the rising generation of the poor has led me to address, I have to no one taken up my pen with more pleasure than to you, my old friend, with whom I formerly passed so many cheerful hours.

I am rejoiced to find that the people in your neighbourhood are thus ready to listen to that strong and pathetic injunction, given by our Saviour a little before his resurrection [ascension], 'Feed my lambs'; and if it were possible for me to afford any hints that might be useful, great would be the pleasure I should receive.

In answer to your inquiries, I shall as concisely as possible state, that I endeavour to assemble the children as early as consistent with their perfect cleanliness, — an indispensable rule; the hour prescribed in our rules is eight o'clock; but it is usually half after eight before our flock is collected. Twenty is the number allotted to each teacher; the sexes are kept separate. The twenty are divided into four classes. The children who show any superiority in attainments are placed as leaders of their several classes, and are employed in teaching the others their letters, or in hearing them read in a low whisper, which may be done without interrupting the master or mistress in their business, and will keep the attention of the children engaged, that they do not play or make a noise. The attending the service of the church once a day has seemed to me sufficient, for their time may be spent more profitably, perhaps, in

---

[28] Robert Raikes, "Original Letter from Robert Raikes to Mrs. Harris, Chelsea, England" in *The History of Sunday Schools, and of Religious Education*, from the Earliest Times, ed. Lewis G. Pray (Boston: W. M. Crosby and H. P. Nichols, 1847), 144-147, accessed May 4, 2016, https://books.google.com/books.

receiving instruction than being present at a long discourse, which their minds are not yet able to comprehend; but people may think differently on this point. Within this month the minister of my parish has at last condescended to give me assistance in this laborious work, which I have now carried on six years with little or no support. He chooses that the children should come to church both morning and afternoon; I brought them to church only in the afternoon. If this should answer better than my plan, on some future occasion I will let you or Mr. Harris know it.

The stipend to the teachers here is a shilling each Sunday; but we find them firing, and bestow gratuities as rewards of diligence, which may make it worth sixpence more.

But the success of the whole depends on the attention paid by people of condition. If persons of some consequences will condescend to officiate as visiters, and by kind words encourage the good among these hitherto despised and neglected creatures, and give gentle reproof to those who stray from their duty, a wonderful effect will in a few months be discoverable. Were I among you, I would call forth the gentlemen to visit the boys, and the ladies to superintend the girls ...

It had been sometimes a difficult task to keep the children in proper order, when they were all assembled at church; but I now sit very near them myself, which has had the effect of preserving the most perfect decorum. After the sermon in the morning, they return home to dinner, and meet at the schools at half after one, and are dismissed at five, with strict injunctions to observe quiet behavior, free from all noise and clamor. Before the business is begun in the morning, they all kneel down while a prayer is read, and the same before dismission in the evening.

To those children who distinguish themselves as examples of diligence, quietness in behavior, observance of order, kindness to their companions ... I give some little token of regard, – as a pair of shoes, if they are barefooted; and some who are very bare of apparel I clothe. This I have been enabled to do, in many instances, through the liberal support given me by my brothers in the city. By these means I have acquired considerable ascendency over the minds of children. Besides, I frequently go round to their habitation to inquire into their behavior at home, and into the conduct of the parents, to whom I give some little hints now and then, as well as to the children.

... It is that part of our Saviour's character which I aim at imitating, — 'He went about doing good.' No one can form an idea what benefits he is capable of rendering to the community by the condescension of visiting the dwellings of the poor. You may remember the place without the South Gate called Littleworth; it used to be the St. Giles's of Gloucester.

By going amongst these people I have totally changed their manners. They avow at this time that the place is quite a heaven to what it used to be. Some of the vilest of the boys are now so exemplary in behavior, that I have taken one into my own service. I mention this as an evidence of what may be done.

But I fear I am growing too prolix, and that I shall cause you to repent the opening of a correspondence with your old acquaintance.

I must now tell you that I am blessed with six excellent girls, and two lovely boys. My eldest boy was born the very day I made public to the world the scheme of Sunday Schools, in my paper of November 3[r]d, 1783. In four years' time it has extended so rapidly as now to include two hundred and fifty thousand children. It is increasing more and more. It reminds me of the grain of mustard-seed ..."

BIBLIOGRAPHY
PRIMARY SOURCES

Gavin, Adrienne E. "Raikes, Robert." *The Oxford Encyclopedia of Children's Literature*. Oxford: Oxford University Press, 2006.

Gregory, Alfred and Robert Raikes. *Journalist and Philanthropist: A History of the Origin of Sunday Schools*. London: Hodder & Stoughton, 1877.

Hawthorne, Nathaniel. "A Good Man's Miracle." Eldritch Press, 1844. (http://www.eldritchpress.org/nh/gmm.html; accessed 13.01.15).

Harris, J. Henry. *The Story of Robert Raikes for the Young*. Philadelphia: Union Press, 1900.

Lloyd, William Freeman. *Sketch of the Life of Robert Raikes, Esq: And of the History of Sunday Schools* (New York: Hunt & Eaton, 1891).

Mayer, Samuel Ralph Townshend. *The Origin and Growth of Sunday Schools in England. Repr., with Additions, from the 'London Quarterly Review.'* London: Beveridge and Co., 1878.

Power, John Carroll. *The Rise and Progress of Sunday Schools: A Biography of Robert Raikes and William Fox*. New York: Sheldon & Company, 1863.

SECONDARY SOURCES

Ferguson, John. "In Honour of Robert Raikes," *Baptist Quarterly* 28 (1980), 342-354.

G. L. Merrill. "Robert Raikes and the Eighteenth Century," in George R Merrill, Marion Lawrence, and Al Hartshorn, *The Development of the Sunday School 1780-1905: The Official Report of the Eleventh International Sunday School Convention Toronto*, Canada, June 23-27, 1905 (Boston, Mass.: Executive Committee of the International Sunday School Association, Fort Hill Press, 1905).

E. W. Rice. *The Sunday-School Movement (1780-1917) and the American Sunday-School Union (1817-1917)* (Philadelphia: American Sunday-School Union, 1917)

Towns, Elmer L. "Robert Raikes: A Comparison with Earlier Claims to Sunday School Origins," *Evangelical Quarterly* 43 (1971), 68-81.

_____. "John Wesley and Religious Education" in *Articles. Paper 16,* 1970. Accessed http://digitalcommons. liberty.edu/towns_articles/16

_____. "Robert Raikes." In *A History of Religious Educators*, edited by Elmer L. Towns. Grand Rapids: Baker Book House, 1975; digital version available at http://digitalcommons.liberty.edu/cgi/viewcontent. cgi?article=1023&context=towns_books.

CHAPTER 18

Johann Heinrich Pestalozzi:

Advocate for Child-Centered Education

JAMES R. MOORE

Johann Pestalozzi (1746-1827)

While the United States was becoming a nation, half way around the world in the small nation of Switzerland, Johann Heinrich Pestalozzi led an educational revolution that would shape child-centered education on the new continent. Early U. S. schooling continued the European tradition of teaching church dogma by recitation and the vigorous discipline of the schoolmaster. Pestalozzi would birth an educational method centering upon the child, emphasizing holistic learning through a caring, parental teacher. His thumbprint on child education continues to be felt today in classrooms (and churches) throughout the world.

HISTORICAL BACKGROUND

Johann Heinrich Pestalozzi arrived as the youngest son into a middle class Protestant family in Zurich, Switzerland on January 12, 1746. Johann Baptiste Pestalozzi, a physician by occupation, and Susanna Hotz Pestalozzi birthed three children. A family of Italian descent, the Pestalozzis had deep roots in Zurich since the mid sixteenth century, but they had not been an active part of civic society.[1]

Citizenship in Zurich was based on ancestry and the Pestalozzis were full citizens. In the mid eighteenth century only five-thousand full citizens resided among the 145,000 Zurich residents. Most of the poor and uneducated population supported the citizenry. Young Johann recognized this social divide that later would shape his educational philosophy and practice.

Tragedy struck the Pestalozzi family in 1751. Johann's father died, leaving five year old Johann and his two older siblings in the care of their mother, and their loyal servant Barbara Schmidt. Barbara, or Babeli, became the primary care-giver and mentor for young Johann's life. He later described his early life as overly protected and isolated from peers, which led to his formation as an introspective, withdrawn, and physically inept young man. Johann's experience growing up in a home with two women led to a high view of women, and the central role of the mother figure as a child's first educator.[2]

A second principle figure early in Johann's life was his grandfather Andreas Pestalozzi. Andreas served as a minister in the nearby Swiss village of Hongg. His ministry was among the very poor. As a child Johann accompanied his grandfather on home visits to poor parishioners; these experiences played a significant role in shaping his educational thinking.

Pestalozzi's primary education included the traditional curriculum of reading, arithmetic, writing, and religion. In 1754 he began his classical studies at *Schola Abbatissanal*. Later he transferred to secondary school *Schola Carolina* and *Collegium Humanitatis* where he studied Latin, Greek, Hebrew, literature, rhetoric, philosophy, and theology.

Admitted to the *Collegium Carolinum* in 1764, Pestalozzi's education focused on

---

[1] Kate Silber, *Pestalozzi: The Man and His Work* (London: Routledge and Kegan Paul, 1965), 3.

[2] Eva Channing writes, "We cannot help being struck with the high esteem in which woman is held by Pestalozzi. In Gertrude he has not only painted the loving wife and mother, the charitable neighbor, and the thrifty housekeeper; but he has made her a pattern of high moral rectitude, endowed her with remarkable executive ability, and given her an intellectual clear-sightedness of a very high order. Thus it is Gertrude alone who originates the improved system of education which is afterward transferred to the [local] Bonnal school." *Pestalozzi's Leonard and Gertrude,* trans. and abrdgd. Eva Channing (Boston: D. C. Heath, 1908. repr. HardPress), v.

philosophy and language. At the *Collegium*, he met professor of history and literature Jean Jacqest Bodmer. Professor Bodmer, while under the pressure of French occupation, advocated a return to the simple life of Swiss peasants. Bodmer formed the Helvetic Society, which Pesralozzi joined, and challenged the corruption present in Swiss life under occupation; Professor Bodmer also published a reformation journal *The Monitor*. The journal did not meet the satisfaction of the French authorities, and Pestalozzi and other members of the Helvetic Society found themselves in jail for a short time.

Pestalozzi's observations of social class as a young child in Zurich, his pastoral encounters of the poor with his grandfather in Hongg, and the social activism practiced while in the Helvetic Society created a desire within him to make working with the poor his life's work. Anderson writes, "Pestalozzi early devoted himself to the cause of the elevation of the poor. The tragic spectacle of the material and mental poverty and wretchedness of a large portion of his fellow human beings became to him almost an obsession."[3]After he discovered his inadequacy at public speaking, he abandoned attempts at the religious ministry and in the legal realm, and determined farming might be a way to revolutionize the social situation.

Johann Rudolf Tschiffeli advocated scientific farming in nearby Berne. In 1767 Pestalozzi decided to study under Tschiffeli in order to learn modern farming methods as a way to enhance the lives of the country peasantry. Pestalozzi soon purchased a sixty acre farm near Birr in Berne canton called Neuhof. In 1769 he married Anna Schulthess, a fellow member of the Helvetic Society and the daughter of an upper middle class Zurich family. His only child, Jean Jacques, named after Jean Jacques Rousseau, was born in 1770. Rousseau's *Emile* reflected the Romantic spirit of the Enlightenment era and had become a favorite among the Swiss youth whose social consciousness extended to the country peasants. *Emile* offered a natural educational guideline which Pestalozzi embraced, and he determined to follow natural educational principles as he raised his son.

Pestalozzi found Rousseau's natural education lacked in several areas. Rousseau was a dreamer,[4] while Pestalozzi applied his educational principles to real life. Rousseau was a pessimist, but Pestalozzi believed life could be improved for both the individual and society

---

[3] Lewis Flint Anderson, ed., *Pestalozzi* (New York: AMS, 1970), 2.

[4] *Pestalozzi's Educational Writings,* ed. John Alfred Green (New York: Longmans, Green, 1912); repr. in *Significant Contributions to the History of Psychology 1750-1920,* ed. Daniel N. Robinson (Washington, DC: University Publications of America, 1977). Pestalozzi wrote, "The contrast between knowing and doing is like that between heaven and earth. Whoever confines his trade to knowledge must indeed take care that he forget not the habit of action." Johann Heinrich Pestalozzi, *The Education of Man: Aphorisms* (New York: Philosophical Library, 1951), 36.

by education. And, Rousseau rejected rational thinking, while Pestalozzi sought to seize ideas of psychological development and science for the good of the learning process. His early educational attempts with young Jean Jacques led to *How Pestalozzi Instructed His Three and a Half Year Old Son* (1774) where he attempted to incorporate a psychology of child development into the learning process. Children are naturally active, and Pestalozzi wanted to seize upon this natural activity for the educational process. Pestalozzi believed the appropriate guiding of natural education could reform not only the child but could also regenerate society as well.

In 1776 he opened a school in his home at Neuhof and invited orphan children ages six to eighteen to attend. When the children, often destitute and in rags, came, they received new clothes and a warm welcome into an educational family. The model of a loving family, with Papa Pestalozzi as the father figure, rather than an authoritarian school master, defined Pestalozzi's educational system. He later wrote, "My point of view led me first of all to make the children feel like so many brothers and sisters, and to regard the house as a real home. On the basis of such a relationship I endeavoured to stimulate more feeling."[5] Pestalozzi's family grew to the point where he "lived surrounded by more than fifty beggar children. In poverty I share my bread with them. I lived like a beggar in order to learn how to make beggars live like men."[6]

Education at Neuhof combined learning with applied experience. Through vocational practices Pestalozzi sought to provide skills for life with the goal to lift persons out of poverty: "My ideal scheme included work in the fields, the factory, and the workshop."[7] While eighteenth century education had been primarily individual instruction, Pestalozzi began "simultaneous instruction" using group methodology. Reading, writing, arithmetic, and moral instruction accompanied chores (such as farming, cheese-making, or gardening) and experiences (such as counting the number of steps to the loft). Children learned in groups with older more experienced students sitting next to and aiding younger learners.[8] Neuhof crystalized several aspects of Pestalozzi's educational thinking: a) a healthy family

---

[5] Pestalozzi in a letter of 1807. John Alfred Green, *The Educational Ideas of Pestalozzi,* Third Impression (Baltimore, MD: Warwick and York, n.d. Reprint, HardPress), 187.

[6] Johann Heinrich Pestalozzi, *How Gertrude Teaches Her Children: An Attempt to Help Mothers to Teach Their Own Children and an Account of the Method,* ed. Ebenezer Cooke, trans. Lucy E. Holland and Frances C. Turner (Syracuse, NY: C. W. Bardeen, Publisher, 1898; repr., Forgotten Books 2012), 343. Note this phrase occurs only in the first edition of *How Gertrude.*

[7] Ibid., 30.

[8] Ibid., 44-45.

life is a necessary foundation for education; b) group instruction is possible; c) both skills and subjects can be taught simultaneously; and d) education can be used to benefit the wider community through the education of its citizens. These early educational insights and methodological changes would lead to a dramatic shift in child education. However, the educational experiment at Neuhof failed financially within two years due to poor administrative management by Pestalozzi.

In 1776 Pestalozzi *Essays on the Education of Children of the Poor* in an effort to secure funds for the Neuhof school and to publicize its work. *Essays,* along with *Evening Hours of a Hermit,* a series of aphoristic reflections on education written in 1780 after Neuhof closed, first appeared in the journal *Ephemerides.* The closure of Neuhof necessitated income for the Pestalozzi family, so he determined to write. The popularity of novels such as *Emile,* led Pestalozzi to write *Leonard and Gertrude,* published in 1781. Immensely popular as an interesting novel, Pestalozzi had hoped it would be accepted as a statement of educational philosophy with a solid moral compass.

The story of *Leonard and Gertrude* illustrated Swiss peasantry life in the small village of Bonnal. Leonard, a mason often out of work, struggles to feed his wife and seven children. His despair leads him regularly to the local tavern, where the conniving Bailiff preys upon his patrons. Gertrude, his loyal and resourceful wife, gathers the courage to visit the lord of the manor, Arner, who receives her with pleasure. Arner is shocked to hear her description of the corruption in Bonnal. He encourages reform through Gertrude and the village pastor and change begins to take place. When Arner visits Bonnal and sees the work of Gertrude and her home school, he vows to extend her educational influence for the good of the whole village. Soon the entire village is a changed community. Gertrude's educational strategy, which began in the home and extended into the school, demonstrates Pestalozzi's view of education as the key to social improvement for all people and civic society and illustrates that education begins in the home among family and moves outward to society.

Pestalozzi's intent for *Leonard and Gertrude* was as a handbook for educational reform; however, it was received with interest but simply as a realistic, but fictitious novel. Thus, he went about rewriting this work and the next variation of was published in 1782 with the title *Christopher and Elizabeth.* In this volume, the father figure, Christopher, reads *Leonard and Gertrude* to his family and leads a discussion about the volume. Though a sequel, *Christopher and Elizabeth* received little recognition.

After nearly two decades of work as an author, and upon formation in 1798 of the Helvetic Republic in Switzerland, Pestalozzi accepted an invitation from the government to direct an orphanage at Stanz. The doors opened on January 14, 1799 and "the number of children increased gradually to eighty, all of different ages; some full of pretensions, others wayside beggars; all, except a few, wholly ignorant."[9] Pestalozzi worked to create an atmosphere of home life for the orphaned children, and an education based on love. His holistic perspective focused education on engagement of the head, hands, and heart.[10] The short-lived Stanz experience ended in June when the French invasion led to the building becoming a military hospital.

While at Stanz, Pestalozzi further worked to develop his natural method of teaching. The prevailing method of education beyond Stanz consisted of lesson recitation and corporal punishment for those who failed to perform, but Pestalozzi desired to create a secure natural atmosphere where the child could learn naturally. Pestalozzi called for use of both the General Method and the Special Method. The first step in education is to create a home-like environment where children feel safe, emotionally secure, and cared for by adults – the General Method. Subsequently, the school, in partnership with the home, builds upon the General Method to further specialized knowledge learning – the Special Method. These two educational axioms served as a foundation for Pestalozzi's educational philosophy.

After Stanz, the Swiss authorities assigned Pestalozzi to an old castle in Burgdorf. Pestalozzi hoped the Burgdorf Institute would serve as a boarding school for poor children, but enrollment included seventy middle class children, and only a dozen poor children.[11] The Institute also provided a context for Swiss teachers to learn the Pestalozzian method of teaching. The Institute grew, and a cadre of teaching assistants was employed. These assistants would carry the Pestalozzian method to their own schools around Europe and the United States. Burgdorf also provided opportunity for Pestalozzi to author the most complete articulation of his educational philosophy and practice, *How Gertrude Teaches Her Children* (1801).

By 1804 the Swiss authorities once again relocated Pestalozzi, this time to Yverdon to reestablish his Institute. He remained at Yverdon until his retirement in 1825 – the longest duration in one location. With a team of teaching assistants, the Yverdon Institute and the

---

[9] Pestalozzi, *How Gertrude*, 41.

[10] Johann Heinrich Pestalozzi, *Letters on Education: Addressed to J. P. Greaves, Esq.* trans. unknown, repr. of 1827 London edition (Syracuse, NY: C. W. Bardeen, 1898), 28. See also Gerald L. Gutek, *Pestalozzi and Education* (Prospect Heights, IL: Waveland, 1968), Chapter VI for a further explanation of this concept.

[11] Solomon Bluhm, s.v. "Pestalozzi, Johann," in *The Encyclopedia of Education* (New York: MacMillan Company & The Free Press, 1971).

Pestalozzi educational family grew to 250. Pestalozzi crystalized his theory of sense impressions or *Anschauung* by the time he arrived at Yverdon. *Anschauung* describes Pestalozzi's complete natural process of educational understanding from initial observation of objects, to their full comprehension. This became the organizing principle at Yverdon, which soon became the most popular boarding school in Europe.[12]

In 1825 Pestalozzi retired to Neuhof to live with his only grandson and to write. He published *Swansong* and continued to promote natural education around the principle of *Anschauung*. After a brief illness Pestalozzi died on February 17, 1827.

PESTALOZZI'S NATURAL EDUCATION

Harnessing the naturalism of the Enlightenment, with both its romantic and scientific rationalism, became an objective in Pestalozzi's educational thinking. Nature's observable patterns follow regular and identifiable laws. These in turn inform the process of education toward development of the child as an individual, and his or her role in civic society.

Pestalozzi had seen poor and orphan children struggle without the necessities of life or a positive parental influence. Against these challenges, he believed emotional security aided the psychological needs of the child (the General Method) before effective knowledge learning (the Special Method) could take place.

A secure environment must first be created in the home, principally by the mother.[13] As she nurtures the young child and attends to his needs, this creates a secure foundation for further learning in the future school context. The mother serves to orient the child to her world, moral standards, and God.

Developing a climate of emotional security was a novel idea during this era. Eighteenth century education viewed religious catechism, corporal punishment, individual instruction, and recitation as the objective of education, with little concern for the child's emotional needs or comprehension of the content. This is a wonderful example of teaching without learning. Pestalozzi's observation on this tendency was insightful. He said, "I saw popular instruction like a bottomless swamp before my eyes; and waded round and round with difficulty in its mire until at last I learned to know the sources of its waters, the causes of its obstructions, and the places from which there might be a possibility of diverting its foul waters."[14]

---

[12] Ibid.

[13] See in particular *Letters on Education: Addressed to J. P. Greaves, Esq.* in which Pestalozzi describes at great length the role of mothers in the nurturing of the young child.

[14] Pestalozzi, *How Gertrude,* 29-30.

Pestalozzi set out to change this mire swamp and create schools that would reflect a loving home. *Leonard and Gertrude* served as a model of this environment. This is a natural education, a bright blossom unfolding from the deep hidden bud.[15] An education contrary to the "artificial method of schooling, forging ahead of the free, slow and patient course of nature and preferring words to things, [giving] man an artificial polish which conceals his lack of inherent natural power. Such a method can satisfy only times like our century."[16]

He envisioned a school where under the guidance of a wise and loving teacher, a student would "develop and strengthen their own 'faculties' and thus evolve into reasoning, self-directing human beings, fitted for usefulness and service in a modern world."[17] Such would provide persons of upright moral character, intelligent and able to serve civic society. Pestalozzi's educational objective was to develop citizens for the betterment of the State, and not simply to create "loyal church members."[18]

ANSCHAUUNG OR SENSE IMPRESSION

Upon securing a safe environment in which the child could naturally develop, Pestalozzi centered his educational theory on observation of the world through sense impressions or *Anschauung*. Observation and investigation of the world is the educational activity through which children learn. In Pestalozzi's theory, group participation and cooperative learning replace the "Socratizing"[19] of the schoolmaster who demands one on one recitation. Children are encouraged to think and understand what they are taught as education shifts from teacher-centered to child-centered. This shift in turn provided future philosophical ground for the child-centered progressive movement and theorists such as John Dewey.

Anschauung, or observation of the surrounding world for educational purposes, may be translated "sense impression," but its translation can be contested and, according to Cooke, "no satisfactory English equivalent" exists.[20] Subsequent to his experience at Stanz, and more fully after Burgdorf, Pestalozzi developed his *Anschauung* theory and describes it at length in *How Gertrude Teaches Her Children*.

---

[15] Ibid., 131.

[16] Robert Ulich, ed., *Three Thousand Years of Educational Wisdom: Selections from the Great Document*, 2nd ed. (Cambridge, MA: Harvard University, 1965), 482.

[17] Ellwood P. Cubberly, *The History of Education: Educational Practice and Progress Considered as a Phase of the Development and Spread of Western Civilization* (Boston: Houghton Mifflin, 1920), 549.

[18] Ibid., 549.

[19] Pestalozzi, *How Gertrude*, 33.

[20] Ebenezer Cooke as quoted in Pestalozzi, *How Gertrude*, 8.

Pestalozzi defines *Anschauung* as "the point at which all instruction begins ... the presence of *the external object before the senses* which rouses a consciousness of the impression made by it."[21] *Anschauung* necessitates a thorough observance of an object and its impression on the pupil. Genuine learning occurs via these sense impressions of objects rather than through simple recitation of words. He said, "I learned from them [children at Stanz] what a disadvantage this one-sided letter knowledge and entire reliance on words (which are only sound and noise when there is nothing behind them) must be. I saw what a hindrance this may be to the real power of observation (*Anschauung*), and the firm conception of the objects that surround us."[22]

When he arrived at Burgdorf, Pestalozzi established a new school and Institute which provided the opportunity to practice this new form of learning.

> I crowed my A B C [*Anschauung*] daily from morn till night ... I wrote whole books ... I sought in all ways to bring the beginnings of spelling and counting to the greatest simplicity and into form, so that the child with the strictest psychological order might pass from the first step gradually to the second; and then without break, upon the foundation of the perfectly understood second step, might go on quickly and safely to the third and fourth. But instead of the letters I made the children draw with their slate pencils, I now led them to draw angles, squares, lines, and curves.
>
> With this work the idea gradually developed of the possibility of an "A B C of *Anschauung*" that is now important to me ...[23]

The A B C of *Anschauung* was the process that based all education on sensory impression beginning with observation of near objects, and moving to far objects. Observation includes form, number, and name.

1. How many and what kinds of objects are before him?
2. Their appearance, form, or outline.
3. Their names: how he may represent each of them by a sound or word.[24]

Pestalozzi defined these elements as the "elementary means of instruction" and the educator purposed to "start from and work within this threefold principle:"

1. To teach children to look upon every object that is brought before them as a unit: that is, as separated from those with which it seems connected.
2. To teach them the form of every object: that is, its *size* and *proportions*.

---

[21] Pestalozzi, *How Gertrude,* 228.

[22] Ibid., 46.

[23] Ibid., 53-54.

[24] Ibid., 145.

3.   As soon as possible to make them acquainted with all the words and names descriptive of objects known to them.[25]

The A B C of *Anschauung* appears logical rather than creative in many ways. Pestalozzi believed in natural progression, a pattern of natural reality completed and understood through education. "So our learning grows from confusion to definiteness; from definiteness to plainness; and from plainness to perfect clearness. ... the clearness of my knowledge depend[s] on the nearness or distance of the object in touch with my senses."[26] As near objects become clear and defined, distant objects in turn become the focus of further learning. These extended learning experiences beyond the home to the school room and beyond the school room to field experiences through field trips, geography, and physical exercises. Described differently, one must know what an object is before they can understand the meaning of the object. A word such as "cow" is simply a nonsense word until one comprehends what a cow is through observation. In similar fashion, it is difficult to understand the word "elephant" until one sees an elephant.

The importance of *Anschauung* cannot be underestimated in understanding Pestalozzi. Not only did it revolutionize his method of teaching, but ours today. The creation of a hospitable affirming environment provides the children opportunity to sense emotional security. In that context they can begin to explore surrounding objects. They describe objects in terms of form – size and proportions and their relationship to one another. As they examine more closely, they see the units present in the object and begin to number them. Then descriptions emerge in terms of names of objects, based not on words themselves or spelling, but on descriptions and related sounds. This mastery of learning names is not identification for its own sake, but a means of understanding. *Anschauung* and Pestalozzi's sensory impression method of education led others to describe him as a sensory realist.

PESTALOZZI AND RELIGIOUS EDUCATION

Christianity to Pestalozzi was a moral religion. As a child of the Enlightenment and its rational naturalistic tendencies, he believed in the innate goodness of humanity and the responsibility of the spirit to subdue the natural flesh. His commitment to Enlightenment humanism is evident in his writings and educational philosophy: "Believe in yourself, O Man — believe in the inner meaning of your being. Then will you believe in God and immortality."[27]

---

[25] Ibid., 146.

[26] Ibid., 143.

[27] Johann Heinrich Pestalozzi, *The Education of Man: Aphorisms* (New York: Philosophical Library, 1951), 88.

332

A clear understanding of morality obtained through education guides people toward their divine destiny. "The animal is destined by the Creator to follow the instinct of its nature. Man is destined to follow a higher principle. *His* animal nature must no longer be permitted to rule him, as soon as his spiritual nature has commenced to unfold."[28] Unfolding of the spiritual nature comes about through education, and education is also the intent of Christianity. "For the ultimate destination of Christianity, such as it is revealed in the sacred volume and manifested in the page of history, I cannot find a more appropriate expression than to say that its object is to accomplish the education of mankind."[29]

The context for educational growth in the spiritual realm begins in the home through the mother, extends to the school–home partnership, with the mutual objective of developing humanness to the full. Educational development is not solely knowledge, but affective as well — growth in feelings of love, trust, gratitude, and obedience, which create dependence on God and originate "in the relations that exist between the baby and his mother."[30] Pestalozzi describes the initiation of the education process with the mother and the increasing independence and redirection of the child's affections well in *How Gertrude Teachers Her Children*:

> These are the first principles of moral self-development, which are unfolded by the natural relations between mother and child. But in them lies the whole essence of the natural germ of that state of mind which is peculiar to human dependence on the Author of our being. That is, the germ of all feelings of dependence on God, through faith, is in its essence the same germ which is produced by the infant's dependence on its mother. That manner in which these feelings develop is one and the same ...

> [A] growing independence makes the child let go his mother's hand. He begins to become conscious of his own personality, and a secret thought unfolds itself in his heart, — "*I no longer need my mother.*" She reads the growing thought in his eyes; she presses her darling more firmly to her heart, and says, in a voice he has not yet heard: "Child, there is a God whom thou needest, who taketh thee in His arms when thou needest me no longer, when I can shelter thee no more. There is a God who prepares joy and happiness for thee when I can no more give them thee.

> Then an inexpressible something rises in the child's heart, a holy feeling, a desire for faith, that raises him above himself. He rejoices in the name of God as soon as he hears his mother speak it. The feelings of love, gratitude, and trust that were developed at her bosom, extend and embrace God as father, God as mother. The practice of obedience

---

[28] Pestalozzi, *Letters*, 51.

[29] Pestalozzi, *Letters*, 177.

[30] Pestalozzi, *How Gertrude*, 284.

has a wider field. The child, who believes from this time forward in the eye of God as in the eye of his mother, does right now for *God's sake*, as he formerly did right for his *mother's sake*.[31]

Pestalozzi's Christianity in a twenty-first century evangelical sense is questionable; however, the vitality of his piety in action cannot be questioned. While Pestalozzi's profession might be lacking, his actions of humanitarian charity for all, and particularly the poor is obvious. Nor do his writings reject or contend with religion; they simply do not describe adherence to a particular religious dogma or understanding.

Johannes Ramsauer, who spent sixteen years with Pestalozzi, first as a student at Burgdorf and later as head teacher at Yverdon, describes with deep appreciation the morning and evening prayers led by Pestalozzi. These grew out of Pestalozzi's character, rather than a mere add-on to the day's activities. As the school later moved to Yverdon, Ramsauer wrote these times of prayer were phased out and increasingly became "a mere empty moralizing" shifting the emphasis of Yverdon from a moral oriented education to an intellectual education.[32]

While Pestalozzi's natural Christianity reflects eighteenth century times, his words and actions provide worthy guidance for the Christian parent. Contemporary parents confront the critical moment when the child says, "I need my mother no more," and the pull of the world — "You are mine now ... The new world becomes his mother, *the new world* becomes his god, *sensual pleasure* becomes his god, *self-will* becomes his god."[33] This too is the time the Christian parent wants to direct love toward God, rather than toward the world.

Christian parents are also fraught with the concern of not wanting "natural education" to run its course and carry the child away from the ways of God. However, we must acknowledge our need to develop a rich Christian home environment and provide a secure context for a positive Christian education from infancy. Only upon such a sure foundation can we expect the child's future to be directed toward God, whether in the church, the public school, or the civic arena.

How might we, as Christian educators, "stimulate" (to use Pestalozzi's word[34]) our children's heart, head, and hands toward God amid a world intent to shipwreck our children's faith? This certainly is the task of Christian educators, whether our work is in the local church, Christian organizations, or the academy.

---

[31] Ibid., , 286-288.

[32] Karl Von Raumer, *The Life and System of Pestalozzi,* trans. J. Tilleard (London: Longman, Brown, Green, and Longmans, 1855. rprt. Kessinger Publishing), 72-73.

[33] Pestalozzi, *How Gertrude,* 288-289.

[34] Ibid., , 290.

PESTALOZZI'S INFLUENCE

Pestalozzi wrote in German, and according to Silber many of his writings remain untranslated due to their complexity in the original German language.[35] Today most of Pestalozzi's works are out of print, while others are largely unknown due to limited circulation. Despite the limited circulation of his written works, Pestalozzi's influence is dramatically seen through those who taught or visited his Training Institutes at Burgdorf and Yverdon. The Institutes attracted a host of teaching assistants and visitors from around the world to Pestalozzi's theory, many of whom went on to establish their own institutes, writings, and educational practices. Some followed Pestalozzi's theory closely, while others quickly adapted it to their own way of thinking.

The shift away from a teacher-centered education to a child-centered education led to the need for normal schools to educate teachers.[36] Teachers themselves needed to understand these new methods of instruction and the theory behind them. Child development and psychology needed to be understood by the teacher. The shift from one-on-one instruction in a large classroom, to age divided small classes with group instruction led to a reconfiguration of the school building itself.

Teaching assistants included Hermann Krüsi who became principle of a Swiss normal school in Gais; Johannes Niederer, Johanne Buss, Karl August Zeller who opened a training school in Zurich; and Joseph Neef who would help bring Pestalozzian theory to the United States. Visitors at Yverdon included Friedrich Froebel, the founder of the kindergarten, who spent two years teaching at Pestalozzi's school, philosopher Johann Herbart, Henry Barnard, William Maclure, and Horace Mann all of whom had extensive influence on modern conceptions of education.

Pestalozzi became widely known in the German states through philosopher Johann Gottlieb Fichte's *Addresses to the German Nation,* written in 1808. Prussia in particular sent teachers to train with Yverdon and in 1804 authorized the Pestalozzian method for their schools.

Pestalozzianism came to the United States in what Gutek describes as "three distinct phases."

1. The introduction by William Maclure and Joseph Neef
2. Henry Barnard's work
3. The development of the Normal School at Oswego, New York by Edward A. Sheldon[37]

---

[35] Silber, *Pestalozzi*, 9.

[36] In additional to the establishment of institutes for teacher training, Pestalozzi also wrote on this need. See in particular "Address to My House, 1818" in Pestalozzi, *Educational Writings*, 210.

[37] Gerald Gutek, s.v. "Pestalozzi, Johann Heinrich (1746-1827)," in *Philosophy of Education Encyclopedia* (New York: Macmillan Publishing and The Free Press, 1971).

In 1806 William Maclure recruited Joseph Neef, a teaching assistant at Burgdorf, to come to the United States. Maclure had visited Burgdorf in an attempt to see how Pestalozzi's method might be used to distribute scientific knowledge to agricultural and working classes. After he secured Neef's services, he established Pestalozzian schools in Pennsylvania and Kentucky. Neef later taught Pestalozzian theory in Robert Owen's communitarian experiment at New Harmony, Indiana from 1824 to 1826. He wrote *A Sketch of a Plan and Method of Education* (1808) and *the Method of Instructing Children Rationally in the Arts of Writing and Reading* (1813), which helped spread Pestalozzi's thoughts in the United States.[38]

Phase two came through the work of Henry Barnard. Barnard was the first U.S. Commissioner on education and a leader in the common school movement. He published *Pestalozzi and Pestalozzianism* (1859) and edited the *Connecticut Common School Journal*.[39]

Edward A. Sheldon and his associates began the Oswego Normal School, which proliferated Pestalozzi's thought in teacher education. Oswego "incorporated Pestalozzi's object lessons, featuring form, number, and name lessons" into their training program. They developed lesson plans widely used throughout the United States. The National Teachers' Association endorsed object teaching in 1865, bringing further attention to Oswego and the Pestalozzian method.[40]

CONCLUSION

Johann Heinrich Pestalozzi, as an advocate for child-centered education in the eighteenth century, continues to influence child education today. The values he espoused that educators continue to embrace include:

1. Children need a safe, secure emotional environment in which to learn.
2. Education begins in the home, and expands to the school, working cooperatively with the home.
3. Education begins with sense observation to describe the immediate world, and expands beyond to the larger world. Observation considers form, number, and language.
4. Attention must be given to a child's psychological development in the education process.

---

[38] Ibid.

[39] Ibid.

[40] Ibid.

5. Instruction thus should center on the child and his or her needs.

6. Education is to be holistic and involve heart, head, and hands.

7. Teacher education, in methods and instruction, is necessary to enable teachers to be best equipped to teach.

While these principles may not be considered explicitly Christian by the Christian educator, they do affirm the value of children made in the image of God, and are worthy guidelines for education in the church and other Christian contexts as Scripture clearly teaches that education begins in the home (Deut. 6:4-8; Prov. 1-9; Is. 28:9-10) and is carried on throughout life.

PRIMARY SOURCE SAMPLE[41]

In this spirit let education be considered in all its stages; let the physical faculties be developed, but without forgetting that they form the lower series of human nature; let the intellect be enlightened, but let it be remembered that the first science which thought and knowledge should teach is modesty and moderation; let the discipline be regulated and the heart be formed, not by coercion but by sympathy, — not by precept but by practice; and above all let it be prepared for that influence from above which alone can restore the image of God in man.

BIBLIOGRAPHY

Bluhm, Solomon. S.v. "Pestalozzi, Johann" in *The Encyclopedia of Education,* New York: Macmillan Publishing and The Free Press, 1971.

Cubberly, Ellwood P. *The History of Education: Educational Practice and Progress Considered as a Phase of the Development and Spread of Western Civilization.* Boston: Houghton Mifflin, 1920.

Downs, Robert B. *Heinrich Pestalozzi: Father of Modern Pedagogy.* Boston: Twayne, 1975.

Green, John Alfred. *The Educational Ideas of Pestalozzi.* Third Impression. Baltimore, MD: Warwick and York, n.d. Reprint, HardPress.

Guimps, Roger De. *Pestalozzi: His Life and Work.* New York: D. Appleton, 1904. Reprint Forgotten Books, 2012.

Gutek, Gerald L. S.v. "Pestalozzi, Johann Heinrich (1746-1827)" in *Philosophy of Education Encyclopedia.* New York: Macmillan Publishing and The Free Press, 1971.

_____. "Johann Heinrich Pestalozzi: Proponent of Educating the Heart and Senses." In *Historical and Philosophical Foundations of Education: A Biographical Introduction.* 2nd ed., 130-156. Upper Saddle River, NJ: Prentice-Hall, 1991.

---

[41] Pestalozzi's view of education, and his high understanding of its regenerative role in the life of the individual created by God, is wonderfully articulated in a letter written in 1819 to J. P. Greaves, a former teaching assistant who was introducing Pestalozzian theory to England. In this letter, he succinctly summarized the nature of education as he saw it – as a requisite part of the total development of a whole person. See Pestalozzi, *Letters,* 172.

_____. *A History of the Western Educational Experience*. 2nd ed. Long Grove, IL: Waveland, 1995.

_____. *Pestalozzi and Education*. Prospect Heights, IL: Waveland Press, 1999.

Heafford, Michael. *Pestalozzi: His Thought and Its Relevant Today*. London: Methuen, 1967.

Holman, Henry. *Pestalozzi: An Account of His Life and Work*. New York: Longmans, Green, 1908. Reprint ULAN Press.

Krüsi, Hermann. *Pestalozzi: His Life, Work, and Influence*. Cincinnati, OH: Van Antwerp, Bragg, 1875. Reprint Carlisle, MA: Applewood Books.

Pinloche, Auguste. *Pestalozzi and the Foundation of the Modern Elementary School*. New York: Charles Scribner's Sons, 1901. Reprint BiblioLife.

Rusk, Robert R. "Pestalozzi." In *Doctrines of the Great Educators*. 4th ed., 208-230. London: MacMillan Press, 1969.

Silber, Kate. *Pestalozzi: The Man and His Work*. London: Routledge and Kegan Paul, 1965.

Ulich, Robert, ed. *Three Thousand Years of Educational Wisdom: Selections from the Great Documents*. 2nd ed. Cambridge, MA.: Harvard University, 1965.

Von Raumer, Karl. *The Life and System of Pestalozzi*. Translated by J. Tilleard. London: Longman, Brown, Green, and Longmans, 1855. Reprint Kessinger Publishing.

PRIMARY SOURCE BIBLIOGRAPHY

Anderson, Lewis Flint, ed. *Pestalozzi*. 1931. Reprint, New York: AMS, 1970.

Pestalozzi, Johann Heinrich. *The Education of Man: Aphorisms*. New York: Philosophical Library, 1951.

_____. *How Gertrude Teaches Her Children: An Attempt to Help Mothers to Teach Their Own Children and an Account of the Method*. Translated by Lucy E. Holland and Frances C. Turner. Edited by Ebenezer Cooke. Syracuse, NY: C. W. Bardeen, Publisher, 1898. Reprint by Forgotten Books, 2012.

_____. *Pestalozzi's Leonard and Gertrude*. Translated and abridged by Eva Channing. Boston: D. C. Heath, 1908. Reprint HardPress.

_____. *Pestalozzi's Educational Writings*. Edited by John Alfred Green. New York: Longmans, Green, and Company, 1912. Reprint In *Significant Contributions to the History of Psychology 1750-1920*. Edited by Daniel N. Robinson. Washington, DC: University Publications of America, 1977.

_____. *Letters on Education: Addressed to J. P. Greaves, Esq*. Translator unknown. Reprint of 1827 London edition. Syracuse, NY: C. W. Bardeen, 1898.

FURTHER READINGS

In addition to primary source readings, and the classic volumes on Pestalozzi noted in the Bibliography, many additional sources have not been translated from the German and/or are out of print and difficult to obtain. Gerald L. Gutek, noted above, is the most recent English writer to write comprehensively on Pestalozzi. His various works are worthy of consideration. Kate Silber's selected bibliography in her 1965 volume includes both German and English works. Roger De Guimps's (1904) biography contains an English listing of Pestalozzi's works in chronological order in Appendix II, and Appendix III provides a number of nineteen century German volumes on Pestalozzi. John Alfred Green's *Educational Writings* (1912) lists an annotated bibliography of Pestalozzi's Chief Educational Writings in

Appendix III with both English and German titles.

There are four comprehensive editions of Pestalozzi's works, all in German. *Pestalozzis sämtliche Schriften* gathered by Pestlozzi's publisher I. G. Cottasche Buchhandlung (Stuttgart and Tübingen) and published 1819-1826 in fifteen volumes, though portions of this collection are the work of Pestalozzi's assistants rather than the master himself. L. W. Seyffarth published two collections *Pestalozzis sämtliche Werke* in 1869-1873; and an enlarged second edition 1899-1902 (Liebnitz). A comprehensive critical twenty-one volume edition *Pestalozzi: Sämtliche Werke* edited by A. Buchenau, E. Spranger, and H. Stettbacher appeared 1927-1964 (Berlin, Leipzig, Zürich). Other volumes of selected works are available in German.

CHAPTER 19

Johann Friedrich Herbart:
Morality as the Task of Education

EDDIE K. BAUMANN
THOMAS HUTCHISON

Johann Herbart (1776-1841)

Johann Herbart was a German philosopher and educator who developed various educational perspectives and practices still commonly used today. He taught that effective instruction requires a working knowledge of the psychology of learning and an understanding of the development aspects of the student being taught. In addition to this, curriculum development practices such as lesson planning and a progressive scope and sequence are educational norms finding their genesis in his work.

HISTORICAL BACKGROUND

Upon his death in 1841, it was eulogized of Johann Friedrich Herbart that his work would not be properly recognized until a century had passed. That recognition came much sooner than predicted. Within twenty-five years, Herbart's ideas became the focus of a small but persistent group of educational reformers, known as "Herbartians," who were highly influential in Germany and the United States for the next fifty years. Extending the ideas of Pestalozzi, whom he highly respected, Herbart not only contributed to the reform of educational practice but also sought to revolutionize pedagogical thinking by focusing on the student and the psychology of learning. Herbart called this combination of artful practice grounded on a systematic psychology of learning "pedagogics." While few educators and almost no laypeople would recognize his name today, Herbart became a founder of the scientific study of education, and his legacy of educational theory and practice can still, albeit indirectly, be seen today.

HIS LIFE

Herbart was born May 4, 1776, in Oldenburg, near Bremen, Germany. His father was a lawyer and administrative official in the town, introverted in temperament, preferring a simple and quiet lifestyle. By contrast, Herbart's mother was highly extroverted and strong-willed; she sought to live life more enthusiastically. The resulting marriage was an unhappy one and would eventually end in divorce. Finding little fulfillment from her marriage, Herbart's mother dedicated herself almost exclusively to her son. Due to an early childhood accident that left Herbart somewhat frail in health, young Johann was tutored at home under the watchful eye of his mother. Subjected to a rigorous curriculum, the young boy learned Latin and Greek, as well as being immersed in classical literature, history and mathematics. The young Herbart also demonstrated a keen aptitude for music, becoming proficient in piano, violin, cello and harp. His love and appreciation for music continued throughout his life and greatly influenced his aesthetic sense upon which much of his moral philosophy was based.

At age twelve Herbart was allowed to attend Latin school, the equivalent of the contemporary elementary school. He showed himself to be a gifted and dedicated student, yet socially aloof in demeanor with his peers and obstinate in his beliefs with his teachers. He would later graduate as valedictorian of his *gymnasium* or high school in 1794. His life-long interest in morality was already evident in his congratulatory address given to the class of 1793 entitled "Some Comments Concerning the Increase and Decline of Morality in States," which later was published.

In 1794 he matriculated at the University of Jena with the intention of studying law, a decision made out of deference to his parents' desire to insure himself a decent living. Quite early in his studies, though, he abandoned law to pursue his passion for philosophy. For the next three years he studied philosophy under the guidance of the gifted Johann Fichte. By 1796, however, Herbart began to distance himself from Fichte and the idealistic philosophy so prominent in German universities at that time in favor of his own realistic philosophy, which proved to be more beneficial for his future educational theory.

In 1797 Herbart left Jena after receiving an offer to become the tutor of the children of a prominent Swiss official. The next three years in Switzerland proved pivotal for Herbart's work in education for two reasons. First, it allowed him the opportunity to develop and field test many of his budding theories of education. Many of these ideas were developed and summarized in the bi-monthly reports Herbart would submit to his employer on the progress of his three sons. Second, while in Switzerland Herbart came into contact with the great German educator Johann Heinrich Pestalozzi and his school in Burgadorf, whose methods on instruction would influence Herbart's own.

In 1802 Herbart entered the University of Göttingen where he earned his doctorate and began his academic career as a lecturer in philosophy. At Göttingen he began by giving lectures on pedagogy and later ethics. It was also during his years in Göttingen that he began to formulate and publish his comprehensive system of philosophy, as well as his ideas on psychology and pedagogy. Herbart's *General Pedagogy*, *Chief Points of Metaphysics* and *Chief Points of Logic* all were published in 1806. He followed these works with his *General Practical Philosophy* in 1807.

In 1809 Herbart was offered a professorship at the University of Königsberg as a successor to the eminent Immanuel Kant. Herbart's appointment to Königsberg was based largely on his reputation as a philosopher and his understanding of education since Prussian authorities were looking for a person who could improve the educational system. While in Königsberg he continued to write, publishing his *Textbook for the Introduction of Philosophy* (1812), *General Metaphysics* (1829) and *Letters on the Application of Psychology to Education* (1831).

In 1833, after being denied the position he most coveted, the chair in Philosophy at the University of Berlin, Herbart returned to Göttingen where he continued to lecture and write; he also established an experimental school where prospective teachers could be trained to use his methods. During this time, Herbart published his *Outlines of Pedagogical Lectures* in 1835 and *Psychological Investigation* in 1841. In his last years Herbart continued to work despite struggling with his deteriorating health. He gave his last lecture on August 9, 1841, and died just two days later.

THEOLOGY OF CHRISTIAN EDUCATION
THEOLOGY

It is difficult to identify an explicitly developed theology in Herbart's work. While religion is included in Herbart's pedagogical model, its place and role is very different from what would be conceived by most contemporary Christian educators. The absence of an overt theological approach may be the best point to represent his position and reflect on his influence.

For Herbart, the development of religious affection or, as Herbart called it, "sympathy," begins as a young child in the home. He believed that specific religious concepts or doctrines should not be introduced to the child at this point, but rather parents should seek to promote a religious consciousness. Herbart argued that the souls of children "have a presentiment of an unseen power," which is to be cultivated for the child by the parents in the home: "For such a child who finds itself in close dependence on its parents and guardians, these visible persons certainly occupy the place which the feeling of dependence assigns to the unseen powers, and just for this reason, the earliest religious instruction is an exceedingly simple expansion of the relation of the parents to the children, as in the same way the first social ideas will be taken from the family."[1]

This early phase of life is necessarily preparatory for later exposure to religion. He explains this writing: "Once the student understands something of man's dependence and limitations, he is ready for religious instruction. Religious interest must have been cultivated early in his life and impressed deeply upon him, so deeply that he will never doubt its basic assumptions and that in maturity he can find in it a haven in every adversity."[2]

These fundamental assumptions parallel his own experience. His first tutor, Hermann Uelzen, was a student of theology and later a pastor. As a result, he "possibly stressed theology and philosophy more than a teacher who had specialized in law or philology would have done, and this bias may account for many of the topics on which the youthful Herbart wrote and spoke."[3] Religious considerations were part of this training, evidenced by an outline for a

---

[1] Johann Friedrich Herbart, *The Science of Education*, as cited in Abraham Friesen, "Johann Friedrich Herbart," in *A History of Religious Educators*, ed. Elmer L. Towns (Grand Rapids, MI: Baker, 1975), 185.

[2] Ibid., 184-185.

[3] Harold B. Dunkel, *Herbart & Education* (New York: Random House, 1969), 5.

paper he prepared as a thirteen year old on "proofs for the existence of an eternal God."[4] This fits his training, for "though a theologian, Uelzen did not teach dogmatically or catechetically. Rather he seems always to have stressed the bases of proof and the grounds for doubt. In other words, particularly if compared with the customary practices of the day, Uelzen's general pedagogical method was essentially that of philosophical inquiry."[5]

THEOLOGICAL HERMENEUTIC

For Herbart, the argument from design was a valid proof for the existence of something supernatural. Still, a detailed explanation or certain knowledge of such a proof cannot be developed from his work. More to the point, his understanding of religion suggests that even if possible, presenting such a proof would violate the goal of producing religious sympathy: "It must be emphasized that Herbart believed the teacher's duty not to teach dogmatic religious content but to nurture religious consciousness, a consciousness which is awakened in the home before any formal instruction begins."[6]

The development of religious consciousness is central to Herbart. Fostered through a child's dependency on parents, there is a subjective awareness of God latent in every student. To further develop religious sympathy, the study of the natural world must precede the examination of history and religion, but this process should not include dogmatic content, which would stifle the student's growth. Accordingly, students should not be introduced to church too early: "From the contemplation of nature the student is led "to a universal teleological search which however must remain in the sphere of Nature." The student is encouraged to keep the Sabbath, to turn his mind to the solace of religion. Once the student has learned to "despise fantastic and mystic jugglery, as well as the affections of mysticism, as being far beneath the dignity of religion," he is encouraged to attend church services."[7]

This approach continues into the teen years, where the teacher allows religious questions to surface naturally, with the content and the authority of the teacher's response being an extension of "metaphysics from physics."[8] While teaching can never go beyond the natural, it must point to something beyond nature. Dogmatisms must be avoided, challenging the student to reflection, even to "the extent of keeping the child out of church if necessary until this subjective assurance

---

[4] Ibid.

[5] Ibid.

[6] Herbart, *The Science of Education*, 144. Cited in Friesen, *History of Religious Educators*, 184.

[7] Friesen, *History of Religious Educators*, 185.

[8] Ibid.

is firm."[9] This also relates to the purpose for religion being included in Herbart's approach to education:

> Education must look upon religion not as objective, but as subjective. Religion befriends and protects, but nevertheless it must not be given the child too circumstantially. Its work must be directing rather than teaching. It must never exhaust susceptibility, and therefore above all must not be prematurely made use of. It must not be given dogmatically to arouse doubt, but in union with knowledge of nature and the repression of egoism.[10]

As a result, Herbart's anthropology is founded more in the centrality of human experience and less on biblical revelation, where human dignity and goals are sourced in naturally unfolding experience. Accordingly, this led to an educational theory that starts with understanding the learner and is developed through the scientific study of the psychology of learning: "Psychology, therefore, provided Herbart with a scientific view of man which aids the teacher in shaping the morally good man. He intended his view of man have no overt religious or philosophical overtones, but lie [sic] conceived the human mind to be part of the soul and therefore made certain metaphysical assumptions."[11]

This leads, ultimately, to the development of a morally good man. Not rooted in an explicit understanding of God or theological content but from the study of man in psychology, the good is sensed as a kind of harmonic resonance of what is recognized as good through aesthetics. This is why it is only after all other instruction that Herbart turns to religion:

> He by no means founds morality on religion, but religion appears to him as a friend and protectress of morality. ... He commends a religion of the inner man, stripped of vain practices. He ridicules children who kneel after the fashion of little girls, holding a prayer-book in their hands with the air of young saints. He scourges religious hypocrites who think to cover and excuse bad deeds by acts of devotion. In his opinion, religious instruction is a general instruction which underlies and permeates all particular faiths; which is essentially Christian, and yet preaches love for even those of a different faith, Religion, as conceived by Herbart, is indeed wide and tolerant; for he requires that it should be strengthened in instruction in the classics by reading the *Dialogues* of Plato; and also that religious instruction should be united with instruction in natural science.[12]

---

[9] Ibid.

[10] Ibid.

[11] Friesen, *History of Religious Educators*, 186.

[12] Gabriel Compayré, *Jean Frederic Herbart and Education by Instruction*, trans. Maria Findlay

CONTRIBUTIONS TO EDUCATION
THE ROLE OF THE LEARNER

Herbart took the position, unusual in his day, to combine the concepts of "education" and "teaching." As Hilgenheger notes, prior to Herbart, such questions tended to be pursued independently. Only as a second step was there any attempt at determining how the process of teaching could be supported by education.[13] Herbart changed this dynamic, subordinated the act of teaching to the goals of education so that the methods used to teach are selected based on the desired outcomes. Thus, teaching becomes the central activity of education, a process that requires knowledge of the student to effectively accomplish the educative goals. As such, teaching (and teachers) must understand those being educated (i.e. students), making the learner and the psychology of learning the starting point for any meaningful discussion of education.

Herbart begins from the basis of a psychology of learning, on the nature of the mind, the soul and the dynamics that bring changes to each. For Herbart, the mind is constructed by experience. The science of psychology must start with an examination of the presentations experienced by the learner in such a way as to develop or form the mind. In this sense Herbart views the mind as a type of *tabula rasa,* rejecting the idea of inherent categories of perception or mental faculties associated with Kant,[14] or the romantic notion of a primitive or inborn "I" which is part of the philosophy of his mentor Fichte. In both Kant and Fichte, the essence of humanity is will, a will that must be free to shape the world and not be constrained by external factors. It is this conception of will, or soul, that Herbart rejects. While Herbart acknowledged the existence of the soul, it is, at birth, amorphous and lacks the ability to act.[15] Through experience the will is formed from the mind and the soul, yet the will's development is completely dependent on factors outside of itself. If these factors fail, the will no longer serves to prompt action, but actions are directed by feelings or desires, separated from and not subject to the mind.[16] This plasticity of the will makes one educable.[17] The "educative instruction," Herbart notes, is designed to make a being moral, and, ultimately, it is the only type of instruction that interested him.[18]

(Honolulu: University Press of the Pacific, 2002), 110-111.

[13] Horbert Hilgenheger, "Johann Friedrich Herbart," *Prospects in Education*, 23 no. 3 (1994): 655.

[14] Harold B. Dunkel, *Herbart and Herbartianism: An Educational Ghost Story* (Chicago: University of Chicago Press, 1970), 49.

[15] Johann F. Herbert, *Samtliche Werke* (Hamburg, 1883-93), 4:363.

[16] Ibid., 2:98-99.

[17] Johann F. Herbart, *Outlines of Educational Doctrine* (New York: MacMillan, 1911), 1.

[18] Dunkel, *Herbart and Herbartianism*, 84.

Despite maintaining a plasticity of the mind, the soul and, eventually, the will, Herbart's psychology is a precursor to what would eventually be known as constructivism. Once the will begins to be formed, it must be stimulated and continue to be molded in ways that appeal to the interest of the student. New ideas are engaged and understood in relation to those that the student already possesses. It is a process similar to the ideas of assimilation and accommodation proposed by Piaget a century later. Herbart called this dynamic process of learning "apperception." Through this process, in the hands of a skilled and competent teacher, the student can be molded toward moral development, the chief end of education.

THE ROLE OF THE TEACHER

By starting with the learner and a psychology of learning, good teachers are no longer those who have achieved a certain mastery of content knowledge; they must also be "pedagogically efficient" — a skill developed through understanding the science of the psychology of learning and practicing the art of teaching.[19] Herbart was impressed by how Pestalozzi engaged students in a type of multi-sensory instruction — giving them materials to handle and encouraging them to think aloud — in order to best make sense of new ideas and enhance their understanding of the world. This understanding, however, is not simply imparting knowledge or shaping aptitudes and skills, but must also serve the goal of developing moral insight and strengthening character.[20] As such, good teachers must be those who also possess a strong sense of moral virtue and character.

Since the goal of education is to act morally through the formation of the will via experience, the art of teaching is engaging the child's attention in activities that will both capture their interest and direct them toward proper action. As Herbart writes:

> Interest means self-activity. The demand for many-sided interest is, therefore, a demand for many-sided activity. But not all self-activity, only the right degree of the right kind is desirable; else lively children might very well be left to themselves. There would be no need of educating or even of governing them. It is the purpose of instruction to give the right direction to their thoughts and impulses, to incline these toward the morally good and true.[21]

The process whereby the teacher directs the learner in the path of virtue begins through taking the learner's initial sensations or impulses and guiding them into a rational morality, As

---

[19] Compayré, *Jean Frederic Herbart and Education by Instruction*, 12.

[20] Hilgenheger, "Johann Friedrich Herbart," 657.

[21] Herbart, *Outlines of Educational Doctrine*, 60.

Herbart notes, "Man's worth does not, it is true, lie in his knowing, but in his willing. But there is no such things as an independent faculty of will. Volition has its roots in thought."[22] The teacher must start with the students' initial perceptions and, through the process of apperception, guide them toward a knowledge of the good. Such knowledge, however, is necessary but not sufficient for morality; therefore, the teacher directs not only the construction of the mind but also the development of the will. Since will is a product of knowledge, that is, it has its foundation in thought, the desire to do the good must be developed alongside and in conjunction with the development of knowledge. The necessity that knowledge plays in the development of morality prompted Herbart to comment, "Imbeciles cannot be virtuous. Virtue involves an awakening of the mind."[23]

CURRICULUM AND METHODS

While Herbart was instrumental in developing the psychology of learning and, like Pestalozzi, focusing the process of education on the learner, his legacy endured after his death in the areas of curriculum and, in particular, instructional methodology. For Herbart, the curriculum (and the instructional techniques used to enhance the learner's acquisition of its content) is where his emphasis on morality and the psychology of the learner came together. He opens his *Outlines of Educational Doctrine* by stating that "pedagogics [pedagogy] as a science is based on ethics and psychology. The former points out the goal of education; the latter the way, the means and the obstacles."[24] As noted, since the mind and the will are both blank and plastic at birth, the enculturation of the student to become a useful and productive member of society needed to be multi-faceted and the teacher should cultivate a myriad of interests. Once cultivated, the many-sidedness of interest could be used in two ways to develop the moral person.

The first of these was knowledge or a comprehension of objects or concepts and their relationships to other knowledge and concepts. The second is sympathy or an interest in the aesthetic relations. As Friesen notes, "whereas knowledge grows out of an interest in the objective, sympathy is interest in the subjective. The latter devotes itself in part to men as human beings . . . sympathy grows out of speculation about and a taste for the first. Sympathy is more difficult to arouse since knowledge can easily become an end in itself."[25]

---

[22] Ibid., 40.

[23] Ibid., 48.

[24] Ibid., 2.

[25] Friesen, *History of Religious Educators*, 184.

Herbart proposed a curriculum that, in many ways, was quite traditional. He did advocate the study of religion, at least in so far as it allowed for the development of dispositions toward Christian charity, humility and gratitude.[26] In addition, he proposed the study of history, mathematics and the natural sciences, geography, one's own language and, additionally, the learning of first Greek and later Latin. While traditional in *what* to teach, Herbart's innovation was in *how* these subjects were to be taught, in essence being the first to develop what would later be called a curricular scope and sequence. For any course, the material was to be presented in a particular order. First is the *descriptive* stage, where the aim is to stimulate the senses in such a powerful way that the resulting mental representations can be retained and easily recalled. In the second stage, called the *analytic*, the teacher breaks down complex concepts into constituent parts and helps the student to analyze these concepts from the perspective of the student's existing knowledge base. In the final stage, the *synthetic*, the teacher leads the student to construct the variety of their experiences into an organized and greater whole.

The development of sympathy, which Herbart viewed as critical to morality, is gained from the study of religion and history. The presentation of these subjects must also follow the prescribed stages in order to avoid misuse. As Friesen notes, "by combining the early stages of historical instruction — the vivid presentation of true stories — with an analysis and understanding of oneself, the student can begin to enter into historical events and sympathize with historical figures."[27] This study can include actual historical figures, presented to the student in an idealized or exemplary form (e.g., when we present George Washington as someone who could never tell a lie). It would also include the study of mythic heroes. For example, Herbart suggested that students begin their reading of history with Homer's *Odyssey* as a way of identifying with the character and actions of Odysseus. Such a process promotes character development by leading first to a grasp of the world of ethical actions, whereby moral sensations are developed out of thoughts and later to the development of principles and patterns of actions derived from these specific sensations.[28]

Just as Herbart prescribed a particular scope and sequence to how the curriculum should be presented, he also advocated a means for how material in a particular lesson should be presented. In this sense Herbart can truly be called the father of the modern lesson plan. Many teachers in Herbart's day (and arguably even now) simply dumped facts on students

---

[26] Herbart, *Outlines of Educational Doctrine*, 220-221.

[27] Friesen, *History of Religious Educators*, 184.

[28] Herbart, *Outlines of Educational Doctrine*, 23.

for memorization. To be successful, students needed to learn the art of rote learning, the understanding of what was learned being of almost no consequence. Such an approach did little to cultivate the moral sensibilities of the student. By contrast, Herbart proposed a four-step approach to presenting content meaningfully to the student. While Herbart's four steps are almost incomprehensible even to professional educators, later disciples of Herbart took his approach and converted it into a recognizable five step sequence of instruction. The five steps are:

- Preparation (stimulating interest in the material)
- Presentation (the descriptive aspect of the material to be learned)
- Association (the analytic process of understanding relationships in the material)
- Generalization (the synthetic process of constructing universal moral principles)
- Application (the lesson's usefulness to decisions and actions)

CONTRIBUTIONS TO RELIGIOUS EDUCATION

It is difficult to state why Herbart would be included in a text on prominent Christian educators, for he cannot be understood as "Christian" in the sense that most religious educators would recognize today. Certainly Herbart's chief objective for education was the promotion of morality and he believed that the ethical teachings of Christianity were, in part, necessary to promote this goal; yet, Herbart was suspicious of organized religion, believing that early associations with a particular creed or denomination produced a one-sidedness that was counter to the multi-sided type of interest necessary to stimulate moral sentiment.[29] As Dunkel notes, "[Herbart's] program of moral education was based, not on religious insight, tradition, or revelation, but on the fundamental ethical ideas."[30] Herbart's faith was more rationally grounded and universal than any particular church. Religion, from Herbart's perspective, has its roots in the dependence of man and his limitations, on the brevity of human life and the fleeting nature of earthly pleasures as compared to joys of frugality and limiting wants. While Herbart was willing to let education make connections with the church, he believed that such connections were to be delayed until the student had developed a fundamental moral aesthetic sense, one universal to religious faith, which would allow the student to avoid the "fanaticism and mysticism" that he perceived in organized religion.

It may well be that Herbart's general philosophy and his ideas of education opposed

---

[29] Ibid., 83.

[30] Dunkel, *Herbart and Herbartianism*, 216.

a general trend in late eighteenth — and nineteenth — century thought that was quite hostile to all forms of creedal Christianity. His rejection of these general trends makes Herbart, albeit indirectly, a defender of the fundamental structure upon which creedal Christianity is based. Johann Gottfried Herder, an eighteenth-century German philosopher and theologian wrote, "We live in a world that we ourselves create." This line captures the spirit of the growing philosophy of romanticism that was prevalent in Herbart's time. While difficult to define, romanticism can be summarized in two main ideas. First is the notion of an indomitable will; so that to be human is to "create values, create goals, create ends, and in the end you create your own vision of the universe."[31] Second, there is no structure to things or, rather, there is no pattern or absolute truth to which one must adapt. From these two propositions a whole new set of virtues develop, where motive is more important than consequences of action and where integrity is measured more by personal sincerity than alignment to a particular set of truths.

Herbart rejected all of these ideas. His theories of education placed considerable responsibility on parents and teachers to guide and shape the moral will of the child since the human soul is amorphous at birth and the will is formed through experiences. This view caused Herbart to reject both the more romantic conception of human nature as basically good and the more biblical idea that human beings are born with an inherent sin nature. Since human nature is essentially neutral, experiences can be directed by the teacher and should be directed toward an appreciation for and, ultimately, a duty to act in ways that are moral. This belief, however, rested on a more fundamental premise — that virtue is founded on knowledge and that possession of this knowledge makes it possible for human beings to know what to do and how to live in a way that produces personal and social harmony. This view of morality, Herbart believed, is consistent with the Christian tradition, but is also one that resonates with classical ideas of virtue, specifically those of the Greeks and the Romans. It is for this reason that Herbart would propose that young people be exposed to the classical myths of Greece and Rome. These myths have universal appeal and teach perennial lessons of virtue and the consequences of impetuous or imprudent actions, moral principles that are also embedded in a rational religion.

While a belief in the malleability of knowledge and the will may sound deterministic or mechanistic, this belief most certainly ran counter to ideas of romanticism and German idealism that were so prominent during Herbart's lifetime. This would help to explain why Herbart's work was not more widely embraced during his life. Also, an approach that places

---

[31] Isaiah Berlin, *The Roots of Romanticism*, ed. Henry Hardy (Princeton, NJ: Princeton, 1999), 119.

the teacher in such a powerful position to form the intellect and affections of the student had tremendous appeal to educators. This appeal, as Dunkel points out, made it particularly enticing to embrace the methodology of Herbart while rejecting the moral objective which he sought to accomplish.[32]

CONCLUSION

As Gabriel Compayré notes, Herbart was among the first who believed and tried to demonstrate that all education depends on instruction and that the ideas and knowledge of virtue must be embedded in a scope and sequence of curriculum designed to promote a happy and ethical life.[33] Yet, a decade into the twentieth century, the influence of Herbart and his disciples was almost non-existent in the United States. The rise of experimental psychology rendered Herbart's more theoretical approach obsolete, and John Dewey's child-centered philosophy, which made learning more important than instruction, replaced Herbart's teacher-centered approach. Despite these trends, schools of teacher education, scope and sequencing of curriculum, making curriculum developmentally appropriate to the student, and providing a format for making content meaningful to the student still exist today. These can all be linked to Herbart, and insofar as Christian educators have mirrored these innovations in the church, the legacy of Herbart continues to exist today.

PRIMARY SOURCE SAMPLE[34]

Part I: The Double Basis of Pedagogics

Chapter 1: The Ethical Basis

8. The term virtue expresses the whole purpose of education. Virtue is the idea of inner freedom which has developed into an abiding actuality in an individual. Whence, as inner freedom is a relation between insight and volition, a double task is at once set before the teacher. It becomes his business to make actual each of these factors separately, in order that later a permanent relationship may result.

9. But even here at the outset we need to bear in mind the identity of morality with its effort put forth to realize the permanent actuality of the harmony between insight and volition. To induce the pupil to make this effort is a difficult achievement; at all events, it becomes possible only when

---

[32] Dunkel, *Herbart and Herbartianism*, 13.

[33] Compayré, *Jean Frederic Herbart and Education by Instruction*, ix – x.

[34] This primary source sample has been quoted from Herbart, *Outlines of Educational Doctrine*, 7-14.

the twofold training mentioned above is underway. It is easy enough, by study of the example of others, to cultivate theoretical acumen; the moral application to the pupil himself, however, can be made, with hope of success, only in so far as his inclinations and habits have been taken a direction in keeping with his insight. If such is not the case, there is danger lest the pupil, after all, knowingly subordinate his correct theoretical judgment to mere prudence. It is thus that evil in the strict sense originates.

10. Of the remaining practical or ethical concepts, the idea of perfection points to health of body and mind; it implies a high regard for both, and their systematic cultivation.

11. The idea of good-will counsels the educator to ward off temptation to ill-will as long as such temptation might prove dangerous. It is essential, on the other hand, to imbue the pupil with a feeling of respect for good-will.

12. The idea of justice demands that the pupil abstain from contention. It demands, furthermore, reflection on strife, so that respect for justice may strike deep root.

13. The idea of equity is especially involved in cases where the pupil has merited punishment as requital for the intention infliction of pain. Here the degree of punishment must be carefully ascertained and acknowledge as just.

14. Where a number of pupils are assembled there arise, naturally, on a small scale, a system of laws and rewards. This system and the demands which in the world at large spring from the same ideas, must be brought into accord.

15. The concept of an administrative system has great significance for pedagogics, since every pupil, whatever his rank or social status, must be trained for cooperation in the social world to fit him for usefulness. This requirement may assume very many different forms.

16. Of the system of civilization only the aspect of general culture, not that of special training, must be emphasized at this point.

17. For the business of education, like idea of perfection, while it does not rise into excessive prominence, stands out above all others on account of its uninterrupted application. The teacher discovers in the as yet undeveloped human being a force which requires his incessant attention to intensify, to direct, and to concentrate.

18. The constant presence of the idea of perfection easily introduces a false feature into moral education in the strict sense. The pupil may get an erroneous impression as to the relative importance of the lessons, practice, and performance demanded of him, and so be betrayed into the belief that he is essentially perfect when these demands are satisfied.

19. For this reason alone, if others are wanting, it is necessary to combine moral education proper, which in everyday life lays stress continually on correct self-determination, with religious training.

The notion that something really worthy has been achieved needs to be tempered by humility. Conversely, religious education has the need of the moral also to forestall cant and hypocrisy, which are only too apt to appear where morality has not already secured a firm foothold through earnest self-questioning and self-criticism with a view to improvement. Finally, inasmuch as moral training must be put off until insight and right habits have been acquired, religious education, too, should not begin too early; nor should it be needlessly delayed.

BIBLIOGRAPHY

Berlin, Isaiah. *The Roots of Romanticism*. Edited by Henry Hardy. Princeton: Princeton, 1999.

Compayré, Gabriel. *Jean Friedric Herbart and Education by Instruction*. Translated by Maria Findlay. Honolulu: University Press of the Pacific, 2002.

Dunkel, Harold B. *Herbart & Education*. New York: Random House, 1969.

_____. *Herbart and Herbartianism: An Educational Ghost Story*. Chicago: University of Chicago Press, 1970.

Friesen, Abraham. "Johann Friedrich Herbart." In *A History of Religious Educators*, edited by Elmer L. Towns, 179-189. Grand Rapids, MI: Baker, 1975.

Herbart, Johann Friedrich. *The Science of Education*. Translated by Henry and Ellen Felkin. Boston: Heath, 1896.

_____. *Outlines of Educational Doctrine*. Translated by Alexis F. Lange. New York: MacMillian, 1911.

Hilgenheger, Horbert. "Johann Friedrich Herbart." *Prospects in Education*, 23 no. 3 (1994) 653-665.

Kehrbach, K., O. Flügel, and T. Fritzch, eds. *Johann Friedrich Herbarts Sämliche Werke in Chronologischer Reihenfolge*. 19 vols. Langensalza: Beyer.

PART V

Educators in the Age of Industrialization
(A.D. 1850-1950)

The American educators whose ideas have been most seminal for modern religious education are **Horace Bushnell** (1802-1876), **William James** (1842-1910), and **John Dewey** (1859-1952). Bushnell, critical of the revival approach to ministering to children in the church, emphasized instead their natural Christian growth in an environment of love. He was optimistic about education's power to reform society. James, probably America's leading psychologist-philosopher in his day, saw the usefulness of religion and philosophy in properly organizing the individual's life. Education requires an individual to determine his relation to the ultimates of the universe, insisted James. He pointed to the crisis that an individual experiences in discovering a meaningful religion. Although Dewey was not a religious educator, his influence on modern religious (as well as secular) education has probably been greater than that of anyone else. With him are associated the concepts of pragmatic education, experimental thinking in education, activity-centered education (learning by doing), and life-oriented religion. For him experience was more vital than knowledge, including Biblical knowledge. He changed the school from a place where children prepare for life to a place where they live. It is to be an embryonic community, busy with occupations that reflect those in the larger society and permeated with the spirit of art, history, and science.

John Henry Newman (1801-1890) was concerned with education on the university level. His ideal was an institution which harmonizes university education with Christian faith. Since religion is part of the universal experience and since the university should prepare students for life in general, not just for their vocations, university education must include religion.

In the years that spanned the late 19th Century and early 20th Century, two "churchmen" used their experience and background for the educating of the everyday parishioner in the church. **C. I. Scofield** (1843-1921) editor of the Scofield Reference Bible, was an influential pastor whose ministry spanned preaching, teaching, and writing. In addition to his ministry from the pulpit, he also was instrumental for the founding of Philadelphia School of the Bible, now Cairn University. In Baptist circles, **Arthur Flake** (1862-1952) pioneered Sunday School Administration as a means of facilitating biblical literacy within the church.

CHAPTER 20

Horace Bushnell:

Advocate of Progressive Orthodoxy and Christian Nurture

SAMUEL J. SMITH

ELMER L. TOWNS

Horace Bushnell (1802-1876)

Disparaged by his critics as a liberal, Calvinist, mystic, and heretic, Horace Bushnell's theology — particularly his model for Christian nurture — has prevailed as a significantly influential model for religious education. His legacy reveals one who attempted to bridge the divides of his time, including the chasm between Orthodox Calvinism and Unitarianism. Though many were confused by his language theory and mediating stance on doctrinal issues, his principles of Christian nurture clearly served as a pilot light that ignited the flame of the twentieth-century religious education movement.

HISTORICAL BACKGROUND

Horace Bushnell was born into a fledgling nation that had been grappling with its identity, not merely as a political entity but also as a moral, ethical, and religious people. In addition to building a distinct government structure, the United States was distinguishing itself from Great Britain with Noah Webster's lexicon, with Benjamin Franklin's practical philosophy, and later with Horace Mann's common school approach to education. Jonathan Edwards' preaching had sparked the First Great Awakening in Colonial Massachusetts, laying a foundation of Puritan and Calvinist principles for the imminent nation, and currents of the Second Great Awakening were well underway. In this New England religious milieu, Bushnell was born and reared — one in which clear divisions had emerged among Orthodox Calvinists, Unitarians, and Revivalists.[1]

EARLY LIFE AND EDUCATION

Life began for Horace Bushnell on April 14, 1802, in Bantam, Connecticut. His father — a farmer, smalltime manufacturer, and justice of the peace — had been attracted to New Methodism with its appeal to human freedom and rejection of predestination. His mother, on the other hand, was reared in the Episcopal Church with its emphasis on sacraments and ritual. Of the two, Bushnell's mother made the greater impact on his spiritual sensibilities. It was neither her doctrine nor her religious traditions, however, that he remembered later in life, but it was rather her character and her "loving instinct."[2] Despite their different religious upbringings, both parents became members of the Congregational Church of New Preston, Connecticut, the town to which the Bushnells moved when Horace was three years of age. They brought up young Horace in a solidly middle class home that was by all accounts a stable family setting, with the exception of a few financial setbacks from ups and downs in their farming and wool-carding businesses.[3] Religion for them was a way of life, fully integrated into the atmosphere of the home — not artificially or nominally, but organically. Although doctrine was indeed instilled at home by recitations of the Westminster Catechism, dogma was not the focal point of their religious life.[4]

It was in this setting where Bushnell grew to young adulthood, becoming an ardent

---

[1] Robert Bruce Mullin, *The Puritan as Yankee: A Life of Horace Bushnell* (Grand Rapids, MI: William B. Eerdmans), 33.

[2] Ibid., 23.

[3] Catherine L. Albanese, "Horace Bushnell among the Metaphysicians," *Church History* 79, no. 3 (2010): 616.

[4] Mullin, *The Puritan and the Yankee*, 23.

outdoorsman and an accomplished angler. His appreciation for nature can be understood more fully in light of his admiration for the poetry and philosophy of Romantic writers such as Samuel Taylor Coleridge, from whom he gained an increased sense of the wholeness and connectedness of nature.[5] For Bushnell, there was no strict dichotomy between natural and supernatural, but God's presence was revealed in nature itself.[6] He claimed that it was from nature that he drew his sense of the divine and that the power of nature led him to prayer.[7]

Bushnell's theological proclivities were displayed as early as age seventeen when he wrote a modest discourse to address some of the problems he observed in Calvinism. Discussing Romans 9, he addressed questions of election, predestination, and the sovereignty of God.[8] At nineteen years of age, he made a profession of faith, joined the Congregational Church of New Preston,[9] and of this experience wrote, "Lord, here I am a sinner. Take me. Take all that I have and shall have ... I am ready to do anything or be anything for thee."[10] After entering Yale College two years later, he began entertaining serious intellectual doubts and seemingly lost his newfound faith.[11] Coleridge's influence had led him to assume that Christianity was understandable primarily by intuition — that its appeal was not so much to the intellect as it was to ethical and spiritual feelings. He thus became convinced that religion appealed primarily to the emotions for its compelling demonstration.[12]

ADULT LIFE: PASTOR AND AUTHOR

After graduation in 1827, Bushnell tried teaching school in Norwich, Connecticut, but the "petty vexations of a pedagogue" drove him to experiment briefly with journalism in New York City, which he found to be a "terrible life."[13] Convinced that neither teaching nor journalism was his calling, he returned to Yale in early 1829 to study law and soon became a tutor in the college. The responsibility of tutors went beyond the academic to include the spiritual development

---

[5] Boardman W. Kathan, "Horace Bushnell and the Religious Education Movement," *Religious Education* 108, no. 1 (2013): 43.

[6] Michael Ryan, "'The Puritan's of Today': The Anti-Whig Argument of *The Scarlet Letter*," *Canadian Review of American Studies* 38, no. 2 (2008): 203.

[7] Mullin, *The Puritan and the Yankee*, 24.

[8] Ibid., 23.

[9] Mary A. Cheney, *Life and Letter of Horace Bushnell* (New York, NY: Harper, 1937), 21.

[10] Mullin, *The Puritan and the Yankee*, 26.

[11] Gary Dorrien, *The Making of American Liberal Theology: Imagining Progressive Religion 1805-1900* (Louisville, KY: Westminster John Knox Press, 2001), 112.

[12] H. Shelton Smith, *Horace Bushnell* (New York, NY: Oxford, 1965), 27.

[13] Mullin, *The Puritan and the Yankee*, 42.

of their students as well, a charge that Bushnell took seriously and carried out with success.[14] Regarding the spring of 1831, Yale Professor Chauncey A. Goodrich wrote, "[It] will long be remembered as one of the most remarkable seasons of refreshing from on high, which has ever been experienced at this college ... The whole college stood waiting in solemn expectation, to see the arm of the Lord revealed."[15] By the end of the semester, it was estimated that as a result of this awakening — eventually known as the "Great Yale Revival of 1831"[16]— nearly half the student body had experienced a spiritual conversion.[17] One of those students was Horace Bushnell.

Late one evening after an arduous period of study, he had what he would later describe as an out-of-body experience. Feeling that his body was floating in the air and that there was no sensation in his hands, he gripped his bed for stability. As his daughter Mary Cheney explained, "He began to believe that he was dead and that this was his voyage to the world of the spirits."[18] Following this renewal experience, Bushnell began to sense a deep concern for the spiritual condition of the young men he was tutoring. He frankly declared to them that he had united himself with followers of Christ and that they should do the same. This bold stance spurred a great number of men on campus to seek a spiritual renewal.[19]

Bushnell's intellectual doubts had disappeared, and the course of his life changed. That very next semester, he entered Yale Divinity School to prepare for the ministry and, soon after graduating at the top of his class,[20] he met Mary Mehitable Apthorp, a student in a Bible class he had been teaching. They fell in love, married, and later had four daughters and one son.[21] Shortly after their marriage, Bushnell was licensed to preach and the following year was called to pastor the North Congregational Church in Hartford — the only church he was ever to pastor. After twenty-seven years of successful ministry, deteriorating health led to an early retirement in 1859.[22] The remaining years until his death in 1876 were spent writing his theological treatises and traveling in search of relief from his tubercular lung disease.[23]

---

[14] Ibid., 43.

[15] Roberta Buckingham Mouheb, *Yale under God: Roots and Fruits* (Maitland, FL: Xulon Press, 2012), 96.

[16] Theodore Dwight Woolsey, "Sketch of the Life of Professor William A. Larned," *New Englander and Yale Review* 21, no. 2 (1862): 325.

[17] Mouheb, *Yale under God*, 97.

[18] Mullin, *The Puritan and the Yankee*, 41.

[19] Mouheb, *Yale under God*, 97.

[20] Dorrien, *American Liberal Theology*, 112.

[21] Michiyo Morita, *Horace Bushnell on Women in Nineteenth-Century America* (Lanham, MD: University Press of America, 2004), 3.

[22] Albanese, "Bushnell among the Metaphysicians," 616.

[23] Kathan, "Horace Bushnell," 43.

THEOLOGICAL FOUNDATIONS FOR CHRISTIAN EDUCATION

It was not until his retirement that Bushnell settled into writing as a primary occupation. Even then, he continued to write as he had been — in a pragmatic voice, as one addressing practical religious problems, not as a theological academician. It was religious praxis that concerned him: the interaction between theory and practice, contemplation and action, thinking and doing, theology and religious life.[24] Problems that most preoccupied both his sermons and his writings dealt with how to find God, how to believe, how to be sure of one's belief, and how to make religion real.[25] For him, the chief role of theology was to make sense of experience.

Though the field of theology has clearly recognized Bushnell as a "religious genius" who demonstrated "sensitivity as a religious analyst," there is disagreement regarding his prominence as a theologian.[26] It is rare, for example, to find references to Bushnell's works among the writings of contemporary theologians.[27] Among those who do acknowledge him are many who recognize an "anti-systematic streak" uncharacteristic of conventional theologians.[28] Others, however, consider him to have been "a theologian as Copernicus was an astronomer" or to have shaped eighteenth-century American theology as Jonathan Edwards shaped the nineteenth century.[29] This status, they argue, is justified because Bushnell is credited with laying the foundation for the twentieth-century religious education movement[30] and earning the title from some as the "Father of American Liberal Theology."[31]

PROGRESSIVE ORTHODOXY

It is a fair question to ask whether or not Bushnell warrants such a designation among liberal theologians. To the progressive clergy of his time, he was perceived as a liberator, the

---

[24] Lee J. Makowski, *Horace Bushnell on Christian Character Development* (Lanham, MD: University Press of America), 2-5.

[25] Mullin, *The Puritan and the Yankee*, 57.

[26] James D. Bratt, review of *The Puritan and the Yankee: A Life of Horace Bushnell*, by R. B. Mullin, *Journal of Religion* 83, no. 4 (October 2003): 627.

[27] Douglas F. Ottati, review of *Horace Bushnell on Christian Character Development*, by Lee. J. Makowski, *Journal of Religion* 81, no. 3 (July 2001): 480.

[28] Bratt, review of *The Puritan and the Yankee*, 673.

[29] Mullin, *The Puritan and the Yankee*, 1-3.

[30] Kathan, "Horace Bushnell," 44.

[31] D. Bruce Lockerbie, *A Passion for Learning: A History of Christian Thought on Education* (Colorado Springs, CO: Purposeful Design, 2007), 296-297.

one who would set them free from the Puritanical tyranny of John Calvin, and — soon after Bushnell's death — liberal theologians solidly hailed him as the reigning "Father of American Liberal Theology."[32] Roger E. Olson, however, described Bushnell as a "mediating theologian," who, on a liberal-conservative continuum, would fall far from the liberal theologians of his time or thereafter.[33] Therefore, Olson, among other scholars of American Christianity and theology, preferred the term "progressive orthodoxy" for Bushnell's brand of theology, as it reflected more accurately how Bushnell creatively bridged the divide between orthodoxy and progressivism while remaining faithful to the gospel.

Always proud of his Puritan heritage, Bushnell often traced the positive influence Puritans had on early American culture, defending them against what he perceived as unwarranted criticism.[34] As a mediating force, though, he was critical both of Calvinist Orthodoxy and of Unitarian Liberalism. He soundly condemned closed-minded attitudes toward doctrine wherever they were found, whether in orthodox or progressive camps. He challenged both Orthodox Calvinists and Unitarians for holding their theological views as ends in themselves rather than critically evaluating them in a meaningful way.[35] While presenting a blend of orthodox Christianity along with liberal notions of the nineteenth century, he always preached that Jesus Christ was the Son of God. This was a clear departure from Ralph Waldo Emerson, whom he admired but whose denial of Christ's divinity was a bridge too far for Bushnell.[36] By holding to the core tenets of the gospel, Bushnell may be considered orthodox; however, it was his adherence to notions of Romanticism that earned his thinking the label of Progressive Orthodoxy.[37]

Where then is Bushnell best situated in his thinking? He would not be aligned with his contemporaries Lyman Beecher and Nathaniel Taylor, both orthodox protestant theologians who viewed God as "a distant being who oversaw a sin-prone humanity that needed guidance from churches in order to attain salvation."[38] Neither would he be categorized among the Unitarians, whom he criticized for their deism, self-perfectionism, and denial of Christ's

---

[32] Mullin, *The Puritan and the Yankee*, 253.

[33] Roger E. Olson, "Remembering the 'Progressive Orthodoxy' of Horace Bushnell," *Patheos Blogs*, August 11, 2012, http://www.patheos.com/blogs/rogerolson/2012/08/remembering -the-progressive-orthodoxy-of-horace-bushnell-part-one (accessed May 4, 2014).

[34] Mullin, *The Puritan and the Yankee*, 15.

[35] Makowski, *Bushnell on Christian Character*, 37.

[36] Lockerbie, *Passion for Learning*, 296-297.

[37] Bratt, review of *The Puritan and the Yankee*, 673.

[38] Ryan, "Puritan's of Today," 2003.

divinity.[39] Though influenced by Romantic ideas, he preached doctrines such as the efficacious death and resurrection of Christ for the forgiveness of the sins of all humanity, which clearly was contradictory to the religious views of the likes of Emerson. Though difficult to categorize because of his tendency to bridge divides, Bushnell may be situated between the Orthodox Calvinists, who at one point tried him for heresy, and the Unitarians, whom he rejected. This difficulty may be attributed to his language theory, which he insisted was key to an understanding of his theological hermeneutic.[40]

THEOLOGICAL HERMENEUTIC: BUSHNELL'S LANGUAGE THEORY

According to Bushnell, those who refused to understand his language theory would misconstrue all of his other assertions. Building on Coleridge's model, Bushnell made a distinction between literal and figurative language. Literal language conveys scientific facts and sensory information about the physical world. It is an instrument of naming things and is simple enough to be used to some degree even among animals. A weakness of literal language is its inaccuracy insofar as it can only communicate physical sensations. Although it holds the ability to name things, it falls short in offering an exact representation of them. Consequently, literal language is incapable of conveying theological truths.[41]

Unlike literal language, figurative language has the capability of conveying thoughts and truths. It requires reflective subjects and, therefore, can only be realized by rational beings. Figurative language expands as thought expands, thus providing limitless possibilities as language and thought interact with signs, images, metaphors, types, forms, and analogies. This dynamic makes figurative language ideal for communicating a sense of the spiritual and is therefore the suitable language of theology.[42]

A point of contention for conservative theologians was that, if the language of thought is always figurative as Bushnell supposed, theological propositions would thereby remain indeterminate. Contemporaries found his talk of spiritual hieroglyphs and *poesis* unsettling, especially as he dared them to embrace the indeterminacy of theological language. By *poesis*, he proposed that theology is a poetic process in the making, that it is not a science, and that there is no one particular interpretation of words used to communicate theological truths. He challenged theologians to practice creativity and imagination, using words as clues to point to concepts beyond the words themselves.[43]

---

[39] Makowski, *Bushnell on Christian Character,* 13, 135.

[40] Dorrien, *American Liberal Theology,* 150.

[41] Ibid., 124-144.

[42] Ibid.

[43] Makowski, *Bushnell on Christian Character,* 23-42.

THEOLOGICAL EVALUATION

In 1849, Bushnell issued a work entitled *God in Christ* which, among other things, claimed that the incarnation and the Trinity are truths derived from Christian experience rather than from dogma. He further suggested that religious truths cannot be known through logical propositions or creeds because they are inherently poetic, appealing to human imagination and feelings. This constituted a radical departure from New England theology of the time. Although the Hartford Central Association of Congregational Ministers, of which Bushnell was a member, did not proceed against him, the Fairfield West Association did. The case was considered by successive meetings of the General Association of Connecticut from 1849 to 1854, and despite the fact that few Connecticut ministers were sympathetic to his views, the association did not formally condemn Bushnell.

The central idea of New England Calvinism in Bushnell's day was the transcendence of God. God's sovereignty was magnified almost to the point of obscuring his indwelling presence in men, which was what Bushnell emphasized. Because God is present in man's world, the child can be expected to grow up within the kingdom of God through participation in the organic life of the Christian family. Bushnell sought to modify a rigid supernaturalism, yet was afraid of the rising tide of naturalistic thought which threatened to undermine Christian faith.[44] He argued against a literal interpretation of scriptural statements about God:

> If God is to be Himself revealed, He has already thrown out symbols for it, filling the creation full of them, and these will all be played into metaphor [and] ... we can say nothing of Christ so comprehensively adequate as to call Him the metaphor of God: God's last metaphor. And when we have gotten all the metaphoric meanings of His life and death, all that is expressed and bodied in His person of God's saving help and new-creating, sin-forgiving, reconciling love, the sooner we dismiss all speculations on the literalities of His incarnate miracles, His derivation, the composition of His person, His suffering — plainly transcendent as regards our possible understanding — the wiser shall we be in our discipleship.[45]

In addition to his denial of the transcendence of God and his rejection of creeds, Bushnell's soteriological views — his notions regarding salvation — were considered heretical by many orthodox theologians of his day. He wrote of Christ's work that it "terminates, not in the release of penalties by due compensation, but in the transformation of character, and

---

[44] Horace Bushnell, *Nature and the Supernatural* (New York, NY: Scribner, 1858), 20-31.

[45] Horace Bushnell, "Our Gospel a Gift to the Imagination," *Literacy Varieties* 3: 249.

the rescue in the matter, of guilty men from the retributive causation provoked by his sins."[46] The death of Christ was not an atonement for man's sin but a moral example to man. To be restored to God, a man should cease to sin. Thus, man's relationship to God is determined by man's character rather than by an act of God's Son. What are the implications of this doctrine for personal religious faith? Bushnell did not believe it necessary to "embrace ... Christ as a sacrifice" or to see Christianity as a "vicarious religion." But he did affirm "that no one ever becomes a true Christian man, who does not rest himself in God, or give himself over to God, in objective faith and devotion, somehow."[47] While Bushnell emphasized the subjective character of religious faith, he also recognized the need for an objective religion saying,

> Therefore, we need, all alike, some objective religion; to come and hang ourselves upon the altar of sacrifice sprinkled by the blood of Jesus, to enter into the holiest set open by His death, to quiet our soul in His peace, clothe it in His righteousness, and trust Him as the Lamb of God that taketh away our sin. In these simple, unselfish, reflective exercises, we shall make our closest approach to God.[48]

Thus, Bushnell vacillated from subjective to objective faith. Perhaps he was concerned about his critics and attempted to invest historic Christian terms and symbols with new meanings and significance.

BRIDGING DIVIDES

Although a controversial figure, particularly for orthodox theologians, Bushnell came to be known for his many attempts to bridge various divides, not just in theology but also in civic and social issues. For example, a rift existed in his Hartford church between Old Light and New Light theological factions, with his two leading deacons on opposite sides of the argument. Rather than permit the division to split the church, Bushnell used his personal skills to negotiate a truce.[49] Some efforts were more successful than others, and at times — especially when navigating issues of slavery and race relations — he confused his audience with seemingly contradictory language.

Dichotomies

Despite the apparent dichotomy of his language theory into literal and figurative language, Bushnell was one who attempted to bridge divides by pointing out unnecessary

---

[46] Horace Bushnell, *Vicarious Sacrifice* (New York, NY: Scribner, 1877), 449.

[47] Horace Bushnell, *God in Christ* (Hartford, CT: Hamersby, 1867a), 264.

[48] Bushnell, *God in Christ*, 267-268.

[49] Dorrien, *American Liberal Theology*, 126.

dichotomies. For instance, rejecting the natural-supernatural dichotomy, he believed both nature and supernature share common roots and harmony in God. He called Christianity the "foster-mother of science," and science the "handmaid of Christianity." The two operate in tandem, he noted, and do not occupy separate spheres.[50] In the same vein, he explained that the doubt-belief dichotomy is false and that one is not antithetical to the other; both are part of the same process.[51] A few of the other divides he attempted to bridge were the faith-reason, science-religion, sovereignty-freewill, Calvinism-Arminianism, and orthodox-liberal divides. "My ruling endeavor," Bushnell proclaimed, "has been in all my investigations of truth to find a form of doctrine broad enough to include, as far as possible, the opposing truths or half-truths which Christian believers are contending."[52]

Orthodox Calvinism and Unitarianism

In Bushnell's day, three factions were represented among the New England churches: Orthodox Calvinists, Unitarians, and Revivalists. Though he defended Orthodox Calvinists in *Christian Nurture*, he refused to accept it *in toto*. He believed that both groups misrepresented Christianity and were only "half-seeing." The major tenets of Orthodox Calvinism included the absolute sovereignty of God; the total depravity of humanity; double predestination, which divided humanity into two groups of the elect and the damned; and a work ethic by which faith may be confirmed.[53]

Gaining strength in the early nineteenth century, the Unitarian movement was a reaction to the Orthodox Calvinists, generally viewing Calvinists as mindless traditionalists. Grounded in Arminian theology, Unitarians emphasized human free will rather than God's sovereignty. Their major tenets included the unity of God, which rejected the trinity as irrational, Jesus Christ as strictly human, and human nature as inherently good. Unitarians were condemned for an epistemology that held reason in higher regard than revelation, which critics claimed gave preference to human wisdom over God's authority. Bushnell dismissed Unitarianism as having drifted into a natural religion based on the humanism of the English Enlightenment.[54]

---

[50] Makowski, *Bushnell on Christian Character*, 45.

[51] Mullin, *The Puritan and the Yankee*, 60.

[52] Ibid., 56.

[53] Makowski, *Bushnell on Christian Character*, 7-17.

[54] Makowski, *Bushnell on Christian Character*, 10-15.

Revivalism

The preaching of Jonathan Edwards had fueled the first wave of revivals that spread during New England's Colonial Era. During the second wave, the United States was a fairly young nation, and Bushnell was a teenager sitting under the ministry of Rev. Charles Boardman, a staunch supporter of revivalism. From the pew, young Bushnell listened as Rev. Boardman preached about how, in the past, God had replenished the church through a gradual process, but now — in this new era of awakening — he was replenishing the church through revivals.[55] Less than a decade had passed when Bushnell found himself transformed by such a revival. Not only was he spiritually transformed by the Great Yale Revival of 1831, but he was also led to point others toward conversion during the movement.

Ironically, Bushnell later became an outspoken opponent of revivalism. It could have been that he perceived his own experience to have been more organic than the synthetic campaigning that centered attention on the stage rather than on the people.[56] It was not so much that he opposed revivals to the point that they should be abolished; he valued them as a means by which God might periodically awaken a church that had dried up and lost its fervor. It was more that he questioned the extremism of the revivalist movement that promoted certain methods of evangelism to exact an expected emotional conversion. Describing his reaction to revivalism, he preached a sermon in 1853 stating, "Things had come to such a pitch in our churches by the intensity of the revival system that the permanent was sacrificed to the casual, the ordinary swallowed up and lost in the extraordinary, and Christian piety itself reduced to a kind of campaigning or stage-affect exercise."[57] Even more disconcerting to him was the movement's neglect of the nurturing role of the family and of the local church congregation. He preferred a more gradual spiritual growth process than was provided by revivalism.[58]

The revivalist mentality presented an expectation that, because individuals were totally depraved anyway, children were born into sin and expected to sow wild oats, particularly through their teen years. The anticipation, however, was that by means of a specific event, the Holy Spirit would place the sinner under such conviction that the misery of the conviction

---

[55] Mullin, *The Puritan and the Yankee*, 22.

[56] Mark H. Senter, "Horace Bushnell, Theodore Cuyler, and Francis Clark: A Study of How Youth Ministry Began," *Journal of Youth Ministry* 2, no. 2 (2004): 39.

[57] H. Shelton Smith, ed., *Horace Bushnell* (New York, NY: Oxford, 1965), 43.

[58] Senter, "How Youth Ministry Began," 39-40.

would lead to a specific event of radical conversion. While not disavowing that legitimate conversions occur in this manner, Bushnell was convinced that the overall expectation was wrong and that it neglected the spiritual nurture, especially of children.[59] He believed that children are "in a sense, included in the faith of their parents, partakers with them in their covenant, and brought into a peculiar relationship to God, in virtue of it ... They are to grow up as Christians, or spiritually renewed persons. As to the precise time or manner in which they are to receive the germ of holy principle, nothing is affirmed."[60] Though unintentional, the revivalist movement had dichotomized the concept of salvation from the family — a divide that Bushnell sought to bridge.

Reacting to this, Bushnell noted that there were two ways of growing the church. The first was through conquest, a coercive means by which the members are amassed rapidly through sudden and emotional conversion. The second alternative, and the one more preferable to Bushnell, was what he called "organic growth," in which the family played the most vital role. This concept of organic growth foreshadowed the imminent religious education movement and became known more specifically as "Christian nurture."

CHRISTIAN NURTURE: BUSHNELL'S THEOLOGY OF CHRISTIAN EDUCATION

Bushnell held a unique doctrine of the family. He considered it a unity, a body, and that "a power over character is inserted therein, which cannot properly be called influence."[61] This power is exerted by parents over children "not only when they teach, encourage, persuade, and govern, but without any purposed control whatever."[62] Bushnell wrote further that the child "sees the world through his parents' eyes. Their objects become his. Their life and spirit mold him. If they are carnal, coarse, passionate, profane, sensual, devilish, his little plastic nature takes the poison of course ... He lives and moves and has his being in them."[63] The parents' power is absolute before the child learns to reason, and it affects the child throughout his life. Bushnell felt that a long line of godly fathers and mothers might induce a religious temperament in the child, producing a godly consciousness and stemming his tendency to compromise his integrity. Character development begins even in early infancy, for it is never too early for good

---

[59] Ibid., 41-42.

[60] Horace Bushnell, "The Kingdom of God as a Grain of Mustard Seed," *New Englander* 2 (1844): 610.

[61] H. Bushnell, *Christian Nurture* (New York, NY: Scribner, 1861), 93.

[62] Ibid., 94.

[63] Ibid., 106-107.

to be communicated. Infancy and childhood are the ages in which children are most malleable to good. Bushnell baptized infants primarily because of his belief in the unity of the family — illustrated in the New Testament by the baptism of entire families — and he accepted them into church membership: "The propriety of this membership does not lie in what those infants can or cannot believe, or do or do not believe, at some given time, as, for example, on the day of their baptism; but it lies in the covenant of promise, which makes their parents, parents in the Lord; their nurture, a nurture of the Lord; and so constitutes a force of futurition by which they are to grow up, imperceptibly, into "faithfuls among faithfuls," in Christ Jesus."[64] This led to Bushnell's view that the child born in a Christian home is to be nurtured, not converted. Bushnell explained his oft-repeated axiom that

> The child is to grow up a Christian and never know himself as being otherwise. In other words, the aim, effort, and expectation should be, not, as is commonly assumed, that the child is to grow up in sin, to be converted after he comes to a mature age; but that he is to open on the world as one that is spiritually renewed, not remembering the time when he went through a technical experience, but seeming rather to have loved what is good from his earliest years. I do not affirm that every child may, in fact and without exception, be so trained that he certainly will grow up a Christian.[65]

Bushnell anticipated orthodox reaction to his view of Christian nurture in a sermon on regeneration. Crucial to his defense was his definition of a Christian:

> But my child is a sinner, you will say; and how can I expect him to begin a right life, until God gives him a new heart? This is the common way of speaking, and I state the objection in its own phraseology, that it may recognize itself. Who then has told you that a child cannot have the new heart of which you speak? Whence do you learn that if you live the life of Christ, before him and with him, the law of the Spirit of Life may not be such as to include and quicken him also? And why should it be thought incredible that there should be some really good principle awakened in the mind of a child? For this is all that is implied in a Christian state. The Christian is one who has simply begun to love what is good for its own sake, and why should it be thought impossible for a child to have this love begotten in him?[66]

Bushnell implied that the child achieves right standing before God by living the "good life."

---

[64] Bushnell, *Christian Nurture*, 166-167.

[65] Horace Bushnell, *Sermons for the New Life* (New York, NY: Scribner, 1867b), 4.

[66] Ibid., 9.

But how can the young child do good when he has no will of his own, or believe when he has no power to comprehend or make rational choices? Bushnell believed that the parents' faith includes faith on the part of the child and that the righteous nature of the parents is transmitted to the child. He argued that if evil can be imputed to children, as the Calvinists believed, righteousness can also be imputed to them. He discerned a natural flow of Christian life from the parent to the child, a flow that continues as the child grows and that finally diminishes as he matures.

> This is the very idea of Christian education, that it begins with nurture or cultivation. And the intention is that the Christian life and spirit of the parents, which are in and by the Spirit of God, shall flow into the mind of the child, to blend with his incipient and half-formed exercises; that they shall thus beget their own good within him — their thoughts, opinions, faith, and love, which are to become a little more, and yet a little his own separate exercise, but still the same in character.[67]

Bushnell also anticipated two more possible objections to his views. He did not hold to a liberal, humanistic concept of human nature, nor did he replace the work of the Holy Spirit in the regeneration of children with the work of parents: "The strong language I have used concerning the organic connection of character between the parents and the child ... is not designed to assert [that there is] a power in the parent to renew the child, or that the child can be renewed by any agency of the Spirit less immediate than that which renews the parent himself."[68] Bushnell distinguished between children of Christian parents and those of unbelievers; the former are to be nurtured, the latter converted.

Bushnell's view of Christian nurture was by no means rejected in all orthodox circles. Charles Hodge, a Princetonian Calvinist, who was one of the best-known theologians of the day summarized the central truth of *Christian Nurture*: "There is an intimate and divinely established connexion between the faith of parents and the salvation of their children; such a connexion as authorizes them to plead God's promises, and to expect with confidence, that through his blessing on their faithful efforts, their children will grow up the children of God."[69] Hodge considered this "the great truth ... that gives [Bushnell's] book its chief value," although he thought the form in which this truth appeared in *Christian Nurture* to be

---

[67] Bushnell, *Sermons for the New Life*, 21.

[68] Ibid., 22.

[69] Charles Hodge, "Bushnell on Christian Nurture," *Biblical Repertory and Princeton Review* 19 (1847): 502.

"strange" and "distorted."[70] Arthur Cushman McGiffert credited Bushnell's *Christian Nurture* with doing "more than any other single factor to break down the extreme individualism of the old Puritanism."[71] Yet others acknowledge this work as the pilot light that later ignited the twentieth-century religious education movement.

CONTRIBUTION TO CHRISTIAN EDUCATION

Bushnell's concept of Christian nurture found a voice at a unique time in the nation; individual states were beginning to adopt educational reforms as churches began rethinking how they propagated religious education. As the Second Great Awakening began to subside in the late 1830s, the common school movement was gaining momentum under the leadership of Horace Mann. In his own effort to bridge the divide between Calvinists and Unitarians while also safeguarding the future of tax-supported schools, Mann — a Unitarian himself — proposed that public schools should not teach sectarian religion. Teachers could present Bible readings without doctrinal commentary and could pray generic Christian prayers, but overall, particular denominational doctrines would not be taught.

The Sunday school movement, which was already well underway, stepped up at this point to carry the torch of teaching biblical doctrine. From the 1790s until the common school movement, Sunday schools had primarily offered basic academic skills for children and even some adults who were too busy working in industrial manufacturing plants during the week to attend school and who were too poor to pay for education otherwise. Influenced by revivalism, however, the purpose and curriculum of the Sunday school evolved. As common schools became more prevalent, Sunday schools surrendered to them the task of teaching basic literacy and ciphering skills and shifted their emphasis to preparing children for the future moment in which they would be converted to the Christian faith.[72] This was antithetical to Bushnell's nurturing model, which called Christian educators to bring up children in the faith and not for some dubious future conversion.

NATURE OF THE LEARNER

Models of education flow from the basic question of the nature of the learner: Are children inherently good or sinful? Innocent or depraved? Romantic notions of the natural goodness of children were spreading in nineteenth-century America from Europeans such as Rousseau, Pestalozzi, Herbart, and Froebel. This impact was seen in the Unitarian definition

---

[70] Ibid.

[71] Arthur Cushman McGiffert, *The Rise of Modern Religious Ideals* (New York, NY: Macmillan, 1915), 277.

[72] Kathan, "Horace Bushnell," 45.

of sin as "a neutral state of incompleteness."[73] Bushnell rejected this definition of sin. Having himself been influenced by the Romantics through the writings of Coleridge and Emerson, Bushnell also refused to embrace fully the Calvinist doctrine that children are totally depraved. From the Calvinist perspective, children should be educated to develop a sense of their own sinfulness, which was a prerequisite for them to come one day to salvation.[74] Bushnell, holding to a more moderate concept of limited depravity, argued that "a self-accusing spirit of sin" hinders redemption rather than advancing it."[75]

Bushnell has been credited with reversing the then traditional practice of regarding a child's nature "in precisely the same manner as adults, with no recognition of any differences in their religious characteristics or in their normal religious experiences."[76] He alleged that learners are living organisms developing through stages — yet another Romantic notion espoused specifically by Rousseau.[77] The most critical stage in the nurturing process, Bushnell noted, is what he termed the "age of impressions." This stage occurs even before the child learns to speak and is when parents can have the greatest impact on the child's character development.[78]

ROLE OF TEACHERS AND PARENTS

By its very emphasis on organicism, *Christian Nurture* clearly was addressed to an audience of parents who would instruct in the home rather than to teachers in a classroom environment. On the question of the role of churches and schools, Bushnell remained vague. Nevertheless, the principles of which he wrote for parents may be applied by any adult in a nurturing role to children. As Lockerbie commented, "No person presuming to love God and love children can be free from this responsibility [of providing children a Christian upbringing] — just as no Christian educator can afford to ignore the influence of Horace Bushnell's *Christian Nurture*."[79]

Bushnell's model of nurture was not strictly a maternal one. He called for both father-centered and mother-centered nurture,[80] and although vague about the specific role of churches and schools, he certainly included them in his concept of "organic unity," which represented naturally-occurring, close relationships. These relationships would involve the

[73] Makowski, *Bushnell on Christian Character*, 48.
[74] Ryan, "Puritan's of Today," 217.
[75] Bushnell, *Christian Nurture*, 212-213.
[76] Sandford Fleming, *Children and Puritanism* (New Haven, CT: Yale University), 185.
[77] Kathan, "Horace Bushnell," 42.
[78] Senter, "How Youth Ministry Began," 40.
[79] Lockerbie, *Passion for Learning*, 296.
[80] Morita, *Women in Nineteenth-Century America*, 6.

family, church, and nation — the family being a microcosm of the church, the church being an enlarged family, and the nation being born out of the church and mirroring its structure. Organic unity was in opposition to the individualism Bushnell found in revivalism. No soul, he felt, acts as an independent entity, but all entities within an organic unity are interdependent. Therefore, the roles of the family, church, and nation are naturally woven together. It would not be the individualism of personal conversion that would spread Christianity through the nation, but it would be the organic unity of family, church, and nation.[81]

INSTRUCTIONAL METHODS

Bushnell did not propose a specific pedagogical method, but he did develop a model of education for parents to implement in the home. He developed five principles in particular:

(1) many things are to be taught "not formally or theologically, but implicitly, in a kind of child's version";

(2) the child's times of interest should be watched for, and religion should not be thrust upon him when it is unwelcome;

(3) the child's questions should be carefully listened to and answered;

(4) teaching should be centered about Jesus Christ, as himself the truth incarnate, and the parent should so live as to make his own life an interpreter of Jesus' life; and

(5) the parent should endeavor constantly "to make the subject of religion an open subject, and [to] keep it so."[82] In connection with the second principle, Bushnell advised parents to play with their children when they desire play and to teach them when they desire instruction. Bushnell urged parents to make use of their child's "instinct of imitation":

We begin our mortal experience, not with acts grounded in judgment or reason, or with ideas received through language, but by simple imitation, and, under the guidance of this, we lay our foundations. The child looks and listens, and whatsoever tone of feeling or manner of conduct is displayed around him, sinks into his plastic, passive soul, and becomes a mold of his being ever after.[83]

Parents were warned by Bushnell not to teach their children

(1) that they are "regenerated in their baptism;"

---

[81] Ibid., 89-92.

[82] George A. Coe, *The Religion of the Mature Mind* (Chicago, IL: Revell, 1962), 376-380.

[83] Horace Bushnell, "Sermons on Living Subjects," in J. L. Hurlbut, ed., *Sunday Half Hours with Great Preachers* (Philadelphia, PA: Winston, 1907), 363.

(2) that they are unregenerate heathens in need of conversion;

(3) that they need to be regenerated because of their faults or their love of play;

(4) that they are "too young to be good; or to be really Christian;"

(5) that they "can never pray, or do anything acceptable to God, till after they are converted or regenerated;" nor

(6) that they must do good works and to build character for themselves.[84]

Parents should be careful not to discourage true piety in their children by

(1) ill-temper, pettishness, and passion;

(2) "too much of prohibition;"

(3) "hard, unfeeling" government or "over-bearing absolutism;"

(4) "an over-exacting manner" or "an extreme difficulty of being pleased;"

(5) "holding displeasure too long, and yielding it with too great difficulty;"

(6) "hasty and false accusations;"

(7) anxiety and over-concern;

(8) the application of "tests of character that are inappropriate to their age"; or

(9) denying to them "an early recognition of their membership in the church, and an admission to the Lord's table."[85] Regarding the issue of family government, which Bushnell explained elsewhere is

(1) "to be government, using authority and maintaining laws and rules over the moral nature of the child";

(2) "to be regarded as a vicegerent of authority, set up by God and ruling in His place";

(3) "to bear rule for the same ends that God Himself pursues, in the religious order of the world"; and

(4) "to secure ... a style of obedience in the child that amounts to a real piety."[86] The home, indwelled by "a domestic Spirit of grace," should be "the church of childhood, the table and hearth, a holy rite ... " In the home, "Christ Himself, by that renewing Spirit who can sanctify from the womb, should be practically infused into the childish mind."[87]

Bushnell's approach to education — exhibiting a greater interest in experiences and imitation than in the transmission of content or in indoctrination — was a forerunner of

---

[84] Bushnell, *Christian Nurture*, 12.

[85] Ibid., 295-308.

[86] Bushnell, *Sermons for the New Life*, xviii.

[87] Bushnell, *Christian Nurture*, 12.

religious educational practice a century later. He "put himself, perhaps unconsciously, into the central current of the great educational reform of the nineteenth century."[88] By directing parents to teach in a manner appropriate to the age of the child, by valuing play, and by addressing the problems of language, Bushnell touched on many issues that developmental psychologists, such as Piaget and Vygotsky, would not introduce into the common pedagogical narrative until the twentieth century.[89]

RELIGIOUS EDUCATION MOVEMENT

It was fifty-six years after the first edition of Bushnell's *Christian Nurture* before William Rainey Harper founded the Religious Education Association in 1903. How, then, may it be argued that Bushnell's teachings served as the pilot light to ignite the religious education movement? Harper was exposed to Bushnell's ideas by Henry Clay Trumbull, a pioneer in the U.S. Sunday school movement. Trumbull often echoed Bushnell's sermons refuting the common notion that children were incapable of having a relationship with God through Christ in their childhood years.[90] According to Trumbull, Bushnell's impression of the Sunday school improved over time.[91] In Bushnell's eyes, the Sunday school deserved much higher regard than did revivals and other attempts to spread Christianity in America.

Delayed acceptance of the Christian nurture model may be attributed to a variety of factors: (1) the prevailing religious traditionalism hindered the acceptance of new ideas; (2) common schools in their infancy were themselves narrow, traditional, and repressive; (3) the notion of developmental stages of learning was absent from the dominant discourse on childhood; and (4) radical conversion was valued over an organic spiritual growth model of salvation.[92] Well into the late nineteenth century, with distinguished preaching from Charles G. Finney and Dwight L. Moody, revivalism continued to be the preferred avenue for church growth. Additionally, with the final edition of *Christian Nurture* released in 1861, the Civil War and Reconstruction may have postponed people from considering new ideas.

By the twentieth century, however, religious teaching had been drastically minimized in the public schools, compelling the church to become more open to new ideas of how to cultivate Christianity among children. Psychologist G. Stanley Hall's work in childhood

---

[88] Coe, *Mature Mind*, 305.

[89] Kathan, "Horace Bushnell," 44.

[90] Ibid., 41-46.

[91] Ibid., 46.

[92] Ibid., 50-51.

development was gaining a great deal of attention among educators both in the public schools and in the Christian arena, and — despite the prominence of Billy Sunday and other evangelists — revivals did not intrigue twentieth-century religious seekers as they previously had done. Eventually, these and many other cultural changes paved the way for Bushnell's ideas to hold great sway over the methods used to educate children within the church.[93] So much so that George A. Coe, widely considered to be the father of the religious education movement, held him up as one of the most important figures in the history of religious education in America: "If it were necessary to give a date to mark the transition to the modern conception of Christian training, we could not do better than to name the year 1847, which saw the first issue of Horace Bushnell's *Christian Nurture*."[94] Of Bushnell's dictum that "the child is to grow up a Christian and never know himself as being otherwise," Paul H. Vieth wrote that it "is now widely known and accepted."[95]

CONCLUSION

Horace Bushnell's optimistic view of human nature burst like a rocket into the black night of what many historians, psychologists, and theologians have referred to as the "pessimism of Calvinism" in New England. He reflected the growing American middle-class confidence in the reforming powers of good men — with the help of natural science and the Industrial Revolution — and its shift away from the dogmatic, creedal approach to Christianity to a more scientific one. Bushnell was a member of the growing American cult of education, believing that education can solve any problem, even the religious ones.

PRIMARY SOURCE SAMPLE[96]

The most genuine teaching, or only genuine teaching, will be that which interprets the truth to the child's feeling by living example, and makes him love the truth afterwards for the teacher's sake. It is a great thing for a child, in all the afterlife, to 'know of whom' he learned these things, and to see a godly father, or a faithful mother, in them. No truth is really taught by words, or interpreted by intellectual and logical methods; truth must be lived into meaning, before it can be truly known. Examples are the only sufficient commentaries; living epistles the only fit expounders of written epistles.

---

[93] Kathan, "Horace Bushnell," 52.

[94] Coe, *Mature Mind*, 305.

[95] Paul H. Vieth, *The Church and Christian Education* (St. Louis, MO: Bethany), 20.

[96] Bushnell, *Christian Nurture*, 370.

BIBLIOGRAPHY

Albanese, Catherine L. "Horace Bushnell among the Metaphysicians." *Church History* 79, no. 3 (2010): 614-653.

Bratt, James D. Review of *The Puritan and Yankee: A life of Horace Bushnell*, by R. B. Mullin. *Journal of Religion,* 83, no. 4 (October 2003): 627-628.

Bushnell, Horace. "The Kingdom of God as a Grain of Mustard Seed. *New Englander* 2 (1844): 610.

_____. *Nature and the Supernatural*. New York, NY: Scribner, 1858.

_____. *Christian Nurture*. New York, NY: Scribner, 1861.

_____. *God in Christ*. Hartford, CT: Hamersby, 1867a.

_____. *Sermons for the New Life*. New York, NY: Scribner, 1867b.

_____. *Vicarious Sacrifice*. New York, NY: Scribner, 1877.

_____. "Our Gospel a Gift to the Imagination." *Literacy Varieties,* 3 (1881), 249.

_____. "Sermons on Living Subjects." In J. L. Hurlbut, ed., *Sunday Half Hours with Great Preachers*. Philadelphia, PA: Winston, 1907.

Cheney, Mary A. *Life and Letter of Horace Bushnell*. New York, NY: Harper, 1937.

Coe, George A. *The Religion of the Mature Mind*. Chicago, IL: Revell, 1962.

Dorrien, Gary. *The Making of American Liberal Theology: Imagining Progressive Religion 1805-1900*. Louisville, KY: Westminster John KnoxPress, 2001.

Fleming, Sandford. *Children and Puritanism*. New Haven, CT: Yale University, 1933.

Hodge, Charles. "Bushnell on Christian Nurture." *Biblical Repertory and Princeton Review* 19 (1847), 502-538.

Kathan, Boardman W. "Horace Bushnell and the Religious Education Movement." *Religious Education* 108, no. 1 (2013): 41-57.

Lockerbie, D. Bruce. *A Passion for Learning: A History of Christian Thought on Education*. Colorado Springs, CO: Purposeful Design, 2007.

Makowski, Lee J. *Horace Bushnell on Christian Character Development*. Lanham, MD: University Press of America, 1999.

McGiffert, Arthur Cushman. *The Rise of Modern Religious Ideas*. New York, NY: Macmillan, 1915.

Morita, Michiyo. *Horace Bushnell on Women in Nineteenth-Century America*. Lanham, MD: University Press of America, 2004.

Mouheb, Roberta Buckingham. *Yale under God: Roots and Fruits*. Maitland, FL: Xulon Press, 2012.

Mullin, Robert Bruce. *The Puritan as Yankee: A Life of Horace Bushnell*. Grand Rapids, MI: William B. Eerdmans, 2002.

Olson, Roger E. "Remembering the 'Progressive Orthodoxy' of Horace Bushnell." *Patheos Blogs*, August 11, 2012. Accessed May 4, 2014. http://www.patheos.com/blogs/rogereolson/2012/08/remembering-the-progressive-orthodoxy-of-horace-bushnell-part-one/.

Ottati, Douglas F. Review of *Horace Bushnell on Christian Character Development*, by L. J. Makowski. *Journal of Religion* 81, no. 3 (July 2001): 480-481.

Ryan, Michael. "'The Puritans of Today': The Anti-Whig Argument of *The Scarlet Letter*." *Canadian Review of American Studies* 38, no. 2 (2008): 201-225.

Senter, Mark H. "Horace Bushnell, Theodore Cuyler, and Francis Clark: A Study of How Youth Ministry Began." *Journal of Youth Ministry* 2, no 2 (2004): 31-51.

Smith, H. Shelton., ed. *Horace Bushnell*. New York, NY: Oxford, 1965.

Vieth, Paul J. *The Church and Christian Education*. St. Louis, MO: Bethany, 1947.

Woolsey, Theodore Dwight. "Sketch of the Life of Professor William A. Larned." *New Englander and Yale Review* 21, no. 2 (1862): 324-340.

CHAPTER 21

John Henry Newman:

Education that Integrates Faith and Learning

BOB DROVDAHL

John Henry Newman (1801 – 1890)

John Henry Newman, also known as Cardinal Newman, had a great influence on the Roman Catholic Church in England and Ireland during the 1800s. Originally, Newman was a priest in the Church of England, attached to Oxford University from which he graduated. He was a leader in the Tractarian Movement, which included 91 tracts arguing for a merger of the Church of England with the Roman Catholic Church. Newman wrote the first and last tracts, and thereafter left the Church of England to be received in the Roman Catholic Church and was eventually granted the title Cardinal by Pope Leo XIII. Newman founded the Catholic University of Ireland, which eventually was called University College of Dublin. Today it is the largest university in Ireland. Newman had a great influence in changing the religious firmament in Ireland from predominantly Protestant to devoutly Roman Catholic.

HISTORICAL BACKGROUND

On July 18, 1851, Paul Cullen, the Archbishop of Armagh, Ireland paid a visit to John Henry Newman in Birmingham, England with a job offer in hand. The invitation was to establish and lead a Catholic University of Ireland in Dublin.[1] Two years earlier, Cullen had convened a gathering of bishops and clergy, known as the Synod of Thurles, to address issues relevant to predominantly Roman Catholic Ireland. One commitment coming out of the synod was the desire to establish a Catholic university there. After securing the Pope's blessing and now ready to move forward on the commitment, the advice to Archbishop Cullen was to "first get Newman."[2] Newman accepted the offer and traveled to Ireland from September 30 to October 8, 1851, to meet with Cullen and the subcommittee assigned to organize the university. On November 12, Newman was officially appointed head of the new Catholic University.[3]

Over the next year, Newman prepared to open the new university. This preparation included laying the conceptual groundwork for the university. Between May and November of 1852, Newman delivered and published nine lectures on the nature of a university education and the relationship between religion and education. These nine lectures, plus additional lectures on particular university disciplines and subject matter Newman delivered between 1854 and 1858, were eventually published in 1873 under the title, *The Idea of a University*. Newman's ideas about Christian education, applied to a university context, have been enormously influential. As one biographer extols, "Modern thinking on university education is a series of footnotes to Newman's lectures and essays."[4]

Before examining Newman's impact on Christian education, we should note that *Christian education* has long carried two meanings. For some, *Christian education* describes a particular worldview on the purposes and processes of education. The focus is a theological perspective on education. For others, *Christian education* refers to educating people in the Christian faith; therefore, the focus is on forming people in Christian faith. Newman's thought and work fits the former understanding. To speak precisely, Newman proposed a Christian theology of (university) *education*, not a theology of Christian *formation*. Newman argued for theology's critical role in a proper understanding of education. In this chapter, we examine the argument he makes in *The Idea of a University*. We begin with a brief biographical sketch

---

[1] Brian Martin, *John Henry Newman, His Life and Work* (New York: Paulist Press, 1990), 92.

[2] Jaroslav Pelikan, *The Idea of a University – A Reexamination* (New Haven: Yale University Press, 1992), 5.

[3] Martin, *John Henry Newman*, 99.

[4] J.M. Cameron, *John Henry Newman* (London: Longmans, Green, 1956), 25.

of Newman's life and explore the cultural contexts which made the argument necessary. Next we analyze the argument's main points by identifying the four key theological principles that shaped Newman's thinking about education. Finally, we consider implications for those working in the field of practical theology, particularly those committed to the teaching ministry of the Church.

THE BIOGRAPHICAL CONTEXT: UNDERSTANDING THE DESIRE TO "GET NEWMAN"

By the mid-19th century, Newman was already established as a substantial Roman Catholic educator and theologian. Though Newman was British by birth and Roman Catholic by conversion, each of these three descriptors – educator, Roman Catholic, and theologian – offers some insight into why Newman was chosen to lead the creation of a Catholic university in Ireland. We consider each in turn.

Newman the Educator

Born on February 21, 1801, into an Anglican family, Newman had a relatively unremarkable upbringing. A serious-minded student, Newman entered Trinity College, Oxford in June 1817, shortly after his sixteenth birthday.[5] Impressed with his hard work during his first year at Trinity, Newman's tutor, Thomas Short, encouraged him to apply for a scholarship. On May 18, 1818, Newman learned that he had been awarded the scholarship and named a Scholar of Trinity.[6] Though Newman studied fastidiously (twelve-hour reading days were common), the success was short-lived. Two years later, he failed to achieve success in his final examinations in mathematics and classics. He left Oxford, but returned in 1821 since he still had use of his scholarship. This time around, Newman's study habits were better balanced and in April 1822, he was elected as an Oriel Fellow. During his time at Oriel (1822-1828), Newman was ordained, became a tutor, and developed his basic views on the essential nature and purpose of a university education. These ideas were further refined in his years as vicar of the University Church of St. Mary the Virgin at Oxford.[7]

Newman the Roman Catholic

Newman's spiritual journey took him from an evangelical conversion experience at age fifteen to a Catholic expression of faith at age forty-four. Newman's conversion experience

---

[5] Martin, 16, 22.

[6] Ibid., 22.

[7] Ibid., 27.

took place in the fall of 1816, a few months prior to entering Trinity College. Part of his conversion experience was a deep sense of God's call on his life. While he was uncertain about the exact nature of his vocational call (he was attracted to missionary work), he was convinced it would require him to live sacrificially. This experience helped set him on a path to ordination in the Church of England, achieved in 1824. This experience also provided a very conservative anchor to Newman's doctrinal commitments. As he later stated, "I fell under the influences of a definite creed, and received into my intellect impressions of dogma, which through God's mercy, have never been effaced or obscured."[8]

The conservative tendencies eventually moved Newman away from both his evangelical commitments and from his Anglican roots and relationships. The latter took hold over a nearly fifteen-year time period, during which Newman worked diligently to purify the Anglican Church against perceived threats from creeping secularism and liberal politics. His efforts were chiefly expressed though the Oxford Movement and the publication of *Tracts for the Times,* a series of ninety publications aimed at returning the Church of England to its apostolic roots. The problem Newman faced was that the three principal arguments undergirding the efforts to purify the Church of England – the importance of tradition, apostolic succession, and separation of church and state – all were equally compelling arguments for the primacy of the Roman Catholic Church. In *Tract 90: Remarks on Certain Passages in the Thirty-nine Articles*, published in 1841, Newman argued that Anglican teachings and "true" Roman Catholic teachings were not incompatible. For this claim, Newman was condemned by the Anglican Church hierarchy. He withdrew from the fray and resigned his post at St. Mary's in 1843. Two years later, Newman became a Roman Catholic and then in 1847 was ordained as a priest.[9]

Though Newman's switch to Roman Catholic faith was personally costly, he entered "full-throttle." In addition to ordination, he busied himself with writing projects and work projects. Chief among the writing projects was his *Essay on the Development of Doctrine,* published in 1845, the same year Newman was received into the Roman Catholic Church. Chief among his work projects was the establishment of the Birmingham Oratory, an intentional community of priests authorized by Pope Pius IX. While at Birmingham, Newman received the invitation to lead the founding of a Catholic university for Ireland.[10]

---

[8] John Henry Newman, *Apologia Pro Vita Sua*, (London: Longmans, Green, and Co., 1904), 2.

[9] Sheridan Gilley, "Life and Writings" in *John Henry Newman*, ed. by Ian Ker and Terrence Merrigan. (Cambridge: Cambridge University Press, 2009), 11.

[10] Ibid., 13-14.

Newman the Theologian

Though he did not consider himself a theologian,[11] Newman's theological works deeply influenced Catholic theology and earned him accolades as "the most important English theologian of the last two centuries."[12] His most important theological work was the *Essay on the Development of Christian Doctrine*. In this book, Newman considers how continuity in Christian teaching can be maintained in the face of many changes in Christian doctrine over the centuries. Newman's argument is largely philosophical; he provides a set of seven criteria by which development can be differentiated from distortion. Later in the chapter, we will see the importance of this theological principle for Newman's approach to higher education. We now turn to Newman's social context.

THE CULTURAL CONTEXT: UNDERSTANDING WHY "GETTING NEWMAN" MATTERED

The Idea of a University provided the position statement that underwrote Newman's great achievement in Christian education — founding the Catholic University of Ireland. Yet this work was not done in a vacuum. Establishing a Catholic university was a response to prevailing cultural trends viewed as inimical to Christian faith and Catholic faith in particular. Industrialization, modernity, the Enlightenment, and other forces of change were sweeping across the landscape, bringing into question traditional understandings of the place of religion in society. We will examine three forces of change Newman addressed.

The Scientific Revolution

It is clear that science, with its findings and attendant principles of experimentation and inductive reasoning, was creating tensions for religion. From Copernicus (1473-1543) to Galileo (1564-1642) to Newton (1642-1727) to Darwin (1809-1882), scientific findings were questioning traditional understandings of the universe's workings. While the story of these tensions could have been told in various ways, opposition from official Christianity led to a "Science vs. Religion" narrative. This dominant narrative included *scientism*, the belief that science could explain all phenomena in the universe. Though the commonly accepted founder of modern science, Francis Bacon, was a devout Christian, subsequent philosophers

---

[11] Ian Ker, *The Achievement of John Henry Newman* (Notre Dame: University of Notre Dame Press, 1990), 96.

[12] Harold L. Weatherby, *Cardinal Newman in His Age* (Nashville: Vanderbilt University Press, 1973), 1.

of science became more antagonistic to religious claims. By Newman's day, many intellectuals had accepted the "science trumps religion" narrative.[13] Through both his intellectual defense and the creation of a Catholic university, Newman hoped to turn the narrative around.

Theological Liberalism

An earlier narrative told a much more harmonious story of science and religion. Science was the appropriate means of studying God's creation. Francis Bacon, often considered the founder of the scientific method, believed there were two books available for humans to study — the book of nature, which revealed the work of God, and the book of scripture, which revealed the will of God.[14] Despite this beginning point, it was not long before God's "work" became an event of the distant past. Belief in a providential God who continued to superintend creation shifted toward deism, with little interest in a living, active God revealed through the created order. Newman considered this form of theology, which he called *physical theology*, the fashion of the day and not worthy of being called a science, since "it is ordinarily nothing more than a series of pious or polemical remarks upon the physical world viewed religiously."[15] Newman believed the doctrinal claims derived from physical theology were so weak that they were tantamount to using the word *God* and meaning nothing by it.[16]

A second theological shift in Newman's day sought to confine religion to the realm of affect and opinion rather than the realm of facts and truth. Newman vigorously objected to a view which he believed was prevalent in Great Britain — the idea "that Religion consists, not in knowledge, but in feeling or sentiment."[17] Newman recognized the logical consequences of such a belief and thought it would be disastrous for the role of religion in higher education. "Where it prevails, it is as unreasonable to demand for Religion a chair in a University, as to demand one for fine feeling, sense of honour, patriotism, gratitude, maternal affection, or good companionship, proposals which would be simply unmeaning."[18]

---

[13] John Henry Newman, *The Idea of a University*, ed. by Frank M. Turner (New Haven: Yale University Press, 1996), xvii.

[14] Francis Bacon, *The Advancement of Learning*, ed. by G. W. Kitchin (London: J. M. Dent & Sons, Ltd., 1973), 41-42.

[15] Newman, *Idea of a University*, 46.

[16] Ibid., 28.

[17] Ibid., 21.

[18] Ibid., 22.

The Secular University

The first half of the nineteenth century saw the founding of many universities characterized by a new trend — they had no professors of theology. This occurred in America, where Thomas Jefferson founded the University of Virginia in 1819 with no theology faculty. In England, the University College London was established in 1826 with no theology faculty and no denominational test for admission.[19] The tipping point was the founding of The Queen's Colleges in Ireland in 1845, which established three colleges in Ireland, none of which offered coursework in theology. The reasons for these trends were varied. In America, constitutional separation of church and state seemed to preclude theological teaching at public institutions. In Great Britain and Ireland, colleges were denomination-specific. Dublin had Trinity College, but it was only for Anglicans. Elsewhere, more "utilitarian" oriented colleges emphasizing technical education and training were established. In these institutions, the liberal arts, including theological studies, were deemed unnecessary. The proposal to establish The Queen's Colleges as a nonsectarian institution was roundly criticized by Pope Pious IX. The wheels were thus set in motion to establish a Catholic university for Ireland. We now turn to Newman's argument against these cultural trends.

ORIENTING PRINCIPLES: BASIC THEOLOGICAL PERSPECTIVES

Newman was well aware of the human tendency to construct worldviews.[20] He believed this capacity separated humans' use of their senses from the "brute's use of them." Newman called this constructive work philosophizing: "the habit of *viewing* ... the objects which sense conveys to the mind, of throwing them into system, and uniting and stamping them with one form."[21] It included actions such as discerning beauty, differentiating accidents and designs, distinguishing rules and exceptions, and connecting causes with effects. Newman considered this method of viewing so natural that we "often put up with insufficient or absurd views or interpretations of what we meet with, rather than have none at all ... We cannot do without a view, and we put up with an illusion, when we cannot get a truth."[22]

---

[19] Gerard Loughlin, "The University Without Question: John Henry Newman and Jacques Derrida on Faith in the University" in *The Idea of a Christian University: Essays in Theology and Higher Education,* ed. by Jeff Astley, Leslie J. Francis, John Sullivan, and Andrew Walker (Milton Keynes, UK: Paternoster Press, 2004), 122.

[20] A person's worldview is typical understood as the basic beliefs and assumptions that orient a person's perspective and interpretation of life.

[21] Newman, *Idea of a University*, 56.

[22] Ibid., 56-57

What was Newman's theological worldview? How did Newman make theological sense of the social and religious events and movements described in the preceding section? Four orienting theological principles seemed to guide his thinking about Christian education. First, Newman accepted the distinction between general and special revelation and the pathway to truth which governed each form of revelation. Second, Newman believed in the power of education to improve human nature, but believed God's grace was needed to perfect human nature. Third, Newman was fearlessly optimistic about all forms of knowledge leading to truth. In contemporary terms, he believed all truth was God's truth. Finally, though he was optimistic about truth, Newman recognized that human knowledge was always an approximation of the truth. Thus he saw most claims to truth as tentative and subject to correction and development. These four interlocking principles comprised the fundamental perspective Newman brought to his idea of a Christian university. After a brief explanation and illustration of each, we will then examine the case Newman makes for a Christian theology of education.

GENERAL AND SPECIAL REVELATION

According to Newman, the importance of this classic theological division rests not in how God's self-disclosing revelation comes to humanity, but in human inquiry regarding these forms of revelation and the knowledge derived from such inquiry. In his lecture on Christianity and physical science (medicine), Newman states, "We may divide knowledge, then, into natural and supernatural ... By the supernatural world is meant that still more marvelous and awful universe, of which the Creator Himself is the fullness, and which becomes known to us, not through our natural faculties, but by superadded and direct communication from Him."[23]

Newman recognized that these two forms of revelation pursued their own distinctive methods of inquiry. Theology operates by deductive logic; physical science operates by inductive logic. Theology relies on received tradition; physical science relies on experimentation. Theology lacks material phenomena upon which to act; physical science has a wealth of information upon which to act. These contrasts resulted in conflict between the two approaches, since "neither of them has been quite content to remain on its own homestead, but that, whereas each has its own method, which is best for its own science, each has considered it the best for all purposes whatever, and has at different times thought to impose it upon the other science,

---

[23] Ibid., 323.

to the disparagement or rejection of that opposite method which legitimately belongs to it."[24] Since Newman accepted this distinction, his solution to the conflict was for the two approaches to show mutual respect while maintaining good boundaries between them. Each should remain in its own sphere. Newman acknowledged that *scientists* and *theologians* have quarreled, but he was convinced that *science* and *theology* could reach a relational plane where quarreling was unnecessary because both revealed God's truth — though in different ways. [25]

Newman appealed to the benefits of both theological and scientific inquiry. This perspective is very similar to the approach taken today in practical theology disciplines such as Christian education. For example, in *Introduction to Practical Theology*, Richard Osmer defines the practical theologian's task as four-fold: 1) A descriptive-empirical task — gathering information that help us see patterns in our experience, 2) an interpretive task — using theory in the arts and sciences to understand these patterns, 3) a normative task – bringing theology understanding and norms to bear on the experience; and 4) a pragmatic task — determining an appropriate response to the experience.[26] Good practical theology respects both theological and scientific inquiry aimed at guiding our responses to God.

GRACE PERFECTING NATURE

Newman believed that secular education — an education without any reference to revealed religion — produced positive outcomes for individuals and society. In his lecture "Knowledge Viewed in Relation to Religion," Newman extolled the role of reason in producing a "Religion of Civilization." Reason, as an agent of human nature, operates historically and teleologically to accomplish a material good in human beings, namely rescuing people from their own passions and self-will.[27] Reason draws "the mind off from things which will harm it to subjects which are worth a rational being; and though it does not raise it above nature ... surely to turn away a soul from mortal sin is a good and a gain so far, whatever comes of it."[28] To illustrate, Newman points to St. Paul's description of the virtue of love in I Corinthians 13 and then laments that "the school of the world seems to send out living copies of this typical excellence with greater success than the Church."[29] Newman concluded that, in his day, a

---

[24] Ibid., 331.

[25] Ibid., 331-332.

[26] Richard R. Osmer, *Practical Theology* (Grand Rapids, MI: Eerdmans, 2008), 4.

[27] Newman, *Idea of a University*, 141.

[28] Ibid.

[29] Ibid., 154.

"gentleman" or a "lady" was a product of civilization, not of Christianity. This is a material good, but not necessarily a spiritual good.

If an educated human nature leads to a morally upright person, of what value is religion for the moral life? Newman argued for a twofold benefit. First, religion reaches to the heart motives of the person: "The world is content with setting right the surface of things; the Church aims at regenerating the very depths of the heart."[30] Newman contrasts humility and modesty to show the difference. Since philosophical morality (Newman's term for secular ethics) focused on exterior morality, it taught the manners of modesty but neglected true humility. He believed ancient civilizations considered humility a defect, not a virtue. In contrast, the Christian religion holds humility as a virtue which "lies close upon the heart itself, and its tests are exceedingly delicate and subtle."[31]

The delicate and subtle nature of true virtue highlights the second benefit of religion for the moral life. Religion keeps "natural" morality from distortion. Modestly becomes a source of pride. Pride becomes self-respect. Self-respecting citizens would never be dogmatic or fanatical. They tolerate religion, because secular ethics have taught them "to look on all forms of faith with an impartial eye."[32] Without the correcting influence of religious truth, Newman concludes that the modest persons "which the cultivated intellect will form ... partly assist and partly distort the development of the Catholic."[33]

Newman's theological understanding of the relationship between nature and grace calls Christian educators to carefully examine the connections between *Christian* and *education*. A classic understanding of Christian education's task divides the work into a content component and a method component. *Content* answers the "what we teach and learn" question; *method* answers "how we teach and learn." If this bifurcation assumes theology is only concerned with the content question, "grace" will have no influence on the "nature" of the educational methods employed. This will surely lead to a distorted Christian education, since there will be no theological critique of educational methods.

ALL TRUTH IS GOD'S TRUTH

Newman concluded his lecture on "Christianity and Scientific Investigation" by urging upon everyone "a great and firm belief in the sovereignty of Truth."[34] Newman surely

---

[30] Ibid.
[31] Ibid., 156.
[32] Ibid., 160.
[33] Ibid., 161.
[34] Ibid., 360.

possessed this firm belief. He was open to truth, regardless of the source. In his introductory lecture laying the foundation for a *Catholic* university, Newman did not hesitate to draw on *Protestant* ideas on liberal education. He explained his reason for this saying, "Let it be observed, then, that the principles on which I would conduct the inquiry are attainable, as I have implied, by the mere experience of life. They do not come simply of theology; they imply no supernatural discernment ... and therefore, though true, and just, and good in themselves, they imply nothing whatever as to the religious profession of those who maintain them."[35] Truth could come not only from other branches of Christianity, but from those outside Christian faith entirely. Newman noted that the Church "has ever appealed and deferred to witnesses and authorities external to herself ... She has even used unbelievers and pagans in evidence of her truth, as far as their testimony went."[36] This concept undergirded his belief that a Catholic university could "pledge to admit, without fear, without prejudice, without compromise, all comers if they come in the name of Truth."[37] For Newman "Truth is bold and unsuspicious,"[38] so the pursuit of truth should be unhindered.

Of course Newman made these claims against the background of tension between theology and the human sciences. He was not blind to points of conflict between science and religion, both historically and in his own day. Newman proposed the concept of an *imperial intellect*, which adjudicated between claims to truth and moved humans along the path of truth. The imperial intellect's "one cardinal maxim ... is that truth cannot be contrary to truth; ... a second is that truth often *seems* contrary to truth; and a third is ... that we must be patient with such appearances, and not be hasty to pronounce them to be really of a more formidable character."[39] Newman used the eighth-century debate about antipodes and the sixteenth-century debate about a heliocentric solar system to illustrate how apparent conflicts between science and religion were eventually resolved. Newman believed great minds needed "elbow-room" to investigate truth according to the methods of their varied disciplines. He was confident that anything proved by "astronomer, or geologist, or chronologist, or antiquarian, or ethnologist, in contradiction to the dogmas of faith, that point will eventually turn out, first, *not* to be proved, or, secondly not *contradictory*, or thirdly, not contradictory to anything *really revealed*, but to something which has been confused with revelation."[40]

---

[35] Ibid., 4.

[36] Ibid., 5. Newman has in mind St. Paul's use of pagan poets in his Mars Hill speech in Acts 17.

[37] Ibid., 344.

[38] Ibid., 54.

[39] Ibid., 347.

[40] Ibid., 351.

This theological conviction reflects the same worldview shown in Scripture's wisdom literature, most notably Proverbs, Ecclesiastes, and Job in the Old Testament. Some would also classify the New Testament letter of James as wisdom literature. The underlying assumption of wisdom literature is that God has created an orderly moral world in which "natural consequences" reward good practices and punish evil practices. Humans are charged with discerning that order and aligning their lives accordingly. While God is the ultimate source, wisdom is gained not by special revelation, but by general revelation. Thus it is accessible to anyone willing to observe and inquire carefully into how life works. For example, one does not need a special word from God to "go to the ant, you lazybones; consider its ways, and be wise" (Prov. 6:6).[41] The truth revealed is God's truth, even though it comes indirectly. Since God is the ultimate source, the proximate source can be anyone who discovers truth. This explains why Proverbs includes aphorisms from non-Israelite sources.[42]

While it may be difficult to establish a direct lineage to Newman's belief in the unity of truth, there is no doubt Christian *higher* education has followed in his footsteps. The idea of "integrating faith and learning" is a widespread and essential identity marker for many Christian colleges and universities.[43]

DOCTRINE AS AN APPROXIMATION OF TRUTH

The epitaph (translated) on Newman's grave reads "Out of shadows and pictures into truth."[44] While the epitaph's meaning is multi-layered, it aptly describes his most important theological principle — the concept of doctrinal development. This principle undergirds his confidence in the unity of truth and his belief that theology and all other disciplines have a mutually influencing relationship. Newman "developed" this concept in *Essay on the Development of Christian Doctrine*, published in 1845, the year he was received into the Roman Catholic Church. Doctrinal development was his hypothesis to account for the difficulty of "want of accord between the early and late aspects of Christianity."[45] Newman was searching for

---

[41] Unless otherwise noted, all Bible references are to the *New Revised Standard Version* (NRSV) (Nashville: Thomas Nelson, 1989).

[42] See Proverbs 31:1, which introduces the teachings of King Lemuel's mother.

[43] In a lead article in *Christian Scholar's Review,* a journal sponsored by 32 Christian colleges and universities, William Hasker identified faith-learning integration as a key aim of the faculty in these institutions. See William Hasker, "Faith-Learning Integration: An Overview," *Christian Scholar's Review* 23 (1992): 238.

[44] "John Henry Newman: A Brief Biography," *The Victorian Web*, http://www.victorianweb.org/authors/newman/jhnbio2.html, paragraph 7 (accessed July 30, 2013).

[45] John Henry Newman, *Development of Christian Doctrine* (Notre Dame: University of Notre Dame

a theological principle that could explain the changes in Christian teaching over the centuries. In addition to a theological defense of doctrinal change, Newman was also defending his own move from Anglican to Roman Catholic. How could he move to a church with "corrupted" teachings?

Newman offered seven *tests* (called *notes* in the 1878 edition) that help discern whether a change in doctrine is *development* or *corruption*. To hypothesize the possibility of doctrinal development, Newman argued that doctrinal claims could never capture the entire truth about God and that doctrinal claims of the church were not the same as dogmatic claims of the church.

Doctrinal claims are an approximation of the truth because they involve the human knowing of an object which is unknowable in its fullness. Human knowing results in ideas formed by the mind's engagement with objects. Newman argues that these ideas are modified as we engage the object in its different aspects, encounter other perspectives, and understand the context of the ideas. He sums up this principle in an analogy: "It is indeed sometimes said that the stream is clearest near the spring. Whatever use may be fairly made of this image, it does not apply to the history of a philosophy or belief, which on the contrary is more equable, and purer, and stronger, when its bed has become deep, and broad, and full."[46] Doctrinal claims are ideas and ideas develop over time. Even though doctrinal ideas may develop over time, the *object* of those ideas will remain out of reach. Humans should pursue doctrinal truth by "following out, as far as man can, what in fullness is mysterious and unfathomable"[47]

One exception Newman made to this principle regarded *dogma*, which he differentiated from doctrinal claims. *Dogma* constituted the authoritative teaching of the church on the fundamental principles of Christianity, which Newman considered "*really revealed*." The contrast may be best demonstrated by an illustration Newman used — the conflict between Copernicus' heliocentric view of the solar system and the traditional (and religious) geocentric view. Newman acknowledges that the witness of Scripture and some authoritative tradition made it seem that a stationary earth and orbiting sun were revealed truth. Yet Newman argued that the church had never made an authoritative decision on the question, nor had she ever formally or authoritatively explained the biblical texts in a way that would contradict contemporary scientific understanding of the solar system.[48]

Press, 1989), 27.

[46] Ibid., 40.

[47] Newman, *Idea of a University*, 347.

[48] Ibid., 354.

Development is so deeply embedded in today's cultural milieu that Newman's concept of doctrinal development may seem self-evident. In addition, contemporary thinkers would quickly acknowledge the power of perspective in shaping our thoughts and ideas. The challenge today is whether any bulwark exists against a philosophical perspectivism that relativizes every truth. Newman's bulwark was a particular understanding of ecclesial authority that not all Christians would accept. Newman could say that anyone who held this belief "has no sort of apprehension, he laughs at the idea, that anything can be discovered by any other scientific method, which can contradict any one of the dogmas of his religion."[49] If Christian educators cannot hold to the infallibility of ecclesial pronouncements, they must think carefully about the limits of perspectivism. Some would argue for Scripture as a final authority for faith and practice. Others would propose various combinations of canonical voices as an adequate bulwark for truth.[50] Still others would rely on a creed or "statement of faith" to separate essential (non-negotiable) from non-essential (negotiable) teachings. Both *development* and *faithfulness* must anchor any theological framework for Christian education.

NEWMAN'S CHRISTIAN THEOLOGY OF EDUCATION: A SUMMARY

The four orienting theological principles just described weave their way throughout the lectures in *The Idea of a University*, Newman's grand argument justifying the place of theology in a university curriculum and explicating the relationship between theology and other disciplines. The opening lecture presents Newman's analysis of a university's purpose — to teach universal knowledge. He then argues that universal knowledge is only attainable if all disciplines contribute to its construction. Disciplines work in a mutually corrective way to build universal knowledge. Newman's second lecture made the case for theology as a legitimate discipline. If so, excluding it from the curriculum necessarily leaves gaps in universal knowledge. Distortions occur as other disciplines seek to fill those gaps. The only remedy is to include all disciplines, so that each has its proper role and boundary. When the truths of disciplines are brought to bear on each other, they stay in their appropriate spheres. These ideas are developed in the third and fourth lectures.

Newman's fifth, sixth, and seventh lectures address the value of learning as its own end, the relationship between knowledge and learning, and the relationship between knowledge and professional skill. In these lectures, Newman argued against the trend towards practical

---

[49] Ibid., 351.

[50] For example, see William Abraham, ed., *Canonical Theism* (Grand Rapids: Eerdmans, 2008).

and applied education — what in his day was termed *useful learning*. Newman returns to theological themes in the last two lectures. In Lecture VIII, he argues that knowledge can, without the aid of theology, *civilize* a person, but theology is needed to cultivate true Christian virtues. In the last lecture Newman considers the duties the church has towards knowledge. In the four lectures given during his tenure as rector, Newman examines particular issues in the relationship between Christianity and the humanities (the first two lectures) and Christianity and the sciences (the last two lectures).

Through these lectures, we see Newman's orienting theological principles at work, making his case for theology's place in the curriculum. While not every argument he marshals would be considered persuasive today, we do witness a Christian educator using all his persuasive power to convince his readers of the importance of theological education and laying out a roadmap for how to accomplish it. Those interested in Christian education can surely benefit from studying Newman's effort in this area.

A CHRISTIAN THEOLOGY OF EDUCATION: NEWMAN'S CONTRIBUTION THEN AND NOW

Christian education concerns the teaching ministry of the church, and Newman's influence on Christian education has been enormous. The story of Christian colleges and universities in America could not be told accurately without addressing the theme of integrating faith and learning. Whether by affirmation or critique, faith-learning integration is an unavoidable topic for anyone engaging the mission of Christian higher education and/or Christian scholars.[51] Newman's *Idea of a University* provided the ground floor for subsequent thinking on the subject. In a broad sense, Newman has contributed to the teaching ministry of the church, since so many branches of the Christian church have established higher education institutions as part of their teaching ministry.

As noted, however, there is a second side to the church's teaching ministry — a theological understanding of education for Christian formation. Does Newman's legacy offer Christian educators insight and perspective on that dimension of Christian education, especially as it is experienced in local congregations? Four contributions might be highlighted. All center on his core convictions, rather than on specific educational theories or practices.

First, Newman was absolutely convinced of the power of education as a transformative influence in people's lives. Newman believed knowledge improved people's social nature and

---

[51] Hasker, 234; See also Douglas Jacobsen and Rhonda Hustedt Jacobsen, *Scholarship and Christian Faith: Enlarging the Conversation* (New York: Oxford, 2004).

theology improved their spiritual nature. In a day when worship, community groups, and service seem to occupy center stage in the life of congregations, leaders in local congregations should pay attention to the place of *education* in congregational life.

Second, Newman was unflinchingly optimistic about the power of truth, which allowed him to be open to truth, regardless of its source. Often it seems like Christian education's primary goal is to protect and seclude students from "secular" sources or to attack those sources with strategic apologetics. In contrast, listen to Newman's attitude toward potential error: "I would venture to recommend to theologians ... a great and firm belief in the sovereignty of Truth. Error may flourish for a time, but Truth will prevail in the end. The only effect of error ultimately is to promote Truth."[52] Christian educators need to instill an attitude of fearlessness in their students.

This optimism allowed Newman to balance certainty of convictions with a strong dose of humility. When faced with ambiguity, conflict, and differing views, Newman advocated committing "the matter to reason, reflection, sober judgment, common sense; to Time, the great interpreter of so many secrets. "[53] Christian educators today need to teach with conviction on essential matters, but may also need to know when to say "I'm not sure" or "There may be more than one correct answer" or "It's okay for Christians to take different views on this topic."

Finally, Newman was convinced that theology was essential to a complete and correct education. He concluded his lecture on "Bearing of Theology on Other Knowledge" with the claim that "Religious Truth is not only a portion, but a condition of general knowledge."[54] In contemporary terms, Newman was arguing not only for the importance of theology as a subject matter in the curriculum, but also for thinking theologically about every subject in the curriculum. Christian educators today must teach students how to see all of their learning theologically, and in doing so, "take every thought captive to obey Christ." (II Cor. 10:5)

PRIMARY SOURCE SAMPLE[55]

... I would now say a word by way of deprecating and protesting against the needless antagonism, which sometimes exists in fact, between divines and the cultivators of the

---

[52] Newman, *Idea of a University*, 360.

[53] Ibid., 351.

[54] Ibid., 52-53.

[55] Two excerpts from the beginning and ending of Newman's lecture, "Christianity and Scientific Investigation," given in 1855 to the School of Science faculty at the Catholic University of Dublin, Ireland, where Newman served as Rector. Newman, *Idea of a University*, 343, 360.

Sciences generally ...

    ... And now, Gentlemen, I bring these remarks to a conclusion. What I urge upon every one, whatever may be his particular line of research, — what I urge upon men of Science in their thoughts of Theology, — what I would venture to recommend to theologians, when their attention is drawn to the subject of scientific investigations, — is a great and firm belief in the sovereignty of Truth. Error may flourish for a time, but Truth will prevail in the end. The only effect of error ultimately is to promote Truth. Theories, speculations, hypotheses are started; perhaps they are to die, still not before they have suggested ideas better than themselves. These better ideas are taken up in turn by other men, and, if they do not yet lead to truth, nevertheless they lead to what is still nearer to truth than themselves; and thus knowledge on the whole makes progress.

BIBLIOGRAPHY

Bacon, Francis. *The Advancement of Learning*. Edited by G. W. Kitchin. (London: J. M. Dent & Sons, Ltd., 1973).

Cameron, J. M. *John Henry Newman*. London: Longmans, Green, 1956.

Gilley, Sheridan. "Life and Writings." In *John Henry Newman*, edited by Ian Ker and Terrence Merrigan. Cambridge: Cambridge University Press, 2009. 1-28.

Hasker, William. "Faith-Learning Integration: An Overview," *Christian Scholar's Review* 23 (1992): 234-248. John Henry Newman: A Brief Biography. "The Victorian Web." Accessed July 30, 2013. http://www.victorianweb.org/authors/newman/jhnbio2.html.

Ker, Ian. *The Achievement of John Henry Newman*. Notre Dame: University of Notre Dame Press, 1990.

Jacobsen, Douglas and Rhonda Hustedt Jacobsen. *Scholarship and Christian Faith: Enlarging the Conversation*. New York: Oxford, 2004.

Loughlin, Gerard. "The University Without Question: John Henry Newman and Jacques Derrida on Faith in the University." In *The Idea of a Christian University: Essays in Theology and Higher Education,* edited by Jeff Astley, Leslie J. Francis, John Sullivan, and Andrew Walker. Milton Keynes, UK: Paternoster Press, 2004.

Martin, Brian. *John Henry Newman, His Life and Work*. New York: Paulist Press, 1990.

Newman, John Henry. *Apologia Pro Vita Sua*. London: Longmans, Green, and Co., 1904.

_____. *Development of Christian Doctrine*. Notre Dame: University of Notre Dame Press, 1989.

_____. *The Idea of a University*. Edited by Frank M. Turner (New Haven: Yale University Press, 1996).

_____. *The Idea of a University*. Edited, with an introduction and notes by Martin J. Svaglic (Notre Dame: University of Notre Dame Press, 1982).

Osmer, Richard R. *Practical Theology*. Grand Rapids: Eerdmans, 2008.

Pelikan, Jaroslav. *The Idea of a University – A Reexamination*. New Haven: Yale University Press, 1992.

Weatherby, Harold L. *Cardinal Newman in His Age*. Nashville: Vanderbilt University Press, 1973.

CHAPTER 22

William James:

The Father of Pragmatic Philosophy and Experiential Education

JONATHAN H. KIM

William James (1842-1910)

William James was one of the eminent American educators whose interdisciplinary ideas still pervade our culture. He was a quintessential American thinker who made remarkable contributions to the fields of philosophy, psychology, education, religion, theology, and literature. In particular, he offered a sustained and informed understanding of the relationship between pragmatism and education to the American public. The work of James is best understood through an analysis of his pragmatic theory of knowledge and its influence on the development of experiential pedagogy.

HISTORICAL BACKGROUND

William James was born in New York City on January 11, 1842, as the oldest of five children to Mary Robertson-Walsh (1810-1882) and Henry James Sr. (1811-1882). His siblings include: Henry James Jr. (1843-1916), a novelist and one of the key figures of nineteenth century literary realism; Garth Wilkinson (1845-1883), an abolitionist who fought against slavery; Robertson James (1846-1910); and Alice James (1848-1892), a well-known American diarist.

Children usually acquire religious interests from their parents. James' interest in religious studies was also largely due to his father, Henry James Sr.'s faith in Christianity. Having been brought up in an Irish Presbyterian Christian household, James Sr. was interested in ministry and attended Princeton Theological Seminary (1835-1837). Though he did not complete a degree there, he met his wife, Mary Robertson-Walsh, a sister of his Princeton classmate, during the course of his studies. Even though James Sr.'s unorthodox and passionate quest for spirituality misled him to a Christian cult later in life, his deep interest in Christianity inspired his children toward a faith in God.

William James was a remarkably talented individual who had both artistic and scientific temperaments. When he was a teenager, he studied painting under one of the leading American artists, William Morris Hunt. In college, James majored in chemistry and physiology at the Lawrence Scientific School of Harvard University. His graduate study was earned in the field of medicine at Harvard Medical School in 1863.

As a scholar, James had a wide range of interests. He was first appointed to teach physiology and anatomy in 1873 at Harvard but could not contain his interests only to these two subject matters. He switched his discipline to psychology and started America's first experimental psychology laboratory at Harvard in 1875. He eventually drifted into philosophy in 1897 and spent most of his remaining years teaching philosophy until his retirement from Harvard in 1907. Though he published countless papers, articles, books, and gave numerous lectures on a wide range of issues, James was never satisfied with where he was and the answers he found. He relentlessly sought to discover the epistemological harmony of philosophy, psychology, education, and religion.[1]

Throughout his career as a writer, James was on a constant quest for new ideas and desire to sort out ambiguities and complexities of life and wrote widely on many topics. His essays, lectures, and books covered many well-known topics including *The Principles*

---

[2] Frank Pajares, "William James: Our Father Who Begat Us" in *Educational Psychology: A Century of Contributions,* eds. Barry J. Zimmerman & Dale H. Schunk (New Jersey: Lawrence Erlbaum Associates, 2003), 5.

of Psychology (1890), *The Will to Believe* (1897), *Talks to Teachers on Psychology* (1899), *The Varieties of Religious Experience* (1902), *Pragmatism* (1907), *The Meaning of Truth* (1090), *Memories and Studies* (1911), *Essays in Radical Empiricism* (1912), and etc. The originality and breadth of ideas contained in his writing were remarkable. In particular, his book *The Principles of Psychology* (1890) became the first psychology textbook ever in America. Due to its depth and breadth, it is still recognized as a seminal work in the field of psychology. Even after his retirement from Harvard, James continued to write and publish until his death in 1910.

WILLIAM JAMES AND RELIGIOUS EXPERIENCE

James was one of the first American psychologists to study the science of religion. While a comprehensive understanding of James' theology may not be possible, we could certainly examine his perspective on religion based on a series of lectures that he gave on the psychology of religious experience, which were published in 1902 as *The Varieties of Religious Experience*. These lectures were one of the first social scientific surveys of religious experience that entailed the human effort to respond to life in a quasi-religious fashion. These lectures detailed many of James' thoughts on the origin, nature, and variation of religious experience. The intent of this study was to respond to academics who were prejudiced by the materialistic dogma of science and rejected the legitimacy of religion. Through these lectures, James desired to validate religious beliefs on the basis of emotional predilection maintained by rational engagement.

While James' thoughts on religious experience have become an invaluable source of knowledge for those studying the psychology of religion, they are highly problematic for Christians. As a pragmatist studying religion phenomenologically, James' basic contention was that religious beliefs are grounded in sense-driven emotional experience and not in rational reasoning. In some situations, emotional experience may stand antecedent to certain ideological beliefs, but it alone cannot provide the inner certainty needed to justify Christian beliefs. Rational reasoning is the primary basis for determining Christian beliefs, which are based on the intellectual understanding of God's truth. Christian religious experience is more or less an outcome of beliefs that are pre-established by a rational assent to the objective truth taught in the Bible. Even though James' pragmatic interpretations of religious experience have shed some light on the role that perceptions, feelings, and acts may play in Christian life, his ideas are contrary to Christian teaching and should not be correlated to Christian beliefs and experiences.

Unless carefully managed, relating psychological theories and Christian beliefs is a task that could easily lend itself to polemic from the moment an attempt is made. With a few exceptions, Christian beliefs do not lend themselves to uniform systematization based on social scientific categories. In most cases, an attempt to establish the validity of social scientific laws in Christian beliefs results in a system of thoughts that reduces the theological essential to what is practical and reframes Christian beliefs to quasi-psychological theories and principles. Far too often, a humanistic interpretation of Christianity becomes the primary basis for explaining Christian spiritual conscience, knowledge, and experience. Since giving the name of "science" to Christian beliefs is undoubtedly problematic, it should therefore be avoided at all costs.

PRAGMATISM AND EXPERIENTIAL EDUCATION

The goal of this section is to present William James' pragmatic theory of knowledge and its influence on the theoretical development of experiential education. Most of the chapters in this book address the theology of education of the individuals who made significant contributions to the field of Christian education — this will not work for James since his theory of knowledge and education was a philosophical rather than a theological venture. James neither initiated nor sought to establish a theological hermeneutics or theology of education with his pragmatic theory. He postulated his belief in pragmatism as a philosophical hermeneutic and articulated it based on an empiricist epistemology to a broader academic audience. It would be erroneous to directly relate his pragmatic theory to Christian beliefs and draw out its relevance to the theology of education. Such an effort would produce an incongruent system of thoughts.

Concerning James' pragmatic theory of knowledge, the term "pragmatism" derives from the Greek noun *pragma*, which means "deed, practice, or activity" (Acts 5:4, James 3:16). One of the well-known Greek synonyms of pragma is praxis — a concept pivotal to James' philosophy of education. As a theory of knowledge, a pragmatic hermeneutics asserts the validity of knowledge based on its utility or practical use. It highlights the primacy of critical reasoning or praxis reflection in lived experience as the basis of epistemological inquiry and justification. In order to understand the rudiments of James' pragmatic hermeneutic, his theory of knowledge is an important foundation, as it relates to his experiential pedagogy.

PRAGMATIC THEORY OF KNOWLEDGE

During the nineteenth century in America, the European speculative theory of knowledge[2] had a philosophical dominance in schools and classrooms. Speculative theory

---

[2] The speculative theory of knowledge is based on the coherence theory of truth whereby knowledge is justified mostly based on deductive reasoning. Whereas, James' pragmatism theory is largely

is a form of rational epistemology, which claimed that reality is a rationally ordered whole, connected and supported by logical necessity. It contended that contemplative abstraction is the only way of gaining knowledge. The entire hermeneutical framework of the theory was built upon the primacy of cognitive insight (*a priori*) devoid of sensory experience (*a posteriori*). Although many educators took the idea to heart, William James had a critical stance toward speculative theory due to its limited account of knowledge and ignorance of human experience. To James, experience was what made knowing possible.

In his assessment of speculative theory, James proposed a new hermeneutical theory based on his pragmatic belief. The main impetus of his pragmatic theory was encountering reality with reflective consciousness, and then, through the activity of critical reflection (i.e., praxis), the perceptual meanings embedded in experience are conceived as ideas in mind. James contended that all knowledge is the product of sense experience (e.g., sight, taste, smell, hearing, touch) and learned by its practicality of the present rather than rationality for the future. The basic tenet of his argument was that knowledge is formed as its values and conceptual categories interact with one another in the course of human reflection-action (i.e., *praxis*).

While James' pragmatic theory has become one of the fundamental theories in understanding the relationship between knowledge and its corresponding roles, his argument partially lacks an explanatory framework for what gives rises to the perception of ideas in the first place. His theory is based on a partial account of the mind. James presupposed that since our capacity to reason is part of our nature, we cannot break free of sense experience. In other words, apart from encountering reality with the five senses, people cannot have conscious awareness and generate ideas. Contrary to what James claimed, our capacity for reasoning could also arise from the mind, detached from sense experience. It is impossible to perceive a new idea purely based on sense experience (i.e. empiricist epistemology) and be totally detached from some type of speculation (i.e. rational epistemology). In order to have holistic knowledge, we need both sense experience and speculative reasoning (or internal mental experience). Although further discussion on the issue is necessary, due to the spatial limitation of the chapter we will move on to our next discussion on the influence of pragmatic theory on the theoretical development of experiential education.

PRAGMATIC HERMENEUTICS AND EXPERIENTIAL EDUCATION
The epistemology underlying pragmatism became the philosophical underpinning of

---

based on the correspondence theory of truth whereby knowledge is justified by inductive reasoning. Philosophically speaking, coherence theory is the polar opposite of correspondence theory.

experiential learning theory (See Figure 1). Long before experiential education was formally recognized as an academic theory in the mid-1900s, William James first developed the theory and taught it. G. Stanley Hall, one of his students at Harvard, further refined the theory and passed it onto John Dewey, one of his students at Johns Hopkins. James paved the way for the development of the theory before it was recognized as one of the foundational ideas in the mid 1900s.

To traditional teachers who viewed learning as the process of static reflection leading to a formulation of abstract ideas, James introduced a theory of experiential learning that gave clear details on how knowledge is derived from the direct encounter of situations via the process of perception, assimilation, validation, verification, and utilization.[3] This perspective is based on James' pragmatic belief in the dialectical unity of thought and action. James explained how learning becomes valid only and insofar as knowledge is utilized toward its end (i.e., *telos*). James explained learning in relation to its purposefulness in the context of lived experience.

Regarding experiential ways of knowing, there are basically two means: semantic and inferential. The former asserts how the applicability of an idea is determined by the procedural meaning it represents. It focuses on the pragmatic value of an idea in its epistemological pursuit. The latter is an evidence-oriented approach. It focuses a subsequent-conduct account of an idea. This approach highlights the operational character of knowledge. James' hermeneutic is based on the latter approach. With a view of the human mind giving actions a more functional role, James highlighted the role that ideas play out in people's lives.[4]

Today, the pragmatic theory of knowledge has become the philosophical underpinning of numerous pedagogical models such as practicum, internship, field education, service-project, cooperative learning, problem-based learning, andragogy, cultural immersion or cross-cultural program, camping/outdoor ministry, inquiry-based learning, and etc. (See Figure 1). These

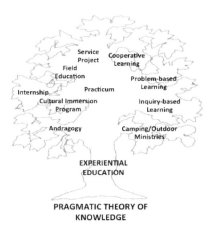

Figure 1: Pragmatism and Experiential Education

---

[3] William James, *Pragmatism: A New Name for Some Old Ways of Thinking* (New York, NY: Longmans, Green and Co, 1907), 121.

[4] Nathan Houser, "Peirce's Post-Jamesian Pragmatism," *European Journal of Pragmatism and American Philosophy* 3, no. 1 (2009): 42.

"learning-by-doing" models of education dominate classroom learning in the twenty-first century. Today's educators owe an immense debt to William James.

CONTRIBUTION TO EDUCATION AND CHRISTIAN EDUCATION

Teacher, learner, and curriculum are the three legs upon which educational philosophy stands. These legs not only support overall pedagogical endeavors, but they are also interdependent and support one another. Though the learner has a considerable amount of autonomy, his/her success ultimately depends on the combined effect of teacher's instructional skills and the quality of the curriculum being used. The success of a teacher depends not only on his/her instructional ability, but also on the efficacy of curriculum and the learner's openness to adapt the knowledge being taught. And, the value of curriculum in essence depends on the teacher's ability to successfully implement its outline as well as the learner's ability to comprehend the curriculum and material. Teacher, learner, and curriculum are inseparably intertwined and support one another. It is within this triadic relationship that education takes place.

Drawing on James' philosophy of experiential education, we now examine in detail his thoughts on teacher, learner, and curriculum. The materials discussed in the remainder of the chapter are primarily based on two of James' books: *Talks on Psychology of Interest to Teachers* (1899) and *The Principles of Psychology (1890 & 1891)*.

ROLE OF THE TEACHER

Answering the questions related to "what is teaching?" and "what does it mean to be a teacher?" is an important aspect for understanding the contributions of James. Those who are involved in teaching often wrestle with these questions. On the one hand, teaching yields amazing results when the right ideas and methods are implemented with the help of the Holy Spirit, but on the other hand, no matter how hard teachers try, sometimes the education fails and students lose interest. Teaching is a complex act that requires an insurmountable preparation and energy, yet the outcome is sometimes unpredictable.

Drawing on decades of experience as a world-renowned scholar and teacher, James offered three pedagogical insights to teachers: transformative teaching, teaching as an art, and teachable moments. Though these ideas are very familiar to teachers today, they were evocative and intriguing in the late 1800s and early 1900s and can be informative to teachers today.

405

Transformative Teaching

Traditionally, the concept of teaching was understood as a process of imparting knowledge fundamental to students' intellectual growth. The most important aspect of this idea would be imparting knowledge that prompts speculative inquiries into discovering objective principles. To James' eyes, the traditional mode of teaching was unacceptable since helping students develop capacities for personal, moral, and spiritual competencies were beyond its aim. James understood that beyond the complexities of teaching content lies creating an environment conducive to transformative learning. Believing personal formation as the chief focus of teaching, he stressed the importance of connecting knowing and being in education. He was interested in the education that transforms the entire being, not just the mind. In stating this belief, James said, "You and I are each all of us educated, in our several ways; and we show our education at this present moment by different conduct."[5] James believed that the quality outcome of education goes beyond the mere accumulation of facts and information; it is determined by a set of transformed belief and character that students will possess. He emphasized that it is critical for teachers to provide students with a continuous process of learning and growth leading to wholeness of being.

Wishing that his teaching would enrich the lives of students and provide them with life changing experiences, James worked on mastering his own pedagogical skills. Because he continually gave his best both inside and outside of the classroom, he was able to impact many lives and was eventually recognized as a magnificent teacher.[6] One author wrote about William James in the following way: "No method stood between James and his students, his teaching was essentially a personal relation infused with his personal qualities. His humor, his playful exaggeration, directness, above all his generosity and comradeship, made him loved by his students as he was by his friends."[7]

Teaching as an Art

The idea of teaching as a science had become a widely accepted view in James' time due to the influence of Johann F. Herbart's (1776-1841) pioneering work on pedagogical science. Claiming that a scientific understanding of how the human mind acquires knowledge is pivotal

---

[5] William James, *Talks to Teachers on Psychology; and to Students on Some Life's Ideals* (New York: Henry Holt and Company, 1906), 29.

[6] Randolph C. Miller, "Educational Philosophy of William James," *Religious Education* 86, no. 4 (1991): 619-634.

[7] Ralph B. Perry. *The Thoughts and Character of William James: Inheritance and Vocation*, vol. 1 (London: Humphrey Milford, Oxford University, 1935a), 455.

to teaching, Herbart integrated the scientific methods of observation and experimentation to teaching and advocated an idea of teaching as a science. In the 1800s, Herbart's idea had a huge impact on educational and religious institutions throughout America and was radically reshaping the pedagogic terrain of education as a whole. Teachers at large, all of whom used to share roughly the similar traditional belief of education, were beginning to incorporate Herbart's scientific pedagogy into their classrooms. The epistemic trust in both public and Christian education was significantly altered by Herbart's ideology.

While James concurred with Herbart in that science complements teaching and provides some basic format for sharing information in the classroom, James believed that pedagogical practice is essentially a work of art that should not be confined to scientific methods nor should be defined by scientific categories. Although the use of scientific methods revealed much about the quality and outcome of education, teaching, for James, was ultimately an art form that requires constant nourishing, practice, creativity, and continual learning. He did not believe that scientific pedagogy would enable students to reach beyond their limits and grow. This thought was occasioned in his 1899 lecture on psychology as a science and teaching as an art. He explained this saying,

> Teaching is an art ... The art of teaching grew up in the classroom, out of inventiveness and sympathetic concrete observation ... To know psychology [or science], therefore, is absolutely no guarantee that we shall be good teachers. To advance to that result, we must have an additional endowment altogether, a happy tact and ingenuity to tell us what definite things to say and do when the pupil is before us.[8]

In the lecture, James contended that if teaching is a science, mastering its content, theories, and methods could easily produce excellent teachers in no time. But since teaching is grounded in aesthetic qualities, it is more of an art that requires incessant preparation, practice, patience, and perseverance. Teaching requires a combination of a mastery of the subject and creativity in the delivery, he said. Ultimately for James, teaching was an artistic pursuit.

Teachable Moments

The phrase, "teachable moments" is often credited to Robert Havighurst for introducing it with his educational theory (1952); however, it was William James who first coined the phrase and introduced it to teachers. In his 1891 lecture, James noted how interest,

---

[8] William James, *Talks to Teachers*, 7.

attention, and habit go together in creating teachable moments for teachers. He explained that teachable moments are the opportune times when students are open and eager to learn. They are significant emotional, intellectual, physical, and spiritual moments during which students are more likely to receive teaching with openness. He explained this in the following, "In all pedagogy the great thing is to strike the iron while hot, and to seize the wave of the pupil's interest in each successive subject before its ebb has come, so that knowledge may be got and a habit of skill acquired — a headway of interest, in short, secured, on which afterward the individual may float ... To detect *the moment of the instinctive readiness* for the subject is, then, the first duty of every educator."[9]

In the lecture, James basically reasoned that teachable moments will allow students to explore and internalize newly received knowledge; thus teachers need to seize the moments and impart knowledge to students.

While James believed that maintaining a high level of proficiency in subject matters and pedagogical skills are essentials to all teachers, their ability to utilize the opportunities that emerge in the classroom for effective teaching was also a very important element to their profession. Though having instincts to detect teachable moments may not come easily for some teachers, when they work at understanding students' needs, motivations, interests and seek to continually create an open learning environment in the classroom, they will eventually develop an ability to appropriate student's readiness for effective teaching.

ROLE OF THE LEARNER

The remnants of James' pragmatic conscience and his leaning toward problem solving as the principal basis of thought prompted him to develop active and analogical learning theories. Historically speaking, the pattern of traditional pedagogy has added much impediment to education in both schools and churches in the 1800s and 1900s. Classroom and Sunday school environments were highly formal and teacher-centric. Additionally, the style and form of learning were obviously highly didactical with the full operational reliance on the use of deductive reasoning. As a result, students who were so used to confusing their learning desires with didacticism became very passive and unmotivated in the classroom.

In responding to the highly didactical classroom ecology, James introduced active and analogical learning theories. He was convinced that these new learning theories would revamp the classroom climate in two ways: first, by bringing forth a learner-centered

---

[9] William James, *The Principles of Psychology*, vol. 2. (London: MacMillan and Company, 1891), 401, 402.

classroom environment; and second, by enhancing learning experience and lead students to the higher level of understanding. These in turn, he believed, would address the limitations of traditional classroom learning and lift students out of their crippling learning environments.

Two pivotal aspects of James' thoughts on education include his active and analogical learning theories which form the foundation for his experiential pedagogy. Both will be summarized below.

Active Learning

When it came down to learning, James was fond of saying St. Augustine's aphorism, "*solvitur ambulando*" (Lat., "it is solved by walking" or "it is learned by active experience"). Believing that people are self-conscious thinkers, James insisted that students should learn actively by seizing "the very first possible opportunity to act on every resolution [they] make, and on every emotional prompting [they] may experience."[10] The concept of active learning theory finds its root in the pragmatic theory of knowledge, which highlights learner's reflective consciousness (i.e., *praxis*) as the primary means of acquiring knowledge. The theory presupposes that: if the inception of new ideas is connected to experiential reflections, it will generate meaningful learning at the core of human conscience.[11]

James was adamantly against the formal mode of teaching, which only emphasized rote learning and devalued students' thoughts and experiences. He reasoned that the consolidation of abstract ideas alone would not help students to learn effectively. While he understood that standard knowledge does need to be taught to children, as they become capable of abstract thinking, teachers needs to incorporate students' thoughts and experiences to their teaching. Listen to James' criticism of traditional pedagogy, "The older pedagogic method of learning things by rote, and reciting them parrot-like in the schoolroom, rested on the truth that a thing merely read or heard, and never verbally reproduced, contrasts the weakest possible adhesion in the mind."[12] James was convinced that the traditional mode of "sit-and-listen" education and rote memorization were not going to help students to learn effectively, so he declared that active learning needs to become a central element of all classroom learning.[13]

---

[10] William James, *Talks to Teachers*, 64.

[11] Ibid., 11.

[12] Ibid., 34.

[13] James H Korn, "The Teaching Spirit of William James," *Teaching Psychology* 30, no. 1 (2003): 44-45.

Analogical Learning

Given James' predisposition toward pragmatism, it should be apparent that he aligned learning more with analogical thinking. Analogical thinking is an aspect of human reasoning that allows individuals to infer relationally similar ideas or objects in recognizing and formulating new ideas in their minds.

The pedagogical significance of analogical learning was no surprise to William James. As a philosopher and psychologist, he understood the limitation of deductive reasoning in the learning process. So in order to make learning more meaningful for students, James introduced the concept of analogical learning theory to teachers. He said, "If the topic be highly abstract, show its nature by concrete examples. If it be unfamiliar, trace some point of analogy in it with the known."[14] According to James, such a shift in thinking was critical in developing learner-centered and experience-driven education.

In regards to analogical learning, James introduced two principles of association, the Law of Contiguity and the Law of Similarity.[15] The former is a principle on mental association, which describes how learning is influenced by a coexisting or subsequent idea (e.g. accompanying sounds, objects, concepts, senses, etc.). The latter is a principle on the organization of ideas, which says that the human mind tends to group similar or resembling ideas into collective entities based on their attributing factors such as shape, color, taste, type, size, and etc. According to the Law of Contiguity, an idea and its mental association are experienced together, whereas with the Law of Similarity, ideas just need to resemble one another in thinking. With the use of these types of analogical reasoning, James believed that students could easily formulate meaningful mental categories and learn.

James was certain that learning will naturally take place when students are taught to think analogically. This type of learning would then arm learners with the skills to create a potpourri of inferential mental categories and will cause them to make personal decisions on what they are receiving from teachers. However, in order to promote analogical learning in the classroom, James believed that teachers need to first modify some of their orthodoxed control in the classroom and encourage students to think openly and critically. As students are given more opportunities to interact and create analogical categories, James believed that they will be able to take charge of their learning and grow. Helping students take a personal responsibility of their learning was what James was after with his idea of analogical learning.

---

[14] William James, *Talks to Teachers,* 111.

[15] Ibid., 80.

ROLE OF CURRICULUM

Having discussed William James' thoughts on teacher and learner, we now proceed to his view of curriculum. As will be insinuated in this section, James' pragmatic belief, in particular his epistemic support of *a posteriori* knowledge[16], was highly influential in shaping his theory and method of experiential learning curriculum. Since James considered experience as the epicenter of all knowing, he believed that all educational curriculums must provide students the learning experiences that are central to their needs, interests, and capacities.[17] By introducing an experiential learning curriculum, James attempted to revamp the traditional classroom pedagogy and create a more learner-centered learning environment.

In the 1800s, the resurgence of progressivism gave rise to experiential education in America. Along with many academics and thinkers, James recognized the limitations of the formal curriculum of his day. As pointed out several times throughout this chapter, the nineteenth century education was highly didactical and highlighted primarily the transmission of the accumulated knowledge of a society as the chief aim of education. So James argued for a non-formal educational curriculum that connects content and process dimensions of learning. Such a curriculum, James believed, would connect students' interests with the ideas being generated, and learning will became highly meaningful to students. James was convinced that meaningful lessons produced inner reflections and led students to transformation.[18] He explained this in the following, "Feed the growing human being, feed him with the sort of experience for which from year to year he shows a natural craving, and he will develop in adult life a sounder sort of mental tissue, even though he may seem to be 'wasting' a great deal of his growing time, in the eyes of those for whom the only channels of learning are books and verbally communicated information."[19]

The conceptual basis of experiential learning curriculum was based on James' premise of *a posteriori* knowledge, which argued for the unity of mind and matter. He suggested that

---

[16] One of the tenets of James' theory of knowledge is claiming the validity of knowledge based on an *a posteriori (experiential)* theory of knowledge. An *a posteriori* (Latin, "from after" or "from what comes after" [observation]) theory explains how knowledge is derived from perception, or deduced from experience via empirical confirmation. What contrasts an *a posteriori* theory is an *a priori* theory of knowledge (Latin, "from former" or "from what is before" [observation]), which argues that knowledge is justified independently of experience, through reasoning alone. From the *a posteriori* and *a priori* theories of knowledge, we derive the expressions of experiential (or empirical) and non-experiential (or non-empirical) knowledge.

[17] Pamela C. Crosby, "Making a Life Significant: William James on Higher Education and Civil Responsibility," *William James Studies*, 7 (2011): 24.

[18] Miller, "Philosophy of William James," 620.

[19] William James, *Talks to Teachers*, 148.

people know what exists in the world (i.e. matter) only as they experience it with their five senses. The term "matter" describes the object of idea or "what" people perceive via experience before it is conceived by the mind. In other words, meaningful knowledge is derived from sense experiences. James wrote, "The intellectual life of man consists almost wholly in his substitution of a conceptual order for the perceptual order in which his experience originally comes."[20]

Due to the introduction of James' experiential learning curriculum in the early 1900s, the quality of education was further enhanced, promoting changes at the foundational level. However, such a change did not come easily. While some were fascinated with James' ideas, others perceived them to be too open-ended and objectionable. His skeptics could not tolerate an unimpeded consideration of students' involvement and questions in the classroom. They believed such an eccentric pedagogy would be liable to infect students with fallacies and confusions as to the fundamental nature of objective teaching that formal education was designed to do. Since people of his day commonly viewed education as a philosophical endeavor, they believed that educational problems, therefore, could not be resolved by an experiential curriculum. James, however, did not give in. He continually challenged his opponents' criticisms and sought to break down the barriers to his integrative work on experiential curriculum. He eventually paved the way toward an unprecedented path of victory that he eventually won later in life. Subsequently, the rise of experiential curriculum brought paradigmatic shifts in schools and churches in the 1900s. Teachers and students began to use dialogs, discussions, questions, and reflection as means for learning.

CONCLUSION

There are several reasons why it is important to understand William James' life and work in order to recognize his significance to both public and Christian education. First, in the early 1900s, people's concern for educational effectiveness rose sharply due to the introduction of James' integrative work on philosophy, psychology, and education. James' lectures and publications created a new wave of educational initiatives that sought to enhance teaching practice and student learning. An increasing number of educators embarked upon more holistic approaches to improve their teaching, and many schools and churches modified their educational philosophies and methods based on James' ideas. Second, due to James' learner-centered philosophy of education, the historic divide between teachers and learners, knowing and being, and theory and practice was abolished. Stemming from

---

[20] William James, *Memories and Studies* (New York: Longmans, Green, and Co., 1911), 51.

this was the emergence of a holistic educational ecology in the classroom. If it were not for James, such a change would have been possible. And finally, James developed the theoretical framework of experiential education. Long before experiential education was popularized as an educational theory under John Dewey (1859-1952), Paulo Freire (1921-1997), and David Kolb (1939-Present), it was William James who first introduced the theory to schools and churches in America. As explained in the chapter, the concept of experiential education was commenced by James' pragmatic theory of knowledge.

William James is one of the foundational figures in the history of American education. His books and lectures are still considered the standard reference material for educators and educational psychologists. But most of all, his pragmatic philosophy is still being recognized as one of the most important achievements in the history of American education. The legacy and scholarship left by James is something that we all educators should remember.

PRIMARY SOURCE SAMPLE[21]

In the last chapter it was stated in as radical a way as possible that the thoughts which we actually know to exist do not fly about loose, but seem each to belong to some one thinker and not to another. Each thought, out of a multitude of other thoughts of which it may think, is able to distinguish those which belong to its own Ego from those which do not. The former have a warmth and intimacy about them of which the latter are completely devoid, being merely conceived, in a cold and foreign fashion, and not appearing as blood-relatives, bringing their greetings to us from out of the past.

Now this consciousness of personal sameness may be treated either as a subjective phenomenon or as an objective deliverance, as a feeling, or as a truth. We may explain how one bit of thought can come to judge other bits to belong to the same Ego with itself; or we may criticize its judgment and decide how far it may tally with the nature of things.

As a mere subjective phenomenon the judgment presents no difficulty or mystery peculiar to itself. It belongs to the great class of judgments of sameness; and there is nothing more remarkable in making a judgment of sameness in the first person than in the second or the third. The intellectual operations seem essentially alike, whether I say "I am the same," or whether I say "the pen is the same, as yesterday." It is as easy to think this as to think the opposite and say "neither I nor the pen is the same."

This sort of bringing of things together into the object of a single judgment is of

---

[21] William James, *The Principles of Psychology*, vol. 1 (New York: Henry Holt and Co., 1890), 330-332.

course essential to all thinking. The things are conjoined in the thought, whatever may be the relation in which they appear to the thought. The thinking them is thinking them together, even if only with the result of judging that they do not belong together. This sort of subjective synthesis, essential to knowledge as such (whenever it has a complex object), must not be confounded with objective synthesis or union instead of difference or disconnection, known among the things. The subjective synthesis is involved in thought's mere existence. Even a really disconnected world could only be known to be such by having its parts temporarily united in the Object of some pulse of consciousness.

The sense of personal identity is not, then, this mere synthetic form essential to all thought. It is the sense of a sameness perceived by thought and predicated of things thought-about. These things are a present self and a self of yesterday. The thought not only thinks them both, but thinks that they are identical....

BIBLIOGRAPHY

Crosby, Pamela C. "Making a Life Significant: William James on Higher Education and Civil Responsibility." *William James Studies*, 7 (2011): 20-25.

James, William. *Essays in Pragmatism*. New York: Hafner Publishing Co. 1948.

————. *Memories and Studies*. New York: Longmans, Green, and Co. 1911.

————. *Pragmatism: A New Name for Some Old Ways of Thinking* 1907. New York, NY: Longmans, Green and Co.

————. *Some Problem of Philosophy*. New York: Longmans, Green, and Co. 1911.

————. Talks to Teachers on Psychology; and to Students on Some Life's Ideals. New York: Henry Holt and Company, 1906.

————. *The Meaning of Truth*. New York: Longmans, Green, and Co. 1909.

————. *The Principles of Psychology*. 1 vols. New York: Henry Holt and Company. 1890.

————. *The Principles of Psychology*. 2 vols. New York: Henry Holt and Company. 1890-91.

Korn, James H. "The Teaching Spirit of William James." *Teaching Psychology* 30, no. 1 (2003): 44-45.

Miller, Randolph C. "Educational Philosophy of William James." *Religious Education* 86, no. 4 (1991): 619-634.

Nathan Houser. "Peirce's Post-Jamesian Pragmatism." *European Journal of Pragmatism and American Philosophy*, 3, no. 1 (2009): 39-60.

Pajares, Frank. "William James: Our Father Who Begat Us." In *Educational Psychology: A Century of Contributions*, edited by Barry J. Zimmerman & Dale H. Schunk. New Jersey: Lawrence Erlbaum Associates, Publishers. 2003.

Perry, Ralph Barton. *The Thoughts and Character of William James*. Vol. 2, *Inheritance and Vocation*. London: Humphrey Milford, Oxford University, 1935a.

————. *The Thoughts and Character of William James*. Vol. 2, *Philosophy and Psychology*. London: Humphrey Milford, Oxford University, 1935b.

Redding, Paul. "Feeling, Thought and Orientation." *Parrhesia: A Journal of Critical Philosophy*, 13 (2011): 41-51.

CHAPTER 23

C. I. Scofield:

Educating for Heavenly Citizenship

JOHN D. BASIE

C. I. Scofield (1843-1921)

Scofield stands as one of the most influential evangelical pastor-educators in the twentieth century. From his powerful teaching, preaching, and writing, to his founding of Philadelphia School of the Bible, Scofield's enduring influence is incalculable. As an extremely gifted evangelical educator and author whose testimony was that of a sinner saved by grace, his kingdom accomplishments and legacy should continue to inspire educators, pastors, and leaders interested in great-commission ministry.

HISTORICAL BACKGROUND

Cyrus I. Scofield was born August 19, 1843, in Clinton, Michigan.[1] His mother died of complications related to his birth, thus, he was raised by his father and stepmother, both people of genuine faith. Scofield grew up in Wilson County, Tennessee, and as a boy had developed an insatiable thirst for knowledge. He read everything he could get his hands on, including Shakespeare and world history. He was schooled primarily at home and toward the end of his high school studies had planned to sit for university entrance examinations; the Civil War began and most southern colleges closed. As a result, Scofield never acquired a formal university-level education.[2]

At the age of sixteen, Scofield served in the Confederate Army as an orderly and frequently carried written messages through dangerous battlegrounds. By the time he turned nineteen, Scofield had braved eighteen battles and minor engagements. Scofield was awarded the Cross of Honor for bravery at the Battle of Antietam.[3] When the Civil War ended in 1865, a twenty-one year old Scofield went to live with his eldest sister in St. Louis. It was during his stay with his sister and brother-in-law that he married Leantine Cerre and decided to go into law.[4] Even though his brother-in-law offered to help him with his education, Scofield insisted on providing for himself. After clerking for several years in a land title office, he entered one of the top law offices in St. Louis in order to formally study law. He passed the bar exam around 1869 and began to gain valuable experience as an attorney in Kansas, where he was serving as legal counsel to a family involved in a land-interest lawsuit. He was elected to the Kansas State Legislature in 1871 where he served two terms. In 1873, President Ulysses S. Grant named Scofield the United States Attorney for the District of Kansas.[5] Scofield resigned only six months later when rumors began to spread about the possibility of his having accepted bribes in some of his court cases.[6]

In 1879, after having returned to St. Louis to continue the practice of law, Scofield began to drink. The severity of his drinking problem was such that his wife and two daughters left him permanently. It was through this trauma that Scofield saw the importance of the

---

[1] Renald Showers, "A History of Philadelphia College of the Bible" (ThM thesis, Dallas Theological Seminary, 1962), 17.

[2] Charles G. Trumbull, *The Life Story of C. I. Scofield* (1920; repr., Eugene, OR: Wipf & Stock, 2007), 1-7.

[3] Ibid., 8.

[4] Showers, "A History of PCB," 17.

[5] Ibid.,18; Trumbull, *Life Story*, 9-22.

[6] Showers, "A History of PCB," 18.

gospel of Jesus Christ, and through the influence of a colleague his conversion experience empowered him to abandon alcohol entirely.[7] Under the discipleship of Dr. James H. Brookes, pastor of Compton Avenue Presbyterian Church in St. Louis, Scofield nurtured a passion for the Bible, and regularly received Bible instruction in Brookes' home. In August of 1880, Scofield was appointed acting secretary of the YMCA in St. Louis and was licensed to preach. Shortly after that, he organized and pastored the Hyde Park Congregational Church of North St. Louis.[8]

In the spring of 1882 Scofield was called to pastor a small church in Dallas, Texas. As a thirty-nine-year-old pastor, Scofield found himself leading a flock of only twelve members. By 1884, the church had grown to seventy-five members, and in that same year Scofield married Miss Hettie Hallwarz, a young woman who had been attending the church. By 1888, the church membership rolls indicated 250 new members since Scofield's arrival as pastor six years earlier.[9] It was during this period in Scofield's life that he was became known as a gifted Bible teacher and was invited regularly to speak at Bible conferences abroad. He was also involved increasingly with Bible studies and evangelistic efforts in Dallas, including in-home Bible study groups, Bible classes in the local YMCA, and training classes for future ministers. In 1888, Scofield launched his writing career with the publication of *Rightly Dividing the Word of Truth*, and in 1890 began a monthly journal known as *The Believer*. About this same time, he also began work on the Comprehensive Bible Correspondence Course, which he personally directed until turning it over to Moody Bible Institute in 1914.[10]

Before moving to Dallas, Scofield became friends with Dwight Moody and had helped Moody with an evangelistic crusade in St. Louis. In 1886, when Scofield was living in Dallas, Moody held a crusade there; as a result of his help, Scofield became part-time superintendent of the American Home Missionary Society for the Texas/Louisiana region.[11] In 1895, Scofield again assisted Moody at an evangelistic campaign in Dallas and soon thereafter was called to the pastorate of the Trinitarian Congregational Church of Northfield, Massachusetts, Moody's home church. As a part of his duties, Scofield presided over the administrative affairs of the two Northfield preparatory schools that Moody founded.[12] By

---

[7] Larry J. McKinney, *Equipping for Service: A Historical Account of the Bible College Movement in North America* (Fayetteville, AR: Accrediting Association of Bible Colleges, 1997), 91.

[8] Showers, "A History of PCB," 19.

[9] Ibid., 19-20.

[10] Showers, "A History of PCB," 20.

[11] Ibid.

[12] Ibid., 21.

the time he left his home church in Dallas in 1895, the membership rolls had swelled to 826 members. Furthermore, during his fourteen years as pastor, the church had commissioned seven men and two women into full-time Christian service.[13] His work at Northfield prospered, and he and Moody became close friends. When Moody died in 1899, Scofield conducted his funeral service.[14]

Of all that Scofield published, his most enduring contribution was the *Scofield Reference Bible*, of which he was editor. In fact, he left the Northfield church to go pastor his home church in Dallas for a second time in 1903, thinking that he would have more time to work on the Bible. However, by the end of that year, he discerned that he would either have to make a choice between the church and the Bible project. Scofield chose to leave the Dallas church a second time and headed to England to work on the reference Bible.[15] He signed a contract with Oxford University Press in 1905 and called upon other experts in getting the project done. Contributors of the project included A.C. Gaebelein; James M. Gray, president of Moody Bible Institute; William J. Erdman, a Presbyterian minister and author; A.T. Pierson, an author and editor; H.G. Weston, president of Crozer Seminary; and Elmore Harris, president of Toronto Bible Institute. The Scofield Reference Bible was completed in 1908 and presented to the public in January of 1909.[16]

Scofield served for a third time in the Dallas church following his return from England in 1905. He served there until 1909 when he accepted Oxford University Press invitation to serve as the editor of the tercentenary edition of the English Bible, which was scheduled for publication in 1911, three centuries after the first edition appeared during the reign of King James. The Dallas church named Scofield pastor emeritus in 1910, a title he held until his death in 1921. In October of 1914, Scofield and his colleague William Pettingill founded Philadelphia School of the Bible. [17] Establishing a Bible institute on the east coast had been a dream of Scofield's for many years, and he was able to serve as the institution's founding president until July 1921 when he died of a heart-related illness.[18]

---

[13] Ibid.

[14] Ibid., 22.

[15] Showers, "A History of PCB," 22.

[16] Ibid., 23.

[17] Philadelphia School of the Bible is now known as Cairn University.

[18] Showers, "A History of PCB," 23, 71-76. Showers points out that Scofield, who had been living in New York while he was president, had suffered from "heart weakness, with his pulse sometimes dropping to thirty beats a minute." Additionally, "As a result of his poor health, Scofield was able to serve the school very little in an active way. He was able to teach occasionally, but his counsel and advice were invaluable" as he and Pettingill met weekly in New York to discuss institutional business (71).

THEOLOGY OF CHRISTIAN EDUCATION
THEOLOGICAL HERMENEUTIC: DISPENSATIONALISM

Although he intentionally kept himself at the margins of the fundamentalist-modernist controversy that was raging in the early 1900s, Scofield clearly identified himself as being with the conservative camp.[19] Perhaps his greatest theological legacy, however, was his highly nuanced dispensational theology, which was central to his understanding of the Bible and which was foundational for the Philadelphia School of the Bible's board, administration, and faculty. It was also a pervasive theme weaved throughout his reference Bible. Although it is a challenge to submit a concise definition of dispensational theology, it is possible to identify the core assumptions of Scofield's dispensationalism.[20] First, he held that there is a strict distinction between Israel and the church. Secondly, he held to a system of biblical hermeneutics that is literalistic.[21] With respect to prophecy, this literalism strongly implied that human affairs on earth as well as culture in general will continue to worsen until Christ returns to rapture the church and all the believers that comprise it. Christ will personally reign on earth for a thousand years, commonly known as the millennium. This will be a time of relative peace and prolonged life on earth as the regenerate and unregenerate alike serve Christ on his throne.[22] The millennium will then be followed by a brief period of

---

[19] Showers, "A History of PCB," 24. The fundamentalist-modernist controversy denotes an early twentieth-century conflict between the fundamentalists (this is an historical term) and the modernists. The fundamentalists believed in the inerrancy and sufficiency of the Bible, whereas the modernists used science and various interpretive methods to call into question many aspects of the Bible's veracity and legitimacy, including miracles. See George M. Marsden, *Fundamentalism and American Culture* (New York: Oxford University Press, 1980).

[20] Mark Noll has pointed out the difficulty in attempting to define dispensationalism's parameters due to its different meanings "to its different exponents, and because outside observers and opponents have isolated different elements as its central teaching." See Mark Noll, *The Scandal of the Evangelical Mind* (Grand Rapids: Eerdmans, 1994), 118.

[21] Ibid. These two criteria were first cited by Charles Ryrie in his 1965 book *Dispensationalism Today*. In *Scandal,* Mark Noll cites a third criterion that I have not cited here, namely that of "a concern for the glory of God rather than simply the outworking of salvation" as God's main purpose in the world. I have included only two criteria since these appear to be the most obvious and widely agreed-upon criteria for dispensationalism.

[22] See C. I. Scofield, "Kingdom Truth" in *Dr. C. I. Scofield's Question Box*, ed. Ella Pohle (Pasig City, TN: LifeLine Philippines, n.d.), 65. Scofield held that, according to Isaiah 65:20, death would still exist during the millennium but that "human life will be prolonged in general." Further, he believed that even though "Revelation 20 proves that the evil heart will still be in man," the unregenerate will be compelled to "instant obedience and subjection" due to the rule of Christ, whereas "the regenerate will serve Christ from the heart."

torment and temptation by Satan, then finally ending in Christ's judgment of all the earth. The assumption that human affairs on earth will grow increasingly worse until Christ's return served as an urgent motivation for the evangelization of as many unbelievers as possible.

John Nelson Darby (1800-1882) is widely credited with bringing dispensationalism to the forefront of American religious life, although its roots may extend as far back as the sixteenth century Swiss Reformer Heinrich Bullinger (1504-1575).[23] For some, even the simple distinction between Old and New Testaments denotes a dispensationalist-type of framework for understanding biblical history.[24] Scofield, however, was the first fundamentalist of the twentieth century to systematize a populist-type biblical history in terms of a dispensationalist hermeneutic. His pamphlet *Rightly Dividing the Word of Truth,* which was written for the educated layperson, provided a logical and coherent attempt at making a biblical case for the church/Israel distinction as well as seven key dispensations in biblical history, which include the following:

1. Man Innocent: This dispensation begins with the creation of Adam in Genesis 2:7 and continues to the expulsion from Eden in Genesis 3:21

2. Man Under Conscience: Extends from the expulsion of Eden to the Flood

3. Man In Authority over the Earth: From post-Flood Noah to the Confusion of Tongues at the Tower of Babel

4. Man Under Promise: From Babel to the Israelite Bondage in Egypt

5. Man Under Law: From Moses leading the Israelites out of Egypt to the crucifixion of Christ

6. Man Under Grace: From the death of Christ through the present day

7. Man Under the Personal Reign of Christ: Following the purifying judgments that attend Christ's return to earth, he will reign over restored Israel and all the earth for 1000 years.[25]

---

[23] For more on the historical development of dispensationalism see William C. Watson, Dispensationalism before Darby: Seventeenth-Century and Eighteenth-Century English Apocalypticism (Silverton, OR: Lampion Press, 2015).

[24] Sydney Ahlstrom argues that the idea of divine dispensations is implicit in the terms "Old and New Testament." With respect to other thinkers who may have contributed to the dispensationalist system, Ahlstrom suggests that Reformers such as Bullinger and Johannes Cocceius (1603-1669) "developed the idea of God's dealing with man through successive covenants." Darby, however, was the thinker who refashioned these older ideas into modern form and emphasized the radical distinction between the church and the coming Kingdom. See Ahlstrom, *A Religious History of the American People* (New Haven: Yale University Press, 1972), 808.

[25] C. I. Scofield, *Rightly Dividing the Word of Truth: Ten Outline Studies of the More Important*

Historian George Marsden explains that these historical epochs represent a key distinctive of the dispensationalist way of thinking. Each epoch, or dispensation, represents a new way in which God tested human beings through a particular plan of salvation. In each case, sinful humanity fails the test, with each epoch ending in divine judgment of catastrophic proportions.[26]

Scofield defined a dispensation as "a period of time during which God deals in a particular way with man in respect to sin, and to man's responsibility."[27] He explained further that what differentiates these dispensations from each other is an indication in Scripture that God's method of dealing with sinful humanity's responsibility has changed. Due to humanity's failure with one method of God's divine action toward human beings, a new method must be devised and tried.[28] As Scofield points out, "Each of the dispensations may be regarded as a new test of the natural man, and each ends in judgment — marking his utter failure in every dispensation."[29] A new dispensation is imminent, claimed Scofield, when we see in Scripture two key marks: miraculous activity and a new prophetic revelation. One of his examples of evidence for this comes from the Old Testament book of Daniel where God reveals to the prophet Daniel the future events of Judah's captivity in Babylon. Although the prophetic revelation component is obvious in this example, the miraculous activity is not, and Scofield's explanation is rather ambiguous.[30] Nevertheless, despite Scofield's poor explanation in this instance, his penchant for the formulaic is evident in the attempt to demarcate clearly each dispensation and is in keeping with the rest of his systematic biblicist understanding of Scripture.

Divisions of Scripture (Old Tappan, NJ: Fleming H. Revell, 1896), 12-16. Sydney Ahlstrom points out Scofield's understanding that the dispensations were marked by but not identical with God's successive covenants. In order, the relevant covenants are as follows: the Edenic covenant (before the fall of man); the Adamic covenant; the Noahic Covenant; the Abrahamic Covenant; the Mosaic Covenant; the covenant of grace through Christ; the millennium. See *Religious History*, 810.

[26] George M. Marsden, *Understanding Fundamentalism and Evangelicalism* (Grand Rapids: Eerdmans, 1991), 40.

[27] C. I. Scofield, *Old Testament*, vol. 1 of *The Scofield Bible Correspondence Course* (1907; repr., The Moody Bible Institute of Chicago, 1934), 17.

[28] While Scofield would not hold to a theological position that limited God's sovereignty nor allowed God to be characterized as less than omnipotent, he does not clearly answer the question of how the previous dispensations failed. Robert Saucy has aided in this shortcoming through some careful thinking that has led to a progressive dispensationalist theology. See his book *The Case for Progressive Dispensationalism: The Interface Between Dispensational and Non-Dispensational Theology* (Grand Rapids: Zondervan, 1993).

[29] Scofield, *Rightly Dividing*, 12.

[30] C. I. Scofield, "Does the Bible Throw Light on This War?" in *What Do the Prophets Say?* ed. C. I. Scofield (Greenville: Gospel Hour, 1918), 12.

According to Scofield's categories, we are currently operating in the sixth dispensation, "Man Under Grace." The church, in this view, is isolated to this particular dispensation, which began with Christ's crucifixion and will end when all believers are raptured.[31] Within the context of the fundamentalist-modernist controversy, dispensationalism's importance was far larger than its system of historical partitioning. The dispensationalist emphasis of biblical inerrancy was particularly strong and served as the doctrinal basis for the movement's understanding of divine truth.[32] All of this has import for how Scofield thought about educational ends versus educational means, and what he thought the ultimate purpose of Christian education was; namely, to evangelize citizens of Earth so that they could become citizens of heaven.

THE INFLUENCE OF DISPENSATIONALISM ON SCOFIELD'S THEOLOGY OF EDUCATION

Although there is no evidence that Scofield ever articulated his own nuanced theology of education, his dispensational assumptions were unwavering in his commitment to producing full-time, future-minded heavenly citizens at the Philadelphia School of the Bible. That is to say, full-time Christian workers whose activities were driven by the urgency of Christ's impending second coming was the goal of his educational endeavors. From the evidence of his sermons and articles, this was his theology of education.

Like many other dispensationalists of his time, Scofield contended that the Kingdom was far from being realized in the Church age. Rather than putting too much hope in human beings and their ability to educate and redeem the world through social progress, the kingdom was a concept that was entirely future-oriented and supernatural in origin. Consistent with the dispensationalist understanding of history, it was untethered from the history and culture of the current era.[33] To put the Kingdom within the context of what Carl Henry called the

---

[31] See Marsden, *Understanding Fundamentalism and Evangelicalism*, 40. In similar fashion to Ahlstrom, Marsden briefly explains that "The first dispensation ended with the human Fall into sin and expulsion from Eden, the second ended with the Flood, the third with the Tower of Babel, and so forth. We live in the sixth era, or church age, also heading toward catastrophe and divine intervention."

[32] Ahlstrom notes that dispensationalism "was much more than a partitioning of history; for its real appeal depended on its doctrinal foundations. In the first place, it insisted undeviatingly on the absolute verbal inerrancy of the Bible was deemed capable of revealing not merely data for the historian and philologist, but divine truth" (*Religious History*, 811).

[33] Ibid., 51. More recent developments in dispensational scholarship have sought to resolve this problem. See Robert L. Saucy, *The Church in God's Program* (Chicago: Moody Press, 1972). Although Saucy holds that the concepts of church and kingdom are distinct — just as Scofield did — Saucy allows that "the church shares in the kingdom as a part of God's purpose to reign upon the earth." As a leading proponent of the view known as progressive dispensationalism, Saucy seeks

"postponement theory," the dispensationalists held that there is "'no kingdom now, but rather a future kingdom.'"[34]

Scofield's dispensationalist assumptions about the kingdom inevitably influenced his understanding of what it meant to form virtuous citizens of earth. In commenting on Christ's outline of the virtuous person in the Sermon on the Mount in Matthew 5, Scofield remarked that "The Sermon on the Mount is kingdom, not church, truth."[35] He went on to explain that, "Christ was preaching the kingdom as "at hand" to Israel, and the great sermon has been called "the constitution of the kingdom of heaven." That kingdom was rejected by the Jews, but will be set up when our Lord returns (Acts 15:16). Then the sermon will be in force as legislation."[36] Scofield explains elsewhere that "at hand" does not indicate a "positive affirmation that the person or thing said to be "'at hand'" will immediately appear, but only that no known or predicted event must intervene." He further explained, "When Christ appeared to the Jewish people, the next thing, in the order of revelation as it then stood, should have been the setting up of the Davidic kingdom."[37] Here, Scofield was being consistent with his own dispensationalist thinking in making the case that Christ, in the dispensation of law, was seeking to bring Israel into congruence with the kingdom of Heaven which was "at hand" by virtue of his physical presence on Earth. With respect to the sermon itself, he held that it laid out principles of the kingdom that were applicable in two ways — literally for Israel under the dispensation of law and morally for the church under the dispensation of grace. Scofield's future orientation with respect to the Kingdom is important as it relates to his work as an educator and preacher. His conviction of the importance of a future Kingdom is likely what helped communicate gospel urgency in his teaching, preaching, and evangelistic endeavors.

---

to avoid the extremes of already/not yet interpretations of the kingdom. He explains that the "two errors of identifying the church with the kingdom or radically separating them are usually associated with a one-sided concept of the nature of the kingdom. Those who would see the kingdom as the church are compelled to stress the abstract aspect of the kingdom, thus viewing it as the present spiritual reign in the hearts of men. Likewise, those separating the kingdom from the church stress the futurity and apocalyptic nature of the kingdom. The kingdom includes both aspects. The church is therefore presently related to the kingdom in its spiritual nature but also looks forward to participation in the glorious culmination in the literal apocalyptic manifestation of the kingdom" (85). Also see Robert L. Saucy, *The Case for Progressive Dispensationalism: The Interface between Dispensational and Non-Dispensational Theology* (Grand Rapids: Zondervan, 1993).

[34] Carl F. H. Henry, *The Uneasy Conscience* (Grand Rapids: Eerdmans, 2003), 42.

[35] Scofield, "Kingdom Truth," 64.

[36] Ibid.

[37] C.I. Scofield, ed. *The Scofield Reference Bible* (New York: Oxford University Press, 1917), 998 n3.

CONTRIBUTIONS TO CHRISTIAN EDUCATION
THE ROLE OF THE TEACHER: PREPARING CITIZENS OF HEAVEN

Scofield's writings indicate that his philosophy of human flourishing lent itself most naturally to a "heavenly" rather than a this-worldly understanding of citizenship. This is an important clue to what he believed teachers should teach students. "For our citizenship is in heaven," he claimed, "from whence also we wait for a Savior, the Lord Jesus Christ: who shall fashion anew the body of our humiliation, that it may be conformed to the body of his glory (Phil 3:20, 21, R.V.)."[38] Furthermore, he clearly stated his view of the relationship between the "earthly" and the "heavenly," which for him was one of contradistinction: "That which is heavenly [is] in contradistinction to that which is earthly. The sphere of the believer's spiritual experience as identified with Christ in nature ... The believer is a heavenly one, — a stranger and pilgrim on the earth (Heb. 3:1; 11:13; 1 Pet. 2:11)."[39]
Making use of his pilgrim metaphor, it is fair to conclude that Scofield believed that believers were heavenly pilgrims on Earth who were not to make their true "home" on Earth, for their home is in heaven. However, this did not mean disengaging from culture or the world in general because the believer's mandate, in Scofield's view, was to evangelize the lost. For Scofield, then, cultural engagement turned out to mean heavenly citizens engaging earthly ones for the sake of evangelizing and converting them rather than to attempt to engender an elusive common good.

In a sermon entitled "Definiteness," Scofield made the case for full-time Christian service by arguing that the "Christian is called a servant, a soldier, a runner, an ambassador, a worker, a priest, a wrestler, and I know not how many other names, all vocal with this one truth, that to come to Christ, to be saved, and then to begin a life of Christian service is an earnest business."[40] In articulating this argument for "a life of Christian service," Scofield was clearly putting forth his view that Christians are duty-bound to engage the culture with the gospel in such a way that the citizens of earth will become citizens of heaven. He shed additional light on his understanding of what constituted worthwhile cultural engagement and the Christian's solution for the world's ills when he said,

> The Christian in this world of want and woe, of sin and despair, of tears and death, is entrusted with the only remedy for all of its ills, absolutely the only one. Men fancy

---

[38] Scofield, *Rightly Dividing*, 9.

[39] C. I. Scofield, "The Church," in Ella Pohle, *Scofield's Question Box* (Pasig City, TN: Lifeline Philippines, n.d.) 31.

[40] C. I. Scofield, "Definiteness," *Serving-and-Waiting* 9, no. 2 (June 1919): 67.

that they will find a remedy for the woe of the world, and the distress and anguish of the world in legislation and education, and in repressive measures, but these invariably break down, and become the tool of selfishness, invariably. God has committed to the

Christians who live in this world in any one generation the only remedy for all that is wrong about them ... We are to bring the free salvation of Jesus Christ to the lost. It is an earnest business. [41]

As this passage shows, Scofield demonstrated doubt in the power of traditional, earthly-minded education to solve the world's problems or to contribute in much of a meaningful way to human flourishing. From the historical backdrop of the fundamentalist-modernist controversy, he was likely saying that education *in and of itself* is ultimately a pointless endeavor with respect to finding that "remedy for the woe of the world," hence the need for an education whose chief end is to train new workers who would bring Christ's free salvation to the world, for the sake of the world, and for the kingdom that comes.

THE ROLE OF THE LEARNER: THE BIBLE AND EVANGELISM

Scofield held that all true believers should be serious learners with respect to biblical knowledge and evangelism. Regarding his conviction on the importance of biblical training for all Christian workers and not just exclusive training for ordination, Scofield once said "This is a layman's age."[42] He was passionate about the gospel message going out to the ends of the earth without the unnecessary delay of formal seminary training.[43] However, he was not anti-intellectual. He held that a careful and proper study of the scriptures was necessary to discern truth from error as well as to keep the essence of the gospel message pure so that evangelism would be effective and souls would be won. He said,

---

[41] Ibid., 67-68. Scofield made this argument partly on the basis of a particular understanding of stewardship, namely that "we cannot forget that we are entrusted with a stewardship for which we must give account. Our time is part of the trust estate. This blessed gospel is part of it. Our money is part of it. We must account for every moment, and for every dollar." (68).

[42] Showers, "History of PCB," 62.

[43] Showers emphasizes the degree to which Scofield was convinced of the need to train lay workers. Scofield said "One hundred years ago practically all of the aggressive activities of the churches of God were in the hands of ordained ministers. A great change has come within fifty years. In every department of Christian work laymen are actively engaged. The purpose of Bible institutions is to train lay workers ... in an age so highly specialized as ours, it is felt necessary that the great host of Sunday School teachers and mission workers shall have clear and competent instruction in the Scriptures and in the best methods of Christian work" ("History of PCB," 62).

There could not be another "gospel." Change, modify, the grace of Christ by the smallest degree, and you no longer have a gospel ... What is a simple child of God, who knows no theology, to do? Just this: to remember that any so-called gospel which is not pure unadulterated grace is "another" gospel. If it proposes, under whatever specious guise, to win favor of God by works, or goodness, or "character," or anything else which man can do, it is spurious. That is the unfailing test.[44]

Like most of his colleagues, Scofield believed that true change in society can be the outcome only of a permanent change in the human heart, namely that of a conversion experience that is the result of nothing other than God's grace — his gift of salvation to sinful man through Jesus Christ. Society was on the downward slide to his way of thinking, and nothing short of the Lord's return would cure society's ills. In a letter he wrote to the attendees of the 1918 Philadelphia Prophetic Conference, he stated as much when he said that he was praying for God to guide their proceedings, "especially in the putting forth of a fearless warning that we are in the awful end of the Times of the Gentiles, with no hope for humanity except in the personal return of the Lord of Glory; and also a statement of the fundamentals of Christian belief, which may form a clear basis for Christian fellowship in a day of apostasy."[45]

For Scofield, the personal salvation of souls had to be the strategy by which society would be transformed. The only social and cultural means that would prove effective for Scofield was evangelism — the proclamation of the simple gospel message. In his view, then, learners were members of Christ's Church who were unwaveringly committed to learning the Scriptures and then spreading the gospel message through evangelistic means. The Church, according to Scofield, was the primary and divinely appointed agent whose mission was to spread the message of the gospel.

The church has but one mission, defined in Luke 24:47, 48; Matthew 28:18-20; Acts 1:8; and the church works most powerfully toward the solution of social problems not by turning reformer, but by preaching the gospel in the power of the Holy Spirit. When Christ was on earth all the social problems — slavery, intemperance, prostitution, unequal distribution of wealth, oppression of the weak by the strong — were at their worst. To cure them He put into the world one message — the gospel, one means — regeneration, one agency, — the Holy Spirit in the church. The best help a pastor can bring to the social problems of his community is to humble himself before God,

---

[44] C. I. Scofield, "The Grace of God," in *The Fundamentals: A Testimony to the Truth*, ed. R. A Torrey and A. C. Dixon (1917; repr., Baker Books, 2003), 3:103.

[45] C. I. Scofield, "To the Philadelphia Prophetic Conference," May 28, 1918, quoted in *Serving-and-Waiting* 8, no. 3 (July 1918): 86.

forsake his sins, receive the filling with the Holy Spirit, and preach a pure gospel in tender love.[46]

In Scofield's view, the Church simply was an "outcalled assembly" based on his understanding of the Greek term "ecclesia." In his understanding there was nothing inherently spiritual about the term itself.[47] What made the New Testament church a uniquely spiritual "outcalled assembly" is the fact that it is not primarily an organization, but rather an organism in a spiritual sense.[48] According to Scofield's interpretation of I Corinthians 12:12, the church "is a living organism in the same way that the human body is a living organism; that it is composed of a Head, Christ in glory; and of living members, the whole number of the regenerate between the two advents of Christ."[49] In drawing the organism/organization distinction, Scofield was making an important assumption, namely that the heavenly nature of the church is to be elevated over its earthly aspects, even with respect to the organizing and governing principles of churches. This is made clear when he argues for the local church model of church government as opposed to the denominational model.

Scripture knows nothing of a church composed of churches — as the Methodist church, the Presbyterian church, etc., meaning many churches united into one church. It is wholly a Roman Catholic perversion retained in Protestant use. Any such "church" must be, like Romanism itself, simply a sect. In every such "church" there survives the papal leaven of a required love of and "loyalty" to, the sect. Innumerable are the evils produced by this utterly unscriptural practice. The multiplication of churches in every village, when one true apostolic church would include easily and naturally all Christians in the place; the reproduction on heathen ground of these wholly unnecessary divisions — these are but a few of the evils. The local church is the beginning and end of divine organization for this age.[50]

Scofield argued that, in order to maintain the purity of her spiritual and heavenly mission, the Church must pursue a path of "separation from the world," as the following statement demonstrates:

[46] C. I. Scofield, "Civic Righteousness," edited by Ella Pohle, *Scofield's Question Box* (Pasig City, TN: Lifeline Philippines, n.d), 36.
[47] C. I. Scofield, "The Church and Churches," in *Things New and Old: Old and New Testament Studies by Dr. C.I. Scofield*, ed. A. C. Gaebelein, (New York: Publication Office "Our Hope," 1920), 257.
[48] C. I. Scofield, *Where Faith Sees Christ* (Greenville: Gospel Hour, n.d.), 30.
[49] Scofield, "The Church and Churches," 269.
[50] Ibid., 274.

It may safely be said that the Judaizing of the Church has done more to hinder her progress, pervert her mission, and destroy her spiritually, than all other causes combined. Instead of pursuing her appointed path of separation from the world and following the Lord in her heavenly calling, she has used Jewish Scriptures to justify herself in lowering her purpose to the civilization of the world, the acquisition of wealth, the use of an imposing ritual, the erection of magnificent churches, the invocation of God's blessing upon the conflicts of armies, and the division of an equal brotherhood into "clergy" and "laity."[51]

His claims here appear to place him in the category of separation as evidenced through his words about politics and governmental structures:

There is such a thing as a mere mechanical separation from the world. We are to remember that a distinction must be made between the world of men — humanity, that God so loved as to give His only begotten Son to redeem, and the world system organized under Satan in its forms social, political and commercial. The individual is in the world, but not of it. It is a scene through which he is passing and his attitude toward it should be that of his Lord and of the apostles.[52]

His doubt about the possibility of a meaningful Christian civic engagement with the world is evident from his own words that "The name Christian is applied to everything. We have even the phrases 'Christian world' and 'Christian nations.' Biblically, one might as well say 'Christian devil' as 'Christian world.' According to Scripture the Christian is 'not of this world,' and no one seriously pretends that any nation is really Christian."[53]

Elsewhere, he explained his view of the Christian's this-worldly involvement in a

---

[51] Scofield, *Rightly Dividing,* 12. There is little doubt that Scofield was here referring to what he and other fundamentalist leaders considered to be the ever-evolving dynamic of the apostasy of American denominationalism, which in turn perpetuated apostasy in the denominational seminaries. Scofield's colleague William Pettingill put it this way: "The vanguard of the great apostasy is in the schools and college and theological (!) seminaries ... it makes a difference what kind of teaching goes on in these schools. Most of them as we have said, are labeled "Christian," but it is to speak mildly when we say that very many of them are anti-Christian to all intent and purpose. They are denominational, for they were established by the denominations and are still controlled by the denominations; but they have long since ceased to be useful in fulfilling the purpose of denominationalism — "they which are approved may be manifest," And in so far they are a swindle and a humbug ... Christianity as a revealed religion is losing its place in the bosom of the professing church itself." See Pettingill's essay "Denominationalism," *Serving-and-* Waiting 1, no. 4 (August 1911): 1.

[52] Scofield, "Civic Righteousness," 35.

[53] Scofield, "What Is Christianity?" *Serving-and-Waiting* 14, no. 1 (May 1924): 31.

more balanced tone. When asked "In what sense is the believer to separate himself from the world?" Scofield replied, "The biblical thought of separation is from whatever is necessarily dishonoring to God. The Christian is separate from the world in that he does not make the world the object of his hopes and ambitions."[54] Most revealing to the discussion of human flourishing and earthly vs. heavenly citizenship is what he said next in his answer, namely, that the Christian "is separate from the unbelievers in that he does not yoke himself with them in a common purpose."[55] Although he did not specifically direct his words here at Christians who were engaged in the political sphere, one could interpret Scofield as meaning that Christians ought not work together with unbelievers to achieve the public common good. When taken with his doubts about the possibility of the world being transformed in absence of the gospel, we are at least led to believe that Scofield probably viewed political efforts at establishing the common good as a waste of time that could otherwise be spent evangelizing the lost.

Scofield did, however, hold that believers had to engage the culture in a specific way in order to live properly as Christians. To re-emphasize, like many of his fundamentalist counterparts Scofield was convinced that the only worthwhile kind of engagement was evangelism. However, he drew a practical connection between evangelism and social service, noting that Christ himself demonstrated the value of serving others: "It seems clear that the Christian could take little part, if any, in schemes for the improvement of the unregenerate world. The whole scene is one awaiting judgment; but as our Lord met throngs of people, He healed the sick and fed the hungry without asking whether they believed on Him or not. In other words, He did works of mercy."[56] From this evidence, the conclusion can be drawn that Scofield believed that Christians should live differently from the unbelieving, unregenerate people around them. Further, he believed that evangelism was the only cure for an unbelieving world and that service to others and "works of mercy" should be done for unbelievers to increase the possibility that converts to Christ would result.

THE ROLE OF CURRICULUM AND METHODS

As was the case for most of the fundamentalists who launched Bible institutes,

---

[54] Scofield, "Christian Conduct," in *Dr. C. I. Scofield's Question Box*, edited by Ella Pohle (Pasig City, TN: Lifeline Philippines, n.d.), 26.

[55] Ibid. He goes on to explain, however, that "In the application of these principles, each believer must under the light of the Word, act upon his own convictions." This caveat leaves some room for interpretation as to what exactly Scofield meant with respect to Christian engagement and separation.

[56] Scofield, "What Is Christianity?", 31.

C. I. Scofield was a pastor, author, and conference speaker; he was a professionally trained educator.[57] The literature that gives insight into his educational methods are scarce; however, one can extrapolate basic principles of his methodology from his theology and his approach to expository preaching. Scofield served as the first president of the Philadelphia School of the Bible; however, William Pettingill was the chief educational architect for the school. In spite of this division of responsibilities, they both agreed that two key concepts should run throughout their curricular approach at the school. The first was the primacy of scripture and Bible training and the second was a practical training in evangelism and Christian ministry.

While Scofield is not typically connected to research on religious educators, he was one of the first pastors who introduced expository preaching in his pulpit. Prior to his ministry, many sermons featured devotional thoughts, exhortations, or evangelistic presentations. In addition to influencing the preaching and teaching adopted by churches across the country, Scofield also was an early pioneer in the field of distance education. He did this through a Bible Correspondence Course managed by Moody School of the Bible.[58] This correspondence course included lessons and examinations aimed at the education of individuals in a biblical, dispensational theology. While not always known as an educator, Scofield's influence on the church through his preaching and teaching ministry situates him as a religious educator worth studying and emulating. Not only does his church ministry justify the study of Scofield as an educator, but he also played significant roles in the formation of Philadelphia School of the Bible as well as influencing his friend Lewis Sperry, Chafer who founded Dallas Theological Seminary.[59] Students would do well to learn from his example

[57] Due to Scofield's growing popularity as a preacher, he began to expand his ministry beyond the pulpit of his church. Soon he began preaching at various conferences around the world. These conferences became quite popular in the late 1800s and early 1900s, but the two most famous were the Keswick Conference in England and the Northfield Conference in the United States. His approach to expository preaching encouraged the attendees in their faith and led them to adopt his methodology. Of the speakers who frequented these conferences, Scofield was perhaps one of the best known. His popularity stemmed from his success of his reference Bible which sold approximately two million copies in the first few years of its publication. For more on the influence of these conferences and the influence of Scofield, see J. Wilbur Chapman, *The Life and Work of Dwight Lyman Moody* (London, 1900); Oswald T. Allis, *Prophecy and the Church* (Philadelphia: Presbyterian & Reformed, 1945), 267; and John Hannah, "Cyrus Ingerson Scofield," *The Dictionary of Premillenial Theology*, ed. Mal Couch (Grand Rapids, MI: Kregel, 1997).
[58] See C.I. Scofield, "Old Testament," in *The Scofield Bible Correspondence Course*, vol. 1. reprint (Chicago: Moody Bible Institute, 1907/1934).
[59] In addition to assisting the founding of Philadelphia School of the Bible and influencing the founder of DTS, there were numerous Bible colleges and institutes influenced by Scofield's dispensationalism and the *Scofield Reference Bible* including the early formation of Liberty University.

and expand on his methodology. In doing so, they will be prepared for a ministry of teaching both in the church and outside.

CONCLUSION

Scofield's dispensationalism was inseparable from the way he wrote, thought, and taught as an educator. As his writings show, the purpose of a Christian education was to save unbelieving citizens of earth so that they could become heavenly citizens. He believed that faithfulness in engaging culture meant evangelizing unbelievers instead of leveraging social programs. For Scofield, the Bible was central to a Christian education, and certainly his legacy through his publications and his institution are evidence of this fact.

PRIMARY SOURCE SAMPLE[60]

Since leaving Los Angeles I have been much in thought about my visit there, and I find that the thing that hulks largest in my mind is not the wonderful city which has sprung up on that coast as by magic, nor the great agricultural and commercial possibilities that center there, but rather the tremendous possibilities of Christian power and usefulness open to the Los Angeles Bible Institute.

Back of you to the eastward and northward lies a great region as yet but slightly developed but certain to become in a very few years the home of teeming millions; there will very largely be emigrant; they will need evangelizing. All experience in the east as well as in the northwest proves that more vigorous means than those in use through the local church will be needed to bring these great populations to Christ. Men must be trained on the ground; trained for rough work, hard work, unselfish work if the great victory for Christ is to be achieved. Here alone is a field bewildering in its immensity and possibilities.

I see the vision of your great building filled with converted young men and young women breathing the atmosphere of consecration, high purity and triumphant faith and going out into these needed fields equipped to teach and preach the gospel. But I see in my vision also an even greater possibility. You at Los Angeles front the pagan world. Just across the sea from you lie the teeming millions of China and other unevangelized sections of heathendom. The great cry is for trained soul-winners adapted to such a work and the opportunity is simply boundless in its scope; and then I think of the millions of Spanish speaking people lying to the southward in Central and South America.

Campbell Morgan calls this the "Continent of Opportunity," and I believe he is right. The success of the Central American Mission alone gives assurance that these peoples

---

[60] "A Letter from Dr. C. I. Scofield," *King's Business* 4, no 7 (1913): 329.

are singularly open to the Gospel. There are at least eight millions of aborigines as yet wholly unevangelized. What a field! And no other Bible Institute in the world is so strategically placed for training workers for these three great needs as yours. How much you need wisdom from above. How much you need sympathy and the effective support of Christians all over this broad land. It is my hope and prayer that these will not be withheld. May God bless you in your great task.

BIBLIOGRAPHY

Ahlstrom, Sydney. *A Religious History of the American People*. New Haven: Yale University Press, 1972.

Allis, Oswald T. *Prophecy and the Church*. Philadelphia: Presbyterian & Reformed, 1945.

Chapman, J. Wilbur. *The Life and Work of Dwight Lyman Moody*. (London, 1900)

Erickson, Millard. *Christian Theology*. 2nd ed. Grand Rapids: Baker, 1998.

Hannah, John. "Cyrus Ingerson Scofield." In *The Dictionary of Premillenial Theology*. Edited by Mal Couch Grand Rapids, MI: Kregel, 1997.

Marsden, George M. *Fundamentalism and American Culture*. New York: Oxford University Press, 1980.

_____. *Understanding Fundamentalism and Evangelicalism*. Grand Rapids: Eerdmans, 1991.

McKinney, Larry J. *Equipping For Service: A Historical Account of the Bible College Movement In North America*. Fayetteville: Accrediting Association of Bible Colleges, 1997.

Moore, Russell D. *The Kingdom of Christ: The New Evangelical Perspective*. Wheaton: Crossway, 2004.

Noll, Mark A. *The Scandal of the Evangelical Mind*. Grand Rapids: Eerdmans, 1994.

Pettingill, William. "Denominationalism." *Serving-and-Waiting* 1, no. 4 (August 1911): 1.

Saucy, Robert L. *The Case for Progressive Dispensationalism: The Interface Between Dispensational and Non-Dispensational Theology*. Grand Rapids: Zondervan, 1993.

_____. *The Church in God's Program*. Chicago: Moody Press, 1972.

Scofield, C.I. "Christian Conduct." In *Dr. C. I. Scofield's Question Box*, edited by Ella Pohle, 20-29. Pasig City, TN: Lifeline Philippines, n.d.

_____. "Civic Righteousness." In *Dr. C. I. Scofield's Question Box*, edited by Ella Pohle, 35-36. Pasig City, TN: Lifeline Philippines, n.d.

_____. "Does the Bible Throw Light on This War? ed. C.I. Scofield, *What Do the Prophets Say?* Greenville: Gospel Hour, 1918.

_____. "Definiteness." *Serving-and-Waiting* 9, no. 2 (June 1919): 67-69.

_____. "Deuteronomic Covenant." In *Dr. C. I. Scofield's Question Box*, edited by Ella Pohle, 87-88. Pasig City, TN: LifeLine Philippines, n.d.

_____. "Kingdom Truth." In *Dr. C. I. Scofield's Question Box*, edited by Ella Pohle, 63-73. Pasig City, TN: LifeLine Philippines, n.d

_____. *Old Testament*. Vol. 1 of *The Scofield Bible Correspondence Course*. 1907. Reprint, Chicago: Moody Bible Institute, 1934.

_____. *Rightly Dividing the Word of Truth: Ten Outline Studies of the More Important Divisions of Scripture*. Old Tappan, NJ: Fleming H. Revell, 1896.

_____. "The Church." In *Dr. C. I. Scofield's Question Box*, edited by Ella Pohle, 30-35. Pasig City, TN: Lifeline Philippines, n.d.

_____. "The Church and Churches." In *Things New and Old: Old and New Testament Studies by Dr. C. I. Scofield*, edited by A.C. Gaebelein, 257-69. New York: Publication Office "Our Hope," 1920.

_____. "The Grace of God." In *The Fundamentals: A Testimony to the Truth*, edited by R.A Torrey and A.C. Dixon, 98-109. Vol. 3. 1917. Reprint, Baker, 2003.

_____, ed. *The Scofield Reference Bible*. New York: Oxford University Press, 1917.

_____. "To the Philadelphia Prophetic Conference," *Serving-and-Waiting* 8, no. 3 (July 1918): 86-87.

_____. "What Is Christianity?" *Serving-and-Waiting* 14, no. 1 (May 1924): 31-32.

_____. *Where Faith Sees Christ*. Greenville: Gospel Hour, n.d.

Showers, Renald "A History of Philadelphia College of the Bible." Th.M. thesis, Dallas Theological Seminary, 1962.

Stanfield, Daniel. "Biography – Dr. C . I. Scofield." In *Bible Sanity.org;* http://biblesanity.org/scofield.htm, accessed May 27, 2014.

Trumbull, Charles G. *The Life Story of C. I. Scofield*. 1920. Reprint, Eugene, OR: Wipf & Stock, 2007.

"Will the Jews Return to Palestine as a War Sequel?" *King's Business* 6, no. 4 (1915): 273-74.

Watson, William C. Dispensationalism before Darby: Seventeenth-Century and Eighteenth-Century English Apocalypticism. Silverton, OR: Lampion Press, 2015.

ADDITIONAL PRIMARY RESOURCES

Scofield, C. I., *A Mighty Wind: Plain Papers on the Doctrine of the Holy Spirit*. Grand Rapids: Baker, 1973.

_____, ed. *What Do the Prophets Say?* Greenville: Gospel Hour, 1918.

_____. "The First Christmas Night." In *No Room in the Inn and Other Interpretations*, edited by Mary Emily Reily, 1-5. Greenville: Gospel Hour, 1941.

_____. "The Heavenly Pattern." *Serving-and-Waiting* 13, no. 12 (April 1924): 605-06.

_____. "Influence of Prophetic Truth Upon Character and Conduct." *Serving-and-Waiting* 12, no. 1 (May 1922): 31-34.

_____. "Israel and the Church." In *Dr. C. I. Scofield's Question Box*, edited by Ella Pohle, 57-61. Pasig City, TN: LifeLine Philippines, n.d.

_____. "Jacob's Well." In *No Room in the Inn and Other Interpretations*, edited by Mary Emily Reily, 41-43. Greenville: Gospel Hour, 1941.

_____. "Miscellaneous." In *Dr. C. I. Scofield's Question Box*, edited by Ella Pohle, 88-89. Pasig City, TN: Lifeline Philippines, n.d.

_____. "The Mystery of Godliness." *Serving-and-Waiting* 9, no. 1 (May 1919): 7-11.

_____. "The New Life." In *No Room in the Inn and Other Interpretations*, edited by Mary Emily Reily, 113-118. Greenville: Gospel Hour, 1941.

_____. "Rationalism." In *Dr. C.I. Scofield's Question Box*, edited by Ella Pohle, 130-33. Pasig City, TN: Lifeline Philippines, n.d.

_____. "Repentance." In *Dr. C.I. Scofield's Question Box*, edited by Ella Pohle, 133. Pasig City, TN: Lifeline Philippines, n.d.

_____. "Science and the Bible." In *Dr. C. I. Scofield's Question Box*, edited by Ella Pohle, 146-49. Pasig City, TN: Lifeline Philippines, n.d.

CHAPTER 24

John Dewey:

Father of Progressive Education

J. GREGORY LAWSON

KEN COLEY

John Dewey (1859-1952)

John Dewey is the father of progressive education. His impact on contemporary secular education is considered unmatched by any other educator. Dewey influenced religious educators by shifting the focus to a student-centered instruction model and curriculum with an emphasis on the importance of experience in learning. Rejecting the Christian foundation of his mother, Dewey would die as an atheist with an evolutionary, pragmatic, humanistic worldview.

HISTORICAL BACKGROUND

The year 1859 proved to be a significant year in the history and development of Western Intellectual History.[1] On October 20, 1859, John Dewey was born to Archibald and Lucina (Rich) Dewey in Burlington, Vermont, as the third of four sons.[2] It was during this same year that Darwin published *Origin of the Species* and John Brown, "the famous abolitionist," conducted a monumental raid on Harpers Ferry, West Virginia, ultimately resulting in the American Civil War (1861-1865), "which began shortly after Abraham Lincoln was elected president."[3] Casil continued saying, "It is accurate to say that the majority of men, women, and children in the United States during the year of John Dewey's birth had few, if any, of the rights all Americans share today."[4] Dewey's birth came in the midst of an era of great social change in the United States which significantly shaped his own view of the world.

Dewey was born into a family experiencing grief. Forty weeks prior to his birth, his family experienced a tragic accident resulting in the death of his oldest brother named John Archibald, who was three years of age.[5] Sharing his dead brother's name, Dewey grew up as a preferred child with a sense of destiny. Martin writes, "He shouldered his responsibilities and learned to enjoy living for his parents first and for others later, until eventually he committed himself to representing the needs of the American people."[6] His early years continued to be a challenge both to John and his parents. His father, Archibald, at fifty years of age answered the call as a Union Soldier, and "sold his grocery business and enlisted as quartermaster in the First Vermont Cavalry."[7] Archibald had a successful military career and remained in active duty until 1865. The war, however, made a deep impression upon the young man and "was an important reference point for his later reflections on the futility of violence in the achievement of human purposes."[8] After the family's brief stay in Virginia toward the end of the Civil War, followed by Archibald's business ventures in both Virginia and Illinois at the conclusion of the war, the family was eventually reunited as a unit in Burlington, Vermont, in 1867.[9]

---

[1] For more on the significance of this era in history see Robert Brett Westbrook, *John Dewey and American Democracy* (Ithaca: Cornell University Press, 1991).

[2] Ibid.

[3] Amy Sterling Casil, *John Dewey: The Founder of American Liberalism* (New York: Rosen Publishing, 2006), 8.

[4] Ibid.

[5] Jay Martin, *The Education of John Dewey: A Biography* (New York: Columbia University Press, 2002), 5-6.

[6] Ibid., 7.

[7] Ibid.

[8] Westbrook, *Dewey and American Democracy*, 3.

[9] Martin, *Education of John Dewey*, 13.

During his formative years, education played an important role in the family. This was due to his mother's influence. Addressing her influence, Westbrook writes, "Her dedication to the education of her sons guaranteed that he would have the resources he needed to work his way out from under her thumb."[10] Lucina came from an educated family, including several college educated men and "was determined that her boys would be the first Deweys to obtain such a degree."[11] She provided numerous reading opportunities for her sons, laying the foundation for John and his brother Davis to enter the University of Vermont in 1875.[12]

When John entered the University of Vermont in 1875, he was only fifteen years old.[13] The University of Vermont was a small college at the time, and Dewey graduated with only eighteen students.[14] During college, he did well enough to graduate Phi Beta Kappa while majoring in moral philosophy, which included courses in political economics, law, history, psychology, ethics, philosophy of religion, and logic.[15] His reading interests went well beyond what was necessary for classroom success focusing on areas of philosophy, literature and sociology; however, his favorite reading "was the British periodical press, and he followed the controversies surrounding evolutionary biology in the *Contemporary Review*, the *Nineteenth Century*, and the *Fortnightly Review*."[16] By this time in his academic career, he was well versed in addressing the major philosophical issues of his day.

After graduation from the University of Vermont in 1879, Dewey taught high school in Pennsylvania and Vermont. Westbrook notes that Dewey had a difficult time in his brief high school teaching career, "He had considerable problems with classroom discipline and began to contemplate a switch to an academic career."[17] This experience served as a catalyst to move Dewey toward analyzing education from both a philosophical and practical perspective. Desiring to be educated at a higher level, particularly in the area of philosophy, Dewey enrolled in a new doctoral program at Johns Hopkins University where he studied "logic, new experimental

---

[10] Westbrook, *Dewey and American Democracy*, 4.

[11] Ibid.

[12] Ibid.

[13] Alan Ryan, *John Dewey and the High Tide of American Liberalism* (New York: W. W. Norton & Company, 1997), 48.

[14] Ibid., 49.

[15] Westbrook, *Dewey and American Democracy*, 5.

[16] Ibid.

[17] Ibid., 8.

psychology, and neo-Hegelian philosophy."[18] His first course was a logic course team-taught by George Sylvester Morris and G. Stanley Hall. One biographer wrote, "It would not be easy to be a student of both — an idealist and an experimentalist — but Dewey tried."[19] While Charles S. Peirce taught at Johns Hopkins during this same time period, Dewey had limited exposure to Peirce even though Peirce's philosophy would eventually become influential in Dewey's philosophical system. In time, Dewey shifted from idealism to pragmatism. While "John Dewey was thought by many to be the greatest of the American pragmatists," it was "Charles Sanders Peirce who originated the pragmatic method."[20] After finishing his doctorate at Johns Hopkins, Dewey followed Morris to the University of Michigan to become a professor.[21]

At the University of Michigan, Dewey met his wife, Alice Chapman. They were married in 1886.[22] In 1887, Dewey published his first book, *Psychology*, which still reflected his interest in Hegelian philosophy.[23] Throughout Dewey's life, publication of books, articles, and essays played an important role in his intellectual development. Southern Illinois University Press has compiled and edited Dewey's writing, which consist of thirty-seven total volumes. Dewey left Michigan after one year to head the philosophy program at the University of Minnesota, but after his friend Professor Morris' sudden death Dewey returned to the University of Michigan where he remained until he accepted a position at the University of Chicago in 1894.[24]

William Rainey Harper was president of the University of Chicago and instrumental in bringing Dewey to Chicago. Westbrook explained some of the motivations for making his change from Michigan to Chicago saying, "Burdened with the costs of raising a growing family, which by this time included three children, Dewey was attracted by Harper's offer of

---

[18] Larry A. Hickman, Stefan Neubert and Kerten Reich, eds., *John Dewey Between Pragmatism & Constructionism* (New York: Fordham University Press, 2009), 5.

[19] Martin, *Education of John Dewey*, 65.

[20] Maureen T. Lapan, *Education on the Brink: Reform Reconsidered* (Hauppauge: Nova Science Publishers, 2003), 29.

[21] Ann Boydston, ed., *The Later Works of John Dewey, 1925-1953: 1938, Logic: The Theory of Inquiry* (Carbondale: Southern Illinois University, 2008), 533.

[22] Schellenberg wrote, "Although Dewey's love affair with Hegelian philosophy continued, another love also became manifest in his early years at Ann Arbor. This concerned an energetic and very bright philosophy student named Alice Chapman." See James A. Schellenberg, *Searchers, Seers, and Shakers: Masters of Social Science* (New Brunswick: Transaction Publishers, 2007), 65.

[23] Ibid.

[24] Ibid.

a salary of five thousand dollars."[25] Ultimately, John and Alice had six biological children and one adopted child. While Dewey's initial desire was to establish a world class department of philosophy, his time in Chicago may best be remembered for his educational experimentation, resulting in "the elementary school created at the University of Chicago to experiment with or test educational and psychological techniques, processes, and experiences."[26] Simpson indicates that Dewey's concern for his own children "turned his academic interests in the direction of philosophy of education."[27] While Dewey's educational philosophy will always be a matter for debate, Hook contends that "the Dewey Laboratory School was the most important experimental venture in the whole history of American education."[28] After a period of infighting at the University of Chicago, the Dewey school was merged with a competing elementary school. Alice Dewey became the principal of the new school but was removed after one year. Westbrook writes, "Both husband and wife immediately resigned from the School of Education, and Dewey also resigned from the philosophy department. Dewey was offered an appointment at Columbia University and began work there in February of 1905."[29] Dewey would remain at Columbia University until his formal retirement in 1930.

Brinkmann explained that Dewey's move from Chicago to Columbia was more than a geographic relocation. "The move to New York marked Dewey's final distancing of himself from idealistic philosophy. Although he would never again be involved in the kind of concrete philosophical — pedagogical experiments he had conducted at the laboratory school, his thinking nevertheless took an experimental, pragmatic, and instrumental direction."[30] During Dewey's tenure at Columbia, he became more involved in political and social issues impacting both the United States and the international community. Villemaire wrote, "At Columbia, Dewey put no educational program forward. Secure in himself, with his own developing philosophy and with his growing worldwide fame, he preferred to be left alone."[31] While Dewey may have preferred to be left alone, he continued to be in demand on a national and international scale as an educational expert.

---

[25] Westbrook, *Dewey and American Democracy*, 59.

[26] Douglas J. Simpson, *John Dewey* (New York: Peter Lang Publishing, 2006), 3.

[27] Ibid.

[28] Sidney Hook, *John Dewey: An Intellectual Portrait* (New York: Cosimo Classics, 2008), 15.

[29] Westbrook, *Dewey and American Democracy*, 112-13.

[30] Svend Brinkmann, *John Dewey: Science for a Changing World* (New Brunswick: Transaction Publishers, 2013), 13.

[31] D. Villemaire, *E. A. Burtt: Historian and Philosopher* (Dordrecht: Kluwer Academic Publishers, 2002), 24.

Dewey spent time lecturing and writing both in China and Japan. In October 1920, Dewey was awarded an honorary doctor of philosophy degree from the National University of China, becoming only the fifth foreigner at that time to have such an honor bestowed.[32] In addition to these international ventures, Dewey also provided educational consultation in many countries that were experiencing rapid social and political change. Acknowledging Dewey's political and social leaning, Martin writes, "In economic terms, Dewey was an ally of the socialist professional unions, and a cooperative commonwealth."[33] Martin continued his description of the development of Dewey's political and philosophical thought which crystallized during his tenure at Columbia:

> He rejected dialectical materialism in favor of experimentalism; class warfare in favor of cooperation; revolutionary change in favor of evolutionary amelioration; party discipline in favor of freedom of thought; and the separation of means from ends in favor of their unity. Above all, he rejected violence as the chosen instrument of change in favor of bringing change about through peaceful evolution. In short, he was a contented socialist but a fierce opponent of Marxism-Leninism.[34]

Dewey's vast international influence was used in many ways, one of which was to benefit the American government during World War II. Martin explained, "Even as late as 1942, after America went to war against Japan, the State Department, convinced of Dewey's still immense influence, asked him to compose a message from Dewey were scattered all over China by U. S. airplanes in an effort to encourage the Chinese to keep fighting against the Japanese invaders."[35] While Dewey was an early advocate of the political and social changes taking place in both China and Russia, he lived to see the violent nature of the communist regimes. Dewey valued the concepts of democracy, freedom of speech, and academic freedom which were greatly limited as the communists gained control.

Throughout Dewey's life, he attempted to be on the cutting edge of educational reform and advancement. This included the use of new technology to get his message across. At the age of seventy, he participated in the shooting of newsreel footage addressing the distinction between education and mere schooling.[36] According to Hickman, "What this little newsreel clip reveals is Dewey's remarkable ability to envision possibilities beyond his

---

[32] Martin, *Education of John Dewey*, 321.

[33] Ibid., 322.

[34] Ibid.

[35] Ibid., 326.

[36] Hickman, *Between Pragmatism & Constructionism*, 4.

own experience, his faith in the intelligence of average citizens, and his openness to the use of new technologies."[37] Scholarship and relevancy were both important components in Dewey's development as an educational philosopher.

Dewey's contributions to education extended beyond the classroom and the international community. He also served as president of the American Psychological Association, American Philosophic Association, and the League for Industrial Democracy. He was involved with the National Association for the Advancement of Colored People, American Federation of Teachers, American Civil Liberties Union, American Association of University Professors, and the New School for Social Research. Dewey was one of the original signers of the *Humanistic Manifesto* in 1933, and he had a close association with Jane Addam's Hull House.[38] In 1937 when Dewey was seventy-eight, "he headed a commission that traveled to Mexico to investigate Joseph Stalin's charges against Leon Trotsky."[39] Active in numerous civil rights struggles, he remained politically and socially active his entire life.

During his long life, Dewey continued to face the future with optimism. Hickman explained that "Despite the cruel losses of two beloved children, harsh criticism of his work, the death of his wife, Alice, in 1927, and dismay at the horrors of the Great Depression and two World Wars, he continued to face the future with great hope."[40] At the age of eighty-seven Dewey married Roberta Lowitz Grant who was forty-two at the time. John and Roberta had shared a friendship for nine years prior to their marriage. The Deweys enjoyed traveling, intellectual discussion, and taking care of their two adopted children. On June 1, 1952, Dewey died at his apartment in New York City at the age of ninety-two.[41]

THEOLOGY OF RELIGIOUS EDUCATION

John Dewey had a major influence on both secular and sectarian education. One author explained, "It would be difficult to find someone in the nineteenth century who had a more profound impact on the educational system of America as a whole and on Christian education indirectly as John Dewey."[42] Further, "His emphasis upon pupil needs, a collaborative learning environment between the teacher and student, and activity-centered

---

[37] Ibid.

[38] Louis Menand, *Pragmatism: A Reader* (New York: Vintage Books, 1997), 181.

[39] Ibid.

[40] Hickman, *Between Pragmatism and Constructionism*, 17.

[41] Ibid.

[42] Michael J. Anthony and Warren S. Benson, *Exploring the History & Philosophy of Christian Education* (Grand Rapids: Kregel, 2003), 334.

learning have shaped modern Christian education in numerous ways."[43] As Dewey's life unfolded, he adopted a humanistic, atheistic, evolutionary view of faith and religion. It is interesting to note that Dewey began his faith pilgrimage in a completely different direction. Campbell writes, "Dewey began his academic career in a traditionally religious fashion; he had been converted as a young man and belonged to congregations throughout the first three and one-half decades of his life. He was active in the Students' Christian Association while at Ann Arbor, and he published in various religious journals."[44] It is evident that Dewey was associated with churches and Christianity, but there is no evidence that he ever had a personal relationship with Jesus Christ. While Dewey may have contributed significantly to contemporary education, his theological beliefs and hermeneutic require a serious evaluation.

Lucina Dewey, John's mother, attempted to provide a spiritual foundation for the Dewey household. John's father Archibald was twenty years older than his wife and failed to provide spiritual leadership in the home. It was Lucina's desire that each of her children receive a higher level education and also to be introduced to and accept the Christian faith. Rockefeller described Lucina's spiritual formation:

> She had been raised a Universalist, but as a young woman she was converted in a revival meeting to the kind of evangelical pietism that was widespread in many parts of the country in the mid-nineteenth century. As a result she abandoned the central Universalist belief that God will eventually save all from sin and damnation, and she joined the Congregational Church. There-after [sic] her personal faith centered around belief in the holiness and goodness of God, the problem of sin, and the doctrine that only those who experience a supernatural regeneration in and through God's grace as revealed in Jesus Christ will be redeemed.[45]

In essence, Lucina had a radical conversion through Jesus Christ. As a result, her life would never be the same, and she attempted to influence her family toward making the same decision.

It appears that Dewey fostered resentment toward his mother's deeply held religious convictions. Ryan contends, "To call it a lifetime of resentment is no exaggeration. Dewey became angrier about his mother's piety as he got older."[46] According to Ryan the negative

---

[43] Ibid.

[44] James Campbell, Understanding John Dewey: Nature and Cooperative Intelligence (Peru: Open Court Publishing, 1996), 269.

[45] Steven C. Rockefeller, *John Dewey: Religious Faith and Democratic Humanism* (New York: Columbia University Press, 1991), 36.

[46] Ryan, *American Liberalism*, 46.

movement away from the evangelical faith was based on the following progression: "In his thirties he merely remarked in an address to a Students' Christian meeting that incessantly examining a child's convictions is as foolish as digging up a seed to see if it is growing ... His mother's efforts eventually alienated Dewey from all moralities that dealt in sin and guilt and by the same token from all understandings of religion that separated the believer from his God in the way traditional Calvinist Christianity did."[47]

Related to the issue of the impact of Calvinism on Dewey, Shook writes, "Dewey's organic idealism healed the dualisms (saved versus damned, spirit versus nature) of the strict Calvinism of his upbringing and confirmed his preference for universal salvation and his identification of religious faith with moral commitment."[48] Dewey indicated "that Hegel's method healed an 'inward laceration' by helping him overcome the 'sense of divisions and separations' inculcated by his evangelical New England upbringing, between mind and body and between nature and spirit that contributed to the growing gulf between philosophy and science."[49] Eventually, even Hegel's philosophy failed to satisfy the deep questions and longings in Dewey's heart and life.

Rockefeller addresses the theological and hermeneutical shift that took place in Dewey's life saying, "There is no explicit affirmation of belief in the God of absolute idealism in *The Study of Ethics* (1894) or Dewey's other published writings thereafter."[50] As far as Dewey was concerned, God began to be "understood as basically a projection of Human values, and the absolute need only be interpreted quite simply as the human community and those aspects of nature that support it."[51] This shift limited Dewey's ability to see the need or have a need for the church, and he began to promote social change through the community and non-sectarian organizations that followed his philosophy. Dewey's theological shift resulted in "actually a short even if critically important, step from Dewey's neo-Hegelian panentheism and social mysticism to a thorough-going humanism and naturalism."[52] The shift to humanism was solidified with Dewey's signing of the *Humanist Manifesto* in 1933.

The *Humanist Manifesto* that Dewey signed contained a complete rejection of the

---

[47] Ibid.

[48] John R. Shook and James Alan Good, eds., *John Dewey's Philosophy of Spirit, with the 1897 Lecture on Hegel* (New York: Fordham University Press, 2010), 14.

[49] Thomas C. Dalton, *Becoming John Dewey: Dilemmas of a Philosopher and Naturalist* (Bloomington: Indiana University Press, 2002), 41.

[50] Rockefeller, *Faith and Democratic Humanism*, 216.

[51] Ibid.

[52] Ibid.

Christian truth taught by his mother and also a rejection of the Bible as God's authoritative word. According to the *Humanist Manifesto,* the universe was not created by God but instead was self-existing. Man is seen as being a part of nature the result of a continuous evolutionary process. The dualism of mind and body is rejected as well as a rejection of afterlife; therefore, the focus should be on improving the current condition. In the humanist mindset, man is the center of the universe and God is rejected. Man is basically good and the biblical concept of sin is rejected.[53] In the next year, 1934, Dewey would solidify his acceptance of the humanistic principles in *A Common Faith,* a book produced based on the Terry Lectures delivered at Yale University. In *A Common Faith*, Dewey wrote, "Faith in the continual disclosing of truth through directed cooperative human endeavor is more religious in quality than is any faith in a completed revelation."[54] In this instance, Dewey blends his pragmatic and humanistic philosophical systems to see truth as being relative based on the human experience and his belief in an ongoing evolutionary process.

The ultimate rejection of Christianity becomes increasingly evident and even hostile later in Dewey's life. Ryan asserts, "[T]he autobiography that his daughter Jane Dewey compiled when her father was eighty years old for inclusion in *The Philosophy of John Dewey* is much angrier."[55] By this point in Dewey's life, there was no room for debate regarding Dewey's rejection of the Christian faith. Ryan concludes, "To call it a lifetime of resentment is no exaggeration."[56] Dewey would die as an atheist with an evolutionary, pragmatic, humanistic worldview. [57]

CONTRIBUTIONS TO EDUCATION

Dewey is widely acclaimed as the most influential educational voice of the twentieth century. His approach to education was a rejection of the prevailing pedagogies of his time and led to the title 'Father of Progressive Education'. Beginning with his dismissal of absolute truth as the metaphysical basis of what students are to be taught, Dewey advocated for change in the way educators viewed their students, the curriculum that was to be presented, the methodologies employed in the classroom, and even the instructional environment itself. "As

---

[53] Jonas E. Alexis, *Christianity's Dangerous Idea*, vol. 1 (Bloomington: Author House, 2010), 186.

[54] John Dewey, *A Common Faith* (Yale University Press, 1934), 26.

[55] Ryan, *American Liberalism*, 46.

[56] Ibid.

[57] Dewey rejected the concept of sin, eternal consequences, and a creator God, replacing this belief system with an emphasis on man's ability to solve his problems through science, education, and experience.

a naturalist, he rejected God and supernatural influences, yet his ideas about learning through experience, student-centered methods, and the educational process have profoundly affected contemporary religious education."[58]

PRAGMATISM AND INSTRUMENTALISM

As previously noted, Dewey's philosophy of education was influenced by the pragmatic thinking of Charles S. Peirce, William James, and George H. Mead. They believed that philosophy should deal with real human problems rather than metaphysical concerns. These pragmatists and Dewey rejected universal or eternal truths. "He believed that human beings can arrive at tentative warranted assertions. These assertions are developed as we test and verify our ideas by acting upon them to resolve problems."[59] Leyda explained Dewey's philosophy saying,

> As a pragmatist, he emphasized the utility of ideas. He called his philosophy 'instrumentalism' since he viewed concepts simply as useful instruments for solving problems. Carrying on in the tradition of earlier pragmatists, Charles Peirce and William James, Dewey believed that all inquiry should take place in a disciplined, experimental manner. Following Peirce, he rejected appeals to traditional belief, external sources of authority, or reason alone as final means of setting beliefs, viewing each as inferior to the experimental method. [60]

Dewey's pragmatism and the notion of *instrumentalism* are evident in his discussion of educational values. Dewey wrote in *Democracy and Education*,

> Since education is not a means to living, but is identical with the operation of living a life which is fruitful and inherently significant, the only ultimate value which can be set up is just the process of living itself ... The way to enable a student to apprehend the instrumental value of arithmetic is not to lecture him upon the benefit it will be to him in some remote and uncertain future, but to let him discover that success in something he is interested in doing depends upon his ability to use numbers.[61]

---

[58] Richard Leyda, "John Dewey," in *Evangelical Dictionary of Christian Education*, ed. Michael J. Anthony (Grand Rapids: Baker, 2001), 201.

[59] Gerald Gutek, *Historical and Philosophical Foundations of Education: Selected Readings* (Upper Saddle River: Merrill Prentice Hall, 2001), 171.

[60] Leyda, "John Dewey," 202.

[61] John Dewey, *Democracy and Education* (New York: Macmillan Publishing, 1964) 239-240.

DARWIN'S INFLUENCE ON DEWEY

Dewey's thinking about education was also impacted by the work of his contemporary, Charles Darwin, whose theory of evolution had much to say about the impact environment has on living organisms. Darwin theorized that various species evolved over generations, in no small part because of their environment. Reflecting on the concept of the organism in interaction with the environment, Dewey reasoned that the human organism had life-sustaining needs and impulses; therefore, "Possessing a highly developed brain, the power of speech, and the ability to create tools, the human being was able to make plans by projecting and weighing the possible results that would be caused by an action. This planning capability, which involved knowing the relationship between cause and effect, was the basis for human intelligence. Humans live in an environment that both supports and threatens life."[62]

This Darwinian view of the makeup of mankind led Dewey to embrace the value of personal experimentation and self-discovery that would become two major cornerstones in his approach to instructional design for the Laboratory School.

SOCIAL REFORM THROUGH EDUCATION

G. Stanley Hall, a contemporary of Dewey, was also an advocate for changes in the education of children; at times Hall was in agreement with Dewey and at times the two disagreed. Both Hall and Dewey rejected the practice of requiring students to sit passively while being expected to absorb large amounts of new information, Both emphasized the importance of connecting with the child's innate curiosity and personal interests as the beginning point for instruction. But unlike Dewey, "Hall argued for the individualization of instruction based on intellectual ability and gender."[63] Dewey was highly critical of Hall's approach of individualized instruction for different ability levels. He believed that education needed to connect the child's interest to the larger community and should emphasize democratic processes and larger social concerns. "For Dewey, the larger social goals included reducing the differences among social classes. Dewey argued that the economic and political power of the few made it impossible for the many either to grow as individuals or to have an impact on the social order." [64]

---

[62] Gutek, *Historical and Philosophical Foundations*, 171.

[63] Fenwick W. English, *The SAGE Handbook of Educational Leadership: Advances in Theory, Research, and Practice* (Thousand Oaks: Sage Publications, Inc., 2005), 499.

[64] Ibid.

SCIENTIFIC METHOD

With this commitment to the larger community in mind, Dewey envisioned learners interacting with each other and their environment in collaborative group problem-solving activities. "Rejecting the possibility of a universal certainty, Dewey argued that we live in a highly uncertain and relative world. In a world of continual change, Dewey advised that we have the possibility to plan and direct our lives by using the scientific method." [65] Problem solving is the way we think most effectively and the most effective approach to teaching and learning. The emphasis on problem solving and the scientific method led to the labeling of his philosophy as 'experimentalism'. His problem solving steps were as follows:

1. We encounter something different or new in experience that blocks our ongoing activity and involves us in a "problematic situation."

2. To begin to solve the problem, we need to locate it in our experience and define it as specifically and exactly as we can.

3. Once we have defined the problem, we can do the research that we need to gather the information that will help us solve the problem.

4. On the basis of the information that we have, we can formulate some tentative hypotheses, informed guesses, about what we can do to solve the problem and what effects our action is likely to have.

5. After choosing the hypothesis we think will solve our problem and give us the effects we want, we need to test it by acting on it. If we used the process successfully, our problem will be solved; if not, we need to identify our mistakes and try again. [66]

As groups of children experiment, explore, and interact with each other, their instructor, and their environment, the richest learning takes place in Dewey's eyes. From 1896 to 1904, the educator/philosopher was given an ideal laboratory in which to test his theories.

CURRICULUM AND METHODOLOGY:
EXPERIMENTALISM (1896-1904) OF THE LABORATORY SCHOOL

The approach at the Laboratory School was based on the philosophy that children learn best as a member of a group in which interaction takes place for the purpose of solving

---

[65] Gutek, *Historical Foundations*, 171.
[66] Ibid.

mutual problems. For Dewey, authentic communities were established as the participants went through three stages:

1. Common tools and objects are used and shared in common activities.

2. The association generated in pursuing common activities produces a sense of identification or membership, which results in communication, talking about common problems and endeavors.

3. Communication leads to the third stage, a commonly shared society and culture — the basis of community.[67]

The curriculum was arranged around three general types of activities: making and doing, history and geography, and science. Dewey felt that there should be continuity between the experiences a child has at home and those that he/she has at school for younger students. This harmony would lead a child naturally into the larger society. The second component, history and geography, was included for the purpose of enlarging a child's perspective of space and time. In the third stage, science challenged students in the areas of interdisciplinary problem-solving. "By using the scientific method in a collaborative group setting, Dewey's students would develop practical intelligence, a sense of reflective inquiry, and the values needed for life in a democratic community." [68]

The physical setting itself was a vital part of the curriculum implementation at the Lab School. "Children were encouraged to work in their schoolyard garden, cooperate in building and furnishing a clubhouse, and make articles in a shop for use in connection with their other work."[69] Other vocation-related learning experiences included preparing a French gourmet meal, participating in the process of making cloth, and studying model houses to aid in the investigation of community life.[70] However, by the 1950s, public support began to turn. "Eventually, progressive education became a pejorative synonym for schooling that catered to the whims of students, majored on trivial life adjustment themes, and left students deprived of the basics."[71]

---

[67] Ibid., 172.

[68] Ibid.

[69] English, *Handbook of Educational Leadership*, 511.

[70] Ibid.

[71] James Braley, Jack Layman, and Ray White, *Foundations of Christian School Education.* (Colorado Springs: Purposeful Design Publications, 2003), 38.

CONTRIBUTIONS TO RELIGIOUS EDUCATION

While his ideas were viewed as progressive and controversial by many, aspects of Dewey's philosophy and pedagogies can be found in the Gospels. The value and importance of each child was emphasized by Christ. In addition, His instruction always began with the schema of His disciples and built upon the learner's prior experience. Jesus frequently engaged His learners in the teaching/learning process, including cooperative learning techniques. So despite Dewey's opposition to Christ and Scripture, it should not be viewed as inconsistent to discover Dewey's concepts in current evangelical educational praxis.

"Emphases on practical applications of knowledge, on the activity of the student, and measurable results from ministry show the influence of Dewey. Curriculum planning has reflected his practical approach to teaching. Virtually all religious education curriculum published today has lesson content grouped into units supported by a variety of activities and projects." [72]

On the other hand, Dewey's rejection of the Creator of both the experiences of his learners and the learners themselves corrupted his philosophy of teaching and learning. His insistence on a philosophy of education purely founded on the capacity of man and devoid of the search for true wisdom found in Scripture would eventually lead to the lessening prominence of his educational theories.

CONCLUSION

For the Christian educator, Dewey provides a theological challenge. During Dewey's early years in the home, his mother, Lucina, attempted to instill strong Christian values into the life of the family. Dewey progressively rejected his mother's teaching and influence as well as the tenets of the Christian faith. He would ultimately advocate an atheistic, evolutionary humanistic worldview. Man would become the center of Dewey's universe and positive change could only take through the goodness of man and the collective experience of humanity. The God of the Bible and salvation through Jesus Christ were rejected. Dewey wished to create a new social order through a pragmatic approach to education. His pragmatism, while laudable in some aspects, was ultimately abandoned by generations that followed because it did not work.

---

[72] Leyda, "John Dewey," 203.

PRIMARY SOURCE SAMPLE[73]
THE NATURE AND MEANING OF ENVIRONMENT.

We have seen that a community or social group sustains itself through continuous self-renewal, and that this renewal takes place by means of the educational growth of the immature members of the group. By various agencies, unintentional and designed, a society transforms uninitiated and seemingly alien beings into robust trustees of its own resources and ideals. Education is thus a fostering, a nurturing, a cultivating process. All of these words mean that it implies attention to the conditions of growth. We also speak of rearing, raising, and bringing up — words which express the difference of level which education aims to cover. Etymologically, the word education means just a process of leading or bringing up. When we have the outcome of the process in mind, we speak of education as shaping, forming, molding activity — that is, a shaping into the standard form of social activity.[74]

THE NATURE OF SUBJECT MATTER

The teacher should be occupied not with subject matter in itself but in its interaction with the pupils' present needs and capacities. Hence simple scholarship is not enough. In fact, there are certain features of scholarship or mastered subject matter — taken by itself — which get in the way of effective teaching unless the instructor's habitual attitude is one of concern with its interplay in the pupil's own experience.[75]

BIBLIOGRAPHY

Alexis, Jonas E. *Christianity's Dangerous Idea*. Vol.1. Bloomington: Author House, 2010.

Anthony, Michael J. *Evangelical Dictionary of Christian Education*. Grand Rapids: Baker Book House Company, 2001.

Boydston, Ann., ed. *The Later Works of John Dewey, 1925-1953; 1938, Logic: The Theory of Inquiry*. Carbondale: Southern Illinois University, 2008.

Braley, James, Jack Layman, and Ray White. *Foundations of Christian School Education*. Colorado Springs: Purposeful Design Publications, 2003.

Brinkmann, Svend. *John Dewey: Science for a Changing World*. New Brunswick: Transaction Publishers, 2013.

Casil, Amy Sterling. *John Dewey: The Founder of American Liberalism*. New York: Rosen Publishing, 2006.

Dalton, Thomas C. *Becoming John Dewey: Dilemmas of a Philosopher and Naturalist*. Bloomington: Indiana University Press, 2002.

---

[73] John Dewey, *Democracy and Education: An Introduction to the Philosophy of Education* (New York: Macmillan Publishing, 1964).

[74] Ibid., 72

[75] Ibid., 183.

Dewey, John. *A Common Faith*. New Haven: Yale University Press, 1934.

English, Fenwick W. *The SAGE Handbook of Educational Leadership: Advances in Theory, Research, and Practice*. Thousand Oaks: Sage Publications, Inc., 2005.

Gutek, Gerald. *Historical and Philosophical Foundations of Education: Selected Readings*. Upper Saddle River: Merrill Prentice Hall, 2001.

Hook, Sidney. *John Dewey: An Intellectual Portrait*. New York: Cosimo Classics, 2008.

Hickman, Larry A., Stefan Neubert, and Kerten Reich, eds. *John Dewey between Pragmatism & Constructionism*. New York: Fordham University Press, 2009.

Lapan, Maureen T. *Education on the Brink: Reform Reconsidered*. Hauppauge: Nova Science Publishers, 2003.

Leyda, Richard. "John Dewey." In *Evangelical Dictionary of Christian Education*, by Michael J. Anthony, 201. Grand Rapids: Baker, 2001.

Martin, Jay. *The Education of John Dewey: A Biography*. New York: Columbia University Press, 2002.

Menand, Louis. *Pragmatism: A Reader*. New York: Vintage Books, 1997.

Rockefeller, Steven C. *John Dewey: Religious Faith and Democratic Humanism*. New York: Columbia University Press, 1991.

Ryan, Alan. *John Dewey and the High Tide of American Liberalism*. New York: W. W. Norton, 1997.

Schellenberg, James A. *Searchers, Seers, and Shakers: Masters of Social Science*. New Brunswick: Transaction Publishers, 2007.

Shook, John R., and James Alan Good, eds. *John Dewey's Philosophy of Spirit, with the 1897 Lecture on Hegel*. New York: Fordham University Press, 2010.

Simpson, Douglas A. *John Dewey*. New York: Peter Lang Publishing, 2006.

Villemaire, D. *E. A. Burtt: Historian and Philosopher*. Dordrecht: Kluwer Academic Publishers, 2002.

Westbrook, Robert Brett. *John Dewey and American Democracy*. Ithaca: Cornell University Press, 1991.

ADDITIONAL PRIMARY SOURCES OF JOHN DEWEY

Dewey, John A. *A Common Faith*. New Haven: Yale University Press, 1934.

_____. *Democracy and Education: An Introduction to the Philosophy of Education*. New York: Macmillan Publishing Company, 1964.

_____. *Experience and Education*. New York: Collier Books, 1963.

_____. *Individualism Old and New*. New York: Capricorn Books, 1962.

_____. *Lectures on Ethics 1900 - 1901*. Carbondale: Southern Illinois University Press, 1991.

_____. *Liberalism and Social Action*. New York: Capricorn Books, 1963.

_____. *Philosophy and Education in Their Historic Relations*. Boulder: Westview Press, 1993.

_____. *The Political Writings*. Indianapolis: Hackett Publishing Co., 1993.

_____. *The Quest for Certainty: A Study of the Relation of Knowledge and Action*. New York: G. P. Putnam's Sons, 1960.

CHAPTER 25

Arthur Flake:

Pioneer of Sunday School Administration

GARY W. WALLER

Arthur Flake (1862- 1952)

Arthur Flake was a pioneer in the administration of the Sunday school as a means for facilitating biblical literacy within the church. His role as the Sunday school innovator for Southern Baptists and his methodology for administrating and growing a Sunday school has led to the growth of the Southern Baptist Convention; the SBC is now the largest protestant denomination. His plan for growth became known as "Flake's Formula" and emphasized envisioning the possibilities, strategic organization, purposeful administration, equipping of the leadership team, and evangelism.

HISTORICAL BACKGROUND

Arthur Flake was born in LaGrange, Texas, on November 17, 1862; however, his family moved to Bell County which is where he spent his early years including his early education. As a young man, he was employed in a dry goods store in Belton. This generated a desire for him to use his sales experience to see the world. From here, he traveled as a sales representative for clothing firms based in Louisville, Kentucky, and eventually New York City. With the experience of sales and traveling, he eventually decided to start a mercantile company in partnership with Mr. Neilson of Oxford, Mississippi. Their mercantile was named, "The Flake and Neilson Company" and it lasted until 1908 when there was a downturn in the economy.

During his years as a salesman, Flake was not living a Christian life even though he had some sort of religious experience at the age fourteen. In 1893, at the age thirty-one, Flake was attending services at Cumberland Presbyterian Church in Meridian, Mississippi. The morning message convicted him of his spiritual condition and he returned that evening to discuss the sermon with the pastor. Later that evening, alone in his hotel room, he submitted his life to Christ.[1]

Because of his traveling schedule, he attended First Baptist Church in Montgomery, Alabama, and Judson Memorial Baptist Church in New York City, where Edward Judson was pastor. Through the discipleship he received from Judson, Flake began to learn to study the Bible, theology, and was encouraged to be consistently involved in the ministry of the church. In 1894, Flake moved his permanent address from New York, New York, to Winona, Mississippi, where he joined Winona Baptist Church; in June of 1895, he married Lena Nelson. Together they had three daughters over the course of their forty-two plus years of marriage.[2]

In 1895, Flake organized the first Baptist Young People's Union in the state of Mississippi. His pastor, T. J. Bailey, was very influential on Flake's growth in church work. Many of the methods that he developed in directing the union later became the foundation for manuals including duties of the leadership officers of the Sunday school.[3] Flake began his work in Sunday school and Baptist Young People's Union in Winona and from 1896-

---

[1] Harold E. Ingraham, *Baptist Leaders in Religious Education*, ed. J. M. Price (Nashville: Broadman Press, 1943), 58.

[2] C. Aubrey Hearn, "Arthur Flake — Beloved Southern Baptist Leader," *The Baptist Training Union Magazine*, Vol. III, No. 2 (February, 1937), 10.

[3] Ibid.

1909, he served in his church as the Sunday school superintendent. As superintendent, he was responsible for the overall administration, growth, and health of his church's Sunday school ministry. Sunday school and Baptist Young People's Union both began as independent organizations outside the control of the local church. Flake felt that for both organizations to achieve maximum potential of effectiveness, they needed to become part of the ministry that is administered by the local congregation. In 1899, he was asked to organize and plan the first Mississippi Baptist Young People's organization for the state and according to the Mississippi Baptist Convention state newspaper, *The Baptist*, on November 30, 1899, he was elected president when the permanent organization was inaugurated.[4]

The concept of Sunday school did not mean much to Flake prior to his election as superintendent of the Winona Baptist Church Sunday school. He began to study Sunday schools and saw various needs that led him to develop practical methods which changed the way Baptists approached the Sunday school methodology. Flake felt that everyone in the community needed to study the Bible to discover God's purpose for life and principles by which to live. Sunday school was a Sunday morning enterprise, normally prior to the worship service, with instruction for all ages. He believed that this instruction should be age appropriate, meeting the needs of believers and nonbelievers. He was so successful that he was sought for advice by churches and denominational leaders throughout the state[5] and eventually he was appointed as an assistant secretary of the Mississippi Baptist State Executive Board. A letter from Flake to Mississippi Baptists, reflecting on his appointment and goals for his new assignment, appeared in *The Baptist*, on September 21, 1899. He included a challenge to regional groups of Baptist churches, called associations, to adopt a training strategy in Sunday school work to assist their respective churches with this great endeavor.

> A Sunday school every Sunday in every Baptist church ought to be our motto. Wherever in this world there are enough Baptist people to organize a Baptist church there ought to be a Baptist Sunday school, and Mississippi Baptist ought not to be satisfied until this is accomplished.
>
> I am sure we are right in having some kind of organization, someone in special charge of the work in the associations to arrange to hold institutes in sufficient numbers that one of them, at least, will be in easy reach of every church in the association. The more local the work, the greater the results to be accomplished, I believe.[6]

---

[4] *The Baptist* (Mississippi), Nov. 30, 1899, 2.

[5] Ingraham, *Leaders in Religious Education,* 59.

[6] Arthur Flake, *The Baptist* (Mississippi), Sept. 21, 1899, 2.

In 1909, J. M. Frost recommended Flake be elected as a Field Secretary of the Baptist Sunday School Board in Nashville, Tennessee.[7] He began his work promoting Sunday schools in Baptist churches throughout the area. In 1912, he was assigned, for a year, to lead the Baptist Young People's Union work of the Baptist Sunday School Board for the area east of the Mississippi River. That one-year assignment lasted for six years.

In February of 1919, he resigned his position at the Baptist Sunday School Board to accept a position on the staff of First Baptist Church of Fort Worth.[8] His time in Fort Worth only lasted until June of 1919 when he was elected to serve once again as a Field Secretary of the Sunday School Board. In the early months of 1920, Flake was selected to serve as the first person in charge of the Sunday School Administration Department of the Sunday School Board for the Southern Baptist Convention.[9]

His leadership of this department would be the crowning achievement of his life. No other denominations had the kind of emphasis on the Sunday school as was found in the early Southern Baptist Churches. Ingraham explained the innovative nature of Flake's ministry saying, "There were no guide posts, no textbooks on what to do, no literature to use. This was pioneer work."[10] Flake quickly recognized the uncharted goal of the Southern Baptist Sunday School methodology saying,

> This new department of the Sunday School Board was recently organized and is just beginning to work at the task of meeting the needs for which it was created. Of course, all these needs are not yet fully known, and the entire scope of the work of the department cannot be stated except in a general way. Time and a rapidly growing Sunday school situation will all along be developing new problems. This department will be on the lookout for them and will adjust itself to meet them as they arise.[11]

Robert Raikes, the father of the Sunday school movement, began in 1780 with a commitment that children needed to learn to read the Bible. Though faced with opposition and challenges

---

[7] Minutes of the Baptist Sunday School Board, Nashville, Tennessee, April 8, 1909, quoted in William Gerald Caldwell, "Arthur Flake's Methodology in the Development of Southern Baptist Life" (DRE diss., Southwestern Baptist Theological Seminary, 1963), 7.

[8] Ibid., March 13, 1919.

[9] Ibid., March 5, 1920.

[10] Harold E. Ingraham, "Arthur Flake — Pioneer," *The Sunday School Builder*, Vol. XVII (October, 1936), 5.

[11] Arthur Flake, "Department of Sunday School Administration," *Superintendent's Quarterly*, Vol. XVI, No. 2 (Third Quarter, 1920), 4.

this pioneer remained focused on the potential of the Sunday school. With a similar commitment, pioneer Flake was focused on establishing Sunday schools that would provide a place for all ages, believers and nonbelievers, to study the Bible. Knowing he would be faced with problems to solve, Flake remained at the task of discovering what would make the Sunday school effective. Flake focused on creating materials to assist church leadership within the Sunday school. Topics addressed included leadership understanding their responsibilities, providing solutions for problems encountered by leadership, and development of standardized methods of work and materials which would be suitable for all Southern Baptist Sunday schools.[12] In 1936, Flake retired from the Sunday School Board stating he felt his health was preventing him from performing at the level required by his responsibilities.[13] He would live to be 89 years old before passing away on July 3, 1952.[14]

THEOLOGY OF CHRISTIAN EDUCATION
THEOLOGICAL HERMENEUTIC

As one reads the writings of Arthur Flake (as well as what others wrote about the Sunday school pioneer), two things are apparent about his foundations for life and ministry: First, he believed the Bible is God's Word. Flake held the Bible in the highest regard knowing it was God's holy text to be read, studied, and applied to one's life. After coming to faith in Christ, the Bible became the most important book for him.[15] Secondly, he believed that man was a sinner in need of redemption. Once a person came to faith in Christ, it is the beginning of a life that should be filled with growth and service to God. These two truths became guideposts for his life and ministry. His time at the Sunday School Board was driven by the desire to assist church leaders to reach people for Bible study that would result in individuals professing their faith, believers growing in the walk with Christ, and serving in a place of ministry.

IMPACT OF THEOLOGY ON EDUCATION

Flake saw that the Sunday school presented an opportunity for the church to do

---

[12] Ibid., 5.

[13] Minutes of the Baptist Sunday School Board, Nashville, Tennessee, June 4, 1936, quoted in William Gerald Caldwell, "Arthur Flake's Methodology in the Development of Southern Baptist Life" (DRE diss., Southwestern Baptist Theological Seminary, 1963), 21.

[14] Ibid., July 23, 1952.

[15] Hearn, "Beloved Southern Baptist Leader," 11.

the work of ministry. Children and adults alike need to be taught to view life from a biblical perspective. Sunday school, with the Bible as the textbook, was the organization that could provide the type of education needed for a nonbeliever and believer alike. Flake explained his views on Sunday school and the role of teachers in the church,

> From a child thou hast known the holy scriptures, which are able to make thee wise unto salvation through faith which is in Christ Jesus" (2 Tim. 3:15). What the Bible did for young Timothy, it will do for the lost pupils in the Sunday schools if they are led to study it ... It is ours to bring the lost pupils in our Sunday schools in touch with the Bible and to inspire them to study it. God will see to it that his Word is honored in their salvation.[16]

In Flake's ecclesiology, the best place for discipleship to take place for new believers was in a Sunday school atmosphere. He said,

> For those who are saved — The Bible is the Christian's food and makes him strong if he studies it. The apostle Paul said to the Ephesian elders: "I commend you to God, and to the word of his grace, which is able to build you up" (Acts 20:32) ... The study of God's Word, the textbook of the Sunday school, is also a safeguard to the Christian. It is his weapon of defense ... It is also the Christian's weapon of offense.[17]

Flake noted that Scripture, in many places, characterizes Christians as *workmen* and *laborers*, which are to fulfill their mission in carrying forward the work that Jesus began by becoming *doers* of the Word.[18] If they are to be effective in their work, then the Sunday school needs to provide training for the workers. Believers are to become busy doing the work of ministry. For Flake, all Christians are to be workers; the Sunday school organization offers members a wonderful opportunity to be involved in serving God.

CONTRIBUTION TO EDUCATION AND CHRISTIAN EDUCATION

In his role as a Sunday school pioneer/leader for Southern Baptists, Flake's main contributions are in the field of educational organization and administration. J.N. Barnette indicates there are at least four significant contributions attributed to Flake.[19] First, he defined

---

[16] Arthur Flake, *Building a Standard Sunday School,* rev. ed. (Nashville: The Sunday School Board of the Southern Baptist Convention, 1950), 89.

[17] Ibid., 90.

[18] Flake, *True Functions*, 46.

[19] J.N. Barnette, "A Philosophy and Science of Sunday School Work," *The Sunday School Builder*

and positioned the Sunday school as the educational ministry of the local church. Historically, Southern Baptists, and other denominations, viewed Sunday school as an independent organization which was consistent with how Sunday school began through Raikes' ministry in England. While others saw the danger in this relationship, it was Flake that saw the possibilities of the Sunday school becoming an agency of the church. He successfully transitioned Southern Baptists to merge Sunday school under the leadership of the church. Churches quickly saw the potential and started using the Sunday school as a vehicle for church work.

Second, he outlined the functions and possibilities of the Sunday school. In his writings and teaching, evangelism was central. Flake showed that if the lost are going to be won, they must first be located, reached for Bible study, and led to worship. Placing evangelism central in the ethos of a Sunday school program directed the attention of volunteers to the unreached in their community. His third contribution was that he formulated a plan for building a Sunday school. He discovered principles to apply to his own Sunday school and then tried and tested them in many other contexts. Out of the evaluation of the principles came five steps that became known as Flake's Formula. Lastly, he evaluated the administration of a Sunday school program. He felt it was important to allow teachers the opportunity to focus on teaching their class; yet, others were needed in the Sunday school that possessed strengths to lead in the overall administrative tasks, such as outreach to prospective members, evangelism, special ministries, and record keeping. These contributions to Sunday school methodology have impacted education within the church across denominational lines for more than a century.

THE FORMULA FOR SUNDAY SCHOOL ADMINISTRATION

In Flake's role as superintendent, he started the process of exploring the administrative principles that encouraged successful growth of a Sunday school. He initiated this exploration in his own church and then applied his formulaic conclusions to various other Southern Baptist churches. His methodology became known as Flake's Formula and it provides a concise outline regarding the steps a church leader could take to effectively reach people for Bible study. This formula can easily be called his most significant contribution to Christian Education. His five formulaic ingredients require that administrators/leaders know their possibilities, enlarge the organization, provide the space, enlist and train workers, and go after the people. Each of these ingredients will be explained briefly below.

(Nashville: Sunday School Board of the Southern Baptist Convention), Vol. XVII (October, 1936), 7-8.

The possibilities of an organization consist of two groups of people, members and prospects. What Flake discovered was that most churches were only concerned about the ones in their respective churches that attended Sunday school. There was no vision for growing the local Sunday school. In order to grow an effective organization, there needs to be a focus on those not enrolled in Sunday school, namely prospects. Many churches view prospects as the mass of people outside of their church. Flake taught that you have to find your prospects through community surveys, referrals, and visitors to your church. For a person to be considered a prospect, the church needs to know some basic information — their name, where they live, age group, and contact information. According to Flake, the number of people in the prospect file (list) should at least equal to the number of people enrolled in Sunday school.

Enlarging the organization means that administrators must facilitate organizational balance in a way that could be maximized for potential growth. According to Flake, the most effective size for an adult Sunday school class was ten in attendance which meant a class might have an enrollment of twenty. For children, the ratio of the number of workers to members was smaller. He noted that most churches were not organized properly to take care of their existing enrollments, leaving no room to reach prospects. The wise Christian education administrator should organize in a manner that leaves room for growth in each class, thus providing a means for fulfilling the great commission mandate.

Educational space is a requisite for a healthy Sunday school program. Flake believed that administrators must provide the space necessary for teachers and pupils to learn effectively. This meant that existing classes and new classes would need a place to meet. As the organization grows through replication, the leadership must find ways to determine where each class should meet. For Flake, that meant building more space and remodeling existing space, unused space such as storage rooms, offices, and offsite space. Today, he would welcome churches who offer multiple services, thus utilizing the space available more efficiently.

Teacher training was also a requisite ingredient for Flake. Leadership development was a key aspect for organizations that were growing. On the average, Flake felt a Sunday school needed one worker for every ten members enrolled. However, it was not enough to have a volunteer fulfilling a role; volunteers needed specialized training and weekly meetings.

Lastly, Flake believed that to grow a Sunday school, leaders needed to go after the people. Based on the first ingredient of recognizing prospects, leaders needed to act on this information and contact and care for those who had expressed interest in the church. Churches using this formula over the past century have experienced amazing result, yet these ingredients are interdependent and must be applied together in one administrative accord.

ROLE OF THE TEACHER

When organizing a Sunday school, Flake found that a team approach produced the best results. Several classes of similar ages would be grouped together in departments. The teams consisted of department leaders (director/superintendent, record keeper, outreach leader) and teachers, and he believed that trained leaders were vitally important for the learning experience because the work of teachers will not rise above the leadership. In one publication on the topic he said, "It is impossible to build an efficient Sunday school with an ignorant, indifferent, untrained, lazy, cold set of officers. No corps of teachers can overcome a handicap like that."[20] This Sunday school pioneer knew one of the keys to an effective Sunday school class was the person that had the responsibility of leading the class — the teacher. For the teacher to be a quality learning guide, they needed to be free of other responsibilities. He discovered that teachers need to give attention to their class while others would be enlisted for leadership, organization, and administrative tasks.

In addition to organizational structures supporting the teacher, the teacher must personally know and understand scripture. He said that in order for a teacher to be successful, "he must know the Bible, he must know the pupil, he must know how to teach, he must know the art of class building, he must have a working knowledge of the science of general Sunday school administration, he must know how to win his lost pupils to Christ, he must know how to build Christian character, he must know the doctrine of his church, he must know how to lead his pupils out into service — and much more."[21] He believed that the "work of teaching a Sunday school class is serious business and calls for the best in every one who undertakes it."[22] The teacher should be one that is aware that the task is a sacred one that involves representing Christ, including lifting up in prayer petitions for class members and those in the class and community that need to be reconciled to God. The teacher is to minister to the needs of the class showing interest in pupils. Preparation and training are of vital importance for the teacher that takes their assignment seriously. "If Sunday school teachers are ever to attain the highest success in their work; if they are ever to realize the greatest and fullest joys which await them, they must love people like Christ loved them."[23] For Flake, the role of the teacher was one filled with great obligation, expectation, and

---

[20] Flake, *Standard Sunday School,* 132.

[21] Ibid.

[22] Flake, *True Functions,* 44.

[23] Ibid.

reward because teachers continued to replicate the example set by Christ as he unselfishly served and cared for others.

ROLE OF THE LEARNER

In spite of the importance of the teacher, the learner/pupil is the deciding factor. Sunday school is a unique educational context and it is operated for the benefit of the learner. Buildings, lessons, and methods are designed to be age appropriate.[24] Each learner must receive personal attention and every effort should be made to make sure learners are not lost in the crowd. However, learners were not subjects upon which to download information. They had their own role to take in the learning process, and there were several things they should be led to do to bring about individual growth and development. First, they must attend regularly — for the learner to receive the full benefit of the lessons, one will need to make a priority of attending weekly. Second, they must study the lesson. Learners, regardless of one's age, will never learn much about the Bible without personal study. If learners are to know much about the Bible and grow in grace, it will have to come through personal effort and study. Teachers should require learners to study during the week. Teachers should make assignments and suggest application of truths during the week. Thirdly, the learner should bring and use his/her Bible. The Sunday school will not function properly as a real Bible teaching school until every learner owns a Bible, brings it to Sunday school, and is led by a teacher who uses the Bible. Next, the learner must actively take part in the lesson. The teacher should give each person an opportunity to express oneself during the lesson. Learning requires appropriation and expression of what is learned. The learner should also make a regular contribution to the church, both in service and in giving. Lastly, learners should attend weekly worship services. If the learner is going to develop to the fullest, they need to understand that teaching of the Word and preaching of the Word go hand and hand, and they are a requisite for living the Word.[25]

CURRICULUM AND METHODS

Flake taught that the Sunday school was a Bible school. The Bible is the textbook to be used in the class. He wanted students to do more than bring their Bible to class; they were to use them in conjunction with the study of the lesson.[26] Class members are to be inspired to study the Bible in a manner that allows them to discover the truths in scriptures. Thus, for Flake, Bible

---

[24] Ibid., 28.
[25] Ibid., 29-33.
[26] Flake, *Standard Sunday School*, 89.

study should be systematic and planned out - whether the study took place in a Christian college, a seminary, or the church. He stated,

> The Bible is a gigantic storehouse of all kinds of riches. Within its vastness there is the solvent for every problem the balm of every wound, and answer to every need the world has ever known. This great truth is the very reason why there must be a plan for its study — a guide for the glorious undertaking of entering its portals with the determined will to perceive and appropriate its message.[27]

In his position at the Sunday School Board, Flake was instrumental in developing leadership development literature, teaching helps, and a Bible study curriculum that would provide a plan for studying the selected Bible passage for the week. The curriculum he created was a guide for personal Bible study. The Bible is more than a history book — it is about life and needs to be applicable and practical in the lives of the students. Flake viewed what he authored as a tool to help teachers lead students to apply to their everyday life the principles discovered in the lesson.[28]

One of the lessons to be learned from Flake's methodology is that curriculum developers should place a high priority on the enlistment of the best scholars and teachers. He explained this reasoning saying, "It is the office then of Sunday school lesson literature to provide the best possible system of helps prepared by the best scholars and teachers available to assist the greatest body of teachers and students in the constant and effective study of the world's greatest Book." Those developing curriculum then have a great responsibility because they are providing a compendium to the greatest book and with that they are taking on the high scriptural expectations of those in this role (c.f. Deut 4:2; Prov. 30:5-6; Matt. 15:14; Rev. 22:18-19).

The True Functions of the Sunday School, authored in 1930, was one of Flake's best known books. This particular book reflected his desire to be practical and helpful to churches as they addressed problems with building effective Sunday schools. His familiar writing style followed that of an outline with subpoints that needed additional explanation and development. On the first page of the opening chapter, he sets forth the theme of his methodology while addressing churches that do not utilize the Sunday school to its fullest capacity.

These conditions exist because the leaders do not have a correct understanding of the

---

[27] Ibid., 67.
[28] Ibid., 69.

true functions of the Sunday school. Its place and work in the churches and its power and usefulness have not been understood and appreciated. Many have sought to define and set out the nature of the work of the Sunday school in a sentence. The place and power of the Sunday school are too great and its activities too varied and wide in their scope for this to be done successfully. These efforts have given rise to many false impressions concerning what the Sunday school is and what it should do, and in an endeavor to limit the Sunday school to these definitions, its work has been greatly hindered ... In this first chapter we shall set out the functions of the Sunday school in brief outline, and in the succeeding chapters we shall study these outlines in detail.[29]

CONCLUSION

After his retirement, Flake was asked for his definition of success. In response to this question he said, "To know that I had put everything there was in me into my assigned task, to encourage and help the most people, arousing in them new hopes and ambitions and inspiring them to devote their gifts and talents to the service of Christ."[30] He was a Christian educator focused on developing people to be involved in helping others. Today's Christian educators would be well served if they would adopt a similar definition of success.

PRIMARY SOURCE SAMPLE

(5) Skill acquired through doing the work

The true science of Sunday school building, in the last analysis, is demonstrated outside the church building in contact with people in their homes and places of business. Out there is the arena in which Sunday school warriors do their fighting ...

A Sunday school teacher or pupil can learn more about Sunday school visiting in one hour of directed visitation in the interest of new members and absentees than he can learn from studying all the things ever written on the subject and never going out ...

Sunday school officers and teachers can learn more about winning lost people to Christ by taking a list of the lost people in the classes and spending one hour some afternoon or evening in visiting them in their homes, speaking a word of sympathy, praying with and seeking to win them to Christ than they can learn from a passive study of all the books written on soul-winning ...

It is important, however, to keep the theory and practice in proper balance. We "learn by doing" provided the doing is directed according to right principles. The practical efforts

---

[29] Arthur Flake, *The True Functions of the Sunday School,* rev. ed. (Nashville: The Sunday School Board of the Southern Baptist Convention, 1936), 11.

[30] Hearn, "Beloved Southern Baptist Leader," 15.

at visitation, at enlistment, at soul-winning, at Sunday school building must all be evaluated according to approved methods. Thus error will be pointed out, difficulties cleared up, and improvements suggested. This will prepare the worker to try again and to profit by his doing.[31]

BIBLIOGRAPHY

Baptist Sunday School Board, Nashville, Tennessee. Minutes of Board meeting, April 8, 1909. Quoted in William Gerald Caldwell, *Arthur Flake's Methodology in the Development of Southern Baptist Life*. Fort Worth, Texas: Southwestern Baptist Theological Seminary, 1963.

_____ Minutes of Board meeting, June 4, 1936. Quoted in William Gerald Caldwell, *Arthur Flake's Methodology in the Development of Southern Baptist Life*. Fort Worth, Texas: Southwestern Baptist Theological Seminary, 1963.

Barnette, J. N. *A Church Using Its Sunday School*. Nashville: The Sunday School Board of the Southern Baptist Convention, 1937.

_____ "A Philosophy and Science of Sunday School Work." *The Sunday School Builder*, Vol. XVII (October 1936): 7-8.

Flake, Arthur. *Building a Standard Sunday School*. Rev. ed. Nashville: The Sunday School Board of the Southern Baptist Convention, 1950.

_____ "Department of Sunday School Administration." *Superintendent's Quarterly*, Vol. XVI, no. 2 (Third Quarter 1920), 4.

_____ "The Place of Lesson Literature in the Study of the Bible in the Sunday School." *The Sunday School Builder*, Vol. 16 (September 1935), 4.

_____ *The True Functions of the Sunday School*, Rev. ed. Nashville: The Sunday School Board of the Southern Baptist Convention, 1936.

Hearn, C. Aubrey. "Arthur Flake — Beloved Southern Baptist Leader." *The Baptist Training Union Magazine*, Vol. III, no. 2 (February 1937): 9-15.

Ingraham, Harold. "Arthur Flake — Pioneer." *The Sunday School Builder*, Vol. XVII (October 1936): 4-5.

_____ *Baptist Leaders in Religious Education*. Edited by J. M. Price. Nashville: Broadman Press, 1943.

PRIMARY SOURCE PUBLICATIONS BY ARTHUR FLAKE

Flake, Arthur, and Carribel Blankenship. *The Department Sunday School*. Nashville: The Sunday School Board of the Southern Baptist Convention, 1924.

_____ *Life at Eighty — As I See It*. Nashville: Broadman Press, 1944.

_____ *Sunday School Officers and Their Work*. Nashville: The Sunday School Board of the Southern Baptist Convention, 1923.

_____ and Emma Noland. *The Sunday School Secretary and the Six Point Record System*. Nashville: The Sunday School Board of the Southern Baptist Convention, 1924.

From October 1920 to July 1936 Arthur Flake was the editor of a monthly magazine titled *The Sunday School Builder*, published by The Sunday School Board of the Southern Baptist Convention. Each edition but two contained an "Editorial" or article from Flake regarding Sunday school work.

---

[31] Flake, *True Functions*, 84-85.

PART VI

Modern Educators

(A.D. 1950 – Present)

Modern educators, have been concerned with the same things as that which has occupied the educators throughout the history of the church, namely how to communicate the message of scripture to a specific population. **Henrietta Mears** (1890-1963) spent her life teaching children the essence of the Bible. Many Christian leaders of the 20th Century credit her investment in their lives as extremely formative. Such leaders are Billy Graham, Dawson Trotman, and Bill Bright. The legacy of **C.S. Lewis** (1898-1963) also lives on in the lives of leaders impacting the church today. Lewis often used apologetics and allegory to communicate his message. He pursued reality through reason and the imagination. While trained as a literary critic, his educational investment will live long beyond the confines of his educational training.

Frank Gaebelien (1899-1983) and **Carl F. H. Henry** (1913-2003) were both concerned with the nature of truth and how truth is communicated in the educational process. Gaebelien was a proponent of the maxim that *all truth is God's truth* and Henry championed Christian education that stood strong on the authority of the truth of scripture. Gaebelien was founding Headmaster of Stony Brook School in New York where he influenced a student who became a leading evangelical Christian educator by the name of Kenneth Gangel (1935-2009).

Donald McGavran (1897-1990) and **Elmer Towns** (1932-) are both associated as educators in the Church Growth Movement. McGavran, a missiologist by trade, brought missional education that took place in an international context and applied it in the church in America. Towns, building on the foundations of McGavran's work in church growth, focused on teachable principles that were common healthy churches. His approach to finding these principles was based on socio-educational research that could apply to the church and was for the church. In addition to his work in the Church Growth movement, Towns was also co-founder of Liberty University, and through Liberty University, we may see the fruition of Carl Henry's vision for a distinctively Christian university asserting the epistemic right to start with a belief in God as a foundation for the educational process.

CHAPTER 26

Henrietta Mears:
Educating God's Children

J. DOUGLAS HANKINS, JR.

Henrietta Mears (1890-1963)

Henrietta Mears was the Director of Christian Education at First Presbyterian Church, Hollywood, California, where she organized the Sunday school to grow to the largest Presbyterian Sunday school in the world. She wrote the innovative Sunday school literature that became Gospel Light Publications, and her Bible survey, *What the Bible Is All About*, has sold over 6 million copies. She was called "Teacher" and considered a mentor by many of the most influential and powerful Christian leaders in twentieth century fundamentalism and evangelicalism, including evangelist Billy Graham, Navigators founder Dawson Trotman, Campus Crusade for Christ founder Bill Bright, U.S. Senate Chaplain Richard Halverson, Radio evangelist and evangelical mogul Charles Fuller, and Hollywood movie stars Dale Evans and Roy Rogers.

HISTORICAL BACKGROUND

Henrietta Cornelia Mears was born on October 23, 1890, into a wealthy family with a rich spiritual heritage. She was the youngest of seven children. Henrietta's great grandfather was Dr. William Wallace Everts who pastored Chicago's First Baptist Church, and helped to found The University of Chicago; he also authored the 1887 book entitled *Pastor's Hand Book*, a staple of seminary reading lists well into the 1950's.[1] Henrietta's father, Ashley, was a successful entrepreneur and lawyer, raising his seven children in a comfortable upper class lifestyle. Henrietta's mother, Margaret Everts Mears, enjoyed the spiritual discipline of praying for no less than one hour at the beginning of each day, a practice that young Henrietta soon adopted.[2] Additionally, Mother Mears trained Henrietta to spend a healthy amount of time and mental energy into the discipline of regular Bible reading and meditation, a discipline that would become the staple of Mears' educational ministry, which began at the age of eleven.[3] Henrietta accompanied her brother on a mission ministry and, upon learning that the mission was lacking in leaders, young Henrietta volunteered to teach the Bible to this group. What began as a volunteer act of obedience became the life-long calling of a Gospel-centered woman.[4]

Henrietta maintained her role of Bible educator throughout secondary school and high school years, leading in various independent Bible clubs, church based vacation Bible schools, backyard Bible clubs, and church based Sunday school classes. This was all the more impressive given a childhood illness that rocked the Mears' household. At age twelve, Henrietta developed muscular rheumatism. This meant that Henrietta had immense pain in her joints and limbs. Henrietta struggled with this disease for two years until, during a

---

[1] Mears' biographer, Barbara Hudson Powers, remembers, "A short time ago when Henrietta Mears was on a speaking engagement in Texas, she stopped by the Baptist Bookstore in Dallas and asked the clerk, 'I was just wondering if you have the *Pastor's Handbook*, written by Dr. W. W. Everts? It was written well over a hundred years ago and I realize that it is very old.' 'Why,' said the clerk, 'that's like stopping at a super market and asking if they have salt and pepper! It may have been written over a hundred years ago, but it's still selling.' 'How amazing,' said Miss Mears, smiling happily as she looked at the copy. 'My grandfather wrote it. Grandfather Everts. He was pastor of the First Baptist Church of Chicago.'" Barbara Hudson Powers, *The Henrietta Mears Story* (Old Tappan, NJ: Revell Company, 1957), 82.

[2] J. Robert Clinton, *Focused Lives: Inspirational Life Changing Lessons From Eight Effective Christian Leaders Who Finished Well* (Springfield, MO: Barnabas Publishers, 1995), 341. See also Powers, *The Henrietta Mears Story,* 106.

[3] Andrea V. B. Madden, "Henrietta C. Mears: Her Life and Influence," (Master's thesis, Gordon-Conwell Theological Seminary, 1997), 8.

[4] Marcus Brotherton, *Teacher: The Henrietta Mears Story* (Ventura, CA: Regal Books, 2006), 37.

particularly intense night of prayer, she was completely healed of this disease.[5] She did not experience any muscular problems again for the remainder of her life on earth. The only other frailty she experienced was poor eyesight, a condition she likened to Galatians 4:13-15, her "thorn in the flesh" that kept her "completely dependent upon God."[6]

The only other subject that captured Mears' attention, apart from the Bible, was the discipline of chemistry. When Mears enrolled at the University of Minnesota in 1908 she decided to make chemistry her major field of study. Mears' university years were a time of immense highs and lows. Her highs included leading a campus women's Bible study that had as many as 60 women in regular attendance.[7] Her lows included the sudden death of her mother in 1910. While grieving the loss, the famed fundamentalist pastor, Dr. William Bell Riley, said to Mears, "Henrietta, I hope the spiritual mantle of your mother will fall upon you."[8] In 1913 Mears graduated from the University of Minnesota with her bachelor's degree and took her first post as a high school chemistry teacher in North Branch, Minnesota. Having successfully taught at both the high school and in a Methodist church's Sunday school department, Mears returned to Minneapolis to teach at Central High School and to Minneapolis's First Baptist Church, under the leadership of Pastor Riley. Riley thought well of Mears and encouraged her to continue following the Lord's direction in Christian education, even giving her space to become a successful Sunday school teacher at his church during her 20s and 30s.

Having garnered success in the First Baptist Church's Christian education ministry, Mears caught the attention of a visiting guest preacher named Rev. Stuart MacClennan, the second pastor of Hollywood Presbyterian Church in Hollywood, California. He began a month long process of recruiting Mears for the now open position of Director of Christian Education. In 1928, MacClennan convinced the 38-year old Mears to travel across country to the warm weather of California and help him build a successful Sunday school program in the First Presbyterian Church of Hollywood, California. The Sunday school program grew from 450 to 1800 by the time of Stuart MacLennan's retirement in 1931, to 6000 by 1953, and to 6500 at its peak — the largest Presbyterian Sunday school in the world at the time.[9]

Several factors led to this growth. Mears located and built new educational space

---

[5] Powers, *The Henrietta Mears* Story, 99.

[6] Ibid., 101.

[7] Earl Roe, *Dream Big: The Henrietta Mears Story* (Ventura, CA: Regal Books, 1990), 75.

[8] Brotherton, *Teacher,* 41.

[9] "Our History," *First Presbyterian Church of Hollywood,* July 11, 2013, http://www.fpch.org/about-us/our-history, (accessed July 11, 2013). See also Powers, 129.

for her students. She also placed an emphasis on leadership development, often times using her college class to recruit new Sunday school teachers and directors. She brought a spirit of soul winning evangelism in addition to verse-by-verse Bible teaching. Not only did she recruit teachers, but she excelled in training and equipping these teachers to minister to their respective students.

When Mears became the Director of Christian Education, most denominations were following the International Uniform Bible Lessons, which covered the Bible every seven years. Also, most Sunday schools divided pupils into classes of beginners (ages 3-5); primaries (ages 6-8); juniors (ages 9-11); intermediates (12-14); youths (ages 15-17); young adults (ages 18-24); and adults (ages 24-up). Mears divided her Sunday school into classes for each age, and as they got older, they were divided boys from girls. When asked why she used age-graded classes, she answered, "I didn't divide them, God did."

Also, most denominational Sunday school literature was built on deductive lessons, i.e., the Bible story was presented, followed by an application. Mears followed an inductive approach to study the verses of the Bible, and based on their principles, applied the lessons to life. In terms of method, Mears organized around an inductive Bible study method, preferring to teach children how to observe, interpret, and apply what the Bible says.

Henrietta was not satisfied with the Sunday school literature supplied by the Presbyterian church so she decided to write her own. For several years she studied every morning from 5:00 a.m. to 8:00 a.m. writing the entire curriculum that would later be known as Gospel Light Publications. The eleventh grade contained fifty-two lessons that surveyed the entire Bible. Later, editors decided this material was suitable for all adults, and made an excellent Bible survey book. When trying to determine a title for the series, one editor described it, *What the Bible Is All About*.[10] This volume has gone on to sell over six million copies.

After having established her own publishing house in 1933, she pioneered and in 1938 she began a retreat called the Forest Home Christian Conference Center, which is still in operation today. Mears spent the remainder of her glory years executing her game plan for Christian education, publishing literature on Christian education, and raising up the future leaders of the Church in America. Out of Gospel Light grew GLINT (Gospel Light International), a foreign mission organization that translated and printed Sunday school literature for foreign mission distribution.

---

[10] Henrietta C. Mears, *What the Bible Is All About* (Ventura, CA: Regal Books, 1953).

Among her spiritual heritage include names such as Dawson Trotman, founder of the Navigators; Bob Pierce, founder of World Vision (a Christian humanitarian organization); Jim Rayburn, founder of Young Life; Billy Graham, Bill and Vonette Bright, founders of Campus Crusade for Christ; and Donn Moomaw, founding member of Fellowship of Christian Athletes. When Mears died in her sleep in 1963 at the age of seventy-three, more than two-thousand people attended her funeral service — an indication of the impact she had on the Kingdom.[11]

Historian George Marsden records that Mears guided five-hundred men into ministry.[12] He also notes that at least one Fuller Seminary professor believed Mears to be the best preacher in southern California. He also suggests that during her lifetime Mears may have done more "to shape west coast Presbyterianism than any other person." Former Fuller Seminary and Gordon-Conwell Seminary president, Harold John Ockenga, wrote to Harold Lindsell of Mears when she was being considered for a faculty position that "no one had done more for Christian education — in young people's work, Sunday schools, publishing, and speaking — than she."[13] Daniel Fuller suggests that Mears had not only been successful in church life and discipleship within the limits imposed on a woman at that time period, but that she was single-handedly responsible for expanding the limits of what local churches could expect from women in ministry leadership.[14] And yet, Mears routinely turned down opportunities to preach in church worship services, citing the Apostle Paul's clear teaching in 1 Corinthians 14:33-35 and 1 Timothy 3:2-7. It is in these kindly rejected opportunities we see the overarching narrative of Mears' life: Henrietta Mears studied, prayed, memorized, taught, and believed the Bible and she aimed to live her life accordingly.

THEOLOGY OF CHRISTIAN EDUCATION

Mears' mission statement for her Sunday school department was, "Teach the Word clearly and correctly to the end that people may come to know Christ as Savior and Lord and

[11] Marion Ann Taylor and Agnes Choi (Ed.), "Mears, Henrietta C (1980-1963)" in *Handbook of Women Biblical Interpreters: A Historical and Biographical Guide* (Grand Rapids: Baker, 2012), 355.

[12] George M. Marsden, *Reforming Fundamentalism: Fuller Seminary and the New Evangelicalism*, (Grand Rapids: Eerdmans, 1987), 89-90, and "Mears, Henrietta Cornella (1890-1963)" in Daniel G. Reid, and others, eds., *Dictionary of Christianity in America* (Downers Grove: InterVarsity, 1990), 722.

[13] Marsden, *Reforming Fundamentalism*, 127. This is Marsden's summation of the letter that Ockenga wrote to Lindsell.

[14] Marsden's summary of an interview with Dan Fuller cited in footnote 27 in Marsden, *Reforming Fundamentalism*, 127.

to grow spiritually, faithful in every good work." This statement is a helpful way of unpacking her theology of Christian education.[15] Her goal through all her ministry was "to know Christ and make Him known."

Henrietta believed that the Bible was not simply one of several literary texts that one would read for personal edification. She capitalized the term "Word" and understood the Bible to be the final and ultimate authority on all matters of life, belief, and reality. Her drive to teach the Bible as the Word of God stemmed from her conviction that the Bible really would transform her students from young Christians to mature disciples of Jesus Christ. There was no substitute curriculum for Christian sanctification.

Additionally, Mears understood her outcome to be nothing short of spiritual growth and transformation. Students were expected to adjust their character and not only their Bible content knowledge. She took Jesus' call in the Great Commission seriously and aimed to teach people all things towards the goal of Christian discipleship and spiritual formation. One of the ways that she observed life change was through Christian service and leadership development. Mears would kindly nudge her students towards reinvesting in her program by stepping into roles of leadership that included teaching, researching, greeting, and song leading. Mears' primary ground for leadership recruitment was her college Sunday school class, which held over one-thousand students. There, she would also see the fruit of Christian Education, fielding questions from students on subjects ranging from the dual nature of Jesus Christ to the practical steps to developing a healthy prayer life. In the college department, Mears saw the culmination of her Christian education efforts as students began to develop in their faith and to pour back into her educational ministry.

THEOLOGICAL HERMENEUTIC

Like many fundamentalists and evangelical leaders living in California in the early twentieth century, Mears rarely mentioned anything like an existential crisis of belief related to her plain reading of scripture. Perhaps this is one of the reasons why she never led her ministry with a developed and official position statement related to authority or hermeneutics. Still, we can observe at least three descriptive characteristics of her views on the Bible by reading through her book, *What The Bible Is All About*, and her speech, "Why We Study The Bible." First, Mears employed something akin to the historical-grammatical hermeneutic in her personal study of scripture. Second, she affirmed something like the verbal-plenary view of inspiration,

---

[15] Helen K. Hosier, *100 Christian Women Who Changed The Twentieth Century* (Grand Rapids: Revell, 2000), 168.

and third, she assumed the perspicuity of scripture and called for anyone and everyone to jump right into studying the Bible. While some of her peers such as evangelist Chuck Templeton pejoratively derided perspicuity as far too "simple," she saw it as the theological equivalent of the scientific method and the prevailing assumption within the discipline of chemistry. Mears held to an unyielding expectation of absolute right and wrong and to a firm belief that absolute truth is self-evident to those who seek to discover truth.[16] Thus, when her friends Dan Fuller and Billy Graham began wrestling with the issue of Biblical criticism in the late 1940's, she encouraged them to consider the "direct correlation between a person's trust in scripture and their effectiveness in ministry"[17] If one wanted to be effective in ministry, one needed to trust the face-value teaching of the Bible.

In addition to presuming that the Bible was self-evidently clear, she also held to the verbal plenary view of scripture. Consider this excerpt from her speech, "Why We Study the Bible:"

> We need to see God's progressive action with men, and how He develops in His revelation to men. When you think that this book was written by 40 authors over a period of 1500 years on every subject under the sun, it seems incredible that there could be any kind of continuity. But you know, if I went and heard a great orchestra and I did not see the leader at all, but that orchestra harmonized and played so beautifully I would know there was a baton somewhere with a leader.[18]

Even though she recognized the unique perspectives and personalities of the various authors of scripture, Mears saw the Bible as speaking with a unified voice, since God was ultimately the author of it all. It is because of this modern presumption of perspicuity that Mears could trust in the Bible's infallible authority.

As Mears taught others to adopt her approach to teaching and learning the Bible, she would essentially describe the historical-grammatical approach. In "Why We Study the Bible," Mears turned to the analogy of a large temple structure to provide a framework for teaching

[16] Templeton told Graham that his (Graham's) approach was "simple" during Graham's crisis of belief, Billy Graham, *Just As I Am* (San Francisco: Harper Collins, 1998), 138. For Mears' belief in absolutes, see Haskin, "The Fabulous Miss Mears," 47.

[17] Laura E. Range, "The 'Grandmother Of Modern Evangelicalism' : The Life And Work Of Henrietta Mears," (Master's thesis, Gordon-Conwell Theological Seminary, 2008), 50. Range points to Mears' statement, "while the blood of the Lamb makes us safe, our trust in God's Word makes us sure," 7.

[18] "Why We Study the Bible," cassette tape of Henrietta Mears' address to Christian education officers, December 1, 1962, Gospel Light Archives, Ventura, CA.

through the Bible. Genesis functioned as the door of the temple. The Pentateuch was the hallway where the portraits of Bible heroes were hung. The history books functioned as the library filled with the promises of God. The Psalms and Proverbs are the music and drama rooms; the Prophetic books are the observatory; the four gospels are the audience room; the Acts and Epistles are the Athletic field; and the book of Revelation is the veranda.[19] Mears used this analogy to help her teachers understand that students of scripture must keep the whole Bible in view and must teach each chapter, verse, and phrase with the narrative in mind.

In helping her students to build this overarching narrative, she taught that they should begin with Genesis and then proceed through to Revelation. Based on the description of the process, one sees something like the historical-grammatical approach to interpretation. Mears expected her teachers to teach entire books of the Bible to students, to lead students to be able to name the chapter, author, date, and purpose, to help students memorize key verses from the chapter, to identify the type of literature, to identify any characters or actors in the scene, to utilize cross references, to take into account geographical and historical locations, and to organize these particulars into an outline with application questions.[20] Additionally, Mears expected her students to read the Bible according to the seven R's: "regularly, rationally, rapidly, reflectively, repeatedly, reverently, and rejoicingly."[21] Each of these R-lettered themes reflected Mears' ultimate pedagogical aim. She wanted a careful method of Bible interaction to produce a rich devotional life with God.

CONTRIBUTIONS TO CHRISTIAN EDUCATION

Mears was one of the earliest educators popularizing the idea that Sunday school should be organized as a "school" is organized and should not be an extension of a children's ministry built upon a philosophy of childcare. She believed in education and that education was not simply a program, but a process that could and should be routine, organized, objective-oriented, and measurable. As such, she valued the teacher and learner relationship and ensured that only qualified and skilled educators were present before the students. Additionally, she structured classes around development-specific learning with kindergarteners learning alongside other kindergarteners and high school seniors learning alongside other high school seniors. Class size also mattered. When the teacher to student ratio became unsustainable,

---

[19] See Range, "Grandmother of Modern Evangelicalism," 48, n. 229.

[20] Ibid, 50.

[21] "Why We Study the Bible," cassette tape of Henrietta Mears' address to Christian education officers.

Mears found new space and a new teacher for her learners. While there are few recorded testimonies of exactly how her students received this instructional method, the list of her admirers speaks volumes about the meaningful nature of her teaching ministry.

CONCLUDING THOUGHTS

Henrietta Mears was a visionary for God. She was a leading evangelical voice for teaching the Bible. She believed in the truth of the Bible and wanted to teach as many people the Bible as possible in the shortest window of time. She may have guided as many as five-hundred men into ministry, but these ministers were an ancillary outcome of her objective to teach tens of thousands of young people how to study the Bible from Genesis to Revelation. She may have been the best preacher in southern California, but that is only because her goal was to communicate effectively and with as much impact as possible for her audience. She may have done the most for Christian education in the area, but it was because she knew that the Lord's calling for her life was to be a Christian educator and she walked comfortably within that narrow calling. And, she may have expanded the limits of what local churches could expect from women in ministry leadership. But again, it was not because she was trying to make a cultural point. She was attempting to lead from within the biblical calling placed on her life by God and under the authority granted to her by her pastors. Henrietta Mears studied, prayed, memorized, taught, and believed the Bible and she aimed to live her life in rich joy and obedience to God through His Word.

PRIMARY SOURCE SAMPLE[22]

The Bible is God's written revelation of His will to humanity. Its central theme is salvation through Jesus Christ.

The Bible contains 66 books, written by 40 authors, covering a period of approximately 1,600 years.

The Old Testament was written mostly in Hebrew (a few short passages in Aramaic). About 100 years (or more) before the Christian era, the entire Old Testament was translated into the Greek language. Remember, our English Bible is a translation from these original languages.

The word "Bible" comes from the Greek word biblos, meaning "book."

The word "testament" means "covenant," or "agreement." The Old Testament is

---

[22] Excerpt from Henrietta Mears, *What the Bible is All About, An Easy-to-Understand Survey of the Bible* (Ventura, CA.: Regal Books, 1983), 13-15.

the covenant God made with people about their salvation before Christ came. The New Testament is the agreement that God made with people about their salvation after Christ came.

In the Old Testament we find the covenant of law. In the New Testament we find the covenant of grace that came through Jesus Christ. One led into the other (see Galatians 3:17-25):

> The Old begins — the New completes.
> The Old gathers around Mount Sinai — the New around Mount Calvary.
> The Old is associated with Moses — the New with Christ (see John 1:17).

The authors of the Bible were kings and princes, poets and philosophers, prophets and statesmen. Some were learned in all the arts of the times and others were unschooled fishermen. Other books soon are out-of-date, but this book spans the centuries. Most books must be adapted to the age level of the intended reader, but old and young alike love this book. Most books only interest the people in whose language they were written, but not this book. And no one ever stops to think it was written in what are now dead languages.

> The Old Testament begins with God (see Genesis 1:1) — the New Testament begins with Christ (see Matthew 1:1).
> From Adam to Abraham we have the history of all people — from Abraham to Christ we have the history of the Chosen People.
> From Christ on, we have the history of the Church.

A historian once noted, "Most people's knowledge of history is like a string of graduated pearls without the string." This statement seems to be especially true of Bible history. Many people know the Bible characters and the principal events but are hopelessly lost when they are called upon to connect the stories in order. Anyone who has experienced the thrill of learning to place the individual characters in their right setting in regard to place and time can realize the difference it makes in the enjoyment of God's Word.

Pick up the "pearls" in the scriptures and string them into order from Genesis to Revelation so that you can "think through" the Bible story.

BIBLIOGRAPHY

Baldwin, Ethel May. *Henrietta Mears and How She Did It*. Glendale: Regal Books, 1966.

Brotherton, Marcus. *Teacher: The Henrietta Mears Story*. Ventura: Regal Books, 2006.

Clinton, J. Robert. *Focused Lives*. Ventura: Regal Books, 1995.

Cox, Betsy. "Henrietta Mears as a Christian Education Director." Master's Thesis, Fuller Theological Seminary, 1961.

Doan, Eleanor. *431 Quotes from the Notes of Henrietta C. Mears*. Ventura: Regal Books, 1970.

Jacobs, Cindy. *Women of Destiny*. Ventura: Regal Books, 1998.

Madden, Andrea V.B. "Henrietta Mears: Her Life and Influence". Master's Thesis, Gordon-Conwell Theological Seminary, 1997.

Mears, Henrietta. *431 Quotes from the Notes of Henrietta C. Mears*. Glendale: Regal Books, 1971.

_____. *What the Bible is All About, An Easy-to-Understand Survey of the Bible*. Ventura, CA.: Regal Books, 1983.

Powers, Barbara Hudson. *The Henrietta Mears Story*. Old Tappan: Revell, 1957.

Range, Laura E. "The 'Grandmother of Modern Evangelicalism': The Life and Work of Henrietta Mears." Master's Thesis, Gordon-Conwell Theological Seminary, 2008.

Roe, Earl O. *Dream Big: The Henrietta Mears Story*. Ventura: Regal Books, 1990.

Zoba, Wendy Murray. "The Grandmother of Us All." Carol Stream, IL: Christianity Today, 16 September 1996.

CHAPTER 27

C. S. Lewis:

Pursuing Reality through Reason and the Imagination

JERRY ROOT

WAYNE MARTINDALE

Clive Staples Lewis 1898-1963

C. S. Lewis was arguably one of the great Christian Educators of the twentieth century. Yet, he did not teach Christian Education. He was a fellow and tutor in Medieval and Renaissance Literature at Oxford University for twenty-nine years. And, for the last nine years of his academic career he was the inaugural professor of the chair of Medieval and Renaissance Literature at Cambridge University. After his conversion to Christianity in 1931, he practiced the integration of his faith in virtually all he studied, taught, and wrote. There are currently seventy-four titles that bear his name, and he published in eighteen different literary genres. His intellectual breadth and academic reach is noteworthy. Through his books, his public lectures, his sermons, his work in Christian apologetics, and his radio broadcasts, he had an educational reach for Christ and His Kingdom extending far beyond the halls of the academy. Though he was not a Christian educator by training or by trade, nevertheless, he must be classified as a Christian educator.

HISTORICAL BACKGROUND

C. S. Lewis was born on November 29, 1898 in Belfast, Ireland. His mother (Flora) had a college degree in Mathematics and his father (Albert) was a solicitor. Lewis's older brother Warren was a career military officer. C. S. Lewis had a very troubled school experience until he was sent to Surry, England for private tutoring with William T. Kirkpatrick. Lewis served in France, in the trenches of World War I, where he was wounded on April 15, 1918. Upon recovery from his wounds, he went to University College, Oxford University where he studied Classics, English, and Philosophy. He began his teaching career as an Atheist but on September 28, 1931, in part through the influence of his friend, J. R. R. Tolkien, Lewis became a Christian. He taught at Magdalen College, Oxford for twenty-nine years. During these years he achieved recognition for his work as a scholar of medieval and renaissance literature. He was part of an informal literary group at Oxford called the Inklings. This group included Tolkien, Charles Williams, Neville Coghill, Lord David Cecil, Hugo Dyson, and others. During his Oxford years he achieved recognition as a writer in Christian Apologetics, Children's Stories, and Science Fiction. On September 8, 1947, after the publication of *The Screwtape Letters*, his picture appeared on the cover of Time Magazine. In 1954, Lewis left Oxford to take up the Chair of Medieval and Renaissance Literature, a position created for him at Cambridge University where he taught until his death. He married Joy Davidman in a civil ceremony in 1956 and a religious ceremony in 1957. She died July 13, 1960. Lewis died in his home in Oxford on November 22, 1963. Virtually all of his books remain in print over 50 years after his death, verifying the significance of his life and work.

THEOLOGY OF CHRISTIAN EDUCATION: TRUTH AND REALITY

Lewis once reminded an Oxford University audience that conditions for pursuit of an education are never perfect. The students were affected by World War II. They wondered why they could justify several years of study while civilization was on the threshold of collapse. Lewis reminded his audience that war does not increase death. He could have added that disease, aging, or accidents do not increase death. The reason: death is total in every generation. If one waited until conditions were perfect, an education would never be pursued. In fact, there would never be an ideal time for culture or education. Not only is it allowable to pursue an education in troubled times, for some it is a duty, for he believed that "Good philosophy must exist, if for no other reason, because bad philosophy must be answered."[1]

---

[2] C. S. Lewis, "Learning in War-time," in *The Weight of Glory and Other Addresses* (New York:

Furthermore, Lewis, standing in the center of the Christian tradition, believed that since the Fall, the soul has been in a state of deformity. In his opinion, "The Normal state of humanity is barbarism."[2] Maturation, while complex, is in part about the conformity of soul (the reason, the emotion, and the volition) to the plumb line of Reality. Because reality is iconoclastic, this conformity is dynamic and ongoing. On this side of Heaven, maturity is something people approximate, not something they achieve. Consequently, the teacher, in the best educational instances, is "trying to make the pupil a good man."[3] There is much at stake in the process. Education is no guarantee one will mature morally. In fact, if there is no growth in character, in the process of knowledge acquisition, education can make one cleverer at self-deception. Lewis wrote, "Continued disobedience to conscience makes one blind."[4] The possibility of rationalization and self-justification is always present. Good education must strive to nurture the student towards character maturation. Of course, there are risks, but neglect in this regard produces the greater liability. It is here the Christian educator has an advantage when the educational need leads naturally, and reasonably, towards faith. Lewis wrote, "If we wish to be rational, not now and then, but constantly, we must pray for the gift of Faith, for the power to go on believing not in the teeth of reason but in the teeth of lust and terror and jealousy and boredom and indifference that which reason, authority, or experience, or all three, have once delivered to us for truth."[5] Faith, therefore, is the power to believe not in opposition to one's reason, but in opposition to one's sin. Character is an end in Lewis's educational scheme, and character cannot be taught in the same way one learns geography or mathematics.

Touchstone, 1996), 48.

[2] C. S. Lewis, *Rehabilitations and Other Essays* (London: Oxford University Press, 1939), 82.

[3] Ibid., 83. Furthermore, Lewis observes, "The purpose of education is to produce the good man and the good citizen, though it must be remembered that we are not here using the word 'good' in any narrowly ethical sense. The 'good man' here means the man of good taste and good feeling, the interesting and interested man, and almost the happy man." *Rehabilitations*, 81. In this regard Lewis stands in a long tradition: Milton wrote, "The end then of learning is to repair the ruins of our first parents by regaining to know God aright and out of that knowledge to love Him, to imitate Him, to be like Him, as we may the nearest by possessing our souls of true virtue, which being united to the heavenly grace of faith makes up the highest perfection." John Milton, "Of Education," in *Areopagita and of Education* edited by George H. Sabine (New York: Appleton-Century-Crofts, 1951), 59.

[4] C. S. Lewis, *A Preface to Paradise Lost* (London: Oxford University Press, 1942), 10.

[5] C. S. Lewis, *Christian Reflections,* ed. Walter Hooper (Grand Rapids, MI: William B. Eerdmans, 1967), 43.

THE HERMENEUTIC OF TRUTH AND REALITY

Lewis began his literary criticism of Milton's *Paradise Lost* with these words: "The first qualification for judging any piece of workmanship from a corkscrew to a cathedral is to know what it is — what it was intended to do and how it was meant to be used." In other words, Lewis observes that "The first thing is to understand the object before you."[6] Truth, therefore, is not reality; truth is what one thinks about reality when he thinks accurately about it. Such accuracy can only be judged by an actual encounter with what is present to the senses empirically, or presented to the mind — as an object of thought — definitionally. However, more can always be known. Truths can be plumbed more deeply and be applied more widely, but all truth begins with a grasp of reality, however faintly it may be perceived. Furthermore, one does not get a last word about any topic, but this does not mean one cannot have a sure word on that topic. In his own writing, Lewis was in quest of the sure word and left his readers free to discover ever more. These two concepts of truth and reality will be further examined below as they represent the major cornerstones of Lewis' theology of Christian education; for, without the pursuit of truth and the possibility of reality, Lewis' passion for education would have been unfounded.

REALITY IS ICONOCLASTIC AND INFUSED WITH THE PRESENCE OF GOD

The next foundation to Lewis's success as an educator is his recognition that one's understanding of Reality must be dynamic. Our notions of it must constantly be modified if our understanding is to develop. Furthermore, Lewis, the Christian educator, saw this real, objective world infused with the Presence of God. He wrote, "We may ignore, but we can nowhere evade, the presence of God. The world is crowded with Him. He walks everywhere incognito. And the incognito is not always hard to penetrate. The real labor is to remember, to attend, in fact, to come awake. Still more, to remain awake."[7] He noted, "I believe in Christianity as I believe the sun is risen not only because I see it but because by it I see everything else."[8] Therefore, any proper understanding of the material world, the world of ideas, and even the complex world inside of oneself, should lead to an enriched sense of the wonder and awe of God as exhibited in the world He has made.

The real world is a complex world. Therefore, Lewis says that "Reality is iconoclastic." This is a theme implicit in every book he wrote, and it reverberates throughout his work as a

---

[6] Lewis, *Preface to Paradise Lost*, 1.

[7] C. S. Lewis, *Letters to Malcolm: Chiefly on Prayer* (London: Geoffrey Bles, 1964), 100-101.

[8] C. S. Lewis, "Is Theology Poetry?" in *The Weight of Glory*, 106.

teacher and communicator of the Christian faith.[9] An iconoclast breaks idols. If a student has an image of God or an understanding of some feature of the world, this understanding may be helpful. Perhaps after reading a book, or hearing a lecture, some pieces of the puzzle of the real world have come together and the picture becomes clearer. But, if the student holds too tightly to that new and present understanding, it will begin to compete against his gaining a bigger grasp of God and His world. The notion once helpful becomes a distraction; in fact, it may become an idol. Lewis rightly observes that God is always kicking out the walls of the temples we build for Him because He wants to give us more of Himself. The idea is not unique to Lewis. It has always been understood where robust, and breathtaking, approaches to education have been valued. Baron von Hugel advised his niece, Gwendolyn Greene, that she should beware of the first clarity on any given matter and press on to the second clarity.[10] There is always more. Similarly, Robert Browning advised in his poem, *Rabi ben Ezra*, "Then welcome each rebuff that turns earth's smoothness rough."[11] One may think he has things nicely figured out and his world is all smooth and round; but the earth is not smooth, it has geography, peaks, and valleys. We should welcome whatever it is that helps us to see the world as it is rather than how we would want it to be. This is a necessary part of education. A changing grasp of reality should never be a threat to either the teacher or the student. Furthermore, one should not be surprised that the acquisition of knowledge is very likely to lead in directions unanticipated. Lewis was eager to follow the truth wherever it led. This is one of the attractions of his writing. He is willing to explore and discover; therefore, his sense of natural curiosity is, once again, giving way to wonder, adoration, and worship.

Perhaps, in his fiction, Lewis makes the point best. Lucy, the most spiritually sensitive of all the children who go from our world into Narnia has encountered Christ. In *that* world, He appears as the great lion, Aslan, in whose mane Lucy loves to bury her face, and in whose Presence she feels divinely comfortable. In *Prince Caspian*, Lucy encounters Aslan for the first time on her return to that world. On seeing Aslan, Lucy exclaims, "Aslan you are

---

[9] For the explicit references see C. S. Lewis, *A Grief Observed* (New York: Faber, 1961), 52; Lewis, *Letters to Malcolm,* 109. Similarly Lewis inscribed these words to Joy Davidman in her copy of *A Great Divorce*, "There are three images in my mind which I must continually forsake and replace by better ones: the false image of God, the false image of my neighbors, the false image of myself. –C. S. Lewis 30 December 1952 (from an unwritten chapter on Iconoclasm). 'Satire is a glass in which the reader commonly sees every face except his own.' –Swift, quoted from memory." Walter Hooper, *C. S. Lewis: A Companion & Guide* (London: Harper Collins, 1996), 61.

[10] Frederic Von Hugel, *Letters to a Niece,* ed. Gwendolyn Greene (Vancouver, British Columbia: Regent College Publishing, 1998), 62.

[11] Robert Browning, *Tennyson and Browning* (London: Thomas Nelson, 1938), 230.

bigger" and Aslan replies, "I am not, but every year you grow, you will find me bigger."[12] That captures well the spirit of Lewis as a Christian educator. He nudges his readers to see God in greater and greater proportion; and to see the world He has made with appreciation for its complexity. Consequently, Christian education ought to be dynamic, but never capricious. Aslan is good, but He is not a tame Lion.[13] Similarly, theology is not God. It is merely an approximation, and sound Christian education must constantly seek to discover better and better approximations.

If Christian education is objective then it must be tethered to the God who has revealed Himself in the world He has made and clarified His self-revelation in Scripture. Sound, orthodox theology is not static; it is dynamic. It is not because God is changing but because a human grasp of God is affected by the limits and weaknesses of human nature. Reality is iconoclastic, and the history of Christianity is freighted with councils and treatises, books, and sermons, each attempting to understand more deeply something of the Infinite. Consequently, the story of theology and its applications in Christian education is more like a tree adding rings than a train passing through stations. Lewis writes that "humanity does not pass through phases as a train passes through stations: being alive, it has the privilege of always moving yet never leaving anything behind. Whatever we have been, in some sort we are still."[14] And, elsewhere, Lewis adds, "But surely arrested development consists not in refusing to lose old things but in failing to add new things?"[15] The maturation process demands a certain rootedness in the past with its traditions and accumulated knowledge. But, if growth is occurring, there must also be new ground explored and new horizons reached. While a new experience may provide a challenge to one's conceptual framework, nevertheless, out of this, development is likely to occur. Orthodox theology has always progressed whenever challenges occurred that demanded change in the conceptual framework. This is supported by the history of the Church Councils. And, this is no less the case in Christian education and Lewis' approach to it.

CONTRIBUTIONS TO CHRISTIAN EDUCATION

The primary characteristics of Lewis' contribution to the field of Christian education

---

[12] C. S. Lewis, *The Lion, the Witch and the Wardrobe* (New York: Macmillan, 1951), 117.
[13] C. S. Lewis, *The Lion, the Witch and the Wardrobe: A Story for Children* (New York: Macmillan, 1950), 64-65.
[14] C. S. Lewis, *The Allegory of Love: A Study in Medieval Tradition* (Oxford: Oxford University Press, 1936), 1.
[15] C. S. Lewis, *Of Other Worlds*, ed. Walter Hooper (New York: Harcourt, 1966), 25.

were, generally speaking, his thinking and teaching on so many topics, expressed in so many genres[16] and venues, with his Christian faith as the means of unity and coherence in his work. Lewis testified to the great value of Christian Liberal Arts, and manifests a substantive apologetic for a Christian Worldview. As for specifics relative to Christian education, Lewis wrote *The Abolition of Man*, his only book that could be categorized as philosophy of education. Nevertheless, much data can be drawn from a wide range of his work to develop some of his seminal ideas about Christian education. The remainder of this article focuses on matters central to the content of Lewis' teaching, as embodied in his written work, in an attempt to discover why he was such an effective Christian educator. Three foundational items are considered regarding Lewis' contributions to Christian education: the role of the educator in which Lewis called his students to adjust their lives to Reality; the role of the learner to recognize that this call necessitated their humble engagement with reality through the imagination; and finally the role of the curriculum to explore reality by connecting the student with truth. These three foundational aspects of Lewis are central to his success as a Christian educator and can guide future educators in following his example.

THE TASK OF AN EDUCATOR: INTRODUCING REALITY

The task of an educator is to call his or her students to honest perceptions of reality. All are born into a complex world and one's orientation to that world begins self-referentially. Therefore a teacher must help the student break out of the dungeon of self and both discover and adjust his notions so that a wider world, and reality itself, may be grasped and understood. Truncated development occurs when this adjustment does not occur. Lewis noted in the Western Canon a significant contrast between two philosophies of education. He wrote that "St. Augustine and Rousseau both wrote *Confessions*; but to the one his own temperament is a kind of absolute (*au moins je suis autre*), to the other it is 'a narrow house, too narrow for Thee to enter — oh make it wide. It is in ruins — oh rebuild it.'"[17] The Rousseau self-referentialism, Lewis believed, leads to utilitarianism and approaches the world and others consumeristically. Things matter, if and only if, they matter to the subject. One projects onto the world what it wants and thereby loses the better Augustinian and Biblical perspective that is nurtured and developed towards honest self-awareness and empathy towards others.

---

[16] The genres Lewis published in include Autobiography, Apologetics, Christian Devotion, Essays, Fairy Stories, Fantasy, Journaling, Juvenilia, Letters, Literary Criticism, Literary History, Literary Introduction, Lyric Poetry, Narrative Poetry, Novels, Science Fiction, Sermons, and Classical Translation.

[17] Lewis, *Rehabilitations*, 194.

Furthermore, self-referential, and therefore false, notions of oneself and the world are likely to result in inappropriate moral choices. A failure to measure one's thought and one's volitional acts by the plumb line of reality will lead to moral chaos and anarchy. Lewis wrote against this form of *subjectivism* propositionally in *The Abolition of Man* as well as depicting its dangers in his fiction.[18] All of his evil characters, in fact, are *subjectivists*.[19] That is, rather than seeking to understand the world as something independent of one's thoughts about it, these characters seek to project onto the world whatever it is they want. Because of this subjectivism and the resulting risk one can be to oneself and others, it is therefore necessary to have guides, teachers, and fellow travelers. With these, a gathered knowledge of the real world can be dialectically processed and thereby the bandwidth of one's understanding of reality can widen.

Breaking free of self-referentialism is vital to encountering the world as it is, with all of its complexity and wonder. Lewis scholar Bruce Edward's noted, "For Lewis every critical posture is always an implicit ontology, a teleology, an eschatology. For in his implicit view of literacy, the critic is always defining the relationship of mankind not only to texts, but also to ultimate matters: the ground of being, the locus of meaning, and the possibility of transcendence. For Lewis, the Christian, this means that literary inquiry is always in some sense apologetics, though of course, rarely explicitly so."[20] What Lewis claims as true he believes has its validation in objective reality. While he holds opinions to be probable, truth claims must have their collaboration with the real world.[21] Therefore, one's observations of the world matter. A teacher who has seen further than the student, or explored more deeply, or read more widely, is a valued resource. Furthermore, such a teacher is likely to be more nuanced. He or she is less likely to make universal claims without substantive support. An educator operating in a Lewisian manner would minimize the number of inflated claims. For instance this kind of a

---

[18] For example, Jadis Queen of Charn saves herself while destroying her world in *The Magician's Nephew*, only to become the White Witch of Narnia making it always winter but never Christmas in *The Lion, the Witch and the Wardrobe*. She is thinks only of herself and seeks to destroy all others who stand in her way. Furthermore, Weston, in Lewis's Science Fiction novels, is also a subjectivist.

[19] For more on Lewis's warnings against subjectivism see Jerry Root, *C. S. Lewis and a Problem of Evil: An Investigation of a Pervasive Theme*, Princeton Theological Monograph (Eugene: Pickwick, 2009).

[20] Bruce Edwards, *A Rhetoric of Reading: C. S. Lewis's Defense of Western Literacy*, Values in Literature Monographs, no. 2 (Provo, UT: Center for the Study of Christian Values in Literature, 1986), 110.

[21] Lewis wrote, "An open mind, in questions that are not ultimate, is useful. But an open mind about foundations either of Theoretical or of Practical Reason is idiocy." In C. S. Lewis, *The Abolition of Man: Or, Reflections on Education, with Special Reference to the Teaching of English in the Upper Forms of Schools* (Las Vegas, Nevada: Lits, 2010), 31-32.

teacher would be unlikely to say something inflated like, "Prague is the most beautiful city in the world." That, is, of course, because it is unlikely the claimant has been to every city in the world. The less inflated claim, "Prague is the most beautiful city I have seen," has, for a teacher in the Lewisian tradition, far more merit. But then, it might fairly be asked, what cities has this person seen? If it is many, and if these examples count significantly as beautiful, the claim has even more substance. But then, the claimant ought to be prepared to offer a definition of beauty and an explanation how that definition may be applied to cities generally, and how Prague figures in the mix specifically. This is necessary if the teacher is to maintain integrity. In this way, Lewis knew that it is reality that shapes honest teaching. The Christian educator ought to strive to understand the very world before him and direct his teaching to help students understand that world as best he or she is able. This idea of tethering one's claims to reality is present in virtually all of Lewis's works of nonfiction. And such an approach is an asset not a liability. A good teacher, whose ideas are tethered to substance, can teach with confidence from knowledge of the real world. He can also guide the student to discover by exploring that real world.

The educator's work is like the work of a gardener. Lewis wrote that "the task of the modern educator is not to cut down jungles but to irrigate deserts."[22] Sensitive to the student's own processes of development, he does not seek to make the student do that which is contrary to his nature. The teacher cultivates in his pupils those characteristics and values consistent with how the pupil is created and also how one ought to conform to reality. Lewis observed that "until quite recent times all teachers and even all men believed the universe to be such that certain emotional reactions on our part could be either congruous or incongruous to it — believed, in fact, that objects did not merely receive, but could *merit*, our approval or disapproval, our reverence or contempt."[23] If justice is rendering to a thing its due, then the role of a teacher to guide the student into a coherent understanding of the universe is an act of justice. Conversely, to abuse the educational privilege is an act of injustice. But this is an old idea; "Let not many of you become teachers, my brethren, knowing that as such we shall incur a stricter judgment" (James 3:1).

This concept of justice as it impacts the role of the teacher in Lewis's educational scheme can be further portrayed. He preached a sermon at Oxford University titled "The Weight of Glory." In this message he noted that there are "no ordinary people." No one has ever met a "mere mortal." Everyone is moving through life progressing towards becoming

---

[22] Ibid., 13. For more on this, see Joel D. Heck, *Irrigating Deserts: C. S. Lewis on Education* (St. Louis, MO: Concordia Academic Press, 2005), 23-48.
[23] Ibid., 14.

either an everlasting horror or an everlasting glory. And each of us is participating in assisting others to one of these ends. This is certainly so for the educator. In this regard, Lewis took seriously his responsibility to his students. He recognized the high privilege and consequences of his role as a teacher. In this way he is a model for all who desire to teach in a manner that is Christian. One thing necessary to the process is to do one's best to understand Reality as it is and as best as one can, within his limits. Lewis writes further, "Aristotle says that the aim of education is to make the pupil like and dislike what he ought."[24] Such a statement is utter madness if there is no reality to support the claim. Therefore, more must be said about the nature of that Reality unique to the Christian educator's perspective.

THE TASK OF THE LEARNER: IMAGINING REALITY

Lewis, eager to learn about the real world was willing to acquire teachers wherever they might be found, even in the imagination. He wrote,

> The man who is contented to be only himself, and therefore less than a self, is in prison. My own eyes are not enough for me, I will see through those of others. Reality, even seen through the eyes of many, is not enough. I will see what others have invented. Even the eyes of all humanity are not enough. I regret that the brutes cannot write books. Very gladly would I learn what face things present to a mouse or a bee; more gladly still would I perceive the olfactory world charged with all the information and emotion it carries for a dog.[25]

One's limits do not have to be a liability if they incline one, with humility and honesty, to gain from the perspective others have of the real world. This is liberating and increases the capacity to explore the questions and curiosities of the heart. It also cultivates wonder, awe, and, in the last resort, worship. Thus, accordingly, Lewis believed that one of the greatest tools in the toolbox of the educator or learner, was the role of the imagination. Since man is limited, and since the world is complex, and since God is infinite, there must always be a place for the imagination in any serious consideration of education that is Christian. Lewis understood this and used the imagination masterfully in communicating about the world as he saw it. The word *definition* means, "of the finite." We define things by their limits and by their function. Something must be small enough to wrap words around and distinguish from other things if it is to be properly defined. If this is so, how does one define God, or the activities of God in the world He has made? Certainly this is, in part, manifest in Jesus

---

[24] Ibid.

[25] C. S. Lewis, *An Experiment in Criticism* (Cambridge: Cambridge University Press, 1961), 140.

teaching about the Kingdom of Heaven and his use of similes to describe what the Kingdom of Heaven is *like*. Jesus teaching made room for parables, figures of speech, symbols, and types. So, too, Lewis wisely models this for his various audiences. In fact, one cannot think about God, let alone engage in Christian education without both respect for and use of the imagination. The medieval theologians understood this and engaged in what they called "the way of analogy" when writing about God. Even scientists, seeking to understand the complexities of the natural world beyond their present grasp, begin their method with hypotheses. These are imaginative exercises. Furthermore, they explain their discoveries using models. The models are not the thing itself; they are imaginative depictions, and these must give way, in time, to more robust models. For both the honest scientist and honest theologian know one cannot grow in understanding without some use of the imagination. This is vital in all forms of education and especially vital for Christian education where encounters with God and His world should be flush with wonder and awe.

Lewis knew growth in understanding necessitated use of the imagination, and he categorized various forms of metaphor to make his point. Lewis wrote of *the pupil's metaphor*.[26] This is when a pupil seeks to advance understanding beyond what he or she presently knows. Thus, a metaphor is suggested, or a simile is advanced: "Suppose it is like this ..." The imaginative depiction grows out of the absence of present knowledge and the quest for more. Lewis also wrote about *the master's metaphor*.[27] This is used by the teacher who, in a given instance, currently knows more that the student. A metaphor, simile, or supposal is suggested by one who knows and is, by means of the imagination, bringing others into the fold of the informed. When Lewis left behind his atheism to become a theist, but before he converted to Christianity, he said he didn't think it was possible to know God personally any more than Hamlet could know Shakespeare. This image was suggested as a pupil's metaphor or analogy. Less than two years later, Lewis became a Christian. He revisited his analogy; only now, as an insider, he sets it forth as a master's metaphor. Hamlet, he explains, could never break out of the play to get to know the author; but Shakespeare, as the author, could have written himself into the play as a character, making the introduction between author and character possible. In fact, Lewis came to believe something like that occurred in the Incarnation when God became man.[28] The imagination is used powerfully here to illustrate both the pupil's and the master's metaphors. Nevertheless, more uses of the imagination must

---

[26] C. S. Lewis, *Selected Literary Essays*, ed. Walter Hooper (Cambridge: Cambridge University Press, 1969), 225.

[27] Ibid.

[28] C. S. Lewis, *Surprised by Joy* (London: Geoffrey Bles, 1955), 223, 227.

be cultivated. If we were courtiers of Elsinore, in Denmark, during Hamlet's day and suddenly encountered a small man in our world wearing Elizabethan tights trying to convince us we lived in a world he created, and he merely showed up to comfort us in light of all the tragedies at court, we might not immediately respond. The work of the imagination will need, yet, further applications. If God is infinite, and His world complex, Lewis makes it clear that the Christian educator's use of the imagination is never final.[29]

But, Lewis warns that while the imagination is a useful tool, like all things human it, too, is fallen and can be put to bad uses. He warns against what he calls the *transforming* imagination. In essence the transforming imagination is little more than what psychologists call "projection." To project onto Reality what we want to find there, to allow our assumptions to prevent us from seeing reality as objectively as one might, engages the transforming imagination. Nevertheless, "an abuse does not nullify a proper use." If we judged any segment of a society by its worst examples nobody could stand. Similarly, if we dismissed all inferior uses of the imagination, we would turn our backs on one of the most important tools necessary for solid spiritual understanding. However, since it is the case that the imagination can be abused, Lewis also recognized that the cultivation of character both in the teacher's life, as well as the nurture of character in the student, becomes an essential part of the educator's work. Here again, Lewis is very helpful as a model and guide.

THE TASK OF CURRICULUM: EXPLORING REALITY

As has been stated, Lewis believed there was a universe that existed independent of one's thoughts about it. There are knowers and things to be known. He told his students, "We have fulfilled our whole function if we help you to *see* some given track of reality."[30] It was not necessary for Lewis to present everything in the world to his students but to help them encounter some slice of reality and guide them in such a way that they might explore it well. After this nurturing, the student is enabled to move on to other areas of exploration to his or her life-long enrichment and fascination. Even in his fiction Lewis bears witness to this fact. In his first book of science fiction, *Out of the Silent Planet*, he wrote, "You cannot see things till you know roughly what they are."[31] Before the primary character of the book, Elwin Ransom, can see certain things, the complimentary development of language has to occur so he can know and understand the uniqueness of Malacandra (or Mars), the world to which he has been kidnapped. Since the inhabitants of that land are not fallen, and since Ransom

---

[29] See Lewis's development of this idea in "Transposition" in *The Weight of Glory*, 72-89.

[30] C. S. Lewis, *Rehabilitations*, 87.

[31] C. S. Lewis, *Out of the Silent Planet* (New York: Macmillian, 1943), 40.

comes from the Silent Planet, Thulcandra (or Earth), some descriptions are difficult. This is because Earth has neglected the language necessary to describe the presence of God manifest in the worlds He has made. It is possible that limits of language can also limit the capacity to see certain things. The Scriptures say, "A natural man does not accept the things of the Spirit of God; for they are foolishness to him, and he cannot understand them, because they are spiritually appraised" (I Corinthians 2:14). Lewis was not the type of teacher who would be likely to abuse his position as a teacher by coercing his nonbelieving students to accept his position on matters of faith. Nevertheless, he could direct any given student to look at a literary text and seek to get inside the mind and emotions of the character, to break out of one's own perspective and try to see how others may have understood circumstances and what the character felt about his world. A materialist in this situation is not doing well to dismiss the supernaturalist without first trying to understand him. For that matter, the supernaturalist is not doing well without trying to understand the materialist; therefore, empathy was a high value for Lewis. In his education, he sought to build empathy in his students by helping them widen their understanding of the very world where each finds himself.

To develop this further, here the medieval *trivium*, which is at the very heart of a liberal arts curriculum, becomes significant. As Lewis observed the *trivium* first taught *Grammar*. This included vocabulary and the use of words or, "the skill of speech." Then the student learned *Dialectic*, or reasoning, "how to talk sense, to argue, to prove and disprove." Three kinds of proof, forming a kind of check and balance in one's understanding was the epistemological objective. These checks and balances were made "from Reason, from Authority, and from Experience."[32] And *Dialectic* and understanding are advanced by these three proofs. And lastly, the *trivium* included *Rhetoric*, the ability to say things well, "the Rhetorician dealt with structure and style." The result of this kind of education was to enable the student to grasp and understand things once beyond his intellectual scope.[33] The increased skill and competency of language benefits the student to see the world before him with greater clarity. This also grants the student the opportunity to grow in empathy as well as increased intellectual sight. Lewis, rightly observed, "In coming to understand anything we must reject the facts as they are for us in favor of the facts as they are."[34]

---

[32] Lewis contends this is not an approach to epistemology peculiar to the Middle Ages for he writes, "Authority, reason, experience; on these three, mixed in varying proportions all our knowledge depends." See Lewis, *Christian Reflections*, 41.

[33] From C. S. Lewis, *The Discarded Image: An Introduction to Medieval and Renaissance Literature* (Cambridge: Cambridge University Press, 1964), 186, 188-190.

[34] Lewis, *Experiment in Criticism,* 138.

In *The Abolition of Man* Lewis built his case for sound education on a foundation of "objective value." He used the word *Tao*, defining it as, "The doctrine of objective value, the belief that certain attitudes are really true and others really false, to the kind of thing the universe is and the kind of things we are."[35] In the appendix to the book Lewis cited examples from a wide range of cultures both east and west and throughout time to show that the *Tao* is not a concept unique to contemporary, western thought. Lewis's brand of objectivity had a history, much older and far more robust than Enlightenment Rationalism. It traces its roots back as far as classical times, and it has a breadth that knows no cultural border.

CONCLUSION

Philosopher Mortimer Adler asks: "If something more than knowledge of straight thinking is needed for good conduct, how is it acquired and how can a man help another to acquire it?"[36] For Lewis, moral development has the opportunity to flourish in a context where the love of God is known. If "perfect love casts out fear" (I John 4:18), then it can be assumed that imperfect love breeds anxiety. Where a student is nurtured in the love of God, by a teacher, error is never a threat but an opportunity to grow. Self-worth is not contingent on performance. Security is in the love of God and therefore one can engage in honest evaluation of cognitive development as well as character development. The love of God provides the atmosphere for maturity to occur properly. Lewis modeled this. His writings reveal his tendency to pursue the truth wherever it would lead. It is fair to say that this is evidence of his relative security in the love of God. In fact, nearly the last words he wrote were sent to an eleven-year-old American girl, and he advised along these lines. He said, "If you continue to love Jesus, nothing much can go wrong with you, and I hope you may always do so."[37]

The questions of any new day are to be approached, not with despair, but optimism and hope. There is a real world before us, and we have the capacity to know some things about it. To grow, we must be willing to let earlier notions of the world give way to more robust ones. And this process never ceases. Therefore, education is not merely and activity for school; it is a lifelong quest. This, too, is fundamental to Lewis's grasp of the Christian educator's work. Imagination is a vital tool in the educator's tool box. It must be wielded with

---

[35] Lewis, *Abolition of Man*, 16.

[36] J. Mortimer Adler, *Great Ideas from the Great Books* (New York: Washington Square Press, 1970), 380.

[37] Lyle W. Dorsett and Marjorie Lamp Mead, ed., *C. S. Lewis: Letters to Children* (New York: Macmillan, 1985), 111.

character and sound judgment and guided by security in the love of Christ. It is by means of these principles so essential to Lewis's teaching and writing that one must classify Lewis as a Christian educator.

BIBLIOGRAPHY
WORKS CITED

Adler, Mortimer J. *Great Ideas from the Great Books.* New York: Washington Square Press, 1970.

Browning, Robert. *Tennyson and Browning.* London: Thomas Nelson, 1938.

Edwards, Bruce L. *A Rhetoric of Reading: C.S. Lewis's Defense of Western Literacy.* Provo, UT: Center for the Study of Christian Values in Literature, 1986.

Heck, Joel D. *Irrigating Deserts: C. S. Lewis on Education.* Saint Louis: Concordia Publishing House, 2005.

Hooper, Walter. *C. S. Lewis: A Companion & Guide.* London: Harper Collins Publishers, 1996.

Lewis, C. S., *The Abolition of Man: Or, Reflections on Education, with Special Reference to the Teaching of English in the Upper Forms of Schools.* Las Vegas, Nevada: Lits, 2010. (reprint from the 1947 New York: Macmillan, edition).

_____. *The Allegory of Love: A Study in Medieval Tradition.* Oxford: Oxford University Press, 1936.

_____. *Christian Reflections.* Edited by Walter Hooper. Grand Rapids: William B. Eerdmans, 1967.

_____. *The Discarded Image: An Introduction to Medieval and Renaissance Literature.* Cambridge: Cambridge University Press, 1964.

_____. *An Experiment in Criticism.* Cambridge: Cambridge University Press, 1961.

_____. *A Grief Observed.* (Pseudonym: N. W. Clerk). New York: Faber, 1961.

_____. *C. S. Lewis: Letters to Children.* Edited by Lyle Dorsett and Marjorie Lamp Mead. New York: Macmillan, 1985.

_____. *Letters to Malcolm: Chiefly on Prayer.* London: Geoffrey Bles, 1964.

_____. *The Lion, the Witch and the Wardrobe* New York: Macmillan, 1951.

_____. *The Lion, the Witch and the Wardrobe: A Story for Children.* New York: Macmillan, 1950.

_____. *Of Other Worlds.* Edited by Walter Hooper. New York: Harcourt, 1966.

_____. *Out of the Silent Planet.* 1943. New York: Macmillian, 1938.

_____. *A Preface to Paradise Lost.* London: Oxford University Press, 1942.

_____. *Rehabilitations and Other Essays.* London: Oxford University Press, 1939.

_____. *Selected Literary Essays.* Edited by Walter Hooper. Cambridge: Cambridge University Press, 1969.

_____. *Surprised by Joy: The Shape of My Early Life.* London: Geoffrey Bles, 1955.

_____. *The Weight of Glory and Other Addresses.* New York: Touchstone, 1996.

Milton, John. "Of Education." In *Areopagita and of Education.* Edited by George H. Sabine. New York: Appleton-Century-Crofts, 1951.

Root, Jerry. *C. S. Lewis and a Problem of Evil: An Investigation of a Pervasive Theme.* Eugene, OR: Pickwick, 2009.

Von Hugel, Frederich. *Letters to a Niece.* Edited by Gwendolyn Greene. Vancouver, British Columbia: Regent College Publishing, 1998.

ADDITIONAL PRIMARY SOURCE MATERIAL

Lewis, C. S. *All My Road Before Me: The Diary of C. S. Lewis, 1922-1927.* Edited by Walter Hooper. New York: Harcourt, 1991.

_____. *Arthurian Torso: Containing the Posthumous Fragment "The Figure of Arthur" by Charles Williams and a Commentary on the Arthur Poems of Charles Williams by C. S. Lewis.* London: Oxford University Press, 1948.

_____. *Boxen: The Imaginary World of the Young C. S. Lewis.* Edited by Walter Hooper. New York: Harcourt, 1985.

_____. *C. S. Lewis's Lost Aeneid: Arms and the Exile*, Edited with an Introduction by A. T. Reyes. New Haven and London: Yale University Press, 2011.

_____. *The Collected Letters of C. S. Lewis: Family Letters 1905-1931*, vol.1. Edited by Walter Hooper. San Francisco: Harper, 2004.

_____. *The Collected Letters of C. S. Lewis: Books, Broadcasts, and the War 1931-1949*, vol. 2. Edited by Walter Hooper. San Francisco: Harper, 2004.

_____. *The Collected Letters of C. S. Lewis: Narnia, Cambridge, and Joy 1950-1963*, vol. 3. Edited by Walter Hooper. San Francisco: Harper, 2007.

_____. *The Collected Poems of C. S. Lewis.* Edited by Walter Hooper. London: Fount Paperbacks, 1994.

_____. *The Dark Tower and Other Stories.* Edited by Walter Hooper. New York: Harcourt, 1977.

_____. (Pseudonym: 'Clive Hamilton'). *Dymer.* London: Dent, 1926.

_____. *English Literature in the Sixteenth Century, Excluding Drama*, Oxford History of English Literature, vol. III. Edited by Bonamy Dobree, Norman Davis, and F. P. Wilson. Oxford: Oxford University Press, 1954.

_____, ed. *Essays Presented to Charles Williams.* Grand Rapids: William B. Eerdmans Publishing Company, 1974.

_____. *The Four Loves.* New York: Harcourt, 1960.

_____, ed. *George MacDonald: An Anthology.* London: Geoffrey Bles: The Centenary Press, 1946.

_____. *God in the Dock: Essays on Theology and Ethics.* Edited by Walter Hooper. Grand Rapids: William B. Eerdmans, 1970.

_____. *The Great Divorce: A Dream.* London: Geoffrey Bles, 1945.

_____. *Hamlet: The Prince or the Poem?.* Norwood Editions, 1976.

_____. *The Horse and His Boy.* New York: Macmillan, 1954.

_____. *The Last Battle A Story for Children.* New York: Harcourt, 1956.

_____. *Letters to an American Lady.* Clyde Kilby, ed. Grand Rapids: William B. Eerdmans, 1967.

_____. *Letters of C. S. Lewis.* Edited and with a Memoir by W. H. Lewis. New York: Harcourt, 1966.

_____. *Letters, C. S. Lewis — Don Giovanni Calabria: A Study in Friendship.* Translated and edited by Martin Moynihan. Ann Arbor: Servant, 1988.

_____. *The Magician's Nephew.* New York: Macmillan, 1955.

_____. *Mere Christianity: A Revised and Amplified Edition With a New Introduction of the Three Books: Broadcast Talks, Christian Behavior and Beyond Personality.* New York: Macmillan, 1952.

_____. *Miracles: A Preliminary Study.* London: Geoffrey Bles, 1945.

_____. *Narrative Poems.* Edited by Walter Hooper. London: Geoffrey Bles, 1969.

_____. *Perelandra.* Oxford: John Lane, 1943.

_____. *The Pilgrim's Regress: An Allegorical Apology for Christianity, Reason and Romanticism.* London: Dent, 1933.

_____. *Poems.* Edited by Walter Hooper. New York: Harcourt, 1965.

_____. *Present Concerns: Essays by C. S. Lewis.* Edited by Walter Hooper. New York: Harcourt, 1986.

_____. *Prince Caspian.* New York: Macmillan, 1951.

_____. *The Problem of Pain.* London: Geoffrey Bles, 1940.

_____. *Reflections on the Psalms.* San Diego: Harcourt, 1986.

_____. *The Screwtape Letters.* London: Geoffrey Bles, 1942.

_____. *Screwtape Proposes a Toast and Other Pieces*. Edited by Walter Hooper. London: Fontana Books, 1965.

_____. *The Silver Chair*. New York: Macmillan, 1954.

_____. *Spenser's Images of Life*. Alistair Fowler, ed. Cambridge: Cambridge University Press, 1967.

_____. (Pseudonym: 'Clive Hamilton'). *Spirits in Bondage: A Cycle of Lyrics*. London: Heinemann, 1919.

_____. *Studies in Medieval and Renaissance Literature*. Edited by Walter Hooper. Cambridge: Cambridge University Press, 1966.

_____. *Studies in Words*. 2nd ed. Cambridge: Cambridge University Press, 1967.

_____. *That Hideous Strength: A Modern Fairytale for Grownups*. Oxford: John Lane, 1945.

_____. *They Asked for a Paper: Papers and Addresses*. London: Geoffrey Bles, 1962.

_____. *They Stand Together: The Letters of C. S. Lewis to Arthur Greeves, 1914-1963*. Edited by Walter Hooper. London: William Collins Sons & Co, Ltd, 1979.

_____. *Till We Have Faces: A Myth Retold*. New York: Harcourt, 1957.

_____. *The Voyage of the Dawn Treader*. New York: Macmillan, 1952.

_____. *The World's Last Night and Other Essays*. New York: Harcourt, 1960.

_____. *Undeceptions: Essays on Theology and Ethics*. Edited by Walter Hooper. London: Geoffrey Bles, 1971.

_____. *Yours Jack: Spiritual Direction from C. S. Lewis*. Paul Ford, ed. New York: Harper Collins, 2008.

Lewis, C. S. and Arthur C. Clarke, *From Narnia to a Space Odyssey: The War of Ideas Between Arthur C. Clarke and C. S. Lewis*. Edited with an Introduction by Ryder W. Miller. New York: Simon and Schuster, 2003.

Lewis, C. S. and Tillyard, E. M. W. *The Personal Heresy: A Controversy*. Oxford: Oxford University Press, 1939.

BOOKS EDITED OR WITH A PREFACE BY C. S. LEWIS

Athanasius. *The Incarnation of the Word of God: Being the Treatise of St. Athanasius "De Incarnatione Verbi Dei" Newly Translated into English by A Religious of C. S. M. V. S. Th*. With an Introduction by C. S. Lewis. London: Geoffrey Bles, 1944.

Bentley, Eric. *The Cult of the Superman: A Study in the Idea of Heroism in Carlyle and Nietzsche, with Notes on Other Hero-Worshippers of Modern Times*. With an Appreciation by C. S. Lewis. New York: The Macmillan Company, 1954.

Brook, G. L. ed., *Selections from Layamon's Brut*. With an Introduction by C. S. Lewis. Oxford: Oxford University Press, 1963.

Davidman, Joy. *Smoke on the Mountain: An Interpretation of the Ten Commandments*. Foreword by C. S. Lewis. Philadelphia: The Westminster Press, 1954.

Farrer, Austin *A Faith of Our Own*. With a Preface by C. S. Lewis. Cleveland: The World Publishing Company, 1960.

Harding, D. E. *The Hierarchy of Heaven and Earth: A New Diagram of Man in the Universe*. With a Preface by C. S. Lewis. New York: Harper Brothers, 1952.

Macdonald, George. *George MacDonald: An Anthology*. C. S. Lewis, ed. London: Geoffrey Bles, 1946.

Phillips, J. B. *Letters to Young Churches: A Translation of the New Testament Epistles*. With an Introduction by C. S. Lewis. New York: The Macmillan Company, 1954.

Sandhurst, B. G. *How Heathen is Britain?* Preface by C. S. Lewis. London: Collins, 1946.

ADDITIONAL RECOMMENDED SOURCES

Aeschliman, Michael D. *The Restitution of Man: C. S. Lewis and the Case Against Scientism*. Grand Rapids: William B. Eerdmans Publishing Company, 1983.

Como, James. *Branches to Heaven: The Geniuses of C. S. Lewis*. Dallas, TX: Spence Publishing Company, 1998.

Holmer, Paul L. *C. S. Lewis: The Shape of His Faith and Thought*. New York: Harper & Row Publishers, 1976.

McGrath, Alister. *If I Had Lunch with C. S. Lewis: Exploring the Ideas of C. S. Lewis on the Meaning of Life*. Carol Stream, IL: Tyndale House Publishers, 2014.

Ward, Michael. *Planet Narnia*. New York: Oxford, 2008.

CHAPTER 28

Frank E. Gaebelein:
Teacher of Truth

ALBERT BECK

Frank E. Gaebelein (1899-1983)

Frank Gaebelein was a key educator in the twentieth-century evangelical movement, active in the arts, letters, and social justice. Gaebelein's main contribution to Christian education came through the publication of *Christian Education in a Democracy* (1951), and *The Pattern of God's Truth* (1954), as well as championing Christian elementary and secondary schooling where Christian teachers and administrators actively integrated faith and learning. The underlying premise for such integration was that all truth is God's truth and thus in agreement with itself, whether such truth was found in nature, the Bible, or the unseen spiritual realm.

HISTORICAL BACKGROUND

Frank Gaebelein was the third son born to noted fundamentalist preacher and writer, Arno C. Gaebelein. Gaebelein completed his undergraduate studies at NYU and earned a master's degree in English and Comparative Literature at Harvard University. In 1921, he became the first headmaster of The Stony Brook School, an evangelical boarding school on Long Island that served as a model for many other Christian schools in the middle years of the twentieth century.

Gaebelein was a prolific writer and, through numerous articles published in the evangelical press, he influenced an emerging Christian school movement. He authored two important books on Christian schooling, *Christian Education in a Democracy* (1951) and *The Pattern of God's Truth* (1954), both published by Oxford University Press. *Christian Education in a Democracy* articulated the scope and nature of a distinctive Christian school movement in American democratic society. *The Pattern of God's Truth*, the more important of the two books, called Christian educators to understand the entire school curriculum in the light of God's eternal truth and thereby integrate faith and learning. Through the 1990s, these books were required reading for teachers seeking certification from the Association of Christian Schools International, the largest Christian elementary and secondary school organization in America.

At age sixty-four, Gaebelein left Stony Brook and joined his friend, Carl F. H. Henry, as co-editor of *Christianity Today*. Around this time, Gaebelein served as an editor for the *New Scofield Reference Bible,* and later became the style editor for the *New International Version Bible* and the general editor of the *Expositor's Bible Commentary*, a project that occupied Gaebelein until his death in 1983.

THEOLOGY OF CHRISTIAN EDUCATION
EPISTEMOLOGY

Theologically, Gaebelein was a rather conventional twentieth-century evangelical. His approach to knowledge was guided by an understanding that historian Mark Noll identifies as *epistemological and methodological common sense*, a belief that one's perceptions reveal the world more-or-less as it is.[1] The inductive method, so useful in determining the facts and laws of nature, was also the method for determining the facts and laws of morality, theology, anthropology, or any other realm of knowledge. A fact was defined

---

[1] Mark Noll, "Common Sense Traditions and American Evangelical Thought," *American Quarterly* 37, no. 2 (Summer 1985): 217-223.

as that which corresponded to reality. Facts were true, and truth was built upon a foundation of facts. Truth was propositional in nature, and for Gaebelein and many other evangelical thinkers, facts came prior to belief or interpretation. Gaebelein wrote, "The intelligent evangelical bases his religious thinking ... on facts ... Christianity is a religion of fact."[2] Facts, when properly understood, should determine one's faith and worldview.

> Who of us, on being suddenly confronted with some startling piece of news, has not exclaimed, 'Is it really true?' Now it is the adverb in this colloquialism that points to the test of truth ... [W]hen we ask whether a thought is 'really' true, we are, almost unconsciously, invoking the criterion of correspondence with reality. Whether it be a matter of science like Einstein's epoch-making equation, E equals MC^2; or whether it be a particular virtue in the intangible realm of character, such as that a man is courageous, correspondence with reality is the criterion of the truthfulness of truth.[3]

ALL TRUTH IS GOD'S TRUTH

Gaebelein's rallying cry that "All truth is God's truth" stemmed from his commitment to the unity of all truth under God."[4] For Gaebelein, truth reflected the character of God, and this divine connection established a basis for understanding the unity of truth. "[T]he most important principle in Christian thought, or, for that matter, in any kind of thought at all ... is the continuity of all truth under God."[5]

God's character provides an objective basis for our understanding and knowledge of truth. "Every idea has both internal and external meaning ... Using 'external' not in its connotation of 'superficial' but rather in its denotation of something outside and beyond us, we see that the external meaning ... has to do with God's truth. That is to say, it is objectively true."[6] In sum, a true idea or fact is true because God is true. Thus, because truth is related to

---

[2] Frank Gaebelein, "An Evangelical's Defense," *North American Review* 232, no. 1 (July 1931): 27.

[3] Frank Gaebelein, "What is Truth?" in *A Varied Harvest: Out of a Teacher's Life and Thought* (Grand Rapids, Mich.: William B. Eerdmans, 1967), 173. Gaebelein stands in contrast to some other evangelicals, particularly those in the Reformed tradition, who prioritize faith over facts. Abraham Kuyper, for example, argued that there were two kinds of people in the world, Christian and non-Christian, and therefore two different sciences and two distinctive ways of knowing. See Abraham Kuyper, *Encyclopedia of Sacred Theology*, trans. John H. DeVries (New York: Charles Scribner's Sons, 1898).

[4] Frank Gaebelein, *The Pattern of God's Truth: Problems of Integration in Christian Education* (New York: Oxford University Press, 1954), 22-23.

[5] Frank Gaebelein, "Truth and Culture," *HIS Magazine* 20 (Feb. 1960): 19.

[6] Gaebelein, *Pattern of God's Truth*, 8.

God, Gaebelein could insist, "What is true, what is really true, can never be otherwise than true. We hear much about the search for truth. It is a noble and exciting thing for a man to dedicate himself to discovering new aspects of truth. But no one can originate or make up truth. Truth is here all the time, to be discovered or to be revealed, as God wills."[7]

THE ATTRIBUTES OF TRUTH

Because truth is rooted in the nature and character of God, truth shares in His divine attributes. For example, Gaebelein insisted that truth was *holy*: "The solemn fact is that truth is holy; inherent in the nature of God Himself, it is ever sacred."[8] Truth was also *immutable*: "Truth is as big as God, because He is truth. Truth remains unchangeable."[9] The immutability of truth provided a touchstone for action in a changing world, a sure guide for how the individual could order his or her life on timeless principles.[10]

Jesus declares himself the Truth in John 14:6. With this equation of Jesus and the truth, Gaebelein insisted that truth was also *personal*. The believer's response to truth is not that of a person to an object, but of one person to another person. "For the Church and for all who serve within its fellowship, it is never truth for truth's sake, in the sense of truth as an abstraction, that is the goal. It is rather truth for the sake of him who *is* the truth and he is also the way and the life. All truth is of God and thus of Christ 'in whom are hid all the treasures of wisdom and knowledge (Col. 2:3).'"[11]

Likewise, truth, rooted in the Triune God, is *authoritative*. To obey truth is to obey God. As Gaebelein's close friend Donald Barnhouse notes, "To give truth its proper position — the position that God Himself gives it — is to subordinate every human opinion to the truth."[12] The postmodern notion that each person could establish his or her own truth had no place in Gaebelein's thinking. To attempt to establish an authority situated in one's own self inverts a person's relationship to truth.

Gaebelein frequently equated truth with the divine quality of *excellence*. The clearest expression of excellence is found in the person of Jesus Christ. "We hear much today about

[7] Frank Gaebelein, "Some Things Can't Be Shaken," *Eternity* 13, no. 11 (Nov. 1962): 13.

[8] Frank Gaebelein, "Dualism of Truth," *Eternity* 5, no. 8 (Aug. 1954): 11.

[9] Gaebelein, "Some Things Can't Be Shaken," 13.

[10] "What a comforting reminder this is in an unstable world! Our God is not only the source of 'every good and every perfect gift'; He is also absolutely unchangeable." Frank Gaebelein, *The Practical Epistle of James* (Great Neck, NY: Doniger & Raughley, 1953), 47.

[11] Frank Gaebelein, "The Sacred Life of the Church," *Christianity Today* 1 (19 Aug. 1957): 21.

[12] Donald G. Barnhouse, *Words Fitly Spoken* (Wheaton, IL.: Tyndale House Publishers, 1969), 10.

the imperative need for the pursuit of excellence in education. It is a worthy purpose to seek excellence in all that we do. Yet by itself the pursuit of excellence is inadequate unless it is always related to the truth, not only abstractly but as it is in Christ."[13] In an essay about the need to pursue excellence in the independent school, Gaebelein noted, "The vision of excellence is ultimately a personal vision ... [T]he best is made known with finality in the Person and words and above all in the saving work of Christ."[14] That which is shoddy, false, or "cheap" in an aesthetic sense lacked truth and authenticity and is a paltry response to the calling of God upon a Christian's life.

As Gaebelein saw it, Christians too often accept falsehood instead of truth. Such acquiescence to falsehood lead to an endorsement of mediocrity among believers. Gaebelein lamented, "Among the rank and file of evangelical Christians, aesthetic standards are generally low. The evidence is abundant ... But, and this also must be said, evangelicals are not alone in the habituation to the mediocre ... A similar kind of cultural illiteracy runs through much of liberal Protestantism, and indeed through most of American life today."[15] To counter this descent into mediocrity, Gaebelein insisted that individuals must become habituated to greatness. Such would occur only when people embrace the truth offered in Jesus Christ as revealed in the Bible.[16]

TRUTH AND ACTION: THE OBLIGATION OF TRUTH

That Truth leads to action was a central theme in Gaebelein's later writings. In *The Practical Epistle of James*, Gaebelein insisted that a commitment to the truth entailed a commitment to *doing* truth. "For the Bible countenances no such gap between doctrine and practice. Rather is the emphasis upon doing the truth." As Gaebelein noted, "To look into the mirror of the Word of God involves an obligation ... Christian truth, 'the perfect law of liberty,' is always in order to practice." A Christian, upon looking into the Word of God, "abides in truth and dwells in it, as it were. Then, remembering what he sees, he goes out to be 'a doer of the word,' and in the very doing he is blessed."[17]

There is an activist impulse in this understanding of truth. To be sure, this was not

---

[13] Frank Gaebelein, "The Christian's Intellectual Life," *Christianity Today* 5 (8 May 1961): 5.

[14] Frank Gaebelein, "Religion and the Independent School: An Inquiry and a Challenge," *The Independent School Bulletin* 61-62, no. 3 (Apr. 1962): 8.

[15] Frank Gaebelein, "Toward a Biblical View of Aesthetics," *Christianity Today* 12, no. 23 (30, Aug. 1968): 4.

[16] Gaebelein, "Religion and the Independent School," 7.

[17] Gaebelein, *Epistle of James*, 51, 52-53.

novel to Gaebelein but a recapturing of the ethical dimension of truth that is essential to Christian doctrine. Much of the modern world, however, has lost its awareness of this ethical imperative of truth. Christian teachers need to recover the ethical and spiritual dimensions of truth and impart such awareness to their students, both through instruction and personal example.[18] "The Bible refers to truth as something to be 'done' ... From Genesis to Revelation emphasis is laid upon 'doing' the truth . . ."[19] For Christian teachers, "doing truth" includes the consideration of how faith and learning could be combined in all facets of the school program.

CONTRIBUTION TO CHRISTIAN EDUCATION
THE INTEGRATION OF FAITH AND LEARNING

Gaebelein's greatest contribution to Christian education was his argument that Christian educators needed to integrate faith and learning. The phrase "the integration of faith and learning" was not used by anyone until 1952 when Gaebelein delivered the W. H. Griffith Thomas Memorial Lectures at Dallas Theological Seminary.[20] He defined faith-learning integration as, "The living union of [education's] subject matter, administration, and even of its personnel, with the eternal and infinite pattern of God's truth."[21] An understanding of the nature of truth is essential to faith-learning integration. "God's truth is of universal scope. This being the case, every aspect of education must be brought into relation to it. So the problem of integration arises — the word, we are reminded, means 'the bringing together of parts into the whole.'" Christian educators need to provide a living example of integrated, holistic education, first to be faithful to the truth of God, but also to serve as a light to others who seek wholeness in the curriculum.[22]

BACKGROUND: FAITH AND LEARNING BEFORE GAEBELEIN

Gaebelein's appropriation of the language of integration was a new way of

---

[18] Gaebelein, "Christian's Intellectual Life," 5.

[19] Frank Gaebelein, *Christian Education in a Democracy* (New York: Oxford University Press, 1951), 42.

[20] While the idea of uniting faith and learning can be found in others (as noted in the earlier essay on John Henry Newman), this particular locution, i.e., "the integration of faith and learning," finds its genesis in the twentieth century with Gaebelein. See Ken Badley, "The Faith-Learning Integration Movement in Christian Higher Education: Slogan or Substance?" *Journal of Research on Christian Education* 3, no. 1 (Spring 1994): 16; D. Bruce Lockerbie, *A Passion for Learning: The History of Christian Thought on Education* (Chicago: Moody Press, 1994).

[21] Gaebelein, *Pattern of God's Truth,* 9.

[22] Ibid., 7.

conceptualizing the relationship between faith and learning. Until the middle of the nineteenth century, Protestants at the forefront of American education took for granted that faith and scholarship naturally converged.[23] Such a supposition was not the integration of faith and learning; there was no conscious attempt by teachers or students to bring together parts into the whole. Contemporary scholars Michael Hamilton and James Mathisen termed this the "Convergence Model" for relating faith and learning. The best of science would always square with the best of theology. Special revelation merely confirmed the reality of scientific discovery but had nothing distinctive to offer in regards to academic starting points, methodology, or conclusions.[24]

When the intellectual rug was pulled out from underneath the feet of Protestant intellectuals by Darwin and other nineteenth-century naturalists, Christians in the academy had to reconsider the way they related faith and learning. The casual assumption that faith and learning necessarily converged in the direction of orthodoxy became untenable. In an attempt to shield the essence of Christianity from secular attacks, many sincere believers widened the chasm between faith and learning, making the split an essential feature of their Christian apologetic. By segregating faith from learning, Christianity was placed beyond the bounds of secular criticism while continuing to provide extracurricular value to the school via moral and spiritual guidance outside of the classroom. But there was a downside to this arrangement. If faith was freed from the dangers of new learning, learning itself was now set free from the faith that had nourished and given it sustenance for nearly two millennia. Hamilton and Mathisen refer to this new arrangement as the "value-added model" for relating faith and learning.[25] Sacred and secular knowledge occupied different spheres and had minimal influence upon each

---

[23] See, for example, Michael Beaty, Todd Buras, and Larry Lyon, "Baptist Higher Education: A Conflict in Terms?" *Baylor Line* (Winter 1997): 43-51; Michael S. Hamilton and James A. Mathisen, "Faith and Learning at Wheaton College," in *Models for Christian Higher Education*, ed. Richard T. Hughes and William B. Adrian (Grand Rapids, Mich.: Wm. B. Eerdmans, 1997), 261-283.

[24] Hamilton and Mathisen, "Faith and Learning," 268-269. Hamilton and Mathisen note the heavy dependence of this model upon the works of such early modern theologians like Joseph Butler and William Paley, but the idea goes back much farther than the eighteenth century.

[25] Speaking particularly to the historic development of Baylor University, Beaty, Buras, and Lyon called this the "Add-On Approach" to Christian Education. "This way of thinking — call it the 'add on' view — suggests that Christian education is comprised of religiously neutral academic activities with some Christian activities added on, like icing on a cake." Beaty, Buras, and Lyon, "Baptist Higher Education," 44.

other.[26] According to the value-added model, nothing distinguished the teaching found at Christian colleges from that offered by their secular counterparts.

BACKGROUND: FRAGMENTATION IN EDUCATIONAL THOUGHT

During the first half of the twentieth century, a growing number of secular educators came to deplore the fragmentation of the American school curriculum. Academic specialization had spread from the universities to secondary and elementary schools, and a sense of social transformation in the wake of the World Wars forced many educators to consider how the curriculum could be rewritten to bring about more holistic education that would unite an apparently fragmenting republic. In 1951, Harvard University appointed a committee to ascertain how universities could meet the objectives of general education in democratic society, and a key point brought forward by the committee was the need for educators to rediscover a unifying factor in education. The members of the Harvard committee determined that while religion had once served as the unifying factor in education, it was no longer a practical source of intellectual unity. To Gaebelein, this statement seemed to be hubris of the highest sort and a challenge to the kind of work he had been doing at Stony Brook for nearly thirty years.[27] Gaebelein wrote *The Pattern of God's Truth* as a direct response to the shortsighted determination of the Harvard committee.

INTEGRATION, SCRIPTURE, AND THE UNITY OF TRUTH

As conceived by Gaebelein, faith-learning integration differed from the convergence and value-added models of Christian education even as it contained elements of both. As with the convergence model, integration requires that faith and learning fit together in a natural order. But integration entails the notion of actively bringing together various parts into a whole, presupposing a prior state of fragmentation or separation. Thus, there was awareness that faith and learning had become separated in education, but there was now a countervailing desire to overcome the gulf that had grown between them. Faith-learning integration implies the restoration of a lost, but previously accessible, unity between academic and spiritual realms.

According to Gaebelein, Scripture alone could bring coherence to the various

---

[26] Hamilton and Mathisen, "Faith and Learning," 270.

[27] Harvard Committee on the Objectives of a General Education in a Free Society, *General Education in a Free Society: Report of the Harvard Committee on the Objectives of a General Education in a Free Society* (Cambridge, Mass.: Harvard University Press, 1951).

realms of knowledge. Gaebelein understood that this would not be a popular position in contemporary America. People would ask, "What has the latter part of the twentieth century got to do with Christ and the Bible?" Gaebelein appreciated such questions, believing that they brought us, "straight up against what may well be the most important principle in Christian thought, or for that matter, in any kind of thought at all. That principle is the continuity of all truth under God. Or, to put it in other words, it is the principle that all truth ... is God's truth."[28] This Christian understanding of truth provided a measure of unity in the midst of diversity, reflective of the Trinitarian nature of the Godhead.[29]

Education requires an awareness of the necessary connection between one truthful fact and another truthful fact, whether spiritual or mundane. Every field of knowledge is connected to every other field of knowledge through the God who created all things. The unity of truth allows, even requires, a holistic approach to knowledge and understanding. A central purpose of Christian education, then, is for teachers to train their pupils to discern the connections within the unity of truth. "We must recognize, for example, that we need teachers who see their subjects, whether scientific, historical, mathematical, literary, or artistic, as included within the pattern of God's truth."[30]

The unity of truth in God meant that truth in one domain had a connection with truth in another. A scientific truth, perhaps regarding the age of the earth, would not disagree with Scriptural truth regarding the creation of the universe. Conflicts might appear on the surface, but substantively, when understood aright, they could not be in disagreement with each other. Overcoming apparent discrepancies between natural and spiritual truth, particularly as revealed in the Bible, requires both faith and human reason to integrate our understanding of multiple true statements into a consistent system of understanding.

As noted earlier, Gaebelein believed that facts were prior to faith in regard to human understanding. Nevertheless, faith is necessary for an individual to properly understand facts in his or her connection to the spiritual realm. The element of faith is essential because truth is ultimately of divine origin. Gaebelein insisted that there was no substantive dichotomy between the sacred and the secular. "In the light of this principle [that all truth is God's truth], the conventional schism between secular truth and sacred truth is wrong. Every truth, no matter in what realm of life it may be found, is of God and under God."[31] It is incumbent upon

---

[28] Gaebelein, "Truth and Culture," 19.

[29] Frank Gaebelein, "What is Truth in Art?" *Christianity Today* 20, no. 23 (27 Aug. 1976): 11.

[30] Gaebelein, *Pattern of God's Truth,* 23.

[31] Gaebelein, "Truth and Culture," 19.

Christian individuals and institutions to seek to develop a holistic, integrated understanding of knowledge, relating fact to fact, truth to truth. If all truth is God's truth, he argued, then Christian schools and colleges committed to both God and truth "must renounce once and for all the false dichotomy between sacred and secular truth. [Such institutions] must see that truth in science and art and literature belong just as much to God as truth in religion."[32]

Gaebelein brought faith-learning integration into the mainstream of evangelical life. Within a few years of the publication of *The Pattern of God's Truth*, the language of integration became a normative way for evangelical educators to conceptualize the unique perspective of Christian education. Gaebelein successfully promoted faith-learning integration for a number of different reasons. By the 1950s, he was recognized as the leading American spokesman for evangelical education. Working under the auspices of the newly formed National Association of Evangelicals, he completed the movement's first and only definitive statement on education with the publication of *Christian Education in a Democracy*. He was the successful headmaster of The Stony Brook School, a premier Christian preparatory school that educated the sons of many leading evangelicals.[33] Gaebelein was a prolific writer, and he frequently contributed articles to widely read magazines like *Christianity Today* and *Eternity* that advanced a vision for faith-learning integration.[34] *The Pattern of God's Truth* continued to receive widespread interest by Christian educators and was published by Moody Press in 1968 and other publishing houses into the twenty-first century. Gaebelein also inaugurated faculty workshops on the integration of faith and learning at Wheaton College, and he lectured at other Christian schools on the matter.[35]

---

[32] Frank Gaebelein, "Portrait of a Christian College," *Eternity* 7, no. 2 (Feb. 1956): 8-9, 44-46

[33] In the middle 1950s, Gaebelein's Stony Brook School was already one of the oldest evangelical schools in the country, even though it was itself only about thirty years old. The paucity of self-identified evangelical or fundamentalist schools did not abate until the 1950s, and then only slowly.

[34] E.g., "Reason and Revelation," *Revelation* 5, no. 6 (June 1935): 231, 258-259; "A Preface to Christian Education," *Revelation* 18, no. 8 (Aug. 1948): 335-336, 374-376; "Christian Education and the Home," *Moody Monthly* 51, no. 3 & 4 (Nov. & Dec. 1950): 149-151, 169, 232-233, 252-254; "Christian Education and Its View of Man," *Our Hope* 57, no. 11 (May 1951): 677-681; "Portrait of a Christian College," *Eternity* 7, no. 2 (Feb. 1956): 8-9, 44-46; "Word of God in Education," *Christianity Today* 4 (9 May 1960): 6-9; "The Christian's Intellectual Life," *Christianity Today* 5 (8 May 1961): 4-6; "Corollaries of Biblical Scholarship," *Christianity Today* 6 (11 May 1962): 7-8; "Towards a Christian Philosophy of Education," *Grace Journal* 3 (1962): 1-28; "Crisis in Christian Education," *Christianity Today* 15 (21 May 1971): 4-7.

[35] Gaebelein began offering the Wheaton seminars in 1969. See Hamilton and Mathisen, "Faith and Learning at Wheaton College," 279. See also, Frank Gaebelein, *The Integration of Truth in Christian Education* (Columbia, S.C.: Columbia Bible College, 1970).

THE METHOD OF INTEGRATION: INTERDISCIPLINARY EDUCATION

For Gaebelein, the Bible is foundational to the Christian school curriculum, for it alone provides the integrative factor in education. Scripture is unique in that it alone is the direct revelation of the God who is Truth. In what appears a somewhat counterintuitive move, Gaebelein therefore argued that Christian schools should do away with a separate Bible department. Instead, a school, "must seek and develop devoted Christian teachers who, along with their competency in mathematics, science, languages, or social studies, are able also to give instruction in Bible." Such teachers did not have to be Bible scholars *per se*, but they should be "individuals whose primary spiritual and intellectual residence is in the Bible."[36]

Integrating faith and scholarship required mental flexibility and an openness to newly discovered truth. A commitment to truth did not entail a backward-looking gaze that sought to recapture a golden Christian past. In regard to education, it would not suffice to merely return to an old model of instruction. "No sensible person would insist on a retreat to the Harvard of the seventeenth century, the Columbia of the eighteenth, or to the colleges of the nineteenth century, Christian as most of them were."[37] A commitment to truth and faith-learning integration looked both forward and back. Instead he wanted,

> To advocate a return to Christianity as the unifying factor of education is not, therefore, to advocate a return to the outworn, a mere nostalgic reversion to that which was once loved and lost. It is rather to urge a deliberate retraction of steps to the place where education long ago departed from eternal reality. Moreover, it is to urge this in the vital context of the present, recognizing the eternal contemporaneity of the living Christ as set forth in the living Word.[38]

THE TEACHER AND THE TRUTH

Christian education requires Christian teachers. "The fact is inescapable; the world view of the teacher, in so far as he is effective, gradually conditions the world view of the pupil. No man teaches out of a philosophical vacuum. In one way or another, every teacher expresses the convictions he lives by, whether they be spiritually positive or negative."[39] There was no room for compromise on this point. Allowing non-Christian teachers in the classroom of a Christian school, whether preschool or university, would lead to secularization of that school. But staffing a school with Christian teachers was not enough. Too often,

---

[36] Gaebelein, *Pattern of God's Truth*, 48-49.

[37] Gaebelein, "Preface to Christian Education," 376.

[38] Ibid.

[39] Gaebelein, *Pattern of God's Truth*, 37.

Christian faculty adopted a secular, non-biblical worldview as a result of their upbringing or professional training. As such, a Christian school must often reeducate its teachers to help them develop a biblical worldview grounded in the pattern of God's truth. "We must go to the root of the problem ... Instead of spending time in discussing side issues, Christian faculties need to investigate the extent to which the secular climate of opinion has drifted into their own minds and colored their own teaching. Such an investigation will be disquieting. It may even result in revisions of cherished presentation of subject matter. But it must be done."[40]

Once the teacher has begun to develop a Christian worldview herself, she must continue to train herself in the truth of God through rigorous, ongoing study of the Bible. The constant, habitual study of the Scriptures will inevitably shape the teacher's mind and thinking. As a result, the teacher can make natural, and not forced, connections between the revealed Word of God and the revelation found in creation.

THE SUBJECT AND THE TRUTH

Gaebelein argued that as teachers become rooted and grounded in the Bible, they would be able to integrate their particular teaching subject into the larger pattern of God's truth. The ease or difficulty of this endeavor would vary by subject matter and was largely dependent upon the effect of sin upon our judgment of that subject. Because of humanity's fallen nature, sin has its greatest impact on the theological and human sciences that, "deal with such living questions as freedom and the relationship of man to man and man to God. In the exact physical sciences, which are further away from the living center, the disturbances through sin become less until in mathematics it dwindles to zero."[41] In other words, mathematics, because it is less influenced by sinful intellect, could stand on its own as revealing truth and did not need to be actively connected with some spiritual fact or program in order to be understood in the pattern of God's truth. On the other hand, our interpretation of human agency, whether in the arts, literature, history, or current events, is much more likely to be tainted by the bias of sinful nature and thus requiring a greater effort at integration with spiritual truth.

---

[40] Ibid., 42-43.

[41] Frank Gaebelein, "Is There Purpose in the Universe? [Review of *The Recovery of Purpose*, by Emile Cailliet]," *Eternity* 11, no. 2 (Feb. 1960): 16.

ELEMENTARY AND SECONDARY CHRISTIAN SCHOOLS

Gaebelein insisted that evangelicals needed to establish primary and secondary schools that taught from a distinctive Christian worldview. Evangelicals had been active in higher education but the foundations of education, elementary and secondary schools had been neglected. "Christian education is top-heavy. It is like an inverted pyramid, resting upon its smallest point. In both number of institutions and number of students its greatest strength is at the top."[42] Such a precarious structure could not long stand.

For Gaebelein, Christian schools were not appendages of the Christian church, nor did they merely provide polite, safe environments for children to learn the same material in the same manner as they would in a public school. Gaebelein lamented, "Some believing parents consider the Christian elementary or secondary school a mere fill or extra, because of the dominance of the public school; and, if the truth be told, others think of it as a sort of educational rescue mission for budding juvenile delinquents and for children who appear to be stupid." But, continued Gaebelein, "Such a view ignores the plain fact that, if we want our children to have a God-centered world view, the foundations must be laid in early youth."[43]

TRUTH BEYOND THE CLASSROOM

Within the Christian school, not just classroom instruction but the entirety of the school program had to be integrated into the pattern of God's truth. Extracurricular activities needed to be evaluated for their compatibility with biblical values, and all activities could be included in the school program as long as they met the standard of reflecting God's truth. Gaebelein offered a principle to help guide in this selection process, which he noted was first "stated by the Apostle Paul in his letter to the Colossians: 'Whatsoever you do in word or deed, do all in the name of the Lord Jesus, giving thanks to God and the Father by him.' For those who are committed to what is good, the criterion is both clear and broad ... everything

---

[42] Gaebelein, *Pattern of God's Truth*, 110.

[43] Ibid., 103. While recognizing the importance of Christian education for children, Gaebelein was not an advocate for the restoration of Christianity in the public school. "However much we believe in evangelical, Protestant education, it would be highly unrealistic to expect that such education be given to all, or to the majority, or even to a very large minority of our youth." America was pluralistic, and the public schools needed to be respected as such. "While for believers Christianity is the final faith, in a democracy it is one of a number of religions. While for evangelicals, historic, Bible-centered Protestantism is the purest form of Christianity, in a democracy it does not enjoy a jot more privilege than Roman or Greek Catholicism, Mormonism, or Christian Science." Gaebelein, *Christian Education in a Democracy*, 17-18.

wholesome, everything happy, everything truly recreative is within their scope."[44] If an activity passed this initial test, then it could be integrated into the life of the school by this simple fact — "work well done, even as a hobby or recreation, effort expended unselfishly, activity that contributes to a life of effective service of God and fellowman — these belong to God's truth fully as much as the most carefully planned course in philosophy or Bible." [45] By pursuing excellence in sports or the arts, a student, coach, or club sponsor could integrate the principle of truth into that activity. Gaebelein called this the criterion of Christian craftsmanship. "The teacher who gives himself to his work in real dedication, the student who is not content merely to get by but goes beyond what is required — these, provided their motive reaches past self-advancement to the glory of God, are practicing the principle of Christian craftsmanship."[46]

CONCLUSION

If there is any criticism to be directed at Gaebelein, it is that his writing, though prolific, sometimes lacked clarity and precision. A twenty-first century reader might wish that he would have better defined his terms, particularly in regard to the nature of truth. Readers will not find an intellectually rigorous response to postmodern thought in Gaebelein's writings, nor should they expect to find such. Gaebelein wrote when the quest for wisdom was centered on the question of what, exactly, constituted truth, rather than the current question of whether or not truth, in whatever form, exists at all.

Yet Gaebelein's ideas on the integration of faith and learning continue to resonate in the halls and classrooms of Christian schools and universities. Faith-learning integration as formulated by Gaebelein reflected a yearning for wholeness and restoration built into the fabric of the universe, something St. Paul touched upon in Romans 8:18-25. The disharmony and frustration of creation will find unity and liberation as it is brought into conformity to the pattern of God's truth. Likewise, the broken pieces of the curriculum will be put together once again, but only as they are brought together in the pattern of God's truth. The pursuit of truth was a pursuit of wholeness. More than that, though, the pursuit of truth was the pursuit of God.

> The solemn fact is that truth is holy; inherent in the nature of God Himself, it is ever sacred. No man who tampers with it is guiltless ... as we go on to struggle with some hard problems, let us do so with a zealous regard for the truth, realizing in deep humility that we may indeed fail to apprehend it in all its sacred perfection, but trusting also that the God of all truth will show us the way to His greater glory in our

---

[44] Gaebelein, *Pattern of God's Truth*, 87.

[45] Ibid., 88.

[46] Ibid., 89.

Christian education.[47]

PRIMARY SOURCE SAMPLE[48]

3. The Problem of Integration

From this brief view of the relevance of our subject, we turn to its analysis. At first glance, there seem to be two separate things before us: 'God's truth' and the matter of 'integration.' In reality, however, the two are closely linked. God's truth is of universal scope. This being the case, every aspect of education must be brought into relation to it. So the problem of integration arises — the word, we are reminded, means 'the bringing together of parts into the whole.' Our aim will be to point the way to a solution of this problem by showing how in some vital particulars Christian education can achieve integration into the all-embracing truth of God ...

An education that has deliberately departed from God and His Word will continue to search, 'ever learning and never able to come to knowledge of the truth,' to use Paul's words to T'imothy.[9] This is why secular education today, including much of our public-school system, is still centrifugal, despite the vain efforts being made to base it on values derived solely from a sociological and naturalistic setting. Having turned its back upon God and His Word and having thus given up its external meaning, secular education is powerless to put together its internal meaning.

Christian education is different. With all its inadequacies, failures, and difficulties, it has something to which to tie itself. For it, too, integration is a problem, but a problem of quite another kind than for secular education. Christian education does not need to keep looking for the integrating factor; it already has this factor. We who believe the Bible to be the inspired Word of God and who take seriously such truths as the creation of the universe by the living God, the lost condition of man, the atonement, justification by faith, the reality of the resurrection, and the fellowship of believers in the Church know the answer to the secularist's vain search. The problem with which these lectures have to do, therefore, is not so much one of discovery as it is one of application.

BIBLIOGRAPHY

Badley, Ken. "The Faith-Learning Integration Movement in Christian Higher Education: Slogan or Substance?" *Journal of Research on Christian Education* 3, no. 1 (Spring 1994): 13-33.

Barnhouse, Donald G. *Words Fitly Spoken*. Wheaton, Ill.: Tyndale House Publishers, 1969.

---

[47] Ibid., 25-26.

[48] Ibid., 7-11.

Beaty, Michael, Todd Buras, and Larry Lyon. "Baptist Higher Education: A Conflict in Terms?" *Baylor Line* (Win. 1997): 43-51.

Gaebelein, Frank E. "The Captivity of Every Thought." *Our Hope* 27, no. 5 (Nov. 1920): 298-301.

_____. *Christian Education in a Democracy: The Report of the N.A.E. Committee*. New York: Oxford University Press, 1951.

_____. "The Christian's Intellectual Life." *Christianity Today* 5 (8 May 1961): 4-6.

_____. "The Dualism of Truth." *Eternity* 5, no. 8 (Aug. 1954): 10-11.

_____. "An Evangelical's Defense." *North American Review* 232, no. 1 (July 1931): 26-32.

_____. "Is There Purpose in the Universe [Review of *The Recovery of Purpose*, by Emile Cailliet]." *Eternity* 11, no. 2 (Feb. 1960): 17-19, 43-44.

_____. *The Pattern of God's Truth: Problems of Integration in Christian Education*. New York: Oxford University Press, 1954.

_____. "Portrait of a Christian College." *Eternity* 7, no. 2 (Feb. 1956): 8-9, 44-46.

_____. *The Practical Epistle of James: Studies in Applied Christianity*. Great Neck, N.Y.: Channel Press, 1955.

_____. "A Preface to Christian Education." *Revelation* 18, no. 8 (Aug 1948): 335-336, 374-376.

_____. "Religion and the Independent School." *The Independent School Bulletin* 61-62, no. 3 (Apr. 1962): 6-10.

_____. "The Sacred Life of the Church." *Christianity Today* 1 (19 Aug 1957): 20-21.

_____. "Some Things Can't Be Shaken." *Eternity* 13, no. 11 (Nov. 1962): 12-13, 37-38.

_____. "Towards a Biblical View of Aesthetics." *Christianity Today* 12, no. 23 (30 Aug. 1968): 4-6.

_____. "Truth and Culture." *HIS* (Feb. 1960): 19-20.

_____. *A Varied Harvest: Out of a Teacher's Life and Thought*. Grand Rapids, Mich.: Eerdmans, 1967.

_____. "What is Truth in Art?" *Christianity Today* 20, no. 23 (27 Aug. 1976): 10-13.

Hamilton, Michael S., and James A. Mathisen. "Faith and Learning at Wheaton College." In *Models for Christian Higher Education*, ed. Richard T. Hughes and William B. Adrian, 261-283. Grand Rapids, Mich.: Wm. B. Eerdmans, 1997.

Harvard Committee on the Objectives of a General Education in a Free Society. *General Education in a Free Society: Report of the Harvard Committee on the Objectives of a General Education in a Free Society*. Cambridge, Mass.: Harvard University Press, 1951.

Lockerbie, D. Bruce. *A Passion for Learning: The History of Christian Thought on Education*. Chicago: Moody Press, 1994.

Noll, Mark A. "Common Sense Traditions and American Evangelical Thought." *American Quarterly* 37, no. 2 (Sum. 1985): 216-238.

Whitehead, Alfred North. *The Aims of Education and Other Essays*. New York: Free Press, 1929.

SECONDARY BIBLIOGRAPHY: GAEBELEIN & EDUCATION BOOKS

Gaebelein, Frank E. *A Varied Harvest: Out of a Teacher's Life and Thought*. Grand Rapids, Mich.: Eerdmans, 1967.

_____. *Christian Education in a Democracy: The Report of the N.A.E. Committee*. New York: Oxford University Press, 1951.

_____. *The Pattern of God's Truth: Problems of Integration in Christian Education*. New York: Oxford University Press, 1954.

ARTICLES AND ESSAYS

Gaebelein, Frank E. "Christian Education and Its View of Man." *Our Hope* 57, no. 11 (May 1951): 677-681.

_____. "Christian Education and the Home [Part 1]." *Moody Monthly* 51, no. 3 (Nov. 1950): 149-151, 169.

_____. "Christian Education and the Home [Part 2]." *Moody Monthly* 51, no. 4 (Dec. 1950): 232-233, 252-254.

_____. "Christian Education: Rethinking the Church's Role." *Christianity Today* 10 (18 Feb. 1966): 3-6.

_____. "From a Headmaster's Study." *Revelation* 5, no. 2 (Feb. 1935): 49-50, 79, 81-87.

_____. "On These We Build Our Schools..." *Christian Teacher* (Nov.-Dec. 1975): 11-13, 30.

_____. "Plan and Scope of Stony Brook School for Boys." *The Presbyterian* 92, no. 50 (14 Dec. 1922): 11, 26.

_____. "Toward a Philosophy of Christian Education," in *An Introduction to Evangelical Christian Education*, ed. J. Edward Hakes (Chicago: Moody Press, 1964), 37-56.

_____. "Towards a Christian Philosophy of Education: The Major Premise of a Christian Education. Part II." *Grace Journal* 3 (1962): 12-18.

_____. "Towards a Christian Philosophy of Education: The Need and Nature of a Christian Philosophy. Part I." *Grace Journal* 3 (1962): 3-11.

_____. "Towards a Christian Philosophy of Education: The Place of Music in Christian Education. Part III." *Grace Journal* 3 (1962): 19-26.

RESEARCH SOURCES
BOOKS AND DISSERTATIONS

Benson, Warren Sten. "A History of the National Association of Christian Schools During the Period of 1947-1972." PhD diss., Loyola University of Chicago, 1975.

Gleason, Daniel M., "A Study of the Christian School Movement." EdD diss., University of North Dakota, 1980.

Lockerbie, D. Bruce. *A Passion for Learning: The History of Christian Thought on Education.* Chicago: Moody Press, 1994.

Lockerbie, D. Bruce. *The Way They Should Go.* New York: Oxford University Press, 1972.

McLeod, Philip. "The Rise of Catholic and Evangelical Christian Schools in the Nineteenth and Twentieth Centuries." PhD diss, Marquette University, 1993.

Simpson, Frances. "The Development of the National Association of Christian Schools." PhD diss., Southwestern Baptist Theological Seminary, 1955.

Wright, Dana. "Ecclesial Theatrics: Towards a Reconstruction of Evangelical Christian Education Theory." PhD diss., Princeton Theological Seminary, 1999.

ARTICLES AND ESSAYS

Eells, Robert J. "Creation, Redemption, and Doing Your Best: Gaebelein's Approach to Learning," in *Christian Approaches to Learning Theory*, Norman De Jong, ed. Lanham, Md.: University Press of America, 1984, 13-29.

Fawcett, Cheryl. "Frank E. Gaebelein: Integrator of Truth." *Christian Education Journal* 3rd ser., 1, no. 1 (Fall 2003): 104-120.

Hull, Gretchen Gaebelein. "Frank Gaebelein: Character Before Career." *Christianity Today* 28, no. 13 (21 Sept. 1984): 14-18.

CHAPTER 29

Donald A. McGavran:

Missionary Educator

TODD BENKERT

Donald A. McGavran (1897-1991)

Donald A. McGavran was an educator, missionary, researcher, author, evangelical statesman, and missiologist. He is best known for his teachings about how churches grow, and as the founder of a school of thought and practice that would become known as the Church Growth Movement. He was the founding dean of the School of World Mission and Institute of Church Growth at Fuller Seminary in Pasadena, California. McGavran spent his life as a missionary educator, researcher, and practitioner of his church growth principles, seeking effective methods to win receptive people to faith in Jesus Christ and sharing the facts of church growth to missionaries and ministers across the globe.

HISTORICAL BACKGROUND

Donald Anderson McGavran was born on December 15, 1897 in Damoh, India to missionary parents John and Helen McGavran. He spent his early years in India on the mission field as his parents served the Lord there. In 1910, as he entered his teen years, the McGavrans returned to the States where they remained during his adolescence and college years. Though he was the son of missionaries, McGavran never intended to enter the ministry himself. The summer before his final year in college, however, he had a spiritual encounter that changed his course. In the summer of 1919, McGavran attended a YMCA camp where he was challenged by John R. Mott and others to follow God's call on his life. During that camp experience, McGavran committed himself to do whatever God might require of him. Later that year, he attended the Student Volunteer Convention in Des Moines, Iowa where he dedicated himself to ministry and the call to be a missionary and carry out the Great Commission.[1]

McGavran began his first term as a missionary in 1923 with the United Christian Missionary Society (UCMS). In his first assignment, he served at the Harda mission station in India where he became the principal of all of its schools. There, McGavran would begin his life as a missionary educator and fulfill what he believed to be God's calling on his life, "Christianization through Christian Education."[2] As he poured himself into his work, McGavran soon became dissatisfied with the methods used in Christian education, both in his own mission and throughout the society's work in India. In particular, he was concerned with the lack of spiritual results among the students of his schools. McGavran set himself to change the situation and addressed the problem in his first publication, *How to Teach Religion in Mission Schools: A Brief Manual of Method*.[3] The book pointed out problems in the current methodology and its detraction from the mission's original vision of Christianization of the Indian people. McGavran's proposals were not merely theoretical. Instead, he provided practical helps for the teacher in both the classroom and personal ministry. His primary aim

---

[1] Vern Middleton, *Donald McGavran, His Early Life and Ministry: An Apostolic Vision for Reaching the Nations* (Pasadena, CA: William Carey Library, 2011), 1-15; Donald A. McGavran, "My Pilgrimage in Mission," *International Bulletin of Missionary Research* 10 (1986): 53. Before he entered the mission field, McGavran would earn his Bachelor of Arts from Butler University, a Bachelor of Divinity from Yale Seminary, and a Master of Arts from the College of Mission in Indianapolis. Following his missions service, McGavran would go on to earn a Ph.D. from Columbia University.

[2] McGavran, "My Pilgrimage in Mission," 56.

[3] Donald A. McGavran, *How to Teach Religion in Mission Schools; A Brief Manual of Method* (Jabalpur, India: Missions Press, 1928).

in this publication was to return Christian education to its evangelistic purpose.

During this first term of service, McGavran's responsibilities and influence grew. In 1928, McGavran became the Director of Religious Education for Disciples of Christ schools in the region. While serving in this position, he formulated a number of teaching and research methods that would characterize his later work in the Church Growth Movement. Vern Middleton notes that, during this time, McGavran established a number of educational principles that he would carry with him throughout his career. These principles would later be practiced on the mission field and then incorporated into the life of his Church Growth Institute.[4]

McGavran's missionary career progressed and, in 1932, his supervisory role expanded from solely religious education to the total missions effort in India. From 1932 to 1935, McGavran served as administrator in the role of executive secretary-treasurer to Indian Missions of the UCMS. During this time, he also served on a variety of missions committees, all of which were devoted to the expansion of the gospel in India. By this time, McGavran had become especially interested in questions concerning effectiveness in missions and in J. Waskom Pickett's research in people movements.[5] During his time as an administrator, McGavran would continue to research effective mission strategy and teach and write about people movements and principles that would lead to church growth. McGavran's desire to see people converted to Christ was developing into a lifelong pursuit of the principles of church growth. From this time forth, his role as a religious educator would focus on the missionary task and the methods and principles that made that task effective.[6]

His tenure as administrator was short-lived. In 1936, unexpectedly, McGavran was not reelected to his position. As a result, he was reassigned to field work among Indian villagers. McGavran recalls that this move was as if the mission had said, "Since you are talking so much about evangelism and church growth, we are going to locate you in a district where you can practice what you preach."[7] For the next seventeen years, McGavran would serve among the Satnami people. McGavran believed that the Satnami were ripe for a people movement and

---

[4] These principles were laid out explicitly in a speech in 1929 and are expounded in Middleton, *Donald McGavran*, 25-29.

[5] McGavran was especially influenced by Pickett's book, *Christian Mass Movements in India* (New York: Abingdon Press, 1933), and its emphasis on group conversion and critique of the mission station approach.

[6] Middleton, *Donald McGavran*, 41-63.

[7] McGavran, "My Pilgrimage in Mission," 56.

he was optimistic that a mass movement toward Christ would take place.[8] While McGavran saw marginal success among the Satnami, it was nothing like the full caste-wide movement for which he had worked and prayed. McGavran would later note that God was teaching him during those years "what methods of evangelism God blesses, and what he does not."[9]

In his time as a village missionary, McGavran's understanding of the principles of church growth developed. Even as he served the Satnami people, he continued to research and write. He never left his role as an influencer of missions thought and practice and continued to advocate his views through his involvement in his own missions organization and as editor of the United Church Review.[10]

A significant shift in his life occurred in 1955 with the publication of his book, *The Bridges of God*. Both before and after its publication, McGavran was involved in numerous field research projects, honing his skills as a church growth consultant and developing research tools to help determine why missions efforts were or were not successful. The principles he discovered were distilled in his book and proved to be revolutionary in his field. The book included such controversial assertions as the distinction between "discipling" and "perfecting," that evangelism was only complete when it resulted in responsible disciples, and the "homogeneous unit principle."[11] Little did McGavran know that the book would birth a movement he would lead for the remainder of his life.

Over the next few years following its publication, McGavran's influence spread. He would become an itinerant professor of missions, teaching his principles of church growth in

[8] For more on McGavran's understanding of people movements see J. Waskom Pickett, *Christian Mass Movements in India* (New York: Abingdon Press, 1933).

[9] McGavran, "My Pilgrimage in Mission," 56.

[10] Middleton, *Donald McGavran*, 62-130.

[11] Donald A. McGavran, *The Bridges of God: A Study in the Strategy of Missions* (New York: World Dominion Press, 1955); Thom S. Rainer, *The Book of Church Growth: History, Theology, and Principles* (Nashville: Broadman & Holman, 1993), 34-36; Middleton, *Donald McGavran*, 122-25,130. McGavran views the verbs "make disciples" and "teaching" in the Great Commission as separate commands that represent successive "stages" of Christianization. He thus coins the terms "discipling" and "perfecting" as separate stages of bringing peoples to faith in Christ and then working to bring about ethical change through relationship to God. McGavran maintains this terminology throughout his writing with a priority for discipling. See McGavran, *The Bridges of God*, 13-16. The "Homogeneous Unit Principle" was a sociological observation by McGavran that people more often come to faith if they do not have to overcome cultural barriers to do so. People "like to become Christians without crossing racial, linguistic or class barriers." See McGavran, *Understanding Church Growth*, 198. McGavran observed that the gospel advanced most quickly and effectively when it did so among homogeneous units — existing familial and social groupings, which he called "bridges of God."

several schools throughout the United States.[12] McGavran developed several courses of study, many of which later became books. His ideas continued to gain traction and in 1959, after being rejected by numerous publishers, McGavran published *How Churches Grow*.[13] This book highlighted the urgency of church growth in what McGavran saw as a world of great opportunity for Christian witness and receptivity to the gospel.

As his influence steadily grew, McGavran sought a wider platform for his church growth principles. He made the decision to resign from the UCMS and approached several schools about establishing an institution for church growth. In 1961, McGavran established the Institute of Church Growth at Northwest Christian College in Eugene, Oregon. Through this new institute, McGavran and his colleagues trained research fellows in the principles of church growth. McGavran spent his summers leading church growth seminars around the nation and conducting field research in church growth. The influence of the Institute and its founder grew as they published a dozen books and the bi-monthly *Church Growth Bulletin*. An additional opportunity arose in 1963 that increased his influence even further. McGavran, along with J. Waskom Picket and Allan R. Tippett, presented his church growth principles at the Iberville Consultation, sponsored by the World Council of Churches in Canada.

In 1965, the Institute moved to Fuller Seminary in Pasadena, California. Fuller established the School of World Mission and Institute of Church Growth with McGavran as its founding dean and he and colleague Alan Tippet as its first faculty members. Commenting on the new development of the institute, McGavran remarked, "The supreme and compelling aim of the Christian mission to the world is to make Christ known to all men as their Divine and only Savior, and to persuade them to become disciples and responsible members of His church. Training missionaries and candidates to carry out this mission is my vision for our new school."[14]

Tippett, too, recognized the significance of the establishment of the school saying, "Not only does it recognize the truth of church growth as the biblical view of the world mission but in establishing this institution it has also proclaimed its readiness to act on the validity of these concepts."[15] He further stated in regard to McGavran as the founding dean, "We all rejoice in

---

[12] Middleton, *Donald McGavran*, 189-238.

[13] Donald A. McGavran, *How Churches Grow: The New Frontiers of Mission* (London: World Dominion Press, 1959).

[14] "Veteran Missionary Leader to Head New Graduate School at Fuller Seminary," *Church Growth Bulletin* 1, no. 5 (May 1965): 70.

[15] Alan R. Tippett, "A Milestone in Church Growth History," *Church Growth Bulletin* 30, no. 2 (November 1966).

the appointment and now the official inauguration, but I imagine he will see this not as a goal in his pilgrimage but rather as a lunching place for new ventures."[16] And that it was. The school began a new phase of ministry for McGavran and became the platform from which the church growth movement would have its greatest impact.

The school grew under his leadership. McGavran would go on to oversee a faculty of influential leaders who would carry the mantle of church growth. In 1970, McGavran published *Understanding Church Growth*,[17] a work that brought together the results of his years of thinking about missions and evangelism. The work would be the climax of a lifetime of research. Looking back, McGavran called his time at Fuller "the best years of my pilgrimage."[18] He would teach at Fuller until the age of 83 and would continue to research and advocate for effective work among receptive peoples until his death in 1991.

THEOLOGY OF CHRISTIAN EDUCATION

McGavran's theology of Christian education was rooted in his theology of mission. Throughout his ministry, McGavran promoted the idea that all Christian education ought to achieve the primary purposes of the Great Commission (Matthew 28:19-20). Education, thus, was a means of fulfilling the purposes of God in taking the gospel to the nations.

THEOLOGICAL HERMENEUTIC

In today's categories, McGavran would be considered conservative and evangelical. Living in an era in which many scholars debated the Bible's content and called its authority into question, McGavran maintained a high view of Scripture. His colleague, Alan Tippet, described McGavran as a biblical missiologist. "The basic pre-supposition of all his writings and debate is the authority of scripture and his view of authority is evangelical."[19] A review of his works reveals that the Bible was the starting point of his theology and that obedience to its demands motivated his thinking and practice.

For McGavran, the Bible was to be believed and, even more so, was to be obeyed. For McGavran, that meant that theology was intensely practical. For theology to be valuable, it must be more than empty philosophy. Theology must be worked out through practical

---

[16] Ibid.

[17] Donald A. McGavran, *Understanding Church Growth* (Grand Rapids: William B. Eerdmans, 1970).

[18] McGavran, "My Pilgrimage in Mission," 57.

[19] Alan R. Tippett, "Portrait of a Missiologist by His Colleague," in *God, Man and Church Growth: A Festschrift in Honor of Donald Anderson McGavran*, ed. Alan R. Tippett (Grand Rapids: William B. Eerdmans, 1973), 20.

obedience. Ralph Winter described the hermeneutic which drove McGavran and the church growth movement saying, "All valid theology must derive from the encounter of the gospel of Christ with the real world."[20]

The primary intersection of this biblical theology with practical obedience was McGavran's conviction that "God wills church growth."[21] Obedience to the command of Christ to "make disciples" meant that every effort must be made to "proclaim Christ and to persuade men to become his disciples and responsible members of His church."[22] This practical hermeneutic led McGavran to champion several concepts derived from his understanding of Scripture and God's desire to "find" people. From his exegesis of the Great Commission passage in Matthew 28, McGavran identified two stages of the missionary command: "discipling" and "perfecting." Discipling referred to the task of bringing persons to faith in Christ and enfolding them in His church. Perfecting was the ongoing process of spiritual development to Christ-likeness. McGavran's priority for discipling grew from his observations of the present world situation. McGavran was convinced that God had, at this unique time in history, made peoples receptive to the gospel. The task of the church was to reap the harvest that God had ripened, a view that became known as "harvest theology" and, later, "effective evangelism." Obedience to the command of Scripture meant that lost people must be found and enfolded into the church.

This view of God's harvest affected McGavran's views of both theology and praxis. His theology of mission required obedience to the Great Commission and effective methods of evangelism. McGavran explained, "To be classed as part of a theology of mission, a particular theology must have as its intent obedience to Christ's command (Matt. 28:19). It must be effective. It must play a major role in bringing men and women to commitment and baptism ... A theology of mission must be biblically true and missionarily effective. Otherwise, it is not a theology of mission."[23]
Further, for McGavran, any valid theology must be a missionary theology because the purpose of God in the Scripture is to redeem all people to Himself. The church growth principles that would become the core of his teaching were based on his conviction that church growth "is faithfulness to God."[24]

---

[20] Ralph D. Winter, "An Insider's View of McGavran," *Mission Frontiers* 12, no. 3 (1990).

[21] Donald A. McGavran, "The Institute of Church Growth," *IRM* 50 (1961): 430.

[22] Tippett, "Portrait of a Missiologist," 38.

[23] Donald A. McGavran, "Particular Theologies and Theology of Mission," in *Contemporary Theologies of Missions*, by Arthur F. Glasser and Donald A. McGavran (Grand Rapids: Baker Book House, 1983), 149.

[24] Donald A. McGavran, "The Discovery of Church Growth," in *Church Growth: Strategies That*

One other note must be made about McGavran's theological hermeneutic. His was an expectant theology. McGavran's theology led him to reject the pessimistic outlook of non-growth and expect positive results from missionary activity. David Liao describes McGavran's view as "optimistic missionary philosophy" which contrasts a "pessimistic, self-defensive, resignation to non-growth."[25] Indeed, McGavran had little patience for those who took a defeatist attitude or rationalized or theologized their ineffectiveness. Rather, McGavran believed not only that God willed church growth, but that God was divinely at work in making people receptive to the gospel.

Throughout his writing, one is struck by his contagious enthusiasm and optimistic outlook. McGavran saw the world around him as receptive to the gospel and that receptivity to be a divinely ordained opportunity to bring men and women to the Savior.

> We live in a ripening world. This is perhaps the most revolutionary and encouraging fact in missions. More populations today are responsive to the Gospel than ever before.[26]

> ...all should be considered as God's wonderful preparation to meet the greatest receptivity men have ever shown.[27]

> We face the most winnable populations which ever existed. More men today want to know about Jesus Christ; more people are being baptized from non-Christian religions; more churches are being built; more congregations are being established; and the mind of Christ is being incorporated more into human society than ever before.[28]

> Today there is unprecedented receptivity to the message of Christ. Today people are more winnable; the nations, the tribes, and the castes of the world are more responsive to the gospel than they have ever been before.[29]

McGavran's high view of Scripture, his desire to obey the commands of Christ, and his observation of God's work in the world led him to become a champion for the principles of

Work, by Donald A. McGavran and George G. Hunter, III. (Nashville: Abingdon, 1980), 26, cf. 19.

[25] David C. E. Liao, "The Orient Awaits an Optimistic Missiology," in *God, Man and Church Growth: A Festschrift in Honor of Donald Anderson McGavran*, ed. Alan R. Tippett (Grand Rapids: William B. Eerdmans, 1973), 16.

[26] Donald A. McGavran, "Have We Lost Our Way in Missions?" *Christian Herald* 81, no. 3 (March 1958): 21.

[27] Donald A. McGavran, "Theological Bed Rock in Mission," *Religion in Life* 30 (1961): 608.

[28] Donald A. McGavran, "Church Growth Strategy Continued," *IRM* 57 (1968): 342.

[29] Donald A. McGavran and Winfield C. Arn, *Ten Steps for Church Growth* (San Francisco: Harper & Row, 1977), 9.

church growth and became the basis for his educational theology throughout his life.

THEOLOGY OF EDUCATION

McGavran's role and practice as an educator was directly influenced by his theology. Throughout his life, McGavran maintained an intense desire to be obedient to the Scripture and particularly the Great Commission. This led him, in his first assignment, to direct the religious educators under his supervision to return to their evangelistic purpose of Christianizing the Indian peoples. Later, this conviction would lead McGavran to a lifelong study of how churches grow.

Early in his ministry, McGavran observed that some missionaries were effective in seeing large numbers of conversions while others, even in similar situations, were not. This observation led McGavran to a life of study of those human factors that lead to effectiveness in missions. Specifically he wanted to answer the questions, "What are the *causes* of church growth? and What are the *obstacles* of church growth?"[30] Thus, a significant part of his role as an educator became the gathering of data about the growth of churches and those methods and practices that enhanced or hindered growth. McGavran developed research methods and quantitative measurements to answer these lifelong questions. He was not content to theorize about church growth, but to identify its real causes and identify strategies that would lead to it. He believed that philosophizing and theorizing about missions was no substitute for research about the "facts of church growth."[31]

As an educator, McGavran did not stop at merely identifying patterns and principles. He called for action. As the leader of what would become the church growth movement, McGavran taught his principles as a matter of gospel obedience. Because God desired church growth and had made people receptive, his role as an educator was to teach church growth principles and call people to effective evangelism. Ineffective practices were not only to be identified, but rejected. Effective strategies were to be adopted. Receptive people were to be harvested. Education was not an end in itself but must lead ministers and missionaries to use effective means for bringing in the harvest of God's ripened fields.

The fact that God was at work in the world making peoples receptive to the gospel caused McGavran to view the task of world evangelization as urgent. He urged missionaries and sending agencies to "win the winnable while they are winnable."[32] McGavran confronted

---

[30] McGavran, "Discovery of Church Growth," 16.

[31] McGavran, "My Pilgrimage in Mission," 57; see also, Gary McIntosh, "The Life and Ministry of Donald A. McGavran: A Short Overview" (paper presented to the ASCG Annual Meeting, November 2005).

[32] McGavran, Huegel, and Taylor, *Church Growth in Mexico*, 134.

evangelicals' satisfaction with anemic growth and challenged them to adopt effective strategies and invest resources to reach receptive peoples. McGavran also became an outspoken critic of the Conciliar movement and its abandonment of evangelism in favor of a social gospel.[33] Through his books, seminars, bulletin, and the Church Growth Institute, McGavran called the Church to see effective evangelism as its greatest priority: "Bed Rock in Mission is bringing our theology and methodology, our priorities and our goals, ourselves, our churches, and our institutions radically and sacrificially under him who died for all, that through his death multitudes might live."[34] For McGavran, all research, thinking, teaching, theorizing about church growth and missions was subservient to the task of reaching the (then) two billion lost people around the world who had "never heard his name effectively."[35]

CONTRIBUTION TO CHRISTIAN EDUCATION

While the heyday of the Church Growth Movement has passed, McGavran's influence remains to this day. Many of our modern church and missions practices and methodologies can be traced to McGavran's quest to find effective methods for evangelism and church growth.[36] McGavran's church growth views have always stirred up significant debate and do so to this day. Some of McGavran's ideas remain controversial. Still, McGavran's key questions about how churches grow and what makes evangelism effective continue to be asked by those concerned with fulfilling the Great Commission. Whether or not one is satisfied with McGavran's solutions or the prescriptions of the Church Growth Movement, his legacy as an educator continues and his principles are valuable for educators today.[37]

THE ROLE OF THE TEACHER

McGavran spent much of his life as an educator – as teacher, supervisor, professor, and dean. He served on the faculty of multiple seminaries and lectured in many more. His

---

[33] See, e.g., Donald A. McGavran, "Will Uppsala Betray the Two Billion?" in *Eye of the Storm: The Great Debate in Mission*, ed. Donald A. McGavran (Waco, Tex.: Word Books, 1972), 56-66.

[34] McGavran, "Theological Bed Rock," 609.

[35] Donald A. McGavran, "Will Green Lake Betray the Two Billion," *Church Growth Bulletin* vii, no. 6 (July 1971): 150.

[36] One can argue that "Church Planting Movements," the current focus of missions agencies on ethno-linguistic people groups, decisions to pour resources into receptive areas, and contextualized churches are all expansions of McGavran's church growth principles.

[37] For more on the lasting impact of McGavran, see Gary L. McIntosh, "The Twenty-First Century Relevance of Donald McGavran," *Great Commission Research Journal* 4, no. 2 (Winter 2013): 216-24.

legacy as a teacher, however, extends well beyond the job titles he has held. One of the greatest lessons educators can learn from McGavran is to pay close attention to the practical outcomes of their teaching. McGavran would instruct teachers to have a view toward action, focusing on practical application and aiming for tangible results. He would insist that teaching be evaluated by its outcome in terms of how students perform outside the classroom. When he spoke of education, McGavran advocated that success in education should not be measured by how much information is retained, but by the resulting actions of students and their effectiveness in the tasks for which they are being prepared.[38] Regarding his own field of missions education, that meant reaching people with the gospel of Jesus Christ. Religious educators today can learn from McGavran to emphasize the practical importance of the subjects they teach and to aim that their students not only grow in knowledge but, more importantly, apply that knowledge to their lives and ministries.

McGavran saw religious education as part of fulfilling God's mission to make disciples (Matt 28:19-20). As a teacher, McGavran always kept the fulfillment of the Great Commission as his goal. His aim was to multiply harvesters in God's ripened fields. Near the end of his life, McGavran challenged fellow educators, insisting "that the courses they teach, the books they write, the lives they live, must be measured by the degree to which their students carry out [the Great Commission]."[39] Were he alive today, he would instruct religious educators in every field of study to always keep the Great Commission in view.

ROLE OF THE LEARNER

For McGavran, the ultimate goal for both educators and learners was effective ministry. McGavran believed that education was a tool for equipping ministers of the gospel to be successful in their mission task. This meant that the role of the learners was not merely gaining knowledge, but acquiring the specific knowledge needed to be effective in their ministry tasks and applying that knowledge practically to their particular situations. The proof of a good education was that the student went on to be effective in evangelism.

McGavran would challenge learners today to go beyond learning principles and general concepts to discover the specific, relevant information needed to become effective in

---

[38] For McGavran, this meant effectiveness in missions work. For example, in his book *Effective Evangelism,* McGavran states, "Seminary courses in effective evangelism must be counted good not merely if they are academically impeccable but if those who take such courses become good harvesters, bringing in many sheaves from the ripened fields." Donald A. McGavran, *Effective Evangelism: A Theological Mandate* (Phillipsburg, NJ: Presbyterian and Reformed, 1988), 15.

[39] Donald A. McGavran, "Missiology Faces the Lion," *Missiology* 17 (1989): 341.

their chosen fields. Each discipline has its own set of questions about ministry effectiveness. McGavran would insist that learners find the answers to those questions and to use solid research methods to do so. As an educator and fellow learner with his students, McGavran was always interested in facts. For his field of church growth, this meant discovering data that showed why some churches were growing and others were not. For his church growth students, the first responsibility of the learner was to discover the "the facts of church growth" through "responsible research."[40]

In his research, McGavran used methods such as historical analysis, quantitative data, field observations, and interviews to gain an accurate picture of why particular missions efforts were or were not effective. As an educator, McGavran expected his students to learn effective research methods and do similar research to discover the facts of church growth. Before his students could graduate, they were required to develop a case history of the development of the church in the place where they served.[41] McGavran found generalizations to be unhelpful and instead insisted on collecting hard data to get an accurate picture of where and how churches were growing.[42] Beyond the classroom, McGavran believed that learning through research should be an ongoing priority, especially for those who engaged in the practice of mission. McGavran believed that significant resources should be allocated to "planned, continuous, purposeful research dedicated to finding out how the Gospel may more effectively be communicated."[43] McGavran would encourage learners today to use solid research methods to discover how they can be most effective in the place where God calls them.

One of the goals of learning is for learners to be able to share what they have gleaned with others. McGavran adopted a collaborative style of learning in which he encouraged the sharing of information among students, researchers, denominations, and mission agencies. As he formulated and wrote about his church growth ideas, McGavran often sought the opinions of his peers. He was comfortable with those who challenged his thinking, and the feedback drove him to further research. Students, likewise, were expected to share the information they gained from their own research by presenting and comparing case studies from the fields in which they served.[44] The data he collected from his own research projects also became the

---

[40] McGavran, "My Pilgrimage in Mission," 57.

[41] Ibid., 158.

[42] Middleton, *Donald McGavran*, 130.

[43] Quoted in Tippett, "Portrait of a Missiologist," 35.

[44] Middleton, *Donald McGavran*, 278.

basis for case studies used in his teaching.[45] Further, McGavran published his own and others' findings through books, articles, and his *Church Growth Bulletin*. McGavran would challenge learners today to share knowledge with one another to further learning and so that all might be effective in fulfilling their ministry tasks.

Ultimately, the purpose of learning the "facts of church growth," was to apply those facts in developing effective mission strategies so that more and more people would become disciples of Jesus Christ. Learning information only had value as that information was applied. Thus, McGavran would challenge learners in the classroom to not only master principles and the body of knowledge of their particular field of study, but to practically and tangibly apply that knowledge in the real life situations of ministry outside the classroom. He would challenge learners to not only do research, but to apply the information gained through research to develop effective, context-specific strategies for ministry. For McGavran, the primary role of the learner was to become effective ministers of the gospel and he would challenge learners today to make this their aim.

CURRICULUM AND METHODS

From early in his ministry, McGavran saw the need for continuing education for educators and missionaries. Long before establishing the Fuller School, McGavran communicated his message of Church Growth and the discipling of the nations through classes, seminars, lecture series, bulletins, journal articles, books, and any other means he could find.

In his first missionary term, as Director of Religious Education, McGavran designed training institutes to help educators hone their skills and enhance their spiritual life. As his church growth ideas developed, McGavran would later seek to educate pastors and ministers through seminars and "Church Growth Institutes." Because the audience of these institutes was limited, McGavran published several of his courses as books and established his *Church Growth Bulletin* so that others could benefit from current research, methods, and church growth principles. His books, especially *The Bridges of God, How Churches Grow*, and *Understanding Church Growth*, held tremendous influence and brought the principles of church growth to an international audience.

His teaching drew from the extensive research he had done around the world and focused on particular ministry situations. Case studies were his specialty. To understand the effects of mission efforts, he compiled case histories of missions and churches for evaluation and

---

[45] George W. Hunter, III, "The Legacy of Donald A. McGavran," *International Bulletin of Missionary Research* 16, no. 4 (October 1992): 158.

discussion. He viewed these case studies as "unvarnished accounts of the growth of Churches."[46] To form the studies, McGavran compiled data from on-site research, primary source material, and authorities in the field in question. He would use the case history to create an accurate picture of what was happening in a particular situation and then have students evaluate each case to discern why churches were or were not growing. Case studies, McGavran reasoned, reduced subjectivity, allowed for evaluation without emotional involvement, and dealt with concrete situations and not mere generalizations.[47]

Whatever methods he used, McGavran's teaching was always intensely practical. He was not satisfied with merely disseminating information or identifying problems. McGavran aimed toward solutions. His writing continually moved toward practical application and often included detailed sections on methodology. His case studies always led to discovering practical means and strategies for church growth. The desired end of his efforts was effective evangelism and obedience to the Great Commission.

It was not until the institution of the Church Growth Institute at Northwest Christian College and later Fuller Seminary that McGavran would be able to develop a full curriculum for his church growth missiology. Building on his previous institutes and seminars, the CGI curriculum centered on church growth principles and how those principles applied in particular contexts. McGavran designed a curriculum that specialized in courses essential to the task of missions.[48] While his Church Growth Institute was unique, McGavran envisioned and advocated for other religious institutions to move toward a curriculum that focused on such practical training of missionaries. In one interview he stated,

> If I were the president of a seminary, or the president of the American Association of Theological Seminaries, or the accrediting association, I would insist that at least 50 percent of the hours be put into the study and practice of the actual transmission of the Christian faith and to the planting of new congregations. I would engage as professors only those who were actually planting churches.[49]

McGavran desired that religious institutions design curriculums to equip effective laborers in the harvest and, thus, to win more people to faith in Christ. Indeed, behind all of McGavran's

---

[46] Middleton, *Donald McGavran*, 158.

[47] Ibid., 154-58.

[48] Ibid., 278.

[49] Donald A. McGavran and Win Arn, "Conversation with a Legend: An Interview with Donald McGavran," in *The Pastor's Church Growth Handbook*, ed. Win Arn, vol. 2 (Pasadena, CA: Church Growth Press, 1982), 190.

educational efforts was a passion to see people brought to a saving relationship with Jesus Christ and enfolded into His church. McGavran did not love statistics or methods; he loved people. He dedicated his life as an educator to reaping God's harvest and bringing as many people as possible to Christ.

CONCLUSION

McGavran was a missionary educator, but he was much more. He not only taught ministers and missionaries; he was a missionary statesman and advocate for Great Commission faithfulness. His ideas sparked a movement that has influenced the way believers approach missions and evangelism for more than fifty years. Beyond the church growth movement, McGavran was a champion for the priority of evangelism at a time when much of Christendom was abandoning the call to go forth with the gospel of Jesus Christ. In his writings, McGavran's heart for bringing salvation to the lost masses of the world is evident on nearly every page. Whatever one's final assessment of his ideas or the church growth movement he kindled, McGavran leaves behind a legacy of passion for the mission of Christ. May we all serve the Lord with such zeal for the Lord's work.[50]

PRIMARY SOURCE SAMPLE[51]

As in the light of Christ we look at the world – its exploding knowledge, peoples, revolutions physical needs, desperate spiritual hunger and nakedness, and enslavement to false gods and demonic ideologies – we realize that Christian mission must certainly engage in many labors. A multitude of excellent enterprises lie around us. So great is the number and so urgent the calls, that Christians can easily lose their way among them, seeing them all equally as mission. But in doing the good, they can fail of the best. In winning the preliminaries, they can lose the main game. They can be treating a troublesome itch, while the patient dies of cholera. The question of priorities cannot be avoided. In this fast-moving, cruel, and revolutionary era, when many activities are demanded, a right proportioning of effort among them is essential to sound policy. And "rightness" – a true and sound proportion in our labors – must be decided according to biblical principles in the light of God's revealed will.

Among other desires of God-in-Christ, He beyond question wills that persons be found – that is, be reconciled to Himself. Most cordially admitting that God has other purposes, we should remember that we serve a God Who Finds Persons. He has an overriding concern that

---

[50] Elmer Towns, one of the editors of this text, was a close friend and mentee of Dr. McGavran and had the privilege of being one of the five speakers at his funeral in 1991.

[51] McGavran, *Understanding Church Growth*, 32-33.

men should be redeemed. However we understand the word, biblical witness is clear that men are "lost." The Finding God wants them found – that is, brought into a redemptive relationship to Jesus Christ where, baptized in His Name, they become part of His Household. He is not pleased when many findable sheep remain staggering on the mountain, shivering in the bitter wind. The more found, the better pleased is God.

Among other characteristics of mission, therefore, a chief and irreplaceable one must be this: that mission is a divine finding, vast and continuous. A chief and irreplaceable purpose of mission is church growth. Service is good, but it must never be substituted for finding. Our Lord did not rest content with feeding the hungry and healing the sick. He pressed on to give His life a ransom for many and to send out His followers to disciple all nations. Nor must service be so disproportionally emphasized at the expense of evangelism that findable persons are continually lost. In the proportioning of service and church planting, the degree of growth being achieved must always be taken into account. God's servants carry on mission in a fast-moving world and must constantly adjust the proportions of service and evangelism, as the Church grows from a few scattered cells to Churches forming substantial majorities of the population, so that maximum finding occurs.

BIBLIOGRAPHY

"Veteran Missionary Leader to Head New Graduate School at Fuller Seminary." *Church Growth Bulletin* 1, no. 5 (May 1965): 70.

Hunter, George W, III. "The Legacy of Donald A. McGavran." *International Bulletin of Missionary Research* 16, no. 4 (October 1992): 158-62.

Liao, David C. E. "The Orient Awaits an Optimistic Missiology." In *God, Man and Church Growth: A Festschrift in Honor of Donald Anderson McGavran*, ed. Alan R. Tippett, 14-17. Grand Rapids: William B. Eerdmans, 1973.

McGavran, Donald A. *The Bridges of God: A Study in the Strategy of Missions*. New York: World Dominion Press, 1955.

_____. "Church Growth Strategy Continued." *IRM* 57 (1968): 335-43.

_____. "The Discovery of Church Growth." In *Church Growth: Strategies That Work*, by Donald A. McGavran and George G. Hunter, III., 13-27. Nashville: Abingdon, 1980.

_____. *Effective Evangelism: A Theological Mandate*. Phillipsburg, NJ: Presbyterian and Reformed, 1988.

_____. "Have We Lost Our Way in Missions?" *Christian Herald* 81, no. 3 (March 1958): 20.

_____. *How Churches Grow: The New Frontiers of Mission*. London: World Dominion Press, 1959.

_____. *How to Grow a Church*. Glendale, CA: Regal, Books Division, G/L Publications, 1973.

_____. *How to Teach Religion in Mission Schools: A Brief Manual of Method*. Jabalpur, India: Missions Press, 1928.

_____. "The Institute of Church Growth." *IRM* 50 (1961): 430-34.

_____. "Missiology Faces the Lion." *Missiology* 17 (1989): 335-41, 352-55.

_____. *Momentous Decisions in Missions Today*. Grand Rapids: Baker Book House, 1984.

_____. "My Pilgrimage in Mission." *International Bulletin of Missionary Research* 10 (1986): 53-58.

_____. "Particular Theologies and Theology of Mission." In *Contemporary Theologies of Missions*, by Arthur F. Glasser and Donald A. McGavran, 137-49. Grand Rapids: Baker Book House, 1983.

_____. "Theological Bed Rock in Mission." *Religion in Life* 30 (1961): 603-09.

_____. *Understanding Church Growth*. Grand Rapids: William B. Eerdmans, 1970.

_____. "Will Uppsala Betray the Two Billion?" In *Eye of the Storm: The Great Debate in Mission*, ed. Donald A. McGavran, 56-66. Waco, Tex.: Word Books, 1972.

McGavran, Donald A., and Win Arn. "Conversation with a Legend: An Interview with Donald McGavran." In *The Pastor's Church Growth Handbook*, ed. Win Arn. Vol. 2. Pasadena, CA: Church Growth Press, 1982.

McGavran, Donald A., and Winfield C. Arn. *Ten Steps for Church Growth*. San Francisco: Harper & Row, 1977.

McGavran, Donald A., John Huegel, and Jack Taylor. *Church Growth in Mexico*. Grand Rapids: William B. Eerdmans, 1963.

McIntosh, Gary L. "The Twenty-First Century Relevance of Donald McGavran." *Great Commission Research Journal* 4, no. 2 (Winter 2013): 216-24.

_____. "The Life and Ministry of Donald A. McGavran: A Short Overview" (paper presented to the ASCG Annual Meeting, November 2005).

Middleton, Vern. *Donald McGavran, His Early Life and Ministry: An Apostolic Vision for Reaching the Nations*. Pasadena, CA: William Carey Library, 2011.

Pickett, J. Waskom. *Christian Mass Movements in India*. New York: Abingdon Press, 1933.

Rainer, Thom S. *The Book of Church Growth: History, Theology, and Principles*. Nashville: Broadman & Holman, 1993.

Tippett, Alan R. "A Milestone in Church Growth History." *Church Growth Bulletin* 30, no. 2 (November 1966).

_____. "Portrait of a Missiologist by His Colleague." In *God, Man and Church Growth: A Festschrift in Honor of Donald Anderson McGavran*, ed. Alan R. Tippett, 14-17. Grand Rapids: William B. Eerdmans, 1973.

Towns, Elmer, Craig Van Gelder, Charles Van Engen, Gailyn Van Rheenen, and Howard Snyder. *Evaluating the Church Growth Movement: Five Views*. Edited by Gary L. McIntosh. Series edited by Paul E. Engle. Counterpoints: Church Life. Grand Rapids: Zondervan, 2004.

Winter, Ralph D. "An Insider's View of McGavran." *Mission Frontiers* 12, no. 3 (1990).

CHAPTER 30

Carl F. H. Henry:

The Pursuit of Veritas and the Christian University

KEVIN L. KING

Carl F. H. Henry (1913-2003)

Carl Henry's influence as a major theological voice in American Christianity started with his publication of *The Uneasy Conscience of Modern Fundamentalism*, which called for a renunciation of the obscurantism of the fundamentalists of his day, and a re-engagement with culture both in terms of social ministries and a renewed commitment to academic excellence. His magnum opus, *God, Revelation and Authority* proposed his theological method, which defended the authority of scripture and challenged evangelicals to live out the implications of the Gospel of Jesus Christ in a robust and vibrant manner. It is here that evangelicalism finds its most definitive defense of biblical authority, inspiration and inerrancy, grounded in Henry's theological methodology — revelational epistemology.

535

HISTORICAL BACKGROUND

Henry emerged onto the theological scene just after World War II. It was a time of transition in many spheres of not only life in the United States, but the world as well. Henry was born January 22, 1913, on Long Island, New York to parents who were immigrants from Germany. Given the growing tensions as the United States entered World War I, the family Anglicized their names (Heinrich became Henry) and the family stopped speaking German. In the Henry household, religion was a matter of private indifference to his parents — his mother was a Roman Catholic and his father a Lutheran. Henry had little in the way of intentional religious instruction. Aside from the nondescript beginning for one who would become a leading evangelical theologian of the twentieth century, the one telling aspect of Henry's early years that would pay dividends in the years to come was his facility with the typewriter.

Henry's typing skills allowed him to land a job at the *Islip Press* (a newspaper on Long Island, NY) and in time would he would eventually become the editor of the *Smithtown Star* (Long Island, NY). Henry's skills as a writer were obviously developed during this period, but two other factors that would play into molding Henry into one of America's greatest theologians were also at work, namely his immersion into the secular world and his conversion. Henry would reflect later in his biography that while working as editor he was immersed into the secular world and had little knowledge of religious things. That would change as he would meet and befriend Mrs. Christy. Mrs. Christy was a widow who served on Henry's editorial team and the two became friends. It was through this friendship that Henry met a man by the name of Gene Bedford. It was Bedford who would introduce Henry to Jesus Christ and, shortly after his conversion, Henry would soon leave the newspaper behind and enroll in Wheaton College as he felt an increasing conviction that he needed to enter college to prepare for full-time Christian service.

As Henry enrolled in Wheaton College in 1935, he could not have known the course that he was about to chart. The time at Wheaton laid a foundation for Henry that he would build on for the rest of his life. It was at Wheaton that Henry met Billy Graham, E. J. Carnell, and the woman that would become his wife, Helga Bender. At Wheaton, Henry studied under Gordon Clark, the man who had a profound influence on the shaping of Henry's theology and his theological method. The time at Wheaton also propelled Henry to further academic study. After receiving his undergraduate degree in 1938, he enrolled at Northern Baptist Seminary and concurrently enrolled in John Dickey Memorial Theological Seminary at Wheaton College. After graduating from both schools in 1941, he received his first doctorate from Northern in 1942, and then enrolled at Boston University in 1942 where he would receive his second doctorate in 1949. Even as Henry was finishing his formal education, he began what would be an amazing literary career that spanned more than fifty years. As influential his writing career would be,[1] even more significant would be Henry's presence and participation in the developing evangelical presence in the United States and beyond.[2]

THEOLOGY OF CHRISTIAN EDUCATION

Henry understood the educational enterprise was purposed to do more than just provide a series of vocational skill sets. In addition to the vocational task, education has traditionally served society as a critical center of not only intellectual, but also, civilizing formation. Henry noted well that a continuing shift has occurred in the great intellectual centers. No longer was attention given to classical learning that emphasized the "great literary works of the past which focused on the perennial problems of philosophy and gave shape and substance to the West's cultural inheritance."[3] Instead emphasis shifted to community involvement and the quest for self-fulfillment. Henry's understanding of a distinctively Christian approach to education attempted to reverse this trend and re-shift attention toward a classical approach to education.

In 1987, Carl Henry summarized his theological position on the purpose of Christian education saying, "Christian education aims to penetrate society with distinctively biblical convictions. It seeks the cohesive integration of all learning and life. It witnesses to the world of the joys and rewards of serving the self-revealed God. These are indispensable facets of our

---

[1] Henry's significant writings played an important role (and will continue to play an important role as they are rediscovered) in the continued shaping of evangelicalism. The following are recommended as an introduction to the remarkable literary and theological program that Henry formulated: *Remaking the Modern Mind* (1946), *The Uneasy Conscience of Modern Fundamentalism* (1947), *The Protestant Dilemma* (1948), *Toward a Recovery of Christian Belief* (1987), and his magnum opus, the six volumes of *God, Revelation and Authority* (1976-1983). See also Kevin King, "The Crisis of Truth and Word: A Defense of Revelational Epistemology in the Theology of Carl F. H. Henry" (PhD diss., University of Pretoria, 2008), 15-58.

[2] Included in the list of Henry's influence upon evangelicalism on the world stage are his roles as a founding member of the National Association of Evangelicals (1942), a founding faculty member of Fuller Theological Seminary (1947), the founding editor of *Christianity Today* (1956), Chairman of the Berlin World Congress on Evangelism (1966), and President of the Evangelical Theological Society (1968-1969).

[3] Carl Henry, "Shall We Flunk the Educator?," in *gods of This Age or God of the Ages,?* ed. Albert Mohler (Nashville: Broadman & Holman Publishers, 1994), 95

evangelical mission in society."⁴ This statement represented the essence of his views in which he clearly outlined his belief that evangelicals should engage their culture on every level with the Christian worldview. He believed that it is not so much that the Christian worldview is one among many options, which technically it is, but cultural engagement with the Christian worldview is rather a visible expression of obedience to the affirmation that Jesus Christ is not "simply a way of truth and life for a beleaguered segment of humanity, but that He *is the Way, the Truth,* and *the Life* for all people."⁵ Henry's view of Christian engagement was for the truth of Jesus Christ to be articulated and applied in every arena of life and that especially included education.

In the remainder of this chapter, I will argue that Carl Henry's approach to education calls for a distinctively Christian understanding of truth that does not seek validation from secular theories. In the following sections, I will describe the method that Henry proposes to base Christian education upon. These methods are namely, (1) the critical assessment of secular philosophical presuppositions to knowing truth, and (2) the articulation of Henry's presuppositions of the distinctive Christian approach to knowing truth. Concluding these foundational methods will be an assessment of Henry's contribution to a theology of Christian education.

THEOLOGY OF EDUCATION

Henry's theology of education is largely a development of the Christian presupposition that all truth is God's truth and God Himself has revealed this truth to us. In this sense, all truth is revelational, be it general revelation or special revelation as contained in Scripture. He believed that Christianity is within its epistemic rights to present its distinctive view of truth and is not compelled to accept secular theories of knowing truth. "If, as scholars have said many times since Augustine, that all truth is God's truth and that in God's light we see light, the whole arena of the liberal arts must reflect the cohesive centrality of Christ. For He is the eternal Logos, the primeval creator of every created thing, the head of the church, and the final judge of men and nations, the one in whom all reality finds its consummatory climax."⁶

More than just providing vocational skills, universities share some of the burden for

---

⁴ Carl Henry, "Reformed Theology and the Molding of Christian Culture," in *gods of This Age or God of the Ages?*, ed. Albert Mohler (Nashville: B&H Publishers, 1994), 232.

⁵ Henry, "Shall We Flunk the Educator?," 101.

⁶ Carl Henry, "Christian Pursuit of Higher Education," *Southern Baptist Journal of Theology 1/3* (Fall 1997), 18.

"civilizing the American student."[7] Classic Greek educational philosophy understood that part of its function was to prepare for moral and intellectual leadership, so as to provide some guidance for what is the good in society and thereby lead to the possibility of a stable and civil society.[8] Education still has that function in Henry's view, but American education is in disarray. As has been stated, education has moved to a more vocational training regimen as opposed to the educating and civilizing the whole person.

Given the comprehensive role that education should play (i.e. knowing truth, the ability to recognize it, and sharing the objective values that make for a stable society), Henry believed,

> Colleges and universities are faltering as the intellectual critical centers of society; some have even become launch pads for social anarchy. The confusion and chaos of society have moved onto the campuses and into the classrooms of our schools; in the name of democratic pluralism major educational institutions forsake the name of God, pride themselves on academic excellence while they neglect objective truth, disagree on ultimate values, and bend to the anti-intellectualistic temper of our times.[9]

Given the rampant commitment to post-modernism, there is no criterion for deciding on truth or falsity. All values are viewed as social constructs and open to constant revision. There are no abiding transcendent realities save the "fact" that there are no abiding transcendent realities. As Henry states it well, " ... the *universitas* has yielded to the *diversitas*."[10]

THEOLOGICAL HERMENEUTIC

It is this milieu that Henry steps into and offers what he considers to be a distinctively Christian approach to education. "Unless Christian education publicly expounds its way of

---

[7] Henry, "Shall We Flunk the Educators?," 97. Here Henry alludes to Allan Bloom in his critique of the education system in *The Closing of the American Mind*. ". . . university officials have had to somehow to deal the undeniable fact that the students who enter are uncivilized, and that the universities have some responsibility for civilizing them." (341).

[8] Carl Henry, "Confronting the Challenge of Paganism," in *gods of This Age or God of the Ages,?* ed. Albert Mohler (Nashville: Broadman & Holman Publishers, 1994), 35. "Secular education legitimates scientific authority over the verdicts of theology and metaphysical morality. Liberal and humanistic learning espouses cultural relativism. Transient secular values now eclipse the Judeo-Christian imperatives." And it is the Judeo-Christian imperatives which served as the foundation for the country and also the earliest nine colleges in the United States, where they not only taught but upheld moral philosophy and ethical standards. "Shall We Flunk the Educators," 92.

[9] Carl Henry, *Twilight of a Great Civilization: The Drift Toward Neo-Paganism* (Westchester, IL: Crossway Books, 1988), 16.

[10] Henry, "Shall We Flunk the Educators?", 91.

knowing God, strenuously proclaims universally valid truth, and clearly identifies the criteria for testing and verifying knowledge-claims we make, then the Christian view of God and the world will survive as but a fading oddity in an academic world that questions its legitimacy and appropriateness."[11]

Henry's theological/philosophical program has three basic planks: (1) the exposing of the weakness of the presuppositions of secular humanism (which forms the underlying foundation to secular educational philosophy); (2) the articulation of the presuppositions of Christian worldview (3) and the role of the Christian educator.

NATURALISM AND THE CRISIS OF AUTHORITY

A chief characteristic of life in the West, in the last half of the twentieth century, was its attack on any transcendent authority. Self- autonomy became the ruling axiom and shared norm in a culture that saw an incredible dwindling of shared norms. The current fixation on self-fulfillment is the natural fruit of the tree that is rooted in secular humanism. Henry cited Locke and Nietzche as but two who recognized the inherent destructiveness of this move away from a transcendent God and to the autonomous self.[12] For Locke, Western culture rested on the sure foundation of theistic belief, and atheism is a threat to its very survival. Nietzsche understood well the implications of the view that "God is dead." Its appropriation "renders inevitable a comprehensive transformation of the whole of Western culture."[13] Henry has not oversold the situation. The competing worldviews (naturalism and Christianity) offer different conceptualities and realities. From early on in Henry's writings, one can see him take on the very foundations of the competing worldviews. In two of his early works, *Remaking the Modern Mind* (1948), and the *Drift of Western Thought* (1951), Henry charts the differences between secular humanism and Christianity. He then followed up this analysis with volume one of his Magnum Opus, *God, Revelation and Authority* (1976) where he argued that there is no neutral ground between humanism and Christianity. Both offer, in terms of ultimate concerns, very different views of the world, the acquisition of truth and knowing truth being one of the chief differences. It is to this difference that we now turn.

---

[11] Ibid., 93.

[12] Carl Henry, "The Crisis of Authority," in *gods of This Age or God of the Ages,?* ed. Albert Mohler (Nashville: Broadman & Holman Publishers, 1994), 46.

[13] Ibid.

KNOWING TRUTH: INCOMPATIBLE ALTERNATIVES

Henry believed that naturalism is at its core fallacious and untrue. And as one follows its trajectory, it leads to potentially disastrous consequences. Henry affirmed this assessment of naturalism that, "the modern naturalistic mind is seriously deranged by false philosophical assumptions about human epistemic power."[14] Henry arrived at this position based on his assertion of his two axiomatic principles, the ontological and the epistemological axiom. The ontological axiom is the true and living God and the epistemological axiom is that all knowledge, is in some sense, revelational. Christians are within their epistemic rights to start with God, just as the naturalist is within his rights to start with matter. In starting with God both ontologically and epistemologically, Christian theism is saying God is the ultimate reality, and knowledge is based in ultimate reality, which is God.

The prime belief of naturalism is that "nature is the ultimate real and that man is essentially no more than an animal."[15] The consequences of this position are immediate and obvious. If nature is the ultimate real, then there is no such thing as objective truth and no objective morality. The effects go beyond these startling denials. The end result is that if nature is all that there is in the end, then there are no "gods, souls, values, or anything else — unsubject to time and change."[16]

Henry notes that this is not the only time in human history where a naturalistic view of the world and humanity was offered as the overriding explanatory hypothesis for life. The ancient Greeks had their own struggle in this regard. It was the overwhelming defeat of the world-life view presented by Democritus that "nature is the ultimate real," by Greek idealism that kept naturalism as a subterranean option. Henry wrote "the idealists discerned that Democritean and Sophistic philosophy offered no basis of a durable Greek culture ... A universe in which everything changes is an unintelligible universe ... "[17]

The naturalistic presupposition that nature is the ultimate real and all reality is in flux exists, but naturalism also posits *a priori* that, in the absence of a transcendent authority, then the only authority is self. Self-assertiveness, self-direction, and self-fulfillment are but three manifestations of this specter of modernism/post-modernism. This view disallows any reality to the supernatural and transcendent. Naturalism asserts:

---

[14] Ibid., 51.

[15] Carl Henry, *Remaking the Modern Mind* (Grand Rapids: Wm. B. Eerdmans Publishing Company, 1948), 22.

[16] Carl Henry, *The Drift of Western Thought* (Grand Rapids: Wm. B. Eerdmans Publishing Company, 1951), 41.

[17] Ibid., 16.

- All reality is reducible to impersonal processes and energy events
- All life, including human life, is transient and its final destiny is death
- Truth and the good are culture-conditioned distinctions that the human race projects upon the cosmos and history.
- The implication is clear: humanity's coming of age requires rejecting all transcendentally fixed and final authority.[18]

Educationally this view has flowered in the several astonishing ways. The first is that by the early 1960s, American educators had largely abandoned the notion of fixed moral values. Consequently, the idea of moral education in the public education system gives rise to the question, "Whose morals?" Second, is the rejection of Plato's view of education as a wedding of the intellectual and moral, and third is the "intolerance of all absolutes except that intolerance."[19]

In light of this brief survey of Henry's critique of the presuppositions of naturalism, which permeate his public educational philosophy, it is quite apparent that a rapprochement is impossible. Naturalism will give no quarter to the Christian worldview. It is openly hostile and at its core antithetical to the Christian view of life and reality. Henry wrote that, "it disputes the Hebrew-Christian view of sin in its totality."[20] It is apparent that in embracing naturalism as the foundation for educational philosophy, we are now reaping the bitter fruit: no coherent and logical way of determining truth and the criteria for its verification. In embracing naturalism as the foundation for educational philosophy, we are now a nation in crisis for truth and authority. On this topic, Henry cited E. M. Adams who says, "The structure of authority is crumbling in our society not so much because of injustice and repression as because of the erosion of its intellectual foundations."[21]

CHRISTIANITY: THE PATHWAY TO TRUTH

Henry affirmed, "The modern naturalistic mind is seriously deranged by false

---

[18] Carl Henry, *Toward a Recovery of Christian Belief* (Wheaton, Il: Crossway Books, 1990), 23.

[19] Carl Henry, "The Shrouded Peaks of Learning," in *gods of This Age or God of the Ages,?* ed. Albert Mohler (Nashville: Broadman & Holman Publishers, 1994), 114.

[20] Carl Henry, "Surmounting the Clash of Worlds," in *gods of This Age or God of the Ages,?* ed. Albert Mohler (Nashville: Broadman & Holman Publishers, 1994), 80.

[21] Henry, "The Crisis of Authority," 51.

philosophical assumptions about human epistemic power."[22] His response to this quote was that the only solution is through cultural therapy that exposes and corrects these errors.[23] This "cultural therapy" is found in part, in Henry's view, through a philosophy of education that is distinctively Christian. A philosophy or theology of Christian education should advocate its distinctive view of truth and the way of knowing it. Henry writes, "It bears repeating that in affirming God's intelligible self-disclosure, the Christian view disputes the naturalistic option not simply in respect to isolated issues, but in its entirety. Christianity propounds a view of God, a view of origins, a view of nature and worth of humanity ... "[24] Henry asks no quarter and gives none with respect to the Christian view of truth and the method for discovering it. He notes that in academia there has been a tendency to soften the Christian distinctives in order to gain acceptability.[25] But in his view this is a fatal mistake, "This outlook [the Christian worldview] has to be embraced in its entirety. There can be no negotiation, no cognitive bargaining; only a robust exposition of the Christian world life view.[26]

Henry is very clear in his understanding of a biblical approach to education. This approach, in part, should reflect an uncompromised transcendent theistic epistemology, the development of a distinctively evangelical university in a major cultural center, and teachers who embody the Christian worldview in terms of "moral integrity and intellectual competency and reliability."[27]

Henry also believed educational philosophy in the West had been led astray. The overriding belief is that people are made for self-fulfillment. The self is the determiner of meaning and life and consequently truth. No longer is truth based on the truths of a Transcendent and self-revealing God. In response to the regnant naturalism in secular education, Henry wrote that "christians should feel no compulsion to taper their transcendent theistic epistemology to the preferences of hostile philosophers."[28] What is the content of this "transcendent theistic epistemology?" Greg Thornbury summarizes it nicely in his book *Recovering Classical Evangelicalism*:

---

[22] Ibid.

[23] Ibid., 51.

[24] Henry, "Surmounting the Clash of Worlds," 81.

[25] Carl Henry, "*Cognitive Bartering on Evangelical Campuses*," in *gods of This Age or God of the Ages,?* ed. Albert Mohler (Nashville: Broadman & Holman Publishers, 1994), 158-165.

[26] Henry, "Surmounting the Clash of Worlds," 80.

[27] Henry, "Christian Pursuit of Higher Education," 13.

[28] Henry, *Toward a Recovery of Christian Belief*, 45.

Henry espoused a Reformation-inspired voluntarism in the best sense of the term. He stressed the absolute dependence of human knowledge upon divine disclosure, whether natural or particular. In other words, according to Henry, we know what we know because God wills both the possibility and the content of that knowledge ... God circumscribes and determines what can be known. Nonetheless, the world remains knowable, because God himself is an intelligent Deity. Contrary to the trajectory of rationalism, no autonomous standard for reason can be offered since reason itself loses meaning apart from the divine character.[29]

Not only is the condition and content for knowledge secured by the self-revealing God, but the mind of man is fashioned in such a way as to discover truth. Contrary to the conditional truth claims that are derived from naturalism, Henry wrote "that the relationship between God's intelligible attributes and human existence in the imago Dei, provides a conduit between the indispensability of logic and human reason with a sovereign personal God, making the existence and the possibility of truth an attainable reality."[30] The Christian distinctive is clear: "There is no neutral, antiseptic path to knowledge. Knowledge, properly defined, is permitted, made accessible, and circumscribed by God himself."[31]

The second aspect of a distinctively Christian approach to education in Henry's view would be the creation of a world class Christian university in a major cultural center. On May 9, 1960, Henry wrote in *Christianity Today* of the need for a Christian university. He later reflected on this same idea in a speech given at Oxford University in 1988. The context of the article was the impending New York City crusade of Billy Graham. Henry asks the question regarding where would the thousands of college students, who were likely to make "spiritual decisions" in the area, be studying. The answer is obvious. They would be studying on secular campuses that were under the influence of naturalistic philosophy. Henry's vision was that a world class research center, located in a major center of cultural influence, that was distinctively Christian in orientation and educational integration, would have the ability to impact the cultural centers of societal influence, such as "journalism, radio, television, business, finance, the arts and other fields."[32]

Owen Strachan summarizes Henry's vision about what a "Christian Harvard" could be:

---

[29] Greg Thornbury, *Recovering Classical Evangelicalism: Applying the Wisdom and Vision of Carl F. H. Henry* (Wheaton, IL: Crossway, 2013), 52-53.

[30] Carl Henry, "The Nature of God," *Christian Faith and Modern Theology*, ed. Carl F. H. Henry (Grand Rapids: Baker, 1964), 86-87.

[31] Thornbury, 55.

[32] Henry, "The Shrouded Peaks of Learning," 109.

1. "Evangelical in urgency," with the gospel at the forefront of all study and research;

2. "Evangelical in doctrine," expressly grounded in biblical and systematic theology;

3. Committed to "academic standards and moral purity," concerned with displaying the kind of life created by the gospel;

4. Grounded in the "importance of personal academic relationships between professors and students," such that holistic intellectual, moral, and spiritual discipleship happens;

5. Achieving "the unification of all the university disciplines in the interest of a Christian world with an eye on tragic cultural crisis of our times";

6. Focused on "the political, economic and social applications of Christianity, and thus expound a consistent criticism of an alternative to socialistic revisions of the social order;"

7. Deeply aware of "the history of thought and systematic orientation to Jesus Christ as the revealed center of history, nature, conscience and redemption;" and

8. Staffed by "a faculty engaged in corporate conversation, research and writing, each making some minimal contribution for the production of textbooks that will enable the evangelical enterprise to challenge the initiative of secular scholars, and to penetrate the collegiate world.[33]

Although Henry's vision was never realized,[34] his goal in this venture was to carry out the implications of the gospel in the influential areas of American society-education, politics, and the mass media. His reflection on this failure is noteworthy:

Evangelicals have forfeited major opportunities — not the least of all, establishment of a quality university in a major metropolitan center. What they lacked in intellectual cohesion was thought by many leaders to be outweighed by their numerical strength and diversity. The eventual cost of such a trade-off may yet be higher than appears on the surface. Few evangelical colleges now fulfill their long-standing promise to teach the Christian world-life view in a way that integrates all the branches of learning. Business

---

[33] Owen Strachan, "Carl Henry's Grand Dream: A Gospel-Driven Christian School," The Southern Baptist Theological Seminary, September 13, 2013, http://www.sbts.edu/resources/towers/carl-henrys-grand-dream-a-gospel-driven-christian-school/, (accessed January 16, 2014).

[34] Henry, "The Shrouded Peaks of Learning," 109. Henry says that main obstacle to the proposed university was not from a lack of money. Rather it was from a lack of a compelling vision that would have forged a consensus, that America needed a world class distinctively Christian university.

and economics majors are displacing philosophy and the other humanities courses as leading majors. Some erst-while seminaries now flaunt an evangelical label but hesitate to affirm comprehensive biblical truthfulness and lack a stable epistemic base.[35]

Henry understood well that evangelicals could not force their commitments upon these centers of power as they reflect a naturalistic worldview. What was and is needed, is a strategy to penetrate these cultural centers of influence with the Christian worldview. This happens at the individual level and then as much as possible in the cultural level. One way for this to take place is for evangelicals to take the initiative in sponsoring ventures that influence and shape the educational, political and mass media centers with Christian principles that demonstrate "truth, justice and *agape* over pragmatism and *eros*."[36]

CONTRIBUTIONS TO CHRISTIAN EDUCATION

While Henry did not systematize a full-length theology of education, one can extrapolate from his work enough of his thoughts to present an emerging analysis of specific aspects of his educational theory. One can see that the insights of Henry on Christian education should continue to be heeded in our day and world. His contributions to a budding theology of education, while not as explicit as some, provide keen insight into the practice, administration, and theology of educators pursuing a distinctively Christian education. In this, it is evident, that Henry had a clear view of the role of the teacher within Christian education. Less obvious are his views on the role of the learner, but in essence, we can see that the learner should reject the persuasive skepticism and selfishness that is characteristic of the age. The philosophical underpinnings of naturalism and its current cultural expression are antithetical to a robust theism. In short, Christian education is a discipline of Christian discipleship.

THE ROLE OF THE TEACHER

The third area that Henry believed was essential to an authentic Christian view of education is centered on the educator. The Christian teacher has a unique and valuable role to play in advancing a Christian view of education. Henry lays out three critical areas that the Christian educator embodies: (1) evangelical integrity, (2) intellectual competence in imparting the bibli-

---

[35] Carl Henry, "Will Christianity Outlive Its Critics?," in *gods of This Age or God of the Ages,?* ed. Albert Mohler (Nashville: Broadman & Holman Publishers, 1994), 199.

[36] Carl Henry, "Besting the Cultural Challenge," in *gods of This Age or God of the Ages,?* ed. Albert Mohler (Nashville: Broadman & Holman Publishers, 1994), 183.

cal worldview, (3) possessing a moral and spiritual life that is expressed in personal holiness and social justice.[37] Henry unapologetically calls for a priority on the unity of thought and life. As a Christian pursues truth and "the good," it is imperative that these pursuits are cohesive and emblematic of an authentic Christ follower. Irrespective of how secular education has excused the incompatibility of thought and morality, this was decidedly not the view that Jesus Christ held. Henry observed that it was Jesus who "shed some light on the complexity of relationships between thought and life. He affirms that the self's moral implications are directly relevant to human thought ("a good tree bringeth forth good fruit," Mt 7:17)."[38]

Intellectual competence in the discipline is a given. But Henry asserted that for the educator to advance a distinctive view of Christian education, it is necessary to demonstrate the cohesive, consistent, and doctrinal interrelatedness of the Christian worldview. As students tend to reflect the strengths and weaknesses of their professors, it is imperative that the Christian educator be able to exhibit Christianity's intellectual power versus the non-biblical alternatives.[39] Again one can see Henry's refusal for cognitive bargaining just to be academically acceptable to those educators who align themselves with alien or non-biblical presuppositions.

The last attribute of the Christian educator is a life that models the life of the Savior. As Christians are called to conform to the image of Christ, so the Christian educator has the added dimension of not only being a fellow believer, but an educator as well. It is well known that educators have immense influence in the lives of their students. The pursuit of the truth and the good life underlies the educational venture. More than just the acquisition of a set of skills or the accumulation of knowledge, the Christian view of education brings the student into greater contact and awareness of the self-revealing God. In this mediatorial role, the Christian educator, who lives a life of personal holiness and engages life in obedience to the commands of our Lord and Savior, also leads the student on the quest for the truth and the good, which is found in a personal relationship with the Lord Jesus Christ.

THE ROLE OF THE LEARNER

As mentioned earlier, the role of the leaner in Christian education is analogous to the role of the disciple. Just as the disciple sits at the feet of the teacher and then applies those

---

[37] Henry, "Surmounting the Clash of Worlds," 79.

[38] Henry, "Christian Pursuit of Higher Education," 14.

[39] Henry, "Surmounting the Clash of Worlds," 79.

teachings to his life, the learner does the same. More than just learning a set of competencies that result in a profession of one's choosing, the learner in Henry's model of Christian education sees his or her role as living out the implications of the Gospel in all spheres of life. Just as the educator lives a life of personal holiness and obedience, the learner does as well. The key mark of differentiation in Henry's view, is that Christian education has as its ultimate goal the redemption of mankind, both on the individual and cultural levels. The learner takes what he has learned and seen modeled in his teacher, and takes the overarching metanarrative of the true and living God who reveals Himself as a means of redemption, and engages his culture in all its dimensions with the life changing message of the Gospel of Jesus Christ.

CURRICULUM AND METHODS

Again, Henry's contribution to the curriculum of the Christian education is the charge for professors to bring a coherent Christian worldview into the classroom. His pursuit of truth in all things implies his curricular approach. In this context, and for Henry, methodology is not as important as a curriculum focused on truth — as revealed through divine revelation.

CONCLUSION

In this chapter it has been argued that Henry calls for a distinctive Christian view of education. He believed that understanding that the Christian worldview and its implications are not compatible, nor do they share common ground on a presuppositional level with naturalism — the regnant philosophy on secular campuses across the United States. It has been shown that the understanding of truth, its reality, its objectivity and its recognition are based in the self-revealing God. The Christian view is the only view that provides the basis for a stable and civil society.

What is the legacy that Henry has left us? First, his writings, spanning over fifty years, are immense and important for they consistently champion the superiority of the Christian worldview and give a basis for an intelligible universe and for man to know himself and his place in the world. Second, Henry advocated for a distinctive view of Christian educational philosophy that would not look for naturalistic presuppositional approval. Christian educators are within their epistemic rights to start with a belief in God and his revelation and need not look for approval in any other place. Third, although not realized in the location that he desired, the call for a distinctively Christian University has not gone unheard. Liberty

University in Lynchburg Virginia, among others, is a viable attempt at living out his view of what should form the core of an unapologetic Christian university. Fourth, the one area of critique might be the lack of just how his view of a Christian worldview works itself out in some areas of study absent of philosophy, history and the like. Just how would Henry's view of a distinctive Christian view of education impact areas of study like math, engineering, etc.? This seems to be the one area that Henry did not address as specifically as the area of presuppositions. Finally, Henry leaves us with the legacy of living in such a way that we are challenged to engage culture with the Gospel of Jesus Christ. The pursuit of knowledge (truth and the good) was a means to an end. For Henry, life was about living out the realities of the life-changing message of the Gospel of Jesus Christ.

PRIMARY SOURCE SAMPLE[40]

In a sense, all knowledge may be viewed as revelational, since meaning is not imposed upon things by the human knower alone, but rather is made possible because mankind and the universe are the work of a rational Deity, who fashioned an intelligible creation. Human knowledge is not a source of knowledge to be contrasted with revelation, but is a means of comprehending revelation ... Thus God, by him immanence, sustains the human knower, even in his moral and cognitive revolt, and without that divine preservation, ironically enough, man could not even rebel against God, for he would not exist. Augustine, early in the Christian centuries, detected what was implied in this conviction that human reason is not the creator of it own object; neither the external world of sensation nor the internal world of ideas is rooted in subjectivistic factors alone.

BIBLIOGRAPHY

Henry, Carl. "Besting the Cultural Challenge" in *gods of This Age or God of the Ages?* edited by Albert Mohler. Nashville: Broadman & Holman Publishers, 1994.

_____. "Christian Pursuit of Higher Education." *Southern Baptist Journal of Theology* 1/3 (Fall 1997), 6-18.

_____. "Cognitive Bartering on Evangelical Campuses" in *gods of This Age or God of the Ages?* edited by Albert Mohler. Nashville: Broadman & Holman Publishers, 1994.

_____. "Confronting the Challenge of Paganism" in *gods of This Age or God of the Ages?* edited by Albert Mohler. Nashville: Broadman & Holman Publishers, 1994.

_____. *The Drift of Western Thought*. Grand Rapids: Wm. B. Eerdmans Publishing Company, 1951.

_____. "The Nature of God." in *Christian Faith and Modern Theology*, edited by Carl F. H. Henry. Grand Rapids: Baker, 1964.

_____. "Reformed Theology and the Molding of Christian Culture" in *gods of This Age or God of the Ages?* edited

---

[40] Henry, *The Drift of Western Thought*, 104.

by Albert Mohler. Nashville: Broadman & Holman Publishers, 1994.

_____. *Remaking the Modern Mind*. Grand Rapids: Wm B. Eerdmans Publishing Company, 1948.

_____. "Shall We Flunk the Educator?" in *gods of This Age or God of the Ages?* edited by Albert Mohler. Nashville: Broadman & Holman Publishers, 1994.

_____. "The Shrouded Peaks of Learning" in *gods of This Age or God of the Ages?* edited by Albert Mohler. Nashville: Broadman & Holman Publishers, 1994.

_____. "Surmounting the Clash of Worlds" in *gods of This Age or God of the Ages?* edited by Albert Mohler. Nashville: Broadman & Holman Publishers, 1994.

_____. *Twilight of a Great Civilization: The Drift Toward Neo-Paganism*. Westchester, IL: Crossway Books, 1988.

_____. *Toward a Recovery of Christian Belief*. Wheaton, IL: Crossway Books, 1990.

_____. "Will Christianity Outlive Its Critics?" in *gods of This Age or God of the Ages?* edited by Albert Mohler. Nashville: Broadman & Holman Publishers, 1994.

King, Kevin. "The Crisis of Truth and Word: A Defense of Revelational Epistemology in the Theology of Carl F. H. Henry." PhD diss., University of Pretoria, 2008.

Strachan, Owen. "Carl Henry's Grand Dream: A Gospel-Driven Christian School," The Southern Baptist Theological Seminary. September 13, 2013, http://www.sbts.edu/resources/towers/carl-henrys-grand-dream-a-gospel-driven-christian-school/, (accessed January 16, 2014).

Thornbury, Greg. *Recovering Classical Evangelicalism: Applying the Wisdom and Vision of Carl F. H. Henry*. Wheaton, IL: Crossway, 2013.

ADDITIONAL PRIMARY SOURCES

Henry, Carl F. H. *A Plea for Evangelical Demonstration*. Grand Rapids, MI: Baker Book House, 1971.

_____. *Answer for the Now Generation*. Chicago: Moody Press, 1949.

_____. *Aspects of Christian Social Ethics*. Grand Rapids, MI: William B. Eerdmans, 1964.

_____, ed. *Basic Christian Doctrines*. Grand Rapids, MI: Baker Book House, 1962.

_____. *Carl Henry: At His Best: A Lifetime of Quotable Thoughts*. Portland, OR: Multnomah Press, 1989.

_____. *Christian Counter Moves in A Decadent Culture*. Portland, OR: Multnomah Press, 1986.

_____. *Christian Faith and Modern Theology*. ed. Grand Rapids, MI: Baker Book House, 1971.

_____. *The Christian Mindset in a Secular Society*. Portland, OR: Multnomah Press, 1984.

_____. *Christian Personal Ethics*. Grand Rapids, MI: William B. Eerdmans, 1964.

_____. *The Christian Vision: Man in Society*. Hillsdale, MI: Hillsdale College Press, 1984

_____. *Confessions of a Theologian*. Waco, TX: Word Books, 1986.

_____. *Contemporary Evangelical Thought*. ed. New York: Channel Press, 1957.

_____. *Conversations With Carl Henry: Christianity for Today*. Lewiston, NY: The Edwin Mellen Press, 1986.

_____. "Evangelical." In *The New International Dictionary of the Christian Church*, edited by J. D. Douglas, 358-59. Exeter, England: Paternoster Press, 1974.

_____. *Evangelicals at The Brink of Crisis*. Waco, TX: Word Books, 1967.

_____. *Evangelical Responsibility in Contemporary Theology*. Grand Rapids, MI: William B. Eerdmans, 1957.

_____. *Evangelicals In Search of Identity*. Waco, TX: Word Books, 1976.

_____. *Fifty Years of Protestant Theology*. Boston: W.A. Wilde Company, 1950.

_____. *Frontiers In Modern Theology*. Chicago: Moody Press, 1964, 1965.

_____. ed. *Fundamentals of the Faith*. Grand Rapids, MI: Baker Book House, 1969.

_____. *God, Revelation and Authority*. 6 vols. Wheaton, IL: Crossway Books, 1983, 1999.

_____. *The God Who Shows Himself*. Waco, TX: Word Books, 1966.

_____, ed. *Horizons of Science*. San Francisco: Harpers & Row Publishers, 1978.

_____. *The Identity of Jesus of Nazareth*. Nashville, TN: Broadman Press, 1992.

_____. "Man's Dilemma: Sin." In *The Word For This Century*, edited by Merrill C. Tenney, 3-20. New York: Oxford Press, 1960.

_____. "The Nature of God." In *Christian Faith and Modern Theology*, edited by Carl F. H. Henry, 89-90. Grand Rapids: Baker, 1964.

_____. *New Strides of Faith*. Chicago: Moody Press, 1972.

_____. *Notes on the Doctrine of God*. Boston: W.A. Wilde Co., 1948.

_____. *Personal Idealism and Strong's Theology*. Wheaton, IL: Van Kamper Press, 1951.

_____. *The Protestant Dilemma: An Analysis of the Current Impasse in Theology*. Grand Rapids, MI: William B. Eerdmans, 1948.

_____, ed. *Revelation and the Bible*. 8th printing, 1980. Grand Rapids, MI: Baker Book House, 1958.

_____. *The Uneasy Conscience of Modern Fundamentalism*. Grand Rapids, MI: William B. Eerdmans, 1947.

_____, ed. *Wycliffe: Dictionary of Christian Ethics*. Peabody, MA: Hendrickson Publishers, 1973.

_____, Everett F. Harrison, and Geoffrey W. Bromiley, eds. *Baker's Dictionary of Theology*. Grand Rapids, MI: Baker Book House, 1960.

_____. and Kenneth Kantzer. eds. *Evangelical Affirmations*. Grand Rapids, MI: Zondervan, 1990.

_____. and Others. *Quest for Reality: Christianity and the Counter Culture*. Downers Grove, IL: Inter Varsity Press, 1973.

CHAPTER 31

Elmer Towns:
Training Champions for Christ

TODD BENKERT

DAVID EDGELL

Elmer Leon Towns, Jr. (1932-present)

Elmer Towns is an educator, writer, and practitioner who has influenced many evangelical leaders through his teaching ministry. Combining the study of Scripture and sociological research, he has taught biblical principles of church growth and Christian spirituality across North America and the world. His primary contribution to Christian education came through his research and writings that have challenged generations of pastors and Christian laymen to study growing churches to learn reproducible principles for evangelism and church growth. He has served in numerous academic institutions, and is co-founder of Liberty University where he has served for over forty years.

HISTORICAL BACKGROUND

Elmer Towns was born on October 21, 1932 in Savannah, Georgia. His parents did not attend church, but he began attending a local Presbyterian church in first grade after being invited by door-to-door salesman and Sunday school teacher, Jimmy Breland. Mr. Breland had a profound influence on the young Towns. For fourteen years, Towns never missed a day of Sunday school. Breland made the Bible come alive through his teaching and influenced Towns to study the Bible and pursue a relationship with Christ.[1] Though he attended Sunday school and learned the Bible through his childhood, his conversion came later. On July 25, 1950, during revival services at a nearby church, he gave his life to Christ. Towns immediately felt the call of God to full-time Christian ministry and enrolled in Columbia Bible College, where the pastors of his church were enrolled.[2]

Towns attended Columbia Bible College from 1950-1953, and it was during this time that he met and married Ruth Forbes on August 21, 1953. While a student, though not yet ordained, Towns began to pastor a small Presbyterian church. The church had been closed by the presbytery, but its remaining members called him to preach and lead the small congregation. During his short time there, Towns led the church back to health and it grew to almost one hundred people.[3]

In 1953, Towns transferred to Northwestern College and graduated with a Bachelor of Arts the following year. After graduation, Towns decided to further his education and moved to Dallas, Texas to begin graduate studies at Dallas Theological Seminary (DTS). While in Dallas, Towns began attending the First Baptist Church of Dallas. He was attracted by the church's Sunday school and outreach ministries and the preaching of its pastor, W. A. Criswell. During his time at Northwestern, Towns had already made a theological shift from a covenantal

[1] It is difficult to overstate the impact Breland had on Towns. Breland served as a spiritual mentor for Towns, who dedicated several books to Breland. In many of his writings, Towns recounts the significant role Breland played in introducing him to the Scriptures and laying the spiritual foundation for his salvation. Breland's influence first inspired Towns to become a teacher. See, e.g., Elmer L. Towns, *Stories from the Front Porch* (Springfield, MO: 21st Century Press, 1996), 25-42; Elmer L. Towns, *Walking with Giants: The Extraordinary Life of an Ordinary Man* (Ventura, Calif.: Regal Books, 2012), 28-38; Elmer L. Towns, *What Every Sunday School Teacher Should Know* (Ventura, CA: Gospel Light, 2001), 15-19. His seventh grade teacher, Margaret Logan, also had a profound impact on Towns and influenced Towns to become an avid reader and writer. See, Towns, *Stories from the Front Porch*, 43-60; Towns, *Walking with Giants*, 50-56.

[2] Towns, *Walking with Giants*, 13-17, 58-64.

[3] Ibid, 64-86. See also, Elmer L. Towns, "The Role of Innovation in Leadership," in *Leaders on Leadership: Wisdom, Advice, and Encouragement on the Art of Leading God's People*, ed. George Barna (Ventura, CA: Regal Books, 1997).

Calvinism of his Presbyterian roots to a more dispensational theology. At Dallas, he made the shift complete. Towns left the Savannah Presbytery, received baptism by immersion, and joined First Baptist Church.[4] His time at First Baptist of Dallas influenced his love for the large church and Sunday school and this experience became his role model for what a church should be.[5]

During his time in Dallas, Towns' writing and teaching ministry developed. In the fall of 1955, while still a student, Towns began writing for *The Missionary Crusader*. The editor, Homer Duncan, had asked Towns what he thought of the newspaper. When Towns answered that his missionary newspaper needed news about missions, Duncan recruited him to begin writing a monthly feature: "The Missionary World at a Glance." Towns would write this monthly column for the next three years.[6] In 1957, because of the influence of this column, the president of Dallas Bible Institute asked Towns to teach introductory courses in missions and philosophy, and it was there that Towns taught at the college level for the first time.[7]

Towns continued in his Master of Theology (Th.M.) studies at DTS and, during the summer break, also pursued a Master of Arts in Education from Southern Methodist University. He completed both degrees in August, 1958. Shortly after graduation, Towns began teaching at Midwest Bible College in St. Louis where he had accepted the position of Assistant Professor of Christian Education. In addition to teaching at the college, Towns offered seminars in local churches and became executive senator of the Greater St. Louis Sunday School Association.

Towns' writing career took another significant step when he self-published his first book. Though Towns did not know anything about publishing, he wrote to meet a need. Seeing that there was no adequate textbook available for his course on youth work, Towns set out to write his own. With help from his students and a mimeograph machine, Towns compiled his lectures into an eighty-two page manuscript entitled *Teaching Teens*. The book was later revised and published by Baker Book House. Towns would go on to write many more books over his long career.[8]

Through a providential introduction, at the age of twenty-seven, Towns became the

---

[4] Stephen R. Towns, "Elmer Towns: A Biographical and Chronological Presentation of His Writings," DMin diss, Fuller Theological Seminary, 1988), 10-11, 153-54.

[5] Ibid., 160.

[6] Towns, *Walking with Giants*, 105.

[7] Ibid., 111; Gabriel Etzel, "A Chronological Presentation of the Writings of Elmer Towns from 1999-2005," DMin thesis, Liberty Theological Seminary, 2005), 77.

[8] Towns, *Walking with Giants*, 118-20; Etzel, "Chronological Presentation," 77-78.

lead candidate to become president of Winnipeg Bible College in Manitoba, Canada. During his interview, Towns laid out a vision for the school to its board, including principles for how it should be governed. He was unanimously elected as president and served there from 1961-65. Armed with a strong sense of God's calling and a firm faith in God's ability to do anything, Towns took on the challenge of leading the college. Though the college never numbered more than one hundred students during his tenure, Towns helped lay a foundation for the school that led to its future growth and influence. His prior involvement with the Accrediting Association of Bible Colleges (AABC) prepared him to lead the school to receiving accreditation and to financial stability. Significantly, Towns helped the school gain official recognition from the Province of Manitoba so that they became the first Bible college in Canada able to offer liberal arts courses. Throughout his time in Winnipeg, Towns continued to teach, write, and speak in conventions and conferences.[9]

Following this position he became an associate professor of Christian Education at Trinity Evangelical Divinity School in Deerfield, IL. While at Trinity, he pursued a Ph.D. in Theology at Garrett Theological Seminary; however, upon completion of the coursework for his Ph.D., the Dean of the School let him know that no professor at Garrett would agree to supervise his dissertation because no one wanted their name to be associated with the research of a "fundamentalist" student. The Dean gave Towns one option: He could write a short thesis over the course of the next week and he would then be given a Masters in Religious Education. Towns took his Ph.D. coursework, completed the thesis in an abbreviated timeline and received the MRE for his efforts all while continuing his teaching load at Trinity.

Faced with Trinity's requirement for its professors to publish a significant work annually and surrounded by distinguished professors such as Gleason Archer, Walt Kaiser, and Carl. F. H. Henry, who were at the top of their respective fields, Towns sought to produce a "cutting edge" book. His big idea came from an off-topic discussion in one of his classes. When Towns recalled his time in Dallas, he made the statement that First Baptist Dallas was the largest in the world with its Sunday school of over four thousand in attendance. Several students quickly jumped in noting other, larger churches and Sunday Schools. A week later, Towns recalled that class discussion and made the decision to research the ten largest churches in America.[10]

Using his resources as Sunday school editor of *Christian Life* magazine, Towns published an article on the ten largest Sunday Schools in America. The article was a huge success and within

---

[9] Towns, *Walking with Giants*, 128-40;

[10] Ibid., 148-53.

two years Towns had expanded the list from ten to one hundred. He would go on to publish his list of the hundred largest Sunday schools for ten years. In the process, he researched and published his first significant work, *The Ten Largest Sunday Schools and What Makes them Grow*.[11] Towns would go on to write numerous books on church growth including *America's Fastest Growing Churches, Great Soul-Winning Churches, The World's Largest Sunday School,* and *The Complete Book of Church Growth*.[12] Towns' renown as "Mr. Sunday School" grew as he preached across the United States and in some of the largest churches in the world.[13]

In the course of his research, Towns interviewed Jerry Falwell, pastor of the ninth largest church in the book. Towns recognized Falwell as a great leader. The two became friends and Falwell later asked Towns to join him in starting a new college. Responding to his invitation and the call of God on his life, Towns joined Falwell as the co-founder of Liberty University. While Falwell cast a faith vision for explosive growth and kingdom impact that would train champions for Christ, Towns crafted the school's structure and philosophy of ministry. Towns laid out a vision of a school built on academic excellence, cutting-edge creativity, and local church evangelism. As Falwell had built a great church, Liberty would be "the extension of the local church at the collegiate level."[14] Liberty began in 1971 with a few part-time faculty and Towns as its only full-time professor.

Falwell led the school to rapid growth in its early years and the student body increased quickly. As the school grew, however, Towns found himself once again spending most of his time in administrative work. Rather than investing in his passion for teaching and writing, Towns was bogged down in the day-to-day details of running a university. "I found myself working harder and harder at things that were secondary to me, and I had less time to do the important things."[15]

---

[11] Elmer L. Towns, *The Ten Largest Sunday Schools and What Makes Them Grow* (Grand Rapids: Baker Book House, 1969).

[12] Elmer L. Towns, *America's Fastest Growing Churches* (Nashville: Impact Books, 1972); Elmer L. Towns, *Great Soul-Winning Churches* (Murfreesboro, TN: Sword of the Lord Publishers, 1973); Elmer L. Towns, *The World's Largest Sunday School* (Nashville: Thomas Nelson, 1974); Elmer L. Towns, John N. Vaughan, and David J. Seifert, *The Complete Book of Church Growth* (Wheaton, IL: Tyndale House Publishers, 1981); for an extensive list of Towns' writing during this time, see Mark H. Senter, III. and Timothy Paul Jones, "Elmer Towns," *Christian Educators of the 20th Century Project*, Talbot School of Theology, Biola University, http://www.talbot.edu/ce20/educators/protestant/elmer_towns (accessed June 2, 2015).

[13] Towns, *Walking with Giants*, 151-58; S. Towns, "Elmer Towns," 15-16.

[14] Towns, *Walking with Giants*, 168.

[15] Ibid., 178-186; quote, 182.

Towns resigned from Liberty in 1973 and moved to Savannah Georgia to pursue his love for writing and teaching. Towns would later describe his time away from Liberty as a "desert experience."[16] Though he had left to pursue teaching and writing, Towns soon found himself back in administrative work. Having first being hired as a consultant, he became the co-founder and later vice-president and academic dean of Baptist University of America.[17]

In 1976, Towns returned to Liberty University where he would stay for the remainder of his career. This time, Towns came as editor-in-chief of all publications. He would write for and manage publications for the university as well as Falwell's television ministry and Thomas Road Baptist Church. Towns would go on to take other administrative roles, serving as dean of Liberty Seminary and later the School of Religion. This time, however, Towns found the balance he needed to pursue his true calling. In 1982, Towns spent his first sabbatical at Fuller Theological Seminary in Pasadena, California where he studied under Donald McGavran and C. Peter Wagner and earned a Doctor of Ministry degree.

Towns continued to be influential in the area of church growth. Towns ushered in a second generation of research on the topic of church growth in America. In 1981, he joined Larry Gilbert and began the Institute for Church Growth. The institute produced more than twenty-five seminar format instructional packets such as, "How to Conduct a Friend Day" and "How to Go to Two Services."[18] Through these packets, Towns provided methods and principles for teaching church growth to ministers across the country. During these years, Towns traveled extensively teaching weekend seminars on Sunday school and church growth methods. He was best known for the seminars "154 Steps to Revitalize Your Sunday School" and "How to Reach the Baby Boomer."[19]

Another milestone in his teaching and writing ministry occurred in 1986, when Towns began teaching the Pastor's Bible Class at Thomas Road Baptist Church. He would teach that class for the next twenty-nine years. The class led Towns to write and teach extensively on spiritual formation and Christian growth. He published numerous books such as *Fasting for Spiritual Breakthrough*, *Praying the Lord's Prayer for Spiritual Breakthrough* and

---

[16] Ibid., 188.

[17] Ibid., 186-92; S. Towns, "Elmer Towns," 18-19.

[18] Elmer L. Towns, "Friend Day," Resource Packet (Lynchburg, VA: Church Growth Institute, 1984); Elmer L. Towns, "How to Go to Two Services," Resource Packet (Lynchburg, VA: Church Growth Institute, 1989).

[19] See Elmer L. Towns, *154 Steps*, Books. Paper 7. 1988, <http://digitalcommons.liberty.edu/towns_books/7> (accessed July 1, 2015). Elmer L. Towns, "How to Reach the Baby Boomer," Resource Packet (Lynchburg, VA: Church Growth Institute, 1990).

The Names of the Holy Spirit.[20] His influence continued to grow as he entered this new era of writing and teaching ministry.

Towns also helped fulfill the vision of Liberty being on the "cutting edge" by helping lead the way in distance learning. In 1985, he supported Ron Godwin who started the Liberty University School of Lifelong Learning, which would later become Liberty University Online. Towns' courses became the first offered through their distance learning program. Within five years, the distance program would grow to 14,000 students. In 2014, Liberty University Online enrolled over 100,000 students online. Towns continued to serve Liberty University in teaching and administrative roles until he retired from these positions in 2013 so he could return to his first loves – research, writing, and teaching.

THEOLOGY OF CHRISTIAN EDUCATION

Towns would describe himself as a fundamentalist. By fundamentalist, however, he means something broader than the independent Baptist fundamentalism in which has spent most of his life and career. Rather, Towns' theology is rooted in five fundamentals of the Christian faith: the authority of Scripture, the deity of Jesus Christ, his vicarious blood atonement, his physical resurrection from the dead, and his coming return.[21] These fundamentals are the core of Christian faith and theology and are not only to be believed, but lived out in practical and experiential ways. Despite various understandings and criticisms of the term, Towns is content to accept the label "fundamentalist" as an adequate description of his conservative theology.[22]

UNITY IN CHRISTIAN EDUCATION

As a religious educator, Towns has had an influence in the greater evangelical world. Though thoroughly and convictionally a Baptist, Towns felt a greater commitment to Christ and his church that lead him to work with other believers outside of his Baptist fundamentalist

---

[20] Elmer L. Towns, *Fasting for Spiritual Breakthrough* (Ventura, CA: Regal Books, 1996); Elmer L. Towns, *Praying the Lord's Prayer for Spiritual Breakthrough* (Ventura, Calif.: Regal Books, 1997); Elmer L. Towns, *The Names of the Holy Spirit: Understanding the Names of the Holy Spirit and How They Can Help You Know God More Intimately* (Ventura, Calif.: Regal Books, 1994).

[21] See, e.g., Elmer L. Towns, "Theologizing: An Analysis of a Method of Formulating Theology" (Ph. D. diss., California Graduate School of Theology, 1979), 15-17; Elmer L. Towns, "We Are Fundamentalist," *Journal - Champion* 1, no. 2 (May 26, 1978): 2; Elmer Towns et al., Lynchburg, VA, "Interview: 2010-7-23," Oral History Project, Liberty University.

[22] When asked in an interview, Towns remarked, "I'm a Fundamentalist and I've neverbacked away from calling myself a Fundamentalist." Towns et al., "Interview: 2010-7-23," 18:06.

circles. In his research, he did not limit himself to Baptists alone, but recognized that God was working among groups that did not share his precise theological views. Towns lived by a "doctrine of blessability," recognizing that God blesses those who disagree with him on nonessential doctrines because of their faith in Jesus Christ and love for Him.[23] Thus, Towns' research, teaching, and influence extended to varying branches of conservative evangelicalism without ever denying his Baptist foundation. Those who affirmed the fundamentals of the Christian faith were brothers and friends from whom he learned and with whom he served.

SCRIPTURE IN CHRISTIAN EDUCATION

A key aspect of Towns' fundamentalism was his belief in the inspiration and authority of Scripture. Whether his focus was Sunday school, Church growth, or Christian living, his writing and teaching were centered on the Bible. Towns' theology was rooted in the Bible as the word of God. He believed that all truth comes from God and that the pursuit of truth, regardless of the subject matter, must begin with theology.[24] Theology involved "gathering data," and thus, Towns has spent his life in researching principles and methods to make the ministry of the church more effective in both evangelism and education.[25] Even as he discovered and articulated new principles, he always came back to the Scripture, and the original principles given by God.

While Towns stood on the authority of Scripture, his view that all knowledge belongs to God led him to embrace the social sciences for his research. Whether writing about church growth or the Christian experience, Towns sought to gather data from both God's revelation in Scripture and in the created world. While God's revelation in Scripture was ultimate, Towns recognized that there were many valuable principles to be learned from God's general revelation as well. Where the Bible does not speak, it is possible to gather data from the social sciences through research. Many principles can be scientifically

---

[23] S. Towns, "Elmer Towns," 150-51.

[24] Elmer L. Towns, "The Relationship of Church Growth and Systematic Theology," *JETS* 29, no. 1 (March 1986): 67; see also Towns, "Theologizing."

[25] Towns described the theological process in terms of "gathering data, weighing them for their importance, arranging them into a consistent system, and then exhibiting and defending the result." As a graduate of Dallas Theological Seminary, Towns was strongly influenced by Lewis S. Chafer and his theology. Chafer defined theology as "the collecting, scientifically arranging, comparing, exhibiting and defending of all facts from any and every source concerning God and His works." Elmer Towns, "The Relationship of Church Growth and Systematic Theology," *JETS* 29, no. 1 (March 1986): 68. See also, Lewis Chafer, *Systematic Theology* (Dallas, TX: Dallas Seminary Press, 1948), Vol. 1, 4.

determined by gathering data from God's natural revelation. Thus, biblical study and scientific research are not competing methods of research with different goals and results. His theological foundations led him not to reject the social sciences, but to embrace them. What one learns from the sciences must be consistent with what is explicitly taught in Scripture; thus, Towns was not afraid to learn from scientific research as he formulated his ideas. Accordingly, scripture was the ultimate authority. He believed that Scripture and science are perfectly harmonious and when there are apparent discrepancies between the two, special revelation should supersede what is known through general revelation.[26] Towns' theology led others within conservative and fundamentalist circles to recognize sociological principles and use them in a way that is consistent with conservative theology and practice.[27]

THE HOLY SPIRIT IN CHRISTIAN EDUCATION

While the content of religious education must be based on principles, the aim of teaching was equally important. For Towns, religious education was more than merely imparting knowledge. Teaching is an act that must result in changing the lives of students and must be done in a way that leads to transformed lives.[28] Effective teaching, too, relied on sound principles and educational methods but there was another dynamic that was essential. Christian education, if it is truly transformative, depends on the Holy Spirit. Only when the Spirit of God is active in the life of the student can true transformation take place. Sound principles and methods are important, but only the Spirit of God can make teaching effective and bring about real change in the life and work of the student.[29] Thus, the goal of education can only be achieved when the Holy Spirit is at work.

---

[26] Towns, "Relationship of Church Growth and Systematic Theology," 68-69; see also Elmer L. Towns, *Understanding the Deeper Life: A Guide to Christian Experience* (Old Tappan, NJ: Fleming H. Revell, 1988), 10; Elmer L. Towns, "Effective Evangelism View," in *Evaluating the Church Growth Movement: 5 Views*, ed. Gary L. McIntosh (Grand Rapids: Zondervan, 2004), 46-48.

[27] Senter and Jones, "Elmer Towns." Senter and Jones consider the "data driven, Bible-based" use of the social sciences by Towns as one of his key contributions to religious education.

[28] Towns defined Christian education as "the process of communicating to students that which is drawn from the content and experiences of Christian sources, with the purpose of producing in students, church, and society, those aims which are implicit in Christian teaching." Elmer L. Towns, "Method in Philosophic Inquiry for Christian Education," *Religious Education* 67, no. 4 (July-August 1972): 260.

[29] Elmer L. Towns, *Evangelize Through Christian Education* (Wheaton, IL: Evangelical Teacher Training Association, 1970), 6; Towns, *Great Soul-Winning Churches*, 8-9.

THE CHURCH IN CHRISTIAN EDUCATION

The role of the church formed a central focus in Towns' theology. Above all else, Towns was a churchman and believed that religious education was to serve and flow from the local church. Towns called himself a "local church enthusiast" and believed that Christian education should be "church centered."[30] Religious education was a basic task of the church.[31] The church was the place where the Great Commission was carried out to make disciples, baptize them, and instruct them in Christ's words. Therefore, the local church is the laboratory for theological education.

Even in his role as a college administrator, Towns affirmed the central role of the church for religious education. During his years at Winnipeg, Towns formulated his thoughts about religious higher education. In an article entitled, "The Bible College is a Church," Towns suggested that pastoral training should take place through the church so that the Bible College, though separate from the church, was a natural extension of it. [32] His maxim, "A Christian College is the extension of a local church at the college level" became a foundational Philosophy for Liberty University as he and Jerry Falwell planned and laid out a vision for the new school.[33] Towns would later credit this church-centric focus as one of the keys to Liberty's success.[34]

CONTRIBUTION TO CHRISTIAN EDUCATION

Towns' contribution to Christian education is considerable. Through his research, Towns demonstrated how the insights of sociological research could serve the church, even as he maintained a fidelity to Scripture and a thoroughly Christian worldview. In his teaching and writing, Towns taught by transcendent principles and led others to do the same. His writings and teachings have impacted pastors and Christian leaders in the United States and across the globe. Perhaps even more impactful is his role in the vision and founding of Liberty University, which he always planned to be more than

---

[30] Elmer L. Towns, *The Bright Future of Sunday School* (Minneapolis, MN: F. C. Publications, 1969), 7.

[31] Elmer L. Towns, *Ministering to the Young Single Adult* (Grand Rapids: Baker Book House, 1967; reprint 1972), 76.

[32] Elmer L. Towns, "The Bible College Is a Church," *The Evangelical Christian* (November 1966).

[33] Elmer L. Towns, "The Bible College Is a Church," *The Evangelical Christian* (November 1966): 24, and (December 1966): 13; quoted in S. Towns, "Elmer Towns," 59. See also, Towns, *Walking with Giants*, 144, 168.

[34] Towns, *Walking with Giants*, 253, note 7:4.

a Bible college, but was meant to be a liberal arts college built upon the truths found in the Bible.

CONTRIBUTIONS THROUGH SOCIO-EDUCATIONAL RESEARCH

One of the most pronounced features of Towns' theology of education is his focus on principles. As Towns collected data from various sources, he would always seek to distill what he gathered into principles that could be taught. Towns distinguished between principles and their application. One would find him often repeating the proverb:

Methods are many,
Principles are few.
Methods may change
But principles never do.[35]

While methods were important, principles were more important. Methods are limited by time and space while principles are "transtemporal and transcultural."[36]

This distinction became important as he taught about Church Growth. "A method is the application of an eternal principle to a contemporary need."[37] Often, a variety of methods could be used to achieve the same result. Many different methods might prove effective, but only when they are based on timeless principles.[38] Towns further observed that certain methods, like Sunday school, proved to be "anointed methods" – methods that God used in significant ways to reach particular peoples at particular places and times. Other methods, like bus ministry and door-to-door visitation, had been effective for a season, but were no longer as impactful in certain cultural contexts. Though the success of a particular method waned, the biblical principles behind the method were still valid. Principles of evangelism,

---

[35] See, e.g., Towns, "Role of Innovation in Leadership," 187; Elmer L. Towns, *Prayer Partners: How to Increase the Power and Joy of Your Prayer Life by Praying with Others* (Ventura, CA: Regal, 2002), 17; Towns, "Effective Evangelism View," 48.

[36] Elmer L. Towns, "Introduction," in *Evangelism and Church Growth: A Practical Encyclopedia*, ed. Elmer L. Towns (Ventura, CA: Regal Books, 1995), 5; c.f., Elmer L. Towns, *Getting a Church Started in the Face of Insurmountable Odds with Limited Resources in Unlikely Circumstances* (Impact Books, 1975), 8.

[37] Towns, *154 Steps to Revitalize Your Sunday School and Keep Your Church Growing*, 7-8.

[38] For example, when writing about church planting, Towns studied ten effective church plants and noted that despite having used different methods, "their patterns are similar because there are certain timeless principles that transcend space and culture." Towns, *Getting a Church Started*, 8.

teaching, spiritual formation, and church growth were timeless; however, when cultural conditions change and people become less responsive to particular methods, God leads church leaders to new methods and applications of biblical principles.[39] Thus, throughout his teaching and writing, Towns focused first on principles and then the effective application of those principles through contemporary communicational methods.

In using socio-educational research in the areas of Christian education and Church Growth, Towns modeled a way for the insights of sociological research to inform the fundamentalist and conservative evangelical movement without compromising biblical fidelity. He saw the church as both a theological and sociological organism. As he sought out fundamental principles from Scripture, Towns also discovered sociological principles that led to greater ministry effectiveness. When researching the Sunday school and church growth, his method of research involved case studies that analyzed churches through descriptive and historical studies of their attendance. He then explored causal relationships to determine factors that churches had in common that had brought about their sustained high attendance.[40] His book *The Ten Largest Sunday Schools,* and other works that followed, articulated a method of church growth that looked for biblical principles along with sociological factors that were important in causing the growth of a church. Towns combined sociological research with a firm grounding in fundamentalist biblical theology and a proper understanding of the work of the Holy Spirit. As a result, the integration of biblical theology and social science research found favor in the life of multiple denominations including evangelical, Pentecostal, Charismatic and Wesleyan congregations.[41]

One of the features of his love for the case study approach was that pastors and churches served as models of innovation and methodology. In both his teaching and his writing, Towns preferred to teach principles and methods by highlighting real-life examples. Thus, his articles on Sunday school and church growth often highlighted a particular ministry. Likewise, he wrote many of his books as a series of case studies from which he drew ministry

---

[39] S. Towns, "Elmer Towns," 151-52; Elmer L. Towns, *Getting a Church Started,* ed. Thomas A. Howe, 3rd ed. (Lynchburg, VA: Liberty University School of LifeLong Learning, 1993), 3; Towns, "Effective Evangelism View," 48; Elmer L. Towns, "Evangelism: Hot as Ever, but Old Methods Are Cooling Off," *Fundamentalist Journal* 3, no. 2 (Feb 1984): 38.

[40] Towns followed a method of case study based on a research model of Good and Scates, *Methods of Research,* Carter V. Good and Douglas E. Scates, Methods of Research (New York: Appleton-.Century-Crofts, 1954.). The method involved using a mixed method of questionnaires, statistical research, and personal interviews. Towns followed a similar pattern in much of his church growth research. Towns, *Ten Largest Sunday Schools,* 147-48.

[41] Senter and Jones, "Elmer Towns."

principles.[42] The leaders and ministries he highlighted served as "models of innovation"[43] and provided examples and motivation to his students and readers.

CONTRIBUTIONS THROUGH WRITING

As an educator, Towns has dedicated a large portion of his career to writing on topics of effective church ministry, church growth, evangelism, Christian leadership, and the spiritual formation of believers. He has influenced the conservative evangelical movement by authoring books that examine reproducible principles and biblical models of effective ministry and methods. Towns is a prolific writer, authoring more than one-hundred-seventy books and two-thousand articles.[44] At the same time, Towns is a well sought-out teacher, having taught in countless churches and one-hundred-eleven different seminaries and colleges around the world.[45]

Towns has made an impact both as a teacher and a writer and the two go hand-in-hand.[46] In nearly every phase of his life, his teaching has been closely related to his writing. His first college teaching assignment came as a result of his writing. Because of his well-researched articles for *the Missionary Crusader*, Towns was hired to teach a missions course at the Dallas Bible Institute. Conversely, his first book was written to serve his teaching. When there was no adequate textbook for his course at Midwest Bible College, Towns wrote one himself. Future works became the teaching texts for his classes. His research interest in Sunday school became the impetus for articles and books. His book, *The 10 Largest Sunday Schools*, was widely successful and afforded him new opportunities to teach in seminars and lectures across the country and these lectures often became the basis for new books.[47]

---

[42] See, e.g., Towns, *Ten Largest Sunday Schools*; Towns, *America's Fastest Growing Churches*; Towns, *Great Soul-Winning Churches*; Towns, *World's Largest Sunday School*; Towns, *Getting a Church Started*; Elmer L. Towns, *10 Sunday Schools That Dared to Change: How Churches Across America Are Changing Paradigms to Reach a New Generation* (Ventura, CA: Regal Books, 1993); Elmer Towns, Ed Stetzer, and Warren Bird, *11 Innovations in the Local Church: How Today's Leaders Can Learn, Discern and Move Into the Future* (Ventura, CA: Regal, 2007).

[43] Towns, *10 Sunday Schools That Dared to Change*, 23.

[44] For an extensive list of his writings, see Senter and Jones, "Elmer Towns." See also, S. Towns, "Elmer Towns"; Etzel, "Chronological Presentation."

[45] "Biography: Elmer Towns," *School of Divinity Faculty*, Liberty University, <http://www.liberty.edu/divinity/index.cfm?PID=12834> (accessed July 15, 2015). For Towns' curriculum vitae, see Towns, *Walking with Giants*, 257-68.

[46] Gabriel Etzel examines the relationship between these two aspects of Towns' ministry in Etzel, "Chronological Presentation," 75-97.

[47] See, e.g., Elmer L. Towns, *8 Laws of Leadership*, Books. Paper 2. 1992, http://digitalcommons.

There was no set pattern for how his teaching and writing might develop. Whenever there was a need for material, Towns set out to provide it. Likewise, whenever Towns prepared to teach, whether for a college course, Sunday school conference, church growth seminar, lecture series, or his pastor's Sunday school class, that preparation found its way into print.[48] Throughout his life, there remained an interdependent relationship between his teaching and writing with each serving the other and both to the end of building up the church in both numerical and spiritual growth.

CONTRIBUTIONS REGARDING THE ROLE OF THE TEACHER

Towns believed the teacher played an important role in the lives of students. On the one hand, Towns always saw the role of "great men" who built and led great churches and institutions. Though he never considered himself as such, Towns followed such men as Jerry Falwell and highlighted other leaders and pastors as models for his readers and students to follow.[49] At the same time, Towns saw the vital role that teachers play in the lives of students. While great leaders served as models of innovation and leadership, great teachers were needed to model principled living and lifelong learning. Teachers lead by example and cast a vision of learning for the student.[50]

A teacher is an influencer whose aim is transformation. The teacher does not settle for deep thinking or thorough understanding of the topic. Rather, the aim of teaching is changed lives and the teacher prepares and guides students toward that end.[51] Every student has great potential to grow in Christ and the teacher has a role in helping him reach that potential. "Christian education is more than an intellectual pursuit. It aims at more than transition of knowledge. Right teaching of the Bible leads to changing attitudes, motives, and the will. Christian teaching involves continual personality adjustment toward spiritual

---

liberty.edu/towns_books/2 (accessed July 1, 2015).

[48] In a light-hearted recognition of the scope of Towns' influence through writing ministry, Ed Stetzer once quipped, "Dr. Towns has no unpublished thought." Towns, *Walking with Giants*, 5.

[49] In the epilogue of his memoir, Towns states, "I've walked among God's giants; I have learned from them and been motivated by them. I've interviewed giants, told their stories, and held them up as examples for others to follow. I've never intended to be a giant, or thought of myself that way. I'm not a giant—though I do want to be a giant-maker." Towns, *Walking with Giants*, 249.

[50] Towns, *10 Sunday Schools That Dared to Change*, 13-14; cf. Elmer L. Towns, "What to Do When You Teach and Nothing Happens," *Christian Life*, November 1976: 92;

[51] Elmer L. Towns, *Fasting for Spiritual Breakthrough Study Guide*, Books. Paper 17. 1998, http://digitalcommons.liberty.edu/towns_books/17 (accessed July 1, 2015).

maturity."[52] Thus, the role of the teacher is to influence students and to help them grow to both spiritual maturity and useful service for the kingdom of God.[53]

In order to achieve that aim, teaching is more than merely conveying information. The teacher must remember that "talking is not teaching" and "listening is not learning."[54] A teacher who merely delivers content through lectures will be ineffective and fail to influence students toward transformation.[55] The teacher must recognize the various factors related to learning including methodology, resources, and the students themselves. The teacher must make whatever adjustments are necessary in order to "create a climate for learning" that leads to changed lives.[56]

CONTRIBUTIONS REGARDING THE ROLE OF THE LEARNER

Learners too have a responsibility to invest in their own learning and put into practice what they learned for Christ and his kingdom. Learning is more than just growing in knowledge, but living out the principles one learns in practical and tangible ways. Towns wrote and taught with the expectation that students would implement what they learned. He taught principles and expected those principles to be applied. He used case studies and personal examples in his teaching and writing so that learners would see principles in action and be motivated to put those principles to work in their own lives and situations.

Thus, one of the roles of the learner is to learn from the example of others. Indeed, Towns himself did not see himself an expert in the principles he taught. Rather, he himself learned from the success of others and then told their stories. Towns served as the "channel" for these stories from which students learned to apply principles in their own contexts.[57] The Sunday school lists that marked the beginning of Towns' influential career were published to motivate readers to reach and baptize more people in their own Sunday schools. Towns sought to motivate churches to put principles into practice, implement new ideas, set numeric goals, grow churches, and start new ones.[58]

---

[52] Towns, *Evangelize Through Christian Education*, 6.

[53] This is true of teachers in the church Sunday School as well as institutions of higher learning. The Liberty University motto, *"Training Champions for Christ,"* is an illustration of that principle.

[54] Towns, *Ministering to the Young Single Adult*, 68; Towns, *Fasting for Spiritual Breakthrough Study Guide*, 6.

[55] Towns, *10 Sunday Schools That Dared to Change*, 13.

[56] Towns, *Ministering to the Young Single Adult*, 68.

[57] See, e.g., Towns, *Getting a Church Started*, 2.

[58] Elmer L. Towns, "Sunday Schools of the Decade," *Christian Life*, October 1977: 30-34; Towns, "Evangelism," 18.

In his writings and in the classroom, Towns sought to motivate students through the examples of others.

The challenge for learners is not merely to learn information or marvel at historical and contemporary examples, but to serve the Lord faithfully in their own sphere. As learners grow in their walk with Christ, they must give themselves to the purposes of God and to serve the Lord faithfully.[59] Towns had an impetus for action and expected learners to attempt great things for God as they put principles into practice.[60] He believed that growth and transformation were the work of God, but that God worked through people who took initiative and were willing to be used by Him.[61] And while Towns believed in the important role of great leaders, he also saw the importance of lay workers and teachers in seeing God's work accomplished.[62] Every learner is to use what he learns to serve God. "There is no such thing as an average Christian. Every believer has a unique contribution to invest for God."[63]

What was true in the Sunday school class was equally true in the university classroom. According to Towns, education at the collegiate level should equip students to cultivate their spiritual gifts for the edification of the church and for vocational service to society. Therefore, students were required each semester to participate in some form of Christian service. In its early years, students were members of Thomas Road Baptist Church and contributed to every area of church life. Each student was required to serve in the ministry of the church and guidelines were followed for dress and conduct.[64] Students practiced serving others together so that they would be ready to serve the church upon graduation. Students attended academic classes to prepare them for professional ministry in the church and vocationally in the marketplace. The expectation was that students not only gain academic knowledge but prepare themselves to serve God wherever he leads. Each student was expected to pursue spiritual maturity, fulfill their role in the Great Commission, and live a life that brings glory to God.[65]

---

[59] Elmer L. Towns, *The Christian Hall of Fame* (Grand Rapids: Baker Book House, 1971), 9-10.

[60] Towns, *Great Soul-Winning Churches*, 9.

[61] Elmer L. Towns, "Sunday Schools 1977," *Christian Life*, November 1977: 30; Towns, *Getting a Church Started*, 12; Towns, *Getting a Church Started*, 1.

[62] Towns, *Evangelize Through Christian Education*, 8; Elmer L. Towns, "50 Fastest Growing Sunday Schools," *Christian Life*, November 1975: 68.

[63] Towns, *Christian Hall of Fame*, 9.

[64] These areas were changed as the school developed and accreditation requirements made Liberty change the church membership requirement. Liberty University still requires Christian service and holds high standards of conduct. This standard is known as the "The Liberty Way."

[65] See Towns, "The Bible College Is a Church"; Towns, *Walking with Giants*, 168, 179-80.

CONTRIBUTIONS THROUGH LIBERTY UNIVERSITY

Though Towns has had a tremendous impact through his teachings and writings, perhaps his most enduring legacy will be that of co-founder of Liberty University. While Towns saw Jerry Falwell as the "great man" with the leadership and vision to build a great university, Towns had a significant role in shaping its structure and core values. Towns' envisioned a school that would pursue academic excellence, cutting-edge creativity, and connection to the local church.[66] Together, they created a "world-class" liberal arts college for Bible-believing Christians and not just a Bible college.[67] From the early days of the school, Towns' vision was for a college that would train students in business, education, sciences, and the arts. The college would train Christian men and women to take part in the Great Commission in the context of their vocational marketplace.

The intention of Liberty University has always been to *Train Champions for Christ*. To this day, the university emphasizes the expectation that professors exist to teach students using the gifts of wisdom and knowledge as they equip students for spiritual maturity, giftedness, and biblical knowledge. Today, Liberty has become what its founders envisioned—a world-class University that prepares Christian men and women to live out their faith in every sector of society.[68]

CONCLUSION

Elmer Towns never considered himself a giant, yet he will be numbered among the great religious educators of his generation. Through his writing and teachings, he has influenced multitudes to accomplish great things for God as they live by biblical principles. Whether one knows Towns as "Mr. Sunday School," as an expert in church growth, as a writer on Christian spirituality, as a conference speaker or college professor, one cannot help but to be encouraged to follow him in his study and imitation of the giants of the Church and of Christ himself. He is a man of principles; he lives by them, and leads others to do the same.

---

[66] Towns, *Walking with Giants*, 168.

[67] They chose to start a liberal arts college rather than a Bible College, intending to prepare not just ministers for missions and evangelism, but preparing Christians to serve in every sphere including the secular professions. From the outset, Liberty found a unique niche in religious education, avoiding both the liberalism of the secular schools and the separatism and narrow focus of the fundamentalist schools. See Quentin Schultze, "The Two Faces of Fundamentalist Higher Education," ed. Martin E. Marty and R. Scott Appleby (Chicago: University of Chicago Press, 1993), 505-13.

[68] Jerry Falwell, *Strength for the Journey* (New York, NY: Simon and Schuster, 1987), 306.

PRIMARY SOURCE SAMPLE[69]

I love the Sunday School and appreciate its influence on my life. I was first introduced to Sunday School when Jimmy Breland, a Sunday School teacher, asked me if he could take me to Sunday School. As a small boy, I faithfully attended Eastern Heights Presbyterian Church in Savannah, Georgia, where I was grounded in Bible content and doctrine. I was taught to bring my offerings in a special envelope.

Because my values in life were taught to me by my mother and reinforced in Sunday School, when I heard the Gospel preached by a Baptist evangelist, I received Jesus Christ as my Savior.

Because our society is changing, some have suggested the age of the Sunday School is past. But the future of Sunday School is bright, and I believe God will continue to use the Sunday School as the evangelistic and educational arm of the church. Still, the Sunday School must adapt to continue its influence. In my seminars, I often challenge audiences, "The Sunday School that has been the steeple of the church must become its foundation."" The Sunday School must not change its purpose but it must go "back to the basics," for the old is again becoming new.

I believe that any church, anywhere, any time, can grow when it is revitalized. That's because I believe in the power of God and the influence of the Word of God. Growing a church is like growing a garden. The ground must be prepared and the seed planted properly at the correct time. The seed must be watered and be exposed to sunshine. These are principles for growing a garden, and when properly applied, new life will spring forth. There are principles for growing a Sunday School. If you apply the principles, your Sunday School will grow.

BIBLIOGRAPHY

"Biography: Elmer Towns." In *School of Divinity Faculty*. Liberty University. Accessed July 15, 2015 <http://www.liberty.edu/divinity/index.cfm?PID=12834>.

Etzel, Gabriel. "A Chronological Presentation of the Writings of Elmer Towns from 1999-2005," DMin thesis, Liberty Theological Seminary, 2005.

Schultze, Quentin. "The Two Faces of Fundamentalist Higher Education," ed. Martin E. Marty and R. Scott Appleby, 490-535. Chicago: University of Chicago Press, 1993.

Senter, Mark H., III., and Timothy Paul Jones. "Elmer Towns." In *Christian Educators of the 20th Century Project*. Talbot School of Theology, Biola University. Accessed June 2, 2015 <http://www.talbot.edu/ce20/educators/protestant/elmer_towns>.

Towns, Elmer L. "The Bible College Is a Church." *The Evangelical Christian*. (November 1966): 24, and (December

---

[69] Elmer L. Towns, *154 Steps to Revitalize Your Sunday School and Keep Your Church Growing*, Books. Paper 7. 1988, http://digitalcommons.liberty.edu/towns_books/7 (accessed July 1, 2015).

1966): 13.

_____. *10 Sunday Schools That Dared to Change: How Churches Across America Are Changing Paradigms to Reach a New Generation.* Ventura, CA: Regal Books, 1993.

_____. *154 Steps to Revitalize Your Sunday School and Keep Your Church Growing.* Books. Paper 7. 1988. Accessed July 1, 2015 <http://digitalcommons.liberty.edu/towns_books/7>.

_____. "50 Fastest Growing Sunday Schools." *Christian Life* November 1975: 28-29, 68-71.

_____. *8 Laws of Leadership.* Books. Paper 2. 1992. Accessed July 1, 2015 <http://digitalcommons.liberty. edu/towns_books/2>.

_____. *America's Fastest Growing Churches.* Nashville: Impact Books, 1972.

_____. *The Bright Future of Sunday School.* Minneapolis, MN: F. C. Publications, 1969.

_____. *The Christian Hall of Fame.* Grand Rapids: Baker Book House, 1971.

_____. "Effective Evangelism View." In *Evaluating the Church Growth Movement: 5 Views,* ed. Gary L. McIntosh, 31-53. Grand Rapids: Zondervan, 2004.

_____. "Evangelism: Hot as Ever, but Old Methods Are Cooling Off." *Fundamentalist Journal* 3, no. 2 (Feb 1984): 17-19, 38.

_____. *Evangelize Through Christian Education.* Wheaton, IL: Evangelical Teacher Training Association, 1970.

_____. *Fasting for Spiritual Breakthrough Study Guide.* Books. Paper 17. 1998. Accessed July 1, 2015 <http:// digitalcommons.liberty.edu/towns_books/17>.

_____. *Fasting for Spiritual Breakthrough.* Ventura, CA: Regal Books, 1996.

_____. *Friend Day.* Resource Packet. Lynchburg, VA: Church Growth Institute, 1984.

_____. *Getting a Church Started in the Face of Insurmountable Odds with Limited Resources in Unlikely Circumstances.* Impact Books, 1975.

_____. *Getting a Church Started.* Edited by Thomas A. Howe. 3rd ed. Lynchburg, VA: Liberty University School of LifeLong Learning, 1993.

_____. *Great Soul-Winning Churches.* Murfreesboro, TN: Sword of the Lord Publishers, 1973.

_____. *How to Go to Two Services.* Resource Packet. Lynchburg, VA: Church Growth Institute, 1989.

_____. *How to Reach the Baby Boomer.* Resource Packet. Lynchburg, VA: Church Growth Institute, 1990.

_____. "Introduction." In *Evangelism and Church Growth: A Practical Encyclopedia,* ed. Elmer L. Towns, 5-6. Ventura, CA: Regal Books, 1995.

_____. "Method in Philosophic Inquiry for Christian Education." *Religious Education* 67, no. 4 (July-August 1972): 259-67.

_____. *Ministering to the Young Single Adult.* Http://Elmertowns.Com/Wp-Content/Uploads/2013/10/ Ministering_to_the_Young_Single_AdultETowns.Pdf. Grand Rapids: Baker Book House, 1967; reprint 1972.

_____. *The Names of the Holy Spirit: Understanding the Names of the Holy Spirit and How They Can Help You Know God More Intimately.* Ventura, CA: Regal Books, 1994.

_____. *Prayer Partners: How to Increase the Power and Joy of Your Prayer Life by Praying with Others.* Ventura, CA: Regal, 2002.

_____. *Praying the Lord's Prayer for Spiritual Breakthrough.* Ventura, CA: Regal Books, 1997.

_____. "The Relationship of Church Growth and Systematic Theology." *JETS* 29, no. 1 (March 1986): 63-70.

_____. "The Role of Innovation in Leadership." In *Leaders on Leadership: Wisdom, Advice, and Encouragement on the Art of Leading God's People*, ed. George Barna, 183-98. Ventura, CA: Regal Books, 1997.

_____. *Stories from the Front Porch.* Springfield, MO: 21st Century Press, 1996.

_____. "Sunday Schools 1977." *Christian Life* November 1977: 30-31, 42-45.

_____. "Sunday Schools of the Decade." *Christian Life* October 1977: 30-34.

_____. *The Ten Largest Sunday Schools and What Makes Them Grow.* Grand Rapids: Baker Book House, 1969.

_____. "Theologizing: An Analysis of a Method of Formulating Theology." PhD diss., California Graduate School of Theology, 1979.

_____. *Understanding the Deeper Life: A Guide to Christian Experience.* Old Tappan, NJ: Fleming H. Revell, 1988.

_____. *Walking with Giants: The Extraordinary Life of an Ordinary Man.* Ventura, CA: Regal Books, 2012.

_____. "We Are Fundamentalist." *Journal - Champion* 1, no. 2 (May 26, 1978): 2.

_____. *What Every Sunday School Teacher Should Know.* Ventura, CA: Gospel Light, 2001.

_____. "What to Do When You Teach and Nothing Happens." *Christian Life* November 1976: 24, 91-92.

_____. *The World's Largest Sunday School.* Nashville: Thomas Nelson, 1974.

Towns, Elmer L., John N. Vaughan, and David J. Seifert. *The Complete Book of Church Growth.* Wheaton, IL: Tyndale House Publishers, 1981.

Towns, Elmer, Ed Stetzer, and Warren Bird. *11 Innovations in the Local Church: How Today's Leaders Can Learn, Discern and Move Into the Future.* Ventura, CA: Regal, 2007.

Towns, Elmer, Lowell Walters, Cline E. Hall, and Ruth E. Sattler, Lynchburg, VA. "Interview: 2010-7-23." Oral History Project. Liberty University.

Towns, Stephen R. "Elmer Towns: A Biographical and Chronological Presentation of His Writings," DMin diss, Fuller Theological Seminary, 1988.

CONTRIBUTOR BIOS

Part I: Educators in Early Church through the Middle Ages (A.D. 1-1500)

The Apostle Paul: Educator of the Early Church

Phil Howard (Ph.D., Trinity International University) is Professor of Ministry Leadership and Spiritual Formation and Chair of the Ministry and Leadership Department at Toccoa Falls College.

Steve Woodworth (D.Min., Gordon-Conwell Theological Seminary) is the Associate Director for the International Theological Education Network (ITEN), which seeks to train indigenous Christian leaders among unreached people groups. In addition to this, he serves as the Secretary for the Academic Planning Committee for the European Training Centre as well as an Instructor of Bible and Religion at Montreat College.

Augustine: Teacher as Mentor

Edward L. Smither (PhD, University of Wales-Trinity St. David; PhD, University of Pretoria) is Dean and Professor of Intercultural Studies at Columbia International University and the author of Augustine as Mentor: A Model for Preparing Spiritual Leaders, Brazilian Evangelical Missions in the Arab World, Mission in the Early Church, and translator of François Decret's Early Christianity in North Africa.

Columba: An Inadvertent Teacher of Wild Peoples

Gwendolyn Sheldon (Ph.D. from the Graduate Center for Medieval Studies at the University of Toronto) focused her dissertation on the conversion of the Vikings in Ireland from a comparative perspective. She is currently a lecturer at St. Michael's College at the University of Toronto.

Anselm of Canterbury: Educating for the Love of God

Byard Bennett (Ph.D., University of Toronto) is Professor of Historical and Philosophical Theology at Grand Rapids Theological Seminary.

Thomas Aquinas: Teaching Theology in the Age of Universities

Daniel Fărcaş (Ph.D., University of Paris IV – Sorbonne) is a historical philosopher who has had two post-doctoral research fellowships. One was at the Institut Protestant de Théologie (Paris, France) and the other at Babeş-Bolyai University (Cluj-Napoca, Romania). Currently he is teaching systematic theology at Liberty University School of Divinity.

Part II: The Reformation Educators (A.D. 1500-1650)

Erasmus: A Return to the Sources of Education

Jason J. Graffagnino (Ph.D., Southwestern Baptist Theological Seminary) is Division Chair of World Missions and Christian Studies and Assistant Professor of History and Christian Studies at Truett-McConnell College in Georgia. He also serves as Assistant Professor of Church History at Liberty University. His dissertation research focused the shaping of the two earliest Anabaptist catechisms.

Huldrych Zwingli: A Christian Humanist Educator

Dongsun Cho (Ph.D., Southwestern Baptist Theological Seminary) is Assistant Professor of Systematic and Historical Theology at Southwestern Baptist Theological Seminary.

Martin Luther: Education for the Preservation of the Gospel and Society

William M. Marsh (Ph.D., Southwestern Baptist Theological Seminary) is Assistant Professor of Theological Studies at Cedarville University. His doctoral work focused on Luther's theological hermeneutic and biblical theology in relation to Christ as the literal sense of Scripture.

Ignatius of Loyola: Solider of the Exercised Mind and Disciplined Spirit

George Thomas Kurian was president of the Encyclopedia Society and the editor of 65 books including 27 encyclopedias, 15 of them multi-volume. His Christian-themed encyclopedias include *Encyclopedia of Christian Education* (3 volumes, Rowman & Littlefield, co-edited with Mark Lamport), *World Christian Encyclopedia* (2 volumes, Oxford University Press), *Dictionary of Christianity* (Thomas Nelson), *Encyclopedia of Christian Civilization* (4 volumes, Wiley-Blackwell), *Encyclopedia of Christian Literature* (2 volumes, Scarecrow Press) and *Encyclopedia of Christianity in the United States* (5 volumes, Rowman & Littlefield, co-edited with Mark Lamport). Kurian was a product of a Jesuit education in India.

Mark A. Lamport (Ph.D., Michigan State University) is professor of practical theology at theological schools in Colorado, Arizona, Virginia, California, Indiana, Belgium, Wales, Italy, and Portugal, and has composed 150 publications in Christian education over 32 consecutive years, including co-editor of *Encyclopedia of Christian Education* (3 volumes, Rowman & Littlefield, 2015) and *Encyclopedia of Christianity in the United States* (5 volumes, Rowman & Littlefield, 2016, and a three volume history and theology of hymnists (with Benjamin K. Forrest and Vernon Whaley, Cascade, 2018).

Philip Melanchthon: Christian Education in the German Reformation

    Martin Klauber (Ph.D., University of Wisconsin) is Affiliate Professor of Church History at Trinity Evangelical Divinity School and an Adjunct Professor of Church History at Liberty University School of Divinity. He is widely published in the areas of Reformation and Post-Reformation History.

John Calvin: Teacher in the School of Christ

    Dustin Bruce (Ph.D., Candidate, Southern Baptist Theological Seminary) is a junior fellow of the Andrew Fuller Center at Southern Baptist Theological Seminary.

    Timothy Jones (Ph.D. Southern Baptist Theological Seminary) is the Associate Vice President of Online Learning for Southern Baptist Theological Seminary and C. Edwin Gheens Professor of Christian Family Ministry.

    Michael S. Wilder (Ph.D., Southern Baptist Theological Seminary) is the Associate Vice President for Doctoral Studies at Southern Baptist Theological Seminary.

Part III: Puritan Educators (A.D. 1650-1750)

John Amos Comenius: Teaching all Things to all People

    David I. Smith (Ph.D., University of London) is Director of the Kuyers Institute for Christian Teaching and Learning, and Director of the Graduate studies in Education at Calvin College. His research interests include the relationship between faith and pedagogy and the thought of John Amos Comenius. He currently serves as senior editor of the *International Journal of Christianity and Education*.

    Joan Dudley (Ph.D., Saint Louis University) is a Spanish teacher and Chair of World Languages at Westminster Christian Academy in St. Louis, MO. She is also an adjunct professor at Missouri Baptist College. Her dissertation on Comenius was titled, *One Pictures is Worth a Thousand Words: A Pictorial Journey Through the "Orbis Pictus" of J.A. Comenius.*

Richard Baxter: Educating through Pastoral Discipleship

    Bob R. Bayles (Ph.D., Trinity Evangelical Divinity School) is Professor of Discipleship and Christian Formation, at Lee University in Cleveland, Tennessee. He has taught spiritual formation, discipleship and leadership in Africa, Korea, China, and Israel at both the undergraduate and graduate levels, and has published several works on spiritual formation and leadership development. He is the father of six children.

    Timothy K. Beougher (Ph.D., Trinity Evangelical Divinity School) served for six years at Wheaton College as Assistant Professor of Evangelism and Associate Director of the

Institute of Evangelism at the Billy Graham Center before moving to The Southern Baptist Theological Seminary where he is Associate Dean for the Billy Graham School of Missions, Evangelism and Ministry and Billy Graham Professor of Evangelism and Church Growth. He has written and edited numerous works related to evangelism, discipleship, and spiritual awakening, including *Overcoming Walls to Witnessing*, *Training Leaders to Make Disciples*, *Evangelism for a Changing World*, *Accounts of a Campus Revival: Wheaton College 1995*, and *Richard Baxter and Conversion*.

August Hermann Francke: Architect of Practical Piety

Tom Schwanda (D.Min., Fuller Seminary; Ph.D., Durham University) is an Associate Professor of Christian Formation and Ministry at Wheaton College.

Mark A. Lamport (Ph.D., Michigan State University) is professor of practical theology at theological schools in Colorado, Arizona, Virginia, California, Indiana, Belgium, Wales, Italy, and Portugal, and has composed 150 publications in Christian education over 32 consecutive years, including co-editor of *Encyclopedia of Christian Education* (3 volumes, Rowman & Littlefield, 2015) and *Encyclopedia of Christianity in the United States* (5 volumes, Rowman & Littlefield, 2016, and a three volume history and theology of hymnists (with Benjamin K. Forrest and Vernon Whaley, Cascade, 2018).

Jonathan Edwards: Influencing the Heart

Michael A. G. Haykin (Th.D., Wycliffe College, and The University of Toronto) is the Director of the Andrew Fuller Center for Baptist Studies and Professor of Church History and Biblical Spirituality at The Southern Baptist Theological Seminary.

Dustin Bruce (Ph.D., Candidate, Southern Baptist Theological Seminary) is a junior fellow of the Andrew Fuller Center at The Southern Baptist Theological Seminary.

Part IV: Post-Enlightenment Educators (A.D. 1750-1850)

John Wesley: Methodizing Christian Education

Mark A. Maddix (Ph.D., Trinity Evangelical Divinity School) is Professor of Practical Theology and Christian Discipleship and Dean of the School of Theology & Christian Ministries at Northwest Nazarene University, and former President of Society of Professors of Christian Education (SPCE)

James R. Estep (Ph.D., Trinity Evangelical Divinity School; D.Min., Southern Baptist Theological Seminary) has taught Christian education for twenty-three years and currently serves as Professor of Christian Education and the Director of the

Lincoln Leadership Institute at Lincoln Christian University (Lincoln, Illinois).

Robert Raikes: Author of the Sunday School Movement

Roderick C. Willis II (Ph.D., The University of North Texas & Dallas Theological Seminary Collaborative Doctoral program in Higher Education & Administration with an emphasis in Christian Higher Education) serves as Senior Research Analyst for the Department of Applied Research & Program Evaluation in the Fort Worth Independent School District and serves as dissertation methodologist on the doctoral faculty at Walden University in the Division of Higher Education and Adult Learning. **L. Philip Barnes** (Ph.D., University of Dublin, Ireland) is Emeritus Reader in Religious and Theological Education at King's College London. His research interests include modernity and religious education, pluralism and religious education, religious education in Ireland, as well as religious conflict and Christian models of political forgiveness.

Johann Heinrich Pestalozzi: Advocate for Child-Centered Education

James R. Moore (Ph.D., Trinity Evangelical Divinity School) is Associate Dean and Associate Professor of Educational Ministries at Trinity Evangelical Divinity School.

Johann Friedrich Herbart: Morality as the Task for Education

Eddie Baumann (Ph.D., University of Wisconsin) is Professor of Philosophy of Education at Cedarville University.

Thomas Hutchison (Ph.D., Marquette University) is Professor of Christian Education at Cedarville University.

Part V: Educators in the Age of Industrialization (A.D. 1850-1950)

Horace Bushnell: Advocate of Progressive Orthodoxy and Christian Nurture

Samuel J. Smith (Ed.D., Oklahoma State University) is Professor of Educational Leadership and director of the M.Ed. in administration and supervision at Liberty University.

Elmer L. Towns (D.Min., Fuller Theological Seminary) is co-founder of Liberty University. He has published extensively in the field of Christian education over the past 50 years.

John Henry Newman: Education that Integrates Faith and Learning

Bob Drovdahl (Ph.D. Michigan State University) is a Professor of Educational Ministry at Seattle Pacific University and is a former president of the Society of Professors of Christian Education (SPCE).

William James: Father of Pragmatic Philosophy and Experiential Education

Jonathan H. Kim (Ph.D., Trinity Evangelical Divinity School) is Professor of Christian Education at Talbot School of Theology, Biola University.

C. I. Scofield: Educating for Heavenly Citizenship

John D. Basie (Ph.D., Baylor University) is a Visiting Assistant Professor of Philosophy at Union University. He is also the Director of the Scholars and Masters Programs at the Impact 360 Institute, an innovative higher education institution affiliated with the Lifeshape Foundation and Union University that emphasizes biblical worldview and leadership studies. He is also founder and principal of Millennial 360, LLC, an academic and career coaching firm targeting college students, graduate students, and young professionals. The title of his dissertation was "Effects of American Fundamentalism on Educating towards a Virtuous Citizenry: The Case of C.I. Scofield and Philadelphia Biblical University."

John Dewey: Father of Progressive Education

Greg Lawson (J.D., Campbell University School of Law; Ed.D., University of North Texas; Ph.D., Southwestern Baptist Theological Seminary) is a professor of Christian Education at Southeastern Baptist Theological Seminary.

Ken Coley (Ed.D., University of Maryland) is a professor of Christian Education and Director of Ed.D. Studies at Southeastern Baptist Theological Seminary. He has taught educational leadership, school administration, and instructional techniques at the graduate school level for the past twenty years and has authored several books and numerous journal articles on these topics.

Arthur Flake: Pioneer of Sunday School Administration

Gary Waller (Ph.D., Southwestern Baptist Theological Seminary; Ph.D., University of North Texas) has served in teaching and administrative roles within seminaries for over twenty years. He was the Associate Dean of the School of Educational Ministries and Dean of Distance Learning at Southwestern Baptist Theological Seminary. Currently he is Assistant Professor of Practical Studies at Liberty University School of Divinity.

Part VI: Modern Educators (A.D. 1950 – Present)

Henrietta Mears: Educating God's Children

> **J. Douglas Hankins** (Ph.D., Trinity Evangelical Divinity School) is a pastor and author. His dissertation was titled, "Following up: Dawson Trotman, the Navigators, and the origins of disciple making in American evangelicalism, 1926-1956."

C. S. Lewis: Pursuing Reality through Reason and the Imagination

> **Jerry Root** (Ph.D., British Open University) is an associate professor and director of the Billy Graham Institute for Strategic Evangelism as Wheaton College. He wrote his master's thesis and doctoral dissertation on C. S. Lewis. He has written extensively on Lewis and has lectured on Lewis at 61 universities in 8 countries.

> **Wayne Martindale** (Ph.D., University of California, Riverside) is Emeritus Professor of English at Wheaton College in Chicago, and has published extensively on C. S. Lewis.

Frank Gaebelein: Teacher of Truth

> **Albert R. Beck** (Ph.D., Baylor University) serves as the admissions and advising coordinator of the Baylor University Honors Program. His dissertation on Gaebelein is entitled, "All Truth is God's Truth: The Life and Ideas of Frank E. Gaebelein."

Donald McGavran: Missionary Educator

> **Todd Benkert** (Ph.D., Southern Baptist Theological Seminary) is a pastor at Eastlake Baptist Church in Crown Point, Indiana and Assistant Professor of Global Studies at Liberty University. The title of his dissertation was "A Biblical Analysis of Donald A. McGavran's Harvest Theology Principle."

Carl F. H. Henry: The Pursuit of *Veritas* and the Christian University

> **Kevin King** (D.Min., Southern Baptist Theological Seminary; Ph.D., University of Pretoria) is Professor of Preaching and Historical Theology at Liberty University School of Divinity. His Ph.D. dissertation research was focused on the doctrine of inerrancy in the theology of Carl F. H. Henry.

Elmer L. Towns: Training Champions for Christ

Todd Benkert (Ph.D., Southern Baptist Theological Seminary) is a pastor at Eastlake Baptist Church in Crown Point, Indiana and Assistant Professor of Global Studies at Liberty University. The title of his dissertation was "A Biblical Analysis of Donald A. McGavran's Harvest Theology Principle."

David Edgell (Ed.D. ABD, Southeastern Baptist Theological Seminary) is a pastor and assistant professor at Liberty University. He is writing his dissertation on the educational philosophy of Elmer Towns.

PICTURE ATTRIBUTION

PART I: EDUCATORS IN THE EARLY CHURCH THROUGH THE MIDDLE AGES (A.D. 1-1500)

The Apostle Paul: Educator of the Early Church – Raphael, St. Paul Preaching in Athens (1515).

Augustine: Teacher as Mentor – Fresco of St Augustine Teaching in Rome, Apsidal chapel, Sant'Agostino, San Gimignano (1464-65).

Columba: An Inadvertent Teacher of Wild Peoples – Painting provided by the Christian Hall of Fame a ministry of Canton Baptist Temple, http://christianhof.org/.

Anselm of Canterbury: Educating for the Love of God – Giovanni Francesco Romanelli (1610-1662), The Meeting of the Countess Matilda and Anselm of Canterbury in the Presence of Pope Urban II (1637-1642), oil on canvas, Galleria dei Romanelli, the Vatican.

Thomas Aquinas: Teaching Theology in the Age of Universities – Fresco of Thomas Aquinas, Triumph of St Thomas Aquinas over the Heretics, Carafa Chapel between 1489 and 1491.

PART II: THE REFORMATION EDUCATORS (A.D. 1500-1650)

Erasmus: A Return to the Sources of Education – Portrait of Desiderius Erasmus of Rotterdam by Hans Holbein the Younger (1498–1543).

Huldrych Zwingli: A Christian Humanist Educator – The Zurich reformer Ulrich Zwingli on a portrait by Hans Asper, 1549.

Martin Luther: Education for the Preservation of the Gospel and Society – Lucas Cranach the Elder (1472–1553), Portrait of Luther as Junker Jörg (1521).

Ignatius of Loyola: Solider of the Exercised Mind and Disciplined Spirit – Painting of St. Ignatius of Loyola by Peter Paul Rubens (1577-1640).

Philip Melanchthon: Christian Education in the German Reformation – Oil painting of Melanchthon by Lucas Cranach the Elder (1472-1553).

John Calvin: Teacher in the School of Christ – Portrait attributed to Hans Holbein the Younger (1498-1543).

PART III: PURITAN EDUCATORS (A.D. 1650-1750)

John Amos Comenius: Teaching all Things to all People – Portrait of Comenius by Fratisek Sestak (1991) and is used with the permission of Comenius University in Bratislava.

Richard Baxter: Educating through Pastoral Discipleship – Used with permission from the Wellcome Library no. 546768i, London. Engraving titled, Six portraits of Eminent Seventeenth Century Men.

August Hermann Francke: Architect of Practical Piety – Ludwig Bechstein, ed., Zweihundert Bildnisse und Lebensabrisse berühmter deutscher Männer, 3rd ed. (Leipzig 1870).

Jonathan Edwards: Influencing the Heart – An engraving from the front-piece of a biography of Jonathan Edwards, Lives of Jonathan Edwards and David Brainerd, Volume 8 of the Library of American Biography (1837).

PART IV: POST-ENLIGHTENMENT EDUCATORS (A.D. 1750-1850)

John Wesley: Methodizing Christian Education – Used with permission from the Wellcome Library no. 9621i, London. Mezzotint by J. Faber, Jr. and J. Williams. John Wesley (1743).

Robert Raikes: Author of the Sunday School Movement – W. J. Townsend, H. B. Workman and George Eayrs, eds., A New History of Methodism (London: Hodder and Stoughton, 1909).

Johann Heinrich Pestalozzi: Advocate for Child-Centered Education – Public Domain Photo by Friedrich Gustav Schöner (1774-1841), original scanned from "Die großen Deutschen im Bilde" (1936) by Michael Schönitzer.

Johann Friedrich Herbart: Morality as the Task for Education – Photo from Georg Weiss and E. Reinhardt Verlag München, Herbart und seine Schule (1928).

PART V: EDUCATORS IN THE AGE OF INDUSTRIALIZATION (A.D. 1850-1950)

Horace Bushnell: Advocate of Progressive Orthodoxy and Christian Nurture – Drawing by Samuel W. Rowse.

John Henry Newman: Education that Integrates Faith and Learning – John Henry Newman reading a book taken from the Sermon Notes of John Henry Cardinal Newman (ca. 1890).

William James: Father of Pragmatic Philosophy and Experiential Education – Public Domain Photo of William James (January 11, 1842 – August 26, 1910). MS Am 1092 (1185), Series II, 23, Houghton Library, Harvard University (1903)

C. I. Scofield: Educating for Heavenly Citizenship – Photo of Cyrus Ingerson Scofield, Bible teacher and creator of the Scofield Reference Bible, c. 1920.

John Dewey: Father of Progressive Education – Original photograph from the John Dewey Photograph Collection (N3-1104, N3-1109), Special Collections, Morris Library, Southern Illinois University at Carbondale.

Arthur Flake: Pioneer of Sunday School Administration – Photo of Arthur Flake, used with permission from B&H, a division of LifeWay Christian Resources.

PART VI: MODERN EDUCATORS (A.D. 1950 – PRESENT)

Henrietta Mears: Educating God's Children – Photo from the Mears Archive. All rights reserved. Used by permission.

C. S. Lewis: Pursuing Reality through Reason and the Imagination – This photo is used with permission courtesy of Jerry Root. It is a photo of C. S. Lewis with the British Royal Air Force Chaplains during World War II.

Frank Gaebelein: Teacher of Truth – Photo of Frank Gaebelein is dated April 21, 1963 and is used with permission from The Stony Brook School.

Donald McGavran: Missionary Educator – Photo of Donald McGavran used with permission from the Ralph D. Winter Research Center.

Carl F. H. Henry: The Pursuit of *Veritas* and the Christian University – Portrait provided by the Carl F. H. Henry Center for Theological Understanding, a ministry of Trinity Evangelical Divinity School (henrycenter.org)

Elmer L. Towns: Training Champions for Christ – Photo of Elmer Towns used with permission from Liberty University.

CPSIA information can be obtained
at www.ICGtesting.com
Printed in the USA
LVOW04*2235130317
527071LV00005B/14/P